Database Design

McGraw-Hill Computer Science Series

Database Design

Second Edition

Gio Wiederhold
Assistant Professor of Computer Science
Stanford University

McGraw-Hill Book Company

New York   St. Louis   San Francisco   Auckland   Bogotá   Hamburg
Johannesburg   London   Madrid   Mexico   Montreal   New Delhi
Panama   Paris   São Paulo   Singapore   Sydney   Tokyo   Toronto

This book was set in Computer Modern Roman.
The editors were Eric M. Munson and Joseph F. Murphy;
the production supervisor was Joe Campanella.
New drawings were done by J & R Services, Inc.
The cover was designed by Jane Moorman.
Halliday Lithograph Corporation was printer and binder.

DATABASE DESIGN

2 3 4 5 6 7 8 9 0   HALHAL   8 9 8 7 6 5 4 3

ISBN 0-07-070132-6

Library of Congress Cataloging in Publication Data

Wiederhold, Gio.
    Database design

    (McGraw-Hill computer science series)
    Bibliography: p.
    Includes index.
    1. Data base management.   2. File organization
(Computer science)   3. Data structures (Computer science)
I. Title. II. Series.
QA76.9.D3W53   1983   001.64 '25   82-20319
ISBN 0-07-070132-6

To Voy

Contents

Preface

Origin

The material in this book is the result of courses given at Stanford University on Database and File Structures since 1971. Initially little coherent published material was available, even though a large number of references could be cited. In particular, no clear definition of the concept of a *schema* was available. Now many practical and scholarly sources for material exist but problems of emphasis and analysis remain.

This book brings together knowledge in the area of database management in a structured form suitable for teaching and reference. The first edition has found broad acceptance in course sequences where quantitative approaches are stressed. Unintended, but gratifying, is the place this book has found as a programmer's reference and analysis guide.

Analyses to predict logical correctness and adequate performance of systems prior to investment in an implementation effort should be expected from professional system designers. An analysis of system development methods assigns a cost ratio of 100 to 1 when errors are found in testing rather than caught in the design stage. Many more cross-references have been added and the extensive index has been further expanded to help the professional reader. The background sections have also been completely redone to reflect the best recent references. Other major changes made are discussed in the objective section.

Much has happened in the database field since the first edition was published. The area has become an accepted academic discipline. Conferences and journals covering the area abound. Selection of material is now more difficult than finding material. At the same time commercial interest in database management has exploded creating a serious shortage of qualified people. Already now the number of professionals working in the database area exceeds the number employed in traditional computing fields as compilers and operating systems. Not everyone working today with databases has the background to deal well with the complexities that can arise, so that complaints of system inadequacies are common.

Much of the literature remains descriptive or presents one-sided experiences, inadequate to provide a basis for the transfer of concepts to diverse applications. An effort has been made here to develop concepts from the wealth of material and to present the subject in such a way that the concepts which evolve can be applied in practice. An engineering attitude to the problems of database organization has been used in order to combine formality with applicability.

I hope that this greatly revised text will continue to fill the needs and that it will help extend and improve the teaching of the data-processing aspects of computer science.

Objective

This book is intended to present the methods, the criteria for choices between alternatives, and the principles and concepts, that are relevant to the practice of database design. No actual systems are described completely, nor are systems surveyed and compared, although specific and realistic examples are used throughout to illustrate points being made. The material provides the basis to allow the reader to understand, recognize the implications, and evaluate database approaches. Databases in this sense are a broader concept than database management systems. The design of a database involves understanding the meaning of the data, the systems chosen, be they database management systems or traditional file systems, just help in the implementation.

This book includes two major parts:

1 The description and analysis of file systems (Chaps. 2 to 6)

2 The description and analysis of database systems (Chaps. 7 to 10)

The first part is intended to provide a solid foundation for the latter part, since the issues arising in database design are difficult to discuss if file-design concepts are not available to draw upon. A number of subjects which pertain to both files and databases, namely reliability, protection of privacy, integrity, and coding are presented in the third part, consisting of Chaps. 11 to 14. If the material is taught in two distinct courses, the third part should not be ignored in either course.

The audience for this book ranges from students of computing who have finished a reasonably complete course in programming to applications and systems programmers who wish to synthesize their experiences into a more formal structure. The material covered should be known by systems designers or systems analysts faced with implementation choices. It probably presents too much detail to be of interest to management outside the database management area itself.

The revision of this book has been major. Nearly every paragraph has been rewritten, and some sections have been completely replaced. The number of tables and examples is also increased. The general outline, however, and the underlying principles could remain the same. Distribution of databases over multiple sites is now considered throughout the book. The equipment table in Chap. 2 deals with the much wider range of storage devices now available. The prevalence of B-trees for indexes has permitted a rewrite of Sec. 3-4 which is more modern and simpler. A new method for dealing with growth of direct-access areas is part of Sec. 3-5. New results dealing with device interference are presented in Chap. 5.

Chapter 7 includes the modern concepts of semantic modeling. A new section, 7-2 deals with the formal semantics now available for database design. Section 7-3 defines the conceptual tools for establishing the structural relationships between files. The entire design process is described step by step in Sec. 7-5. The introduction of commercial relational database implementations permits now a consistent description of these systems in Sec. 9-2. The performance of databases using relational operations can be predicted using the information introduced in Sec. 9-3.

The concept of using transactions to access the database is used throughout but has a major impact on the handling of reliability issues in Chap. 11 and integrity maintenance in Chap. 13. New sections have been added there.

Design Methodology

This book presents a comprehensive collection of database design tools. In order to employ them, a strategy of problem decomposition, followed by a structured design process is advised. A top-down design requires the underlying primitives to be understood. Since this book starts with the basics, the design process is initiated with concepts from Chap. 10.

The categorization of database approaches given in Chap. 10 helps to set the initial objective for a database. Chapter 7 provides the means to construct a model which integrates the requirements of multiple applications which share the database. The schemas in Chap. 8 provide methods to describe the model in machine-readable form. Existing database systems, described in Chap. 9 and referenced in Appendix B, suggest available implementation alternatives.

If the database is to be directly supported by a file system, the basic file choices in Chap. 3 and their combinations shown in Chap. 4 provide the alternatives. The data representation can be chosen using the material of Chap. 14.

The performance of the chosen approach can be predicted following the outline shown in Chap. 5. Factors relevant to specific database systems or file systems appear where they are discussed, but the terminology and variable definitions are consistent throughout, so that cross-referencing is simple. The structural model defined in Chap. 7 provides the framework for the translation of application loads to the load to be handled by the database. Transaction performance in database systems is estimated using the performance analyses for the prevalent approaches from Chap. 9. An optimal file design may be selected after application of the load parameters to the performance formulas from Chaps. 3 and 4. The formulas also require the hardware description parameters introduced in Chap. 2.

Problems of reliability, protection, and integrity (Chaps. 11, 12, and 13) require a close scrutiny of the available operating system. The long-term maintenance of a database is guided by considerations presented in Chap. 15.

Curricula

Modern curricula give increased emphasis to files and databases. This book matches the suggested courses well. The material of Chaps. 1 to 6 covers course CS-5 (Introduction to File Processing) and Chaps. 7 to 14 cover course CS-11 (Database Management System Design) as specified in the report by the ACM Curriculum on Computer Science [Austing et al[78]]. The quantitative approach taken in this book causes that algorithmic and analytic material assigned to courses CS-6 and CS-7 is included as well, albeit limited by relevance to databases. I do not agree with the recommendation that students write a database management system during CS-11; this is apt to be an exercise in trivializing real issues. Design and performance prediction of a nontrivial database application is part of the course taught at Stanford and enables a broad exposure to important concepts beyond programming. I agree with Ralston and Shaw[80] that mathematical competence is necessary for a computer science student.

The text provides all the material for the file and database subjects of Courses C1, C2, C3, C4, and D2 specified in the Curriculum Recommendations for Graduate Professional Programs in Information Systems [Ashenhurst[72]]. The author feels, however, that these courses are easier to teach using a depth-first approach to the subjects versus the breadth-first approach advocated in the proposal. I have been impressed by constructive comments received from readers who used the book for self-study.

In many schools files and databases are still neglected, possibly because of a shortage of teachers. Students who enter industry or commerce with a bachelor's-level education in computing or data-processing feel this void sharply. It is now reasonable to expect that students majoring in computing and computer applications should be familiar with this subject area [Teichrow[71], Sprowls[75]]. Projections regarding the future use of computers give a considerable weight to the importance of the database area [Dolotta et al[76]], so that we can expect an increasing demand for educational services in this area.

Terminology

We are grateful that the terminology in the area of database and file management is becoming more consistent. Within this book a major effort has been made to define all terms and to use only one term per concept. Some terms were changed since the first edition because usage developed differently than I had foreseen. All terms are listed in the index. In order to aid both experienced readers and users of the references, Appendix A cites common alternate terminology and compares it with the terminology used in this text. The introductory chapter is mainly devoted to definitions. It is assumed that subjects such as programming and basic functions of operating systems are familiar to the reader.

Most of the program examples throughout the text use a simple subset of PL/1. The variable names are chosen so that they will aid in the comprehension of the programs; they are printed in lowercase. Keywords which are to be recognized by the translating programs appear in uppercase. The programs are designed to be obvious to readers familiar with any procedure-oriented programming language. A number of introductory PL/1 texts [Hume[75], Richardson[75], Mott[72]] can be used to explain features that are not recognized. Some PL/1 texts, unfortunately, omit the statements required for the manipulation of data files.

Most of the examples shown to illustrate features of design approaches or systems are based on actual systems but are of necessity incomplete. An effort has been made to note simplifying assumptions. The same should be done in students' design assignments, so that awareness of real-world complexities is fostered without overwhelming the design with trivia.

Exercises

The exercises listed in each chapter have been kept relatively simple. It is strongly suggested that an analysis of some of the systems described in the referenced literature be used for major assignments. Many of the problem statements in fact require such material. The analysis or comparison of actual systems may seem to be an excessively complex task, but has been shown to be manageable by students when the material of this book has been assimilated. Appendix B provides references to a large number of systems implementations. A knowledge of calculus will be helpful when doing some of the problems, but purely graphical methods will provide adequate results.

The primary exercise when this course is being taught at Stanford is a design project. Early in the course students prepare an objective statement for a database application of interest to them. Some individual research may be needed to obtain estimates of expected data quantities and transaction load frequencies. The students prepare a structural model describing their database while Chap. 7 is being covered. The project is fleshed out with a schema description and a performance prediction of selected important transactions for the application.

References

Source material for this book came from many places and experiences. References are not cited throughout the text since the intent is to produce primarily a text and reference book which integrates the many concepts and ideas available for database design. A background section at the end of every chapter cites the major sources used and indicates further study material. The references have been completely updated for the second edition and provide a generous foothold for students intending to pursue a specific topic in depth. Use of the references can direct research effort toward the many yet unsolved problems in the area.

The bibliography has been selected to include some important material for each of the subject areas introduced. The volume of database publications is now such that a comprehensive bibliography is beyond the scope of a textbook. Only sources that are easy to obtain, such as books and journals, have been chosen. Papers which appear in conference proceedings containing much relevant material are cited only by author and proceedings, and do not appear individually in the bibliography.

Typically only one or two early publications and some instances of recent work in an area are cited. To provide a complete view references in the recent material have to be traced. Trade publications, research reports, theses, and computer manuals are referenced only when used directly, although much relevant information can be found there. Up-to-date information on computer systems is best obtained from manufacturers.

I apologize to the authors of work I failed to reference, either due to application of these rules, or because of lack of awareness on my part. A large annotated bibliography is being maintained by me and has been made available. I look forward to distribution of the bibliography in computer-readable form since it is too large to be effectively scanned without computer assistance.

Acknowledgments

Parts of the first edition were carefully reviewed by John Bolstead, Frank Germano, Lance Hoffman, Eugene Lowenthal, Tim Merrett, Joaquin Miller, Richard Moore, Dick Karpinski, Bernard Pagurek, Donn Parker, Jean Porte, Gerry Purdy, Diane Ramsey-Klee, John Rhodes, Justine Roberts, Diane Rode, Hank Swan, and Steve Weyl. Thomas Martin and the members of the SHARE Database Committee provided many ideas during mutual discussions. The second edition has had comments by innumerable students, as well as by many colleagues. I thank especially Anne Beetem, Bob Blum, Ramez ElMasri, Sheldon Finkelstein, Jonathan King, Joaquin Miller, Toshi Minoura, Witold Litwin, Bob Paige, Domenico Saccà, and Kyu Young Whang for their reviews and corrections.

I received support from the National Library of Medicine during the preparation of the first edition [Wiederhold[77]]. Experience was obtained in part during evaluations funded by the National Center for Health Services Research. Subsequent support came from the Defense Advanced Research Projects Agency (contract N-39) for research in Knowledge Based Management Systems. This research provided the basis for many of the concepts presented here. I have also benefited from the computer services at Stanford University, some of which are supported by the NIH Division of Research Resources. The TEX program, developed by Donald Knuth[79], was used to prepare the plates for printing. Arthur Keller provided the initial typesetting macros and advice. Peter Ullman, Chris Tucci, John and Randy Wiederhold managed the photo-typesetting. The ability to prepare beautiful copy under full control of the author is both an opportunity and a responsibility. I hope to have carried them adequately. Jayne Pickering read the proofs several times to insure that my editing matched my intentions. Any errors in content and format remain my responsibility, and I welcome all kinds of criticism.

This book would not have been written without the inspiration, support, and just plain hard work by my wife, Voy. The appreciation she has received from her students, and users of computer manuals she has written, has encouraged me to attempt to present this material in as straightforward a fashion as she has been able to present PL/1 programming.

                                                                                    Gio Wiederhold

Chapter 1

Definitions and Introduction to the Subject

The order and connection of ideas is the same as the order and connection of things.
Baruch (Benedict de) Spinoza
Prop. VII from Ethics, Part Two.

When we talk informally about a *database*, we refer to a collection of mutually related data, to the computer hardware that is used to store it, and to the programs used to manipulate it.

By mutually related we mean that the data represents knowledge about a specific enterprise, say a company, a university, or a governmental institution. The data may also be related because it deals with a certain problem area, perhaps about a disease which is of concern to the staff of a number of hospitals. The data should be organized so that it can be processed to yield information.

The organization of the data in a database has to represent the underlying meaning or semantics of the data correctly and efficiently. In conventional programs the structure of data is arranged for the convenience of the program. A database contains data to be used by many and diverse programs. The organization of a database can hence not be solely determined by decisions made while programming specific functions.

This chapter begins by defining the concept of a file, since files are the major physical units into which a database is organized. The second section discusses operations or tasks performed when using a database. In Sec. 1-3 we develop a classification of data management which will provide the structure for all subsequent material. We then take familiar concepts from programming and relate them to the presented classification. This sequence is intended to provide a link between our existing programming experience and the approach taken in this presentation of database-management methodology. In Sec. 1-8 a list of application areas is given as an aid for the selection of a topic for analysis to be followed throughout the text.

You may have learned nothing new after you have read this chapter, but the framework established will allow us to proceed through the book in an orderly fashion.

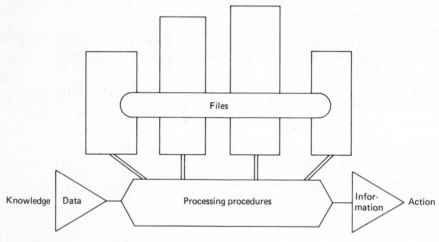

Figure 1-1 A database.

1-1 FILES

A database is a collection of related data. The data storage for a database is accomplished by the use of one or more files. All files of one database are accessible from one computer or from any interconnected computer if the database is distributed over several computers. Procedures in these computers are used to enter data, store data in files, and process the data in response to requests for information. A *file* is defined to be a collection of similar records kept on secondary computer storage devices.

Typical of *secondary storage* devices are disk drives with magnetic disks, but there are a number of alternatives. A *record* is defined at this point to be a collection of related *fields* containing elemental data items. A more formal and detailed definition will be developed in Chap. 3. A data item is typically represented by a value which is part of a description of an object or an event. Computational processes can manipulate such values.

1-1-1 Size

To warrant the attention and the approaches discussed in this book, the database should be reasonably *large*. We will concentrate on topics that are applicable to large external files. This outlook limits the choice of algorithms that can be applied. Collections of data that can be processed in their entirety in the directly addressable memory of a computer, its primary storage, allow techniques that will not be covered here. The use of the term database also implies that a variety of people are involved. Data entry may be done by people far removed from the users and the data may contain information suitable for several purposes. The quantity of data to be handled may range from moderately large to very large. These measures of size depend on the hardware and on operational constraints which may apply in a given environment.

Large implies a quantity of data which is greater than a single person can handle alone, even when aided by a computer system. The actual quantity will vary depending on the complexity of the data and applications. An example of a large database is the integrated personnel and product data system in a manufacturing company of about 6000 employees, with more than 300,000 records of 21 types [Emerson in Jardine[74]].*

A very large database is an essential part of an enterprise and will be in continuous use by many people. At the same time it will require many storage devices. A very large database presents particular problems in its management, since it cannot be turned off without affecting the operation and well-being of the enterprise into which it is integrated. A formal definition of a very large database is one where the time required for making a copy is greater than the permissible interval between update transactions performed to keep the database up to date. An example of a very large database is found at a telephone company with 5 million subscribers [Karsner in Kerr[75]]. Much larger yet are databases at the social security administration and other national systems.

To have a copy of the contents of a file frozen at a certain instant in time is important for many purposes, including periodic analysis of data, backup for reliability purposes, and auditing. To avoid problems, it is best not to permit a file to be modified while it is being copied. In a very large database these two considerations conflict. This definition imposes certain design constraints on the systems which we will be discussing.

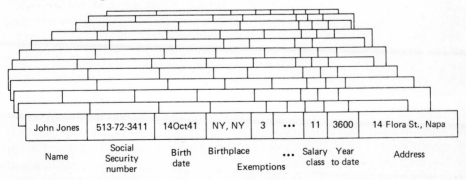

John Jones	513-72-3411	14Oct41	NY, NY	3	•••	11	3600	14 Flora St., Napa
Name	Social Security number	Birth date	Birthplace	Exemptions	•••	Salary class	Year to date	Address

Figure 1-2 A payroll file.

*Superior number next to reference indicates the year of publication.

1-1-2 File Organization

Files not only are characterized by their size but are further distinguished by their organization. Differences in the organizations of files lead to great differences in performance when storing and retrieving records. The evaluation and comparison of file organizations is an important aspect of this book.

Six basic file organization types will be analyzed in detail in Chap. 3, and Chap. 4 will show some of the possible combinations and permutations of these basic file types. A database often requires more than one type of file.

1-1-3 Input-Output

When reading or writing files, data is transferred between storage and memory devices of the computer system. When reading input or writing output, data enters or leaves the computer system. A database is concerned with the data which remains within the scope of the system. Data which is written onto tapes, although the tapes are dismounted, securely stored, and later mounted and read again, can be part of the database. Data which is taken out, made accessible for modification, and reentered has to be considered new input, since its consistency is not assured.

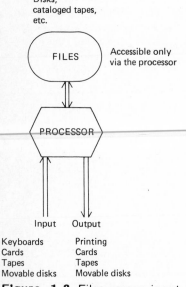

Examples of devices used for files are nonremovable disks and drums, removable disks that are normally kept mounted, dismountable master tapes or disks kept at the computer site, archival tapes and disks kept in remote vaults for protection, and sometimes card decks containing master lists that are loaded into the system when needed.

Devices used for input and output are terminals and all those machines that read or write media as cards, paper tape, printed reports, microfilm output, and tapes or disks that are shipped between computer systems.

Figure 1-3 Files versus input-output.

In many computer systems the distinction of files versus input and output is not clearly delineated. The subject of input and output is at best as complex as the database area and will not be covered in this text. We will simply assume that an *operating system* is available which provides adequate input and output capabilities, including access via on-line terminals where appropriate, when we talk about database systems.

We will not discuss file organizations that are based on input and output facilities. These tend to regard data as a continuous stream of characters. *Stream files*, as defined by PL/1, and their equivalents in other systems, are based on the reading and writing of continuous lines of text. Continuous text streams are important for communication but are not suitable for data manipulation. The word "file" will also not be used to refer to the hardware used to store the data comprising the files.

1-2   COMPUTATIONS ON A DATABASE

In the first section we considered some of the static aspects of a database, namely, the storage of data as files, records, and fields. We now will look at a database from a dynamic point of view. The dynamic behavior of programming structures has been studied whenever operating systems have been analyzed. The terminology used in this chapter follows Tsichritzis[74]. The term *computation* is used to denote a section of an application which manipulates the database. Most of the computations which are used to manipulate a data collection are conceptually simple. We recognize four kinds of computations related to databases:

1   The building of the data collection
2   Updating of data elements in the data collection
3   Retrieval of data from the data collection
4   Reduction of large quantities of data to usable form

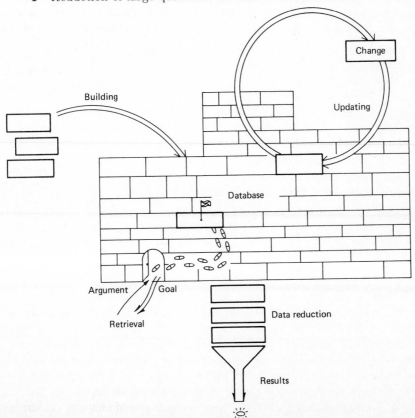

Figure 1-4 Computations with a database.

A database application will use all four kinds of computations, but certain applications will stress one kind more than others. The kinds are sketched in Fig. 1-4. One may note that the only computation which uses the calculating powers of the computer is the reduction of data to yield information.

The building of a database includes data collection, data coding, and data entry. This kind is often the most costly part of a database operation.

The updating of a database includes inserting new data, changing stored data values when necessary, and deleting invalid or obsolete data.

Update activity varies much among types of applications. A static database, one not receiving updates, may be used in a retrospective study where all the data is collected prior to analysis. A dynamic or volatile database is encountered in applications such as reservations systems.

Data retrieval can consist of the fetching of a specific element in order to obtain a stored value or fact, or the collection of a series of related elements to obtain data regarding some relationship which manifests itself when data are joined. To fetch a specific data record the database will be entered using a *search argument*, which will be matched with a *key* in the database records. The argument of a search is sometimes called the *search key*; in general the context clarifies the distinction.

In computing, the usage of the word key is unfortunately the opposite of the concept associated with a key in common household usage: a person who desires something from a house uses a key which will unlock the latch of the proper house; here a person uses the argument to match the key of the proper record.

Data reduction is needed when the relevant data volume exceeds the capability of the requestors. In a static database this kind of activity tends to dominate. In dynamic databases data reduction is used primarily for period summaries and trend analyses. When the desired information is diffused throughout the database, it may be necessary to access most of its contents in order to summarize or abstract the data. Statistical summaries, annual business operating statements, or graphical data presentations are examples of frequently used data reduction techniques. Data reduction is very demanding of database performance.

Conceptual descriptions of computations for a particular problem frequently can be written in a few lines; the procedures to implement them may be diagrammed on a one-page flowchart and programmed in a short time. Yet the effort required to bring a database system into operation frequently involves expenditure of large amounts of time and money. The causes for this discrepancy will be discussed later in this book but may well be obvious before that point.

1-2-1 Processes

The operating system which schedules the execution of a computation requested by a user may decompose the computation into a number of distinct *processes*. Processes are the basic computational units managed by an operating system. The various processes of a single computation may require different units of the computer's hardware and may be executed in parallel. Various types of operating systems will require different properties from the processes they manage. In Sec. 1-7 we will review the types of commonly available operating systems. The scheduling and performance of processes, and hence of the computations that were specified, determine the performance of database systems.

1-2-2 Process Sections

A process itself can be decomposed into a number of sections. A *section* is the collection of program steps during which the operating system does not have to worry about the process. When a process stops, requests data from a file, requires a new allocation of storage space, and so on, the operating system has to intervene. When, for instance, a record from a file is requested, the operating system has to assure that the record is not currently being modified by another process. A section of a process which presents such interaction potential is known as a *critical section*. Figure 1-5 sketches a process with its sections.

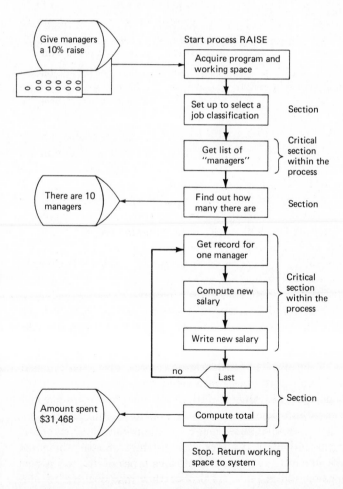

Figure 1-5 Sections of a process.

The design and performance of typical sections which manipulate the database are the subjects of Chap. 3. There we will consider that the sections are not affected by activities being carried on simultaneously in the same or adjacent databases. Interactions will be encountered beginning in Chap. 5, and Chap. 13 will be devoted to the problem of resolving interference between parallel critical sections.

1-3 A HIERARCHICAL VIEW OF DATA

Database problems can be initially approached from two points of view. There is the comprehensive view, in which the database is seen as a component of an overall system involving people, organizations, and communication; in contrast there is the microscopic view, in which the database is a collection of the hardware bits and bytes provided by computer technology. In between these two extremes is subject matter of this book. A database is viewed as a structured representation of data which describe a subset of the real world. This representation is implemented using files, records, and references between these records. Figure 1-6 presents the structure in the form of a pyramid to symbolize the breadth of the base required to obtain information.

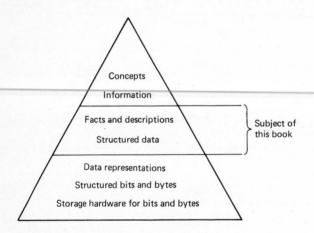

Figure 1-6 Database levels.

The technical aspects of database implementations can be discussed independently of the informational significance of the data value stored. The fact that this book will only casually touch on the value of data is not intended to imply that people who actually implement information processing systems should ignore these considerations in their particular applications. It is clearly irresponsible if computer professionals ignore the ramifications of the task at hand or their contribution to the social and human environment. A number of textbooks deal with the proper use of information for business and governmental operations and decision making [Davis74, DeGreene73, Gotlieb73, Westin71].

This text also avoids subjects on the engineering side of the database domain, the design and construction of data storage devices. Although the architecture and performance of computer hardware is central to the evaluation of database systems, very little discussion of hardware-design alternatives will take place. Obviously, familiarity with the hardware that provides the building blocks of computer systems is beneficial to the system developer. Again, textbooks are available for the computer engineer at many levels of sophistication [Hill[73], Siewiorek[82]]. A sufficiently large body of material is available between these two extremes to keep us busy for some time.

Table 1-1 presents the various areas of discussion and places them in relationship to each other. The table also lists some of the fields of study which provide background or further material appropriate to the levels presented. The reader is not expected to be knowledgeable in all these areas; they are listed merely as navigational aids.

The term *naming* in the table is used to mean the creation of symbolic references to data with minimal concern as to location and form. The term *addressing* is used to denote the exact specification of position and representation. We see in Table 1-1 that as we descend to more primitive levels, naming is replaced more and more by addressing.

A Comparison   A comparison can be made here between the levels presented in Table 1-1 and the operation of a railroad.

1 The *conceptual level* concerns itself with the idea of value added due to the transportation of the goods and their relevance to the economic structure.

2 The *descriptive level* concerns itself with scheduling, train sizes, and equipment combinations required to move goods at a a reasonable cost and with adequate flexibility.

3 The *organizational level* concerns itself with the building of trackage, the operation of marshaling yards, and the operational efficiency of the complex.

4 The *material level* concerns itself with the design of locomotives, freight cars, signaling mechanisms, rails, and ties, and all the myriad of pieces of equipment required to actually run a railroad.

Description and Organization   This text considers the two central levels shown in the diagram: the descriptive level and the organizational level.

On the *descriptive level*, we present the processes carried out to satisfy demands for data according to its meaning or utility relative to some problem. We have to specify the data in terms which aid their selection by such processes. The content of data elements is quite important. Database systems provide tools to relate data elements according to their meaning. Because of this concern we analyze this level using tools that employ logic and formal semantics. There are also issues that required some intuition or common sense for their resolution.

On the *organizational level*, we present the processes which locate and move data according to demands of efficiency. Descriptions of data may be manipulated at this level as well as the data themselves. Here it is not the content but the size and the position of the data element which is of concern. File systems provide tools to fetch records containing data according to relative position or name. This level is analyzed using quantitative tools in order to provide good performance estimates.

Table 1-1a   Levels of Database Structure: conceptual and descriptive

---

Level 1   At the *conceptual level* we deal with *information*, data with sufficient significance to make us act. Information has the essence of newness and nonredundancy so that its acquisition increases our knowledge.

A: Some processes used to obtain information:
Cross tabulation
Exception reporting
Mathematical and statistical analysis
Linear and dynamic programming
Deductive inference

B: Intellectual tools for managing information:
Intuitive or formal models of the application area
Formalized conceptual relationships
Theory of semantics
Heuristic processes

C: Requirements for the production of information:
Named and described data
Means to collect needed data comprehensively or representatively
Means to analyze such data, intellectually or automatically

Level 2   At the *descriptive level* we deal with *data*, a collection of text or numbers describing items or events.

A: Processes used to obtain and manipulate data:
Data collection
Data organization
Data selection and retrieval

B: Intellectual tools for data manipulation:
Logic
Data modeling
Computer science concepts of syntax and semantics
Knowledge of formal languages and meta-languages
Propositional and relational calculus

C: Requirements for large-scale data manipulation:
Named files
Named or addressable records
Addressable data elements
Catalogs and descriptions of available facilities
Facilities to obtain resources from the system
Procedure libraries

The two central levels are highly dependent on each other. The descriptive level can easily specify requirements that the organizational level cannot reasonably supply using any given set of hardware. On the other hand, a file organization that expands the basic hardware capabilities only minimally may impose restrictions that prevent the descriptive level from being effective. The separation of the two inner levels assures that logical requirements are kept distinct from the performance issues.

Table 1-1b   Levels of Database Structure: organizational and material

---

Level 3   At the *organizational level* we deal with *data representation*, data removed from context, but named and processable.

  A: Processes used to encode data and manipulate the encoded data:
  Encoding and decoding
  Storage layout definition
  File management
  Space management and cataloging
  Moving and comparing of fields containing coded data
  Control of errors

  B: Intellectual tools for the design of data representation and manipulation:
  Information theory
  Arithmetic processes
  Programming languages
  Knowledge of computer architecture and component performance

  C: Required for the representation of data:
  Storage devices for encoded data
  Hardware facilities to move addressed fields between memory and storage
  Capability for comparison of encoded data

Level 4   At the *material level* finally we find *hardware*, the equipment used to provide unformatted addressable storage.

  A: Processes used to obtain hardware:
  Engineering design
  Production

  B: Tools required for the engineer who is designing hardware:
  Knowledge of electronics, physics, and logic
  Experience in production practice

  C: What the engineer in turn has to rely on:
  Availability of components, devices, and measurement tools
  Availability of production facilities

The applications of a database will be a reflection of the decision maker's concept of the information problems and will vary over time as the needs, the analysis tools, and the insight of the users of the database mature. During this time the operating systems and computers which support the database may evolve and change. We therefore want a clean separation or interface between the levels.

In order to ensure that the separation of levels is not evaded, systems which attempt to support the concept of distinct levels may hide the structural detail of lower levels from users at the higher levels. This idea of *information hiding* can remain valid only when lower level functions are reliable, complete, and reasonably efficient. The independence of the descriptive and organizational levels is also referred to as *data independence*.

1-4   CURRENT PRACTICE

The previous section discussed database concepts in an abstract fashion. Experience has to be placed into the framework which has been developed. Some examples will help relate programming practice to database concepts.

1-4-1 A File Program

To illustrate the use of a file, we will use a simple program to carry out the actions that were presented in Fig. 1-5. The program is not intended to be especially good or bad, but rather typical.

Example 1-1   A transaction program for a database

```
/* Transaction program to give a 'raise' to a class of employees */
  raise:PROCEDURE(message);
        DECLARE message CHAR(200);
     s1 :DECLARE emp_list(5000) INITIAL((5000)0);
     s2 :DECLARE workspace(20);
        DECLARE class CHAR(8), pct INTEGER;
        class = SUBSTR(message,6,8);  pct = SUBSTR(message,17,2);
/* get record listing employees of this class */
     s3 :OPEN FILE(job_classification) DIRECT;
     s4 :READ FILE(job_classification) KEY(class) INTO(emp_list);
        CLOSE FILE(job_classification);
/* count how many employees are eligible for the raise */
        DO i = 1 TO 5000 WHILE emp_list(i) ¬= 0;  END;
        no_employees = i - 1;
     s5 :PUT SKIP EDIT(no_employees, class) ('There are ', I5 / A8);
/* prepare to give raises */
        OPEN FILE(payroll) SEQUENTIAL UPDATE;
        total_increase = 0;
        DO j = 1 TO no_employees;
     s6 :  READ FILE(payroll) KEY(emp_list(j) ) INTO(workspace);
/*   increase salary field of record */
          increase = workspace(18) * pct / 100;
          total_increase = total_increase + increase;
          workspace(18) = workspace(18) + increase;
          REWRITE FILE(payroll) FROM(workspace);
        END;
/* report total cost of all raises */
        PUT SKIP EDIT(total_increase) ('Amount spent $', F(8,2));
      END raise;
```

The DECLARE statements, s1 and s2, define working areas for a copy of each of the two types of records used within the program. All items of one record are related by being kept in adjoining cells on the file and in the declared arrays. The OPEN statements name the files and specify their usage. When they are executed the name of the requested file is found by the operating system (OS) in a directory of file names. The programmer who wrote the program expects that the file, from this point on, is under exclusive control of this program until the file is released by a CLOSE statement. The execution of the OPEN statements can involve a number of sections within the OS, and may take a relatively long time.

The READ statement s4 fetches the particular record named by the title class = 'Managers', as specified by the input message of Fig. 1-5, to obtain a list of employee numbers. The print statement s5 reports the number of employees found for this class. The READ statement s6 names a particular record of the file identified with the employee and moves a copy of this record into the workspace. The system will have to look up and compute the proper record address in the files corresponding to the identification. It will use primary or core storage for the workspace. The address for the workspace is determined during program compilation and loading.

The program now can extract information, such as the salary, by addressing fields in the copy of the record. The copy of the record is modified to reflect the employee's raise. The comment provides some help in understanding the content of the addressed fields. The final REWRITE completes the update of a record in the file. For its proper operation, it depends on the record address that was determined by the file system during the execution of the READ statement. The file system must have saved this address at the time of the READ for use in the REWRITE.

Naming Versus Addressing In this example the records on the file have been specified using a *name*, namely, the title or the employee_number. The file system performs some computational procedure to determine an actual address for the corresponding record and then fetches the record. It remembers this address for any file which is to be updated in order to perform a later REWRITE properly. Within the record fetched, the program located data by providing *addresses*; for instance, the salary field was addressed as position 18 of the workspace. When an address is used, the programmer controls position and size of the data unit.

1-4-2 Operating System Control

Facilities of an *operating system* were used above to handle the major units of data, the files. This has provided independence of the program and the specification of the storage hardware. The writer of the transaction processing program expects that there exists somewhere an expert who controls the actual placement of the records of the file in storage. The expert directs the file system, which is generally a part of a computer operating system. The expert is restricted to select among facilities provided within the computer system by the vendor. Operating system alternatives are summarized in Sec. 1-7.

Statements outside the programming language are used to provide information to the operating system regarding the program. These statements form the *control language* for the operating system. The lack of communication between the programming language and the control language is often a barrier to effective utilization of computer systems.

A control language statement for the above example may read as shown in Example 1-2.

Example 1-2 Control language for "raise" transaction

```
FILE(data):(NAME('payroll'), DEVICE(diskdrive), LOCATION(disk5),
   ORGANIZATION(fixed records(80 bytes), indexed, sequential)
   BUFFERS(2), SIZE(60 tracks), etc.
```

The statement above has been made prettier than most control languages permit in order to aid comprehension. Once this statement is processed, the payroll file is available to the program throughout the entire computation.

It is not clear if the payroll file belongs exclusively to the program during the entire computation, during the period between OPEN and CLOSE statements, or only during the interval between READ and REWRITE statements. The answer depends on the operating system in use, and the alternatives are discussed in Chap. 13. The question of exclusive ownership is a concern when multiple programs share access to data. For instance, another transaction, to add up all the salaries in order to prepare a budget, should wait until the entire raise transaction is completed if inconsistent results are to be avoided.

The knowledge required for applications programming may be separate from the knowledge to write control language statements; but in order to write effective database systems, both aspects have to be understood. In order to design the entire database application, considerably broader knowledge is required. The analysis of retrieved data requires a different type of expertise than that required for the design, organization, or collection and updating of the data. In order to manage an entire database, a specialist in database administration may be needed, as shown in Chap. 15.

1-4-3 Modularity

As database applications become more complex and better understood, formal separation of functions takes place. We use the term *module* for a small but integrated set of programs which deals with some definable subtask and has well-defined interfaces to the other modules of a larger programming system. The user programs which operate on the database will often be *transaction* modules. These will use *file-access* program modules, and they will themselves be used by higher-level modules, which carry out the user's information-generation requirements. The raise program, for example, is a module which implements one transaction type of a larger payroll system and is called upon when the message entered says raise. The OPEN, READ, REWRITE, etc., statements are calls invoking modules of the file-access system. The OPEN is passed directly to the operating system. The data moving statements will also generate some operating system commands. A high degree of modularity is needed in database processing because:

1 Projects are undertaken that are of a size where many people have to work together, and individuals take on more specialized functions.

2 Many projects may make use of a single database or of some part of it, and the specification of the database becomes the sum of many requirements.

3 The information in a database has a value that makes unlimited access by everyone involved unreasonable. In order to provide protection of access to private data, the access processes are controlled by the operating system.

In the example above, all of the program was written by someone who was aware of the application. The control-language statement may have been generated with the assistance of a specialist. The system (invoked by the file access statements OPEN, READ, and REWRITE) was written by someone not aware of the application, at an earlier time and at a different place. The operating system was designed in concert with the computer hardware.

The example is not intended as an indictment or blessing of PL/1 as a programming language. No computer language exists that forces structuring of database programming according to the levels we discussed, although there are a number of languages which make structuring truly difficult.

1-5   DESCRIPTIONS

In order to permit implementation and use of a system by a number of people some documentation will have to exist to describe both the static aspects, the *database structure*, and the procedural aspects, the *computations*, which carry out the data transformations.

A picture of the data in terms of files, records, fields, and the relation between items of data contained in these elements is appropriate for the static aspect. Concepts to guide the development of such descriptions are presented in Chap. 7. Such a data-structure definition may take the form of a document to be used by the people who program the file operations on this database. It is even better to materialize the structure definitions in the form of a collection of computer-readable codes, a *schema* which guides file processes automatically. Much of the content of this book will be concerned with the design and use of such schemas. Examples of schemas are presented in Chap. 8.

The procedural description may be given as a formula, a description of program sections to be executed, or a flowchart. In many commercial programming groups much effort is put into *systems analysis* which prepares process descriptions in minute detail for subsequent implementation by coders. It is easy for errors to develop because of communication problems between systems analysts and coders. The analyst may assume that the coders are aware of conditions which are beyond their knowledge. Coders, on the other hand, may program for cases which cannot occur. The determination of critical sections is often a source of difficulty. No formal methods are yet adequate to fully verify correctness for interacting processes. We therefore prefer detailed static data descriptions for the development of databases.

Static versus Procedural Descriptions   The static and procedural aspects often occur together when we describe files. For many simple data-processing problems, however, no process descriptions are needed. In those cases the computation is indirectly described by providing two pictures of a file, specifying the form and contents before and after the computation. This method is also applicable to the movement of data between two separate files of a database. The programmer uses the before and after layout charts to write the code. Dispensing with the coding entirely is the intent of *report generators*, which accept the description of the source files and a layout of the output report which is desired. Most processing steps are implied and created by the report generator system. The same idea is the basis for many high-level query systems where an information-retrieval request is stated as a formula and its resolution is the task of a retrieval system. Aspects of these approaches will be presented in Chap. 9.

At other times one may find that the data organization is implicitly defined by a listing of the steps of the process which puts the data into the database. Much analysis is needed when new programs want access to data that have only been defined procedurally. The two choices available are implied in the existence of two terms for the description of storage structures: *file organization* versus *access methods*.

Special data elements, described and kept in the database, can be used to control program dynamics. A data element of a database could state that a particular file has been completely updated by some computation. Such information can be used to assure a correct execution sequence of programs that share data. Data elements kept with each record may specify that certain records have not been updated yet, maybe because of lack of input data, such as hours worked by some employees. Some computations could be programmed to decide not to proceed at all in that case; other processes would not be impeded unless they require one of the records which have not yet been brought up to date. We refer to data which are not input but describe the state of the database for the control of computations as *control data*.

We see that there is a relationship between the quality or completeness of our description of the data and our ability to specify the program sections which are combined to form data-processing computations.

Flowcharts   In order to describe complex processes and data flow, we sometimes have to resort to a graphic description of the dynamics of an algorithm, a *flowchart* as shown in Fig. 1-7. In these we will distinguish three types of activity:

Control flow, the sequence of instruction executed by the processing unit under various conditions. This sequence is described when flowcharts are used to document a programming algorithm.

Control-data flow, the flow of data elements whose effect is on the control flow of the computations. Typical examples are counts, references, control switches that indicate whether an operation is permitted, whether an area is full or empty, and so forth. These may be set by one program and used by another program.

Data flow, the flow of the bulk of the coded data as it is moved, merged, and processed to generate information for the benefit of the users of the system. This flow is typically between files, memory, and input or output devices.

The last two activities are sometimes difficult to distinguish, since often some control data are extracted during data processing. In many cases, however, the distinction is helpful. Figure 1-7 indicates the three types of flow in the process of using a library.

With modern techniques of programming, including the use of higher-level languages, well-defined modules, well-structured processes, and documented standard algorithms, the need for description of the program flow has lessened. Detailed descriptions of file and program state are much preferable unless process interactions are unusually complex.

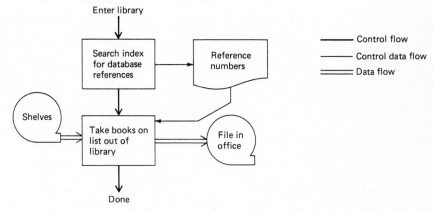

Figure 1-7 Flowchart notation.

1-6 BINDING

Many people in data processing still accept that the contents and the structure of the database have to be fully determined before procedures that operate on it can be written. This assumption defeats one of the major advantages that can be accomplished when we consign processes to computer technology. When designing and implementing a database system, it is desirable that methods be employed that allow development and change, so that we are not wholly dependent on perfect foresight. The fact that all our data and procedures can be manipulated by computation should make it possible to add data and relationships to the database at a later time. The operations involved in such a change may not be trivial, but a system that takes advantage of such growth possibilities can avoid obsolescence.

Whenever a decision is implemented which defines a fixed relationship between data elements, the number of choices available from that point on is reduced. Some knowledge has been used to make processing feasible. The process of fixing data or processing relationships is referred to as *binding*. At the final stage of data processing all relationships needed to generate information have to be bound. Methods that delay the binding of data definition and structure through the use of schemas are discussed in Chap. 8.

Binding Time The concept of binding is in common use to distinguish compiling, *early binding*, versus interpretive, *late binding*, processes. The range of binding choices in the database area is considerably greater than in the area of programming. Binding frequently takes place years before a new database system produces its first results.

Binding choices can be illustrated by expanding Example 1-1. Let us assume that an employees classification is not found in a single file (`job_classification`), but that there is a file for each department, and the names of these files are in an array `dep_class_filename`. Statements s3 to s5 then become a loop which appends the lists together.

Example 1-3 Using departmental files for the 'raise' transaction

```
        . . .
      no_employees = 0;
      DECLARE dep_emp_list(1000) INTEGER, dep INTEGER,
          dep_class_filename(100) CHAR(8) EXTERNAL, filename CHAR(8);
s3:   DO dep = 1 TO no_depts;
          dep_emp_list = 0;
          filename = dep_class_filename(dep);
          OPEN FILE(job_classification) TITLE(filename);
s4:       READ FILE(job_classification) KEY(class) INTO(dep_emp_list);
          CLOSE FILE(job_classification);
s4a:      DO i = 1 TO 1000 WHILE dep_emp_list(i) ¬= 0;
              no_employees = no_employees + 1;
              emp_list(no_employees) = dep_emp_list(i);
s4b:      END;
      END;
s5:   PUT SKIP ...
```

This program is bound to the assumption that an employee, including a manager, is listed in only one department file. This constraint will have to be enforced when the departmental employee lists are created. Otherwise, if one manager becomes responsible for two departments, `raise` will give this manager a 21 percent raise instead of the 10 percent raise. Inserting after `s4a` the statements

```
      /* check for duplicated employees */
      DECLARE id INTEGER;
      DO id = 1 TO no_employees;
          IF dep_emp_list(i) = emp_list(id) THEN GO TO s4b;
      END;
```

releases the binding and resolves the problem at the time that `raise` is executed. An analysis of the program's execution will show that now retrieval processing takes much more computational effort. Late binding can be especially costly because it is done at a critical time, when the answer is needed, and because it has to be done on an element-by-element basis, rather than once and for all when the structure is defined.

Early binding may be chosen because it can provide considerable initial efficiencies. In a database a significant amount of binding occurs when the designer specifies the position of data elements within the files. Later modifications of bound structures will be extremely awkward and often cause inefficient processing when the opposite was intended. When new data types or relationships are to be added, a major reorganization of the file structure and modification of the associated programs may be required.

To avoid the cost of a major change a programmer may decide to put additional data elements into positions originally intended for other purposes. This situation is analogous to the making of machine-language changes in the output of compilers. Such situations are no longer acceptable in programming because of the low cost of recompilation; in the area of file management, the patching of file structures is still common. An example of such a patch is given in Example 1-4.

Example 1-4   A database patch

Given that the records of a personnel file have fields as follows:
```
name,address,sex,salary,military_service,date_employed;
```
and a field for maternity_leave is required. The records are used by many programs, even though only a few of them use the military_service field. The patch adopted is to use this field for maternity_leave whenever the sex field indicates a female employee.
```
IF sex='F'THEN maternity_leave = military_service;
```

In this example the decisions made at an earlier binding time determine the implementation of later system features. The patch will cause further problems as progress in sexual equality invalidates the assumptions made.

The lack of proper programming methodology and the pressures to patch rather than to do changes properly are a cause of frustration in many computer shops. The consequences are often cynicism and low productivity of professional personnel. Much of the design guidance presented in this book has as objective that decisions in regard to binding will be made in a knowledgeable manner. Both the users and the system maintainers have to be satisfied. The choice of binding time made by a database designer reflects a compromise between efficiency and flexibility.

1-7   CLASSIFICATION OF OPERATING SYSTEMS

Databases can be established using any of the large variety of operating systems that are available. Operating systems provide a variety of services, of which the major ones can be classified as:

Process scheduling
File-system support
Input and output support
Usage measurement

File systems include programs to maintain directories of files and assure their long-term security and programs invoked by the users to access, that is, read and write, the files during computational tasks. This book will be concerned with access to file systems, but as little as possible with the specific operating system aspects. Some aspects of usage measurement are discussed in Chapter 15, and the other two areas are briefly summarized here. This review is not intended to explain the material but is needed only to establish the vocabulary used throughout this book.

Scheduling is a system process which allocates the resources available to user processes or to jobs containing a sequence of processes that are submitted for execution on a computer. The resources consist of the computing capability provided by the Central Processing Unit (CPU), the core memory which contains the process, the file storage, and the input and output capability including the control of user terminals. The scheduling system will of necessity consume computing resources themselves in direct proportion to their complexity.

1-7-1 Batch Processing

Sequential scheduling of computations, or *batch processing*, assigns all available resources of the computer to one single process while it is running. Figure 1-8 provides diagrams of this scheduling method and other methods discussed in the remainder of this section. Only a few jobs will be able to use all the available resources effectively when we use the single job-stream batch method.

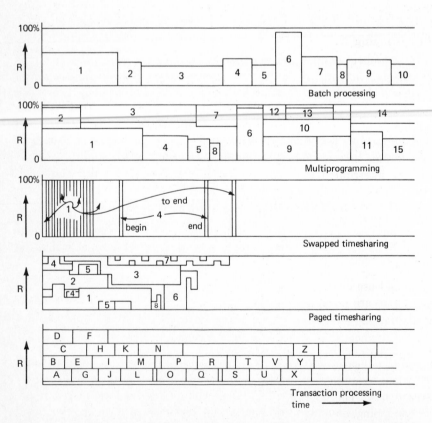

Figure 1-8 Resource allocation for five modes of system operation.

The sketches present the allocation of one resource. Actually all the resources mentioned above participate in the execution of a computation. When use of one resource reaches its limit, the full utilization of the other resources by the computations is prevented.

A typical example of unequal utilization occurs when reading data which are to be processed. Reading may proceed at the maximum speed of the input device, but the central processor (CPU) uses only a few percent of its capacity to perform the immediately required computations on the data. Subsequently a large summary calculation takes place, and the reading device waits for a new set of instructions from the CPU.

1-7-2 Multiprogramming

Multiprogramming attempts to utilize resources more effectively by allowing sharing of the resources among a number of computations according to their current requirements. If a computation cannot use a resource, it will give up its claim so that the operating system can start a process which has been waiting to use the resource. Individual computations will take longer, but if the resources can be distributed better among the computations, the total productivity will be larger. Some amount of processor capability will be taken from the total available in order to effect the switching between computations.

1-7-3 Timesharing

Timesharing splits the computations into slices in an attempt to strike a balance between the productivity of users and the system. Note that the users which interact on-line, at a terminal, are also a critical resource. They perform unfortunately very slowly but are quite demanding when they require computation. Fast response for on-line users is provided by limiting the competing computational slices to a small fraction of a second by means of a timer-driven interrupt.

New processes that users want to initiate are put in a queue with the processes that have been interrupted, and are executed in turn. The time between successive turns depends on the number of active users, the size of the slices, and the time it takes to switch from one slice to the next. A very critical resource in timesharing systems with many simultaneous users is the core memory, so that during inactive periods the users' processes may be "swapped" out of memory and kept on disk or drum storage. This storage space is generally not part of the storage space available to data files.

Timeshared use of CPU and core provides effective resource utilization when the computations are short. Many database operations deal with users at terminals, and timesharing permits the process to be inactive while the user responds. A computation which is longer than one slice will take longer to complete than it would have in batch mode, since all other active users will get their slices interposed. This computation hence ties up resources for a longer time. A database user often has files assigned exclusively to the computation, and these are now not available to the other users. The active user is well served, but the system incurs costs of slicing and swapping, and the periods of file assignment are longer, which may hold up others.

1-7-4 Paging

Since a single slice of a timeshared computation rarely makes use of all the available core memory a further division of the memory into pages improves sharing of this resource and reduces swapping volume. Pages for programs used by multiple users, such as database systems, may be shared. The number of pages actually required will vary from slice to slice. The pages are generally brought in on demand. Pages which show heavy recent usage are kept in core memory if possible. *Paging* capability can also aid the allocation process when multiprogramming in general.

1-7-5 Transaction Processing

The most important operating system approach for interactive databases is called *transaction processing*. This method assumes that the computations are naturally small, in terms of both space and time. The database system software is assumed to be already available, so that the users' computations consist mainly of calls to the database for reading and writing, and a limited amount of numeric and logical computing. Such a computation is called a *transaction*. Transactions are started as soon as possible after the user requests them and are permitted to run as long as necessary to fulfill their computational requirements. When a transaction comes to a point where it has to wait for a response from terminals or for data from files, it may yield to the system to enable another transaction process to be started or resumed. At times a transaction may avoid yielding to prevent release of a file which is not in a well-defined state. A transaction still ties up resources like files that have been exclusively assigned to it, but its total computation time will not have been lengthened by slicing and swapping. When a transaction is finished, it will inform the system, which can then free all allocated resources. Example 1-1 was written to show a typical transaction program.

A transaction is also formally defined as a computation which, after completion, leaves the database in a well-defined state, or at least not in a worse state than before. A failure during the execution of a transaction requires that the database be restored to its original state, Sec. 11-3 presents the required mechanisms. If only well-behaved transactions operate on a database, the integrity of the database will always be maintained. For example, if a transaction is to update a **salary** and increment the **budget** amount in a database, it will do either both or neither, so that the sum of the **salary** amounts will always match the **budget**.

A transaction-oriented environment often exercises close control over the computations to prevent one faulty computation from locking up the entire system. Limits are applied to program size, execution time, number of file accesses, and locking actions for exclusive use of files. This control is applied when the computation is specified or bound. At execution time little checking is performed and hence the operating system can be considerably less complex. A computation which grossly exceeds reasonable limits of resource consumption can be abruptly terminated. Typical design constraints are 25 calls to the database system, 2 seconds total execution time, and 25 pages of memory [Inmon[79]]. Many database actions can be handled most effectively in a transaction processing environment.

1-7-6 Sharing and Distribution

Any form of resource sharing is associated with a considerable overhead for operation and management. If there is no significant benefit to the use of shared resources, a dedicated system that is of just adequate size is preferable. Such a system will, of course, not be able to cope well with irregular high-intensity demands. Mixed systems, having local and distributed capability as well as access to central shared resources, are of great interest to system designers. A distributed system will have data and processing tasks that are of mainly local importance executed at a local computer. Requirements for data and processing that cannot be carried out locally will generate requests to remote computers. A logically remote computer may be another local computer or a specialized device attached to a central computer. Design issues of distributed computation will be covered specifically in Secs. 2-4-4, 5-3-3, 5-4-4, 7, 9-7-1, 11-3-1, 11-3-4, 11-5-4, 13-2-6.

1-8 APPLICATIONS

Application areas that employ database systems currently include:

Manufacturing with inventory management, Bills-of-Material processing, and production equipment scheduling

Government at all levels with records on taxpaying individuals and property

Financial institutions with lists of individual accounts, assets, and convertibility of funds

Service industries with lists of service capabilities and allocation schedules

Medical services with patient records, disease histories, problem classification, treatment effectiveness data

Economic models with production and consumption data for allocation and planning

Scientific research with collections of previously gathered data used to determine future research directions

Offices which are automating their document management

Libraries cataloging abstracts and indexes of their holdings

The background and references section cites some examples from each category. It will be useful to gain some understanding of the uses to which these systems are put, in order to obtain a perspective of the problems discussed. We note that information systems based on data in text form, often used for automated library support, tend not to use structured data but depend greatly on searches for keywords in titles, abstracts, and author lists. This book deals mainly with structured data, so that it is less relevant to applications that are based on content analysis.

The management of inventories in manufacturing, particularly where products consist of many parts and subassemblies, has been one of the earliest and most productive areas of database systems. A particular objective of these *Bills-of-Material* systems is the proper accounting and order scheduling of parts that are components of diverse end products and hence particularly critical. We will draw many examples from personnel files, since their contents and function are frequently self-evident. More interesting and potentially more significant applications are in food and energy resource planning.

Definition of an Application of a Database In any application of computers, the purpose of the effort should be spelled out in detail. Only then can one identify and judge the relevance of the data elements contained in the files, the processes required to manipulate the data, and the file structures which will enable the processes to be effective. Knowledge of the environment is needed to determine the value of the produced information. We also have to know the response time intervals required to ensure timely delivery of the system outputs. All these items provide the data for system analysis and the subsequent selection of the hardware. The dynamics of the application environment will provide useful information to decide the degree of formalization of the data organization and the corresponding binding times.

A statement of objectives and constraints, which specifies the goal and environment of the application, is an essential part of any project carried out in practice. Such a statement should also be presented with any project carried out as an exercise within the scope of this book. A frequent error in the formulation of objectives is the inclusion of the method or technology to be used as part of the objective. A proper place for such an account is the section which describes the results of the system analysis.

Objective statements which imply that the desire to *computerize* was the reason for development of a database should send a shiver down the spine of any computing professional. If the choice of methods or technology has been intentionally limited, a separate section of the objective statement should clarify such conditions.

1-9   REVIEW

We will treat files and databases which use files as an extension of the storage capability of a computer system. Their data contents remain under the control of the system. Since the user will never directly see the stored data, they can be organized and formatted by the system. This allows optimal use of resources. New information which enters the system or results that leave the system are handled via a separate input or output mechanism. Within the data storage organization, we distinguish two levels: the file system and the database system. The file system operates without knowledge of the contents of the data, whereas the database system will select data on the basis of the expected contents.

1-9-1 Overview of the Material to Be Presented

The chapters following will discuss the level of hardware and file systems, and we will continue with database structures only in Chap. 7. Chapter 2 will describe available hardware and reduce its complexities to a small number of quantifiable parameters. In Chapter 3 we will develop evaluation formulas based on these parameters which can be used to analyze appropriate basic file organizations. Chapter 4 will introduce more complex file designs. The design process, beginning from user requirements, is presented in Chap. 5. A central measure of goodness of a design is the overall economic utility of the services provided by the file system. Some primary elements of positive performance are economy of storage, speed of access to information, and speed and ease of update of data.

The database topics begin with database models, in Chap. 7. The description of models by schemas, the structure of database management systems, and their information-retrieval methods follow through Chap. 10. Related factors required for a successful database system include flexibility, as well as reliability, privacy, and integrity. These are discussed in Chaps. 11, 12, and 13.

This breakdown of the database problem into manageable subjects makes an analytic approach possible. A synthesis of preceding material is attempted in Chaps. 5 and 15. Chapters 6 and 14 discuss areas that are not of primary concern in this book but which contribute material important to database system analysis.

BACKGROUND AND REFERENCES

The structure of information systems has emerged slowly. A prophetic paper, published originally in 1945 (Vannevar Bush, reprinted in Kochen[74]), predicted machines for information retrieval, and in 1948 Shannon[62] published a paper defining the concept of information in a formal sense. Storage devices capable for databases became available in the early sixties, and some early systems such as MEDLARS for medical documentation (Katter[75]), SABRE for airline reservations (Desmonde[64]), and other systems for governmental planning (Clark[67]) were initiated. Expectations of effective use were tempered by disappointments and reassessments (Aron[69], Lucas[75], and in Riley[81]).

In parallel a scientific approach to database problems began to be concerned with the concepts of data and data structure (Steel[64], Mealy[67], Bachman[72], Senko[77], Kent[78], Lucas[81], and Tsichritzis[81]), and this, influenced by the developing ideas of structure in programming (Dykstra[71], Dahl[72], Parnas[72]), has led to an approximate agreement of structural levels; a taxonomy is given in Booth[73]. Lindgreen[74] has suggested a primary stress on the information-management level in database design.

The SHARE and GUIDE organizations of IBM computer users collaborated on a study of database requirements; a SHARE database conference (Jardine[74]) summarized effectively the state of the art in applications and systems. Another product of these user groups is a projection of growth and problems in the eighties (Dolotta[76]). Textbooks are now available which describe (Sanders[74], Kroenke[78], Atre[80]) or analyze (Davis[74], Everest[82]) management-oriented applications.

Applications The popular computing literature (DATAMATION, etc.) as well as specialized journals in every field of science carry regularly articles on automation which often involve databases. In the management area the HARVARD BUSINESS REVIEW carries regularly relevant material. Murdick[75] has collected a number of relevant early papers.

Databases are found in local (Mantey[75]) and national (Mendelsohn[71], Sibley[74], and Ghosh in Furtado[79]) government. The directions in office automation are surveyed in Ellis[80]. The use of computer databases in banks (Cannellys[67]), insurance (Allen[68]), utilities (Liu[68]), for sales support (Lucas[75]), in manufacturing of aircraft (Fulton[80]), computers (Mallmann[80]), and for the general Bill-of-Materials problems (see Bachman in Jardine[75]), as well as fashion design (Kunii[75]) has been described.

Databases have been applied in agriculture (Kendrik[80]), the social sciences (Bisco[70]), environmental control (Ouelette[75]), and to the study of history (Schneider[75]). The use of computers in information systems oriented toward bibliographic data is described in books by Salton[75] and Lancaster[79]. Chemical data (Anzelmo[71]) have long been cataloged, and applications in clinical medicine have a long history (Allen[66], Davis[70], Yourdon[72], Weyl[75], Barnett[79], Wiederhold[81]). Motivation for scientific databases is provided by Lide[81]. This list can be extended further by use of references in the works cited.

Operating Systems   Many of the system problems faced in the database area were first encountered in the design of operating systems. Textbooks in this area are BrinchHansen[73], Tsichritzsis[74], and Haberman[76]. The ACM COMPUTING SURVEYS is an excellent source for analytic material and further references. Transaction-processing systems have received less attention until recently; they are described in Martin[67], Yourdon[72], Davis[74], and Holt[75]. Clark[66] describes the data management in IBM-OS, using a large variety of arrows to distinguish control, the various types of control data, and data flow. Distributed systems are covered by Tanenbaum[81] and Davies[81].

Basic algorithms, such as sorting, table look-ups, and the manipulation of data structures as lists and trees in core memory will have been encountered by most readers. An introductory reference is Stone[74] and a thorough analysis of most techniques is found in Knuth[73F,S]. COMPUTING SURVEYS is also a useful resource here.

EXERCISES

1 Write a statement of objective for one of the applications mentioned in Sec. 1-8. Select a subject area with which you are familiar and in which you are interested. Many other exercises in this book can be based on the same application.

2 Provide a list of data elements which you think would be included in the application presented above, and justify their value with a short sentence for each.

3 Identify which elements are likely to have a dynamic relationship or function and hence will cause definitional problems.

4 Inspect a file-oriented program that you have access to and select statements which typify some of the classifications given in Table 1-1.

5 Rewrite the control-language statement presented in Example 1-2 in the language of the computer system you have available.

6 Write a query to the database with the patch shown in Example 1-4 which would produce an error.

7 Discuss the desired binding time for elements of a specific file-oriented program.

8 Classify the operating system you have available according to the categories of Sec. 1-7. List aspects of your system which you consider especially good or poor for database-system implementation.

9 Give an example of a very large database as defined in Sec. 1-1-1.

Chapter 2

Hardware and Its Parameters

On a clean disk you can seek forever

Thomas B. Steel Jr.
at SHARE DBMS Conference, July 1973

This chapter will summarize the basic types of hardware used to store data files: cards, tapes, disks, and drums. These descriptions will provide background for the understanding of their operation and performance; in other words, the concern here is what the devices do rather than how they do it.

This chapter contains two major interrelated sections: the first section contains a review of the types of hardware available, and the second section discusses the parameters used to describe hardware. Along with basic performance data, cost estimates are provided since the benefits of good performance cannot be separated from the expenses associated with powerful devices.

Section 2-3 presents hardware-related programming concepts, and the chapter concludes with a short discussion of storage system architecture. After this chapter there will be very few direct references to hardware in this book, since we will be able to describe all types of current hardware with a limited number of parameters and concepts.

New or improved storage devices are continually being developed, and any description reflects the state at the time of writing. The reduction of hardware descriptions to a small set of parameters makes it possible to use the analysis and design procedures in the remainder of the book also for devices which are not described or even not yet developed. The use of recent devices will make the problems in subsequent exercises more interesting. Values of parameters for the types of hardware discussed are given in Table 2-1. The abbreviations used in formulas can be found on the inside covers and in Appendix D.

2-1 BASIC HARDWARE CHOICES

Since this section lists the varieties of hardware and Sec. 2-2 defines the parameters needed to describe their performance, some cross referencing may be necessary when encountering new terms in the section below.

2-1-1 Mechanical Storage

Some use is still made of mechanical storage for data, using storage media which were already developed before the turn of the century:

>One such medium is the Hollerith or IBM *card.* These cards store data by having holes punched to encode a character per column. Cards with 80 columns of 12 bit positions each are the most common, other cards exist with 90×6 positions, and special cards are in use for attaching to inventory items.
>
>*Paper tape* is still used at times for storing communication messages and to record raw data from measuring instruments. Holes, punched into eight *tracks* across according to the ASCII code (see Fig. 14-1), record data and a *check* bit.

These paper storage media can be used only once for the recording of data. The punching devices, being mechanical, are slower yet than the readers, which typically use light-sensitive sensors.

2-1-2 Magnetic Tape Storage

In traditional data processing operations magnetic tape was predominant. Two categories, typified by cassettes and reels of tape, offer distinguishable capabilities. Tapes and all other magnetic surface devices have identical performance characteristics when reading or writing. Figure 2-1 illustrates the principle of magnetic digital recording.

>Limited amounts of data can be stored by the use of *cassette* or *cartridge tape.* The magnetic tape in these packages is 0.150 inch (3.8 mm) or 0.250 inch (6.4 mm) wide and typically 300 feet (100 m) long. A single track of data bits is recorded along the tape, and a parallel track may be used for timing or addressing information. The low cost of purchase and storage of tapes makes their use attractive for local or intermediate storage requirements.
>
>Industry-compatible *magnetic tape* is $\frac{1}{2}$ inch (12.7 mm) wide, comes mainly in lengths of 2400 feet (732 m) on large ($10\frac{1}{2}$-inch, 267-mm) reels, and contains seven or nine tracks across its width. Table 2-1 assumes 9-track tape on 2400 foot reels, having a density of 800 bits-per-inch (bpi) (31.5 bits-per-mm), which uses *non-return-to-zero* encoding, as illustrated in Fig. 2-1. A *phase-encoding* method permits 1600 bpi (63 bits-per-mm). A gap of 0.6 inch (15 mm) separates blocks of data to permit starting and stopping of the tape between read or write operations.

Tape units which provide densities of 6250 bpi (246 bits-per-mm) have a smaller gap and provide the highest performance currently commercially available.

The term *bits-per-inch* or bpi refers to the linear density of bits in each track, so that the full width of the tape carries that many characters per inch of its length. On 9-track tape, a character is encoded into 8 bits, providing for 256 distinct symbols. The 8-bit unit, whether used to represent characters or a binary number, is usually called a *byte*. The extra track is used for error-checking information. The tape format which supports 6250 bpi includes a group code transformation, using five recorded bits for four data bits and an error-correcting byte in every eighth position, so that the actual recording density is about 9000 bpi (355 bits-per-mm). Error-checking and -correcting techniques are described in Sec. 11-2.

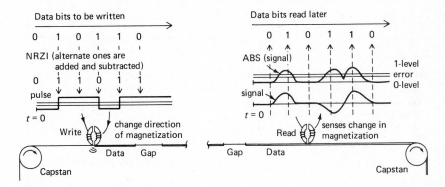

Figure 2-1 Digital-tape recording.

Conventional tape units have very poor random-access qualities. The time to read through an entire tape is on the order of 4 min for reels containing 30M* characters each. Many tape units allow tapes to be read in both forward and reverse direction. In order to reach a data item at an arbitrary, but known, position starting the search at another random position, a search procedure will have to read, on the average, a third of the length of the tape. This means that, even when using the ability to read in either direction, this operation will take more than 1 min.

High-density tape units using 1 inch (25.4 mm) or 2 inch (50.8 mm) wide tape have been manufactured and are being developed further. Techniques from video recording are influencing the design so that a high density of storage is achieved by writing data tracks across the tape. The distance between tracks is now determined by the relationship of the head assembly speed across the tape and the forward speed of the tape itself, rather than by the spacing of the parallel heads, as shown in Fig. 2-2. Searching can be performed using the audio and synchronization tracks along the tape edges. Search speeds of 1000 inches per second (in/s) (25.4 m/s) are being used whereas the conventional units move tape at 75 in/s (1.9 m/s) to 225 in/s (5.7 m/s).

An example of use of such a high-speed and high-density tape, made by Ampex, can store 5600M characters per reel and search in 28.8 s through a complete reel

---

* We will use the letter **M** to stand for mega, or one million, and **K** for kilo, or one thousand.

for a block identifier. When a block is found, the tape speed is lowered and data is read using transverse scanning. Helical scanning, as used in home TV recorders, is employed by the tape library shown in Fig. 2-19.

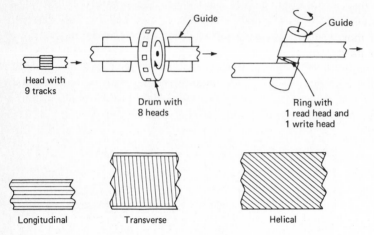

Figure 2-2 Tape-recording methods.

2-1-3 Rotating Magnetic Storage

The primary type of storage devices to provide large quantities of easily accessible storage for a computer system is the *magnetic disk*. It, and related *direct-access devices*, dominate database storage. We have the choice of removable media (disk packs) and nonremovable media; there may be either movable access mechanisms or fixed magnetic heads.

Diskpack Drives Most popular is the *diskpack drive*. Here a set of disks, numbering from 1 to 11, is packaged together in a stack. Multiple disks are separated by spacers from other disks in the stack. The disks are covered with a ferromagnetic oxide, similar to that deposited on tape, and these surfaces are hardened to withstand accidents and the heavy duty expected. The pack of disks can be placed on a spindle and each surface can be read by a recording head mounted on one of a set of arms that moves in or out, relative to the center of the disks, to find a specific track. The disks rotate continuously once started, and the heads may read or write information on the disk surfaces. Figure 2-3 presents a sketch of one platter mechanism of a two-platter disk drive. The entire unit has four heads, one for the top and one for the bottom surface of each disk. The drive listed in Table 2-1, an IBM 2314 type unit, has a stack of 11 disks rotating together. The top and bottom surfaces of the stack are not used, so that 20 recording surfaces are available for data. On some types of disk drives one of the recording surfaces is used to provide timing or position information.

Cylinders All recording heads in a disk drive move in or out together, but only one head may actually transfer data at any one time. No further physical movement of the arm is required to reach any one of the sets of tracks (20 in the

2314) that are radially equidistant from the center but on different surfaces. For these tracks the time required to switch from track to track is only due to electronic switching delays and is negligible. This set of tracks forms a hypothetical cylindrical surface at right angles to the physical access directions. Since we often use such a set of tracks together, we will use the term *cylinder* to describe the tracks which we can use without motion of the access mechanism. A disk unit will have as many cylinders as one of its disk surfaces has tracks. Data written sequentially will fill all the tracks of one cylinder before the mechanism will be stepped to the next cylinder.

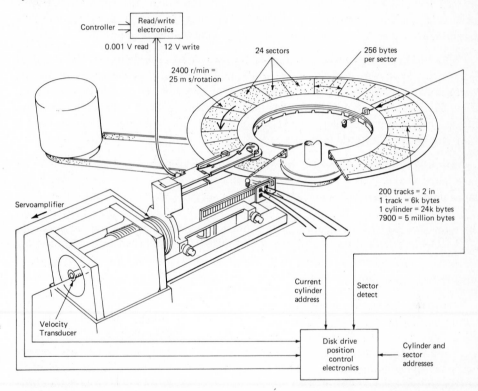

Figure 2-3 Part of a HP 7900 two-platter disk drive. *(Courtesy of Hewlett-Packard Co.)*

Many varieties of the basic design of a disk drive can be imagined. A number of alternatives giving either higher performance or lower costs, have been implemented and others are under development. In order to increase performance, there are disk units that have multiple moving heads and there are disks that have both fixed and moving heads.

In many modern devices, referred to as Winchester drives, the head and disk assembly is enclosed in an airtight and dust-free capsule. The clean environment permits closer tolerances and higher recording densities. Disk drives are now (1982) available which can store 2500M characters per pack while in 1970 28M was the highest capacity available in a disk unit of the same physical size and design.

A development in the direction of lower costs is exemplified by the flexible or *floppy* disks, circles of 7.8 inch (19.8 cm) diameter, cut out of coated Mylar material, and kept within an 8.0 inch (20.8 cm) envelope. Holes in the envelope permit access for spinning, writing and reading, and sensing the position of the disk. After the disk is inserted into the drive unit the disk may be spun via a pressure clutch. The disk is spun only while in use. The reading head touches the flexible disk during access, which permits a relatively high recording density but increases wear.

A generic name for all these devices is *direct-access storage drive* or DASD, but the term disk drive seems more convenient and adequate. Even though disk packs and disks are removable, it often happens that the disks containing an active database are never removed unless hardware maintenance is required.

Fixed Disks and Drums Another form of a disk storage unit is the so-called *fixed disk*. The term "fixed" refers to the fact that the disk cannot normally be removed from the disk unit. These units may or may not be equipped with moving arms. Some units have multiple heads for each surface, since the fixed disk position allows closer alignment tolerances. Each of these heads will then move only over a limited number of cylinders.

Head-per-Track Devices In another type of fixed disk design, the disk units have actually one head per track, so that there is no access arm to be moved and hence no delay required to move the heads to a specific cylinder position. The heads will be staggered over the surface since tracks will be closer to each other than the minimum possible separation of the magnetizing elements within the magnetic heads. Geometrically differently arranged, but logically identical to head-per-track fixed disks, are *magnetic drums* where the heads are mounted facing a cylindrical magnetic surface which is rotated past them. This head arrangement is sketched in Fig. 2-4.

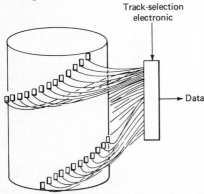

Figure 2-4 Diagram of a magnetic drum.

Head-per-track devices have very good access-time characteristics but provide relatively less storage since moving-head devices will typically access more tracks. We will use the term magnetic drum to refer any head-per-track storage units, disregarding whether they have disk or drum shaped recording surfaces.

2-1-4 Large-Capacity Storage Devices and Development

To provide mass storage at low cost, two approaches are followed:

    1 Increased storage capacity per unit to reduce storage cost per character

    2 Reduction of dependence on manual operation and mechanical parts to achieve more reliability and compactness

Magnetic disks are nearing their limits of storage capacity because of limits in the size of the magnetizable area, which is determined by the surface coating and by the physical dimensions of the read-write heads. Mechanical limitations are due to the positioning of head assemblies over tracks, even when feedback controls are used which align heads dynamically over the track being read. At the same time the great manufacturing experience with these disks makes their production costs low, and hard to match by other devices.

Increased storage capacity can be achieved by increasing the size of the units, but this adds mechanical delays to the storage systems. In order to increase data-storage capabilities without also increasing bulk, the space required to store each single bit of data has to be reduced. The use of tape or other thin media has the advantage that data surfaces, when not in use, can be densely packed.

Magnetic Strip Files attempted to combine the economy of magnetic tape with the accessibility of disks. Very wide magnetic-tape strips are assembled in cartridges. These cartridges are placed under a mechanism which selects the desired strip, moves it past a set of reading heads, and at completion of the reading cycle redeposits the strip back in its cartridge, as shown in Fig. 2-5. An NCR CRAM file of this type provides access to about 120M bytes at about $560 for a million bytes with an access time of 114 milliseconds. The mechanical complexity of these types of units has halted their development.

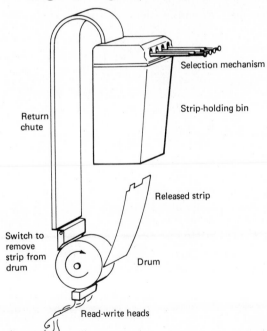

Selection mechanism

Strip-holding bin

Return chute

Released strip

Switch to remove strip from drum

Drum

Read-write heads

Figure 2-5 A strip file.

An approach to achieve an even larger, but slower accessed, on-line storage capacity is seen in *automated-tape libraries*. These are available both for conventional $\frac{1}{2}$-inch-tape reels and for extra-wide-tape strip cartridges. A mechanical picker mechanism selects the tape, carries it to the tape unit, and puts the reel on the tape unit so that it can be read conventionally.

Optical Technology The use of light rather than magnetism to store data has the advantage that the required area per bit is much smaller than the area per bit required for magnetic recording. Some large storage devices based on microfiche technology have been used for some time. Their cost and the maintenance required for the automated developing process have discouraged widespread use.

Storage devices based on laser technology have also been developed. In one system a bit is recorded by the laser burning a miniscule hole into the opaque coating of a Mylar strip. To read the data, a beam of light at a lower level of energy is guided to the bit position and will be transmitted if a "1" has been recorded. Other laser-based devices have been demonstrated but have not gained acceptance.

Optical disks in units without much mechanical complexity have been manufactured using photosensitive material written directly by intense light. Development of semiconductor lasers of adequately high power may make *write-once* optical disks feasible. The availability of disks for video entertainment raises great expectations in that area. Data areas of these devices can written only once, but read many times. We present some techniques for write-once storage in Sec. 11-3-3.

Semiconductor Technology The rapid development of integrated circuitry has made semiconductor technology attractive. We see applications that were based on secondary storage handled now completely in primary memory, and thus leaving the realm of databases. At the same time, new applications for secondary storage devices become feasible as their capacity increases.

Semiconductor storage can be organized in ways that differ from random access memory in order to serve specific database requirements. If cheaper devices or higher densities become possible, alternatives for databases will emerge. Very large arrays of storage cells may, for instance, be accessed only from the edges. The data will be shifted to the edges where amplifiers and connectors extract the data. Another alternative considered is to have the data processed within the arrays so that only results will have to be transferred out of the semiconductor chips. Economies can accrue because the space required for access paths to the data and for control of individual bits of storage can be minimized. One specific architecture of this type, *associative memory*, is presented in Sec. 2-4-2.

Semiconductor technology proposed for secondary storage includes charge-coupled devices, shift registers, and MOS circuitry. These devices compete currently mainly with drums and head-per-track disks. Electronic drums have the advantage that data transmission can be stopped and reinitiated without loss of data or the time needed for another revolution due to mechanical inertia.

A development which originated at Bell Telephone Laboratories is based on electrical control of small magnetic charge domains on ferrite surfaces. Under the influence of a magnetic field the surface charges, which are otherwise randomly distributed, will form electromagnetic *bubbles* a few thousandths of an inch in size. These can be rapidly moved along pathways by pulsed electric currents in conductors which have been deposited on these surfaces. These bubbles can be generated and detected by semiconductors. There are some operational similarities with disk drives, but the surfaces and the reading and writing mechanisms stay fixed while strings of data-carrying bubbles are moved along the surfaces between the sensing and the generating mechanisms.

2-1-5 Core Storage

Rarely used for data storage, but essential for processing, is *magnetic core* or semiconductor memory. By interpreting the term "core" as "central", rather than as a description of a doughnut-shaped ferrite ring, we can retain the term core memory for our main processing memory. Core memory is assumed to be volatile, i.e. removal of power on purpose or by accident will cause a loss of memory contents. This memory contains the instructions of the programs and the data elements while they are being used.

Core memory is randomly addressable at a level of one or a few characters at a time. These units, *words*, are of limited size to allow the processor to manipulate all bits simultaneously through the use of parallel circuits. This type of memory also is relatively fast, so that it can serve to tie other devices, which operate at different rates, together into one data-processing system. Data-storage units which depend on mechanical motion have considerable inertia so that they are not started, stopped, accelerated, or decelerated to suit processing needs. They operate asynchronously, and when they have completed a data transfer to memory, other devices and processes can use the results. Data obtained from storage devices are kept temporarily in buffer areas allocated in core memory. We will discuss buffering in Sec. 2-3-4.

In Table 2-1 values are given for two types of core memory. The data under "on-line" represent a modern fast processor memory; the data under "off-line" refer to a relatively cheap bulk storage memory. Both types may be properly considered on-line memories, although the system designer would attempt to concentrate processing in the faster memory. The costs of both types is decreasing rapidly.

2-1-6 The Cost of Storage

The performance of a system cannot be considered independently of its cost. We consider this aspect primarily in Chaps. 5 and 15. In Sec. 5-3 storage costs are assessed, and in Sec. 5-4 considerations which include the entire storage architecture, including the devices which connect the disks, etc., to the processors, are presented.

When the volume of data is large, infrequently used data may be kept *off-line*, on tapes or disks that are mounted by operating personnel when needed. In all other cases we will want to have the data available without manual intervention, i.e. *on-line*.

The cost of keeping data on-line shown in Table 2-1 consists of the cost of the storage medium, the cost of the device that can read and write the data, and the estimated cost of its connection to the computer's processing unit. The cost of keeping data off-line includes the cost of the materials themselves as well as the costs for properly conditioned space for one year. The values in the table combine all costs and are reduced to a cost per year using normal lease and maintenance rates. It is obvious that these values are only estimates.

In recent years hardware costs of storage devices and media have fallen by about 20% per year. The purchase cost for disk storage has been projected to decrease from $65/Mbyte in 1981 to $17 in 1985 and $5 in 1989. At the same time personnel and maintenance costs continue to rise. A design for a new system should include a formal projection of all of these costs for its lifetime.

Table 2-1   Performance and Cost Parameters of Some Storage Devices

Device:	Card	Mag.tape	Floppy	Disk devices — Pack	Disk devices — Giant	Disk devices — Fixed	Core	Units
Manufacturer		IBM	Shugart	IBM	IBM	DEC	Univac	
Model[a]	80 col	9 track	851 8"	2319[b]	3380	RS-64	1106	
Type		800 bpi	Double	Stack	Module	Single	Core	
Year[c]	1889	1954	1970	1962	1980	1956	1948	
Physical configuration:								
	Individual	Reels	Mylar	11 plates	Winch.head/track		cabinet	
	cards	of tape	$k=2$	$=20$	$=2 \times 15$	$=2$		Surfaces
	80 cols.	2400 ft	cyl$=77$	$=200$	$=2 \times 885$	$=32$		Tracks
Cost per year:								\$/M char.
Off-line	12	1.2	17	20	1		130K[d]	
On-line	1.2M	150	200	600[e]	20	8K	320K	
Capacity:								Char.
per track[f]	80	3K	8192	7294	50K	4K		
Min block	80	6	256	2	32	64	1	
Max block	80	45M	1024	7294	50K	4K	196K	
per device	16K[g]	33.7M	1.26M	29.1M	2520M	128K	1M	
Gap size	40	600	60	200	524	167		Char.
Block access time:								ms
Seek (s)	60M	90K	141[h]	60	16	0.26[i]		
Latency (r)	0.8	250	83.3	12.5	8.3	16.67		
Transfer rate(t):								Char./ms
Write	0.3	120	62	312	3000	125	8K	
Read	1.0	120	62	312	3000	125	8K	
Block transfer time (btt)[j]:								ms
(for B char.:	80	2400	1024	2400	2400	2400	2400)	
Write	267	50	34	7.7	2	19	0.3	
Read	80	50	34	7.7	2	19	0.3	
Rewrite(T_{RW})[k]		40	167	25	16.6	34	0	

[a] Model refers to the actual device described.

[b] A later model of the IBM 2314. Similar disks are made by other manufacturers, often with smaller seek times.

[c] Year refers to the first year of use for the general type of

[d] Value applies to another, more appropriate model (**Ampex** ECS).

[e] Cost in 1962, now approximately \$120 for 3330-type disks, see also Sec. 2-1-6.

[f] Data on track size and transfer rate assume 8-bit characters (char.), also called *bytes*.

[g] To permit cards to be entered in this table we assume that they are read on a 1000-card-per-minute reader with a capacity to read 4000 (2 boxes of) cards without operator intervention. Card output assumes use of a 300 cards-per-minute punch.

[h] Includes 50 ms to load the heads after having been idle.

[i] Electronic switching time.

[j] These values are based on the given block size B, and can be modified significantly by software sytem choices. They are included to simplify comparision of processing times.

[k] The rewrite delay estimates are based on assumptions stated in Sec. 2-3-7.

2-2 BASIC HARDWARE PARAMETERS

The hardware for databases will now be discussed in quantitative terms. This will provide parameters to use when evaluating alternate file organizations. The parameters used in this book are oriented mainly toward disk and drum devices. Equivalent parameters can be obtained for most other types of storage hardware if some operational assumptions are made. We will capture the salient features of a wide variety of hardware and hardware oriented system choices with half a dozen parameters, summarized on page 63 in Table 2-5.

Random-Access Time   The average time to reach a specific known position, which contains the data item that is wanted, from an undetermined previous position, is the most critical single parameter. This delay is referred to as the *random-access time*. The choice of this term is not particularly felicitous, since the time required to access data is certainly not random. The term is in use because direct access to data occurs in a sequence not determined by the device.

The random-access time is best broken down into two constituents, *seek time* and *latency*. The former refers to the positioning delay, for instance, the movement of the head mechanism of a disk, and latency is the rotational delay incurred until the data can be read. The time required for the actual reading or writing depends on the size of the unit of data, or *block*, and on the data-transfer rate of the hardware. So, before proceeding with an analysis of the time needed to get the data, we will present how the hardware organizes the data into blocks.

Blocks and Sectors   As can be seen in Table 2-1, the capacity of a track can be quite large. Copying such a large quantity of data into memory can take a long time and much memory space. It is hence common to divide a track into a number of *blocks*. A block becomes the unit of data being transferred. The division of a track into blocks may be implemented completely by hardware; such hardware units are termed *sectors*. There will be a fixed number of sectors, typically 10 or 16 per track, each capable of holding a fixed number of characters. In other disk units a track can be divided into sectors by a software-controlled formatting operation, which writes markers onto the disk to define the block boundaries. These markers are recognized by the hardware during normal read or write operations.

This division of a track into fixed blocks by formatting is sometimes called *soft sectoring*, and the alternative devices are said to use *hard sectoring*. If the size of a hard sector is inconveniently small, it is still possible to routinely use a number of sectors together as one block. If soft sectoring is not supported by hardware, system software may yet divide a track into smaller units, so that a reasonable block size is obtained.

A block then is a collection of coded characters or values, of a fixed size within a computer system or part of a system, which is moved as a unit between the storage devices and the core memory for processing. Once the right block is found, it will be read completely in order to obtain the error checking-and-correction information for the block. A block, be it composed of a sector, a number of sectors, a formatted (or *soft*) track sector, a track, or a software-defined portion of a track, will be the prime hardware data unit considered throughout this book. The data units that programs manipulate, and submit to the file system for reading or writing, are called *records*. Section 2-2-4 will discuss the transformation of blocks and records.

Block Size   Most files and databases use one single, predefined block size. Use of the same block size on different devices with differing track sizes can cause loss of storage space, but a careful selection of a block size which fits well into all devices can minimize this loss. The fixed block size reduces complexity in the device-oriented programs. The user programs will still have to deal with a variety of fixed and variable records.

The selection of the optimal size of a block depends on many factors, and in turn the size affects file system performance in a critical fashion. This chapter will discuss the factors which directly relate hardware performance to block size, but throughout the first half of the book the block-size parameter B will appear.

Records, the data units required for processing, vary in size from a few to thousands of characters. A large block size implies that more irrelevant data is moved around and that more core storage is required. A small block size means that more separate block-access requests have to be made to collect the data required for a task. The trade-off of these inefficiencies depends on the needs of the application and the design of the processing programs. Section 4-2-4 presents an optimization analysis for the block size for indexes.

We can now discuss hardware performance in terms of accessing blocks within tracks, and tracks and cylinders within disk storage units.

2-2-1 Seek Time

The *seek time* is the time required to position the access mechanism over the proper track. Figure 2-6 shows the seek times required to move over various track distances for a moving-head disk, here an older model of the IBM 2314. The relationship of distance traveled and time taken for this travel is seen to be not very linear.

On many modern disks the seek times can be approximated by a relationship of the form $s_c + \delta i$, where s_c is an initial startup time and i is the distance traveled, measured in terms of intertrack spaces traversed. Many disk units are designed so that the time to move to the nearest track, s_1 or $s_c + \delta$, is less than the time for one revolution. This minimizes the delay for reading cylinders sequentially.

To avoid the pain of actually evaluating travel distances for individual disk accesses we will use an average seek time s whenever a seek is encountered. Often an average value for the seek time is provided by the manufacturer. It should be based on a uniform access distribution over all tracks. A lower average seek time can be obtained if important and highly active files are placed on a few adjoining cylinders. In such cases it can be useful to calculate the corresponding expected average seek time.

Derivation of an Average Seek Time   To demonstrate the computation of the average seek time, the assumption of random distribution of track access will be used here, but other distributions can be handled similarly. In the case of a uniform random distribution, the likelihood of travel is equal from any cylinder to any cylinder. The distribution of distances to be traveled will not be equally likely.

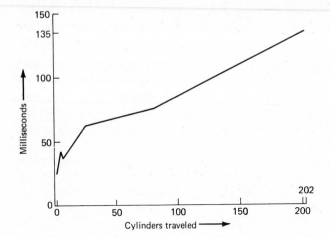

Figure 2-6 Seek times for an IBM 2314 model 1.

Starting from the extreme cylinders, the heads may have to traverse all of the disk, whereas from the center track, they never have to travel more than half the distance. Figure 2-7 illustrates this effect. It shows for some of the 200 possible starting cylinders *cyl* the distances that the reading head may travel to the left (**l**) or to the right (**r**).

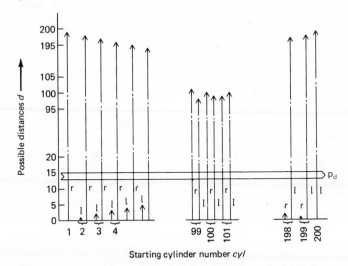

Figure 2-7 Travel possibilities for disk heads.

A seek to the left of distance i, $i = 1 \ldots 199$, is possible from initial positions $cyl \geq i + 1$; and a seek to the right of distance i is possible from $cyl \leq 200 - i$.

For a disk with j cylinders, a distance i, left and right, can be traveled from positions cyl if $cyl \geq i + 1$ and also if $cyl \leq j - i$. No travel will occur if the starting point is equal to the destination cylinder.

We will compute the probability of each distance to be traveled by counting the event, left and right, for each cylinder position. There are a total of $j(j - 1)$ actual travel combinations between the j cylinders, and we are assuming that they are all equally likely. We note that the probability of no travel is $pd_0 = 1/j$.

For any given distance i, $i = 1\ldots j-1$, the probability of travel of this distance pd_i is then

$$pd_i = \sum_{cyl=i+1}^{j} \frac{1^\dagger}{j(j-1)} + \sum_{cyl=1}^{j-i} \frac{1^\dagger}{j(j-1)} = 2\frac{j-i}{j(j-1)} \qquad i = 1\ldots j-1 \qquad \text{2-1}$$

This probability distribution is shown in Fig. 2-8a. The product of these seek distance probabilities and the time required to travel any of these distances gives the expected seek time distribution. The expected average seek time s for this device, with the assumption of random access, is

$$s = \sum_{i=1}^{j-1} s_i \, pd_i \qquad \text{2-2}$$

where s_i is the seek time for distance i. A result is shown in Fig. 2-8b for the disk head travel times s_i presented in Fig. 2-6.

Devices with arbitrary seek delays can be evaluated using Eq. 2-2. The case of exclusive usage of fewer cylinders can be computed by limiting the range of i to the number of cylinders that are in use. A nonuniform travel distribution is handled by replacing the nominators($\dagger$) in Eq. 2-1 with functions of cyl and i which define the usage pattern for a particular situation.

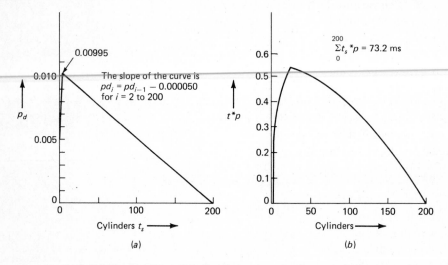

Figure 2-8 (a) Probability distribution of seek distances from random cylinder to random cylinder. (b) Probability distribution of random seek times.

Controlling Seek Times   The value of s may be effectively reduced by various programming techniques. We indicated already that when a file occupies a limited number of consecutive cylinders the average movement will be less as long as there is no other file activity on the same unit. For a large file this can mean distributing the file over multiple disk units. This will also provide overall access overlap between the two access mechanisms.

An alternating use of two files on the same disk will result in average seek times that are a function of the distance in terms of cylinders between these files. This could lead to substantially larger average seek times. In multiprogrammed and timeshared computer systems the probability of multiple use of a disk unit at any time appears large, especially when there are many users relative to the number of available disk drives. Transaction systems attempt to minimize this effect.

Whenever voluminous data can be accessed without interruption and in the same sequence that they are stored on the tracks, a seek needs to occur only once per cylinder. This seek will also require only minimal motion. The cost of seeks per disk access will then be a fraction of the average seek time. We will quantify that effect in Sec. 2-2-5 as a factor in the *bulk transfer rate*.

After the desired track has been located by the seek, it is still necessary to determine where the head is relative to the actual block on the track, since that is the unit we wish to transfer. The begin point for the tracks or of the actual blocks on the disk will be sensed by the access mechanism. There will be a rotational delay before the data can be read or written.

2-2-2 Rotational Latency

After the reading and writing mechanism of a disk drive or similar mechanism is positioned at the correct track, a further delay is incurred to reach the desired block on the track. The various delays between the completion of the seek and the actual transfer of data are referred to as the *rotational latency r* of storage units.

One type of delay occurs because the reading of the recorded data cannot commence at an arbitrary point. This is because we cannot synchronize the single stream of bits coming from the disk with any desired point in memory, until some identification marker is found. Sometimes a track begin point must be reached first, and then it still is necessary to proceed to the desired block. In most devices with fixed sectors a sector count is maintained so that the next complete sector can be transferred, if it is the desired one. If the sector was just missed, most of a revolution will pass before data transfer will take place. In software-controlled formats a block-identifying area or count area is read to determine which of the blocks that pass by is the desired one. A track-begin identifying area (*home address*) is used by programs only when a track has to be reformatted into new block areas.

We will first consider the case where a block can be recognized at its own begin point, so that as soon as the desired block is below the reading heads, the data transfer can commence. Then the average value of the rotational latency r is one half of the time required for one rotation of the disk, or

$$r = \frac{1}{2} \frac{60 \times 1000}{\text{rpm}} \qquad\qquad 2\text{-}3$$

where rpm is the number of disk revolutions per minute, and the latency r is specified in milliseconds. Typical rotational speeds are 2400 and 3600 rpm, leading to values of r of 12.5 and 8.33 ms.

Latency with Reading of Track Identifiers   Some disks have at the beginning of each track a field which permits verification that the positioning mechanism is at the desired track or cylinder. Then the above estimate has to be modified to account for the additional delay before data blocks can be transferred. The expected distance between the track begin point amd the data is dependent on the number of blocks per track. The average time required to reach the track identifier is r, and the average distance from the track begin to the beginning of the blocks, given b blocks per track, is $\frac{1}{2}(b-1)/b$ of the track length. In terms of the previous value of r we find a new total latency:

$$r' = r + \frac{1}{2}\frac{b-1}{b}\,2r = r\left(2 - \frac{1}{b}\right) \qquad\qquad 2\text{-}4$$

If there is only one block per track, the block is found at the beginning of the track and the latency remains r. For many and small blocks this value becomes nearly double the standard latency. This value of the latency is always applicable when writing into unpreformatted areas, since then no block recognition is possible. This occurs often in FORTRAN-based systems, since the standard for this language does not include file–definition capabilities, so that sector sizes are not defined prior to first use.

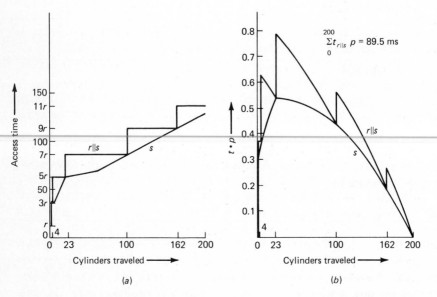

Figure 2-9 (a) Combined effect of rotational latency and seek. (b) Probability distribution of access times.

Seek and Latency Combined   Sometimes the values provided by computer manu-facturers have rotational delays factored into the seek times given. Such data, while being essentially honest, tend to blur the correct evaluation of specific system performance. Figure 2-9a portrays the combined effect of the two components, seek and rotational latency, for the IBM 2314 shown, with a one-block-per-track allocation. We expect a delay of r to find a block on the current cylinder and, since in this case a new record coincides with the beginning of a track, additional delays of entire revolutions due to seeks from other cylinders. The expected combined seek and rotational latency time provides only a few discrete choices, here r (no seek), $3r$, $5r$, $7r$, $9r$, or $11r$. By combining this fact again with the previous probability distribution for seek distances, we can obtain for a total expected access time an aggregate as shown in Figure 2-9b.

Certain disk units allow the seek process to continue automatically until a specified sector on the desired cylinder, included as part of the seek destination address, is found. The published seek time then may include the average rotational latency. Such *sector addressing* can reduce significantly the load on the channel which connects the disk unit and the main processor. In this chapter we ignore this type of design. In Chap. 5, where the total load of an application on a computer system is discussed, we will encounter such disk control mechanisms as class 5 devices.

Write Verification   In order to verify that information just written has been correctly recorded, an immediate reread may be performed after a write operation. A reread operation will carry out a comparison of the data from memory and the data just written and indicate mismatches. The operation causes the disk unit to be busy for one more revolution.

In current practice verification by rereading is performed infrequently. Errors on disks tend to be more often caused by poor handling of disks subsequent to the writing process than by writing failures or poor quality of the disks. We will ignore the effect of rereading in our analyses and trust that its effect can be easily inserted when rereading of written information is done.

2-2-3 Track Length and Track Capacity

The amount of data that can be read or written with one access determines the effectiveness of the random-access operation. If the entire track can be transferred as one single block, the largest possible block determines the *track length*. Otherwise the track length is equal to the product of the number and the size of the sectors provided per track by the hardware. The length of a track may be given in terms of bits, characters, or words. The entries in Table 2-1 are standardized by using characters, generally of seven or eight bits in length. On many disk units with hard sectors multiple sectors may be read as one block. Blocks will always have to fit within a single track, so that the track length places an upper limit on the block size. If yet larger units of data are required by an application, multiple blocks have to be used.

We have already introduced the fact that the contents of a track is frequently divided, by formatting or by software, into a number of blocks of length B each. At every break between two blocks there is a *gap* to permit the head mechanism to prepare for the next operation. The space required for this interblock gap, G, reduces the actual storage capacity, as is shown in Table 2-2. With high recording densities the gaps replace hundreds of characters. Small block sizes increase the number of gaps, causing significant amounts of wasted disk or tape storage. Large block sizes do make heavy demands on core memory-capacity and on transmission capability while transferring unrequired, but adjacent, data.

The gaps between blocks of tape depend on the tape system used. The older six-data-track tapes used 0.75 in (19 mm) and at their highest recording density, 800 bpi, had a value of G of 600 characters. Eight track tapes require 0.6 in (15 mm), or 960 characters at 1600 bpi; and the 6250 bpi tapes have a gap of only 0.3 in (7.6 mm), but this leads to a gap G of 1875 characters.

Formatted disks can have complex gaps. The gap on an IBM 3330-type disk consists of the equivalent of

1 Space equivalent to about 135 characters

2 A variable-length block-identification field, which may be considered useful space

3 A space between this identification field and the actual block of about 58 characters in length. This space allows for switching from reading – for the identification – to writing of data.

The total gap size G is hence about 200 characters for this device, more values appear in Table 2-1. The block-identification field is used by software to keep a name for the block.

**Table 2-2   Actual Storage Capacity of Tapes and Disks
for Various Formatted Block Sizes in Terms of Total Characters**

Capacity for	Characters per block B				
Device	$1^\dagger$	80	200	1000	3000
Tape 800/6	37.9K	2.67M	7.58M	14.2 M	18.9 M
Tape 1600/8	47.4K	3.25M	10.1 M	22.3 M	33.7 M
Tape 6250/8	94.5K	6.75M	22.1 M	60.5 M	107.0 M
Floppy disk	45.6K	1.06M	1.29M	1.386M	1.386M
Disk 6 (2311)	118K	4.16M	5.40M		
Disk 11(2314)	288K	12.8 M	20.0 M	24.0 M	24.0 M
Disk 11(3330)	730K	37.1 M	68.4 M	83.6 M	91.2 M
Disk giant(3380)	79.6 M	2 119.75M	2 272.68M	2 442.6 M	2 389.5 M

† Blocks of one character length are hypothetical for many devices. A minimum number of characters is often required to generate proper redundancy-check information. The USASI standard for tape specifies a minimum block size of 18 characters for information interchange.

Block Size and Track Capacity The reduction in capacity illustrated in Table 2-2 is caused mainly by the gaps between the blocks, and to a some extent by the loss when fitting these blocks into the track dimensions of the disks. In order to reduce the loss associated with a poor fit of blocks into the track size, as seen in the last two columns for the disks, block sizes which make optimal use of the track capacity for the device may be used. An odd block size will, however, create problems when different devices are used within one system or when storage units are replaced by newer devices. The desire to use identical block sizes on different devices will cause a compromise to be made. Optimal space utilization over many device types leads to small block sizes. Systems with a single hardware determined block size for all devices may use blocks of only 128 or 256 characters.

Block Pointers In order to refer to a block, we have to construct an address identifying the device and the position of the block on the device. Such a reference address is known as a *block pointer*. A block pointer provides a unique name for every block in a system. We will use block pointers in the remainder of this section but will discuss the implementation of block pointers in Sec. 2-3-3. The block identification field seen on soft-sectored disks is used by file-system software to keep a name for the block, and hence is a form of block pointer. The size of block pointers will be denoted by the symbol P.

2-2-4 Records and Blocking

Records are our actual units for data storage on the logical or file level. The fitting of records into blocks is referred to as *blocking*. Records may be of a fixed size, or may be variable in length, as required by the application. We denote the size of a record by R.

Since evaluation of files has to concern itself with performance in terms of records rather than in terms of blocks, we will now analyze blocking and derive some parameters which relate hardware and block based parameters to records. The basic parameter is the *blocking factor*, denoted by Bfr, which gives the number of records expected within a block. Three important methods of blocking are discussed next. When the methods require that all records fit within blocks, we call them *unspanned*. Unspanned blocking applies to fixed- and to variable-length records.

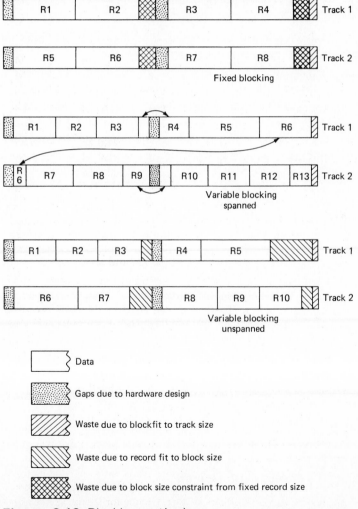

Figure 2-10 Blocking methods.

Fixed blocking An integer number of fixed-length records are placed within a block as shown in Fig. 2-10. We observe that for unspanned fixed blocking the blocking factor Bfr is an integer constant. Any unusable space in a block is wasted.

$$Bfr = \lfloor B/R \rfloor \qquad\qquad \langle \text{fixed†} \rangle \text{ 2-5}$$

Variable-length spanned blocking Records are packed into sequential blocks, and are broken at block boundaries. The continuation is indicated by a pointer to the successor block. *Spanning* is difficult to implement. Records that actually span two blocks are expensive to search and the resultant files are difficult to update.

Variable-length unspanned blocking Only entire records are placed within a block. There is wasted space in most blocks because of the inability to use the remainder of a block if the next record is larger than the remaining unused space. The number of records per block varies if the records are of varying lengths. Records cannot exceed the blocksize.

The value of Bfr for both types of variable-length blocking will be also affected by the marking scheme used to separate records, as discussed below.

Record Marks When manipulating records, it is necessary to know where records begin and end within the blocks. For fixed blocking, only the (constant) record length has to be known to be able to locate records within a block. When records of variable length are packed into blocks, data for marking the record boundaries within the block has to be added to separate the records. When spanned records bridge block boundaries, some reference to the successor block is also needed.

The external specification of the file format, obtained at the time of execution of an OPEN statement, will give the blocking type and marking convention in use. For fixed blocking only the fixed record length R has to be given. For variable length records three techniques, shown in Fig. 2-11, are available to mark the records.

The blocking descriptor may be a separator marker between the records, which can be recognized when searching through a block. Such a marker has to be unique so that data within the record cannot be mistaken for an end-of-record marker. When data are stored in the form of character strings, standard end-of-record characters are available to delineate records within blocks. These character codes are often derived from communication technology; examples are CR, GS, RS, and US shown in Fig. 14-1.

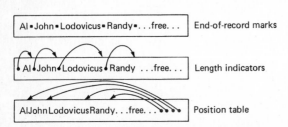

Al ▪ John ▪ Lodovicus ▪ Randy ▪ . . . free. . .	End-of-record marks
▪ Al ♦ John ♦ Lodovicus ♦ Randy . . . free. . .	Length indicators
AlJohn Lodovicus Randy. . . free. . .	Position table

Figure 2-11 Marking of variable-length records.

†We use ⟨condition⟩ to distinguish cases where a variable is derived in more than one equation.

Another method used to mark the record positions within blocks is the use of a length indicator preceding every record. The beginning point of the next record can be reached by skipping over the body of the current record. A third method uses a table within each block giving all the record positions in a block.

We can now compute Bfr for variable-length blocking. Each record requires one marker entry, and we assume that the size of one marker entry is about equal to the size of a block pointer P. For spanned blocking a block pointer of size P to its successor block may be included in each block, so that the pieces of a spanned record can be easily retrieved. Then

$$Bfr = \frac{B - P}{R + P} \qquad \langle\text{var-spanned}\rangle \text{ 2-6}$$

With unspanned variable-length blocking an average of $\frac{1}{2}R$ will be wasted because of the fitting problem, but no successor pointer is required. Here

$$Bfr = \frac{B - \frac{1}{2}R}{R + P} \qquad \langle\text{var-unspanned}\rangle \text{ 2-7}$$

Waste   A result of having gaps between blocks, unused space within blocks, and various markers, not all the space provided by the devices can be used. Since this factor is significant, we calculate now the *waste per record W* due to these factors.

The waste due to gaps W_G will equal the gap size G per block divided by the number of records per block, or *blocking factor Bfr*:

$$W_G = G/Bfr \qquad \text{2-8}$$

There is also waste due to unused space from blocking in each block. This is also allocated to each record as W_R.

With fixed blocking the record sizes are generally set to minimize the amount of waste, and the wasted space per block is certainly less than one record R. The bounds on W_R are hence $0 \leq W_R < R/Bfr$. We find fixed blocking frequently when records are small, and we recall from Sec. 2-2-3 that gaps are often large. For fixed blocking the waste per record is then

$$W = W_G + W_R \qquad \text{often} \qquad W \approx G/Bfr \qquad \langle\text{fixed}\rangle \text{ 2-9}$$

We will now consider the cases of variable length record blocking. The waste due to record fitting and marking has already been discussed in the evaluation of the blocking factor Bfr. For spanned blocking all the space in a block is usable and the total waste per record is

$$W = P + (P + G)/Bfr \qquad \langle\text{var-spanned}\rangle \text{ 2-10}$$

and for unspanned blocking we expected a half record loss per block, so that

$$W = P + \frac{\frac{1}{2}R + G}{Bfr} \qquad \langle\text{var-unspanned}\rangle \text{ 2-11}$$

Since Bfr is also a function of R, we note that in this last blocking method the waste increases quadratically or $O(R^2)$ with the record size. With a small value for P, and with Eq. 2-7 substituted, $W \approx \frac{1}{2}R^2/B + RG/B$. The waste due to fitting is now quite significant when records are relatively long relative to the block size. This factor has to be taken into account when estimating total storage capacity and effectiveness of data transfer. In order to arrive at an accurate estimate in critical situations, the actual distribution of record sizes should be considered. A discussion of tools to perform such analyses is presented in Chapter 6.

We recall that the size of a record, when spanning is not supported, is restricted to the block size. If this size is not adequate for an application, the problem of proper blocking is passed on to the next higher level of the system. Such inadequacies of the lower-level file systems make other parts of the system more complex and violate the modularity concepts discussed in Sec. 1-4-3.

2-2-5 Transfer Rate

We have up to this point discussed the two constituents of the random access time, the seek time and the rotational latency. When the proper track and rotational position is reached, the actual data block still has to be read or written from or to the disk. This third constituent of a data-transfer operation depends on the speed of actual data transfer. The rate or speed with which data can be transferred is known as the *transfer rate t*. It is measured throughout this book in terms of characters per millisecond or, equivalently, Kcharacters/s or also Kbytes/s.

The basic transfer rate is dependent on the design of the device used. On most devices the read and write rates are identical, although exceptions exist for mechanical and optical recording schemes. On disks the transfer rate is a function of rotational speed and recording density. Manufacturers often provide a raw transfer rate in terms of bits/second, which then has to be adjusted for the number of bits required to encode and check a block of 1000 characters.

The time to read a record of R characters is

$$T_R = R/t \qquad \text{ms} \qquad\qquad\qquad 2\text{-}12$$

and the time required to transfer an entire block is equal to B/t. Since the transfer of a block is such a frequent operation, we will write for the *block transfer time*

$$btt = B/t \qquad\qquad\qquad 2\text{-}13$$

Whereas the transfer rate is determined by the device, the block transfer time is also determined by the block size B. Since blocks can never be larger than tracks, we note that $btt \leq 2r$. In practice we see values of btt ranging from 1 to 20 ms.

Bulk Transfer Rate The transfer rate t given in the literature provided by a manufacturer is the instantaneous rate during the actual transfer. When transferring large quantities of data sequentially, there are periods when gaps and other nondata areas are being passed. At the end of each cylinder a seek will occur, during that time no useful data are transferred. In such cases, with continuous sequential reading or writing, the use of a *bulk transfer rate* can simplify performance analyses. We will now quantify the two factors which affect bulk transfer, and then combine them into a new parameter, the bulk transfer rate t'.

Effect of Gaps and Blocking on the Transfer Rate The effect of unused space due to gaps and due to blocking of records into blocks was expressed previously in terms of waste per record. We ignore any special gaps that some devices have at the beginning of a track and include only the gaps between blocks considered in computing W. The effect of this waste on the bulk transfer rate can be evaluated by considering an entire cylinder, with k tracks and nrt records per track. Reading of an entire cylinder takes a period of $k\,nrt(R+W)/t$ ms, and during that time $k\,nrt\,R$ data characters are transferred. The actual transfer rate for a entire cylinder of data is now computable in terms of W as

$$t_{cyl} = \frac{k\,nrt\,R}{k\,nrt(R+W)/t} = t\,\frac{R}{R+W} \qquad \text{characters/ms} \qquad \text{2-14}$$

The value of W for various types of blocking is provided by Eqs. 2-9 to 2-11.

Effect of Seeks on the Transfer Rate In reading even larger quantities of data sequentially, we will have to cross over cylinder boundaries. One minimal seek is required once per cylinder. Even though seeks may be infrequent, the required correction may still be far from negligible because of the relatively long seek times on many units. On disks with few surfaces, seeks will be needed frequently.

In order to account for the effect of seeks, we will consider the seek frequency and seek time, and use the combination to predict an effective seek time per block s'. The assessment requires some understanding of the operating environment. In a multiprogrammed environment, competition may exist for the seek mechanism, so that a full seek time delay s may be incurred frequently, up to once per block. The effective delay per record is then $s' = s/Bfr$. But when interference is limited or can be controlled, the expected delay is much less. In the case where there is no interference at all, only a minimal seek delay will occur at the end of a cylinder. We will hence use the number of surfaces k to determine the size of a cylinder in terms of tracks and then determine a minimum seek delay. To evaluate seeks per record, the number of records per track nrt is also needed; the entire cylinder contains $k\,nrt$ records.

In general, but not necessarily, a seek to the next track (s_1) requires less than the time of one revolution ($2r$). The desire to keep $s_1 < 2r$ caused in fact the mechanical complexity which led to the complex seek-time curve shown in Fig. 2-6. Since we continue the reading of records at the beginning of the next track of the new cylinder, we have, if $s_1 < 2r$, a seek delay per cylinder of $2r$. We recall from Eq. 2-14 that one revolution can be expressed in terms of the time to transfer all records from a track, so that $2r = nrt(R+W)/t$. Combining these terms we find a minimum seek delay per record $s' = 2r/(k\,nrt) = ((R+W)/t)/k$.

The seek overhead per block for continuous reading s' is now bound by

$$\frac{1}{k}\frac{R+W}{t} \leq s' \leq \frac{s}{Bfr} \qquad \qquad \langle\text{bounds}\rangle \ 2\text{-}15$$

As a practical estimate, the seek time overhead per record, while reading sequentially, may be taken to be equal to the lowest value ($2r = nrt(R+W)/t$), but occurring at every track boundary, so that

$$s' \approx \frac{2r}{nrt} = \frac{(R+W)}{t} \qquad \qquad \langle\text{estimate}\rangle \ 2\text{-}16$$

Measurements indicate that this estimate is often still conservative and that in most computing systems interference is modest. If this factor is of great importance to the eventual success of the system, measurements of sequential read performance may be made, on the system to be used, to assure that the estimate is met.

Any assumptions of this type, regarding expectations of less than average seek times and seek frequencies less than once per block, should be well documented in any evaluation, so that effects of changes in the operating environment will not lead to unexpected and disastrous performance degradations.

Calculation of the Bulk Transfer Rate We obtained Eq. 2-14 above for the bulk transfer rate within one cylinder. For multiple cylinders we add the seek delay per record s' to the transfer time per record and its waste within a cylinder $(R+W)/t$, and obtain the bulk transfer rate

$$t' = \frac{R}{(R+W)/t + s'} \qquad \text{characters/ms} \qquad\qquad 2\text{-}17$$

where s' is chosen to reflect the operating environment as detailed in the reasoning leading to Eqs. 2-15 and 2-16.

To combine the two factors for the case of no interference, we consider the time to read an entire cylinder with k tracks and nrt records per track. During this time $k\,nrt\,R$ characters are transferred, and during this time the access mechanism passes each of the k tracks. The lower bound in Eq. 2-15 is based on the loss of an additional revolution once per cylinder for a seek and causes an effect per record of $s' = ((R+W)/t)/k$ or per cylinder of $nrt(R+W)/t$. The time per cylinder is the sum $T_{cyl} = k\,nrt(R+W)/t + nrt(R+W)/t = (k+1)nrt(R+W)/t$. The bulk transfer rate for the entire cylinder is hence

$$t' = \frac{k\,nrt\,R}{T_{cyl}} = t\,\frac{k}{k+1}\frac{R}{R+W} \qquad \langle\text{no interference}\rangle\ 2\text{-}18$$

A similar reasoning can provide the bulk transfer rate for the estimated value of the seek effect given in Eq. 2-16. Now $T_{cyl} = k\,nrt(R+W)/t + k\,nrt(R+W)/t = 2k\,nrt(R+W)/t$ and

$$t' = \frac{k\,nrt\,R}{T_{cyl}} = \frac{t}{2}\frac{R}{R+W} \qquad\qquad \langle\text{estimate}\rangle\ 2\text{-}19$$

We can compare this estimate with the value of t_{cyl} given in Eq. 2-14 and note that the seek interference halves the estimate of the bulk transfer rate, and doubles the time for sequential data-transfer operations. Factors in this estimate involved the interference per block and the seek distances expected. Since larger blocks take a longer time to transfer, a change in block size will not affect the estimate directly, although the total seek delays may be less.

Transfer of data at the bulk transfer rate, as computed above, can of course be obtained only if we do not have to delay the reading in order to perform major computational tasks. We will describe in Sec. 2-3-4 the conditions for computational interference required to make this transfer rate valid. In this section we considered the access interference by other, concurrent, tasks. In either case a system environment which creates significant interference will cause delays in the transfer operations, and such delays will in turn increase the opportunity for interference. The effect of interference on the bulk transfer rate quantifies one of the reasons for operating in a transaction-oriented operating system, as described in Sec. 1-7.

Use of the Bulk Transfer Rate The bulk transfer rate accounts for all minor factors when reading through sequences of records. It has been obtained for the actual data record size R, so that it can be applied to the units of concern to the user programs. When we apply the bulk transfer rate to entire blocks, only the actual size of the data in a block $Bfr{\times}R$ has to be taken into account, since the waste due to gaps and record fitting has been accounted for in the formula for t'. Whenever the instantaneous transfer rate t is used, gaps have to be accounted for when reading from block to block.

If a single record is to be read from a random file position, an entire block of size B has to be transferred from the file. The single block is read, following a seek and latency to arrive at the block, with a transfer rate t. Gaps between blocks can be ignored. In summary:

> **Sequential accessing of records** Use the bulk transfer rate t' applied to the record size R.
>
> **Sequential accessing of blocks** Use the bulk transfer rate t' and the actual data quantity per block $Bfr{\times}R$ or, if neccessary, the transfer rate t and all of $B + G$ to compute the processing time per block.
>
> **Random accessing of records or blocks** Since an entire block has to be read use the transfer rate t and the block size B after s and r to compute the transfer time per block, giving a total of $s + r + B/t = s + r + btt$.

When blocking, the fitting of records into blocks, generates little waste, we can ignore the difference between the net $(Bfr{\times}R)$ and actual (B) block sizes. The use of B where $Bfr{\times}R$ would be more appropriate will lead to more conservative values when estimating performance. There is little waste with spanned blocking or when fixed records fit precisely into the blocks. In those cases, the number of records per block, the blocking factor Bfr, can always be taken to be equal to the block size divided by the record size (B/R).

2-3 BLOCKS AND BUFFERS

We already have developed the concept of a block in the preceding section and will only review the definitions before proceeding with a number of subjects related to the management of blocks.

2-3-1 Blocks

A *block* is the unit of information actually transferred between the external storage devices and a working area, the *buffer*, in the core memory of the computer. The requirements imposed on buffer management to achieve good file performance will be one of the subjects to be discussed.

We presented three basic methods of placing records in a block:

Fixed blocking

Variable-spanned blocking

Variable-unspanned blocking

The effect of the blocking method shows up mainly in the quantity W, the wasted space per record. If, in subsequent chapters, the blocking method is not noted, use of the variable unspanned method can be assumed for variable-length records and fixed blocking for fixed-length records.

Mixed Blocking Techniques Sometimes blocking methods are not kept consistent throughout a file. An example of such an inconsistency exists in some file systems in regard to updating. To avoid complex update programs, new records are written unspanned into a file which is otherwise spanned, or blocking may be avoided altogether when updating. A traditional file access method, IBM-ISAM, uses this technique. The analysis of such files becomes more complex than the methods shown in the examples in the next chapters.

A mixed blocking strategy also can be employed for other reasons. In an operating system that provides a paged, virtual memory environment, it can be desirable to use pages as the basic unit of data transfer. Since the size of records, when using unspanned blocking, is limited to the size of a block, multiple pages may actually be combined into a block for file purposes. We find this approach used by IBM-VSAM, where a *train* of pages is the basic working unit (see Fig. 2-12). Within the train, records may span across pages, but between trains, no spanning takes place. Since the entire train is read or written together, for many considerations the entire train acts like a single block. More interference is possible, even when the pages are maintained in sequence. The total gap space, of course, will be greater than the gap associated with a block composed of a single unit; the blocking factor and wasted space per record are now

$$Bfr = \left\lfloor \frac{B - nppt\,P - \frac{1}{2}R}{R + P} \right\rfloor \qquad \langle \text{VSAM train} \rangle \ 2\text{-}20$$

$$W = \frac{G + \frac{1}{2}R/nppt + P}{Bfr} + P \qquad \langle \text{VSAM train} \rangle \ 2\text{-}21$$

where $nppt$ is the number of pages per train. Other aspects of this file-access method will be discussed in a detailed example in Sec. 4-3 (also see Fig. 4-15).

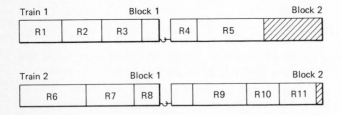

▨ Waste due to record fit to train size

Note that a train is not necessarily equal to a track.

Figure 2-12 Train arrangement of multiple pages per unspanned block.

2-3-2 Density and Locality

Other considerations which can affect blocking decisions are related to the growth of a file. Updating of information in a file may require that new records have to be inserted into the file or that longer records replace earlier, shorter records. The various types of file organization discussed in Chap. 3 all have their own method of handling insertions. Some of these methods will extend blocks by linking new blocks to the old ones using block pointers. Since the successor blocks are assigned at later times, they will not be accessible by sequential reading but require access to another point of the disk, and additional seek and rotational latency time.

Loading Density If we expect many update operations, we may actually leave some free space distributed within the file for future needs. Each block that is assigned when a file is created or enlarged will initially have some unused space. The fraction of space initially utilized is called the *loading density*. If sufficient free space is available within a block, data can be added without an interspersed random access. When all the free space has been used, a new block has to be fetched and linked into the file, but this block will also have space for several more updates. A disadvantage of a low loading density is, of course, that more blocks have to be read to get the same amount of data when the file is not yet full.

Equilibrium Density A system where the records themselves grow and shrink is forced to move and reallocate records within the blocks. Depending on the design of the file structure, some or much of the space for the file may become fragmented and unusable. Space no longer used can be allocated for reuse to retain the benefits of a low loading ratio. The density expected after a long period of operation is the *equilibrium density*.

Locality A record will be obtained with minimum delay if it is placed close to its predecessor. When a series of records has to be fetched, the clustering of the series is the most important factor in performance. A similar consideration is encountered in paging systems where it is desirable that all core storage references be located within a small number of pages. If this is achieved, there is strong *locality*. If serial references are far apart so that it is costly to get the next record, the locality is weak. Locality applied to records in a file is shown in Table 2-3.

Table 2-3   Locality

Strong locality

    Record is in the same block and the block is available in core.
    Record is in the next available block on the same cylinder.
    Record is on the same cylinder.
    Record is on a current cylinder of another device.
    Record is on adjoining cylinders.
    Record is on a known cylinder.
    Record is on an unknown cylinder, position to be computed using data in core.
    Record is on an unknown cylinder, position to be found by accessing an auxiliary file.
    Record is on a device not currently on-line.

Weak locality

If the data that are to be used during some transaction exhibit strong locality, we say that we are dealing with a clustered data structure. *Clustering* applies to data in one or more files, and we will encounter this term mainly in the design of databases which include many files.

In a system where there is a variety of devices, the considerations which determine strength of locality will become more complex. We will not attempt to define the strength of locality as a single, quantitative term, but we do use locality as a useful concept in file design.

2-3-3 Block Pointers

The *block pointers* that have been used to link blocks to each other require some more elaboration. We use block pointers to address a specific data field in secondary storage. To refer to a unit of data on a disk, a *physical address* will have to specify up to six components:

1 The number of the physical device
2 The number of the cylinder
3 The number of the surface
4 The sector or block number
5 The record number within the block
6 The field or character number within a record

The physical address composed of a sequence of such segments is both unwieldy and inadequate. Simple integer arithmetic applied to a segmented address will lead to bad values.

Another problem with a segmented address is due to the fact that different types of physical units in a computer system will have a different number of cylinders, surfaces, and blocks. This means that multiple address formats have to be manipulated within one system.

A further problem occurs when diskpacks can be exchanged on a physical device. In that case a physical address does not correspond to a specific item of data.

A final problem is that record sizes and field sizes are application dependent, so that the maximum number of these components in terms of the next higher components is not fixed. In most systems a *block* is the smallest fixed unit under control of the operating system.

Relative Addresses   An alternative to physical addressing is the use of a *relative address* over the entire file domain. Relative block, record, and character addresses are all used in practice. A relative address is an integer ranging in value from zero (or one) to the maximum number of blocks within the domain of the system which controls the storage of data. Figure 2-13 shows a sample system. There will be a unique translation of a relative address to a physical address and vice versa, which allows access to the physical devices to be carried out by operating system routines when a relative address is given. The application of such an algorithm is shown in Table 2-4.

Symbolic Addresses   It is also possible to assign a *symbolic address* or *block identifier* to every block or record. There is now no computable relationship between a symbolic address and its value. An address table will provide the physical or relative address for every block in use, and a look-up procedure is executed to obtain the block address whenever a block is requested.

The block identifiers can be integers which select the table entry, or can use key-to-address transformation techniques as *hashing*. Such methods are commonly used for the linkage of records in the ring-file structures presented in Sec. 3-6.

The use of an address table provides a flexible assignment of blocks to storage. Blocks or records can be moved, and the address table changed appropriately, so that references to the data which use the symbolic identifier remain valid.

Use of Pointers   We find hence three techniques used to refer to blocks or records of files. We will use the term *pointer* for any value used to reference a block or record. Any one of three pointer types:

> Symbolic block or record identifier
> Relative block or record address
> Physical hardware address

provides a means to identify a block or a record uniquely. Whenever a specific record is wanted, a pointer is provided to the file programs which fetch the data from storage. The alternate is to retrieve data in physical sequence. Then a pointer may be provided as a second output to identify the record which was retrieved. When data are stored, a pointer is also provided for subsequent retrieval.

Programs which are at a level closer to the hardware tend to use addresses more; higher-level software will use symbolic references more. A single level of software should, for consistency, use only one pointer type throughout. In the illustrations we will show mainly relative addresses.

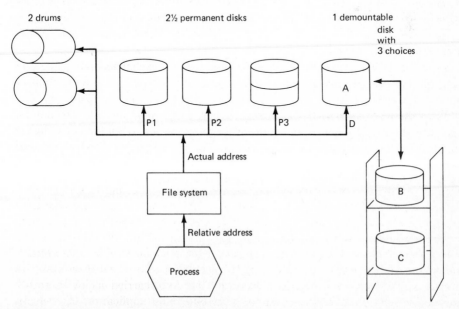

Figure 2-13 Relative block addressing.

Table 2-4   Relative Block Addressing

Equipment in the domain of the file system

Number	Type	Cylinders per unit	Tracks per cylinder	Blocks per track	*Total*
2	Drums	1	128	16	4 096
2.5	Permanent disks	400	20	8	160 000
1	Disk drive with choice of 3 packs	200	20	4	48 000
					212 096

Relative Block Address($RBA = 0$ to $212\,095$) allocated to the devices as follows:

Allocated RBA Range		Device type no.	Hardware address computation
$RBAbeg$	$RBAend$		
0 to	2 047	Drum 1	track$=\lfloor RBA/16 \rfloor$, block$=RBA \bmod 16$
2 048 to	4 095	Drum 2	track$=\lfloor (RBA - RBAbeg)/16 \rfloor$, block$=(RBA - RBAbeg) \bmod 16$
4 096 to	68 095	Disk P1	cylinder$=\lfloor (RBA - RBAbeg)/(20\times 8) \rfloor$, track$=\lfloor ((RBA - RBAbeg)\bmod(20\times 8))/8) \rfloor$, block$=(RBA - RBAbeg) \bmod 8$
68 096 to	132 095	Disk P2	etc.
132 096 to	164 095	Disk P3	
164 096 to	180 095	Disk D,pack A	cylinder$=\lfloor (RBA - RBAbeg)/(20\times 4) \rfloor$, track$=\lfloor ((RBA - RBAbeg)\bmod(20\times 4))/4 \rfloor$, block$=(RBA - RBAbeg) \bmod 4$
180 096 to	196 095	Disk D,pack B	etc.
196 096 to	212 095	Disk D,pack C	etc.

To refer from one record to another record, a field of the referencing record will be used to hold a pointer. The field size for a pointer P has to be large enough to hold a value adequate to address all possible records or blocks; in the example of Table 2-4 this requires six digits. A pointer field which is empty is denoted by Λ.

When the pointers associated with addressing techniques are used within a file to represent cross references, the resulting structure becomes complex and has to be managed with care. If blocks or records are not moved freely, relative addresses allow efficient use of pointer fields and accessing of data without requiring the look-up of a symbolic identifier. We can consider that the files have been bound with differing intensity or strength, depending on which pointer type is used.

2-3-4 Buffers

The area into which a block from the file is read is termed a *buffer*. The management of buffers has the objective of maximizing the performance or the utilization of the secondary storage systems, while at the same time keeping the demand on CPU resources tolerably low. The use of two or more buffers for a file allows the transfer of data to be overlapped with the processing of data.

Buffer Requirements Buffers can occupy a large fraction of the core memory resources of a system. Let us look at a simple medium-sized computer system where 30 users on terminals can manipulate files. A typical data-processing operation may involve three files. For each file one may use one or two buffers. Then 90 or 180 blocks will be occupying core buffers. If each block has a length of 1000 characters, 180 000 characters of the core memory are used for buffers, while the total core size may be 250K to 1M characters. Even in systems where core memory is backed up by paging storage on disk or drums, those pages which are involved in data transfer of files have to be kept resident in core memory. The demand made by a file system on core storage for buffers is hence an important part of the resource usage of a file system. The high cost of core storage relative to disk storage, as shown in Table 2-1, makes good buffer management very important.

Buffer Management In order to optimize the allocation of limited core buffers, a buffer-scheduling algorithm assigns buffer spaces to users as needed. As shown in Example 2-1, blocks requested more than once will use the same buffer. Any core memory not currently in use by other processes may be made available for the buffer manager; but when the requests exceed the available space, the buffer-scheduling process may have to delay a user process or deallocate buffer space of a lower priority process. Deallocation may also be done on the basis of low usage.

If buffer management is to be performed in a paged multiprogramming environment for the entire system, a separate buffer-managing program can be omitted. The paging program will have to take account of the need to keep active buffers resident. In either case, separate management or paged management, it will be useful to match the sizes and boundaries of the buffers, used by the file system, and the pages, used by the operating system, in order to minimize fragmentation of core memory.

Example 2-1   Block Request Processing by a Buffer Management Program

---

```
Q: Check if the block is already in core using a table look-up process.
   If yes, then give the process a core pointer to the
           buffer which contains the block.
   If no, then allocate a buffer,
           initiate reading of the block into the buffer, and
           delay the process by putting it into an operating system queue.
           The process is restarted at a suitable time beginning at point Q.
```

If only one record out of a block is needed, the remainder of the buffer space could be immediately released for other uses. Frequently it is beneficial to keep the contents of the entire block available. This will allow updating of the record and subsequent rewriting of the block with the surrounding records. If the remainder of the block has not been kept available, the block has to be read again before rewriting can take place. Also, if the process at the next request wishes to read a successor record, retention of the block can avoid the rereading from file which improves file-system performance.

Throughout the following evaluations we keep at least two buffers available in core, as well as directory and other critical information from other blocks which have been read previously. If the algorithms require more buffer space, the descriptions will state this fact explicitly. Two buffers, when used correctly, provide high performance in a file system when reading sequentially.

Double Buffering   The availability of two buffers permits reading into one buffer while processing the previous buffer contents. This is a prerequisite for the use of the bulk transfer rate t' for sequential reading; Fig. 2-14 illustrates the algorithm in detail. It is clear that the computational time required for processing one buffer must be less than the time used by the disk units to fill the other one. This algorithm is hence valid as long as the computational time required to process the records of one block $c_{block} = c\,Bfr$ is relatively small in comparision with the block transfer time, that is

$$c\,Bfr < btt \qquad \text{or} \qquad c\,Bfr < \frac{B+G}{t} \qquad \text{or} \qquad c < \frac{R+W}{t} \qquad \text{2-22}$$

The gaps between the blocks provide some leeway, (G/t), but it should be realized that the sending of the process wake-up message and buffer switching also requires time. This time is the *overhead* caused by buffering. We prefer hence the safer condition, $c\,Bfr < btt$.

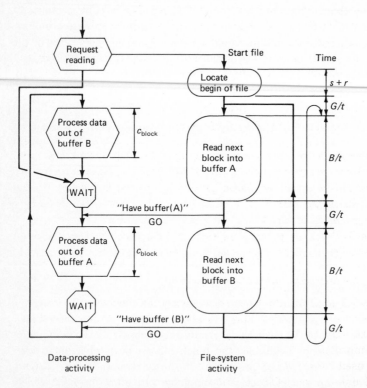

Figure 2-14 Use of two buffers for sequential reading.

The areas indicated as "Wait" are the periods, $btt - cBfr$, that the CPU is idle relative to this computation. Operating systems which provide capability for multiprogramming will attempt to allocate this time to other processes. In order to terminate the entire process, a file system will have the capability to pass the message " `No more blocks on the file.` " to the process requesting sequential data.

If the condition of *small computational time* is violated, the previous buffer is not free to be refilled and we will lose one revolution or $2r$ prior to reading the next block. This loss is very significant if this case, $cBfr > btt$, happens regularly. With two buffers, and $r > c_{block} > btt$, this loss is incurred for every two buffers, and the effective bulk transfer rate is reduced to

$$t' = \frac{2B}{2r + 2btt} = \frac{B}{r + btt} \qquad \text{if} \qquad r > cBfr > btt \qquad \text{2-23}$$

In most cases this causes a reduction of processing speed by several factors.

If $c_{block} > r$, it becomes reasonable to assume a random delay based on search and latency with an average value $c + r$ for every block, so that

$$t' = \frac{B}{c + r} \qquad \text{if} \qquad cBfr > r \qquad \text{2-24}$$

The use of more buffers to hold more blocks in core will, within the limits imposed by the computation time c, allow for a short time bulk-transfer rates higher than as shown in Eq. 2-22. Eventually all buffers will be filled and file reading will have to stop. While sufficient buffers are available, the rate of sequential reading or writing is then constrained by two factors, computation and device speed (Eq. 2-14),

$$t' = \min\left(\frac{R}{c}, \, t\,\frac{R}{R + W}\right). \qquad \langle\text{limit}\rangle \ \text{2-25}$$

The purpose of buffering is to achieve this minimum. Since the assumption of unlimited buffers is rarely true, the benefit of having more than two buffers is mainly to even out the effects of computation times that vary greatly, but where on the average $c \approx (R + W)/t$. Irregular computation can be caused in multiprogrammed systems by competing computations.

The requirement for two buffers becomes even stronger when blocks containing spanned records are to be processed, as discussed in Sec. 2-2-4.

2-3-5 Techniques to Improve Bulk Data Transfer

In many data-processing applications entire files have to be read periodically. Typical of such processing is daily account balancing, weekly preparation of payrolls, or extraction of data subsets for further analysis. Buffering provides the most important tool to improve sequential performance. We will present here three techniques that are used to further improve sequential processing. In the analyses of Chap. 3 we will not assume that these techniques are being used, since we concentrate there on transactions applied to individual records.

Alternate-Block Reading Where data are often read sequentially but core-memory constraints do not allow two buffers per file, there is yet a chance to avoid paying the full latency cost $2r$ for successive blocks. Figure 2-15 illustrates the method which can be used. By changing the relative addressing algorithm to arrange serial blocks on a track in an alternating pattern, the next block can be accessed after one block's worth of rotational delay. The interblock delay is $(B + G)/t$, so that the time to transfer and process one block is $btt + (B+G)/t \approx 2(B+G)/t$. The bulk transfer rate for this arrangement is then

$$t''_{\text{one buffer}} = \frac{1}{2} t'_{\text{two buffers}} \qquad\qquad 2\text{-}26$$

when using an alternate-block arrangement.

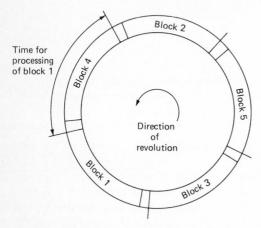

Figure 2-15 Alternate-block arrangement.

Scatter Block Reading A seek which commences the reading of a train of many sequential blocks can in some systems avoid the full latency time r to begin transferring data from a cylinder. If the file system can read any block of the train as it appears at the reading head, identify it, and deposit it in a buffer for later processing, useful data can be transferred as soon as some block can be read. We expect to have at least enough buffers available for every block on the track, so that any block appearing on the selected track can be read. The average latency delay is now equivalent to $\frac{1}{2}$ block or

$$r'' = \frac{1}{2}\frac{B + G}{t} \qquad\qquad 2\text{-}27$$

This type of operation is called *scatter reading*.

If the identification of the block can be carried out prior to the reading of the block, the block number i can be deposited into the buffer numbered i. Otherwise the file system will maintain a table with (`block_no, buffer_no`) entries and will direct record requests to the appropriate buffer.

The computational algorithms will still process the data records in a logically sequential order independently of the order in which the blocks were read. There are also instances where data can be processed in any order. For instance, if the sum of all values of a certain field within the records is required, the processing sequence is immaterial. Then scatter reading of blocks can allow significant reductions in reading time.

The algorithm also can be used for writing of data. *Gather writing* picks buffers from core memory as the appropriate blocks appear at the heads of the disk unit.

Track Stagger Staggering the begin point of tracks of successive cylinders provides minimization of the effect of rotational latency encountered when reading information sequentially. The amount of stagger is determined by the time required to perform a seek operation to an adjacent cylinder s_1. The amount of stagger has to be adequate to account for the mechanical variability in the seek time. Looking at Fig. 2-16, one can derive that the stagger ϕ in degrees should be

$$\phi = \frac{360}{60 \times 1000} \text{ rpm } \max(s_1) \qquad\qquad 2\text{-}28$$

where rpm is the number of revolutions per minute and the seek time for a one track distance s_1 is in milliseconds.

Stagger is especially useful if the seek time to an adjacent cylinder is much less than the rotational latency. For the examples used earlier the seek time for one track was just less than $2r$, so that the appropriate amount of stagger was $\phi \approx 360° = 0°$. Devices with few tracks per cylinder will also benefit more than disks with many surfaces.

Where no hardware track stagger capability exists, but sector addressing is available, the effect can be accomplished through sector renumbering by file software. Staggering between cylinders is easiest if done using the relative block-addressing mechanism, analogous to the method used to provide alternate-block reading within cylinders.

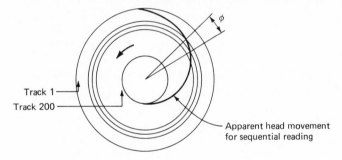

Figure 2-16 Stagger of track-begin points.

2-3-6 Updating Blocks

Updating of data in a block requires more time than either the read or write operation alone, since at least one read and one write is required. To append a record to the file, it has to be inserted into an existing block containing predecessor records unless that last block happens to be full. This last block may have yet to be read only to determine that it is full, unless counters, kept in a file directory in core memory, keep track of the status of the last block written. Change of an existing record will always require the block to be read so that all other records, and other fields of the changed record, are available.

After the reading of a block, the new record is inserted into the core memory buffer containing the block and the block is rewritten. In most instances it is necessary to rewrite the block into its original position so that the file structure remains unchanged. If the insertion of the record in the core buffer for the block is fast, it will be possible to rewrite the block during the next disk revolution. Such a rewrite operation will take one revolution or approximately

$$T_{RW} = 2r \qquad \text{if} \qquad c_{update} \ll 2r \qquad\qquad 2\text{-}29$$

This assumption is generally made throughout the text. This condition is not as restrictive as the one required to continuously read sequential data (Eq. 2-22), since $2r = nbt\,btt \gg btt$ for multiple blocks per track $(nbt > 1)$, and $c_{update} < c\,Bfr$ for one record being changed at a time.

For devices other than disks the rewrite time has to be specifically analyzed. For magnetic-tape units with the capability to *backspace* a block, the value $2r$ can be replaced by two block transfer times and two delays to account for the gaps, or $T_{RW} \approx 2(B+G)/t \approx 2B/t'$. Some typical values of T_{RW} are given in Table 2-1.

Conditions for Rewriting in One Revolution A more rigorous limit on the allowable value of c for disk rewrites can be deduced by inspecting Fig. 2-17. The assumption that $T_{RW} = 2r$, for the rewriting of a single block i, is valid when the time required for computation and update c is such that the following relation will be true:

$$T_{RW} = 2r \qquad \text{if} \qquad c < 2r\frac{(nbt-1)(B+G)+G}{nbt\,(B+G)} \quad \text{or if} \quad c < 2r\frac{nbt-1}{nbt} \qquad 2\text{-}30$$

If there is more than one block per track $(nbt > 1)$ and the system is designed so that the update has sufficient priority, this condition will generally be true.

If a rewrite is not accomplished in time, a second revolution is lost, so that $T_{RW} = 4r$. When there is a fluctuation of the computational time, sometimes one, at other times two or more, revolutions will be lost. The use of the average value of c in the analysis will give erroneous results, since the relationship between c and T_{RW} is not linear. Chapter 6 will present methods to evaluate such cases. If there is other use of the disk unit, a new search is required when the computation is completed and

$$T_{RW} = c + T_F \qquad \text{if} \qquad c \gg 2r \qquad\qquad 2\text{-}31$$

where T_F is the time to fetch a record without any benefit of prior conditions.

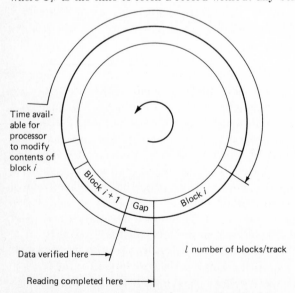

Time available for processor to modify contents of block i

Block $i + 1$

Gap

Block i

Data verified here

Reading completed here

l number of blocks/track

Figure 2-17 Rewrite-time considerations.

2-4 STORAGE ARCHITECTURE

We have, in the preceding sections, taken a variety of hardware types and a number
of basic, low-level, file-software implementation choices and distilled their effect into
a small number of parameters: seek time s, rotational latency r, and transfer rates
t and t'. We will use these parameters in the next chapters to produce measures
of file-system performance. In Sec. 5-4 we consider overlap of operations based on
these parameters.

Summary of Hardware Parameters   We will now summarize these parameters, in the context in which they were derived, namely, the evaluation of the
performance of files and databases which use the prevalent disk and drum devices.
We will then discuss the applicability of these parameters in more complex hardware
systems, where these parameters must be reassessed with care.

Table 2-5   Hardware Parameters for Disks

Parameter name	Unit	Code	Function	Condition
Seek time	ms	s	Mechanical delay	Device requires positioning
Latency	ms	r	Rotational delay	Block access or $1/2$ reaccess
Transfer rate	char./ms	t	Block transfer	Hardware speed
Bulk transfer rate	char./ms	t'	Sequential transfer	Requires buffering
Block size	char.	B	Fixed transfer unit	Hardware or system specified
Blocking factor		Bfr	Records per block	Blocking method and fit

The time to transfer a block having B characters, after positioning and latency
delays, is $btt = B/t$ ms. The random-access time to a block is then $s + r + btt$,
but a block being read sequentially is transferred in a time B/t' ms. A shorthand
notation for the time to reaccess a block, typically done to rewrite it with changed
data, is $T_{RW} = 2r$.

We note that the bulk transfer rate t' requires determination of the waste W
due to blocking and gaps G and consideration of a unit seek s_1 or a latency loss $2r$
whenever a cylinder break occurs. Buffering requires establishing that $c\,Bfr < btt$.

These, and other assumptions made, require periodic verification during the
design of a database system and the evaluation of its performance. The sections
where the parameters are derived may have to be reread to assure that the formulas
remain applicable in specific situations. We do not include a table of formulas here,
since that could encourage their erroneous application. The index can be used to
locate the page where the derivation of the *primary* form of the parameter begins.

It is clear that this simple parameterization leaves some holes uncovered in the
system-design process. In the remainder of this chapter we will raise some warning
signs, so that we can avoid distracting the reader from the principal subjects in
the chapters ahead. Whenever the simple hardware model used previously does not
hold, a system-design process has to reevaluate the results obtained in this and the
following chapters. The general methodology employed, however, should remain
valid.

Virtual Memory On many large operating systems the range of addresses available to refer to core memory is adequate for many file requirements. Typical addressing limits in large computers range from $5 \times 2^{18} = 1.280M$ to $2^{32} = 4096M$ characters. Only part of the memory space is real; the remainder is virtual and brought in by paging from backup drums and disks when referenced, as reviewed in Sec. 1-7. The use of *virtual memory* to support files is analyzed in Sec. 4-5. We find that the fundamental considerations developed here continue to hold, although the programmer will have less control over the actions of a file system based on virtual memory facilities.

2-4-1 Differences among Storage Devices

The relative importance of the hardware parameters differs among the various types of hardware. We emphasize in the next chapters disk-drive units, without ruling out other devices. This means that we stress the effect of the seek time.

Disk versus Drum Drums, and disks without moving heads, as well as most semiconductor memories do not require a seek. When the seek time s is zero, the effect of rotational latency and transfer rate becomes more important than the discussions imply. All the formulas developed will still hold when $s = 0$. The benefits of double buffering, for instance, continue to hold, and are in practice significant even when $c\,Bfr > btt$.

Disk versus Tape The methods discussed also apply to the use of tape for files. The track size of disks is simply taken equal to the tape block size when required. The extremely high value of the expected random seek times effectively removes some choices for file structure. Most tapes can be read in both the forward and the reverse direction and this provides the effective random seek time. If reverse reading is not possible, other values for the seek times will have to be substituted, depending on the method used to find a record. The simplest approach then is to rewind the tape and then seek forward. Better strategies can be used if the current position of the tape is remembered and used. Then tape may be spaced forward or backward to achieve minimal seek delays.

To find a predecessor block on a disk unit the strategy is to wait until the disk has rotated forward to access the block again on the same or on a predecessor track. On a reversible tape unit such a block can be read immediately in reverse mode. Otherwise it is possible to backspace over the block and then read or write it forward. This assumption was made for the rewrite time in Sec. 2-3-5.

We can incorporate the effect of rewrites for tape to the formulas of Chap. 3 by setting the value of the latency r to the block transfer time for tape. Similarly the single cylinder seek s_1 can be kept as $\approx 2r$. These simplifications introduce errors in the value of s for the seek times, but the effect is in most cases negligible because of the long seek times when tape is used.

Multilevel Access Devices Devices as strip files and other mass storage devices often have a two-level seek mechanism. A short seek is required to reach a strip position for a strip which is in the reading mechanism. A long seek is required when the strip has to be fetched from its archival container. An average seek time has to be computed, using the methods shown in Sec. 2-2, which takes into account the pattern of access to the file to obtain the proper balance of short and long seeks. If applications differ greatly in their use of the file, more than one seek time parameter may have to be computed.

2-4-2 Associative Hardware

In the devices presented up to this point we have accessed data by providing a specific address for the data to be manipulated. An alternative is to have the hardware look for data that satisfies certain requirements. An effect of this idea is that now searches to many records can proceed in parallel. *Associative addressing* locates records by matching one or several *key* fields of the stored records with a search argument. Multiple records may simultaneously satisfy the search request. To state this in a simple form: The search request does not specify *where* but rather *what* it is we are looking for.

We note also that associative hardware implements methods to access records which are described otherwise within this book in software terms. The use of specialized hardware typically increases performance but reduces flexibilty and capacity.

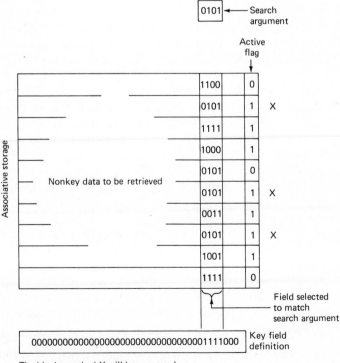

The blocks marked X will be processed.

Figure 2-18 Associative memory.

Associative Memory Associative memory uses semiconductor devices that are arranged into arrays with long word lengths – we will call them again blocks – in a manner that permits comparisions to be executed on all or many of these blocks in parallel. The data records are stored one per block within the associative memory. Within the data records are fields which may be selected as retrieval keys. A match register is used to define which parts of a record are to be taken as key fields, as shown in Fig. 2-18. The block size and match register will be fixed by the hardware design, and limits record sizes and field arrangements within the record. Every block may have an active flag to indicate if it is to participate in the next operation.

A search operation presents a search argument, which will select all blocks having active records with a matching key value, setting a marker X for these blocks. Subsequent operations will fetch a marked record at a time to the processor, resetting the marker, until all records are processed. Other associative operations may be available which permit such simple operations as incrementing, summing, shifting, or replacement to be applied to defined fields of all marked records in parallel. Such associative memories have been built only on a small scale, or used in highly specialized applications, for instance, processing of data obtained from radar observations. The evaluation of their performance is not covered in this book.

Associative Storage Storage devices have been built which permit associative searching for a value stored on its tracks. This capability can relieve the processor and its memory. Speed is gained if the search can proceed in parallel for multiple heads. For traditional high-capacity disks parallel reading is difficult to accomplish, since the entire head assembly is normally synchronized to follow a single, selected track. Tracks of drums, bubbles, and charge-coupled devices are easier to use in parallel. A microprocessor may be associated with every head, and each microprocessor can test and select data in parallel, so that all tracks of an entire cylinder are searched at the same time. The possible degree of parallelism is hence equal to the number of tracks per cylinder.

To retrieve data associatively, all track processors are loaded with a search program and a search argument. When a processor finds matching data, it may set a mark, or it may transfer the record to the central processor for further manipulation. If the central processor is just receiving a record from another track processor, a delay and possibly a second revolution will be needed.

The track processors can have relatively sophisticated programs, so that multiple and conditional matches can be performed on each record, without involving the central processor. Less data will need to be transferred. The record formats may also be variable, since the track processors can decode the record and field marking schemes that are used. Work in this area is progressing, although the degree of speedup is limited to the parallelism of the device reading mechanisms.

File Processing with Associative Hardware The use of associative storage and associative memory in a single system should improve substantially the cost of important processing algorithms (see Sec. 7-3) for database systems. Often matching records from multiple files have to be brought together for data analysis, for instance, `Sales by Region` and `Population_centers by Region`. An associative system would permit matching records to be brought together for analysis without expensive intermediate sorting **by region**, or repetitive searching, as is commonly done now. A speedup yielding linear performance $O(n)$, versus the best sort performance $O(n \log n)$ is hoped for. Such systems have not yet been demonstrated.

2-4-3 Multistage Storage Systems

Up to this point we have mainly discussed devices where the storage unit feeds data directly into the main memory. Storage systems exist which move the data through an intermediate stage between files and CPU. The intermediate stage may be a specialized processor or a faster, but smaller, storage unit. An example of such a system is a slow disk that uses small high-speed drums as intermediate storage.

Disk-Staging Tape Libraries Some automated tape libraries (see Sec. 2-1-4) are used only to load and unload disks rapidly. Their effectiveness is based on the observation that data files are used intensively for limited times, and then remain unused for long periods. These complex storage systems require again assumptions of usage patterns during the derivation of performance parameters which should be documented and verified when a specific data organization is being designed or evaluated.

Figure 2-19 shows a tape-cartridge library used for disk backup. Each cartridge contains 700 feet of 2.7-inch-wide tape. Data are recorded in helical format (see Fig. 2-2) with each diagonal track containing 4096 bytes across the tape. The tape is moved in steps from track to track. The data is transferred to a disk cylinder by cylinder in eight cylinder units. The intermediate disk unit is an IBM 3330 disk drive. One cartridge contains up to 202 cylinders, half the capacity of a 3330. The software system addresses the cylinders of the cartridge library as if the data were actually stored on many on-line 3330 disks.

Figure 2-19 Picker mechanism of an IBM 3850 tape-cartridge system.

File-Control Processors   In the large CDC systems the file devices are controlled by a peripheral processor, which obtains the data blocks to be read, verifies correct transmission, and then retransmits the blocks which have been read to the main processor.   As in the associative storage systems, data may be pre-analyzed and reduced within the the peripheral processors, so that less data has to flow to the central processor. The process is sketched in Fig. 2-20.

The proper analysis of performance of these systems becomes more complex than the cases of direct data transfer considered up to now. While there are some obvious delays in the system, the ability to reduce data and optimize placement of records can compensate partially for the delays. Since the main processor does not need to know where the data actually reside, the peripheral processor can control the file allocation. Active files or records can be placed on faster devices, or on devices which have less total load and interference. In order to perform this optimization the order of accessing data has to be predefined or usage prediction may be done dynamically based on usage monitoring. Alternate blocking and stagger may also be used.

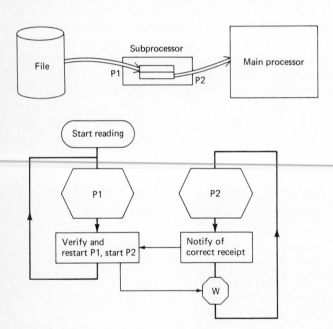

Figure 2-20 Indirect file access.

2-4-4 Distributed Systems

We have concentrated up to this point on approaches where the storage system is connected, directly or indirectly, to one central processor. There are a number of situations where the use of a central processor is not the best solution. Reasons for distributed processing include:

Functional A system carries out a number of distinct functions, and it is desirable to develop and manage these functions separately. If the activity within a function is greater than the interaction between functions, a system where functions are distributed to specialized processors will be more manageable.

Geographical If groups of users are located in distinct sites, it may be efficient if substantial local processing can be carried out on a local processor.

Performance Retrieval from local nodes avoids communication delays. Highly specialized nodes can provide high performance for certain functions, without having to alter other aspects of a data system. *Back-end* database processors or *front-end* communication systems are examples of such specialized nodes.

Autonomy When, in an organization, responsibility over business or scientific areas has been delegated, a corresponding delegation of control over the related information is implied. This may be achieved by distribution of the data, so that access privileges, quality-control responsibilities, reliable communications, and access convenience correspond to the pattern of responsibility.

Reliability If parts of a data system can be isolated, much of the system can continue to function while one processor or its storage devices have failed.

Growth If the demands on a data system grow, adding a new node can provide additional capacity without replacement of the entire previous system.

Networks In order to permit multiple processors to be integrated into one system, a communication network has to exist among the nodes. If the processors are close to each other, as close as they are to their storage devices, they could communicate at rates similar to the highest disk or drum transfer rates, about 1M characters/s. As distances increase to span buildings, the effective rate is reduced by a a factor of 10 or more, and using telephone lines by a factor of more than 100. Transmission of data over public dial-up lines is at best about 1K characters/s. We note that in distributed systems the interprocessor transmission delays become dominant.

Distribution It is hence important to distribute processing in such a manner that local processing reduces demands on the communication network. The processors in the network may be controlled by individual users or may be system subprocessors. We define subprocessors as processors carrying out highly specialized tasks in response to an overall system scheduler, for instance, the maintenance of an important file. Requests originate from a source user processor. At this processor the transaction request is analyzed and, if necessary, forwarded to other processors or to subprocessors. Other user processors may be needed because these users may maintain data required for a particular transaction. The logical capabilities of subprocessors are used to eliminate the need to pass data containing no information to the user machine. Frequently data blocks are fetched from a file only to obtain pointers to other blocks; and in these cases a capable file processor can carry out a large fraction of the work. Some specialized subprocessors may be used to merge and analyze data retrieved from one or more such file processors. Yet other processors in a network will carry out switching functions between the other nodes. The work of all the individual processors is still analyzed as before, but the range of design alternatives is greatly increased.

No comprehensive systems of this type exist today, but many components are available. In order to enable general solutions, it will be necessary to develop high-level data request and response protocols. We will discuss this issue in Chap. 10. In order to avoid excessive data transfer and to increase reliability in distributed systems, some information will be replicated in multiple nodes. We will deal with problems of this type in Secs. 11-3-1 and 13-2-5.

2-4-5 Directions

New approaches to data storage will continue to be developed. Many of these will be driven by innovation in hardware, and will not have been included in these discussions. The ongoing reduction in the cost of primary memory will permit some applications to avoid secondary storage entirely, or to use secondary storage only for backup purposes, but larger and growing collections of data will continue to strain current and future systems.

Since few truly novel systems have yet attained operational status, little experience is available to judge system-design alternatives. Alternate system organization strategies are often tried by industry while academic institutions provide analysis and evaluation. A detailed analytic evaluation of new and complex systems is often beyond the current state of the art, although many of the engineering level techniques for performance analysis presented here, combined with simulation and fundamental experiments, can direct further work and avoid expenditure of effort in fruitless directions.

BACKGROUND AND REFERENCES

Storage technology had its beginnings in card and paper-tape filing systems. The original Hollerith card was dimensioned on the basis of the dollar bill in 1890. The dollar and its value have shrunk since then, but storage costs have decreased even faster. Half-inch digital tapes were first used in 1953. Later in the fifties, UNIVAC computers used metal tapes and strong operating personnel. The recording density has increased by a factor of 100 since that time.

In 1956, the first disk units were used on RAMAC (Random Access Memory Accounting Computers), machines which required users to insert wires to specify the logic of their programs. Two read-write heads on one access arm were moved up or down, and inserted between a stack of 20 fixed disks. Seek times were often many seconds. Removable diskpacks appeared in 1962, and in 1973 diskpacks with integral head assemblies became available. The capacity increase from RAMAC disks with 5M bytes to 1 200M bytes for 3380-type units exceeds the advances seen in tape technology. Recording technology is described in White[80].

More than 30 different types of disk units are now on the market. Surveys of available devices appear regularly in the trade literature and are also obtainable from companies specializing in market surveys. Specific information regarding computer hardware is best obtained from manufacturers; frequently their promotional literature omits some of the parameters needed for a proper performance evaluation. A regular feature of computer publications is a projection of future hardware availability and costs; an example is Chi[82].

Prices of computing equipment can be obtained from the price schedules prepared for the General Services Administration (GSA[57,...]). Sharpe[69] provides an analysis of storage-device economics. Often obsolete equipment is used beyond its economic lifetime, GAO[80] cites examples.

An overview of storage technology (semiconductor, tape, disk, bubble, optical devices, automated libraries) is found in Hoagland[75] and Hoagland[79] discusses fundamental limits. Instructive descriptions of hardware-design considerations appear regularly in the IBM *Journal for Research and Development*; see, for instance, Mulvany[74] on the design of a diskpack system with an integral access mechanism. Design decisions leading to the IBM 3330 sector-addressing scheme are considered in Brown[72].

Developments in magnetic technology are covered in the IEEE *Transactions on Magnetics*; instances are Pugh[71], which provides an overview of storage devices and their use, and Michaels[75] on a bubble mass memory. Mallinson[76] presents a comprehensive tutorial and bibliography on magnetic recording. The use of a strip file is presented by Terdiman[70]. Bobeck[75] tells all about bubbles; Chang[78] and Doty[80] assess them for databases. The *Bell System Technical Journal* has many original papers in this area beginning with Thiele[69].

Papers describing new systems and technology appear regularly in the proceedings of the AFIPS conferences; Kuehler[66] presents the IBM photodigital mass storage unit; Gentile[71] describes tape files based on video techniques, and Johnson[75] describes the automatic-tape library which provides backup to disks. An issue of COMPUTER is devoted to optical storage; see, for instance, Copeland[82]. New architectures are presented annually since 1975 in the *Workshops on Computer Architecture for Non-Numerc Processing*, published by the ACM special interest groups SIGARCH, SIGMOD, and SIGIR.

A database computer using video mass storage is described by Marill[75]. Canaday[74] proposes a back-end computer for file control, and Epstein[80] introduces an implementation. The topic is surveyed by Maryanski[80].

Research efforts toward database machines using associative storage, for instance Ozkarahan[77] and Lin[76], are surveyed in a collection edited by Langdon[79]. Their principles are discussed in Su[80] and Hawthorn[82] provides a comparative analysis. King[80] has doubts about their effectiveness. System examples are found in Appendix B. An early associative memory system is described by Rudolph[72]. Addis[82] describes the language for CAFS, an associative file storage device produced by ICL. Shaw[80] proposes a system combining associative memory and storage which would use new algorithms to carry out database operations. The effectiveness of database machines was questioned by King[80].

Distributed systems are introduced in Tanenbaum[81] and developed in Davies[81]. Madnick[75] and Gardarin in Lochovsky[80] present proposals for distributed database architecture. Badal in Lochovsky[80] presents a global analysis for these systems. Their reliability is considered in Bhargava[81].

Programming for OS-360 files is taught by Chapin[68]. The relatively low-level programming and performance analysis methods presented have seen little formal publication; some are documented in IBM GC20-1649. Knuth[73S] reviews general aspects of disk-performance analysis. Gaynor[74] calculates seek times; Anzelmo[71] and Inglis[73] discuss record packing; Premchand[74] analyzes buffering; Salasin[73] evaluates record fetch costs; Weingarten[68] and Waters[72,75] discuss file placement to optimize access. Baber[63] evaluates record access on tape. Ghosh[76] concentrates on optimal sequential placement.

Other techniques are part of programming lore, noted at best as a paragraph in some system description. Many of these are specific to certain hardware combinations and have not been presented here. On large machines users have little control of the storage system, but on smaller personal or network computers there are many opportunities to improve storage-system performance.

EXERCISES

1 Derive the result stated in Sec. 2-1-2 for the average distance to be traveled when accessing tape randomly (one-third of the length of tape is used).

2 Why is the surface area available a concern when building a magnetic storage device? What is the advantage of many reading heads?

3 Read a manufacturer's description of a disk file or a storage device not now included and determine the parameters for Table 2-1.

4 What is the seek time for tape using the simple approach of Sec. 2-4-1? Assume that rewinding over b blocks requires $btt(5 + b/10)$.

5 Design a better method to seek tape blocks when a backspace operation, but no read backward operation, is available. Backspacing over a block takes as long as reading a block btt.

6 Compute the bulk transfer rate for an IBM 2314 transferring blocks of 300 chars.

7 Determine the net transfer rate seen by the user for this 2314 if for each block 1.0 ms of computation is required and three buffers are available.

8 Solve the same problem (by simulation?) if the computation time is evenly distributed between 0 and 3 ms.

9 Do the calculations from Exercises 6 to 8 for a system using a peripheral processor to transfer the file.

10 You are computing per block for $c_{block} = 7$ ms, while the file is being read sequentially and double-buffered. The values of btt and r are respectively 10 and 20 ms. A new computing application on the system runs with high priority and uses 50% of the CPU. How much is your program slowed down?

11 Calculate the average seek time for a file on a mass storage device having a seek time distribution as shown in Fig. 2-21.

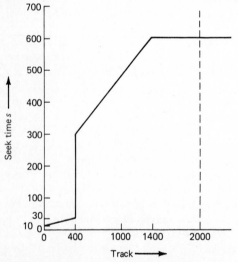

Figure 2-21 Mass storage seek-time distribution.

Chapter 3

Basic File-System Organization

This thinker observed that all the books no matter how diverse they might be, are made up out of the same elements: the space, the period, the comma, the twenty-two letters of the alphabet. He also alleged the fact which travellers have confirmed: In the vast Library there are no two identical books. From these two incontrovertible premises he deducted that the Library is total and that its shelves register all the possible combinations of the twenty-odd orthographical symbols (a number which, though extremely vast, is not infinite): in other words, all that is given to express, in all languages. Everything: the minutely detailed history of the future, the archangels' autobiographies, the faithful catalogue of the Library, thousands and thousands of false catalogues, the demonstration of fallacy of the true catalogue, ...

Jorge Luis Borges
from "The Library of Babel", a story in the "Labyrinths"

3.0 INTRODUCTION

The basic features desired of systems that store large amounts of data are fast access for retrieval, convenient update, and economy of storage. Important secondary criteria are the capability to represent real world information structures, reliability, protection of privacy, and the maintenance of integrity. The design of databases requires analysis for the prediction of performance, and this requires that the file organization can be easily abstracted. All these criteria tend to conflict with each other. The choice of the method of file organization determines the relative suitability of a system according to all these criteria. We will initially evaluate files according to the basic criteria. A good match of the capabilities provided by the file system to priorities assigned to the criteria, as determined by the objectives for the database, is vital to the success of the resulting system.

The number of possible alternatives in the organization of files is nearly un-limited. In order to make the selection process manageable, we describe and measure, in Secs. 3-1 to 3-6 of this chapter, six basic file-design alternatives. Most structures used in practice either fall into one of these categories or can be reduced to combinations of these methods. The selected methods are also reasonable in terms of the secondary criteria, i.e., they are fairly reliable and easy to analyze and implement.

The six types are the pile, the sequential file, the indexed-sequential file, the indexed file, the direct file, and the multiring file. The choice of these six has been influenced by the fact that all these basic models are closely related to systems in actual use. In other words, the collection of these six is not intended to repre-sent a mathematically minimal set of independent file organization methods. The collection does cover all common techniques.

The previous definition of a file can now be expanded to state that *a file not only consists of similar records but also has a consistent organization.*

With each description a simple performance evaluation is given. The accom-panying formulas use a consistent notation; the inside covers or Appendix C can be used to find the significance of the abbreviations employed. The formulas should be viewed as concise descriptions of the behavior of the files under normal conditions. The student should try to understand the formulas and may use them for reference purposes but should not attempt to remember them or apply them blindly. We ignore the programming complexity of the alternatives. A final comparative rating of performance characteristics for the six types of files is given in the introduction to Chap. 4. In the remainder of this initial section various general aspects of file-organization methods are described.

3-0-1 File Directories

Associated with a file may be a header or a directory record. This record contains information describing the position and the format of the records comprising the file. Different types of file organization put different requirements on the contents of the file directory. Much of the information that is kept in the directory is associated with storage allocation and with database concepts, and for that reason directory records are not discussed as part of the subsequent file analyses.

Typical data elements kept in a directory include the name of the file, the owner, the begin point, the end point, the amount of space allowed, and the amount of space actually used. It is worth noting here that the collection of the directory records for a number of files may in turn form a file. The owner of the directory file is typically the operating system for the particular computer. If multiple computers are used, the directory may be partially replicated in all computers so that the right computer can be selected if a particular file is needed.

A practical procedure to deal with directory records is to read these records once, when a computation begins using the file, and to retain the information for further reference. This process is referred to as the *opening* of a file. A corresponding process at termination of the use of a file, the *closing* of the file, will update the file directory if changes in the file have occurred that should be reflected in the directory.

3-0-2 File Descriptions

With each description of a file organization, new definitions will be encountered that are relevant for the subsequent file-organization methods. This implies that it is best to follow the material of this chapter in the sequence presented.

Each file-organization method is described and analyzed in conjunction with one specific record organization. While the combination presented is common in practice, it should be realized that many other combinations are valid. Such alternative combinations will produce different formulas for the performance parameters. The derivations are sufficiently simple to allow readers to evaluate other alternatives on their own.

Quantitative measures are necessary to evaluate file-system performance. For the four tasks outlined in Chaps. 1 and 2, seven measures of performance are needed. These seven measures are provided for each of the six file-organization methods. The seven measures used are:

R : the amount of storage required for a record
T_F : the time needed to fetch an arbitrary record from the file
T_N : the time to get the next record within the file
T_I : the time to update the file by inserting a record
T_U : the time to update the file by changing a record
T_X : the time needed for exhaustive reading of the entire file
T_Y : the time needed for reorganization of the file

To simplify cross referencing, we use corresponding section and paragraph names in this introduction and in the six sections which follow.

The six operations on files are executed by combining seeks, reads, and writes of blocks, so that the measures to be derived are based on the hardware parameters obtained in the preceding chapter. The use of generalized parameters provides a certain amount of independence from the physical specifics of the hardware, so that the analysis of file methods can proceed without considering details of the possible hardware implementation. The critical decisions in the evaluation of file performance in specific cases are reduced to the four questions below:

Is a seek required, or are we positioned appropriately; i.e., is s to be used?
How is the record located; i.e., is the latency 0, r, or $2r$?
Are we transferring only data blocks, or are we spacing through a file;
                      i.e., do we use t or t' for the transfer rate?
Are we measuring the net quantity of data or the space required;
                      i.e., do we use R or $(R + W)$ as a measure?

In a system we will have to consider the sum of all these operations. If we produce information, rather than operate an archive, the read frequencies should exceed the number of updates of files and records by a considerable ratio, perhaps 10:1 or more. Hence we are often willing to use data organizations which provide fast retrieval, even when this makes insert and update operations more complex. In this chapter we will measure the cost of these operations in terms of time required. In Chap. 5 storage and time requirements are reconciled by using financial measures.

Table 3-1   A Dense, a Sparse, and a Redundant File

(a) A dense file: data base course attendees

	Student No.	Class	Credits	Incompletes	Current work	Age	Grade type
1	721	Soph	43	5	12	20	PF
2	843	Soph	51	0	15	21	Reg
3	1019	Fresh	25	2	12	19	Reg
4	1021	Fresh	26	0	12	19	Reg
5	1027	Fresh	28	0	13	18	Reg
6	1028	Fresh	24	3	12	19	PF
7	1029	Fresh	25	0	15	19	Reg
8	1031	Fresh	15	8	12	20	Aud
9	1033	Empl	23	0	14	19	PF
10	1034	Fresh	20	3	10	19	Reg

(b) A sparse file: data base course attendees

	Student No.	CS101	CS102	Bus3	EE5	IE101	Exp. years
1	721	F72	F73		W73		
2	843	F72	W73				
3	1019		S72	S73			1
4	1021		S72			F73	
5	1027	F73		S73			
6	1028				W73		1
7	1029	F73	W73				
8	1031	F73					
9	1033						3
10	1034					F73	

The column group spanning CS101, CS102, Bus3, EE5, IE101 is headed "Courses taken".

(c) A redundant file: data base course attendees

	Prerequisite	Student No.	When taken	Years exp.	Acc. credits	...	Grade type
1	CS102	721	F73		43	...	PF
2	CS102	843	W73		51	...	Reg
3	CS102	1019	S72		25	...	Reg
4	CS102	1021	S72		26	...	Reg
5	CS102	1029	W73		25	...	Reg
6	Bus3	1019	S73		25 [3]	...	Reg
7	Bus3	1027	S73		28	...	Reg
8	EE5	721	W73		43 [1]	...	PF
9	EE5	1027	W73		28 [7]	...	Reg
10	IE103	1021	F72		26 [4]	...	Reg
11	IE103	1034	F73		20	...	Reg
12	Exp.	1019		3	25 [3]	...	Reg
13	Exp.	1028		1	24	...	PF
14	Exp.	1033		1	23	...	PF
15	none	1031			20	...	Aud

Note: the superscripts indicate records where redundant data already appeared.

Record Size   In order to gain economy of storage, we wish to store the data with a minimum of *redundancy*. Redundancy of data elements also increases the effort required when values of data elements have to be changed, since we expect all copies of a data element to present a consistent view of the world. Redundancy exists when data fields are duplicated, or when the description of the contents of the data fields is repeated with every entry.

Table 3-1 shows a dense file, a sparse file, and a redundant file. Each of these files presents information in a form useful for a particular purpose. These files are structured, and the descriptions of the data fields appear only once, in the heading of the files. When data are quite diverse, the rigid definition of fields will cause many fields to be empty and will lead to large, sparsely filled records. Section 1 presents a less structured organization, which can be advantageous for heterogeneous data.

Fetch Record In order to be able to use data from a file, a record containing the data has to be read into a processor. Fetching a record consists of two steps: locating the position of the record and then the actual reading. We use the term *fetch* when the retrieval of the record is *out of the blue*, that is, no operations to prepare for a simpler locate and read sequence have preceded this fetch. To read data efficiently, we have to locate the element to be read fast. A simple address computation, similar to the determination of the location for an array element in core memory, seems most desirable but leads to inflexibility in terms of data storage whenever the data is not tabular in nature or the entries in the table are not dense, so that entries cannot be directly located on the basis of a subscript value. The use of look-up tables or indexes helps in data retrieval when the position cannot be directly computed, but their existence increases redundancy. A look-up table, helpful in obtaining access to the other files, is shown in Table 3-2.

Table 3-2   A Look-up Table

Name	Student No.	Prerequisite entries (variable in number)			
Allmeyer, John	1031	15			
Bushman, Wilde	1028	13			
Conte, Mary	843	2			
Erickson, Sylvia	1034	11			
Gee, Otto	1021	4	10		
Heston, Charles	721	1	8		
Hotten, Donna	1029	5			
Jason, Pete	1027	7	9		
Makale, Verna	1019	3	6	2	
Punouth, Remington	1033	14			

Get-Next Record Isolated data rarely provide information. Information is mainly generated by relating one fact with another; this implies getting the next record according to some criterion. While Fetch can be characterized as an *associative* retrieval of a data element based on a key value, Get-Next can be characterized through a *structural* dependency. A successor record can be obtained most efficiently when related data are kept together, that is, when the *locality* of these data is strong. Since there may be multiple dimensions to data relationships, but only one efficient access sequence or *clustering* through the physical devices in which the data reside, a highly redundant storage design can help; or a liberal use of pointers to provide linkage to successor records can provide assistance. The reading, or writing, of records in a particular order is referred to as *serial reading*.

If serial reading is simplified by a physical ordering of the records, we can read the file containing these records *sequentially*. Table 3-1*c* shows the use of redundancy to simplify grouping of records that identify the prerequisite courses.

Insert Record Many files require the regular insertion or addition of new data records in order to remain up to date. Writing into a file is more costly than reading the file. Adding records is easiest if they can be placed at the end of a file, extending the file. When a record has to be put in a specific place within the file to permit future clustered access, other records may have to be shifted or modified to accommodate the insertion.

When data is stored redundantly, multiple write operations will have to be carried out to perform a complete file update operation. If the number of `Credits` of student `1019` has to be changed in the file shown in Table 3-1*a*, only one record is changed; but in the file of Table 3-1*c* three operations are required.

Each write into a blocked file will require the reading of a block in order to merge the data from the surrounding records before rewriting the entire block.

Appending Records Insertions to the end of the file, *append* operations, are frequent and handled differently in some systems. The address of the last block of the file is nearly always kept in the directory to make the end of the file easy to locate. A sequence of *append* operations may be performed without successive read and rewrite operations, since a block needs to be written only when full or when a batch of appends is completed. New blocks, allocated to extend the file, do not have to be read. The relative frequency of encountering a block boundary, which determines the frequency of block writes when appending, is $1/Bfr$. For this case of record insertion a separate evalution, based on these factors, could be made. Other considerations, however, argue against batching of appends.

With batching of appends an intervening failure of the computer system will cause multiple appends to be lost. If these append operations are part of distinct transactions, this approach violates the integrity constraints of a transaction. A *rewrite* of the block for every insertion of a record, including an append, is hence done for every transaction. When each append is a single transaction, no benefits are derived from batching.

We will ignore the difference of appends and general insertions in the analyses that follow and assume that a read and a rewrite of a block are used for all new records.

Update Record When data within a stored record have to be changed the new, updated record is created using the remaining data from the previous instance of the record. The old data and the changes are merged to create a new record, the new record is inserted into the position of the old record within the block, and the block is rewritten into the file. If the record has grown in size, it may not be possible to use the old position. The old record will then have to be invalidated and a new record inserted in an alternate appropriate place. Records in the look-up table shown in Table 3-2 will grow in size if a prerequisite is added.

Invalidation of the old record is actually done by rewriting the old record with a special field having a marker {`valid`, `invalid`} changed, or by filling the old record space with `NULL` characters or a message as "`* Deleted  ...   *;`". We will refer to such a marker as a *tombstone*.

For a variable spanned organization two blocks will have to be read, updated, and rewritten whenever the record spans blocks. The frequency of that event is also $1/Bfr$.

Read Entire File Some application functions require the reading of the entire file. Here again we prefer a dense, nonredundant file to avoid excessive time and errors due to the multiple occurrence of the same data item. If this cannot be achieved, the process of exhaustive reading has to maintain additional information either within the file or in separate tables. There is, for instance, no simple way to use the file shown in Table 3-1c to count the number of students or to compute the average credits accumulated by them.

Reorganization of a File Finally, it may be necessary to clean up files periodically, removing deleted and invalidated records and reclaiming the space for new data. Reorganization is especially important for files that have had many records inserted and deleted at random positions or when records were updated with new fields so that old records were invalidated. The frequency of this operation is not only dependent on application requirements but varies greatly with the type of file organization used. This operation, called *file reorganization*, has many similarities with the process of garbage collection encountered in some computer-language systems which provide dynamic storage allocation.

In a more informal manner we will use the term *retrieve* for both fetch and get-next, and use the term *access* to denote any reference to a file. The word *search* is used sometimes to describe the file activity for access prior to the read or write of a block.

3-1 THE PILE

The initial method presented is a minimal method. This method, the *pile*, is rarely practical but forms a basis for evaluation of more structured methods. Data in a pile is collected in the order that it arrives. It is not analyzed, categorized, or forced to fit field definitions or field sizes. At best the order of the records may be chronological. The records may be of variable length and need not have similar sets of data elements.

3-1-1 Structure and Manipulation

Some restrictions, though, will have to be observed to allow processing of data in order to extract information. A record has to consist of related data elements, and each data value needs to have an identification of its meaning. This identification may be an explicit name, a code, or a position which indicates its *attribute* type, such as `height` in Fig. 3-1. If multiple identical domains exist in a record, the attribute type also specifies the relationship to the object or event described by the record: `height of doorway`, `height of tower`. We will use in pile files an explicit name for the attribute description, since this matches best the unstructured form of the file.

Example 3-1 Data Element
        `height = 95`
In this example, the value of the data element is `95` and the descriptive name is `height`.

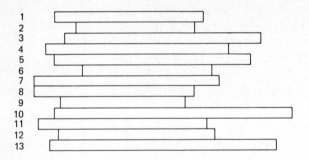

8 | name = Hagstrohm, age = 36, height = 5'7'', weight = 148, } { = 233;

Figure 3-1   A pile file with a representative record.

The set of two entries in Example 3-1 is referred to as an *attribute name-value pair*.

Just one such pair does not make a significant record. We need a number of such pairs to adequately define an object, and then, if we want to associate factual data regarding this object, we will want to attach to the record additional attribute pairs that contain further data.

Example 3-2   Data Record
```
name=Hoover, type=Tower, locale=Serra⊔Street⊔(Stanford), height=95;*
```

When information is to be retrieved we select records by specifying some attributes in a *search argument* and retrieve other attributes as the *goal data*. The attributes of a record to be matched to the search argument of the fetch request are the key attributes. The terms *key* and *goal* define two parts of the record for a query. Different requests may specify various combinations of attributes, so that we do not wish to preassign attributes to the role of key or goal data. The key identifies the record wanted in the file, and the goal is defined to be the remainder of the record.

The number of attributes required for a search is a function of the *selectivity* of the key attributes. Selectivity is the measure of how many records will be retrieved for a given value of an attribute. When we select a subset of the file according to the value of an attribute, we have partitioned the file into a potential goal set, and a set to be rejected. *Partitioning* can take place repeatedly using other attributes, until only the desired goal set is left.

The selectivity can be given as an absolute count or as a ratio. After the first partitioning, we can imagine that we have a file with a smaller number of records. It is important to isolate this subset of records in such a way that it will not be necessary to search all of the original data for a match according to the second attribute specified. The second search should be measured in terms of a selectivity ratio, which is applied to the partition of records produced by the previous search.

---

*We use ⊔ when it is desirable to indicate explicitly the presence of a blank character

Partition sizes are computable by multiplication of the file size n by the selectivity ratio if the selectivity of the first search specification is independent of the second search. Successive application of all other search specifications narrows down the possibilities until the desired record, or set of records, is obtained.

Estimation of Selectivity Using Example 3-2, the specification `Tower` applied to a file containing all objects in this world, or at least all towers, would restrict our search to the 10^7 towers in this world (assumption: one tower per 300 people and 3×10^9 people in this world). The name `Hoover` may have a selectivity ratio of 4×10^{-6} (fraction of Hoovers in the world, extrapolated from the San Francisco telephone book, combined with the assumption that half the towers are named after people), so that the second search attribute would yield 25 possible records. (Assumption: as many towers are named after Hoovers as after other family names). A third specification (the street name) should be sufficient to determine which tower is desired, or the nonexistence of a tower answering the given request.

If there are no attribute pairs left in our record beyond those required for the search, the only information retrievable is the fact that this object exists in our files. This frequently is an adequate goal. In the example, the height of the tower still is available as a goal-data element.

Example 3-3 Complex Attribute

```
..., addr.=(place=Serra␣Street, town=Stanford␣U.,
                         county=Santa␣Clara, state=California), ...
```

An attribute value may in itself be divided into a number of attribute name-value pairs to permit structural organization of the record, as shown in Example 3-3.

Throughout the remainder of this book, we will assign to the symbol a the total number of attribute types in the file under consideration, and to the symbol a' the average number of attributes occurring in a record. If the record in Example 3-2 is representative for the file, then a' for that file would be 4. In Example 3-3 we find 5 attributes. We do not need to know the value of the total attribute count a of an entire file in the pile organization.

3-1-2 Use of Piles

Pile files are found where data are collected prior to processing, where data are not easy to organize, and in some research on file structures. They also provide a basis for performance comparison within this text.

Data banks that have been established for military intelligence sometimes have this form, since the potential usage of a record is difficult to assess. In this type of application many attribute types may exist which defy a priori compartmentalization. Many manual data collections, such as medical records, also have the form of a pile. In pile files, data analysis can become very costly because of the time required for retrieval of a statistically adequate number of sample records.

Since much of the data collected in real-world situations is in the form of piles, we can estimate processing efforts needed to create more efficient file organizations for retrieval by analysis of the transformation from a pile.

3-1-3 Performance of Piles

The following performance parameter values can be associated with a pile organization.

Record Size in a Pile File density in a pile is affected by two factors: negatively, by the need to store the attribute names with the data, and positively, by the fact that nonexistent data need not be indicated at all. The effect is a relatively high density when the material collected is heterogeneous or sparse, and a relatively low density when the data are dense and the same attribute names occur in successive records. Since name and data are of variable length, two separator characters (= and , or ; in the examples above) are stored to mark each data element. We will denote the average length of the description of an attribute as A, and the average length of the value portion as V. For Examples 3-2 and 3-3 above A is 5 and V is 9 bytes.

Using these definitions we can state that the expected average record length will be

$$R = a'(A + V + 2) \qquad\qquad\qquad 3\text{-}1$$

Appropriate values for a', A and V will have to be based on an adequately sized sample. Techniques to reduce the values of A and V by encoding are discussed in Chap. 14.

Fetch Record in a Pile The time required to locate a record in a pile is high, since all the records may have to be searched to locate a data item that has a single instance in the file. If it has an equal probability of appearance anywhere in the file, we consider that at least one, and maybe all (b) blocks will have to be read. The expected average then is the sum of all the times to reach and read any of the blocks, divided by the number of choices, or

$$\text{Average blocks read} = \sum_{i=1}^{b} \frac{i}{b} = \frac{1}{2}(1 + b) \quad \approx \frac{1}{2}b \quad\quad \text{if} \quad\quad b \gg 1 \qquad 3\text{-}2$$

The time to read this number of blocks sequentially is then, using the notion of bulk transfer developed for Eqs. 2-17 and 2-19,

$$T_F = \frac{1}{2} b \frac{B}{t'} \qquad\qquad\qquad 3\text{-}3$$

Figure 3-2 illustrates the process. We now restate the sequential fetch time per record, using the fact that the file size can be expressed as either bB or nR:

$$T_F = \frac{1}{2} n \frac{R}{t'} \qquad\qquad\qquad 3\text{-}4$$

The use of the bulk transfer rate t' is appropriate here, since we read the file sequentially from its begin point, passing over gaps and cylinder boundaries, until we find the block containing the desired record.

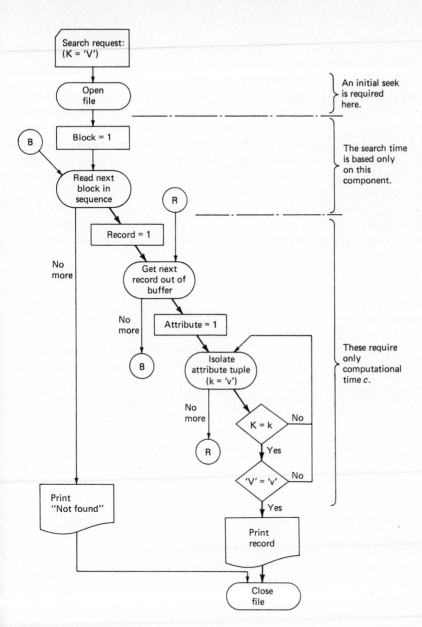

Figure 3-2   Search through a pile.

Batching of Requests   To avoid the high processing cost due to long search times, one can collect search requests into batches, since a batch of many requests can be processed in one pass through the entire file. The average search-length factor will increase from the value $1/2$ above to $3/4$ or $7/8$ for two or three requests. For more requests, this factor will approach 1, so that we simply state for the expected cost of executing a batch of L

fetch requests

$$T_F(L) = 2T_F \quad \text{for} \quad L \gg 1 \qquad \langle\text{batch}\rangle \text{ 3-5}$$

While this lowers the cost per item searched to $2/L\,T_F$, the responsiveness to an individual request is now twice the original value of T_F. In addition, there is delay due to the amount of time required to collect an adequate batch (L) of requests. Such batch operations are typically done on a daily cycle to make them profitable. Here the search costs are reduced as indicated above, and the expected delay is one day for any request. If many requests are processed in one batch, an efficient data-processing algorithm for the record content is required to ensure that the condition of Eq. 2-22 or $c < R/t$ still holds. Batching of requests applies also to other file organizations.

Get-Next Record of a Pile Since no ordering of records is provided in a pile, the potential successor record may be anywhere in the file. Since the position is not known, the time required to find an arbitrary successor record is also

$$T_N = T_F \qquad\qquad 3-6$$

We have to assume that information from the previous record is required to search for the successor record. If the specification of required attributes for the successor record were known initially, the search for this record could be made during the one combined fetch using the method for batched requests described above.

Insert into a Pile The time required for inserting a new record into a pile file will be fast because of its lack of structure. The address of the end of the file is known, a new record is simply added to the end, and the end pointer is updated. To obtain dense packing of records, the last block is read into core memory, the new record is appended, and the block is rewritten. The time required will be then

$$T_I = s + r + btt + T_{RW} \qquad\qquad 3-7$$

When disregarding block boundaries and batching of appends, as argued in Sec. 3-0, and using Eq. 2-29 we can simplify:

$$T_I = s + 3r + btt \qquad\qquad 3-8$$

We find, as we all know from personal experience, that a pile is very easy to update.

Update Record in a Pile Updating of a record consists of locating and invalidating the old record, and writing a new, probably larger, record at the end of the file, so that

$$T_U = T_F + T_{RW} + T_I \qquad\qquad 3-9$$

If only a deletion is to be made, the T_I term drops out. Deletion is actually effected by rewriting the old record space with a *tombstone*.

Read Entire Pile An exhaustive search in this file organization requires reading the file to the end. It is hence only twice as costly as a specific search, at least if the order in which the records are read does not matter:

$$T_X = 2T_F = n\,\frac{R}{t'} \qquad\qquad \langle\text{sequential}\rangle\ 3\text{-}10$$

If, however, we wish to read this file serially according to some attribute, the repetitive use of n individual fetches would cost $T_X = n\,T_F$. This extremely high cost is avoided by sorting the records according to the attribute of the search argument prior to processing. Records without a matching attribute may be deleted prior to the sort. The sorted file will provide sequentiality of the attribute values. The resulting file is no longer a simple pile.

Sorting It is well known (i.e., Knuth[73S]) that sorting can be performed in $O(n\,\log_2 n)$ steps. When sorting files the $\log_2 n$ term is related to the number of passes over the file taken by the sort; it is generally an integer. Each pass steps sequentially through the files. An initial pass over the file to be sorted arranges the records within each block of the file into sorted order and distributes the blocks for merging. Subsequent passes merge the sorted blocks into sorted sequences of blocks of increasing length until the sequence is of the length of the file. Although the files will be distributed over multiple devices their total size remains constant. A typical sort step involves a sequential read and a sequential write of one record. Each pass is evaluated based on the number of blocks b and the bulk transfer rate t'. An estimate of the time required to perform a sort on an entire file is now

$$T_{sort}(n) = 2b\,btt + 2b\lceil \log_2 b\rceil btt = 2n\left[1 + \log_2\left(\frac{n}{Bfr}\right)\right]\frac{R}{t'} \qquad 3\text{-}11$$

This estimate will be adequate for most cases. Since many systems have very specialized and efficient programs for sorting, it can be useful to determine the value of T_{sort} in a particular system from documentation or by experimentation.

Using a sort to put the file into serial order leads to an exhaustive search of

$$T_X = T_{sort}(n) + T_X(sequential) \qquad\qquad \langle\text{serial}\rangle\ 3\text{-}12$$

which will be considerably less than $n\,T_F$ for any nontrivial file.

Reorganization of a Pile If the pile file is updated with tombstones to mark deleted records, as described above, then periodically a removal of the invalidated areas is desired. This is accomplished by copying the file, excluding records marked with tombstones, and reblocking the remaining records. If the number of records added during a period is o and the number flagged for deletion is d, the file will have grown from n to $n + o - d$, so that the time to copy the file will be

$$T_Y = (n + o)\frac{R}{t'} + (n + o - d)\frac{R}{t'} \qquad 3\text{-}13$$

Here $\qquad o = n_{insert} + v$

The number of records d to be removed during reorganization is

$\qquad d = n_{delete} + v$

where n_{insert} is the number of records inserted, n_{delete} the number deleted from the pile, and v the number of records that were updated. The values of o and d are dependent on the file organization, so that this and later formulas using these parameters cannot be directly compared.

It also is assumed here and in the other evaluations of the term T_Y that the reading and the writing during the reorganization do not cause additional seeks by interfering with each other. This means specifically that if moving head disks are used, separate disk units must be used for the old and the new file. It also requires that sufficient buffers are available to fully utilize the disks. Overlap of disk operations is further considered in Sec. 5-4. Since reorganization is mostly scheduled to be done at times of low utilization, this condition can frequently be met.

3-2 THE SEQUENTIAL FILE

This method provides two distinct structural changes relative to the pile organization. The first improvement is that the data records are ordered into a specific sequence, and the second improvement is that the data-attributes are categorized so that the individual records contain all the data-attribute values in the same order and possibly in the same position. The data-attribute names then need to appear only once in the description of the file. Instead of storing attribute name-value pairs, an entire set of values, a column, is associated with each name. Methods to manage the attribute names will be encountered in Chap. 8 when the concept of a schema is introduced. This organization looks similar to the familiar tabular output that is generally associated with computers.

3-2-1 Structure and Manipulation of Sequential Files

To provide a sequence for the records, we define a key for every record. One or more attributes will become the key attribute(s) for the records in the file. The set of values for the key attributes typically identifies the object described by the record, i.e., the license number of a car or the name of a person. We expect to be able to identify records uniquely on the basis of their keys. The records in the file are then maintained in order according to the key attributes. One key attribute will provide the primary, high-order sort key, and if this attribute does not uniquely identify the object, then secondary and further key attributes can be specified until the order is completely determined. Serial reading of the file in this order now can be performed sequentially. In Table 3-1a and b the student number provides such an attribute, but in Table 3-1c there is no single field usable as a key. Two attributes, prerequisite and student number, can be combined to form a key.

Sometimes artificial fields containing sequence or identification numbers are added to obtain unique key attributes. The partitioning of the file, discussed with the pile file description, now is performed explicitly: the identification number is chosen to be unique for all the records and hence partitions the file into n individual records. Unfortunately, a separate computation may be needed to determine the identification number pertaining to the desired data.

With these structural constraints, and the attendant increased efficiency in tabular-oriented processing, a great deal of flexibility is lost. Updates to a sequential file are not easily accommodated. The fact that only the key attribute determines the sequence of the records introduces an asymmetry which makes sequential files unsuitable for general information retrieval. The common procedure to handle insertions to a sequential file is to collect them in a pile, the *transaction log file*, until the pile becomes too big and then to perform a *batch update*. This is done by reorganizing the file. At that time the transaction log file is sorted according to the same keys used for the main file, and the changes are merged into a new copy of the sequential file.

	Name	Age	Height	IQ
1	Antwerp	55	5'8"	95
2	Berringer	39	5'6"	75
3	Bigley	36	5'7"	70
4	Breslow	25	5'6"	49
5	Calhoun	27	5'11"	80
6	Finnerty	42	5'9"	178
7	Garson	61	5'6"	169
8	Hagstrohm	36	5'7"	83
9	Halgard	31	5'6"	95
10	Kroner	59	5'5"	145
11	McCloud	26	5'8"	47
12	Miasma	27	5'2"	75
13	Mirro	38	5'8"	52
14	Moskowitz	23	5'7"	50
15	Pop	38	5'3"	53
16	Proteus	41	5'8"	152
17	Purdy	37	5'9"	48
18	Roseberry	38	5'7"	70
19	Wheeler	23	5'8"	67
20	Young	18	5'8"	89

Figure 3-3 A sequential file.

A sequential file is restricted to a limited and predetermined set of attributes. A single description applies to all records, and all records are structurally identical. If a new attribute has to be added to a record, the entire file has to be reorganized. Every record of the file will be rewritten to provide space for the new data item. To avoid this problem, one finds that sequential files are sometimes initially allocated with space to spare; a few columns are left empty.

The fixed record layout is easy to construct by processing programs. Since similar information is found in identical positions of successive records, data-analysis programs are easy to write. The record written to the file is often simply a copy of the data in processor storage. Sometimes data are transformed by the processing languages so that files are written using a single data type, perhaps ASCII characters, but kept in binary form in memory to simplify computation. Strong support is given to such record-oriented data through PICTURE specifications in COBOL, FORMAT statements in FORTRAN and PL/1, and RECORD declarations in PASCAL.

Example 3-4   Record Declaration

```
DECLARE 1 payroll_record,
          2 name,
           3 initials CHAR(2),
           3 last_name CHAR(28),
          2 date_born CHAR(6),
          2 date_hired CHAR(6),
          2 salary FIXED BINARY,
          2 exemptions FIXED BINARY,
          2 sex CHAR(1),
          2 maternity_leave FIXED BINARY,
                etc.
          2 total_wages FIXED BINARY;
 ...
 ...
WRITE FILE (payroll_file) FROM (payroll_record);
```

The record layout which will appear on the file in the example shown is a direct representation of the DECLARE statement in the program. The declarations also imply fixed element and record lengths.

3-2-2 Use of Sequential Files

Sequential files are the most frequently used type of file in commercial batch-oriented data-processing. The concept of a *master file*, to which *detail* records are added periodically, has been basic to data-processing since its inception. This concept transfers easily from manual processing to computers, and from one computer to another one. Where data are processed cyclically, as in monthly billing or payroll applications, the effectiveness of this approach is hard to achieve by other methods. Data kept in sequential files is, however, difficult to combine with other data to provide ad hoc information and access to the file has to be scheduled if the requested information has to be up to date.

In order to combine data from multiple sequential files, sorts are performed to make the records of the files cosequential. Then all required data can be found by spacing only forward over the files involved. A sequential file can be in sequence only according to one key so that frequently the file has to be sorted again according to another criterion or key in order to match other sets of files.

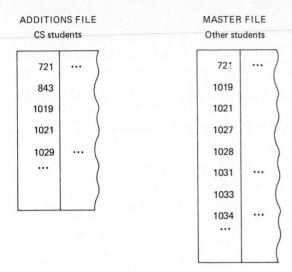

Figure 3-4 Cosequential files.

3-2-3 Performance of Sequential Files

The performance of sequential files ranges from excellent to next to impossible depending on the operations desired.

Record Size in a Sequential File The file storage requirement for sequential files, using a fixed record format, depends on the number of all the possible attributes a. The description of the attributes appears only once per file, and thus the space required for the attribute names can be neglected. The names may appear outside the file itself, perhaps only in program documentation. However, space will be used for values even when attributes have an undefined value or are unimportant in combination with other attributes. The last two entries shown in Example 3-4 illustrate such an attribute dependency where for the category `sex` = `Male` the next attribute value, `maternity_leave`, will probably be `NULL`. The fixed record size is the product of the number of fields and their average size.

$$R = aV \qquad\qquad\qquad 3\text{-}14$$

If many values are undefined, the file density will be low. If the value a' is close to the value for a, the file density will be high. Some methods to reduce storage costs for sparse data $(a' \ll a)$ will be discussed in Chap. 14. If insertions are expected, space for the transaction log to hold up to o new records of length R must also be allocated in an associated area.

Fetch Record in a Sequential File The common approach to fetch a record from a sequential file consists of a serial search through the file. The time required to fetch an arbitrary record can be significantly reduced if we have a direct-access device and use a direct access-technique. In a sequential file direct access can be applied only to the attribute according to which the file has been put in sequence.

We describe two direct methods for access to a sequential file organization, binary search and probing, after Eq. 3-17.

When the search argument is not the key attribute used to sequence the file, the search is always sequential. The process is similar to the search through a pile file. Since the total size of the file will be different from the size of a pile file due to the difference in record organization, the relative performance will depend on the attribute density a'/a as well as on the relative length of attribute descriptors A and data values V. Half the file will be searched on the average to fetch a record, so that

$$T_F = \frac{1}{2}n\frac{R}{t'} \qquad \langle\text{main file}\rangle \ 3\text{-}15$$

For small files this time may be better than the direct methods presented below.

If the file has received o' new records into a transaction log or overflow file, this file should be searched also. The entire overflow file has to be processed to assure that any record found in the main or in the earlier part of the overflow file has not been updated or deleted. This file will be in chronological order and processed sequentially. With the assumption that the overflow is on the average half full ($o = \frac{1}{2}o'$), we obtain

$$T_{Fo} = o'\frac{R}{t'} = \frac{1}{2}o\frac{R}{t'} \qquad \langle\text{overflow}\rangle \ 3\text{-}16$$

as the term needed to process changes made to the main file.

We cannot expect that the simple systems which use sequential files will search through both the main file and the log file in parallel. The total fetch time, if both parts of the file are searched sequentially, is the sum

$$T_F = \frac{1}{2}(n + o)\frac{R}{t'} \qquad\qquad 3\text{-}17$$

where o is the capacity of the transaction log file.

Binary Search   A well-known search technique for memory can be adapted to provide an alternate access method for sequential files. The binary search begins with a direct access to the middle of the file, and partitions the file iteratively according to a comparision of the key value found and the search argument. Whenever a block is fetched, the first and the last records in this block will be inspected to determine if the goal record is within this block. The number of fetches does not depend on the number of records n, but rather on the number of blocks $b = n/Bfr$.

We find, using the expected number of block access for the binary search $log_2(b)$ (Knuth[73S]), that

$$T_F = log_2\!\left(\frac{n}{Bfr}\right)(s + r + btt + c) + T_{Fo} \qquad \langle\text{binary}\rangle \ 3\text{-}18$$

The term for processing time c is included here, since until the record range in a block has been checked, it is not known which block is to be read next. The efficiencies obtained when reading the file sequentially using alternate buffers have been lost in this case. The value of c may well be negligible compared with the other times involved, but the bulk transfer rate t' is always inappropriate. The overflow term remains unchanged.

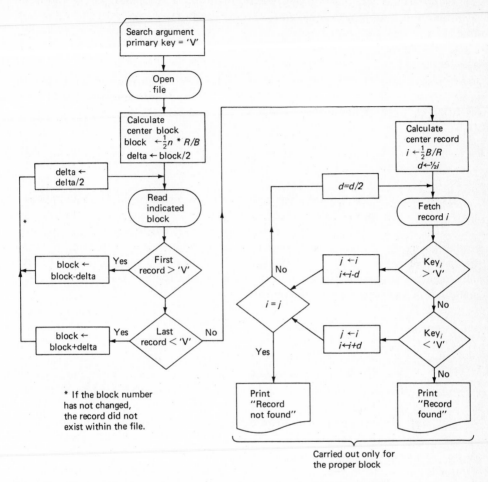

Figure 3-5 Nested binary search in a blocked sequential file.

Probing A third access method for sequential files, *probing*, is more difficult to quantify. It consists of an initial direct fetch, or probe, to an estimated position in the file, followed by a sequential search. If only forward sequential searches can be executed efficiently, the initial probe will be made to an estimated lowest matching key position, so that having to read backward is rare. Only one seek is made, and the number of blocks read sequentially is based on the uncertainty of the probe.

Likely values for an initial probe have been based on the leading digits of a social security number, if its value is used as a key, or on a percentile expectation for leading characters of names, if names are the key. Names beginning with the letters "E", for instance, may be found after $0.2446n$ records in a file sequenced by name (see Table 14-4). With a 3% uncertainty for the distribution the probe may actually begin at the block numbered $\lfloor 0.2146n/Bfr \rfloor$. More refined techniques to access records directly are used by the indexed and direct file organization methods described in later sections.

Get-Next Record of a Sequential File In a sequential file, a successor record is immediately accessible and may well be in the same block. If there is a frequent need for successor records, the file system should be programmed so that it does not discard the remaining records in the block but keeps the buffer with the contents of the current block available. The probability of finding a successor record in the same block is determined by the number of records per block Bfr : in $1/Bfr$ of the cases the next block is required. If the processing speed satisfies the condition of Eq. 2-22, the expected time to get the next record is only

$$T_N = \frac{btt}{Bfr} = \frac{R}{t'} \qquad\qquad 3\text{-}19$$

Insert into a Sequential File Insertion of a record into the main file requires insertion into the proper place according to the key. The sequence would not be maintained if new records were to be added to the end. For very small files, records beyond the point of insertion can be moved up to make space for putting the new record in place. This effort involves locating the insertion point by a fetch, and subsequently reading and rewriting of the remainder of the file. Each phase involves again half of the blocks of the file on the average, so that

$$T_I = T_F + \frac{1}{2}\frac{n}{Bfr}\left(btt + T_{RW}\right) = n\frac{R}{t'} + n\frac{r}{Bfr} \qquad \langle\text{in place}\rangle\ 3\text{-}20$$

where the assumptions from Eqs. 3-15 and 2-29 are made. This method is feasible for data files only if insertion occurs rarely, for instance, for a list of **departments** of a company. Successive insertions can be combined and handled at the same cost.

The usual method for insertions is to collect new records into a transaction log file and, at a later time, execute a batch update. We will use o to indicate the number of records collected for deferred insertion. The actual cost of extending the file is hence a function of the time required to append the records to the transaction log file and the cost of the reorganization run. Append methods costs were considered for the pile; we use the conservative method (Eq. 3-8) and write each record immediately to the log. The cost of the reorganization T_Y is allocated below to the o records that are collected into the transaction log file between reorganization periods. The reorganization time T_Y and the overflow count o are defined below.

$$T_I = s + 3r + btt \quad + \quad \frac{T_Y}{o} \qquad\qquad \langle\text{into log}\rangle\ 3\text{-}21$$

The response time that the user senses when a record is inserted includes only the initial append terms.

The definition of sequential files does not allow insertion of larger records than the original record stored. Problems of variable records and spanning in insertion and update are hence avoided. The transaction log file can also serve other functions, as described in the chapter on reliability, Sec. 11-4.

Update Record in a Sequential File A new record is created from retrieved data and new attribute values. If the key value does not change, the record could be rewritten into the main file. If the key value changes, the update is similar to the process of inserting a record but also involves the deletion of a record at another position in the main sequential file.

Since the main file is not otherwise touched in this method, it is best to use the transaction log file also for record update. The updated record and a flag record indicating deletion are appended to the transaction log file and used for subsequent fetches and in the reorganization process. The flag record will include the key and a tombstone. Both records should be added to the transaction log at the same time; the cost of adding two records at a time to a block is not much more than adding a single one. Deletion of a record generates only one entry. Then

$$T_U \approx T_F + T_I \qquad\qquad 3\text{-}22$$

If there are d record deletions and v record updates, $d + 2v$ records have to be added into the count o, the size of the transaction log file. A sequence of updates can avoid the T_F cost, and use T_N instead. Multiple updates to the same record will create multiple entries in the log file. Since complex updating is rarely done using this file organization, we will skip further evaluation of updating performance.

Read Entire Sequential File An exhaustive processing of the file consists of sequentially reading the main and the transaction log file. This means that data will be processed serially for the key used to establish the physical sequence of the file. The transaction log file should be sorted first to establish this sequence. Both files can then be read sequentially so that

$$T_X = T_{sort}(o) + (n + o)\frac{R}{t'} \qquad\qquad 3\text{-}23$$

given that all conditions for the use of t' hold. We find from the comments in the preceding paragraphs that, defining the number of insertions as n_{insert} and the size of the prior main file as n_{old},

$$o = n_{insert} + 2v + d \quad ; \qquad n_{new} = n_{old} + n_{insert} - d$$

The value of the transaction count o includes here insertions, twice the number of records to be changed, and the number of records to be deleted.

We assume that the exhaustive search processes the file in sequential order; otherwise the main file may also have to be sorted. If serial processing is not important, the transaction sort can be omitted. If the transaction log file is relatively large ($o \not\ll n$), it may be best to reorganize the file first. The records can be analyzed during the reorganization, so that $T_X \to T_Y$, as analyzed below.

Reorganization of a Sequential File Reorganization consists of taking the old file and the transaction log file and merging them into a new file. In order to carry out the merge effectively, the transaction log file will first be sorted according to the same key field used for the old file. During the merge the sorted data from the transaction log file and the records from the old sequential file are copied into the new file, omitting any records which are marked for deletion in the transaction log file. The time required for the reorganization run consists of the sort time for the transaction log file plus the merge time. Merging requires the sum of the times to read both files and write a new sequential file

$$T_Y = T_{sort}(o) + n_{old}\frac{R}{t'} + o\frac{R}{t'} + n_{new}\frac{R}{t'} \qquad 3\text{-}24$$

or if the number of records being deleted, $d + v$, can be neglected:

$$T_Y = T_{sort}(o) + 2(n + o)\frac{R}{t'} \qquad 3\text{-}25$$

The time required to sort a file of size o is given as $T_{sort}(o)$ and can be estimated using Eq. 3-11, provided with the analysis of exhaustive reading of a pile file.

3-3 THE INDEXED-SEQUENTIAL FILE

The indexed-sequential file design attempts to overcome the access problem inherent in the sequential file organization without losing all the benefits and tradition associated with sequential files. Two features are added to the organization of the sequential file to arrive at this third file organization type. One additional feature is an index to the file to provide better random access; the other is an overflow area to provide a means to handle additions to the file. Figure 3-6 shows a particular example of an indexed-sequential file. We find in this figure the three important components: the sequential file, the index, and the overflow area. The sketch also has a number of details which will appear in later discussions.

3-3-1 Structure and Manipulation of Indexed-Sequential Files

This file organization allows, when reading data serially, sequential access to the original record areas of the file. This is accomplished by reading the sequential parts of the file. Records which have been inserted are found in a separate file area, similar to the transaction log file used above, but integrated into this organization. They are located directly by following a pointer from their predecessor record. Serial reading of the combined file proceeds sequentially until a pointer to the overflow file is found, then continues in the overflow file until a NULL pointer is encountered; then reading of the sequential file is resumed. In order to fetch a specific record, the index is used.

The Index An index consists of a collection of entries, one for each data record, containing the value of a key attribute for that record, and a pointer which allows immediate access to that record. For large records, the index entry will be considerably smaller than the data record itself. The entire index will be correspondingly smaller than the file itself, so that a smaller space will have to be searched. The index is always kept in sorted order according to its key attribute so that it can be searched rapidly.

Indexes become effective when files are quite large, so that the index requires many fewer blocks. The search process within a large index itself is aided by again indexing subsets of the index, here perhaps groups of social security numbers with the same initial three digits.

Example 3-5   Index

We have an employee file sequenced by social security number:

Rec#	Social Sec#	Name	Birthdate	Sex	Occupation	...
1	013-47-1234	John	1/1/43	Male	Welder	...
2	028-18-2341	Pete	11/5/45	Male	Creep	...
3	128-15-3412	Mary	6/31/39	Female	Engineer	...

To find employees we establish an index file as follows:

013-47-1234	1
028-18-2314	2
128-15-3412	3

In practice the subsets are determined by the size of buffers, blocks, and tracks available to the file system. In Fig. 3-6 the subsetting of the index is based on the number of index entries (8) which fit into a block. Successively higher levels of the index become smaller and smaller until there remains only a small, highest level index that can be kept in core memory. It will be shown later that there is rarely a need for many levels of indexing.

Indexes have been implemented in a variety of ways. We will consider here a static, multilevel index. A dynamic technique, called a *B-tree*, will be presented with the indexed files of Sec. 3-4. Another alternative to multilevel indexing is to provide for a binary search on the index file. Binary searching was discussed when sequential files were evaluated in the preceding section. Section 4-1-2 presents some simpler index schemes that have been used. We continue here the discussion of this, the most common type of indexed-sequential file.

A Primary Index   The index for an indexed-sequential file is based on the same key attribute which has been used to determine the sequence of the file itself. For such a primary index a number of refinements can be applied. One of these is indexing only the first record in every block, the use of *block anchors*, and the other is keeping most of the index on the same cylinder as the data records, *cylinder indexes*.

Block Anchors   The benefit of the index is to rapidly access a file block. Individual records in a block can be found by a search within the block, so that it is not necessary to keep in the index an entry for every record, but only a reference to one record per block. The referenced record is called an *anchor point*, and only the anchor's key value and the block pointer are kept in the index. Natural anchor points are based on blocks, tracks, or cylinders. In Fig. 3-6 the choice of anchor point is the first record of a block.

The cost of searching within a file block for a record is minimal, since the entire block is brought into memory whenever required and can be kept available in a buffer. A block will contain a number of records equal to *Bfr*. The number of entries in a block anchored index is hence n/Bfr, and the size of an index entry is $V + P$.

When only block anchors are kept in the index, it is not possible to determine by checking the index alone if there exists a record corresponding to a specific argument. The appropriate data block has to be read also. To determine if the value of a search argument is beyond the last entry in the file, the last data block will have to be fetched, since the anchor point refers to the first record in this block.

If records are often inserted at the end of the file, it can be more convenient to keep
the key value of the last record in each block in the index instead of the key for the first
record. The appropriate block for a given search argument is then found in the index
through a less-than-or-equal match.

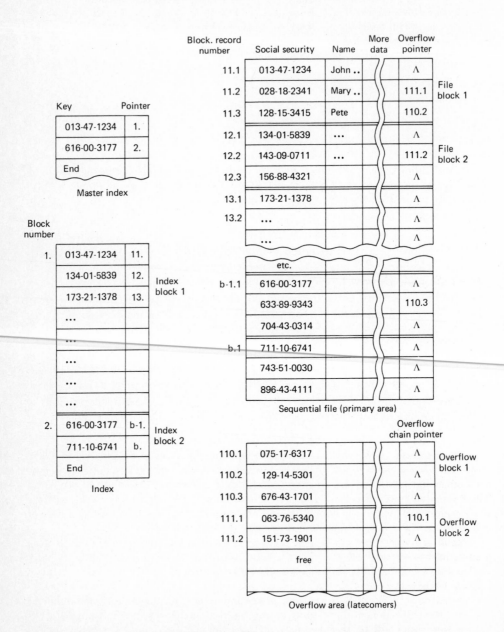

Figure 3-6 An indexed-sequential file.

Cylinder indexes   Since much of the overhead of fetching a block is due to the seek time required to reach a particular cylinder, a reduction of seek effort can be made by placing the subset of the index according to hardware boundaries. A two-level index is typical for this method. There will be a master index which contains only key attribute values and addresses of cylinder anchors. On the initial track of each cylinder there will be a cylinder index using tracks, blocks, or records for that particular cylinder as anchors. No seek delay will be incurred between cylinder-index and data records. Example 3-7 will evaluate this type of index.

The Fanout Ratio of an Index   An important parameter of an index is the referencing capability of a block of index entries, the *fanout*. The fanout y is the quotient of the block size B and the space required for each entry, $V + P$,

$$y = \left\lfloor \frac{B}{V + P} \right\rfloor \qquad\qquad 3\text{-}26$$

To evaluate the number of levels of indexing that might be required, we will take an example of a fairly large file (one million records) and a block-anchored index. In order to estimate the access time to fetch a record, we need to know how many levels of index are needed for a file of this size. Example 3-6 does this for a general block-anchored index, and Example 3-7 evaluates for the same file the case of a block-anchored index kept on the same cylinder as the referenced data.

Example 3-6   Hardware-Independent Index Design
Given is a block size B of 2000 bytes, a value size V of 14 bytes, a pointer size P of 6 bytes, and data records having a total length R of 200 bytes. With this blocking factor Bfr of 10, the 10^6 records require 10^5 data blocks and hence as many index pointer entries. The size of the index entry is here $14 + 6 = 20$ bytes, and the block size B is still 2000.

Now Eq. 3-26 gives a $y = 100$, so that the 10^5 lowest-index-level entries occupy 10^3 blocks which can be pointed at by 10^3 second-level index entries. This second-level index will occupy a total of $20 \times 1000 = 20\,000$ bytes. The latter number is still excessive for core storage, so that a third index level to the second index level will be created. Only $20\,000/2000 = 10$ entries occupying 200 bytes are required at the top level. The term *master index* refers to this topmost level. The index levels are numbered from 1, for the level closest to the data, to x (here 3) for the master level.

A record-anchored index for the same file would have been Bfr or 10 times as large but will use the same number of levels, as can be seen by recomputing Example 3-6 for 10^6 index entries. Its master level will have more entries, of course.

Example 3-7   Hardware-Oriented Index Design
Using a disk with cylinders of 19 tracks capable of holding 14 000 bytes each and $B = 2000$, we find on each cylinder $19 \times 14\,000/2000 = 133$ blocks. Index entries which match sequential hardware units do not need a pointer field, since entry 1 simply corresponds to block 1, etc. The index to the data on one cylinder, level 1, will require one entry per block, at most $133V = 1862$ bytes or one block on each cylinder, leaving 132 blocks for data.

There also will be the second-level index to the cylinder indexes; its size in this organization depends on the number of cylinders required for this file. The data file occupies $\lceil n/Bfr \rceil = 10^6/10 = 10^5$ blocks or $\lceil 10^5/132 \rceil = 758$ cylinders. The index to the cylinders does not require a pointer field either, since it simply has one entry per sequential cylinder. In practice, when using cylinder-resident first-level indexes, the second-level index will reside within each diskpack. Given diskpacks of 200 cylinders, each index to the cylinder for one pack will use $200\times14 = 2800$ bytes. If block sizes cannot be increased for the second-level index, each pack will use $\lceil 2800/2000 \rceil = 2$ blocks to refer to all its cylinders, and an access to the second level requires two block reads. With two buffers the loss of one revolution can yet be avoided.

The master index for the entire file will have one entry per diskpack, or four entries for this particular file.

We find in these examples that the hardware-oriented indexing structure has a higher fanout ($y_1 = 132$, $y_2 = 200$) and hence a smaller master index ($y_3 = 4$) than a general, symmetric index structure. There is also no seek between the cylinder index and the data. The second-level index is larger and requires additional block reads *btt* for retrieval, and perhaps additional buffer space as well. The actual values will depend on blocking size and file size. The hardware-independent index structure is more flexible to adapt to specific file requirements.

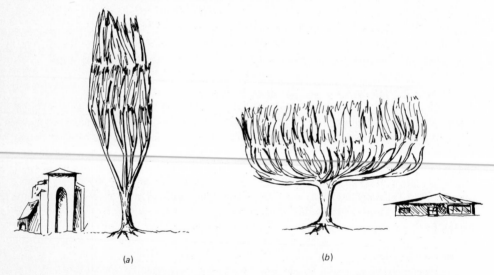

(a)   (b)

Figure 3-7 Italian and Monterey cyprus. (a) Low fanout. (b) High fanout.

The Shape of Indexes It can be seen that the trees for these index organizations are very broad, rather than high. The term used to measure the breadth of a tree was the *fanout ratio y*. Broad trees have few levels and provide rapid fetch access. The number of indexing levels or *height of an index tree x* is estimated for indexed-sequential file by evaluating the exponential growth

$$x = \lceil \log_y \lceil n/Bfr \rceil \rceil \qquad \text{easily computable as} \qquad \lceil \ln \lceil n/Bfr \rceil / \ln y \rceil \qquad 3\text{-}27$$

but should be verified for a specific design, since its value is so critical to performance. Values of x found in practice range typically from 1 to 3. Larger values occur only when the size of the key attribute V is unusually great; in Sec. 4-2-1 we will describe techniques to keep the effective V small. In Fig. 3-7 we illustrate symbolically a small and a large fanout ratio. The trees are not presented in the traditional computer science upside-down fashion, so that the process to fetch a leaf on the tree starts in the figure from the bottom, at the root. The fanout ratio is a very important parameter in the analysis of indexed file organizations and will be encountered frequently.

Master Index in Core   During processing another reduction of access cost is common: the master index (level x) remains available in core memory once it has been read. The lower levels (levels $x-1 \ldots 1$) of the index will be used from disk. With this scheme we require a total of x accesses to disk blocks to fetch data records in the main file.

The Overflow   In order to insert records into the file, some free space has to be allocated. We can place insertions to the file in a separate file, or can reserve space in every block for insertions, or can reserve space on every cylinder for inserted records. A separate insertion file requires a separate access with seek and latency overhead at any point where an insertion had been made. We looked at this technique for the simple sequential file and want to do better now. Allocating space in every block is feasible only if blocks are large and insertions are well distributed; otherwise, it is too easy to run out of space in some blocks. In general this approach requires dynamic space allocation, a file organization with that degree of complexity is described in Sec. 4-3.

Keeping spare space in every cylinder provides a reasonable compromise. This is the method chosen in the typical indexed-sequential file organization. Locating an overflow record will require rotational latency but not a seek. To insert a record the cylinder address is obtained from the index by matching the attribute key value of the new record to the entry for the nearest predecessor. The new record is placed in the next sequential free position in the cylinder overflow area.

Linkage to Overflow Records   The records in the overflow areas should be found both by **Fetch** and by **Get Next** operations. In both cases the search process begins from the predecessor record and then follows pointers.

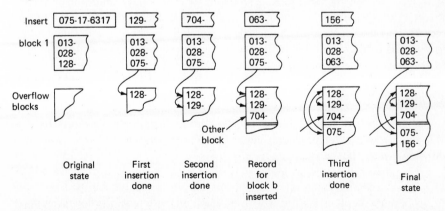

Figure 3-8 Insertions of records into a block of an indexed-sequential file.

Pointers to overflow records are placed with the predecessor records in the primary data blocks (see Fig. 3-6). The key of the inserted record is not kept there; only the pointer is put into the sequential file, so that a search for any intervening record is directed to the overflow area. This procedure avoids modification of the index to reflect the insertion but adds one block reading time to every fetch for an overflow record. A request for a nonexistent record will also require going to the overflow file if the search argument follows the key of a primary record with an overflow indication.

Chaining of Overflow Records   In order to locate multiple overflows, pointers are placed in the records in the overflow areas. All overflow records starting from one source are linked into a *chain*, possibly through many blocks of the overflow area. A new record is linked into the chain according to its key value, so that sequential order is maintained.

When the fetch has to proceed via many overflow records, in a large number of blocks, following the chain to a specific record may actually be less efficient than simply searching the overflow area exhaustively. On the other hand, serial processing is greatly simplified when we can follow the chain. In order not to lose the records from the sequential file buffer when processing, a separate overflow buffer should be available.

Push-through   Instead of having one overflow pointer per record in the data file it is common to use only one pointer per block. This method maintains the key sequence in the blocks of the primary file. New records are inserted after their proper predecessor; successor records are pushed toward the end of the block. Records from the end of the primary block are pushed out into the overflow area.

Figure 3-8 illustrates the *push-through* process using the same insertion sequence which led to Fig. 3-6. The final state of the file is shown in Fig. 3-9. The index is identical, since block positions do not change. Pointers are depicted in the form `block.record` number.

Now only one overflow pointer is required per primary block and only one jump is made to the overflow file per block. The chains will be longer than if each record had its own successor chain in the overflow area, by a factor of *Bfr*. This means that a fetch of a record placed in the overflow area will, on the average, take longer, but serial access is not impaired. If the access time between the sequential file area and the overflow file area is greater than the access time between overflow blocks (i.e. the two areas are not on the same cylinder), then serial processing will be faster when using push-through.

Size of Overflow Areas   Cylinder overflow areas have to be carefully dimensioned. If insertions cluster in certain areas, the corresponding cylinders will need large overflow areas. If the system provides a space allocation so that all cylinder overflow areas are of equal size, as most do, then much space can be wasted in cylinders that are not receiving many insertions. An escape hatch can be the provision of a secondary overflow area that is used when any cylinder overflow area itself overflows. Now the objective of avoiding seek time is lost for the records placed in the secondary overflow area; specifically, serial access will be quite slow.

Some methods to estimate the size of overflow areas required, given a specific distribution of record insertions, can be found in Chap. 6, and an assessment of insert versus inquiry frequencies is presented in Chap. 5.

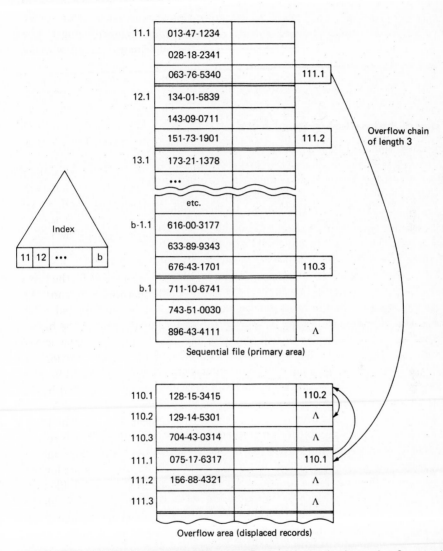

Figure 3-9 Indexed-sequential file overflow with push-through of records.

Reorganization At or before the point in time when the overflow areas themselves overflow, a file reorganization is required. Reorganization can also be needed when, because of the creation of long chains, the fetch or serial processing times become excessive. Such a reorganization consists of reading the file in the manner that would be used when doing serial processing and writing it anew, leaving out all records that are marked deleted, and writing all new and old remaining records sequentially into the main areas of the new file. During this processing, the reorganization programs will create new indexes based on new anchor point values.

The frequency of such reorganization is dependent on the insertion activity within the file. In practice one finds time intervals ranging from a day to a year between reorganization runs. Since a reorganization run can take a long time, the reorganization is generally performed before the file is actually full to avoid unpleasant surprises at busy times. It may simply be scheduled on a periodic basis or be done in the next convenient period after the overflow area exceeds a certain limit of entries. In Sec. 6-5 an algorithm for determining reorganization time will be presented.

3-3-2 Use of Indexed-Sequential Files

Indexed-sequential files of the basic type discussed above are in common use in modern commercial processing. They are used especially where there is a need to keep files up to date within time frames that are less than the processing intervals which are possible with cyclical reorganization of sequential files. Since individual records can be inserted and retrieved through the index, so that a limited number of block accesses are required, this type of file is suitable for *on-line* or terminal-oriented access. This is not feasible with the pile and sequential file types.

At the same time sequential access is relatively simple and efficient. Without overflows, after a reorganization, sequential access is practically identical to that of the sequential file. An indexed-sequential file can, for instance, be used to produce an inventory listing on a daily basis and be reorganized on a weekly basis in concert with a process which issues notices to reorder goods for which the stock is low.

Indexed-sequential files are also in common use to handle inquiries, with the restriction that the query must specify the key attribute. Typical of these are billing inquiries based on account numbers. Sometimes copies of the same data are found sequenced according to different keys in separate indexed-sequential files to overcome this restriction. Updating cost and space requirements are multiplied in that case.

The effects of the specific design implemented for an indexed-sequential file are frequently not understood by the users, so that many applications which use indexed-sequential files take longer to process data than seems warranted. In situations where files receive updates in clusters, the generated chains can take very long to follow. Often clustered updates are actually additions to the end of a file. By treating these separately, or by preallocating space and index values in the indexed-sequential file during the prior reorganization, the liabilities of appended records can be reduced. Within one indexed-sequential file method the options are often limited, but a number of alternative indexed-sequential file methods are available from computer manufacturers and from independent software producers.

The restriction that only one attribute key determines the major order of the file, so that all other attribute values are not suitable as search arguments is common to all sequential files. Indexing of multiple keys is presented in Sec. 3-4, there a different scheme of index management is used and the sequential file is abandoned. Sometimes multiple indexed-sequential files are combined to provide access by more than one key.

3-3-3 Performance of Indexed-Sequential Files

The performance evaluation of indexed-sequential files is more complex than the evaluation of the two preceding file organization methods because of the many options possible in the detailed design. We will base the evaluation on a simple form similar to the most common commercial designs.

The index is parallel in sequence to the data file itself. The first-level index is anchored to blocks of data, and a second-level index has one entry per first-level index block. The first-level index, its data areas, and the corresponding overflow area are all kept on the same cylinder. Push-through is used when records are inserted into a block. Records in an overflow area are linked in key order to provide serial access. Records to be deleted are not actually removed, but only marked as invalid.

An additional field for a tombstone in each record of the main file is used for a deletion flag. A pointer is maintained for chaining within the overflow area. For both functions a pointer position is allocated in every record. We permit records of variable length in our analysis, although only few systems support such records.

After a reorganization the main data areas and the index areas are full and the overflow areas are empty. No change of the index takes place between reorganizations, which simplifies the insertion procedure. All areas are blocked to an equal size B. The total file may occupy multiple cylinders.

Record Size in an Indexed-Sequential File In the sequential part of the file, a record requires space for a data values and for a possible tombstone. The number of records that exist initially or after reorganization is n. Additional space is allocated for o overflow records. For any record

$$R = aV + P \qquad \qquad 3\text{-}28$$

In addition, there exists an index with entries to locate the file blocks. The first-level index contains one entry per data block, so that for this level

$$i_1 = \frac{n}{Bfr} \qquad \qquad 3\text{-}29$$

entries are required. The sizes of successive levels of the index are determined by the fanout y, which in turn is determined by the block size B and the size of each index entry $V + P$, as shown in Eq. 3-26. On the next higher index levels there will be one entry per lower level index block, so that

$$i_{level} = \left\lceil \frac{i_{level-1}}{y} \right\rceil \qquad \qquad 3\text{-}30$$

until one block can contain all the pointers to the lower level index. The number of blocks bi required for any index level is

$$bi_{level} = \left\lceil \frac{i_{level}}{y} \right\rceil = i_{level+1}$$

The total size of the index is then, using the value 1 for bi_x, the root block

$$SI = (bi_1 + bi_2 + \ldots + 1)B = (i_2 + i_3 + \ldots + 1)B \qquad \qquad 3\text{-}31$$

The total space per record, including space allocated to overflows, is then

$$R_{total} = R + \frac{o}{n}R + \frac{SI}{n} \qquad\qquad 3\text{-}32$$

The space used for the file remains constant during insertions, until a reorganization frees any deleted records and moves the overflow records into the main file.

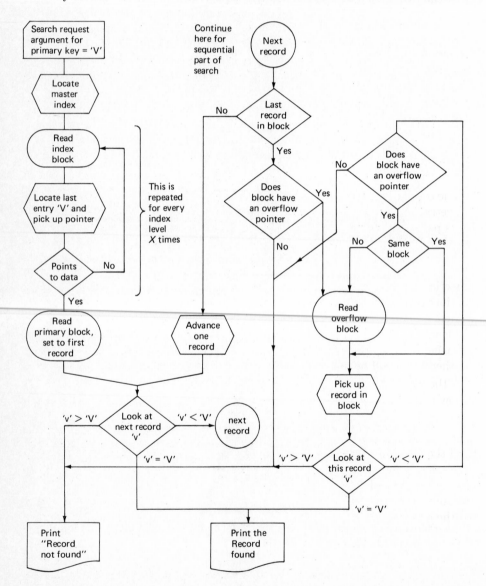

Figure 3-10 Fetch a record in an indexed-sequential file with push-through overflow.

Fetch Record in an Indexed-Sequential File To locate a specific record, the index will be used. The master index will not require a disk access, since it will have been placed into core storage when the file was opened. We will also assume that the remaining index levels reside on the same cylinder as the data. The primary fetch process will consist of a look-up in the master table, a seek to the cylinder, a read for each remaining level of the index, and a read of the data block, requiring

$$T_{Fmain} = c + s + (x - 1)(r + btt) + r + btt \qquad 3\text{-}33$$

However, if insertions have occurred, the procedure may fail to find a record because it has been pushed into the overflow file area, and the search will have to continue to the overflow area. The probability Pov that the desired record is in the overflow area depends on the number of insertions o' that the file has received, since it was reorganized to hold n records in the main file. For a fetch where any record is equally probable the overflow probility per stored record is

$$Pov = \frac{o'}{n + o'} \qquad 3\text{-}34$$

The overflowed records are attached in a chain to the block which the primary fetch retrieved. Under conditions of uniform distribution and with fairly many records per block $(Bfr \gg 1)$ the length of each chain can be estimated as

$$Lc = Pov\, Bfr \qquad 3\text{-}35$$

In practice overflow chains may have quite unequal lengths; for instance, **append** operations create chains connected to the last block only, unless special mechanisms are used for appends. In Sec. 6-1-5, Example 6-4, we develop estimates of the chain-length Lc for random insertions, leading to Poisson distributions. Statistical approaches to estimating chain lengths become essential if push-through is not used, since then there will be many more smaller chains to be considered.

If the overflow is kept on another cylinder, a seek $s^\dagger$ is required whenever any overflow record is accessed, and then the first record of the chain is obtained

$$T_{Foverflow} = Pov\,(s^\dagger + r + btt) \qquad 3\text{-}36$$

Any of the $Lc - 1$ further records from the chain are probably on different blocks but on the same cylinder. An estimate of the number of the additional records accessed to locate the desired record is $((Lc - 1) + 1)/2$ and this is equal to the number of additional blocks to be accessed. This operation is done only if any record is fetched from the overflow

$$T_{Fchain} = Pov\,\frac{Lc}{2}\,(r + btt) = \frac{1}{2}Bfr\,Pov^2\,(r + btt) \qquad 3\text{-}37$$

This factor, although including the squared term Pov^2 may remain significant, since the derivation assumed high values of Bfr.

An adequate estimate for record fetch in common indexed sequential file configurations and usage is obtained by combining Eqs. 3-33, 3-36, and 3-37 to give

$$T_F = T_{Fmain} + T_{Foverflow} + T_{Fchain}$$

$$= c + s + xr + x\,btt + Pov\,(s^\dagger + r + btt) + Pov^2(\frac{1}{2}Bfr)(r + btt)$$

$$= c + \left(1 + \frac{o'}{n+o'}^\dagger\right)s + \left(x + \frac{o'}{(n+o')} + \frac{Bfr}{2}\left(\frac{o'}{n+o'}\right)^2\right)(r + btt) \qquad 3\text{-}38$$

If overflow areas are placed on the same cylinder, the $s^\dagger$ term due to Eq. 3-36 drops out, and if $n/o' \gg Bfr$ the term due to Eq. 3-37 drops out. We are left with

$$T_F = c + s + \left(x + \frac{o'}{n+o'}\right)(r + btt) \qquad \qquad \langle\text{simple}\rangle\ 3\text{-}39$$

Estimation of Fetch Time We use the same file size presented in Examples 3-6 and 3-7, so that x is 3. If reorganizations are made when the overflow area is 80% full, the average value of o' will be 0.4o. If we consider a case where an overflow area equal to 20% of the prime file has been allocated, then $o' = 0.20 \times 0.4\,n = 0.08\,n$. Using the relations above, and a Bfr of 10,

$$Pov = \frac{0.08}{1.08} = 0.0741 \qquad \text{and} \qquad Lc = 10 \times 0.0741 = 0.741$$

With these assumptions we arrive at an average fetch time of

$$T_F = c + 1.0741s + 3.0645(r + btt)$$

Nonuniform insertion distributions can increase T_F considerably.

Get-Next Record of an Indexed-Sequential File In order to locate a successor record, we start from the last data record and ignore the index. We have to determine whether serial reading can be done sequentially or whether we have to go to another area. A number of possibilities exist depending on the locations of the predecessor and of the successor record. The six cases distinguished are illustrated using the record numbers of Fig. 3-9. The process is flowcharted in Fig. 3-11.

Path Choices for Next Record We consider again block-anchored overflow records, and begin with the most likely case

a The current record is in a main data file block and the successor record is in the same block, and hence already available in a core buffer (e.g., the current record is 11.1, 11.2, 12.1, ...).

b The current record is the last one in the block, there were no insertions, and the successor record is in a following block on the same cylinder.

c The current record is the last one in the block, and there have been no insertions, but the record is in a new block on another cylinder. Given that there are β blocks per cylinder, and the file begins at a new cylinder, this would happen between records $\beta.3$ and $(\beta + 1).1$, $2\beta.3$ and $(2\beta + 1).1$, once for each cylinder occupied by the file.

d The current record is the last one in the block, but there has been an insertion, and the successor record will be in an overflow block (the current record is 11.3 or 12.3).

e The current record is an inserted record, and the successor is found following the chain to another overflow block on the same cylinder (current record is 110.1 or 111.1).

f The current record is an inserted record, and to get to the successor record a new data block has to be read (current record is 110.2, 110.3, or 111.2).

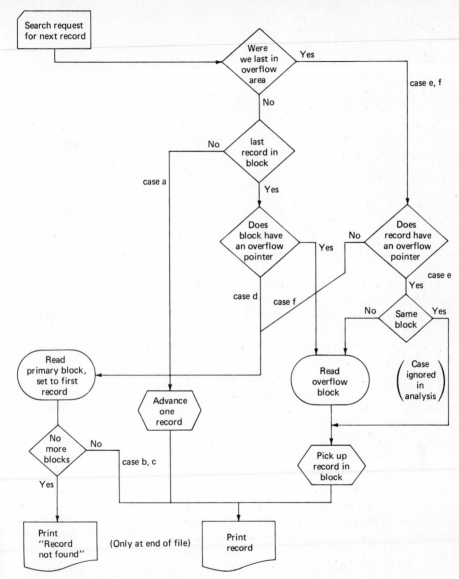

Figure 3-11 Get the successor record in an indexed-sequential file.

Note that the flow in this figure overlaps Fig. 3-10 to a great extent.

We will evaluate each of these cases using probabilities of the events which lead to their occurrence. The following notation is chosen to define the more likely condition of each event:

Pd: the current record is in a primary data block $= 1 - Pov$

Pb: the successor record is in the same block $= 1 - 1/Bfr$

Pm: there has been no insertion into the block $= 1 - Pov$

Pc: the next block is in the same cylinder $= 1 - 1/\beta$

Pl: the current overflow record is not the last of the chain $= 1 - 1/Lc$

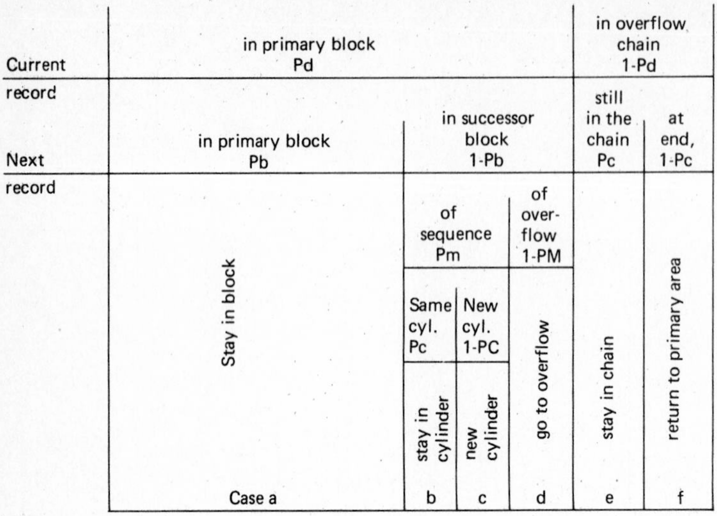

Current record	in primary block Pd				in overflow chain 1-Pd	
Next record	in primary block Pb	in successor block 1-Pb			still in the chain Pc	at end, 1-Pc
		of sequence Pm		of over- flow 1-PM		
		Same cyl. Pc	New cyl. 1-PC			
	Stay in block	stay in cylinder	new cylinder	go to overflow	stay in chain	return to primary area
	Case a	b	c	d	e	f

Figure 3-12 Conditions in the search for a successor record.

Figure 3-12 indicates the conditions based on Fig. 3-11. By applying the appropriate combinations of probabilities to their costs, we obtain for the cases considered

$$
T_N =
\begin{aligned}
&(Pd)(Pb)(c) + &&/* \; case\,a \; */\\
&(Pd)(1 - Pb)(Pm)(Pc)(r + btt) + &&/* \; case\,b \; */\\
&(Pd)(1 - Pb)(Pm)(1 - Pc)(s + r + btt) + &&/* \; case\,c \; */\\
&(Pd)(1 - Pb)(1 - Pm)(s^\dagger + r + btt) + &&/* \; case\,d \; */\\
&(1 - Pd)(Pl)(r + btt) + &&/* \; case\,e \; */\\
&(1 - Pd)(1 - Pl)(s^\dagger + r + btt) &&/* \; case\,f \; */
\end{aligned}
\qquad 3\text{-}40
$$

The seek terms in cases d and f, marked with a †, disappear when the overflow areas are kept on the same cylinders as the corresponding data blocks. The probabilities Pm and Pl can be rewritten in terms of n and o' using Eq. 3-34.

Equation 3-40 was obtained by a detailed case analysis, but as is typical, the result can be made practical by consideration of the relative importance of the terms. If we neglect the core search time c for records within the block, if cylinder seeks can be ignored (i.e., β is large, so that the value of $Pc \approx 1$), and if the overflow areas are on the same cylinders as the data blocks ($s^\dagger = 0$, cases e and f combine, and Pl can be ignored), then

$$
T_N \approx \left(\frac{1 - Pov}{Bfr} + Pov\right)(r + btt) = \frac{n + o'\,Bfr}{(n + o')Bfr}(r + btt)
\qquad 3\text{-}41
$$

We note that the chain length Lc does not affect this approximation for T_N, but overflows still increase the estimate.

Insert into an Indexed-Sequential File Adding a record to the file will always cause an addition to the overflow chain, either because of push-through or because the new record follows serially a record already in the overflow chain. Each insertion requires the reading and rewriting of a predecessor data or overflow block, since a pointer will have to be inserted or changed and also a read and rewrite of the overflow block for the pushed or inserted record. The probability of using the same overflow block for both is small if records are randomly inserted into a large data file. We avoid a detailed case analysis now by using the previous result for T_F and making some further assumptions. The fetch time for the predecessor is equal to T_F, the overflow block is on the same cylinder and requires $r\,btt$ to be reached, and each rewrite will take one revolution $T_{RW} = 2r$ (given the conditions of Eq. 2-30), so that

$$T_I = T_F + T_{RW} + r + btt + r + T_{RW} = T_F + 5r + btt \qquad 3\text{-}42$$

The effect of the length of the overflow is incorporated into T_F.

Update Record in an Indexed-Sequential File An updated record of equal size and identical key can be placed into the place of the previous version of the record, so that the process can be evaluated as a fetch followed by a rewrite with a cost of T_{RW}

$$T_U = T_F + T_{RW} = T_F + 2r \qquad \langle\text{in place}\rangle\ 3\text{-}43$$

Deletion of a record, done by setting a tombstone into the record, is also done using this process. Equation 3-43 is always appropriate for systems which disallow both the updating of key fields and variable-length records.

In the general case, the previous version of the record has to be deleted and the new record inserted appropriately. The old record is rewritten with the tombstone; the key and pointer fields are kept intact so that the structure of the file is not violated. Then

$$T_U = T_F + T_{RW} + T_I = 2T_F + 7r + btt \qquad \langle\text{in general}\rangle\ 3\text{-}44$$

If the cases which permit in-place updates are recognized by the file system, then T_U is to be computed based on the mix of in-place and general updates.

Read Entire Indexed-Sequential File An exhaustive search of the file has to be made when the search argument is not the indexed attribute. The file may be read serially by following the overflow chains for every block, or if seriality is not required, the entire data area on a cylinder can be read sequentially, followed by sequential reading of the entire overflow area. In either case the index can be ignored unless it contains space-allocation information.

Most systems provide only the ability to read serially, so that

$$T_X = T_F + (n + o' - 1)T_N \approx (n + o')T_N = \frac{n + o'\,Bfr}{Bfr}(r + btt) \qquad \langle\text{serial}\rangle\ 3\text{-}45$$

The assumptions leading to Eq. 3-41 are valid here.

In the alternative case the evaluation would consider the effective transfer rate, neglecting the delay when skipping from data blocks to overflow blocks. Unused overflow blocks will not be read, so that o' can be used to estimate the size of the overflow areas read. Now

$$T_X \approx (n + o')\frac{R}{t'} \qquad\qquad \text{(sequential) 3-46}$$

Reorganization of an Indexed-Sequential File To reorganize the old file, the entire file is read serially and rewritten without the use of overflow areas. As a by-product a new index is constructed. The prior index can be ignored, since the file is read serially. Two additional buffers in core are needed to collect the new data and index information. These outputs can be written sequentially. Then

$$T_Y = \frac{n + o'\,Bfr}{Bfr}(r + btt) + (n + o' - d)\frac{R}{t'} + \frac{SI}{t'} \qquad\qquad 3\text{-}47$$

We assume that o' new records are in the overflow areas; however, the value of o' will be larger at reorganization time than in the cases considered in Eqs. 3-34 to 3-45. The value of o' will still be less than o, the number of records for which overflow space has been allocated. Following the discussion of reorganizatioon in Sec. 3-3-1, we may assume $o' = 0.8\,o$. Such a value would be justified if the reorganization policy were as follows:

> Reorganization of a file is to be done the first night the overflow area exceeds 75% utilization where the average daily increase of the overflow area is 10%.

A simpler assumption that $o' = o$ will provide a conservative approximation for the number of overflow records to be processed.

3-4 THE INDEXED FILE

When there is no requirement for sequentiality to provide efficient serial access, an *indexed file* can be used. In an indexed file the records are accessed only through one or more indexes. Now there is no restriction on the placement of a data record, as long as a pointer exists in some index that allows the record to be fetched when the goal data from the record are wanted. One index will be associated with one key attribute, and indexes can exist for all attributes for which a search argument can be expected.

With the loss of sequentiality relative to a primary key attribute, a gain in flexibility is obtained which makes this organization preferable to the indexed-sequential file organization in many applications. The actual physical placement of records in indexed files can be determined by secondary considerations, as ease of management or reliability. The availability of indexes on more than one attribute greatly increases the potential for use of the data in information retrieval and advanced processing systems. Variable-length records are common in these applications.

The flexibility of indexed files has created a great variety of actual designs. We will evaluate again a specific approach which is becoming increasingly common, based on the use of *B-trees* for the indexes. The variety of designs has unfortunately also created a diversity of terminology, often quite inconsistent, so that anyone intending to evaluate a specific approach to indexed files will have to translate terms used in describing such systems into standard concepts.

Figure 3-13 shows schematically three indexes into a `Personnel` file, for the attributes `Names`, `Professions`, and `Chronic_diseases`. Each of the variable-length spanned records of the file can be located by giving a name or profession value. The third record, in block 2 at position 35, has a field with the attribute name `Chronic_diseases` and can also be located via that index.

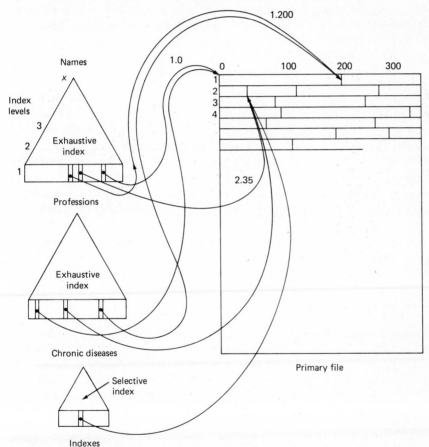

Figure 3-13 Record linkage in an indexed file.

Inverted Files A file for which indexes have been created is sometimes referred to as an *inverted file*. This term has its origin in bibliographic indexing and will be used rarely and carefully in this book. Sometimes a copy of a sequential file, when sorted according to another key attribute, has been called an inverted file. The term *fully inverted* generally implies a file where all attributes have indexes.

One older use of inversion is the creation of a single index to all the words in a body of writing. The index has as entries all the unique words (types) in the file, and is essentially a vocabulary. With each entry there will be pointers to all the instances (tokens) in the text where the words appear. If the pointers are augmented by a sample of the text, the result assumes the form of a *concordance*. The language used for the text is, of course, not restricted to English. An excerpt from a concordance is shown in Fig. 3-14.

Following our concepts a text file has only one type of attribute, *words*, and the index has multiple entries per record, one for each word. Partial inversions may exclude high-frequency words or other words not of interest, such as initials of authors. The term *indexing* in a bibliographic context is the selection or creation of significant attribute values for subsequent retrieval. These may be placed with the text sections so that there is now a second attribute type.

The terms inverted index, inverted list, inverted file, and partially inverted file are also used inconsistently in the literature, and frequently imply indexing as described in the remainder of this book.

Sample of text

Key-attribute value   Pointer

```
. quant vit pasmer  Rollant, / dunc out tel doel unkes mais n'out si grant. / Tendit sa mai 2223
la sele en remeint quaste. / Mult ad grant doel  Carlemagnes li reis, / quant  Naimun veit 3451
c. / Co dist li reis: "Seignurs, vengez voz doels, / si esclargiez voz talenz e voz coers,  3627
chevaler." / Respont li quens: " Deus le me doinst venger!" / Sun cheval brochet des esperu 1548
ad mort  France ad mis en exill. / Si grant dol ai que ne voldreie vivre, / de ma maisnee,  2936
d sanc. / Franceis murrunt,    Carles en ert dolent. /  Tere  Majur vos metrus an present.    951
ent, / e cil d' Espaigne s'en cleiment tuit dolent. / Dient  Franceis: "Ben fiert nostre gu 1651
alchet ireement, / e li  Franceis curucus e dolent; / n'i ad celoi n'i plurt e se dement,   1825
ma gent." / E cil respunt "Tant sy jo plus dolent. / Ne pois a vos tenir lung parlement:   2035
sil duluset; / jamais en tere n'orrez plus dolent hume! / Or veit  Rollant gue mort est su 2023
devers les porz d' Espaigne: / veeir poez, dolente est la rereguarde; / ki ceste fait, jan 1104
e vient curant cuntre lui; / si li ad dit: "Dolente, si mare fui! / A itel hunte, sire, son 2823
pereres cevalchet par irur / e li  Franceis dolenz e curucus: / n'i ad celoi ki durement ne 1813
aienur, / plurent e crient, demeinent grant dolor, / pleignent lur deus.  Tervagan e Mahum  2695
perere,' co dist Gefrei D' Anjou, / "ceste dolor ne demenez tant fort! / Par tut le camp f 2946
ance ad en baillie, / que me remembre de la dolur e l'ire, / co est de  Basan e de sun frer  489
amimunde, / pluret e criet, mult forment se douset; / ensembl'od li plus de xx. mil humes,  2577
out mais en avant. / Par tuz les prez or se dorment li  Franc. / N'i ad cheval ki puisset e 2521
ad apris ki bien conuist ahan. /  Karles se dort cum huse traveillet.  Seint  Gabriel li a 2525
poeent plus faire. / Ki mult est las, il se dort cuntre tere. / Icele noit n'unt unkes esca 2494
it le jur, la noit est aserie. /  Carles se dort, li empereres riches. /  Sunjat qu'il eret  718
ent liquels d'els la veintrat. /  Carles se dort, mie ne s'esveillat. AOI. /  Tresvait la no  736
le cel en volent les escicles. /  Carles se dort, qu'il ne s'esveillet mie. / Apres iceste,  724
s  Deu co ad mustret al barun. /  Carles se dort tresqu'al demain, al cler jur. / Li reis  2569
et les os, / tute l'eschine li desevret del dos, / od sun espiet l'anse li getet fors,     1201
gemmet ad or, / e al cheval parfundement el dos; / ambure ocit, ki quel blasme ne quil lot. 1588
eruns a or, / fiert  Oliver derere en mi le dos. / Le blanc osberc li ad descust el cors,  1945
ros; / sur les eschines qu'il unt en mi les dos / cil sunt seiet ensemble cume porc. AOI.  3222
re joe en ad tute sanglente; / l'osberc del dos josque par sum le ventre. /  Deus le guarit 3922
ele les dous alves d'argent / e al ceval le dos parfundement; / ambure ocist seinz nul reco 1649
t li ber. / De cels d' Espaigne unt lur les dos turnez, / tenent l'enchalz, tuit en sunt cu 2445
a fuls: / de cent millers n'en poent quarir dous. /  Rollant dist: "Nostre ume sunt mult p 1440
s e l'osberc jazerenc, / de l'oree sele les dous alves d'argent / e al ceval le dos parfund 1648
tet en ad, ne poet muer n'en plurt. / Desuz dous arbres parvenuz est . . . li reis. / Les c 2874
Dedesuz  Ais est la pree sult large: / des dous baruns justee est la bataille. / Cil sunt 3874
agne, ki est canuz e vielz! / Men escientre dous cenz anz ad e mielz. / Par tantes teres ad  539
t vielz, si ad sun tens uset; / men escient dous cenz anz ad passet. / Par tantes teres at  524
```

Figure 3-14 Sample of a concordance. (From Joseph J. Duggan, "A Concordance of the Chanson de Roland"; Ohio State University Press, Columbus, 1969.)

3-4-1 Structure and Manipulation of Indexed Files

There may be as many indexes as there are attribute types in the file. An index for an attribute of an indexed file consists of a set of entries, one for every record in the file. The technique of using block-anchor points to reduce index size, which was used in the indexed-sequential file, is not available here, since index and data are not cosequential.

The entries are ordered as determined by the attribute values. Each entry consists of the attribute value and a pointer to the record. In indexed files successor records are reached using the next index entry rather than by sequentiality or via pointers from the predecessor record. Each index may require multiple levels, as seen in an indexed-sequential file.

The data record format may be similar to any of the previous organizations. Records containing attribute name-value pairs, as seen in the pile file, are the choice permitting greatest flexibility; otherwise structured records may be employed. Since the pointers in the index specify the block address and record position for every record, there is essentially no restriction on record size or on the placement of records within a specific block. Records can be inserted wherever the file system finds sufficient free space.

A directory of attributes is needed to locate the index corresponding to an attribute name. We will discuss such facilities in Chap. 8, since these directories serve more than just the needs of the file systems. For our evaluations we assume that such a directory is read into a core memory buffer when the file is opened, and can be rapidly searched. Since many indexes may be required, we do not expect to find master indexes in core.

Exhaustive and Selective Indexes   Indexes may be *exhaustive*, that is, have pointers to every record in the file; or *selective*, that is, have only pointers to records where the attribute value is significant. Significance can mean simply that a value exists (is not undefined or zero) or that the value has a good partitioning effectiveness.

An example of a selective index could occur in a personnel file which includes health data. Only indexes to current or chronic diseases are maintained, although a more complete record is kept for statistical or individual purposes in the data file itself. This was shown symbolically in Fig. 3-13 as a `Chronic_diseases` index; here `NULL` or `Healthy` data values do not lead to entries. Another selective index for a health attribute could point to all individuals with a `cholesterol_level` greater than `250`, if frequent reference to this fact is made, for instance, in meal preparation.

If there is not even one exhaustive index, there is no easy way to list each record once. Now a space allocation table is required to allow the file to be properly maintained. Such a table gives an accounting of all the space allocated to the file. If the file is read serially according to this table, a record ordering similar to the pile file may be perceived.

Maintenance of Indexes   The major problem in the use of indexed file is caused by the need to update all the indexes that refer to a record whenever a record has been added or deleted or is moved. Single indexes have to be changed when a single data field value of an indexed attribute has been updated. In indexed-sequential files dynamic updating of the index was avoided through the use of pointer chains to insertions. With indexing for multiple attributes such overflow chaining is not feasible; each record would need many overflow pointers. The pointers would have to link a new record to many predecessor records. The alternative is to update the actual indexes as the file changes, but a dense index structure as used with indexed-sequential files would require for each insertion or deletion of an index entry the rewriting of the entire index.

An Index Structure for Dynamic Updating – B-trees   In indexed files every change of an indexed attribute will require the insertion, deletion, or both, of an index entry into the appropriate index block. To make such changes feasible, we reduce the density of the index. Extra space is left initially empty in each index block, and now one insertion will affect only that index block. The blocks can accommodate a number of insertions, and only when the block is full is another block obtained. Half of the entries from the full block are distributed to the new block. There has been a trade-off made here, space has been given up in order to have reasonable maintenance of the index.

A method based on this solution is the *B-tree*, and we will describe a specific version of this algorithm useful for index trees. A B-tree has index blocks which are kept at least half full; the effective fanout y_{eff} is hence between y and $y/2$ as shown in Fig. 3-15.

The original B-tree was defined with space for y pointers and $y-1$ values, and kept at least $y/2 + 1$ pointers in a block. The value corresponding to the first pointer (v_1) in a block is the value (v_n) in the entry associated with this block in the next-higher-level index block. In the index-file approach presented here, we keep this value redundantly. This simplifies the formatting of entries, permits index blocks to be accessed independently of their ancestor blocks, and has little effect on the analyses when y is reasonably large.

The insertion and deletion algorithms for B-trees maintain the condition that index blocks are at least half full. New entries are inserted into the first-level index blocks until the limit y is reached. The next entry to be inserted will require the allocation of a new, empty index block, which is then initialized with half of the entries taken from the block which was full: the block has been *split*. The entry which forced the split can now be inserted into the appropriate level one index block. At the same time a new entry has to be created for the new index block at the next higher level, containing a pair $\{\,v_{n+1}, p_{n+1}\,\}$. The value v_{n+1} is the former $v_{y/2+1}$ taken from the split block, which is now v_1 in the new block.

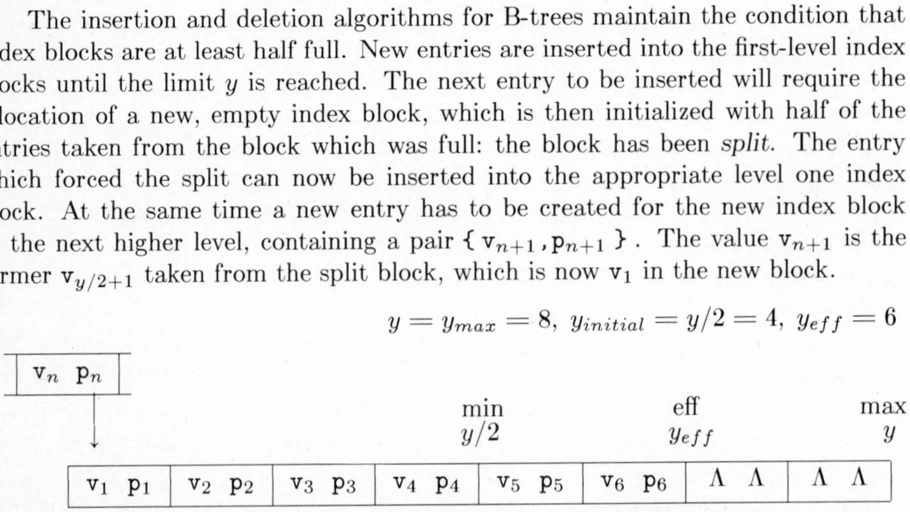

$$y = y_{max} = 8, \; y_{initial} = y/2 = 4, \; y_{eff} = 6$$

Figure 3-15   Block of a B-tree index after two insertions.

The next-level block may in turn be already full and also require such a split. If the top or root block is full, a new root block is created and initially filled with two entries, one for the previous root block and one for its new partner. The tree has now grown by one level. We note that the root block only may have fewer than $y/2$ entries; y_{eff} may be anywhere from 2 to y but will ignore the effect due to this one block in our analyses.

This insertion algorithm maintains the value of y_{eff} in the desired range; the deletion algorithm below does the same. For a file receiving only insertions the average y_{eff} for the entire index will become $0.75\,y$, but we will henceforth use a result of Yao[78], which specifies that under conditions of random insertions and deletions the B-tree eventually achieves a density of $y_{eff}/y \to \ln 2 = 0.69$. Then

$$y/2 \leq y_{eff} \leq y \qquad \text{or} \qquad y_{eff} \to \ln 2 \times y = 0.69\,y \qquad \text{3-48}$$

where y is again defined as in Eq. 3-26 as $\lfloor B/(V + P) \rfloor$. In order to simplify the analysis, we also assume an initial loading density of 0.69.

When an entry is deleted, an index block may be left with less than $y/2$ entries. Its partner should now be inspected. If the total number of entries in both is less than y, they should be combined. An entry in the higher-level index block is now also deleted, and this deletion may propagate and even lead to the deletion of an entry in the root block. If the root block has only one entry left, it can be deleted so that height of the tree is reduced by one. If the total of two blocks is exactly y, then it is best not to combine the blocks to avoid excessive costs if deletions and insertions alternate.

Many systems use alternate deletion strategies, either to simplify the programs or to reduce effort. Perhaps index blocks will not be checked until one has fewer than $0.69/2y$ entries or will not even be combined at all. In the last case index blocks will be deleted only if they become empty.

An alternate and improved insertion strategy is *presplitting*. When the search for an index entry is made from the root to the lowest level, each index block read is checked; any index block which is already full ($y_{eff} = y$) is immediately split. This assures that the block at the next level up will never be found full, so that no split has to propagate from the lowest to the higher levels.

The number of levels of indexing required is a function of the number of index entries y_{eff} that appear in one index block. In order to evaluate the height of the B-trees we will assume here that stability has been achieved and that all index levels partition their data evenly. Given that one index will refer to n' records, where n' is determined by the expected number of records having an indexable attributes, we find, similarly to Eq. 3-27,

$$x = \left\lceil \log_{y_{eff}} n' \right\rceil \qquad \text{3-49}$$

The search process is flowcharted in Fig. 3-16. We note that because of the reduced density and fanout the height of the index B-trees is greater than the height of a dense index. The height x will be one level greater in many practical cases. A greater increase occurs only in large files with small fanouts, say, $n' > 10^6$ and $y < 12$. With large fanouts there will be wide ranges of n' where the index height is the same for a dense index and a corresponding B-tree.

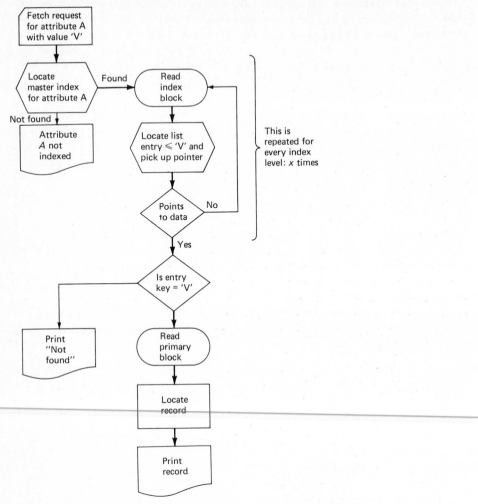

Figure 3-16 Fetch using one index of a multi-indexed file.

Deferred Updating of Indexes The algorithms to maintain dynamic indexed files do generate many more block accesses and rewrites than those used for indexed-sequential files. It can be impractical to attempt to change all indexes immediately after a record has been changed. High-priority fetch requests using the file may need to be processed before all indexes are brought up to date.

The continuous maintenance of indexes can also be quite time-consuming. A batch of updates may have to rewrite the same index block again and again. Hence we find systems where indexes are created from a file for a particular analysis but are not kept up to date when the file changes. Sometimes indexes are updated only periodically, which causes recent information not to be accessible. This approach is akin to a periodic file reorganization.

Deferred Updating The updating of the indexes may be done at times when the computer is relatively idle. If such updating can be performed incrementally, a periodic wholesale reorganization can be avoided so that the file is kept available, although retrievals may not include recent changes. Such index updating will be done by a process which is kept active at a low priority until it is completed. It is necessary to keep the old record in place until assurance exists that all referring indexes have been updated.

Updating while the file is otherwise active requires careful sequencing of update operations and the maintenance of status information on incomplete updates. Approaches to monitor concurrent file operations and maintain reliability will be discussed in Chaps. 11 and 13. Deferred updating of derived data is presented in Sec. 8-3-4.

When index update is deferred, a retrieval may not find recently inserted data but may also retrieve data that has been previously deleted or changed. A new record will not be retrieved by a request based on attribute values until the relevant index has been updated. An index that is out of date will also include references to recently obsoleted data. This problem can be avoided by marking the old record with a tombstone. If the record has been moved, the marker can also provide an indication of the new location.

Many applications can operate with deferred updating. When queries involve management decisions for planning, say, analysis of a `sales` pattern, use of data which is at most a few hours obsolete will not matter. These types of analysis transactions tend to access many records so that a relaxation of their access requirements can be very beneficial to the overall system.

A counterexample is a `sales` transaction which actually commits to deliver specific items from stock. Then an index update may have to be forced to assure the stock counts are up to date. A relatively higher priority may be assigned routinely to a process which updates important attribute indexes than the priority given to other index-update processes. If the priority given is higher than the priority of certain retrievals, these retrievals will always find up to date information.

3-4-2 Use of Indexed Files

Indexed files are used mainly in areas where timeliness of information is highly critical. Examples are found in airline reservation systems, job banks, military data systems, and other inventory type applications. Here data are rarely processed serially, other than for occasional, maybe only yearly, stocktaking.

When an item of information is obtained, e.g., a free seat on a certain flight, the data should be correct at that point in time, and if the item is updated, i.e., a seat is sold on that flight, that fact should be immediately known throughout the system.

Multi-indexing of such information makes it possible that one can find the same data by flight number, by passenger name, by interline transfer record, and so forth, without file reorganization or data redundancy. There is now, of course, redundancy between the contents of the index and the data.

Other instances where indexed files are desirable occur when data are highly variable and dynamic. The flexibility of the record format and record placement available with indexed files does not exist in other file systems. Much of Chap. 4 is devoted to specific alternatives and examples of indexed and related files.

The use of indexed files is increasing, specifically on more modern systems, where new software is being developed. There is also more literature in this area than about any other file organization.

3-4-3 Performance of Indexed Files

The performance of indexed files is easier to evaluate than the performance of the preceding indexed-sequential file designs. B-trees have a very predictable behavior since all single indexing operations require an effort based on the height of the index tree. The critical design decision is the selection of the attributes that are to be indexed. The space required for exhaustive indexes for all attributes will easily exceed the size of the original file. In practice, there are always some attributes for which indexing is not justified. We have noted that attributes that have low partitioning effectiveness are poor candidates for indexing. Not having indexes for these attributes, or the use of selective indexes, will reduce the size of the index space and accelerate updating, but will not affect the other performance factors, as long as no searches try to use omitted indexes.

> The evaluation which follows considers a completely indexed file, so that all existing attributes of every record are indexed. There will hence be a indexes with up to n, say n', entries. Each index is a B-tree, and the main data file has the form of a pile file. The records are then of variable length and have a variable number of attribute name-value pairs. Insertions are placed into the pile file itself and cause updating of all indexes.
>
> We also assume that steady state has been achieved, so that the density of the index is assumed to be stable at $dens = y_{eff}/y = 0.69$. This means that deletion is done so that partners have never jointly fewer than y entries. The actual space requirement for the index entries is now $1/0.69 = 1.45$ of the net requirement, and also that the height of the index tree may be greater than the height of a denser index.

Record Size in an Indexed File   The space required for the data portion of such a file is identical to the space required for a pile file as derived for Eq. 3-1. In addition, there will be a indexes to provide an index for every attribute. Since the data attributes are sparse, there are only a' attribute entries per record; the average index contains

$$n' = n\,\frac{a'}{a} \qquad\qquad 3\text{-}50$$

index entries referring to data records, each entry is of size $V_{index} + P$ and the size of one index is estimated as

$$SI_1 = n'\,\frac{(V_{index} + P)}{dens} = 1.45\,\frac{n\,a'}{a}(V_{index} + P) \qquad \langle\text{one index}\rangle\ 3\text{-}51$$

Higher-level index blocks are ignored here; for instance, the second level would add only $SI_2 \approx SI_1/y_{eff}$ bytes. The total space needed for all indexes becomes then

$$SI_{total} = a\sum_{1}^{x} SI_i \approx 1.45\,n\,a'(V_{index} + P) \qquad\qquad 3\text{-}52$$

The space requirement per record is equal to the sum of data and index space. No overflow area exists. We will again consider only the lowest level index entries.

Since all attribute values which exist in a given record are indexed, the space allocated to a record is

$$R_{total} = R_{main} + a' R_{index}$$
$$= a'(A + V + 2) + 1.45\,a'(V_{index} + P) \qquad \text{3-53}$$

for index and data.

The value field in an index V_{index} is often not of the same size as in the data so that it should be estimated separately. The value field in an index may, for instance, be required to be of fixed length to allow fast searches through the index, so that V_{index} will be larger than the average value field V in a data record. On the other hand, if there are frequently multiple records related to a certain attribute value (for example, the attribute category is **profession**, so that we have many entries in this index for an attribute value like **welder**), then one value entry may serve many pointers. Techniques discussed in Sec. 4-2-2 can reduce key value sizes of indexes further, so that often $V_{index} < V$. If V_{index} can be assumed to be equal to V, then

$$R = a'(A + 2.45V + 1.45P + 2) \qquad \text{if} \qquad V_{index} = V \qquad \text{3-54}$$

based on Eqs. 3-48 and 3-53.

Additional index blocks will be used for index levels above 1. In most designs, that additional number amounts to only a small percentage of the storage space, as will be shown in Example 3-8.

Example 3-8   Calculation of Levels for an Indexed File

Consider a **personnel file** of $n = 20\,000$ **employees**, containing an inventory of their **skills**. Each **employee** has an average of 2.5 **skills** so that for this particular index a'/a is actually greater than 1. The skills are given a code of 6 characters. To find an employee record, an 8-digit pointer is used which occupies 4 character positions, giving $V + P = 10$ bytes per index entry.

The blocks in the file system are $B = 1000$ characters long, so that $y = 100$ index elements can appear per block.

$$n' = n\,a'/a = 20\,000 \times 2.5 = 50\,000$$
$$b_1 = n'/(0.69y) = 50\,000/69 = 725$$
$$b_2 = b_1/(0.69y) = 725/69 = 11$$
$$b_3 = b_x = b_2/(0.69y) = 11/69 = 1$$

Estimating x directly, we obtain the same result:

$$x = \lceil \log_{69}(20\,000 \times 2.5) \rceil = 3$$

An estimate for the space was given by Eq. 3-51, $SI_{skill} = 1.45n\,a'/a(V + P) = 725\,000$ bytes, and used to derive Eq. 3-53. The space requirement for this index is actually $SI_{skill} = \sum b_i B = 737\,000$ bytes, because of the higher-level indexes.

Fetch Record in an Indexed File The expected fetch time for an indexed file is similar to the time used for an indexed-sequential file. However, no overflow areas exist, and hence the term that accounts for the chasing after overflow records is eliminated. Since there will be, in general, several index subfiles, we can no longer assume that these indexes and the data will both occupy the same cylinder. The indexes will be of the larger record-anchored variety and also will contain space for insertions, so that their height x will be greater. We add the accesses for index and data and find

$$T_F = x(s + r + btt) + s + r + btt = (x + 1)(s + r + btt) \qquad \text{3-55}$$

where x is given by Eq. 3-49.

If each index can be kept compactly, on a single cylinder, then some seeks can be avoided so that

$$T_F = 2s + (x + 1)(r + btt) \qquad \langle\text{compact index}\rangle \text{ 3-56}$$

Get-Next Record of an Indexed File The search for a successor record is based on the assumption that the last index block is kept available in a buffer, so that only a new data record has to be fetched.

$$T_N = s + r + btt \qquad \text{3-57}$$

This holds as long as the effective fanout ratio $y_{eff} \gg 1$, since the probability that the current index block contains also the pointer to the next record is $Pd = (y_{eff} - 1)/y_{eff}$.

If indeed a successor index block is needed, the second-level index block has to be accessed to locate the successor. If the second-level block is not kept in a core buffer as well, two block accesses are needed with a frequency of $1 - Pd$. The frequency of having to access a third- or higher-level index block is generally negligible.

Insert into an Indexed File To add a record to an indexed file, the record is placed in any free area, and then all a' indexes referring to existing attributes for this record have to be updated. The insertion process will have to find for each index the affected index block by searching from the root block of each index, and rewrite an updated index block at level 1; we will call this time T_{index}. With a probability of $Ps = 1/(y/2) = 2/y$ there will be a block split. A block split requires the fetch of a new partner block, some computation to distribute the entries, and the rewriting of the the new block and the ancestor block with a new entry, all this in addition to the rewrite of the old block; the incremental time is T_{split}.

Summing the times for data block fetch and rewrite, for the following a' indexes down x levels, for first-level index rewrites, and for the possible split, we find

$$T_I = T_{data} + a'(T_{index} + Ps\, T_{split})$$
$$= s + r + btt + T_{RW} + a'\left(x(s + r + btt) + T_{RW} + \frac{2}{y}(c + s + r + btt + 2T_{RW})\right)$$
$$= \frac{2}{y}c + \left(1 + a'\left(x + \frac{2}{y}\right)\right)(s + r + btt) + \left(1 + a'\left(1 + 2\frac{2}{y}\right)\right)T_{RW}$$

$$\text{3-58}$$

Keeping indexes within a cylinder can reduce the time by requiring only one seek per index. If all indexes are small so that $x = 2$, further ignoring the cost of splitting ($y \gg 1$) and using $T_{RW} = 2r$ gives a less forbidding estimate

$$T_I = (1 + a')s + (3 + 4a')r + (1 + 2a')btt \qquad \langle \text{simple} \rangle \text{ 3-59}$$

In the absolutely worst case the insertion could cause all index blocks to overflow so that they all have to be split. The delay of even several splits could be quite disconcerting to a user entering data on a terminal. Presplitting reduces the likelihood of multiple splits in one index. With deferred updating only one index access and the actual record rewriting is noted by the user.

Update Record in an Indexed File An update of a record in an indexed file consists of a search for the record, the update of the data record, followed by a change of those indexes for which the new record contains changed values. An update changes one data record and a_{update} indexes. The new field values may be far removed from the old ones, so that the new index entries are in blocks other than the old ones. Now each index update requires the search for and rewriting of two index blocks, the old one and the new one, doubling the term $T_{index} + Ps\,T_{split}$ found in Eq. 3-58. The new index block may require a split because of the insertion and the block used previously may have to be combined because of the deletion of an entry. We assumed that deletion is as costly as insertion and use below T_{split} for either operation.

The pile organization of the data file leads us to expect that the old data record will be invalidated and a new copy will be inserted ($T_{newcopy}$). The pointer value for all indexes will then have to be updated so that the remaining $a' - a_{update}$ indexes also have to be fixed. Fixing the pointer requires finding the blocks and rewriting them; no splits will occur here; this term is $T_{fixpointer}$. We collect all the costs.

$$
\begin{aligned}
T_U = {}& T_F + T_{RW} + T_{newcopy} \\
& + \quad 2\,a_{update}(T_{index} + Ps\,T_{split}) \\
& + \quad (a' - a_{update})(T_{fixpointer}) \\
= {}& (x + 1)(s + r + btt) + T_{RW} + s + r + btt + T_{RW} \\
& + 2\,a_{update}\!\left(x(s + r + btt) + T_{RW} + \frac{2}{y}(c + s + r + btt + T_{RW})\right) \\
& + (a' - a_{update})(x(s + r + btt) + T_{RW}) \\
= {}& (x + 2)(s + r + btt) + 2\,T_{RW} \\
& + a_{update}\!\left(x(s + r + btt) + T_{RW} + \frac{4}{y}(c + s + r + btt + T_{RW})\right) \\
& + a'(x(s + r + btt) + T_{RW})
\end{aligned}
\qquad \text{3-60}
$$

Making the same simplifications used to obtain Eq. 3-59, we find that a simple update for a modest file will take approximately

$$T_U = (4 + 2\,a_{update} + 2\,a')(s + 2r + btt) \qquad \langle \text{simple} \rangle \text{ 3-61}$$

If the updated record does not have to be moved, the $a' - a_{update}$ indexes do not have to be changed, and now the same simplification gives

$$T_U = (4 + 4\,a_{update})(s + 2r + btt) \qquad \langle \text{in place} \rangle \quad 3\text{-}62$$

Small Value Changes   When an update changes an attribute value by a small amount, further savings will occur if both old and new index values fall into the same index blocks. In that case one search and rewrite may be saved. The ratio between out-of-index block and within-index-block changes is difficult to predict and depends on the behavior of the attribute change. For instance, if the attribute type is a person's **weight**, we can expect the within-index-block case to be predominant. If the update changes a value from undefined to a defined value, only a new index entry has to be created. If we define Pi to be the probability of out-of-index-block updates, we find for a single update, given all the conditions leading to Eq. 3-62,

$$T_U = 2(3 + Pi)(s + 2r + btt) \qquad \langle \text{single change, in place} \rangle \quad 3\text{-}63$$

In the general case we have to assume the index changes will be randomly distributed among the blocks of an index. Given an average loading density of 69%, there will be

$$b_1 = 1.45\,\frac{n}{y}\,\frac{a'}{a} \qquad\qquad\qquad 3\text{-}64$$

primary index blocks for one attribute; then the probability, given random data changes, of requiring another index block is $Pi = (b_1 - 1)/b_1$. For a specific attribute the specific values of V and a'/a should be used, so that y and b_1 are appropriate. For large files and frequently occurring attributes Pi will be close to 1, so that Eqs. 3-60 to 3-62 remain appropriate.

However, Eq. 3-62 is of interest if Pi can be shown to be low because of the behavior of data value changes for updated attributes. A number of important cases exist where the database monitors changes in the operation of some physical process. Changes in **pressure**, **temperature**, or **flow** occur mainly gradually, and the data may be acquired at high rates, so that file performance could be critical.

We observe that updating is, in most cases, yet costlier than insertion and that techniques for deferring part of the update process may be quite beneficial to gain response time for the user.

The uniform behavior assumed for insertion and update patterns represents the best behavior in terms of index growth over the long term. Updating tends to be periodically heavy in one area, and then concentrate again on other attributes. These irregularities can specifically affect system behavior. The analysis of these conditions requires statistics of update behavior which we do not have available here, and we will not evaluate their effect. If there exists a good understanding of the frequency of attribute changes and of the value-change ranges, a more precise estimate of update cost can be made, using the concepts discussed above.

Read Entire Indexed File   The basic fully indexed organization is poorly suited for exhaustive searches. When necessary, such searches may be accomplished by using the space-allocation information, or by serial reading of the file using some exhaustive index. An exhaustive index is created when the referred data element is required to exist in every record. A brute force approach using such an index will cost

$$T_X = T_F + (n-1)T_N \qquad \text{3-65}$$

If one can follow the space-allocation pointers, seeks need to be done only once per block, so that here the read time for a consecutively allocated file would be equal to the time needed to read a sequential file. If the blocks are distributed randomly or found from the space allocation in a random fashion, then, neglecting the time needed to read the space-allocation directory,

$$T_X = \frac{n}{Bfr}(s + r + \frac{B}{t'}) \qquad \langle \text{by blocks} \rangle \text{ 3-66}$$

In this approach the records appear in a logically unpredictable order. A reduction in actual search efficiency may be due to the processing of empty spaces created by previous deletions.

Reorganization of an Indexed File   Indexed files are not as dependent on periodic reorganization as are the previous file organizations. Some implementations of indexed files in fact never need to reorganize the files. Reorganization may be required for the data file in order to recover unusable fragments of space from deletions. A specific index may require reorganization to recover from updating failures or from having poorly distributed index entries due to clustered insertions or deletions. Index reorganization can be done incrementally, one index at a time. The largest, lowest level of an index will have b_1 blocks as given in Eq. 3-64. The number of higher-level blocks is much less, as was shown in Example 3-8.

In order to reconstruct one index, the data file is read. A reorganization of an index separately would propagate any existing errors in the index. It is best to use the space-allocation directory, not only for speed but also to assure that every record is read. Since the records will not appear from the data file in the proper logical sequence for the index attribute, it is best to collect them in a dense temporary file having n' small $(V + P)$ records, then sort this file, and then generate the index blocks sequentially.

$$T_{Yi} = T_X + T_{sort}(n') + \frac{SI}{t'} \qquad \langle \text{one index} \rangle \text{ 3-67}$$

Estimates for these terms were given as Eqs. 3-66, 3-11, 3-50, and 3-51. The sort will be rapid if the space required for sorting $n'(V + P) = 0.69\,SI_1$ is small relative to memory capacity.

If the data file is reorganized, all the index pointers become invalid. An effective way to reorganize data and the indexes is to read the old data file and write the file anew and reconstruct the indexes. The time requirement then is

$$T_Y = 2T_X + a\,T_{Yi} \qquad \langle \text{data and indexes} \rangle \text{ 3-68}$$

We cannot expect to have sufficient memory to process all indexes, so that here a total of a sort files will be generated during the processing of the data file. Some assumptions made in Eq. 3-11 about sequentiality will then not hold.

3-5 THE DIRECT FILE

The direct file is not a development of the previous file-organization methods but attempts to exploit the capability, provided by disk units and similar devices, to access any block of known address. To achieve direct addressing, the key of the record is used to locate the record in the file. Direct access is diagrammed in Fig. 3-17.

The earliest direct-access disk files were used by electromechanical accounting machines which would use a number, punched on a card, to determine where the remainder of the card contents was to be filed. Modern direct-access methods transform the key with a computational algorithm before it is used as an address. The direct-access method is fast, since it avoids intermediate file operations, but the method forces the data to be located according to a single key attribute.

We can compare direct access with an indexed-sequential file in that access is provided according to a single attribute; however, records within direct files are not linked to their predecessor or successor records. The direct file methods use a computation τ to provide the record address for a key, whereas indexed file organizations search indexes to determine the record corresponding to a given key. Index B-trees used extra space to reduce the effort of insertion. The direct file will use extra space in the main file $(m > n)$, keeping some record spaces empty, in order to reduce the probability and cost of conflicts when inserting more records into the file.

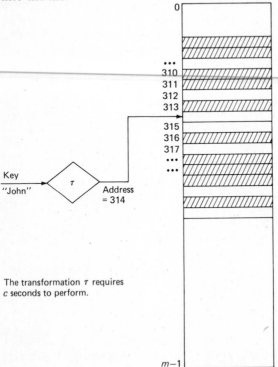

Figure 3-17 Record accessing in a direct file.

3-5-1 Structure and Manipulation of Direct Files

In simple implementations of direct access, identification numbers are assigned to the data records that provide a relative address into the file. Thus, employee Joe is designated as 257, and that tells us directly that his payroll record is to be found as record 257. We will list a number of problems with the use of file addresses to identify data records, and then present the common methods used currently.

Problems with use of direct file addresses   There are problems when using actual disk addresses in terms of numeric continuity and response to system changes. Thes are solved by using relative addresses as shown in Sec. 2-3-3, but several other problems remain:

> Identification numbers for a person or object may be needed in more than one file; in fact, different subsets may be required, causing one individual or item to carry a variety of numbers.
>
> To reuse space, the identification number has to be reassigned when a record has been deleted, causing confusion when processing past and present data together.
>
> Natural keys are names, social security numbers, or inventory numbers where groups of successive digits have meaning. Such keys are long, longer than is needed give a unique address to each record. In general, the number of people or items which may be referred to by *natural* keys is much larger than the number of records to be kept on the file. In other words, the key address space is much larger than the file space, and direct use of the key would fill the file very sparsely.

Key-to-Address Transformations   The solution to the problems associated with the use of keys as file addresses involves the use of a computational procedure that translates the key attribute values into relative addresses within the file space. Each candidate relative address identifies a *slot* into which a record may be placed. There should be at least as many slots as expected records. The procedure is hence based on the number of slots in a file. A different procedure is used to compute the relative addresses from the identifying key of a person in the Employees file and from the same key in the Sales_personnel file. The procedure depends also on the type of key. Such computations are called *key-to-address transformations*. Two categories of these computations may be distinguished, *deterministic proce-dures* which translate identification fields into unique addresses, and *randomizing techniques* which translate the keys into addresses which are as unique as possible but do not guarantee uniqueness.

Figure 3-17 shows the access to a direct file for a new record with key "John". The key-to-address transformation algorithm τ applied to the string "John" has generated the relative record address "314". The same key-to-address transforma-tion is applied to a search argument when a record is to be fetched.

A *deterministic procedure* takes the set of all key values and computes a unique corresponding relative address. Algorithms for such transformations become difficult to construct if the number of file entries is larger than a few dozen. Adding a new entry would require a new algorithm, since the algorithm is dependent on the distribution of the source keys; hence only static files can be handled. The replacement of a computational algorithm with a table makes the problem of transformation more tractable: we have invented again the indexed file! We will not discuss deterministic direct access further.

The *randomizing transformations* translate the key value into relative addresses within the file using a randomizing algorithmic procedure. A uniform distribution of addresses is desired, since this will place an equal fraction of the keys into each and every slot.

The problem with randomizing transformations is that they will generate some identical addresses from different source keys, so that more than one record may be directed to the same place in storage. Such an occurrence is called a *collision*, and we will discuss later in this section what is to be done in that case.

The randomizations may be designed to try to preserve the order of the records, or it may be designed to maximize the degree of uniqueness of the resulting address. Most transformations take the latter as their only goal. The first class of transformations are called *sequence maintaining*; the other algorithms are referred to as *hashing techniques*. A family tree of key-to-address transformations is displayed in Fig. 3-18. A simple technique is illustrated in Example 3-9.

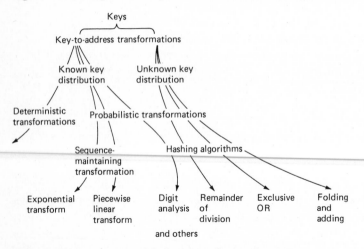

Figure 3-18 Key-to-address transformation types.

Example 3-9   Key-to-Address Transformation
A randomizing transformation for a personnel file uses the social security number as the key. We assume that the value of the low-order digits of these numbers is evenly distributed and hence there is a high probability of deriving out of these digits a unique number for every employee. If one wants to allow space for 500 employees, the value of the key may be divided by 500, leaving a remainder with values between 0 and 499. Obviously identical addresses can occur:

```
Al     or    322-45-6178    giving    178
Joe    or    123-45-6284              284
Mary   or    036-23-0373              373
Pete   or    901-23-4784              284
```

Here Joe and Pete will both be assigned to a record number 284; the records for Joe and Pete will collide if both are placed directly into a file.

Key and File Address Space A key value may range over a large number of possible values, limited only by the maximum size of the key field V. The number of legal keys is up to 10^V for a numeric key, 26^V for a simple alphabetic key. For a social security number the key space size is $999\,999\,999$. The number of records n to be kept, and the record space of the file, will be much less for all users outside of the Social Security Administration itself. The available file address space can be defined in terms of the record capacity or number of slots m of the file. The number of actual records put in the file cannot exceed the number of available slots; hence, if the key uses *base* distinct symbols,

$$base^V \gg m \geq n$$

Since many of the key-to-address algorithms depend on a numeric key value, it may be desirable to convert alphabetic keys into integers. If a value from 0 to 25 (`lettervalue`) can be assigned to the 26 letters used, a dense numeric representation can be obtained without any loss of information, using a polynomial conversion as

```
/* Letters to Integers; applied to the key given in array 'letter'*/
   numeric_value = 0;
   DO i = 1 TO number_of_letters;
     numeric_value = numeric_value * 26 + lettervalue(letter(i));
   END;
```

Numbers and blanks occurring in keys require appropriate expansion of this routine, and computer-word overflow has to be considered.

Now the actual key-to-address translation can take place, using the remainder-of-division algorithm described below and assigning $m \approx 1.5 \times n \to 751$ slots for the 500 employees

```
/* Slot number for the key; uses Remainder of Division by a prime */
   rel_address = MOD(numeric_value, 751);
```

The file system uses relative addressing, as detailed in Sec. 2-3-3, to translate the sequential slot numbers given in `rel_address` from their range of 0 to $m-1$ into the physical addresses of the devices, probably disk units, used for the storage of the data. Sequentiality of the storage blocks is immaterial for direct access.

For files it is desirable to compute block addresses instead of addresses of specific record slots. Records with the same block address will be placed sequentially into the block. The *Bfr* slots available in such block comprise a *bucket*. The effect of using buckets is considered below when collisions are discussed.

Linear Growth of File Space A method, termed *linear hashing* [Litwin[80]], can avoid the reduction of the fetch performance of a direct file which occurs if the number of records n grows substantially during the existence of the file. The problem of file growth is that an increased density $dens = n/m$ leads to higher rates of collisions, as quantified by Eqs. 3-69, 3-73, etc.

The direct file grows through insertion of records, and an inserted record may cause a collision. To reduce the probability of ever-increasing collisions we let the hashing space grow also, by appending blocks linearly to the end of the hash space. For collisions which still occur overflow blocks are used. We will use m_0 to indicate the initial, basic allocation, and let m_0 be a power of 2. The current allocation m_1 begins with m_0. THe simplest growth policy is to increase the allocated space m_1 by one slot for every collision; this will ensure that in the long term the collision rate is constant. The actual space allocation in a file is by buckets which have Bfr slots, so that the file is actually made to grow from $m_1 \Rightarrow m_1 + Bfr$ every Bfr collisions.

Whenever a new block is assigned it is populated by splitting a block, but the split is assigned differently from a split seen in B-trees. The block to be split is **not** the block where the collision occurred, but in linear hashing the block to be split is the *lowest numbered* block not yet split. This scheme avoids auxiliary tables to indicate which blocks have been split, only the current limit m_1 has to be known.

The method for addressing and the method for splitting cooperate. The block to be split has `rel_address = m1 - m0` so that the first block to be split corresponds to `rel_address = 0`. The address computation uses the same type of key-to-address transformations but uses for the space parameter m twice the initial allocation m_0, so that an extra high-order bit is available. The generated address is reduced to the current range $0, \ldots, m_1$ by an additional statement

```
IF rel_address > m1 THEN rel_address = rel_address - m0
```

This corrects the addresses of all blocks not yet split: $(m_1 - m_0), \ldots, m_0$.

A collision creates an overflow but can also indicate the need to append a new block. In that case a new block is allocated and the current `m1` is incremented. The block at $m_1 - m_0$ is now to be split. The hash addresses of the records in that block and any overflows attached to that block are recomputed using the incremented value of m_1. All those records will either have the original address (the high-order bit was zero and their `rel_address = m1-m0`) or will have the new address `m1`, referring to the new block! The records which now belong into the new block are moved and both the split block and the new block are rewritten.

When the file has grown to twice its size $(m_1 = m)$ the hashing function is adjusted by another bit: m and m_0 are doubled, and the process can continue with $m_1 = m_0$. Methods to actually allocate these blocks are presented in Sec. 6-5.

A Short Survey of Key-to-Address Transformation Methods Of the many techniques which have been proposed and evaluated, only some are used for files.

Distribution-dependent methods depend on some knowledge of the distribution of keys for the expected records. If we have, for instance, assigned random numbers to identify 1000 samples of some experiment being recorded, we can expect that any three digit positions of the sample identification will be randomly distributed, and suitable as direct-access keys. The liabilities of distribution-dependent transformations are major, since a change in key distribution can cause these methods to generate many more collisions than previously. A benefit of some distribution dependent key-to-address transformations is that they can allow maintenance of sequentiality. Such a *sequence-maintaining key-to-address transformation* achieves this goal by letting the addresses produced increase with increasing keys. Serial access is made possible in this case. Otherwise basic direct files do not have the capability for serial access. Two distribution-dependent methods are *digit analysis* and *sequence maintaining transformations*.

The three hashing methods presented here (*remainder-of-division, exclusive-OR, folding-and-adding*) randomize the properties of the digits of the key to a uniform distribution. Operations such as arithmetic multiplication and addition, which tend to produce normally distributed random values (see Sec. 6-1), are undesirable when hashing.

The *digit-analysis-method* attempts to capitalize on the existing distributions of key digits. An estimate or a tabulation is made for each of the successive digit positions of the keys of a sample of the records to be stored. The tabulation lists the frequency of distribution of zeros, ones, twos, and so on. The digit positions that show a reasonably uniform, even distribution are candidates for use in the slot address. A sufficient number of such digit positions has to be found to make up the full address; otherwise combinations of other digit positions can be tested. In Example 3-9 the three low-order digits of a social security number were considered to be uniformly distributed. Similar use can be made of character-string keys.

A *sequence-maintaining-transformation* can be obtained by taking an inverse of the distribution of keys found. This inverse function is applied to the keys. The addresses generated will maintain sequentiality with respect to the source key. In a *piecewise-linear-transformation* the observed distribution is approximated by simple line segments. This approximation then is used to distribute the addresses in a complementary manner. An *exponential transformation* is presented in Example 6-1 as an illustration of the evaluation of the uniformity of obtained addresses. These approaches are valid only if the source key distribution is stable.

The *remainder-of-division* of the key by a divisor equal to the number of record slots allocated m was used to obtain the desired address above. The remainder does not preserve sequentiality. The remainder of division is in some sense similar to taking the low-order digits, but when the divisor is *not* a multiple of the base (10 in Example 3-9 above) of the number system used to represent the key, information from the high-order portions of the key will be included. This additional information scrambles the result further and increases the uniformity of the generated address.

Large prime numbers are generally used as divisors since their quotients exhibit a well-distributed behavior, even when parts of the key do not. In general, divisors that do not contain small primes (≤ 19) are adequate. If the address space m_0 is a power of two then $m = m_0 - 1$ is often suitable. Tests [Lum[71K]] have shown that division tends to preserve, better than other methods, preexisting uniform distributions, especially uniformity due to sequences of low-order digits in assigned identification numbers, and performs quite well.

The need to use a division operation often does leads to programming problems. The key field to be transformed may be larger than the largest dividend the divide operation can accept, and some computers do not have divide instructions which provide a remainder. The remainder then has to be computed using the expression

```
rel_address = key - FLOOR(key/m) * m
```

The explicit FLOOR operation is included to prevent a smart optimizer from generating address=0 for every key which would lead to all records colliding. Costly divisions can be avoided by replacing them by multiplication of the reciprocal of m, but the behavior of the result may differ.

The *exclusive-OR* (**x-or**) operation provides a very satisfactory randomization and can be used when key lengths are great or division is otherwise awkward. The **x-or** operation is available on most binary computers or can be obtained by statements as

```
        DECLARE (rel_address,keypart1,keypart2) BIT(19);
    x_or: PROCEDURE(arg1,arg2); DECLARE(arg1,arg2) BIT(*);
          RETURN( (arg1 ∨ arg2) ∧ ( ¬ (arg1 ∧ arg2)) );
          END x_or;
    ...
    rel_address = x_or(keypart1,keypart2);
```

As the example shows, the key is segmented into parts (here 2) which match the required address size. Using this operation results in random patterns for random binary inputs. If the segments contain characters, their boundaries should be avoided. For instance, **x_or('MA','RA')** will be equal to **x_or('RA','MA')**, so that "**MARA**" will collide with "**RAMA**". Care has to be taken also where the binary representation of decimal digits or characters is such that certain bit positions always will be zero or one. Both problems can be controlled by making the segment sizes such that they have no common divisor relative to character or word sizes. This operation is generally among the fastest computational alternatives provided by the hardware.

Folding and adding of the key digit string to give a shorter string for the address has been often used. Alternate segments are bit-reversed to destroy patterns which arithmetic addition might preserve. A carry from a numeric overflow may be added into the low-order position. This method is available in the hardware of some large Honeywell computers.

Probability of Success with Randomization Methods   We assess now the performance risks in randomization. A graphic or quantitative understanding of the processes of transformation can aid in developing a feeling for the effects of various methods to achieve random distributions [Peterson[57]]. The number of ways to transform n keys into m addresses is huge; there are in fact m^n possible functions. Even for the most trivial case, say, $n = 4$ records and $m = 5$ slots 625 transforms exist. Of these, however, only $m!/(m - n)! = 125$ would avoid any collisions while loading the file. It would obviously be most desirable to find one of these. On the other hand, we have $m = 5$ possibilities for a total collision; all records wind up in the same slot, and in those instances, the expected number of accesses for a fetch, using a chain, would be $(n+1)/2 = 2.5$; the remaining 495 transforms cause one or two collisions.

Since the randomization method is chosen without any prior knowledge of the keys, the selection of any reasonable method out of the m^n choices gives a probability of that method causing no collisions ($o_0 = 0$) of only $p_0 = (m!/(m - n)!)/m^n = 0.2$. On the other hand, the probability of selecting one of the five worst methods for this case, which would lead to $c = n - 1 = 3$ collisions and $o_{max} = 1 + 2 + 3$ extra accesses, is only $p_{max} = m/m^n = 0.008$. The remaining three cases of one collision, two collisions in two slots, and two collisions in the same slot can be analyzed similarly and are shown in Fig. 3-19. Given the assumption that we have just an average randomization, we find that we may expect an average of $p = \sum_c p_c o_c = 0.30$ additional accesses per record loaded.

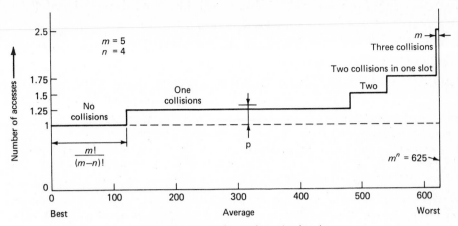

Figure 3-19 Fetch-length distribution.

We expect at the final point that $o = \sum_c p_c c = 1.05$ records collided and were not loaded within the main file; they have to be placed somewhere else. The file is expected to contain $n - o = 4 - 1.05 = 2.95$ records. The collision probability for the next insertion is $1 - 2.95/5 = 0.41$.

The distribution will have a similar shape for other values of m and n. The number of steps rapidly increases with n and m so that the distribution function becomes smooth. Estimates for the number of collisions in the general case are derived in Sec. 6-1, but the intent of this discussion is to show the relative unimportance of the specific choice of randomization method, as long as it is chosen to be outside of the obviously worst areas. It might be mentioned here that a change of keys, that is, a new set of data to be randomized, will completely reorder the position of the m^n functions in the figure, but the form of the distribution remains the same.

Summary of Key-to-Address Transformations It is obvious from the above that many choices exist for transforming keys of records to record addresses. We find also that the average performance of reasonable transformations is such that perfectly good results are obtained with less than perfect methods. Cute methods, as deterministic and sequence-maintaining schemes, carry in fact a high risk of failure when conditions change.

Since the placement of the records is determined by a computation, only one attribute of the record can be used for retrieval. Another inherent restriction due to the computation is that data records are expected to be of fixed length.

Records of randomized direct files can be accessed only via one precise attribute value and not by range, and not serially. To locate the next record in key sequence requires knowing or guessing the value of the key, and this violates our definitions for **Get-Next** operations. Guessing a successor key would, in the great majority of fetches, result in a *record-not-found* condition. In practice this choice is excluded from consideration.

Some solutions to the problems listed here are shown in Sec. 4-6; they all carry additional access costs. All randomizing methods may create identical addresses, even when the source keys differ. Now we consider what may be done in that case.

Collisions When a randomizing key-to-address transformation produces identical addresses for distinct records, we have a collision. In Fig. 3-20 a new entry `Shostakovich` collides with an earlier entry `John`. The resolution of the collisions will occupy us in this section.

The more slots a file has relative to the number of records to be stored, the lower the probability of collisions will be. While we will evaluate such probabilities in detail subsequently, we note that at typical B-tree density ($m/n = 1.45$), we incur a rate of collisions that is quite bearable; even without buckets, we expect collisions less than 35% of the times we access the file.

To determine whether such a collision has occurred, we have to compare the key value found at the computed address with the key value given.

Consider using a file constructed from Example 3-9. The algorithm computed for `Pete`, with `social security number = 901-23-4784`, a slot number of `284` but this does not necessarily provide a space for `Pete`'s record. The content of the slot itself has to be tested. The slot can be empty, it can contain an older record for `Pete`, or it can already contain a colliding record for `Joe` or someone else.

On insertion the slot at the computed address is fetched and tested whether it is empty. To indicate that a slot in the file is `Empty`, the field to be used for the key may be set to `NULL`. Insertion into an empty slot is straightforward. If the slot is full, there is a collision. If in the file multiple records may have the same key, the record to be inserted can be stored according to the collision resolution scheme used, but typically records of direct files are to be *unique*.

Uniqueness is assured by matching the key fields of the file slot and the request. If the new and old key fields do not match, it is a true collision. If key fields match on insert, the record found may have to be replaced; the implied operation is an update of possibly all attributes but the key.

A similar process is followed for the search argument when a record is to be fetched. If nonunique records, i.e., records with duplicate keys, are to be retrieved, a count is needed to find all matches to the search argument. We will avoid duplicate keys here. The corresponding outcomes are now:

Condition	Insert	Fetch
slot_key = NULL	ok to insert	no record found
keys match	replace record if permitted	record found
keys do not match	look for another free slot	go to successor slots

We will now discuss methods of handling collisions, first from the point of view of inserting a new record to a direct file.

Collision Resolution Three strategies are in use to resolve collisions, sometimes in combination. Two methods, *linear search* and *rerandomization*, which use the main file for storage of the records which have collided, the *overflow*, are referred to as *open addressing* techniques. Figure 3-20 shows the third alternative, the use of a separate *overflow area* for such records. The performance of all three methods is significantly improved if first a search through the current block or *bucket* is made.

Search in the Bucket An important aspect in the management of overflows from collisions is the grouping of slots into buckets. A typical bucket is equal to one block, as shown in Fig. 3-21. A search through successive slots in the bucket is used to locate space for the new record. Only computational time is required to access the records within a bucket. Only when the bucket itself is filled will one of the three alternative overflow methods require a disk access. If the bucket is of block size B, there will be space for *ovpb* collisions in the block, where

$$ovpb = \left(1 - \frac{n}{m}\right)\frac{B}{R} \qquad\qquad 3\text{-}69$$

namely, the fraction of free space times the number of slots per block. We can use the blocking factor *Bfr* for B/R if we are careful to remain aware that we

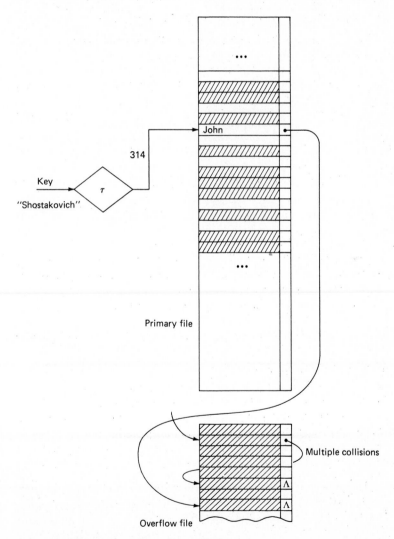

Figure 3-20 Direct file with collision.

are talking here about slots, and not records. The cost of most collisions is now drastically reduced. An analysis of the effect of the use of buckets is unfortunately quite complex. Figure 3-23 gives results for the use of buckets with a linear search in the file. We find for the earlier example ($m/n = 1.45$) and $Bfr = 8$ a reduction in collision cost from 35% to 5%.

   Bucket Addresses   When buckets are used, the entire block is made available when a record is required. Now a shorter address can be used. If there are Bfr slots in a bucket, the address space reduces from m to m/Bfr and the size of an address pointer will be $\log_2 Bfr$ bits less.

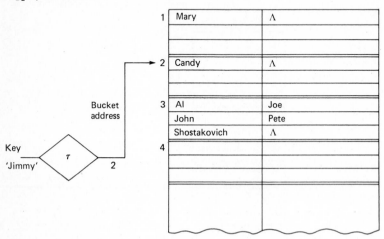

Figure 3-21 Buckets.

   Linear Search in the File   When an overflow out of the bucket does occur, the search can continue to the next sequential block. This avoids the costs of seek times to new areas but tends to cluster overflows together. The linear search method for overflow slots is predominant for direct files, since it is simple and, one hopes, infrequently invoked. As long as the number of entries is less than the number of slots available ($n \leq m$), a record space will eventually be found. Since the availability of a free slot can be determined a priori, no alternate termination method is required.

   The problem of clustering is that, when an area of the storage space is densely used, fetches need many search steps. Additional insertions tend to increase the size of the dense area disproportionally. Clustering has been shown to be quite detrimental even for moderately loaded direct files; an example how clusters develop is shown in Fig. 3-22.

   Rerandomization in the File   To avoid or to distribute the clusters one may assign the bucket for the overflow at a random position in the file. A new randomizing key-to-address computation, taking other identifying data or using an alternate algorithm, computes a new slot address in the same file space. Rerandomization, when applied to devices such as disk files, causes a high overhead, since generally a new seek is required. Further collisions can occur, and the procedure may have to be repeated a number of times. A randomizing procedure cannot easily guarantee that it will ever locate an empty space. Rerandomization techniques are used commonly when hashing in primary memory, but for files they appear less beneficial. They probably should also be evaluated carefully when it appears that memory is used, but the operating system uses paging to storage for memory management.

Use of an Overflow Area   The third method of handling collisions is to put all records which cause a bucket overflow into a separate file with a linkage from the primary record, similar to the overflow chains used in indexed-sequential files. If such a separate overflow area is established, no clustering will take place. An overflow still causes a new seek but avoids the repeated block fetches which can occur with the previous two methods. A difficulty here lies in the allocation of sufficient overflow space, since the number of collisions is not absolutely predictable. The overflow area may fill while the main area has much free space.

The cost of overflows out of the main file can be lowered again by allocating overflow areas on each cylinder. This requires modification of the key-to-address transformation to account for the gaps in the primary addressing space. If buckets are already used, it may be better to use this space to reduce the density per bucket.

Linkage to Colliding Records   Once the block for an overflow is located, the record is yet to be found. Overflow records in successor blocks can be found either by simply matching all successive records in the block to the search argument, or by locating the candidate records by use of a chain before doing the comparison.

Without a chain the search for a record or for a free slot for an insertion terminates when an empty slot is reached. This approach constrains the deletion of records, as discussed below. In a densely loaded file it may take many accesses to find an empty slot, because many intervening slots may be filled by records belonging to the set associated with a different primary bucket address. To identify an arbitrary stored record as a member of the set of colliding records for a specific prime bucket, the key of stored record accessed has to be transformed to the corresponding address, which is then matched to the initial bucket address. If the addresses are equal, this record belongs to this *collision set*.

The use of a pointer chain avoids accessing records which do not have the same computed bucket address. Now fetches can be limited to the set of colliding records. The use of chain also improves fetches where the record is not in the file, since the search terminates when the chain pointer is NULL, rather than going on to a free slot.

For insertions it is best to use any free slot in the nearest bucket. If chains are used, the inserted record must be linked into the chain. The linkage of records into the chain at the current block improves locality. This is probably more effective than trying to keep records in sequential order by key or by access frequency.

Deletion from Direct Files   Deletion of a record involves some additional considerations. We have to assure that the freed slot does not hinder subsequent fetch usage, and we also would like to have the slot available for reuse to avoid excessive reorganizations.

We will first consider the cases where a chain is used to link the records of a collision set. The use of a chain requires that deletions mark the slot Empty and also that the chain is reset so that any successor records can still be retrieved. If there is more than one record

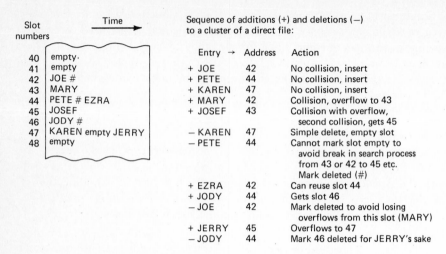

Sequence of additions (+) and deletions (−) to a cluster of a direct file:

Entry →	Address	Action
+ JOE	42	No collision, insert
+ PETE	44	No collision, insert
+ KAREN	47	No collision, insert
+ MARY	42	Collision, overflow to 43
+ JOSEF	43	Collision with overflow, second collision, gets 45
− KAREN	47	Simple delete, empty slot
− PETE	44	Cannot mark slot empty to avoid break in search process from 43 or 42 to 45 etc. Mark deleted (#)
+ EZRA	42	Can reuse slot 44
+ JODY	44	Gets slot 46
− JOE	42	Mark deleted to avoid losing overflows from this slot (MARY)
+ JERRY	45	Overflows to 47
− JODY	44	Mark 46 deleted for JERRY's sake

Slot numbers, Time →

40	empty·
41	empty
42	JOE #
43	MARY
44	PETE # EZRA
45	JOSEF
46	JODY #
47	KAREN empty JERRY
48	empty

A search in this cluster, as it appears now, will require an average of

$$\frac{2(\text{MARY}) + 3(\text{EZRA}) + 3(\text{JOSEF}) + 3(\text{JERRY})}{4(\text{number of entries})} = 2.75 \text{ comparisions.}$$

An optimal distribution, as sketched below, for these entries would require:

41	empty
42	MARY
43	EZRA
44	JOSEF
45	JERRY
46	empty

$$\frac{1 + 2 + 2 + 1}{4} = 1.5 \text{ comparisions on the average}$$

Rearrangement of members of chains when deleting can improve the search time experienced in the cluster above.

Figure 3-22 Operations on a file without chaining and with open addressing.

in the collision set, the predecessor record has to be rewritten with the pointer value from the deleted record. Subsequent insertions should use free slots close to the primary bucket, so that the search path does not become longer and longer.

Open addressing methods can be used without a chain. In that case a search for a record to be fetched or for a free slot for an insertion terminates when an empty slot is reached. This means that deleted records cannot just have their slot set to Empty, but have to adjust the file to avoid breaking a subsequent search.

Either a tombstone has to be set which indicates that this record, although deleted, still is on the path to successor overflow records, or the last record of the collision set has to be moved to fill this freed slot. In this latter case the slot can still not be marked Empty, because it may be crossed by some other collision set. Its tombstone, however, can indicate Deleted, and the slot is available for reuse.

Figure 3-22 illustrates what can happen in these clusters of collision sets when we use open addressing, no chains, and sequential search for slots for overflows. Some deleted record spaces can be reused, but the path length for fetches and inserts includes all spaces not explicitly marked empty. After many deletions and insertions there will be many slots which hold markers and no data. This increases the number of slots to be scanned when searching. The effective density of the file is hence greater than n/m, and this can considerably reduce the performance of a direct file.

A partial, block-oriented, reorganization can collect sufficient information about the collision to set deleted slots which are not within any collision set to **Empty** in order to break these clusters. A complete reorganization would rehash all the keys in the block and place the records in order by computed address.

3-5-2 Use of Direct Files

Direct random access is an invention specific to computers and has been used to access data on the earliest disk files. Direct files find frequent use for directories, pricing tables, schedules, name lists, and so forth. In such applications where the record sizes are small and fixed, where fast access is essential, and where the data are always simply accessed, the direct file organization is uniquely suitable. Simple access means here use of a single key for retrieval, and no serial access.

Direct files also play an important role as a component of more complex file organizations. We will find many uses of direct files in Secs. 4-6 and 4-7.

3-5-3 Performance of Direct Files

The performance of direct files has been more thoroughly analyzed than the performance of any of the preceding methods. The initial parameter in these evaluations is the number of record spaces or slots m that are available for the storage of the n records. The number of records that still cause collisions is denoted here as o.

We will first analyze a simple direct-access structure with the main file having buckets that hold only a single record and with a separate overflow area to contain up to o records that caused collisions. The records are of fixed length, and contain a single pointer field to allow access to any successor records due to overflows. With the fixed record format the attribute names are not kept within the records, so that space is only needed for the a data values of size V.

Access to the single overflow area will require a seek. There are no identical keys, i.e., all stored records are unique, so that all collisions are due to the randomization. The number of records stored n is still smaller than the number of slots m, so that a perfect distribution would not lead to any overflows and hence keep $o = 0$.

We let overflow records be found via a chain of pointers starting from the primary area. The overflow chain is maintained so that blocks containing overflow records are accessed in sequence. This avoids accessing the same block more than once in a chain.

We will, when appropriate, also make comments which pertain to direct files using open addressing and to the use of multirecord buckets, since these methods are used frequently.

Record Size in a Direct File The space required for a file S_F as described above is

$$S_F = m(aV + P) + o(aV + P) \qquad \text{3-70}$$

or per record,

$$R_{effective} = \frac{m + o}{n}(aV + P) = \frac{m + o}{n}R \qquad \text{3-71}$$

The required overflow space is based on the fraction of collisions p, as discussed below, but should also consider the expected variability of that estimate, so that this area will in practice never overflow between reorganizations. For a file with many records the expected variability is small, and o can be safely dimensioned to be 25% to 100% greater than pn. The estimation of the needed overflow size o is elaborated in Sec. 6-1-5.

Fetch Record in a Direct File   In order to predict an average for time to locate a record in a direct file, we must determine the probability of collision p, since the predicted fetch time is simply the time required for randomization, the time for the single direct access, plus the average cost of the case of a collision

$$T_F = c + s + r + btt + p(s + r + btt) \qquad \langle \text{basic case} \rangle \; 3\text{-}72$$

An analysis which estimates the collision cost p for this design is given in Sec. 6-1-5, leading to Eq. 6-15. The result of the analysis shows that for direct files, single-slot buckets, and using separate overflow areas for collisions, the expected value of p is

$$p = \frac{1}{2}\frac{n}{m} \qquad \langle \text{with overflow area} \rangle \; 3\text{-}73$$

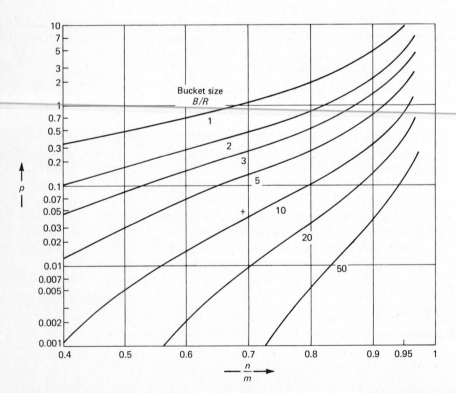

Figure 3-23 Overflow cost for multirecord buckets, open addressing, and linear search.

Effect of Open Addressing In open addressing with a linear search clusters of collisions can occur. The detrimental effect of clusters increases rapidly with the file density n/m, as seen in Fig. 3-23 for the bucket size $B/R = 1$. Knuth[73S] has derived, using the arguments of an "average" randomly selected randomization discussed above, that the number of additional accesses becomes

$$p = \frac{1}{2} \frac{n}{m-n} \qquad \langle \text{with open addressing} \rangle \ 3\text{-}74$$

The result for bucket sizes $B/R > 1$, as derived by Knuth[73S], is complex and hence is presented in graphical form as Fig. 3-23. The overflow cost is based on the initial probability of an overflow plus all further overflows to be accessed, so that under poor conditions $p > 1$.

It should be noted that no overflow area is required when open addressing is used, so that for the same total amount of storage the value of m may be appropriately larger. Increasing m to $m + o$ will not compensate fully for the increased number of collisions, as demonstrated in Example 3-10.

Measurements of direct files have produced results which are in close agreement with Eqs. 3-72 and 3-73 [Lum[71]]. The values shown in Fig. 3-23 have been experimentally verified by Deutscher[75] using the remainder of division algorithm to compute the addresses. Even for poorly distributed keys the results became valid when bucket sizes $B/R \geq 5$.

Example 3-10 Collision Costs

We can now evaluate the effect of collisions. We will provide 50% more primary space than the amount required for the expected records themselves, i.e., $m = 1.5 n$. For the basic direct file – only one record space per bucket and a separate overflow area – we obtain a collision cost of

$$p = \frac{1}{2} \frac{n}{1.5 n} = 0.3333 \qquad \text{or about 33\% extra accesses}$$

due to collisions when the file is fully loaded. A reasonable overflow area in this case may be based on $1.5 p$, giving $o = 0.5 n$.

With open addressing, using the same primary space m and still bucket sizes equal to R, the value of p becomes

$$p = \frac{1}{2} \frac{1}{1.5 - 1} = 1.0 \qquad \text{or 100\% extra accesses}$$

Adding the space no longer required for the overflow area o to the space for the main file m reduces this estimate to

$$p = \frac{1}{2} \frac{1}{1.5 + 0.5 - 1} = 0.5 \qquad \text{or 50\% extra accesses}$$

The use of multirecord buckets has a greater effect. If the record size $R = 200$ and the block size $B = 2000$, the bucket size can be made equal to $Bfr = 10$; this change increases only the computational overhead for a block retrieved into memory. We will *not* add the overflow space to the main file, so that $m = 1.5 n$. We obtain from Fig. 3-23

$$p = 0.03 \ \text{for} \ \frac{n}{m} = 0.66, \ Bfr = 10 \qquad \text{or about 3\% extra accesses}$$

Since now only 3% of the fetches will have to access another block, a linear, sequential scan for overflows is reasonable.

Locating the Successor Block In linear searching, if the decision to read the next block can be made immediately, no revolution needs to be wasted. In general, however, one revolution is required to read the next block if the read decision is based on the contents of the predecessor block, so that the access time for an overflow is $T_{RW} + btt$ or $2r + btt$. Alternate-block accessing, as shown in Fig. 3-24, can reduce this delay to $2\,btt$, leaving a time $c < btt$ for the comparisons within a bucket. This technique does not require any general block renumbering, since the decision where to place overflows is specific to the procedure for direct-file access.

We find overflow records in successor blocks by use of a chain. The search for a nonexistent record can be terminated at an end-of-chain flag. Multiple records may be found within the same block. In linear search we can expect, without clustering, $(m-n)/m\,Bfr$ free slots in a block, and these are available for insertion. A failure to find the record in a successor block p_2 is then

$$p_2 \approx p^{\frac{m-n}{n}} Bfr \qquad\qquad \langle\text{linear search}\rangle\ 3\text{-}75$$

which makes the event quite rare. When needed, successive blocks are accessed using the chain of records extending from the primary bucket.

When a separate overflow area is used, the probability of not finding the successor block in the same bucket is higher and can be evaluated based on the number of blocks used for the overflow area. This value is

$$p_2 \approx o'/Bfr \qquad\qquad \langle\text{separate overflow area}\rangle\ 3\text{-}76$$

We will ignore p_2 in the fetch evaluation below, since we will always choose methods with a low primary collision cost p.

In summary, the fetch time for the various cases becomes

$$T_F = c + s + r + btt + p\,t_{overflow} \qquad\qquad \langle\text{all cases}\rangle\ 3\text{-}77$$

where the choices for p are given above and the values for the overflow cost are

$$t_{overflow} = s + r + btt \qquad \text{for a separate overflow area}$$
$$t_{overflow} = r + btt \qquad \text{for separate overflow areas on the same cylinder}$$
$$t_{overflow} = 2r + btt \qquad \text{for linear searching, sequential blocks}$$
$$t_{overflow} = 2\,btt \qquad \text{for linear searching, alternate blocks}$$

and c depends on the complexity of the hashing algorithm and the bucket size.

Fetch for a Record Not in the File In a fetch for a nonexistent record, we will be forced to follow the chain search until we find a NULL pointer. This time is greater than the time required for fetching an existing record, since we expect to find records on the average halfway into the chain. This condition occurs also when insertions are considered (T_{Iov}), since all the records of an overflow chain have to be tested to locate an empty slot for insertion.

The effect can be estimated by setting the term $p\,t_{overflow} \approx 2\,p\,t_{overflow}$ for the fraction of records(not_in_file) in Eq. 3-77 above.

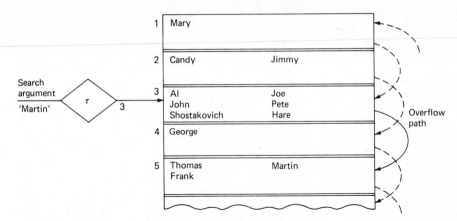

Figure 3-24 Alternate bucket overflow accessing.

Get-Next Record of a Direct File   No concept of serial access exists within the direct file which uses randomizing for its key-to-address translation. If the key for the next record is known, a successor record can be found using the same procedure used to find any record.

$$T_N = T_F \qquad\qquad 3\text{-}78$$

If the key for the next record is not known, no practical method exists to retrieve that record.

For direct files using linear key-to-address translations, which do maintain a serial ordering, the successor record is found by sequential reading, skipping over any unused slots. The probability of finding the record in the next slot can be estimated using the density of the main file n/m. A low density reduces performance here. If a separate overflow area is used, and the probability of overflow is significant, a case-analysis approach, as used for an indexed-sequential file (Eq. 3-40), may be neccessary.

Insert into a Direct File   To insert a record into the file, an empty slot has to be found which can be reached according to the key. The key-to-address transformation generates a prime bucket address. The bucket must be fetched and checked to determine whether there is a free slot for the record. We will consider now again buckets of only one slot and the use of a chain of records which collided. The probability of the initial slot being filled p_{1u} has also been derived in Sec. 6-1-5, Eq. 6-18 for the case of a separate overflow area:

$$p_{1u} = 1 - e^{n/m} \qquad\qquad \langle \text{overflow area} \rangle\ 3\text{-}79$$

If open addressing is used all records are in the file and we can simply use the density:

$$p_{1u} = \frac{n}{m} \qquad\qquad \langle \text{open addressing} \rangle\ 3\text{-}80$$

For multiple records per bucket the value of p_{1u} can again be best determined from Fig. 3-23.

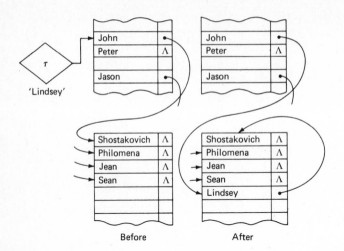

Figure 3-25 Overflow record linked as second chain member.

The insertion cost can be computed as the sum of the expected cost for the case where the primary slot is empty, which has the probability of $(1 - p_{1u})$, and the cost for the case where the primary slot is filled, a probability of p_{1u}. In both cases the primary block is fetched first. If the slot is found empty, the record is placed into the empty slot, and the block rewritten; otherwise the existing record is kept and one of the overflow procedures discussed has to be followed.

When a *separate overflow area* is used, the procedure is to link the new record as the second member of the chain, as illustrated in Fig. 3-25. The block with the primary record is still rewritten, now with the existing record and the latest address in the overflow area in its pointer field. The new record is placed into the overflow area at position **last** with the pointer value obtained from the primary record. The two rewrites require

$$T_I = c + s + r + btt + T_{RW} + (1 - p_{1u})(s + r + btt + T_{RW}) \qquad \langle \text{simple} \rangle \ 3\text{-}81$$

If duplicate records with the same key are not permitted, all in the bucket records have to be checked prior to insertion of the new one. This means that the entire chain must be followed. The cost considerations for the fetch of a nonexisting record apply $p(\texttt{not\_in\_file})$ and the search time for checking involves the same terms used in (Eq. 3-77). When the end of the chain is reached (pointer is **NULL**), a block with the selected prior record and the new inserted record is rewritten. If the block where the search terminated is full, an additional block fetch and rewrite is required. The probability of this event is only $1/Bfr$. The primary block is not rewritten unless it is the terminal block.

$$
\begin{aligned}
T_I = \ &c + s + r + btt \\
&+ 2\, p_{1u}\, t_{overflow} + T_{RW} + \frac{1}{Bfr}(s + r + btt + T_{RW}) \qquad \langle \text{with checking} \rangle \ 3\text{-}82
\end{aligned}
$$

The cost of following the chain is similar for overflow areas and for open addressing.

If buckets with many slots per bucket are used, the secondary overflow probabilities p_2 reduce rapidly and the chains will be short. We can consider here simply that insertion requires a fetch, and a rewrite. In open addressing there is a probability based on the density that the inserted record does not fit into the block found. Now

$$T_I = c + s + r + btt$$
$$+ p_{1u} t_{overflow} + T_{RW} + \frac{n}{m}(s + r + btt + T_{RW}) \qquad \langle\text{large buckets}\rangle \quad 3\text{-}83$$

Use of a separate overflow area would affect the last term, as seen in Eq. 3-82. The use of chaining affects mainly the value of c.

The considerations leading to Eqs. 3-81 and 3-82 apply also if we wish to optimize the record placement into blocks of the overflow area. Here the simple procedure of Eq. 3-80 is not adequate and the chain will have to be followed until a suitable block is encountered.

When the combination of open addressing, single-slot buckets, and no chaining is used, the entire set of colliding and all the associated clusters (see Fig. 3-22) have to be passed to find a free space. No satisfactory formulation for the linear searching required in this case is known to the author. A low density n/m is important to keep p_{1u} reasonable. Knuth[73S] suggests that

$$T_I \approx \frac{m}{m - n}(s + r + btt) \qquad \langle\text{open addressing, one slot buckets}\rangle \quad 3\text{-}84$$

when rerandomization instead of sequential search is used. A special technique for inserting a batch of insertions is given in the discussion leading to Eq. 3-89.

Update Record in a Direct File The process of updating the record consists of finding the record and rewriting it into the original slot, so that

$$T_U = T_F + T_{RW} \qquad\qquad 3\text{-}85$$

When the key changes, a deletion and a new write operation has to be performed.

Deletion requires the same effort when records are not chained. Depending on the method used for linkage, a tombstone may have to be set. If chaining is used, and it is desirable to set the slot to `Empty` to make it available for another collision set, then the preceding record has to be rewritten with the linkage pointer obtained from the deleted record.

Read Entire Direct File An exhaustive search for a file using a randomizing key-to-address translation can be done only by searching through the entire space allocated to the file, since the discrete transformations from a sparse set of key values do not allow serial reading. The search is costlier, since the file space also contains empty and deleted slots. The area used by the overflows will also have to be checked. A separate overflow area will be dense, except for deletions, but

$$T_X \approx (m + o)\frac{R + W}{t'} \qquad\qquad 3\text{-}86$$

In practice direct files are rarely used when reading of the entire file is an expected operation.

Reorganization of a Direct File   Reorganizations are mainly required if the total number of records to be kept has grown and no provisions were made for extension of file space; linear hashing was presented in Sec. 3-1 as a method to accomodate growth.   Growth causes the density n/m to exceed the design goals. Reorganization allocates a larger space to the primary area for the file; the randomizing procedure has to be rewritten or adjusted. All data have to be copied using an exhaustive search and reloaded into new slots. The terms T_X and T_{Load} defined below should be estimated using the old value of m for T_X and the new value of m for T_{Load}.

Reorganization is also beneficial when many deletions have occurred so that search paths have become tangled and long. For large collision sets which are not chained, this effect can reduce performance sufficiently to make a reorganization warranted.

If the file cannot be removed from service for a long time, i.e., a high *availability* is desired, an incremental reorganization can reorganize a single cluster (defined as the space between two empty slots) at a time. Otherwise a reorganization will read and reload the entire file

$$T_Y = T_X + T_{Load} \qquad\qquad 3\text{-}87$$

where T_{Load} is the loading time discussed below.

Loading a Direct File   The most obvious way to load or reload a direct file is to rewrite the records one by one into the new space; then

$$T_{Load} = n\,T_I(n) \qquad\qquad 3\text{-}88$$

with a continuously changing value of $T_I(n)$ as n/m increases. Initially there should be scarcely any collisions. The evaluation with Fig. 3-19 was based on loading the file. A first-order estimate to compute the average T_I can be based on a density of $\frac{3}{4}n/m$. Loading still requires much effort; every record will require at least one random block access, and if open addressing is used, the new file will develop clusters as it fills.

A two-pass procedure can be used to reduce the effect of clusters. In the first pass records are stored only if they have primary slots; any colliding records are placed into the remaining empty slots of the file during a second pass.

A major reduction in loading cost can be accomplished by sorting the file to be loaded into the direct file sequence, i.e., by computed address. To do this, the key-to-address transformation is applied to all the record keys of the records to be loaded into the file, and the address obtained is attached to the records. The records are then sorted based on the attached address. Equation 3-11 indicated the speed of a sort operation. The sorted file is then copied without the addresses into the space for the direct file; slots which do not have a matching address are skipped, and colliding records are placed into successor slots. This writing time is equal to the sequential exhaustive read time, so that

$$T_{Load} = c + T_{sort} + T_X \qquad\qquad 3\text{-}89$$

The advantage of a substantially reduced loading time is that reorganization can become a valid alternative to more complex schemes used to combat clustering and to manage deletions in a dynamic environment.

Using the technique of sorting by address, leading to Eq. 3-89, to reload the direct file space permits the entire reorganization to be performed at a cost of

$$T_Y = c + 2T_X + T_{sort} \qquad\qquad 3\text{-}90$$

Batch Insertion The reloading method can also be used to add a batch of insertions into the file. The batch would have to be quite large. If we use n_I to denote the size of the batch, this insertion method would be profitable only if $n_I > (T_Y/T_I)$.

3-6 THE MULTIRING FILE

The three previous file-organization methods dealt with the problem of finding individual records fast. This last of the six basic methods, the *multiring* file, is oriented toward efficient processing of subsets of records. A subset is defined as a group of records which contain some common attribute value, for instance, all **employees** who speak **French**. The multiring approach is used with many database systems; in this chapter we consider only the file structure of this approach.

Subsets of records are explicitly chained together through the use of pointers which define some order for the members of the subset. One record can be a member of many such subsets. Each subset has a header record which is the origin for the chain. A header record will contain information which pertains to all its subordinate member records. The header records for sets of subsets can also be linked into a chain.

The particular type of chain which will be used to illustrate this approach is the *ring*, a chain where the last member's pointer field is used to point to the header record of the chain. Similar file structures are called *threaded lists* or *multi-lists* in the literature, and can be implemented either with rings or with simple chains. The rings being considered here can be nested to many levels of depth, by letting member records become the header records of subsidiary rings. This capability does not necessarily exist in threaded lists or multi-lists.

Figure 3-26 shows a simple hierarchically linked ring structure. The individual records in this example could be formatted as shown in Fig. 3-27.

An example of the type of query for which this organization is well suited is

"List all employees in Thule"

A search in a multiring file is made by following a chain for an attribute type until a match is found for the search attribute value. Then a new chain is entered to find the subordinate attribute records. This process is repeated if neccessary until the desired record or set of records is found. For the example the location ring is read until the record for **Thule** is found; then the three **employees** living there could be listed.

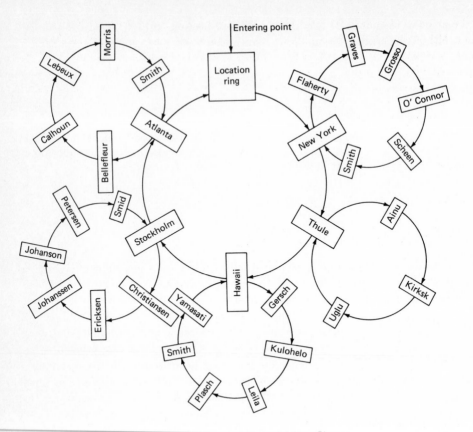

Figure 3-26 Record linkage in a simple multiring file.

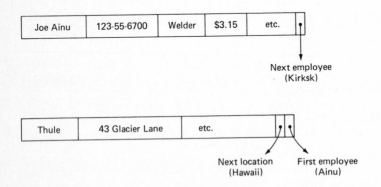

Figure 3-27 Records in a ring structure.

Depiction of Multiring Files In order to simplify the presentation of these rings, we will use boxes and a specially shaped arrow to indicate rings and their relationship. The concept of the arrow to depict $1 \rightarrow m$ relationship of the one master record to many subsidiary member records is due to Bachman[66]. The shape of the arrow is chosen to denote the fact that many rings will exist at the terminal point, although only one box is shown. A simple arrow is used to indicate an *entry point*, a ring whose header record is immediately accessible. Such rings will be cataloged and will provide an initial point for processing queries. Figure 3-28a depicts the structure of the sample shown as Fig. 3-26 with an entry point using direct access.

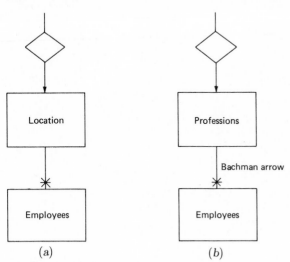

(a)   (b)

Figure 3-28a and b Two employee files.

Interlinked Rings Another query of interest, which should be answerable from this file, might be

"List all welders in our company"

Using the structure shown in Fig. 3-26, this would require an exhaustive search, traversing the **department** ring and each **employee** subsidiary ring in turn. Figure 3-28b shows the ring structure which would allow answering this second query effectively.

It is obvious that the redundant **employee** files should be combined, which can be accomplished by replacing the data field for **profession** with another linkage field, as shown in Fig. 3-29. The actual ring structure with these two relationships has already become quite complex, but practical implementations can include many more rings.

If we expand the above example by segregating the **employees** in the various **locations** into specific **departments**, allow access also in order of **seniority**, add a **warehouse** at each **location**, and keep **stock** information available, then the structure diagram will be as shown in Fig. 3-30. If the actual connecting pointers had to be drawn, the picture would look like a bowl of spaghetti.

Relationships between rings are not necessarily hierarchical. Linkages may be implemented that relate members of the same ring (Fig. 3-31), that provide multiple pathways between records, or that relate lower rings back to higher-order rings.

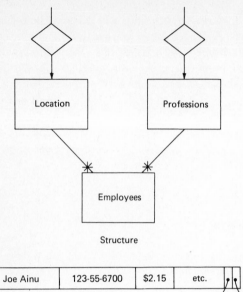

Structure

Record

Next
welder

Next employee
in Thule

Figure 3-29 Interlinked rings.

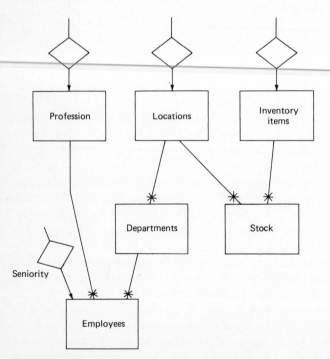

Figure 3-30 Complex hierarchical structure.

Two examples of multiple pathways are shown in Fig. 3-32, which may be helpful to readers who understand football.

Not all constructs are allowed or implementable in practice. The ease with which the membership arrows can be drawn hides the complexity of underlying structure very effectively. Loops and other nonhierarchical relationships between records may require a variable number of pointer fields in the records and are hence undesirable. In Fig. 3-31 an implementation may limit the spouses relationship to one entry. The visit_history relationship may be best implemented using a search argument from children to an index for clinics. A database approach which permits some of these alternatives is described in Sec. 9-6.

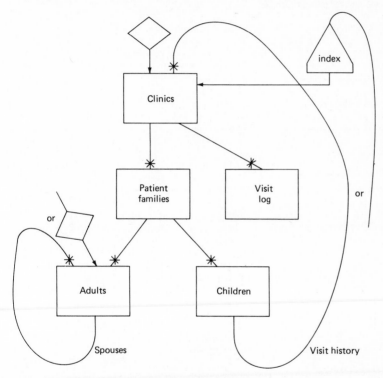

Figure 3-31 Loops in ring structures.

As the structures become more complex, the query processor may have to choose among alternate access paths to retrieve a record or a subset, and the choices may have quite different costs. A query applied to the structure shown in Fig. 3-30 as

"Find an employee in Thule who can weld"

can be processed beginning at the location or at the profession ring. The appropriate records will be found at the intersection of any department at that location and the welder ring.

The effectiveness of a process in locating a record depends strongly on a good match of the attribute pairs forming the query argument with the structure of the file. If the file is not organized appropriately, the process cannot proceed efficiently, and user intervention may be needed. For instance, if there is no **profession** ring, the path for the query above would have to begin at the entry point for **location**. Since the **location** record does not give a clue about the **profession**, an exhaustive search would be necessary through all **department** rings at this **location**. In an interactive environment, the system might have asked at this point,

> "Which department do you suggest?".

The process of finding the best path for a query to such a database has been termed *navigation* by the principal developer of this file-design concept [Bachman[73]].

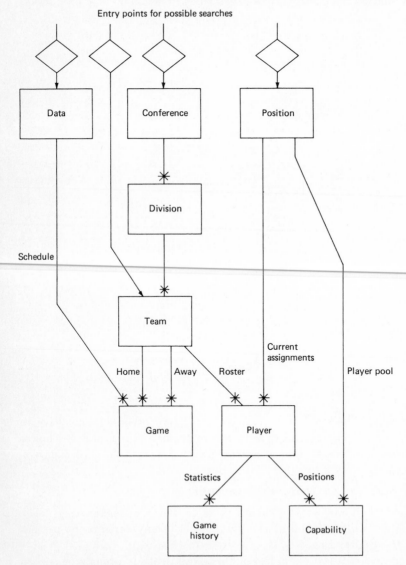

Figure 3-32 NFL football database.

3-6-1 Structure and Manipulation of Multiring Files

In a multiring file all records will have similar structures, but their contents and size will be a function of the rings to which they belong. A multiring file may have a considerable number of distinct record categories. We note here a violation of the earlier definition of a file: the records now are not identical in format, and ring membership as well as file membership has to be known before processing.

Record Formats The precise format of a record depends on the combination of ring types of which the record is a member. The attribute-value pairs could be self-identifying, as seen in the pile file; but typically they are not, and each record will have a record-type identifier. In Fig. 3-33 the field **t** identifies this record as being an **employee** record. Each record of type **t** will have similar data fields and seven pointer fields. This identifier will allow reference to an appropriate record format description, stored with the general description of the file.

To link the records into their rings, many pointers will appear in a typical record. A record can belong to as many rings as it has pointers. A given pointer position in the record format is, in general, assigned to a specific category of rings. In the example above, **profession** may be such a category and **welder** one specific ring of that category. If an instance of a record is not a member of a certain category ring, there will be an unused pointer field containing a **NULL** entry (Λ), as shown in Fig. 3-33.

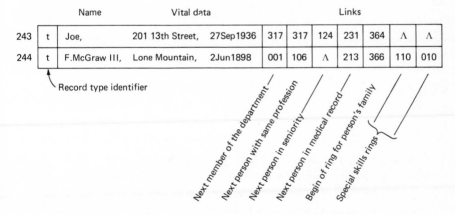

Figure 3-33 Record field assignments for a ring file.

There can also be **NULL** data fields, but since there are many types of records for specific purposes the overall file will be relatively dense. If all data fields are filled, and no redundant data are kept, the number of fields used is commensurate with the parameter a' which was used to enumerate the number of valid attributes for a record. The use of header records in fact reduces the redundancy of attributes found in files without the structure provided in the multiring file.

Header Records Each ring will have a header. This header is either an entry point, a member of another ring, or both. The header for the ring of department **employees** will be the list of **departments**; the header for the ring of **welders** will be a member of the ring of **professions**; and the **employee**'s record may be the header for a ring listing family members. When a ring is entered during a search, the point of entry is noted so that when this point is reached again, the search can be terminated.

As shown in the examples above, the typical multiring file organization avoids redundancy of data by placing data common to all members of a ring in the header of the ring. For example, the name and other data about the **department** of an **employee** appears only in the header record. A negative effect is that, in the basic ring design, whenever record is to be fetched based on a combination of search arguments, the match of all search arguments with data values applicable to the record cannot always be performed using only the attributes kept in the record or in the header records accessed during the search. Two alternatives can be used:

A *parallel search* through all rings identified in the search argument can be made, terminating at the records at the intersection of these rings.

An *initial search* can be made according to the attribute with the best partitioning effectiveness. The records collected are then checked for appropriateness by locating the header records for the other attribute types needed and rejecting records with inappropriate data values.

This latter process applied to the simple structure of Fig. 3-20 yields the steps shown in Example 3-11.

Example 3-11   Searching through a Nonredundant Multiring File

---

```
Query:
  Find an Employee with Location ='Thule' and Profession='Welder'.

        Enter Location chain;
        For each member record determine if key ='Thule';
        When found follow Employee chain;
            /* every record is also a member of the profession chain  */
            For each Employee record follow the profession chain;
            When its header record is reached,
                then inspect for key ='Welder'
                If the profession header indicates the desired profession,
                    then the Employee member record is selected for output;
            Continue with the next Employee record;
        When the its header record, the Location = 'Thule' is reached,
            then the result is complete.
```

The importance of the final pointer to the header which transforms a chain into a ring is clear here, but the cost of obtaining data from the header can still be great. Hence it may be desirable to still keep important descriptive data redundantly in the record, or to expand the structure to allow easy access to header records. Auxiliary constructs for that purpose are presented in Sec. 4-7.

Ring Membership The design decisions that select the attributes for which rings should be established are similar to the decisions which determine the attributes to be indexed in a multi-indexed file. The cost of following the chains increases linearly with chain sizes. The sizes of individual chains can be reduced by increasing the number of chains and the number of levels in the structure of the file.

Increasing the number of levels (x) reduces the expected chain lengths (y), since the number of partitions for the lowest-level (1) records increases. If all chain lengths in the file are equal, the expected chain length according to one hierarchy, say `locations, departments, employees` of Fig. 3-30, is

$$y = \sqrt[x]{n} \qquad \qquad \text{(equal chain lengths) 3-91}$$

since the product of all the chains (`#locations * #departments_per_location * #employees_per_department`) is $y^3 = n$. This effect is shown graphically in Fig. 3-35. Numerically Eq. 3-90 is equivalent to stating that $x = \log_y n$, similar to the number of levels found for indexes (i.e., Eq. 3-48). However, in this file organization the partitioning of the file by attributes and hence the number of levels determines the chain sizes; whereas the computed fanout determines the number of levels in an index.

We consider now the case where the desired record can be recognized without having to trace back to alternate headers. The search time for a lowest level record decreases then proportionally to the xth root of the record count n and increases proportionally to the number of levels x.

Example 3-12   Cost of Searching through a Multiring File

Query: 'Find the welder with social security number = 123 45 6789'.
 Given the multiring file of Fig. 3-30 with the following record counts:
        10000 employees with 10000 social security numbers,
        and 50 professions (of equal size, 200 members each);
        also 20 locations with 10 departments of 50 employees each.
    The first search alternative is to enter the employee ring at the
        entry provided for ordering by seniority and search for the
        employee by social security number,
            takes 5000 block accesses.
    The second search alternative - by profession and then
            within a profession -
            takes $25 + 100 = 125$ expected block accesses.
        The optimum for two levels is $2\frac{1}{2}\sqrt{10000} = 100$
    A third alternative - by location, department, and then employee -
            takes $10 + 5 + 25 = 40$ block accesses
        but is only possible if location and department are known.
        The optimum for three levels is $3\frac{1}{2}\sqrt[3]{10000} = 33$

The block fetch counts seen are much greater than the expected number when indexes are used; the retrieval of successor records, however, is more economical in this structure than it is when using indexed files.

An attribute which does not partition the file into multiple levels, such as a `social security number` which has a perfect partitioning effectiveness, is not very useful as a ring element in a `personnel` file, since to find someone in this manner we would expect to require $n/2$ fetches. Finding a specific `welder`, however, is done fairly efficiently by searching down the `profession` chain and then through the `welder` chain. The file designer hopes that both these chains will partition the search space effectively; the optimum is attained when both chains are equal in length, namely, $\sqrt{n}$. In practice this is of course never quite true.

If we wish to summarize data for all the `welders`, we can expect $25+200=225$ accesses. This number of records probably cannot be obtained more efficiently by any of the preceding methods. In order to gain a complementary benefit in access time, locality of rings has also to be considered in the file design.

Some attributes, such as `profession`, can be naturally enumerated as a number of discrete categories, e.g., `welders, bookkeepers`. Such a categorization will have a powerful partitioning effect, and the file will match well the natural structure of the data. Attributes that do not represent discrete data, e.g., `weight` or `height`, do not provide effective partitioning unless they are artificially categorized. Such artificial categories for an attribute `height` may be

{`<150cm, 150-154cm, 155-159cm, 160-164cm, ..., >189cm`}.

If continuous variables like these are used as secondary categories, so that the memberships of each of these rings is reasonably small, a simple ordering within the ring may be all that is necessary. Ordering of members of a ring is frequently used.

Clustering of Rings Records which are frequently accessed together are obviously best stored with a high degree of locality. One single ring can, in general, be placed entirely within one cylinder so that all seeks are avoided when following this particular *clustered* ring.

When frequent reference to the header record of the ring is needed, that header record may also participate in the cluster. Now the ring at the next-higher level will be difficult to cluster, unless the total space needed by all member records and their ancestors is sufficiently small to be kept on one or a few cylinders. With success traversal according to a clustered hierarchy will take very few seeks. In substantial files a given record type at a lower level will require many cylinders, and traversals of rings other than the clustered ring will require seeks.

A possible assignment for the data of Fig. 3-30 is sketched in Fig. 3-34. Locating an `employee` via `department` will require only a few seeks within the `department` ring, to find the `employee` ring for the `department`. If there are many `employees` in some `department`, there may be some cylinder breaks in the ring. Finding an `employee` by `profession` may require seeks between nearly every `employee` record. `Stock` in a warehouse is found with few seeks for a given `location`; these rings are apt to be long, and will require some seeks at cylinder break points. In order to relate `stock` to the `inventory` data will take seeks between records, but these rings may be short if there are few `locations`. A peek at Fig. 9-16 can convey an impression of the complexity of optimal clustering assignment in a realistic situation.

In a dynamically changing database, optimal clustering is difficult to maintain and its benefits should be partially discounted. A reorganization may be needed to restore clusters.

Ring structures have been implemented in practice with a number of important additional features. We will mention several of these in Chap. 4; they all will make the analysis of file performance more complex.

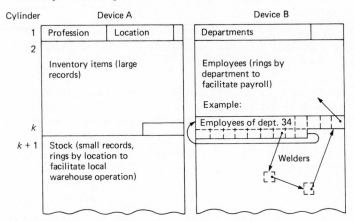

Figure 3-34 Assignment of rings to storage.

3-6-2 Use of Multiring Files

The concept of related master and detail records can be traced to traditional data-processing procedures. Multiring structures are the basis for some of the largest databases currently in use. Management information systems where much of the system operation involves tabulating, summarizing, and exception reporting have been implemented using these multi-linked lists. Examples of such operation were shown in the introduction to this section.

Some problems in geographic and architectural space representation also have been approached with a multiring approach. Current developments in integrated multifile systems depend greatly on the capabilities provided by ring structures. A problem with the multiring structure is that a careful design based on prior knowledge of the data and usage pattern is required before a multiring file can be implemented.

3-6-3 Performance of Multiring Files

The performance of a multiring system depends greatly on the suitability of the attribute assignments to particular rings. In the evaluation below, we will assume that the file structure is optimally matched to the usage requirements.

We will analyze the performance for access to lowest level records in a hierarchy of rings. Each record can be adequately identified when accessed, so that no tracing from a candidate goal record to its header records is required. The record formats are fixed within a record type.

In each record, there will be a fixed number of data and linkage fields, denoted as a'_{data} and a'_{link}, respectively.

We also assume an ideal partitioning of the file by the attributes, so that the rings on the various levels are of equal size. We neglect benefits to be gained by locality management of the rings, or clustering. The effects of these two factors may balance each other.

Record Size in a Multiring File Since many distinct record types will exist in a multiring file, an accurate estimate is obtained only by listing all types, with their respective frequency and size. In a file designed for minimal redundancy we expect that in the most frequent lower-level records

$$a'_{data} + a'_{link} \leq a' \qquad\qquad \langle \text{nonredundant} \rangle \text{ 3-92}$$

since each data element is either explicitly represented or found by reference to some header record; one linkage pointer can replace a number of attributes.

If there is complete duplication of information in attribute fields and linkage fields to permit rapid selection of individual records, but still no empty fields, then

$$a'_{link} \leq a'_{data} = a' \qquad\qquad \langle \text{redundant} \rangle \text{ 3-93}$$

Linkages to the same header record are not included.

In practice we find values in between these ranges, and relatively few linkage fields. Some important data fields will be kept redundantly to avoid excessive header referencing. A reasonable first order estimate is to let

$$a'_{data} + a'_{link} = a' \qquad\qquad \langle \text{estimate} \rangle \text{ 3-94}$$

if the files have been carefully designed to satisfy a known query pattern.

The size of a data field is again averaged at V, and a linkage field contains pointer values of size P. One field of size P is prefixed to each record to allow identification of the record category. Then for an average record

$$R = P + a'_{data}V + a'_{link}P \qquad\qquad \text{3-95}$$

If the records are members of relatively few rings, the size difference of data values and pointers will not matter, so that with the estimate of Eq. 3-94

$$R \approx a'V \qquad\qquad \langle \text{estimate} \rangle \text{ 3-96}$$

Again, individual record categories will vary about this estimate, and where R is used to estmate Bfr and block retrievals the specific values are needed.

Fetch Record in a Multiring File The time to fetch a record is a function of the number of chains searched and the length of the chains. We assume that the record contains enough data so that when it is found according to one particular accessing sequence, it can be properly identified. The record hence is found by searching strictly down a hierarchy of x levels. We hence have to consider here only one ring membership per record type.

The length of a ring (y) depends on the size of the file, the number of levels, and how well the file is partitioned into the rings, as shown in Fig. 3-35. An estimate for the ideal case was given in Eq. 3-91. The lowest level (1) contains a total of n records in all its rings together, discounting other record types at higher levels or other hierarchies in the file.

If a single record is to be fetched, the number of hierarchical levels should be matched by the number of search arguments, a_F, in the search key. Example 3-12 illustrated this interdependence.

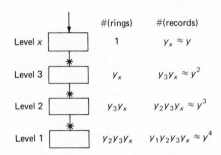

	#(rings)	#(records)
Level x	1	$y_x \approx y$
Level 3	y_x	$y_3 y_x \approx y^2$
Level 2	$y_3 y_x$	$y_2 y_3 y_x \approx y^3$
Level 1	$y_2 y_3 y_x$	$y_1 y_2 y_3 y_x \approx y^4$

Figure 3-35 File size at four hierarchical levels.

If there are fewer search arguments in the key, an entire ring, i.e., a subset of the records of the file, will be retrieved; if there are more arguments, there is redundancy, and attributes unproductive in terms of an optimum search strategy can be ignored. For a standard fetch the condition $a_F = x$ holds, and with Eq. 3-91

$$a_F = x = \log_y n \qquad \qquad 3\text{-}97$$

In order to traverse one level, we expect to access $\lceil y/2 \rceil$ records, using the same reasoning which led to Eq. 3-4. In order to locate a record at the lowest level, the most likely goal, we will traverse x rings so that $\frac{1}{2}x\,y$ records will be accessed. Assuming random placement of the blocks which contain these records,

$$T_F = \frac{x\,y}{2}(s + r + btt) \qquad \qquad 3\text{-}98$$

Using the expected number of levels, a_F for the hierarchy used by the query, and the corresponding value for y

$$T_F = \frac{a_F \sqrt[a_F]{n}}{2}(s + r + btt) = fna(s + r + btt) \qquad \langle\text{in query terms}\rangle \ 3\text{-}99$$

where fna represents the terms based on the values of a_F and n. We see that this relation is critically dependent on the optimum structure of the data, since the query format matches the relationships inherent in the file structure. Auxiliary rings or linkages will have to be employed if the search length for some foreseen and important search attribute combinations becomes excessive. Unplanned queries are difficult to satisfy with this structure.

Table 3-3 lists values for fna given some typical values for n and a_F.

Table 3-3   Values for the File-Access Factor fna

	fna		
a_F	$n =$ 10 000	$n =$ 100 000	$n =$ 1 000 000
1	5 000	50 000	500 000
2	100	318	1 000
3	33	72	150
4	20	36	72
5	20	25	32
6	18	24	30

fna = file-access factor
a_F = number of levels of rings in the search hierarchy
n = number of records on the level to be accessed

The search time may be reduced when important rings are placed, so that they tend to cluster on a single cylinder. Large databases of this form have also been implemented on fixed-head disk hardware where no seeks are required, so that the term $s = 0$.

Get-Next Record of a Multiring File The next record, according to any of the linked sequences, can be found simply by following the proper chain

$$T_N = s + r + btt \tag{3-100}$$

It should be noted that in this file organization serial ordering exists for multiple attributes. The "next" record can be a record according to several (a_{link}) attribute types. The only other basic file organization that provides multiattribute serial access is the multi-indexed file.

If serial access via one particular ring is frequent, the records for one ring can be clustered within one cylinder, as discussed above. Then $s = 0$ when accessing members of that ring. Getting a next record tends to be an important operation in data processing using this file structure, so that multiring files will often use clustering. It is wise, however, to evaluate the effect conservatively.

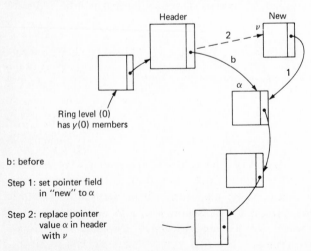

Figure 3-36 Insertion into a ring.

Insert into a Multiring File Adding a record to a multiring file is done by determining a suitable free space for the record, locating all predecessors for the new record, taking the value of the appropriate links from the predecessors, setting it into the new record, and placing the value of the position of the new record into the predecessor link areas.

The total effort, except for placing the record itself, is hence proportional to a'_{link}. Some effort can be saved at the bottom levels when the chains are not ordered. The sum of the fetches in all hierarchies into which the record is linked, the predecessor rewrites, and the placing of the final record is basically

$$T_I = a'_{link}(T_F + T_{RW}) + s + r + btt + T_{RW} \qquad\qquad 3\text{-}101$$

The cost of inserting a new record is obviously quite high, especially if the record is a member of many rings. In Sec. 4-7 structures that allow faster location of the predecessor records are shown. Fig. 13-3 shows alternative insertion methods.

Unordered Attributes If the records are ordered by attribute value, the chain has to be searched for the correct insertion point. If the chain connects identical attribute values, such as all **welders**, then only the header record has to be read, modified, and rewritten. For rings where the order does not matter, new records can also be inserted in the initial position. This will result in an inverse chronological sequence. Such a sequence is also desirable for fetching single records, since recent data are found rapidly. The process is illustrated in Fig. 3-36.

This linking has to be carried out for all a'_{link} rings of which the new record is a member. For each ring which is maintained in unordered form $y/2 - 1$ block accesses can be saved in insertion or update. We will not account for this saving in the evaluations, but the term can be subtracted if appropriate from Eqs. 3-101, 3-103, and 3-104.

Update Record in a Multiring File If only data fields are to be changed, the update requires only finding the record and rewriting it. We can assume that updated records do not change type and keep the same length. Then

$$T_U = T_F + T_{RW} \qquad\qquad \langle\text{unlinked attributes}\rangle\ 3\text{-}102$$

for data field changes. If the record to be updated is initially located via a **Get-Next** operation, as is frequent in this type of file, the initial T_F can be replaced here, and in Eqs. 3-103 and 3-104, by T_N.

Updating of records can also require changes to the linkage. Only linkages whose values have changed need to be altered, since the updated record and its predecessors can be rewritten into the original position. Two cases exist here, since a new predecessor can be either in the same ring or in another ring, although at the same level, as the current predecessor.

If the changed value for one linkage is still within the type of the search attribute used to locate the record, then the point where the new record is to be inserted will be in the same ring and will require only $\frac{1}{2}y$ expected accesses of records in the ring. If, for instance, **stock items** of a given type are kept sorted within their ring by **weight**, a change due to a new design can require an item to shift position within the ring. To achieve such a shuffle, the new and the old predecessors have to be located for every link that is to be changed. We assume conservatively that a circuit of length y around each ring is needed to find both.

To relink the updated record into a new place within the ring, the pointers of the three records are interchanged:

```
The new predecessor is set to point to the updated record.
The old predecessor is set to point to the former successor record
                    of the updated record.
The new record is rewritten after all the new predecessor records
                    have been read, since its successor links are
                    copied from the new predecessors.
```

For this final rewrite no reading is required, but the position has to be recovered, requiring $s + r$ before the updated block can be written (btt).

The total for this case includes the initial fetch, the search for the predecessors of a_U links, the rewrite of these new and old predecessor records, and the final repositioning and rewrite of the new record. All this requires

$$T_U = T_F + a_U(y(s + r + btt) + 2\,T_{RW}) + s + r + btt \qquad \langle\text{links in ring}\rangle \text{ 3-103}$$

If, during the search for the old position of the record, a note is made of each predecessor and also if the new position is passed, the accesses to locate one of the predecessors and sometimes the accesses required to find the new predecessor record can be eliminated. The term y can then be reduced to $\frac{1}{2}y$ or even to 1 for one of the links. Since a_U is often 1 or small, the difference can be significant.

If updates cause ring membership changes within the same ring type, the new insertion positions have to be located. An example of this case is an `employee` who changes `departments`. This could be done by searching from the top, as was necessary in the case of record insertion. It may be faster to go to the header records using the ring, and then search through those header records for the desired place (`'Hawaii'`). The predecessor in the old ring (`'Calhoun'`) has also to be located and rewritten with a pointer to the previous successor (`'Morris'`). This process is illustrated in Fig. 3-37. The insertion place (`'Kulahelo'`) still has to be found.

We denote the number of links requiring access outside the current ring by a_W. The first choice, searching for the header records of a_W links from the top of the hierarchy, again requires a_W fetches of time T_F. For updates less than three levels from the top (level numbers x, $x-1$, and $x-3$), it is advantageous to locate the insertion point from the top. The general approach is to navigate via the headers.

Using the header requires, for each changed outside link, finding the current header, finding the new header, and finding the new insertion point. A fourth scan of a ring is required to find the old predecessor, needed to achieve unlinking. The expected accesses in each ring are again $y/2$. The entire process requires for all fields together $a_W\,4\,y/2$ accesses. The entire process now takes

$$T_U = T_F + a_W(2\,y(s + r + btt) + 2\,T_{RW}) + s + r + btt \qquad \langle\text{links outside of ring}\rangle \text{ 3-104}$$

In practice there may be both a_U links that can be updated within the ring and a_W links that require the complexity of ring changes. In that case both terms apply with their factors.

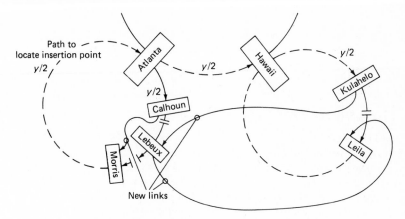

Employee 'Lebeux' is transferred from 'Atlanta' to 'Hawaii'

Figure 3-37 Finding a new linkage point.

Read Entire Multiring File Exhaustive searches may be carried out by serially following any of a variety of possible linkages. A proper understanding of the file design is required to assure that no records will be read more than once. The cost will be relatively high, since the process will have to follow the linkages given in the records. The alternative, searching sequentially through the space, may not be easy, since the records have a variety of formats, and the description of a record type is necessary to make sense of the fields obtained.

Reading according to the chains requires, in addition, that a header record is accessed for each subsidiary ring. Both the old and the new header record is needed to move between two rings, but it should be possible to keep a stack of x old header records in primary memory. Then

$$T_X = n\left(1 + \tfrac{1}{y}\right)(s + r + btt) \qquad\qquad 3\text{-}105$$

Reorganization of a Multiring File Reorganization is not required as part of normal operating procedures. This is made obvious by the fact that a database system based on multiring files, IDS, available since about 1966, did not have an associated reorganization program available until 1975. Only when reformatting of record types is required will such records have to be rewritten. This may require only a partial reorganization of the file, since the changes are limited to rings of the levels using those records types. If one ring can be processed in memory at a time the costly rewriting of pointers found in updating can be avoided. The entire ring of y records is read, rearranged, and then rewritten at a cost of $y(s + r + btt) + c + y(s + r + btt)$. To fetch the rings to be reorganized we access the headers with one fetch and subsequent get-next operations.

A reorganization of n' records of one level, according to this incremental approach, is then

$$T_Y(n') = c + T_F + \frac{n'}{y}T_N + 2\,n's + r + btt \qquad\qquad 3\text{-}106$$

where, if the reorganization takes place at level λ from the top (level $= x - \lambda + 1$), an estimate for $n' \approx y^\lambda$.

BACKGROUND AND REFERENCES

The basic file designs presented here can easily be traced to early developments in data processing. A pile is, of course, the most obvious data collection. Most of the pieces of paper that cross our desks are self-identifying documents, which can be processed without reference to an external structure description. Ledgers and card files are the basis for sequential files; they are often divided into pages or folders with headings. Sequential indexes and rings provide a partitioning of a file to accelerate access. Multiple indexes, based on title, authors, and subject, can be found in any library. Only direct access seems to be a concept specific to computer technology.

All the file organizations have corresponding algorithms and structures applicable to core memory, but their use within a homogenous space affects the access parameters so that the evaluation of the relative value of the algorithms and their options leads to quite different results. An example is found in hashing, although paging effects often invalidate the assumptions made for memory-oriented performance. The six basic methods discussed in this chapter will be summarized in the introduction to Chap. 4.

These methods have been analyzed at several levels of abstraction. A pile file is described by Glantz[70] and partitioning is exploited by Yue[78]. Lomet[75] describes the use of tombstones. Severance[72] considers sequential files and buckets, and the difference between fetch and get-next operations. Heaps[70] does batch fetching in sequential files. Gildersleeve[71] is devoted to sequential files, and programming to use them is described by Germain[67]. The problem of merging co-sequential files has often been analyzed, a recent example is Levy[82]. Chapin[68] includes also the programming of indexed-sequential files. Further information is available in the literature of software suppliers (see Appendix B). Seaman[66] and Lum[73] treat indexed-sequential files analytically, and Ghosh[69] proposes to use probing instead of lower-level indexes. Allen[68] describes an application using large indexed-sequential files. Indexed-sequential files were considered in Brown[72] to comprise such a significant fraction of disk usage that the IBM3330 disk design was greatly influenced by their behavior.

The construction of index trees has been frequently discussed in the computer science literature. It is important to realize when using this literature that the index trees found in storage file have very high fanout ratios and do not contain the data within themselves. Trees containing data are discussed in Sec. 4-4. Landauer[63] considers dense dynamically changing indexes, and Sussenguth[63] evaluates indexes in core storage. Bose[69], Welch in King[75], and Larson[81] evaluate access to indexed files using formal and mathematical models.

The B-tree algorithm was presented and evaluated by Bayer[72O,S]. Comer[79] provides an excellent summary and Knuth[73S] includes some file-oriented considerations. Yao[78] analyzed the density of B-trees under random insertions and deletions. Yamamoto[79] and Rosenberg[81] consider strategies for optimal behavior. Aho[79U] evalutes their use in relational databases. Ghosh[69] combines B-trees with probing. The technique of presplitting is described in Guibas[78].

Peterson[57] and Heising publicized randomized direct access for files. Schay[62, 63], Buchholz[63], Hanan[63], and Heising[63] analyzed direct access with chaining and open addressing. Amble[74] discusses optimal chain arrangements for direct access files. Open addressing with linear probing has been further analyzed by Morris[68], Kral[71], and Knuth[73]. VanDerPool[73] analyzes for the steady state the optimal file design for various storage cost to processor cost ratios, both for a direct file using a separate overflow area and for the case of open addressing. Gurski[73] considers digit selection by bit, IBMJ20-0235 describes digit selection, Kronwal[65] presents the piecewise-linear-distribution algorithm, and Sorensen in King[75] presents an evaluation of distribution-dependent hashing methods. Waters[75] defends and analyzes linear transformations. Summaries of hashing techniques are given by Maurer[75] and by Knott[75]. Many papers concentrate on the choice of hashing algorithms and the expected fetch chain length.

Concurrent access of direct primary and overflow areas is proposed by Groner[74]. Bays[73] presents rules for reallocating entries to new, larger, direct access file areas, Fagin[78] uses tables to locate extensions and avoid multiple seeks for collisions, and Litwin[80] develops this approach and adds linear hashing. Batch updating of a direct file is suggested by Nijssen in Codd[71]. Prywes[63] proposes multiple chains for files, and Bachman[64] describes the multiring approach; the CODASYL standards encouraged numerous applications of this system. Lang[68] presents another ring implementation and many illustrations are found in Kaiman[73]. Further aspects of ring structures can be found in the descriptions of database systems, and more references to specific file methods will be found with Chap. 4.

The desire to recognize communalities among the several file methods is expressed by Bachman[66]. Hsiao[70] defines file concepts formally and applies the definitions to retrieval in pile, indexed-sequential, indexed, ring, and redundantly inverted files. Bayer[74] compares B-trees with direct access. Wedekind in Klimbie[75] compares dense indexes and B-trees and favors indexes. Stonebraker[80] presents the alternatives used in INGRES. Dodd[69] surveys sequential and various ring and chain techniques. File methods have been compared by many, including Chapin[69] (sequential, indexed-sequential, direct, and hierarchical), Collmeyer[70] (single and multilevel indexes, and directly accessed indexes) and Teory[82] (sequential, serial, direct, indexed-sequential, trees and tries, indexed rings, and hierarchical indexes). Cardenas[77] alo considers hierarchical indexes and in Cardenas[73] uses actual data files and considers cost functions for a single-level multiple index, a ring structure, and a single multiple-level index. Lum[73] describes results of parameterization of IBM OS file-access methods to predict file behavior. The model developed by Senko[73] allows description of file-design methods. File systems which implement various methods are described by Judd[73]. Martin[75] describes many file operations in detail and provides design guidance.

EXERCISES

1 Suggest ways to further reduce the redundancy in the dense file of Table 3-1.

2 What is the difference between writing a block and inserting a record? What is the difference between reading a block and fetching a record?

3 Program the algorithm for a continuous-search described as the topic of *Batching of Requests* in Sec. 3-1-3. Test it using a fetch-request arrival rate that is derived from a random-number generator which interrupts a pass through the file

10 times on the average. The file can be simulated by an array in core memory. Report the result. Refer to Sec. 6-2 for a description of a simulation process.

4 Give the expected insertion time per record inserted into a pile file where $R = 0.7B$ and spanned records are used (Sec. 3-1-3).

5 Determine the time for a batch insertion into a pile (see Sec. 3-1-3). What conditions are required for your result to be valid?

6 To speed retrieval of name records from a sequential file, you want to use probing. Where would you look for data to build the required table? How big a table would you use?

7 Write in a high-level language the procedure to actually insert a record into an unspanned and into a spanned blocked sequential file. Discuss the buffer requirements for both cases.

8 Discuss the collision probabilities when linear hashing is used.

9 When reorganizing a sequential file, it is possible that a new record on the transaction file is indicated to be deleted by a later transaction. What does this require when sorting the transactions and merging the files? Draw the flowchart for the merge process.

10 Choose three out of the attributes shown for indexing a personnel file:
`Name, age, sex, job, number of dependents, salary of dependents, salary`
and explain why you chose them.

11 Flowchart and compare the performance of a binary search through an index with the multilevel approach for indexed files.

12 Find a file system where you study or work or in the literature and determine the seven measures of performance $(R, T_F, T_I, \text{etc.})$ for its organization.

13 You have a large direct file using separate overflow chains. You are aware that 10% of your records are used 50% of the time and the other 90 You assume that within both groups the access distribution is uniform (equally probable).

Describe the processes required to keep the average access to records as fast as possible by ordering overflow records. Calculate the gain or loss in total efficiency versus the unordered organization for a file of 10 000 records with a primary allocation of 12 000 slots.

14 Sketch the actual ringstructure for Fig. 3-29.

15 Evaluate the average access time for a direct file using buckets of three records, linear search for free record space, and 20% excess capacity.

16 Using the sketch of a database system, shown in Fig. 3-38, make a flowchart for a program to answer complex questions. Such questions may involve references to multiple files as well as usage of multiple indexes. Since the sketch is not complete, you have some freedom in the implementation of details. As in all other questions list any assumption made in a table to be appended to the answer to this question.

17 Mark in the flowchart made in (16) a dozen possible error conditions and make a table with entries giving suitable diagnostic messages for each error condition and a code indicating if the error is the user's (U), the database manager's (M), or the hardware and software system's (S) responsibility.

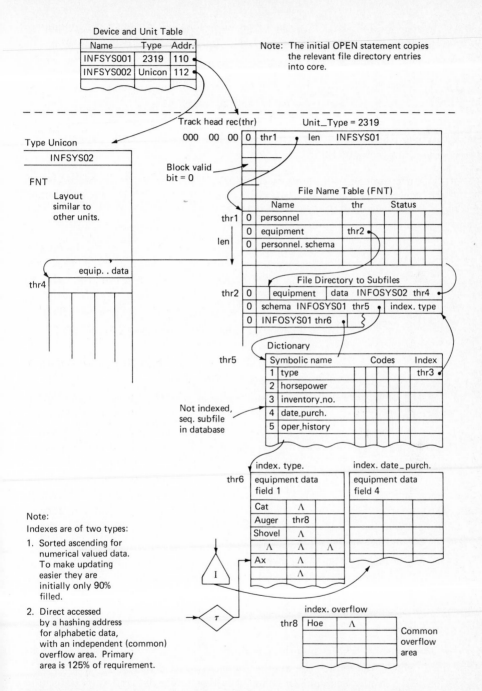

Figure 3-38 Structure of a file system to support database operations. The initial OPEN statement copies the relevant file directory entries into memory. Access structures are of two types: (I) B-trees and (τ) direct.

18 Derive a predictive formula which can be used to give an estimate of the length of an inquiry response time from the inquiry parameters and the file dictionary only, using again the above file design.

19 Evaluate the formula derived above for the following query:
"`Find an unmarried man between 25 and 30 years old`
`with recent experience operating Caterpillar D-10 equipment.`"
where the operating history is given in an equipment file and the personnel data are provided in a personnel file.

20 Discuss the equilibrium density for the six file structures presented.

21 Calculate the total space required for a file as shown in Fig. 3-39, using record-anchored indexes.

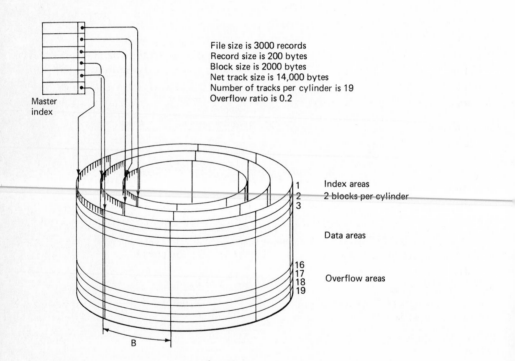

File size is 3000 records
Record size is 200 bytes
Block size is 2000 bytes
Net track size is 14,000 bytes
Number of tracks per cylinder is 19
Overflow ratio is 0.2

Master index

1
2   Index areas
3   2 blocks per cylinder

Data areas

16
17
18   Overflow areas
19

B

Figure 3-39 Illustration of indexed sequential file layout.

Consider a design where the primary index level is placed on the same cylinder as the data, which will reduce the nember of seeks needed to access the data. The calculation will initially evaluate the capacity of one cylinder and then determine the number of cylinders required.

Parameters to be used are:

$R = 200$ (including the linkage pointer of 6 bytes length), $B = 2000$, $V = 14$, $P = 6$, blocks per track $= 7$, surfaces per cylinder $k = 19$, and overflow allocation $= 20\%$.

Chapter 4

Hybrid File Organizations

Even the question whether one did right to let WESCAC thus rule him, only WESCAC could reasonably be asked. It was at once the life and death of studentdom; its food was the entire wealth of the college, the whole larder of accumulated lore; in return it disgorged masses of new matter – more alas than its subjects ever could digest . . .

John Barth
Giles Goat-Boy, vol.1, first reel

In this chapter we illustrate some of the varieties of file designs that can be obtained by combining the basic methods described in the previous chapter. Such combinations can satisfy requirements that are not fulfilled by the basic methods.

We will show in Sec. 4-1 some simple structures which save space or retrieval time when the data or problems have a well-defined structure. In Sec. 4-2 index construction techniques will be presented, leading to an example of a complex indexed-sequential file in Sec. 4-3. In Sec. 4-4 tree-structured files with data within an indexlike structure are presented, leading to hierarchical files with an example in Sec. 4-5. Sections 4-6 and 4-7 discuss combination-based or direct access and ring structures. The final two sections discuss files based on virtual storage and phantom files.

The information presented in this chapter is more diverse than the contents of Chap. 3. Techniques described in earlier sections will often be applied again in combination with other file methods. Many techniques improve the data-retrieval capability by adding redundancy but this increases the amount of space required and makes updates more difficult. The aggregate performance of a system depends on the balance of update and retrieval usage, and will be presented in Chap. 5.

Summary of Previous Results We will review briefly the six basic file designs which were discussed in detail in Chap. 3.

The *pile file* provides a basic unstructured organization which is flexible, uses space well when the stored data vary in size and structured, is easy to update, quite awkward for fetching specific records, and amenable to exhaustive searches.

The *sequential file*, containing a collection of ordered fixed records, is inflexible, efficient for the storage of well-structured data, difficult to update, awkward for finding single records, and very suitable for efficient exhaustive processing.

The *indexed-sequential file* adds a single index to the sequential organization. The result is a file which can be efficiently searched and updated according to one attribute, but is otherwise still fairly inflexible. The file is reasonably efficient for the storage of well-structured data, and suitable for exhaustive processing.

The *multi-indexed file* removes the constraint on sequentiality and allows many search attributes. It is quite flexible, reasonably efficient for data storage, permits very complex updates at some cost, allows convenient access to specific records but is awkward for exhaustive processes. Much storage may be occupied by the indexes.

The *direct file* is quite inflexible because of its mapping requirements, has some storage overhead, allows updates at some cost in complexity but provides efficient record retrieval according to a single dimension. Serial and exhaustive searches are, in general, impossible.

The *multiring file* provides for a number of record types with many interconnections. Redundant and empty fields are reduced, but some space is required for the linkage pointers. Updates may be performed at a moderate cost. The ring organization provides flexible, but not always fast, access to single records and allows great flexibility for exhaustive or subset searches.

Table 4-1   Grades of Performance for the Six Basic File Methods

File method	Space Attributes Variable	Space Fixed	Update Record size Equal	Update Greater	Retrieval Single record	Retrieval Subset	Retrieval Exhaustive
Pile	A	E	A	A	E	D	B
Sequential	F	A	D	F	F	D	A
Indexed-sequential	F	B	B	D	B	D	B
Multi-indexed	B	C	C	C	A	B	D
Direct	F	B	B	F	B	F	E
Multiring	C	B	D	D	B	A	B

A = excellent, well suited to this purpose
B = good
C = adequate
D = requires some extra effort
E = possible with extreme effort
F = not reasonable for this purpose

Only the multi-indexed file and the multiring files provide the capability for access to data according to more than one dimension. These two methods provide the basic building blocks for file designs providing multiattribute access whenever there are many records. Table 4-1 above lists these conclusions in a summary form.

Reasons for Combining the Basic Methods It is obvious that there are frequently requirements that are not well supported by any of the organization types described up to this point. Typical requirements may include the need to collect variable-length records while preserving sequentiality, or the desire to take advantage of the speed of direct access while requiring retrieval according to more than one attribute.

Not all possible solutions will or can be listed. Many of the methods described here have been implemented in practice; others are shown in order to provide a logical continuity or to suggest alternate approaches. For most of these methods, no comparative formulas will be provided. We hope that the reader, using the approaches of Chap. 3, will be able to develop formulas to estimate any file organization method that is encountered in this chapter or in actual practice.

Review of Terms In this section we frequently refer to the *search argument* and to the *key* and *goal* portion of the record. These terms are used particularly when files are used for data retrieval. The term search argument denotes the attribute type and value known when a record is to be retrieved. The *key portion of the record* is the field to be matched to the search argument. The fields of the record to be retrieved by the fetch process are known by the term *goal*. In an example, the search argument may be "`social security number=134-51-4717`"; the key in the specified attribute field of the record contains the matching value "`134-51-4717`", and the goal portion of that record contains the `name` and `salary` for the employee.

The key is generally intended to identify one record uniquely, so that there is a simple functional dependence from key to record. A key may comprise multiple attribute fields of the record in order to achieve a unique relationship. An example of the need for multiple fields might be the title of a book, which may not identify a book uniquely without specification of author or publisher and date of publication.

It should be understood that another instance of a retrieval request can have a different composition. Then the search argument may comprise a different set of attributes; these may have been previously part of the goal, and the goal can include the former key values.

4-1 SIMPLE FILES

We will take a step backward in this section and present some file mechanisms which are simpler than any of the six presented in Chap. 3. Such simple files are sometimes the only ones provided on small computers or on systems which were not designed to provide data-processing services. The simple files presented are in general not adequate for databases. A better file organization can be constructed on top of some of them if a database is needed and no alternative file support exists. The extra software layer will typically diminish performance but is required to provide database software without excessive code to deal with file inadequacies.

We deal first with some simple index types. If the attribute values used for indexing are restricted to integers, a simplified indexing scheme can be used.

4-1-1 Immediate Access

No structure to assist access was provided in the earliest direct files. An index number given by the user specifies a relative record position. Translation of a key to an index number, density of the file, and avoidance of collisions is left to the user of the file. Index numbers are integers of a limited range. The specifications for many FORTRAN implementations of *direct* access input and output limit themselves to this level of service. FORTRAN statements defined for this purpose include

```
DEFINE FILE 17(n,R)
   . . .
WRITE (17 ' key) data
```

The number 17 following the keywords DEFINE FILE is the *name* for the file; FORTRAN restricts even the file names to integers. The parameter n specifies the maximum size of the file and R the maximum record length. The values given for n, R, and **key** must be integers, with **key** $\leq$ n. If the **data** field exceeds R, the record written will be truncated; if it is less, the unused space will be filled with blanks, or its contents left unpredictable.

In IBM FORTRAN systems, two additional parameters are provided:

```
DEFINE FILE 17(n,R,code,nextkey)
```

The **code** specifies usage; U is for an unformatted file to be stored while a **code** of E indicates formatting for input-output. The variable **nextkey** specifies an output parameter, which is set to the key value of the next existing record in the file in order to simplify serial processing.

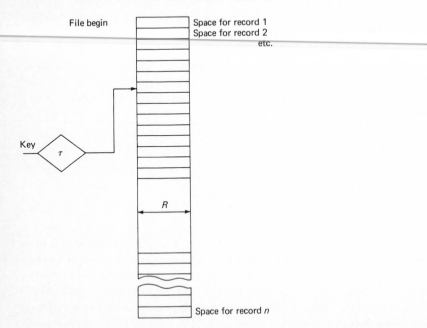

Figure 4-1 File using an integer key with all record spaces allocated.

Preallocated Space If, in the implementation, the entire space for all the expected records has to be allocated in advance, the simplest direct organization can be used. The only transformation τ required by the system to locate a record given a key is the following:

```
record_address = filebegin + (key-1) * R
```

as indicated in Fig. 4-1.

If data are of variable lengths, then the user has also to program blocking routines. In essence, the file system provides the user with a software-sized block, calling it a *record*. Some systems add the further restriction that the size of this record has to be equal to the system block size. Now most user records will require blocking routines if space utilization is a concern. Such systems frequently are found in microcomputers, and in simple timesharing systems.

The required system software is of course minimal, and also quite reliable. A subsystem developer may not want more than these basics from the system. Users may choose to add the logic described for indexed-sequential, B-trees, or direct files to their programs if their requirements make this addition necessary. On larger systems immediate access may be available as a optional building block for file designers unhappy with standard file organization methods.

4-1-2 Simple Indexes

The addition of an index to such a file provides flexibility of space allocation, so that the file can be incrementally or sparsely filled. Used record spaces can be identified by a marker in the index to provide the capability to omit, insert, and update records. Figure 4-2 shows such an arrangement.

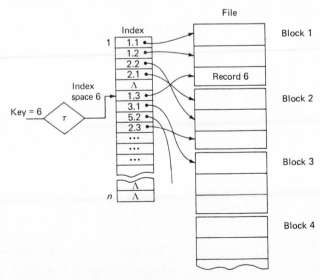

Figure 4-2 Fixed indexes pointing to a dynamic record structure.

A distinction now can be made between WRITE and REWRITE operations to prevent loss of previously stored data due to errors in the calculation of the key value. A function FREE can be provided to allow the user to test the status of a record space.

```
        IF ( FREE(17,key) )  GO TO 20
C       A record with this key exists already in the file
```

Space for records is taken out of blocks as required. The entire index is predefined, and allocated at least to an extent that the highest existing record is included. Where records do not exist, the index entry value is Null. The actual attribute value or key does not appear in the index since the proper index entry is found by the computation

```
index_address = indexbegin + (key-1) * P
```

which is similar to the one used for the immediate access to the record without indexes. In fact, we have for the index a structure identical to that for the file in Fig. 4-1. The storage overhead is reduced for nondense files, since we expect that the index entry, only a pointer of size P, is much smaller than the actual record.

In this organization the indexes are relatively simple to maintain. Data records are easily read and written. Updating of records, however, can involve the invalidation of record spaces so that a list of the record spaces that are available for reuse has to be maintained.

It is easy to permit the storage of variable-length records, since the access algorithm does not depend on a fixed value of R. A record-marking scheme as described in Sec. 2-2-4 will be employed. However, if deletion or updating of records of varying size is to be allowed, space management becomes more complex. Compression and expansion of the file has to be provided, or a periodic reorganization will be required. Since only one index is maintained, few problems occur when a record has to be moved to another position during an update or a reorganization. In practice most systems of this type do not allow for variable-length records nor do they warn the user that the effects are unpredictable.

4-1-3 Indexing of Buckets

The index organization shown above also can be used to support more complex environments. Since this mechanism can provide facilities for variable-length records, it also can be used to store sets or *buckets* of small records. The concept of using buckets allows the use of variable-length records in most file-organization methods.

Since file storage is organized in terms of blocks, these buckets are defined again so that they match block sizes as effectively as possible. Not all the records in a key range for a bucket need to be present. Records can be packed and searched sequentially in the block or area assigned to the bucket. For example, the records numbered 1 to 60 could be assigned to a bucket using the first index entry, 61 to 120 to the second entry, and so on. The buckets accommodate defined partitions of the index range. If many long records are placed into a bucket, it may overflow. This type of file is hence a hybrid of features found previously in the direct and the indexed file organizations.

In these fixed indexes the anchor points always have the same source key values, while in indexed files the anchor keys were those of entries appearing at the file system partitions. The lowest level index needs to contain only one entry per bucket, so that the index size is again reduced. The proper allocation to buckets depends on the expected average record length, the block length, and the desired performance ratios between file density, sequential access, random access, and updating of the file.

An indexed bucket organization can be very useful for files consisting of program or data text. The records here are small and of variable length, but the variation between typical pages of text is not very great. Both fast sequential access, for processing and searching, as well as reasonable access to specific lines to be edited are required. Keeping the density low provides all these features.

A bucket which contains a page of text can be expected to fill several blocks. These blocks are exclusively assigned to an index entry. Multiple blocks for one index entry can be chained sequentially from the initial block referenced by the index entry. Figure 4-3 sketches this organization. This file now can be read sequentially with a low overhead.

Space will remain unused in the last block of a sequence of blocks containing data for one bucket. Relatively fewer blocks will be filled incompletely if the buckets use chains consisting of multiple blocks. Better use of space causes increased fetch processing time, since the number of accesses to locate a record increases for many of the records. An insertion into a long chain can be particularly expensive. Careful allocation of continuation blocks to increase locality will reduce the frequency of seeks and also the expected rotational latency incurred when fetching or inserting.

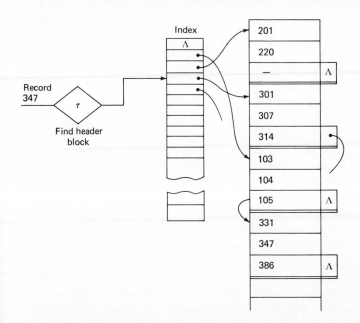

Figure 4-3 Bucket indexes with linked overflow blocks.

If we denote the chain length in terms of blocks as bch we find that

$$T_F = (x + \frac{bch + 1}{2})(s + r + btt) \qquad \text{4-1}$$

Here x is again the depth of the index and $s + r + btt$ the components of the random access time. If record sizes and record quantities per bucket are random, half a block per chain will be wasted. Thus, the waste per record in the chain is

$$W = \frac{\frac{1}{2}B}{bch - \frac{1}{2}} \frac{1}{Bfr} = \frac{R}{2bch - 1} \qquad \text{4-2}$$

The index space SI is preallocated to contain m bucket pointers of size P. The value of $m = n_{max}/(bch\,Bfr)$, typically $m < n$. The space used per record R' is then

$$R' = \frac{SI}{m} + R + \frac{R}{2bch - 1} \approx P + R + \frac{R}{2bch - 1} \qquad \text{4-3}$$

where R is the actual record size. The storage required for the index, SI, is reduced when the bucket size and hence the value of bch increases.

When such files are used for the storage of textual data, the line numbers can provide the basis for block address computation. The index entry is found by computing the quotient of the line number and the estimate of lines that can be stored in the block or blocks expected per bucket, as shown in the example below:

Given is $B = 1000$ and $bch = 2$. The expected bucket loading capacity is then 1500 bytes. The text averages 75 characters per line; hence one bucket should be assigned for each set of 20 lines.

4-1-4 Transposed Files

In some applications there is a frequent requirement to access all values of a given attribute. An example is the selection of the *average person*, where first the sum of all values of a given attribute has to be computed before a specific record can be selected.

If the file is relatively small and storage is affordable, the creation of a duplicate data file, in transposed form, may be the easiest solution to the problem of minimizing exhaustive search times for specific attributes. Only one record is fetched per attribute from a transposed file, and this record contains the values of this attribute for all entities, e.g., persons, in the file.

A transposed file contains one record per transposed attribute type from the main file, and each record has a number of data values which is equal to the number of records in the main file as shown in Fig. 4-4. If all attributes are transposed, the transposed file will be equal in size to the main file.

A transposed file is oriented to aid selection or evaluation of data according to a dimension which is orthogonal to the data entry or update dimension. Use of transposition presents opportunities for the discovery of trends or functional dependencies among attributes which are otherwise not obvious. Many research-oriented data processing tasks will take transposed data and group, select, and correlate the values found. When transposed files are used for statistical purposes, the updating or re-creation of the transposed file may be done only periodically. This process is analogous to a file reorganization.

The potentially very long records, $R = nV$ for one attribute, can easily exceed the limits of available analysis programs in terms of storage space. The processing time required for such long records also will become more significant. The analysis of very large quantities of data will also require consideration of the numerical stability or accuracy of the analysis algorithm used. The assumption made in most other examples that the computational time can be neglected is not valid when processing records from transposed files.

A record of a transposed file shows much similarity with the lowest level of an exhaustive index. A transposed file, however, stands more on its own; it does not need to contain pointers from the transposed file to the main file. It may be convenient to use a transposed file as input to a program which generates indexes to the main file. If the record positions of the main file cannot be computed, the transposed file can contain one record with values of all the original source record positions.

Transposition of a File The effort needed to transpose a large file with many attributes is large. The most obvious procedure is to construct one transposed record during one exhaustive read of the file. To transpose all of a file in this manner will require a time equal to $a \times T_X$ for the a passes over the file. If blocks for multiple transposed records (buf) can be built up in core at a time, only $\lceil a/buf \rceil$ passes over the file are required.

Floyd[74] describes two transposition algorithms which take on the order of $\lceil \log_2 w \rceil$ passes where w is the greater of n or a. The simpler algorithm generates records increasing gradually in size to n; the second algorithm is given as Example 4-1 and generates each transposed record as a sequence of pieces of size a and requires only three buffers of that size.

New record number	Field ID	Original record number										
		1	2	3	4	5	6	7	8	9	10	
1	2	55	39	36	25	27	42	61	36	31	59	Ages
2	3	5'8"	5'6"	5'7"	5'6"	5'11"	5'9"	5'6"	5'7"	5'6"	5'5"	Heights
3	4	95	75	70	49	80	178	169	83	95	145	IQs

Figure 4-4 The file from Fig. 3-3 transposed.

Transposition Program The program shown as Example 4-1 on pages 176 and 177 transposes a source file using $\lceil n/a \rceil (2 + \lceil \log_2 a \rceil)a$ fetches and as many insertions. Most of the operations are not sequential and will require a seek. The benefit of this procedure will become substantial when $a/buf \gg 10$.

Example 4-1   Floyd's second transposition algorithm

```
/* Program to transpose a source file of 'n' records of length 'a'.
   The input and output files are sequential.
   The program contains  three distinct sections:
        1. Copy groups of 'a' records to a work file, resequencing
   all but the first record of a group in inverse order.
   Values in these records are circularly shifted so that the
   first column elements form a diagonal.
   The last group is padded with zeroes.
        2. Record pairs within groups are selected, and within
   each pair alternate entries are transferred to rotate columns
   by 1,2,4,8,.. using powers of two in log2(a) passes per group.
        3. When all groups are rearranged, the work file is copied to
   the output file with a final adjustment shift for each record.
file_transpose: PROCEDURE(source,transposed,n,a);                   */
        DECLARE(source,transposed,work) FILE;
        DECLARE(spacein,spaceout,save)(a);
        DEFAULT RANGE(*) FIXED BINARY;  DECLARE(MOD,MIN)BUILTIN;
     /* The transposition proceeds in groups of 'a' records */
        groups = (n-1)/a+1;  amin1 = a-1;  record_in = 0;
     /* Perform sections 1 and 2 for each group and leave re-  */
  g_loop: DO group = 1 TO groups;       /* sults on the work file */
     /* Copy and rearrange a group for permutation */
  loop_1:   DO out_rec_pos  =  a TO 1 BY -1;
            IF record_in<n  THEN READ FILE(source) INTO(spacein);
                      ELSE spacein = 0;
            record_in = record_in+1;  base_out = a*(group-1)+1;
     /* Shift records to align columns so that transposition
                              can proceed in parallel blocks */
            CALL movearound(out_rec_pos);
            record_out = MOD(out_rec_pos, a) + base_out;
            WRITE FILE(work) KEYFROM(record_out) FROM(spaceout);
            END loop_1;
     /* Set up number of passes to permute one group */
            order = 1;  order2 = 2;
  loop_2:   DO WHILE( order<a );
     /* Permute records by order = 1,2,4,8, ... */
            CALL rearrange(base_out);
            order = order2;  order2 = order*2;
            END loop_2;
          END g_loop;
     /* Now copy the result from each transposed group to the */
  loop_3: DO shift = 0 TO amin1;                    /* output file */
     /* Each record contains 'groups' segments of length 'a'*/
    a_loop: DO rec = shift+1 BY a TO base_out-1;
              READ FILE(work) KEY(rec) INTO(spacein);
              CALL movearound(shift);
              WRITE FILE(transposed) FROM(spaceout);
              END a_loop;
          END loop_3;
```

```
/*    Dick Karpinski helped with checkout and structuring */

/* Subprocedures */
   /* Procedure to copy records, elements are circularly shifted */
   movearound: PROCEDURE(move);
           DO i = 1 TO a;      /* note that last (a) precedes 1 */
              j = MOD(i-move-1, a)+1;  spaceout(j) = spacein(i);
           END;
        END movearound;
   /* Subprocedure to pair alternate records */
   rearrange: PROCEDURE(beg_rec);
       /* The record pairs exchanging data will be:
           pass=1: (last,1),(last-1,last),(last-2,last-1),...;
           pass=2: (last,2),(last-2,last),(last-4,last-2),...;
           pass=3: (last,4),(last-4,last),(last-8,last-4),...;etc.*/
           rec_in, rec_save = beg_rec + order;
       /* Loop through all 'a' records in the group */
   t_loop: DO transfer_count = 1 TO a;
              IF rec_in=rec_save
                  THEN DO;  rec_out = rec_in-1;
       /* This record is saved to provide data for its partner */
                      READ FILE(work) KEY(rec_out) INTO(spaceout);
                      save = spaceout;  rec_save = rec_out;
                      END;
                  ELSE DO;  rec_out = rec_in;
                      spaceout = spacein;
                      END;
              rec_in = MOD(rec_out+amin1-order, a) + beg_rec;
       /* Use saved record when it comes */
           IF rec_in=rec_save THEN spacein = save;
                  ELSE READ FILE(work) KEY(rec_in) INTO(spacein);
       /* Shift data values from 'spacein' to 'spaceout' */
           CALL transfer;
           WRITE FILE(work) KEYFROM(rec_out) FROM(spaceout);
       /* Terminate when all records have been processed */
           END t_loop;
        END rearrange;
   /* Subprocedure to move alternate elements in records selected
                                 by the rearrange procedure */
   transfer: PROCEDURE;
       /* Elements to be moved from 'spacein' to 'spaceout' are for:
           pass=1, order=1: 2,4,6,8,etc.
           pass=2, order=2: (3,4),(7,8),(11,12),etc.
           pass=3, order=4: (5,6,7,8),(13,14,15,16),etc. */
           DO i = order BY order2 TO amin1;
             limit = MIN(i+order, a);
           DO j = i+1 TO limit;  spaceout(j) = spacein(j);
           END;
        END transfer;
   /* This completes the file transposition program */
      END file_transpose;
```

4-2 MULTILEVEL INDEX STRUCTURES

Some issues associated with indexed files were not considered in the previous chapter. One of these is due to the complexity associated with long and variable-length attribute values in the key. The next section will deal with abbreviation of index keys, and Sec. 4-2-2 will deal with alternate index structures which can also ameliorate the problems of long keys. Serial processing by means of an index is considered in Sec. 4-2-3. There is an interaction of the processing of keys and the optimal block size; the trade-off is evaluated in Sec. 4-2-4. Finally, Sec. 4-2-5 presents the interesting issues of retrieval of records by multiple attributes using indexes.

4-2-1 Key Abbreviation

The keys used to identify data records can be very long. Examples of long keys which can be encountered are names of individuals, technical terms, names of diseases, and addresses. Long keys, when kept in various levels of an index as well as in the goal records themselves, not only waste space but reduce the number of entries that can be kept in one index block. The reduction of fanout will require more levels of indexing and hence increase the processing time significantly.

With long key fields and a large index, there will be long sequences with identical high-order parts of the key field. On the other hand, the low-order parts of the keys may not aid at all in the discrimination process between records. The key field can be shortened by judiciously abbreviating the keys. Abbreviation of long keys may be made before records are put into a system, or may be performed completely within the file system. Some key abbreviation algorithms are designed to be convenient in either case.

External Key Abbreviation In order to introduce the topic of key abbreviation, we will present a scheme oriented toward manual use. This scheme also randomizes the key values, so that buckets used to store the records are evenly filled. The abbreviation has hence also a hashing objective.

Hashing techniques are difficult for human interaction; the computed addresses tend to be unintelligible. In Fig. 4-5 we have the example of a mailing label, with a code which is intended to be understandable by clerks who have to deal with subscription renewals and delivery complaints of newspapers and magazines. The file is accessed based on the coded file address in the top line. We see that the zip code, the characteristics of the name, and the street address are used to obtain an abbreviated key. This method is similar to a sequence-maintaining hashing technique but can also be carried out manually. The method used does not guarantee uniqueness unless a sequence digit is added.

```
60282HGS5155POT31

Edgar R. B. Hagstrohm
           - —·····
155 Proteus Park
—— - ··
Chicago, Ill 60282
```

A mailing label code. The underlined parts of the address are included in the code. Counts are given for the dotted characters. A sequence digit 1 is appended.

Figure 4-5 Abbreviated address key.

In many European countries identifiers for individuals are constructed using similar techniques. When such an abbreviated key is constructed at a later time, the sequence digit is not known, so that no unique transformation can be made. In that case multiple records have to be retrieved and checked using further information, in a manner similar to the handling of collisions in a direct file organization. A trade-off will have to be made between the length of the abbreviated key and the number of key collisions.

Internal Key Abbreviation Abbreviation techniques are often essential within the file system. Adequate fanout requires that we deal well with potentially long keys. For character-string fields abbreviation by deletion of segments of low-order blanks is common. Keys can be much more abbreviated, however, since keys should not need more bits than needed to discriminate among the n items in the file. A theoretical minimum is a length of $\log_2 n$ bits, and within one index block only $\log_2 y$ bits should be needed for the key.

When processing data automatically, it is necessary that only one record be selected in response to a fetch request. In the technique used externally a sequence digit was used to assure uniqueness. A file system has to abbreviate the key so that any record, given a unique key, say the full **name and address** of a subscriber, can be uniquely identified by that key alone. This will also avoid collisions. Automatic abbreviation is feasible when the keys appear in a sorted sequence. The portions of the key which do not discriminate between adjoining keys can then be deleted.

In order to benefit from internal abbreviation the index has to be able to handle variable-length keys. The record marks which are needed to indicate key and record boundaries reduce the effect of the abbreviation.

Variable-length keys Variable-length keys can occur naturally or be due to an abbreviation algorithm. Naturally occurring variable-length keys, for instance, people's names, should in any case be allocated to variable-length fields, since a fixed allocation of adequate space for the longest key may be prohibitive. Key abbreviation is hence not costlier and is always desirable for variable-length keys. Figure 4-6 shows a problem due to a fixed-length abbreviation: in which volume would you find a "**Canoe**"?

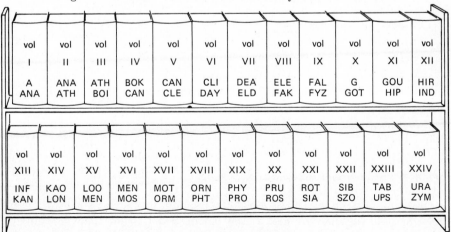

Figure 4-6 Volumes of the 1890 Encyclopaedia Britannica.

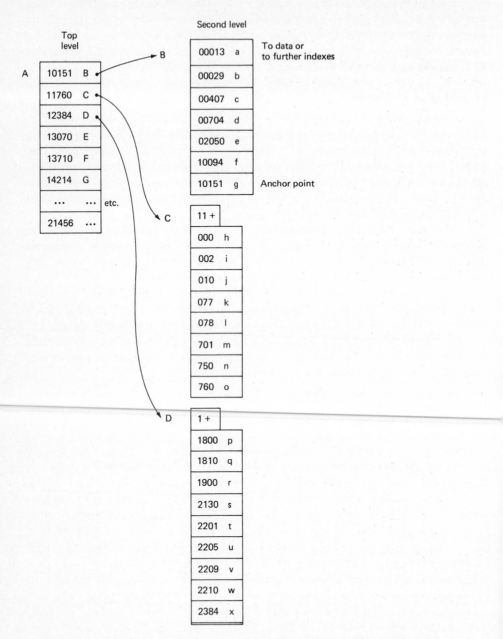

Figure 4-7 Part-number index with block-based key abbreviation.

Figure 4-7 illustrates opportunities for abbreviation of long keys. The index shown uses the highest value of the key as the block anchor point. The keys in our examples are numeric and letters indicate block addresses. We will show how to delete redundant high-order and low-order segments of keys.

High-Order Key Abbreviation If it is known from a higher level index that all index entries in a block refer to keys within a certain range, the high-order digits will be identical and this *high-order segment* can be deleted. In Fig. 4-7 the two leading digits of entries in block C of the second-level index were redundant, and were deleted from the individual entries. In block D only one digit could be deleted, but in both cases the number of entries per block and the fanout ratio y has increased.

It is desirable to keep in a header portion of each index block the value of the high-order segment to allow reconstruction of the key from data within the index block. Key abbreviations may be also applied to individual entries within blocks, as is shown in Example 4-2 for blocks B and D. Now the entries are also variable within a block.

Example 4-2 High-order key abbreviations

B : 000+13=a,+29=b,00+407=c,	D : 118+00=p,+10=q,11900=r,1
+704=d,0+2050=e,10+094=f	2+130=s,1220+1=t,+5=u,+9
,+151=g;	=v,12+210=w,+384=x;

The stored segments are separated by markers $\{+ = , ;\}$ as indicated. The high-order segment is repeated in front of a + symbol whenever the truncation changes. Some analysis is needed to make the truncation optimal for the entire block.

If the key is of known length, the value and length of high-order segments omitted may be implied by the length of the remainder, as shown in Example 4-3.

Example 4-3 High-order abbreviation for keys of known length

B : 00013=a,29=b,407=c,704=d	D : 11800=p,10=q,900=r,2130=
,2050=e,10094=f,151=g;	s,201=t,5=u,3=v,10=w,384
	=x;

Low-Order Key Abbreviation Similarly, the right-hand side of keys may frequently be shortened. Indexes where the attribute is a potentially long string of characters, such as a name, sometimes arbitrarily limit fields to a fixed number of characters. When keys are poorly distributed, records may no longer have unique keys in the index.

This method can be seen in the volume headings of an encyclopedia as shown in Fig. 4-6. Three characters here did not provide enough discrimination between Volumes 1 and 2, 2 and 3, and 15 and 16.

Instead of arbitrary limits, the contents of an index block can be inspected to determine how many low-order digits can be safely deleted. In the earlier example (Fig. 4-7), the two low-order digits of the first index level (block A) can be deleted without loss of discrimination. For insertion omitted digits are taken to be zeros. The third character is required only because of the density of entries in the range between 13 000 and 14 000.

The alternate version of block D shown in Example 4-3 has both a high-order and low-order abbreviation applied to the entries. The dash (-) indicates the boundary for the low-order segment.

Example 4-4 High-order and low-order abbreviation for keys

```
D :  118-0=p,-1=q,119=r,213=s
     ,220-1=t,-5=u,-9=v,221=w
     ,23=x;
```

Low order key abbreviation has the disadvantage that the actual data file has to be accessed in order to determine whether a record corresponding to the full key exists. A search for a nonexistent record, via a record-anchored but abbreviated index, will require one more access. Without the abbreviation, the lack of the record is recognized when the index entries do not yield a match. When using block anchors, the file has to be accessed in either case.

Repeating Keys In indexes where the keys are not *unique*, so that more than one record for a given key can exist, it can be profitable to avoid restating the key. With the flexible key organization obtained with abbreviated keys, such a facility is easy to implement, as shown in Example 4-5.

Example 4-5 Abbreviation of repeating keys

```
E :  1241-1=y&z,-2=...
```

Two records, stored at **y** and **z**, both have a key value of **12411**.

Abbreviating Pointers If the goal records occupy only a part of the file space, then the pointers to the goal record may be similarly abbreviated. The high-order segment of the pointer in any block can be significantly shortened, especially in the case where the indexed entries are used to point to a sequential file in index order. Similar benefits of increase in fanout ratio and reduction of levels of indexing can be expected.

Use of Abbreviated Index Entries Abbreviation of keys is effective when keys are relatively long and files are big. Often one level of index can be saved. When there is no need to access data serially, a key-to-address translation algorithm can perform the same service without the complexity and computational overhead of variable-length keys. Since the keys are denser in the record-anchored indexes associated with multi-indexed files, key abbreviations can play an important role there. The abbreviation of pointers complements abbreviation of the keys and can lead to further savings.

4-2-2 Index Blocks Structured as Trees

The abbreviated keys require considerably more processing time c than would be required if a simpler index entry format were used. Measurements have allocated 14% of total database CPU usage to abbreviation and expansion of keys. If the indexes are kept on high speed disks, the computation time may exceed the time available because of the access delays. Since index blocks are not accessed sequentially this does not affect the assumptions made for the bulk transfer rate made in Sec. 2-3-4, but the heavy demand on CPU resources is significant.

In a multiprogrammed environment the CPU can be used for other processes and be too valuable to spend on excessive index abbreviation. Processing all the keys in sequential order requires accessing about $cix = \frac{1}{2}y$ entries for comparison with the search argument. The approaches described in this section reduce cix by replacing the sequential key structure of the entries in the current index block with a tree. The use of rapid search in an index block regains computational time lost because of abbreviation. We recall that the motivation for abbreviation is to increase the fanout ratio, which reduces the number of seek operations in the tree as well as the index space.

This section presents three alternate tree structures for indexes. When entries are of fixed size and not abbreviated, a conventional binary search or probing, as shown in Sec. 3-2-3, also provide rapid access to entries within an index block.

Jump Index Search A simple scheme groups the y index entries within one block into a number of sections to provide a second level. The number of sections is chosen to be about equal to $\sqrt{y}$. An initial search pass *jumps* from section to section and compares one entry in each section. A subsequent pass searches within the proper section through the $y/\sqrt{y} = \sqrt{y}$ entries found in a section.

The expected number of comparisons of sections and entries is $\frac{1}{2}\sqrt{y}$ each, so that the total number of comparisons cix expected is

$$cix = 2\left(\tfrac{1}{2}\sqrt{y}\right) = \sqrt{y} \qquad\qquad \langle\text{jump search}\rangle \; 4\text{-}4$$

which is the minimum obtainable with two passes and linear searching. The number of comparisons $\sqrt{y}$ to find an entry is within a factor of 2 of the optimum, a binary search, for typical values of y. This additional pseudo-level does not require redundant entries of the key or pointers, only a means to locate the sections.

If the records are of fixed length the location of the sections in the index block is computable. Otherwise $\sqrt{y}$ section pointers can be used in each index block to define a two-level tree. These section pointers have to be distinguishable so that will not interfere with sequential processing of index entries. An implementation is shown in Sec. 4-3-3 and Fig. 4-18.

A Binary Arranged Index Tree We presented the algorithm for binary search within a sequential file in Sec. 3-2-1, Fig. 3-5. Since entries in an index block are always sequential, a binary search can be used here too if the entries are of fixed size. For entries of arbitrary length a method which uses explicit successor pointers can permit a binary search to be used.

Figure 4-8 shows block D from the earlier example in Fig. 4-7. The entries are arranged by level, so that the search begins at the middle value. Two fields per entry direct the search algorithm to the next index entry to effect a binary partitioning. In this example, the maximum number of comparisons is four, and the expected number is $25/9 = 2.78$. In a sequential search, $(1 + 9)/2 = 5$ comparisons would be expected. In general, the tree search will require on the order of

$$cix = \log_2 y \qquad\qquad \langle\text{binary search}\rangle \; 4\text{-}5$$

comparisons. This is significant when there are many entries per index block.

The index shown has grown in size because of the pointers which relate the index entries to the tree structure. Of these pointer fields, $y + 1$ will be empty. In the example the comparison is based on the whole value of the key and some opportunities of high-order key abbreviation are lost.

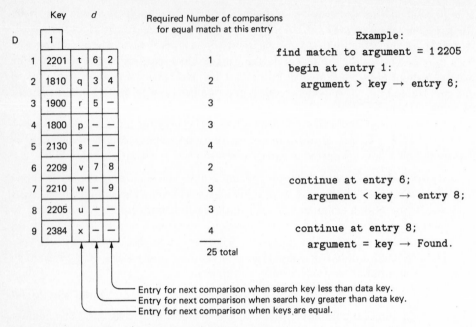

Figure 4-8 Index arranged as a binary tree.

A Trie An alternate arrangement into a binary tree can be achieved by basing the partitioning decision on individual digits of the key. A base comparison value partitions the key digit value into two subsets. The method produces also an abbreviation of the key, since entries are represented by only one digit. The digits of the key to be used are chosen to provide the best partition of the search space, but the number of comparisons will generally be greater than the number for a binary search, since we cannot guarantee that the space will be optimally partitioned. Exact matches, which would lead directly to data, are also excluded now. The destination after a comparison can be either a goal record or another comparison entry. Files based on this idea are named *tries* (pronounced "try-s").

Figure 4-9 shows an index trie for the same index block D. The first digit (which anyhow could be omitted from the block) will of course not play a role, but even the second digit never provided a useful discrimination. The expected number of comparisons in this example is $29/9 = 3.22$, and in large indexes the improvement over sequential searching will again be significant. In this method we can also make very effective use of the pointer fields by allowing both index entry numbers (**digits**) and goal block addresses (**letters**).

These tries, because of the binary decisions made, are best implemented in practice by basing the comparison on a single bit, rather than on a digit. In this case no column with base comparison values has to be provided, since the conditions are always only "=0" or "=1".

The number of entries in a block of a trie leading to y records n_e is determined by the number of decision nodes $n_d = \lceil y/2 \rceil$ and their ancestors in the tree $n_d - 1$, and hence $n_e \approx y$. The space required for the key segment of a binary trie entry is composed of the bit position of the key and two internal references. An entry for a five-character (40-bit) key and up to 500 entries per block will require only $\lceil \log_2 40 \rceil + 2 \lceil \log_2 50 \rceil = 24$ bits or 3 bytes, plus extra space for the external pointers. Trie entries are hence apt to be smaller than index entries, and there will be a corresponding increase in fanout.

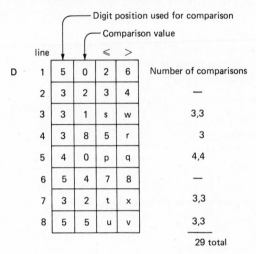

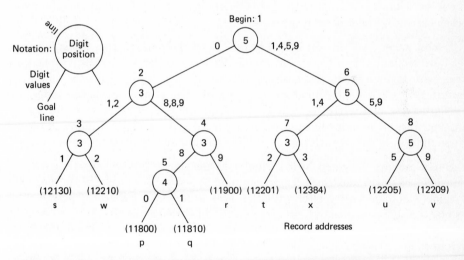

Figure 4-9 Index arranged as a trie.

Indexes based on trie structures as shown are suitable only for record-anchored indexes, with entries pointing to each individual record, since an exact match is implied. Intermediate search arguments will not provide a sensible result. If the digits used for the branching decisions are chosen only from left to right, the unpredictability of the match is avoided; and then the method might be used with an index containing entries which point to block-anchor points in the primary file or refer to lower-level index blocks.

4-2-3 Serial Processing via Indexes

The ability to perform a serial search has to be considered in the design of indexed files that may be serially accessed. Since an index provides an ordering for the data records, it is possible to find pointers to successor records by scanning through an index blocks at level 1. Making sure that serial access works well affects the management of indexes.

Serial access is required for `Get_Next` and `Read_Exhaustive` operations. Long sequences of repeated `Get_Next` operations occur when a subset is to be retrieved. If the attribute that is indexed can have nonunique values, many entries may have to be retrieved for a single search argument, say,

      FIND Houses with 3 bedrooms

An important requirement in many data-analysis tasks is to retrieve subsets specified by a *range*. An example of retrieval by a range of values is a query such as

      FIND Houses priced 31 000 → 33 000

These are the types of queries for which serial access capability through an index is essential. We will first consider access within a block, then access between blocks, and finally the use of the pointers obtained to fetch goal data.

The pointers we obtain from the index entries are commonly referred to as *tuple identifiers* or TIDs; the source for this term is found in Chap. 7; see Table 7-1. We assume that the number and size of the TIDs for one query is such that we can collect them in core storage and sort them, prior to accessing any of the data blocks containing the desired results.

Serial access within an index block In the B-tree structure the entries on level 1 are sequential in a block and provide for easy collection of TIDs. Sequential entries with faster random fetch access are provided by the jump search method shown in Sec. 4-2-2; internal pointers are used to permit variable-length entries.

Neither the binary tree nor the trie presented in Sec. 4-2-2 provides for serial searching within the index blocks. A further linkage is required within each block if these indexes have to provide a set of TIDs in serial order by entry value.

Serial access between index blocks When the entries in a block have been exhausted, the next index entry has to be found in a successor block. Since the next key value is not known, no fetch using a search argument equal to the next key is possible; the successor has to found by navigation through the tree.

At the end of a lowest-level index block, a new search from the second level is required to find the next block. At each level the search requires an entry from the superior level to find the successor block when the end of a block is reached. This search requires a stack of information about the current status of index blocks at all levels.

A linkage of index blocks on the same level of the tree can avoid this pain. The solution using lower-level linkage of index blocks is shown in Fig. 4-10. The linkage pointers will have to be maintained with care. For a B-tree the pointers are reset when a lower level block is split. The pointers also identify the partner block to be checked when deletions reduce the number of entries in the block below a certain minimum.

Accessing data blocks The pointers we obtain from processing of index entries can be effectively used to reduce the number of block accesses to the data file. By putting the pointers in order by block number we can assure that each block will be accessed only once; if possible, we will fetch multiple goal records out of one block. This technique becomes especially important when processing multi-attribute queries, as will be shown in Sec. 4-2-5.

We need to know the number of block fetches b_G required to retrieve n_G goal records in TID order from a large file of n_{file} records with Bfr records per block. The file uses hence $b_{file} = n_{file}/Bfr$ blocks. We will first consider the extreme cases. For small results ($n_G \ll n_{file}$) the value of $b_G = n_G$ since one block fetch will fetch one result record. For large numbers of n_G the value of $b_G \to b_{file}$, if the retrieval is carried out in TID order, since nearly every block will be accessed once; at $n_G > n_{file} - Bfr$ this is absolutely true.

In the important intermediate region, where many but much less than all records are selected from the goal file, some blocks will yield multiple records and others will not be needed at all. An estimate of the number of block fetches required to retrieve n_G records in TID order from a file of n records with Bfr records per block, for the cases $n_G \leq n_{file} - Bfr$, is computable as [Whang[81]]

$$b_G = \frac{n}{Bfr}\left(1 - \left(1 - \frac{Bfr}{n}\right)^{n_G} + \frac{Bfr}{n_G^2}\frac{n_G(n_G-1)}{2}\left(1 - \frac{Bfr}{n}\right)^{n_G-1}\right.$$
$$\left. + \frac{1.5}{n_G^3 Bfr}\frac{n_G(n_G-1)(2n_G-1)}{6}\left(1 - \frac{Bfr}{n}\right)^{n_G-1}\right)$$

4-6

This formula is a good approximation in the range of values seen in databases of the computationally difficult function required to produce an exact result [Yao[77]]. To a retrieval time computed on the basis of this technique the computation time c, required for sorting of the TIDs in core prior to file access, has to be added.

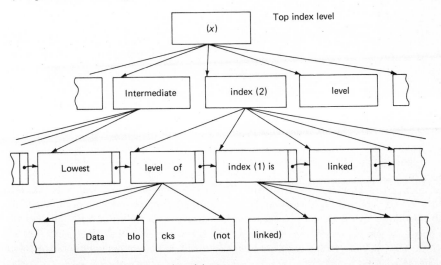

Figure 4-10 Linked lower level indexes.

Serial linkages in alternate file organizations In the case of the indexed-sequential file, which we examined in Sec. 3-4, serial access according to a single attribute was established through the location of the data records themselves and through a linkage for any overflow records. Files with multiple indexes establish multiple serial access paths within the indexes themselves. The optional extra linkage between blocks at the same level, presented above, increases update costs when new blocks are allocated but simplifies serial access. Serial access remains indirect, and data records are fetched according to the pointers found in index entries. The alternative, multiple direct linkages of data records themselves, is used in the design of the multiring file.

Since indexes are small, it is easier to achieve a high degree of locality for indexes than for data records. If few records are to be obtained per serial retrieval, multiple indexes with linkages will perform better than multiring structures. For retrieval of subsets the indirection of access makes use of an index costlier than following a ring.

4-2-4 The Interaction of Block Size and Index Processing

Up to this point we have used the block size as a given parameter in the design of indexes. In many cases this is a valid assumption, but it is instructive to see how changes in block size affect the performance of an index. The size of an index entry will be denoted below as Rix, and the number of index entries by nix. The positive effect of large block sizes is a high fanout ratio ($y = B/Rix$, from Eq. 3-26), which reduces the number of levels required. The number of levels x is again determined by $x = \log_y nix$ (Eq. 3-27). The detrimental effects of large block sizes are the increased block transfer time $btt = B/t$, the increased computational effort cix to locate the appropriate index entry in a block, and the cost of core-storage occupancy. Figure 4-11 shows the combined effect of all these factors except the core-storage occupancy for a fairly large index. The fetch time within the index is computed as

$$T_{Fix} = \lceil \log_y n \rceil (cix + s + r + y\frac{Rix}{t})$$
4-7

where $cix = c\frac{1}{2}y$ ⟨linear search⟩

and $cix = c\log_2 y$ ⟨binary search (Eq. 4-5)⟩

Not presented is $cix = \sqrt{y}$ ⟨jump search (Eq. 4-4)⟩

which is in between, but close to the binary search.

The optimum length for index blocks in the case shown, a 2314-type disk, is 4000 bytes. The steps in the function are an effect of the discrete assignment of index levels. The lower, continuous curve represents use of optimal index processing; approaches were described in Sec. 4-2-2. The time needed to inspect an index entry is taken to be 40 microseconds(μs). Abbreviated entries will take longer to process and will raise the left side of the curve, especially if linear searches are made through the index blocks, but their use will also decrease the size of an average index entry, so that the same fanout will correspond to a smaller block size. Devices with a shorter seek time will favor shorter block sizes, while devices with a higher transfer rate will cause minimal values of the fetch time to occur with larger blocks.

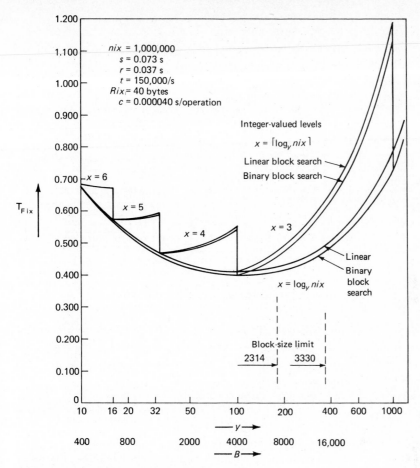

Figure 4-11 Fetch time versus fanout.

4-2-5 Partial-Match Retrieval

Indexes provide multiattribute retrieval, that is, access via any of several attributes. We also have to consider queries where several attributes are combined. Such a query is termed a *partial-match query*, since several of many (a) attributes of the record are to be matched. A partial match query with four attributes terms is shown in Example 4-6.

An important use of indexes is the reduction of search effort for partial-match queries. For each attribute {style, price, bedrooms, location, ...} indexes are available; each key value found will point to many records.

Example 4-6   Partial-Match Query

```
LIST houses WITH style    = 'Colonial',
            AND  price    = 31 000  → 33 000,
            AND  bedrooms = 3,
            AND  location = 'Wuthering Heights';
```

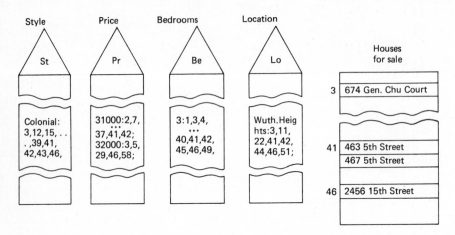

Figure 4-12 Multiattribute indexing for partial-match queries.

Merging of Multiple Indexes To restrict the retrieval to one or a few goal records, all arguments in the query are first processed against their indexes. Each index produces a list of identifiers (TIDs) for the candidate records. Example 4-5 showed an efficient encoding for multiple records per key.

These lists of TIDs are then merged according to the expression given by the query, using boolean functions to select the TIDs for those goal records which satisfy all query arguments. The process is sketched in Fig. 4-12.

Only the goal records needed for the response are eventually retrieved. The cost of processing a partial-match query can be estimated by expanding Eq. 3-54. We use a_Q indexes, merge the lists, and retrieve n_G goal records using b_G (Eq. 4-6) block accesses.

$$T_F(a_Q, n_G) = a_Q x(s + r + btt) + c + b_G(s + r + btt) \qquad 4\text{-}8$$

We made here the assumption that each subset of TIDs of the a_Q selected subsets was fetched from one block. If more index blocks are required some additional serial access costs are incurred; the linkage scheme for index blocks presented in Sec. 4-2-3 will minimize incremental costs.

The merging of TIDs is aided by sorting the TIDs initially, so that the retrieval of the blocks containing goal records is conveniently carried out in TID order. The value of b_G has an upper bound of n_G, but no block has to be accessed more than once. A good estimate of b_G as a function of n_G, n, and Bfr is given in Sec. 4-3-2 as Eq. 4-6.

In the next section we will discuss schemes that reduce the factor a_Q of Eq. 4-8 by creating additional indexes. If two or more attributes occur together in partial-match queries, it is possible to construct a single index for those specific attributes. Partial-match retrieval using other schemes is shown in Secs. 4-1-4, 4-6-4, and 4-7-5. Other aspects of the process of information retrieval are discussed in Chap. 10.

Partial-Match Indexes An index is not necessarily based on a single attribute, but can be based on entries that contain the catenation of several attribute values of a record. The number and size of the keys and hence the size of a combined index will be larger, so that the fanout may be less than the size of a single attribute index; but with effective index-abbreviation schemes, the increase will be moderate. In Fig. 4-12 it may be wise to combine `Style` and `Bedrooms`, since `Bedrooms` has a very low partitioning power. This combination is denoted St‖Be. If it is desirable to have access capability via one index for *all* queries which specify the logical intersection of attributes, then, in the same example another eleven combinations are required in addition to the four single attribute indexes (Fig. 4-13a).

The number of combinations for a indexes will be $2^a - 1$. The number of indexes can be much less, since an index ordered on a catenation of multiple attribute values $v_1, \ldots, v_a$ is also ordered for attributes $v_1, \ldots, v_{a-1}$. An index for a attributes can hence also serve to answer queries for one of the combinations of $a-1$ attributes, one of the combinations of $a-2$ attributes, etc. An index for another combination of $a-1$ attributes can similarly serve simpler queries. An assignment of a minimal set of indexes is shown in Fig. 4-13b.

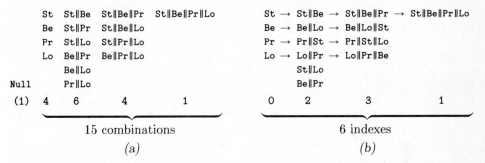

St	St‖Be	St‖Be‖Pr	St‖Be‖Pr‖Lo		St	→	St‖Be	→	St‖Be‖Pr	→	St‖Be‖Pr‖Lo
Be	St‖Pr	St‖Be‖Lo			Be	→	Be‖Lo	→	Be‖Lo‖St		
Pr	St‖Lo	St‖Pr‖Lo			Pr	→	Pr‖St	→	Pr‖St‖Lo		
Lo	Be‖Pr	Be‖Pr‖Lo			Lo	→	Lo‖Pr	→	Lo‖Pr‖Be		
	Be‖Lo						St‖Lo				
Null	Pr‖Lo						Be‖Pr				
(1) 4	6	4	1		0		2		3		1

$$\underbrace{\qquad\qquad\qquad\qquad}_{\text{15 combinations}} \qquad\qquad \underbrace{\qquad\qquad\qquad}_{\text{6 indexes}}$$

(a)   (b)

Figure 4-13 Partial-match indexes. *(a)* Combinations of indexes for four attributes {St,Be,Pr,Lo}. *(b)* A minimal set of indexes for the four combinations.

In minimal case the first index serves four combinations; three indexes serve three combinations each, and two combinations of two attributes remain. Only six indexes are required now. In general

$$nic(a) = \binom{a}{\lceil\frac{1}{2}a\rceil} = \frac{a!}{\lceil\frac{1}{2}a\rceil!\lfloor\frac{1}{2}a\rfloor!} \qquad\qquad 4\text{-}9$$

indexes will be required. This number is still quite large even for a modest set of attributes a, e.g., $nic(9) = 126$. It is possible to reduce the number of indexes further if some merge operations among indexes are acceptable.

Fewer combinations of attributes need be stored if for some queries a merge of two or more distinct TID lists is permissible. Then the a attributes will be partitioned into d sets with a_i attributes so that $\sum_{i=1}^{d} a_i = a$. The attributes will be partitioned to let frequent queries require only one set. The number of needed combinations reduces drastically. For $d = 2, a = 9, a_1 = 5, a_2 = 4$ the number of indexes becomes $nic(5) + nic(4) = 16$; for $d = 3, a = 9, a_1=a_2=a_3 = 3$ the number of indexes is $3\,nic(3) = 9$, the original number, although each index will carry more keys. The increased cost of updates will still discourage extensive use of combinatorial approaches for partial-match queries.

4-3 AN IMPLEMENTATION OF AN INDEXED-SEQUENTIAL FILE

A practical example of a comprehensive indexed-sequential file system is provided by IBM in their Virtual Storage Access Method (VSAM). The term *virtual* refers only to the fact that the programs used to implement VSAM depend on the virtual addressing provided by IBM's 370 type of computers. The approach is a hybrid of techniques presented in Secs. 3-3, 3-4, and 4-2.

We can describe the file design, using the terminology developed in the previous section, as follows:

> VSAM is an indexed-sequential file organization. The single index and the data file uses a B-tree algorithm. The index has a fixed number of levels, thus limiting the file size, albeit to a very large number of records. Anchor points are the keys with the highest value in a train of blocks. There is high- and low-order abbreviation of keys as well as abbreviation of pointers. The variable-length elements of the index are described by count fields which specify the original key length and the amount of low-order abbreviation. The lowest-level index is linked to maintain seriality.

In addition, a number of practical considerations have been given much attention in the design, and we will discuss some of these in detail.

It also is possible to use the structure of VSAM files while bypassing the processing procedures in order to provide record retrieval by *relative byte addressing* as presented in Sec. 2-3-3. The conversion of record keys to relative byte addresses is a user responsibility. Of interest here is the use of VSAM which corresponds to the normal use of full VSAM facilities to obtain indexed-sequential access to variable-length records.

When evaluating the performance of a VSAM file, the fact that the unit moved from disk to core consists of an entire train rather than just one block has to be considered. First the cost of moving a train of sequential blocks has to be estimated; then this result can be used with care in the relations based on variable-length unspanned blocking; Eqs. 2-20 and 2-21 provide the basic parameters.

4-3-1 Space Allocation

When a file is established, a large *portion* out of the available disk space is allocated to the file based on estimated future file-space requirements. The intent of such a *bulk allocation* is to keep the records closely together, so that the locality within a portion of a file is high.

When all the trains in a portion have been used, but space for a new train is required. a new portion will be allocated and an entry for this portion inserted at the top level of the VSAM B-tree; this level is called the *directory*. The first (low-order) half of the trains will be copied to the newly allocated portion, and the space from the trains moved will be put in a list (see Sec. 4-3-5) of free trains for reuse in the original portion.

A new portion is also obtained by a bulk allocation, but it may be smaller. It will not necessarily be close to the old portion. Benefits of locality are important for sequential processing of the data. Benefits of locality will of course be lost when other users intersperse file requests on the same device. A disadvantage of bulk allocation is that substantial storage space may be unused if the file size cannot be accurately estimated.

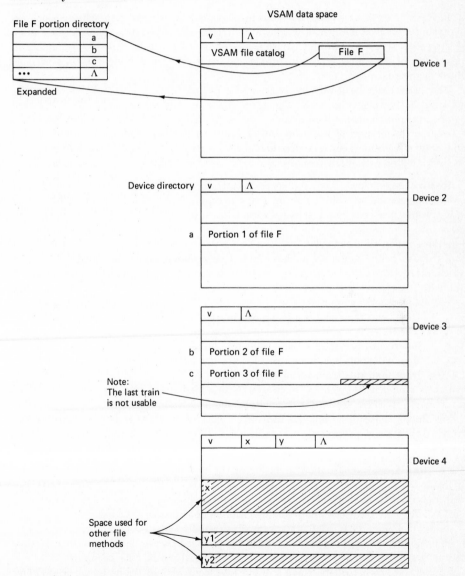

Figure 4-14 VSAM space allocation.

Directory   A directory to the allocated portions is kept as part of an entry for every VSAM file in a VSAM file catalog. The directory is limited to 256 entries. A possible allocation is shown in Fig. 4-14. The size of the allocation to the initial and to any further portions is determined by the expected maximum file size, as estimated from parameters given at the original file definition time. These parameters also are kept in the file catalog entry. The entire catalog contains many file descriptions and is itself a VSAM file.

The allocation within the portions is also done using the B-tree algorithm. The blocking and insertion of records into trains will be presented below.

Blocking   VSAM uses the *train* concept presented in Sec. 2-3-1 to achieve blocking. Each train has a fixed number of blocks, also determined at the time of initial allocation, and is treated as one logical unit. Within a portion there will be space for a number of trains. Some of these may be in use; others may be free. Trains in use contain a variable number of records.

The records may be of variable length and may span blocks within a train. A partially filled train is shown in Fig. 4-15. The actual data records are packed into the forward area of the train; the three-byte markers giving the length of these records are stored in reverse order in the rear of the train. Adjoining records of equal size are controlled by a single, double-sized marker. A control field for the entire train gives the amounts of space used by the markers and left free.

Record Insertion   The free space in a train can be used to insert records and position information without requiring index manipulation. The new record is merged into its proper position. Some shifting within the train will nearly always take place to achieve this. The markers may have to be shifted too. Since they contain only the length, old markers retain their values.

If there is insufficient space in the train, a free train will be requisitioned. The B-tree algorithm is carried out in three steps, performed in a sequence which reduces vulnerability of the data in case of system malfunction.

1   The records comprising the first half of the full train are copied into the new train, and the new train is written out to disk.

2   The index is updated to include the new train at the appropriate point; the last record provides the key value for the index entry.

3   The old train is adjusted by shifting the latter half of the records to the front, and this train is rewritten.

During this sequence, the record which was to be added is put into the correct position, and the length markers are set for the old and the new train.

We already have discussed the measures taken when there is no free train in the portion, so that a new portion has to be allocated. Both overflow handling algorithms are B-tree based; they differ mainly in terms of the size of the units that are being manipulated.

Loading Density   To allow updating of the files without immediately forcing the splitting of trains and portions, the initial file density is specified at < 1. Here the B-tree algorithm is used for an indexed sequential file, trading space in order to avoid deterioration of performance due to insertions. Reorganization is not normally needed.

A file which undergoes much updating will eventually achieve an equilibrium similar to the equilibrium conditions described in Eq. 3-47. We used the result that space utilization will approach 69% so that we expect the trains eventually to be 69% occupied.

In addition, there will be some storage loss from unused trains in portions. The directory to the trains in one portion provides for the allocation of initial free trains. Trains which are freed are made available for reuse only within the same portion, so that also here a space utilization of 69% is expected when equilibrium conditions are reached. It will take a very long time to achieve this equilibrium, since portions will not be split frequently if the initial loading density and train allocation was generous. However, a specific portion can overflow while there is yet much space in all but one of the trains.

If trains are initially filled to 60% and portions to 90%, the initial storage utilization will be $0.60 \times 0.90 = 54\%$. After a number of updates equal to 40% of the initial loading, the storage utilization will be $1.40 \times 0.54 = 75\%$. This is the expected density for the trains under random insertions only. For this case we can expect that now many trains are filled, but also that little portion overflow has yet occurred. Beyond this point portions will overflow more frequently, and the portions will also achieve this density. Eventually the total storage density will approach the limit of $0.75 \times 0.75 \rightarrow 0.5625$, or 56%. If insertions and deletions both occur at high rates, the eventual equilibrium density may become as low as $0.69 \times 0.69 \rightarrow 48\%$.

If better utilization of space in a highly dynamic environment is desired, a reorganization can be used to reload the file to a desired density.

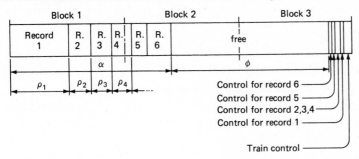

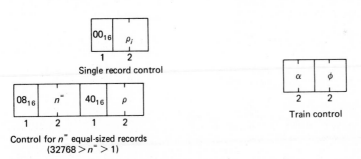

Figure 4-15 Record allocation within a train.

4-3-2 Addressing

A relative address space is set up for every file. The address begins with the initial portion and continues through all further portions allocated to the file. The components used to construct the address are shown Fig. 4-16. The size of some of the components is established for the life of the file, using estimates of future file size which are provided by the user or estimated by the system at file-creation time.

If no records are inserted, deleted, or replaced by records of differing size, the relative address of a record will remain the same. Such addresses then can be used to access data records in a VSAM file directly. The addresses are used in an extension of VSAM to provide multiple indexes. A primary file will contain the actual data records, and secondary files have lower-level entries which refer to the records of the primary file.

Relative addresses can be obtained by a program as a by-product of any operation on a record of the file to enable such usage. With relative addressing sequential access can be carried out more rapidly. Any change of record arrangements due to updates or insertions will, however, invalidate such addresses.

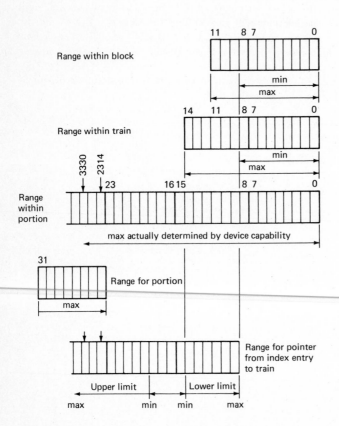

Figure 4-16 The components of the relative byte address.

Limits Any implementation of a file has limits. Many limits here are related to the assignment of components of the relative address used for pointing, as shown in Fig. 4-16. The size of the entire address is limited to 32 bits, so that the size of a file is limited to $2^{32} \approx 4.29 \times 10^9$ bytes. A portion is limited to one device. Up to 256 portions may be allocated, so that a file has to grow by substantial increments if it is not to run out of portions. Block may be {512, 1024, 2048, or 4096} bytes long, and a train is limited to a total of 32 768 bytes. The size of a record is limited to the space available in one train. There are some other implementation limits to allow simple fixed sizes for the marker fields seen in Fig. 4-15.

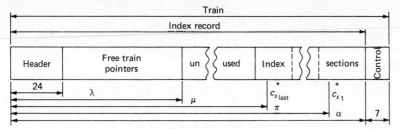

Complete index record

The header describes the remainder of the train format.

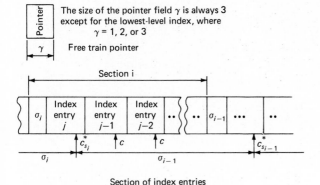

Header contents

The base value for data trains δ is 0 in all but the lowest-level index since all other indexes are kept within one portion ϵ is the pointer to the next index train

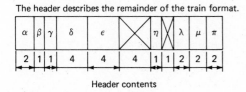

The size of the pointer field γ is always 3 except for the lowest-level index, where
$$\gamma = 1, 2, \text{ or } 3$$

Free train pointer

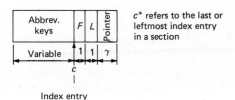

Section of index entries

c^* refers to the last or leftmost index entry in a section

Index entry

Figure 4-17 Components of an index record.

4-3-3 Index Manipulation

A multilevel index is used to access the data records. The index is considered to be a separate but related file. The index entries at the lowest level point to the beginning of the train, but the value associated with each index entry is the highest or last value in the train. Every train in a portion has an index entry, but entries for free trains do not have a key value and are collected at the end of the index.

The assignment of fields within a single index train is given in Fig. 4-17. The index entries in a train are grouped into section to accelerate the search within a block. In order to appreciate the issues addressed in a specific B-tree implementation, we will describe the VSAM index in more detail.

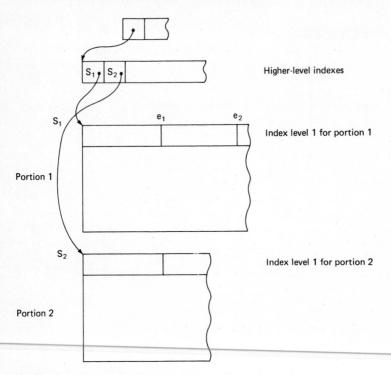

Figure 4-18 Index levels in VSAM.

Levels We indicated earlier that the number of index levels x is fixed for a VSAM file. Three levels are easily identifiable; the grouping of index entries into sections provides intermediate levels. It is convenient to regard $x = 3$.

If the file uses multiple portions, the level 1 index will be split into corresponding pieces. In the example sketched in Fig. 4-18 these pieces have been located adjacent to the corresponding data portions, which can help to obtain good performance. Locating the pieces of the index on separate or on devices with a smaller access time than the data can increase the fetch performance even more.

The next higher index level (2) provides at the same time information regarding the location of the allocated disk portions and the indexes. It encompasses the portion directory discussed in Sec. 4-3-1.

If a portion is split, a new level 1 index is built for the new portion, the old index is changed to indicate the trains that are now free, and one new entry is made in the second-level index. Since there is a limit of 256 portions, index level 2 is limited to 256 entries, and one third (x) level block provides the root. If the root block is frequently referenced, the paging scheme should keep this block in memory, providing fast access.

Blocking of the Index   The index file uses trains of a size appropriate to its own needs. One index record appears to fill one train completely, but within each record there are three types of fields: a header, entries for free trains, and index entries. There may be unused space between the two variable-length areas to allow for changes in the contents of the index record. Figure 4-17 shows the various components of an index record.

The index entries are again stored from right to left within an index record. They are grouped into a number of sections to reduce the index search time. The significance of the various fields is indicated through the matching Greek-letter symbols. In order to read or write programs to interface with the file structure at this level of detail, the reference manuals should be used.

Key Abbreviation   Since VSAM deals with general keys, often long names, effective abbrevation of keys is neccessary in order to have a fanout which can address all records in a file using only the fixed three levels. Table 4-2 shows a set of keys and how they would appear in abbreviated form.

The key abbreviation algorithm uses two count fields, each of fixed size, to describe the extent of abbreviation. The first field (F) indicates the number of characters omitted from the high-order part of the key, and the second field (L) indicates the number of characters remaining after both high- and low-order abbreviation. The high-order part of a key can be reconstructed by using the preceding entries. The initial entry establishes the range for the first data block. The F value of the first entry and the L value of the last entry will always be zero.

The low-order part is reconstructed with highest possible values in the character collating sequence. For clarity we assume this character to be "Z". All records to be inserted subsequently with keys from the begin value to the reconstructed boundary value for the first train (BEZ... in the figure) will be added to this first train. The boundaries for all subsequent trains are similarily established once the abbreviation has been done. Note that in the entries, when fewer characters are required to define the next entry, the size of the actual key entry will be zero.

Table 4-2   VSAM Key Abbreviation

Source Key	Key	F	L	Remarks			
BADE	BA	0	2	Begin value			
BERRINGER	E	1	1	first train:	BAA.....	to	BEZ.....
BIGLEY	I	1	1	second train:	BFA.....	to	BIZ.....
BRESLOW	RES	1	3	third train:	BJA.....	to	BRESZ...
BRETSHNEV	T	3	1	fourth train:	BRETA...	to	BRETZ...
BRODY	O	2	1	fifth train:	BREUA...	to	BROZ....
BRUCKNER	none	2	0	sixth train:	BRPA....	to	BRZ.....
BUHLER	U	1	1	seventh train:	BSA.....	to	BUZ.....
CALHOUN	CALH	0	4	eighth train:	BVA.....	to	CALHZ...
CALL	none	3	0	ninth train:	CALIA...	to	CALZ....
CROSS	none	1	0	tenth train:	CAMA....	to	CAZ.....

This example shows the abbreviations if there were only one record per data train. In practice one extreme record per train is chosen as anchor. The anchor in VSAM is the immediate successor record, that is, the first record in the next train. Otherwise it could not be determined if a reference to "BIGLOW" would be an existing entry in the third train or a new entry in the second train.

When the index is used, the entries have to be searched serially. The number of matching high-order characters is counted. If the number of characters that are provided in the index is equal to the number matched, the proper index entry has been found. A proper match occurs also when the search-argument character in the current position is smaller than the matching index-entry key character, or if the index key entry is abbreviated so that no further key character is available.

Index Search   The number of index entries within a train, y, can be substantial, and the basic procedure to reconstruct the keys for matching is very time-consuming. In order to reduce the search time, a jump search, as described in Sec. 4-2-2 is implemented, leading to $cix = \sqrt{y}$ (Eq. 4-4). The index entries within one train are grouped initially into $\sqrt{y}$ sections. After insertions and deletions the sizes of the sections may differ from this optimum.

The key for the last index entry in each section, the section key $c^*_{s_j}$ of Fig. 4-17, is abbreviated less, to permit reconstruction for jumping from the preceding section key $c^*_{s_{j-1}}$. The first search pass uses this section key and skips from one to the next section using the section length indicator σ_j to find the proper section. When the section has been found, a search pass for the appropriate entry is restricted within that section. This additional pseudo-level does not require repeated entries of the key or pointers, only a reduced key abbreviation for the section keys.

Pointers   Pointers are also abbreviated. The index pointers on level 1 to the data trains include only the displacement within a portion in terms of trains. For instance, if there are 300 trains in one portion, $\gamma = \lceil 300/2^8 \rceil = 2$ 8-bit bytes suffice for the pointer entry. To calculate the byte address of the train, the contents of the pointer field is multiplied by the train size and the beginning address of the portion δ is added.

4-3-4 Sequential Access

In VSAM the index has to be read to process the data trains serially. To obtain high-performance serial access, the use of higher levels of the index is avoided. The linkage pointer (ϵ) is used to locate successive lowest-level index trains, and the data trains are fetched using the pointers of the index entries.

After many dynamic changes of a VSAM file the trains will no longer be in a physical sequence. Within each train, however, the record sequence has been maintained. For large trains fewer seeks is required, but train size will be limited because of buffer capacity and the limits imposed by the relative addressing scheme. A file with portions covering multiple cylinders will have its trains distributed over them, so that seeks during serial access still can add substantially to the time required to read the file.

Locality Control   There are some optional features to increase search performance through improved locality. One of these features allows replication of the index on a track of a rotating device so that the average rotational latency for reading of the index can be reduced. Other options provide for the close location of index file components and the data file itself to minimize seek times. Index and data can also be placed on separate devices to provide overlap of access. This is especially useful when processing the file serially.

4-3-5 Programming

Programmers who use a file-access method can operate on one of three levels:

- They can write instructions to manipulate the file on the basis of understanding the logical functions to be executed.
- They can attempt to also understand the underlying physical structure in order to produce programs that are efficient within the perceived system environment.
- They can use attractive features of the file system and attempt to bypass or disable parts of the file-system support which do not suit them, and replace these parts with programs of their own invention.

Each of these choices has associated costs and benefits, and the decisions should be made based on documented evaluations of the trade-offs which were considered. The cost of the first alternative may be inadequate performance and the cost of the third alternative may be intolerable inflexibility.

A philosophy in structured programming, *information hiding*, advocates the imposition of the first approach by not revealing the underlying structure of system programs. This is sometimes unintentionally aided by the lack of clear system documentation. The author prefers to work with a good knowledge of the available tools and use them to a maximal extent. When programming tools are inadequate and have to be rejected, good documention of the reasons, not only of the resulting system, will help successors maintain the programs and may also give guidance to the developers of newer tools.

Statements   The operations that are basic to the use of VSAM and similar methods include the following statements.

An OPEN statement is to be issued before the file can be processed. The OPEN statement is used to specify the file name, the type of operations to be performed, and optionally, a *password* to be verified. The OPEN statement also specifies the area or areas where the parameters for further processing requests will be found. The catalog, the file listing all files, will be searched to locate the file. The device or devices which contain index and data will be accessed and directory information extracted. A check to ensure the use of the right versions of the index files and the data file is made by matching the contents of a field in each file directory which contains the most recent update times. Buffer storage for file processing also is obtained and initialized.

A CLOSE statement is used to indicate that processing of the file is completed. The CLOSE statement empties any outstanding buffers and updates the file directory.

A GET statement is used to read data from the file. Before its execution the search argument and other parameters are placed into a parameter area which specifies what is to be read. The parameters to be set for indexed access include the key value and indicate whether an exact or a less-than-or-equal match is desired. The position and length of the area into which the record is to be placed have to be specified. An area for receiving error messages should also be provided. A further parameter states whether the process will wait until the reading is completed. Otherwise the process can continue computation while the system executes the GET process asynchronously. The calling process can check later if the system process is complete. The length and address of the record read will be placed into the parameter list upon completion.

The advantage of using a separate fixed area for the parameter list is that only parameters that change have to be respecified when the next GET is issued. To provide more flexibility of operation, it is possible to generate new or to modify existing request parameter areas during program execution by means of GENCB and MODCB statements.

The PUT statement initiates the writing of a record, again using parameters contained in the specified parameter area. When writing, the length of the record has to be set into the parameter list prior to execution of the statement. The parameter area can be separate since its address is specified as part of a GET or PUT operation.

The ERASE statement causes deletion of the indicated record.

The POINT statement provides a capability to reset the current-record pointer for serial GET and PUT statements.

The CHECK statement is used to determine whether a previous asynchronous operation has been completed.

The ENDREQ statement can be used to terminate an outstanding request. This will cancel an operation which is no longer desirable, perhaps because of a detected error or because a parallel operation has delivered the desired data already.

Escape Procedures   Optional parameters allow the specification of program segments which are to be executed when the file system performs certain operations or senses certain conditions in the file. One use of these escape procedures is to compress or expand data records in order to save file space. Others can be used when End-of-file conditions occur. Considerable modification of the basic operations is possible when these escape hatches or exits are used.

These facilities are also exploited to create multi-indexed files within VSAM. Upon insertion of a record into the data or primary file an escape procedure will initiate updating of all secondary indexes.

The programmer who uses escape procedures has access to all the options and the underlying code at the same structural level. Now the distinction between the three levels of programming described above is not very explicit, and good intentions can easily come to naught. Programs which are invoked as escape procedures may introduce errors which are not visible when the program which invokes the file services is checked out. These escape hatches can also easily be misused to violate system security.

4-4   TREE-STRUCTURED FILES

Up to this point we have discussed indexed organizations where the index was *distinct* from the data portion of the file. In this section, we will describe file organizations where the goal portions of records are lifted into the index structure itself. A block of such a file is sketched in Fig. 4-19 and can be compared with the block of an indexed file shown in Fig. 3-15. The position of the entire record is determined by the position of its key. The tree-structured file organization is sketched in Fig. 4-20.

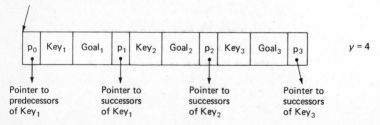

Figure 4-19 A block of a tree-structured file.

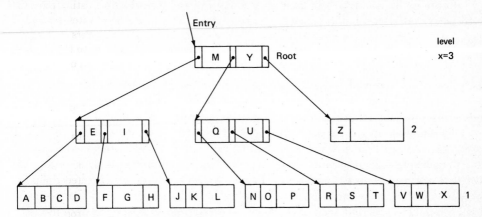

Figure 4-20 A tree-structured file.

Since the goal records are placed into a single tree, this organization is akin to the indexed-sequential file. Seriality is established according to only one attribute. The process of processing the records of the file serially is a generalization of *inorder traversal* for binary trees [Knuth[73F]]. Example 4-7 sketches the algorithm.

Example 4-7   Obtaining Records Serially from a Tree

```
proceed: go to the left subtree,
             if not terminal block
                 then → proceed,
                 else process the block,
          go up to the root for this subtree,
             if there is a record,
                 then do; process the record,
                     go to the next subtree,
                     → proceed, end;
             else do;
                     if this is the root for the entire file,
                         then → done,
                         else → proceed, end;
    done:       ...
```

A tree-structured file will be *balanced* if the number of levels is equal or nearly equal for all branches of the tree. A balanced tree will require on the average fewer block accesses to locate a record, given that record requests are uniformly distributed.

4-4-1 Evaluation of a Tree-Structured File

The major advantage of this structure is the nonredundancy of storage. The goal record is directly associated with its key. Key fields appear only once, they are not replicated at other levels.

In the evaluation which follows we assume that the records are densely packed into blocks, although not spanned. Update performance would be better if a non-dense B-tree scheme were used, but the reduction in density reduces the effectiveness of the tree structure.

We now find goal records throughout the levels of this file and at different seek distances from the root index. A disadvantage of the tree-structured file is that the fanout can be significantly reduced versus the fanout of an index so that many more seeks may be required to retrieve an average record of a large file.

The increase in the expected number of block retrievals depends on the ratio of key sizes to goal sizes, which controls the reduction of the fanout factor. Some access benefit is gained because some records (7 out of 26 in Fig. 4-20) are closer to the root and hence easier to retrieve. This factor will only outweigh the reduction in fanout if the goal records are extremely small. This happens when the tree is is used as an index tree but then another access is required to access the data file. An operational benefit of trees is that keys are stored in only one place, and hence are easier to update.

Records can be of variable length, since the access algorithms do not depend on a specific number of records per block. In order to simplify the analysis, a fixed value for R will be used below, which will provide adequate results if there are many records per block ($R \ll B$).

The fanout ratio is given by

$$y = \left\lfloor \frac{B-P}{R+P} \right\rfloor + 1 \qquad\qquad 4\text{-}10$$

found by inspection of Fig. 4-19. Even though the lowest level does not require further pointers, space for such pointers is frequently allocated, since this simplifies further growth of the file. Then the fanout ratio y is the same at level 1.

We assume now that the file is filled at the top levels ($x, \ldots, 2$), rather than at level 1 as shown in Fig. 4-20, and hence is balanced. This will provide the shortest access paths to the data. The number of records at each level is again determined by the number of blocks on a level and by the fanout ratio. Note that here, as with the original B-tree, the number of records in a block is one less than the fanout.

$$n_{level} = (y-1)b_{level} = (y-1)y^{x-level}$$

If the tree is balanced, only the bottom level (1) will be partially filled; it will contain the remaining records, computed by subtracting the records on levels $x \to 2$ from the total file size n

$$n_1 = n - (y-1)\sum_{i=x}^{2} y^{x-i}$$

We assume at least a two level tree here, i.e., $n > y - 1$. To find the number of levels in the tree, we follow Eq. 3-48. For $y \gg 1$ an estimate for x is

$$x_{est} = \lceil \log_y n \rceil \qquad\qquad 4\text{-}11$$

The exact height of the tree can be obtained by summing the number of records at the successive levels $n_{level=x}, n_{x-1}, \ldots$, and stopping when all records are stored.

the expected, i.e., average, fetch time can be computed by taking the fetch time for the n_{level} records at each level and allocating this over the n records in the file. The access path increases from 1 for $level = x$ to x for the bottom level, and this accounts for the first factor in the summation below

$$T_F = \frac{s + r + btt}{n} \left((y-1) \sum_{i=x}^{2} (x - i + 1)\, y^{x-i} + x\, n_1 \right) \qquad \text{4-12}$$

The fetch time in a tree structure is not constrained by consideration of integer–level numbers, as were the indexes shown earlier. Also, if the tree is used as an index, the pointers in the tree to the remote goal data can exist at various levels. The smooth curve in Fig. 4-11 is hence appropriate to describe the fetch time to fanout relationship seen here.

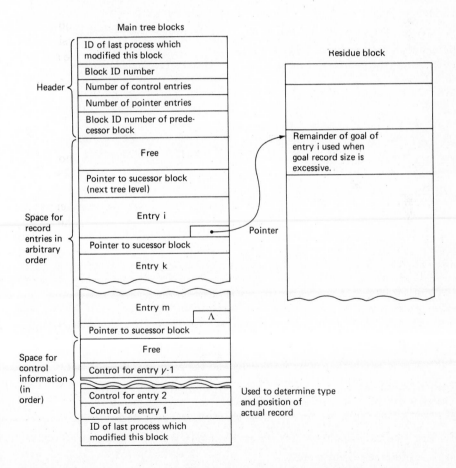

Figure 4-21 Contents of blocks in the SPIRES system.

**Example   4-8   Comparison of performance of two tree-structured files
and similar B-tree indexed and indexed-sequential files**

We will evaluate a tree-structured file and two alternative indexed files each for two cases,
a short and **b** long records. We will use similar parameters as were used in the example
of a personnel file given as Example 3-9 of Sec. 3-4.

In case **a** we will assume that an **employee** goal record contains only a **social
security number** of nine characters (V_K) and a **skill code** of six characters (V_G), so
that $R = 15$; in case **b** we use a still modest record length of $R = 180$ characters.

The remaining parameters required are

$$n = 20\,000 \text{ records}, \quad B = 1\,000 \text{ characters}, \quad P = 4 \text{ characters}.$$

1   Tree-structured file

For the tree-structured file we assume a dense packing of records, and use Eqs. 4-9, 4-10,
and 4-11. To verify that x_{est} is indeed equal to x, we also present the contents of each
level of the files.

Case a

$$y = \left\lfloor \frac{1000-4}{15+4} \right\rfloor + 1 = 53$$

$$x_{est} = \lceil \log_{53} 20\,000 \rceil = \lceil 2.49 \rceil = 3$$

Case b

$$y = \left\lfloor \frac{1000-4}{180+4} \right\rfloor + 1 = 6$$

$$x_{est} = \lceil \log_6 20\,000 \rceil = \lceil 5.21 \rceil = 6$$

The files are then constructed as follows:

Level	Blocks	Records	Pointers	Blocks	Records	Pointers
6				$= x : 1$	5	6
5				6	30	36
4				36	180	216
3	$= x : 1$	52	53	216	1 080	1 296
2	53	2 756	$\le 2\,809$	1 296	6 480	$\le 7\,776$
1	331	17 192		2 445	12 225	
Total	385	20 000		3 964	20 000	

Hence $T_F =$

$$\frac{1 \times 52 + 2 \times 2756 + 3 \times 17192}{20\,000}(s + r + btt)$$

$$= 2.86\,(s + r + btt)$$

$$\frac{1 \times 5 + 2 \times 30 + \ldots + 5 \times 6480 + 6 \times 12225}{20\,000}(s + r + btt)$$

$$= 5.53\,(s + r + btt)$$

2   B-tree index to a data file

One of the alternatives to a tree-structured file is a file accessed via a B-tree index. Here
we can consider two further cases, one where the file is record-anchored, as required
for multi-indexed files, and one where the file is block-anchored, which is adequate for
indexed-sequential files as VSAM. When the file is record anchored the record size does not
affect the fetch time, but in the block-anchored case the short records of case **a** require
only $\lceil n/Bfr \rceil = \lceil 20000/\lfloor 1000/15 \rfloor \rceil = 304$ blocks and corresponding pointers, whereas
the longer records require $\lceil 20\,000/\lfloor 1000/180 \rfloor \rceil = 4000$ pointers for the data blocks. The
fanout in the index is determined by the density and the entry size $V_K + P = 13$

Record-anchored	Block-anchored	
Cases a and b	Case a	Case b
$y = \left\lfloor \frac{0.69 \times 1000}{13} \right\rfloor = 52$	also $y = 52$	$y = 52$
$x = \lceil \log_{52} 20\,000 \rceil = \lceil 2.51 \rceil = 3$	$x = \lceil \log_{52} 304 \rceil = 2$	$x = \lceil \log_{52} 4\,000 \rceil = 3$

Fetching a record requires one more
access to the file; hence $T_F =$

$$(x + 1)(s + r + btt) = 4(s + r + btt) \qquad 3(s + r + btt) \qquad 4(s + r + btt)$$

3   A dense index to a data file

The tree-structured file presented as alternative **1** of this example uses blocks densely and will hence be much harder to update than the B-tree file of alternative **2**. As a third alternative we will evaluate a dense index, one that is also hard to update. The same considerations of record anchors versus block anchors apply, but the fanout is greater. With block anchoring this case is the indexed-sequential file design presented in Sec. 3-3.

Record-anchored	Block-anchored	
Cases a and b	**Case a**	**Case b**
$y = \lfloor \frac{1000}{13} \rfloor = 76$	also $y = 76$	$y = 76$
$x = \lceil \log_{76} 20\,000 \rceil = \lceil 2.29 \rceil = 3$	$x = \lceil \log_{76} 304 \rceil = 2$	$x = \lceil \log_{76} 4\,000 \rceil = 2$

Fetching a record requires also here one more access to the file; hence $T_F =$

$$(x+1)(s+r+btt) = 4(s+r+btt) \qquad 3(s+r+btt) \qquad 3(s+r+btt)$$

if no overflows have occurred.

Summary In comparing these three methods applied to this problem, we see that the best performance is obtained for short records with the tree structure, but that this method is the worst for long records. The indexing methods discussed in Chap. 3 are more robust but cannot match the instances where the tree structure is optimal.

To complete Example 4-8, we will list for the six cases the fetch time and file space.

Record size	Short $R = 15$	Long $R = 180$
Tree-structured file	$T_F = 2.86, b = 385$	$T_F = 5.53, b = 3964$
B-tree index on one attribute	$T_F = 4, b = 698$	$T_F = 4, b = 4269$
block-anchored	$T_F = 4, b = 311$	$T_F = 3, b = 4080$
Indexed-sequential	$T_F = 4, b = 573$	$T_F = 4, b = 4269$
block-anchored	$T_F = 3, b = 310$	$T_F = 3, b = 4054$

If the records are long, a tree structure still can be employed for the keys themselves by removing the nonkey portions of the records, the goal portions, into a separate file. Elements in this file are found by pointers so that some of the considerations developed for overflow of files are valid here. One extra access will be required to fetch the goal record; so there is an advantage only when operations that operate solely on the key are frequent. Such is the case when keys are used to produce counts or subset TID pointers.

To close this subsection, we show a block layout for a tree-structured file system used for information retrieval (Fig. 4-21), which attempts a compromise by splitting large records into a node segment (located within the tree), and a residual segment, kept in a separate file, to be accessed indirectly.

Fields of the record which remain in the node segment benefit from immediate access. The key, of course, will always be placed within the node segment and will not be replicated in the residual part. The record-marking scheme uses a position table as shown in Fig. 2-11.

4-4-2 Balancing Trees

In tree-structured files the performance of the file can degrade after insertions and deletions are made, since insertions are connected to their ancestors. For instance, insertions of records **F1, F2,** ... in Fig. 4-20 will increase the file height $x \rightarrow 4$, and the path length to these records will also be 4.

In order to retain the performance of indexed and tree-structured files, it is desirable that the tree be *balanced*. An optimally balanced tree has only path lengths to terminal nodes of size x or of size $x - 1$. Inspection of Eq. 4-10, which predicted the search time, will show that any other distribution of the records will lead to higher expected search values.

The strict B-tree algorithm also leads to balanced files, although irregularity of insertions and deletions causes a reduction in density and thus longer path lengths, but the effect is bounded by the condition that $y_{eff} \geq y/2$. In tree-structured files balancing has to be explicitly done, either during update operations or by reorganization. Balancing has been extensively analyzed for *binary trees*.

Binary trees   A tree where each record contains only one value and two branches $(y = 2)$ is of interest for two reasons:

- The structure is appropriate for core storage because of its simplicity, and hence is also useful within a block of file storage.
- The behavior of dynamically changing binary trees has been investigated both theoretically and statistically.

A basic record in a tree is called a *node*. Figure 4-22 shows a binary tree equivalent to the file tree of Fig. 4-20. Analyses of conventional binary trees, based on core storage, typically assume equal access costs between linked nodes. The analysis of performance trees, when they are placed on files where multiple nodes fit into one block, has to consider that the access cost along sequential branches in a block is much less than the access cost along pointer branches. Only if locality is so poor that all nodes will reside on distinct blocks will access costs be equal. The equivalent analysis for binary file trees has to take differential access costs into account.

Algorithms to keep trees balanced are covered extensively in Knuth[73S], and their performance is presented by Karlton[76]. For certain file trees useful results can be derived from the analyses of conventional binary trees.

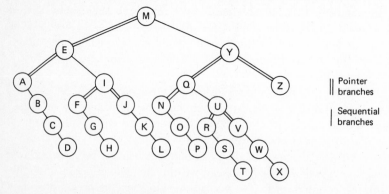

Figure 4-22 Binary tree.

Maintenance of Trees Problems in tree balancing occur mainly when updating the file. Some of them have been discussed in Sec. 4-3-3. B-trees do not require rebalancing unless either a higher loading density than the equilibrium density is desired or when a simple deletion algorithm does not fill the nodes adequately.

If a file is reorganized, it can be more efficient to generate a new tree sequentially for each level instead of performing n insertions. After y_{eff} entries are written into a block for level 1, one entry is taken for level 2, etc. This procedure may also be advantageous for batch updating.

If a certain pattern of growth is expected, the reorganization algorithm can make decisions which will lessen the effect of unbalanced growth. This is typically done when most update activity is expected to occur at the end of the file. Extra index blocks at the end of each level may be preallocated.

When multiple indexes are to be created, the input to an index creation process can be the output of a transposition procedure as described in Sec. 4-1-3.

4-5   HIERARCHICALLY STRUCTURED DATA

In the previous section, we discussed the use of trees to store data that were sequentially indexed. All data records were of the same type and could be moved between levels as dictated by considerations of access efficiency. Treelike structures have found more appropriate use where data have a natural hierarchical organization. Figure 4-23 shows a data structure which is naturally hierarchical in concept.

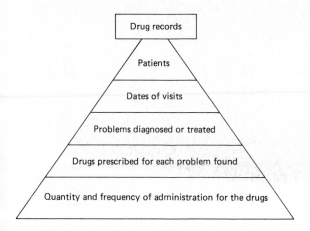

Figure 4-23 A hierarchical data structure.

We have already encountered hierarchical data structures when multiring files were presented in Sec. 3-6. In this section hierarchical structures based on trees will be described. A classical example of such data is a genealogical tree or an organizational hierarchy.

A list of assemblies, subassemblies, parts, and material, in a manufactured product, is an important hierarchical structure found in many database applications. This example, also called a bill-of-materials database, is shown in Fig. 4-24. The alternative, a translation of the hierarchy into a long, composite key, does not provide a convenient model to the user: the key for "dial" is

Products‖washing_machine‖control‖dial .

A nomenclature which is common and nonsexist is also shown with the tree in Fig. 4-24.

We distinguish hierarchical structures that form proper trees from structures that form banyan-type trees or *networks*. The latter case arises when the goal records can be accessed via more than one path. In the bill-of-materials example, this condition would occur if a certain type of "Switch" is used in several of the subassemblies and only one record is to contain all the data for this switch. The record "Switch" would then have three parents. In a hierarchical file, every record has only one parent.

4-5-1 Criteria for Hierarchical Data Files

In tree-structured files access is optimized by generating a well-balanced tree. Since the records are similar throughout the file, the fanout ratio is made equal at every level. A hierarchical file is structured by the data; the number of levels and the fanout is controlled externally. We have distinguish now the fanout y, which is a data-structure-oriented value, from the number of entries per block, which is based on the mechanical blocking factor Bfr. In order to be able to process hierarchical data structures effectively, certain structural conditions are to be met.

One requirement is that there will be a reasonable fanout at each level. The number of children for one record should not be so small that too many levels would be required to find level 1 data. Neither should there be so many children that the search for a specific child will be difficult.

Another condition is that an equal level number implies an identical record type. This means that it is not desirable to change the hierarchy for the "Spin Dryer" in Fig. 4-24 by inserting a level below which distinguishes electric from gas dryers, if this is not to be done for all products.

Since this type of file structure is so closely related to the data structure for an application, we will present hierarchical files by means of a detailed example of a simple system.

4-5-2 MUMPS

As an example of an implementation of a hierarchical file we will describe the file system which supports the requirements of the MUMPS language. This language is oriented toward interactive computing on small systems. It was standardized in 1976 by the ANS institute [O'Neill[76]] and is finding increasing use. The syntax and user interface are close to those found in BASIC language systems. A unique feature is that a hierarchical file-management scheme is embedded in the language, so that it is frequently used for database implementations.

MUMPS operates in an interpretive mode, and hence no declaration of any variables is required. The MUMPS language allows great flexibility in the assignment

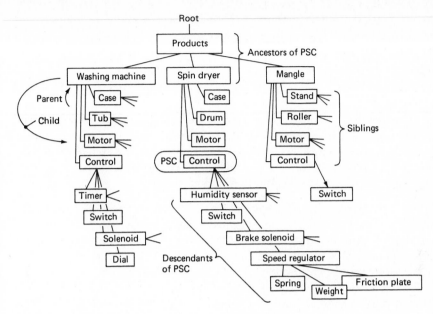

Figure 4-24 Nomenclature in a hierarchy.

of values to variable names. All data are represented by strings of up to 255 characters. Size limits are imposed on strings used in computations. A class of variables called *globals* are always fetched from and stored onto data files. To distinguish global variables in the language from program local variables, they are prefixed with the symbol "↑" or "^".

The names of MUMPS global variables are stored in a directory level of the user's file space, so that the name of a data file is permanently associated with the name of the global program variable. There is no control language to associate a file name from a system directory to a reference file name used within a program, but the language provides indirection so that any string can be used to address globals. Integer subscripts are used to provide keys for the globals, they have a permissible range from 0 to 999 999 999.

If there is a single value associated with a global, as is the case in this write statement,

        SET ↑username='Penelope'

then the string 'Penelope' will become the value of the global named **username**. Single globals of this type appear in the top level of the hierarchy. They provide a useful means for the communication of status variables, as **DONE** in Fig. 4-25, between program segments. To store one patient name with a key of **patno** into a **drug** global file which will have many patients, a subscript is used, as

        SET ↑drug(patno)='Manuel Cair'

To read the value of the name of patient identified by **hospno**, one writes

        SET name=↑drug(hospno)

The number of subscripts ns used determines the level number in the hierarchy, $level = x-ns$. Note again that the subscripts are not used for address computation, but as search arguments and keys for the hierarchical global files.

The flexibility of MUMPS is seen in Fig. 4-25 where the field for drug frequency on level 1, item 2, has been set to a data element of a different type by

```
...   SET icdno=49390
      SET ↑drug(patno,dateno,icdno,1,3)='PRN'
```

using a string data value, indicating *as needed*, here rather than the usual numeric data element specifying a frequency.

An analysis of MUMPS files also provides an example of the capabilities which can be provided by systems that are considerably less massive than those that support the elaborate indexed-sequential files discussed earlier.

Storage Structure   To begin with an example, we consider the following structure used for records in a clinic pharmacy. The description which follows will assume a B-tree data file approach followed in modern implementations. Since MUMPS does not need statements to define variables and storage, we will use a PL/1 notation to document the intended data.

Example 4-9   A Hierarchical Data Structure

```
DECLARE
    1 drugrecord,
        2 patients (n1),
            3 patient_number,
            3 patient_name,              } 2
            3 visit_dates (n2),
                4 treated_problem (n3),
                    5 drugs_prescribed (n4),
                        6 drugname,
                        6 quantity,      } 3
                        6 frequency;
```

This structure implies a hierarchy which provides storage for `n1` patients with *2* data values {`patient_number, patient_name`} each and a subtree for `n1`×`n2` visits, `n1`×`n2`×`n3` problems, and `n1`×`n2`×`n3`×`n4` drugs with *3* data elements per drug. Conventional languages and their files will have to allocate excessively large amounts of storage to accommodate the possible maximum array sizes.

If 500 patients may be seen in the clinic per day, if patients might have 100 visits and might have 20 diagnosed problems, and if treating a problem can require up to 10 drugs, then the array space required for the data items on each level is

$$1 + 500 \times 2 + 500 \times 100 + 500 \times 100 \times 20 + 500 \times 100 \times 20 \times 10 \times 3 = \quad 31\,051\,001$$

At some point in time there may actually be 450 patients seen in a day, the average number of visits is 8, the average number of problems per visit is 2.3, and the average number of drugs used for a problem is 1.2, so that only

$$1 + 450 \times 2 + 450 \times 8 + 450 \times 8 \times 2.3 + 450 \times 8 \times 2.3 \times 1.2 \times 3 = \quad 42\,589$$

data fields would be occupied at that time, and more than 31 000 000 will be empty.

We wish to avoid these null entries because of the storage cost, and even more because of the processing cost incurred when fetching and rejecting empty fields. The hierarchical structure provides a method to achieve compact storage.

A MUMPS data file stores each data value in a distinct *segment*. The relationship of segments will be explained using the nomenclature of Fig. 4-24. A segment is identified through its position in the hierarchy of ancestors and by a key which distinguishes multiple children of one parent. The segments which are logically part of one record are not stored together. Segments of different records that are at the same level are stored together. Those segments on one level that belong to the same parent are arranged to form a continuous *segment sequence*. A logical record can be constructed by assembling from each level the segments that are related by a parent-child binding. Among multiple children the child with the desired identification can be chosen. For example, a record of Fig. 4-24 is made up of keys and data found at each level from `Product` to `Dial`.

A segment forms a triplet or quadruplet {level, key, value, and/or child}. The level is implied. Table 4-3 describes the stored components of a segment.

Table 4-3   Components of a MUMPS Data Segment

Function	Code	Typical value
Key (integer)	V_{key}	5 chars.
Type identification for the value field combination	Pid	1 char.
Data string value (if entered)	V_G	15 chars.
Pointer value to children (if entered)	P	2 chars.

Multiple children of the same parent, *siblings*, are appended to their particular segment sequence in order of arrival. Siblings which do not fit into the initial block referenced are put into successor blocks. Blocks are split as required. A linkage between blocks, as presented in Sec. 4-2-3, is maintained to assure rapid access to all segments of a sequence.

The actual implementation of the conceptual hierarchy is shown in Fig. 4-25. The position of the segment sequence with all children is defined by a single pointer from the parent. The key for a data item is part of the segment, so that a search for a sibling is done at the same level used to keep sibling data. The number of pointers in a block is relatively high, since a segment contains only one or zero data elements, and hence is quite short. The actual format of the segments is described later. We will now consider the data found in this file structure.

Contents of the File   An entire hierarchical structure is known by one global variable name kept at level x, here ↑`drug`. The variable names stored are limited in length to 8 characters to provide a high density of segments per block (Bfs_x) at the top level. There are no names associated with the variables at the lower levels, and extrinsic documentation is required to explain the meaning of levels in the hierarchy.

At level $x - 1$, we find the patient number as key and the name as data. At level $x - 2$, the date itself provides the key, and no actual data field is required. To permit use of the date as a key, the vlue of the date is represented in storage as an integer, say, 31271 for 3DEC71. Patient `Cair` has had three visits recorded.

Hybrid File Organizations

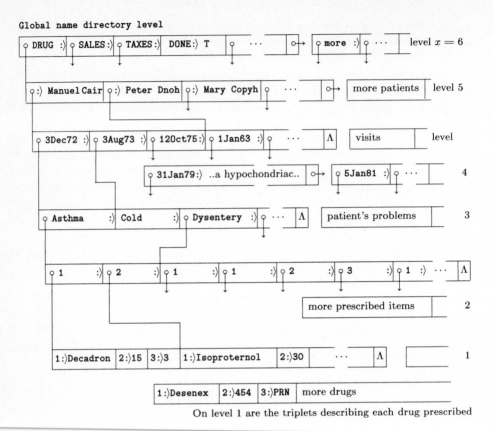

On level 1 are the triplets describing each drug prescribed

Figure 4-25 MUMPS data storage.

The pointer field of the date segment allows retrieval of the problem list on level $x-3$. A problem name could be kept as data; here the problem is identified through a standard coding method. A suitable key might be the ICDA code (International Classification of Disease) which assigns numbers of the form xxx.xx to diseases. For a value of this code, 493.90, the key would be 49390. We have again a segment without an explicit goal field. Patient Cair had only one problem treated at his 3Dec72 visit.

Level $x-4$ contains as key a sequence number of each drug given in the prescription for this problem. For each drug there is a pointer to a segment sequence on level $x-5$. Cairs prescription for Asthma had two items; on a later visit for a Cold nothing was prescribed.

At this final level we find the actual data segments for a drug. In our example this segment sequence has always three segments with keys of 1,2,3 and associated data fields. These segments have no further pointers.

To retrieve drug data, we have available as keys the patient number, the visit date, the problem number, and the drug sequence number. The fetch statement to get the name of the drug would read

    SET drugname=↑drug(patno,dateno,problemno,drugno,1)

and would require the 6 steps shown in Example 4-10 for execution. Intermediate level data, such as the patient name, can be found with fewer accesses.

Example 4-10   Navigating Down a Hierarchy

```
Access the initial block containing the global names,
   search for 'drug',
   read through successor blocks until global='drug' found,
Follow pointer to first level x-1 block ,
   search for patient segment  key=patno .
   /* If we have many patients, many blocks may have to be searched. */
When found follow pointer in segment to date level block,
   search for visit date  key=dateno .
When found follow pointer in segment to problem level block,
   search for problem number  key=problemno .
When found follow pointer in segment to prescription level block,
   search for drug number  key=drugno .
When found follow pointer in segment to drug data level block,
   and then search for drug data segment  key='1' .
When found pick up data field ('Decadron') out of segment.
```

As in all hierarchical files the natural structure of the data has a great effect on file performance. Within a single level the length of the segment sequence y is a very critical parameter. This length is determined by the number of siblings on one level and is not controlled by file-system procedures. If Bfs denotes the average number of segments in one block; a B-tree implementation will permit

$$Bfs = 0.69 \frac{B}{V_{seg}} \qquad \langle \text{MUMPS B-tree} \rangle \ 4\text{-}13$$

where V_{seg} is the segment size.

When there are, on the average, few siblings, the fanout is low $(y < Bfs)$ and the number of levels of the file increases. Sibling segments within a segment sequence, i.e., having the same parent, need not be kept in any particular order.

To locate all siblings in arbitrary order requires only sequential access to segments in a block and, if the sequence y extends beyond the block, serial access to the successor blocks on that level. To minimize the cost of accessing long sequences, most MUMPS systems do attempt to maintain locality of blocks when a block split occurs. The system may avoid spanning a segment sequence, which fits into one block, over two blocks. Such an optimization is possible since the segments are not sequential but the space versus time trade-off is quite complex.

4-5-3 Evaluation of a MUMPS File

Following the general description of the MUMPS file structure, we will evaluate a typical organization in greater detail so that some criteria for proper utilization of MUMPS capabilities become clear.

Chains The number of seeks or block fetches is determined by the number of levels and the length of the chains at each level. Figure 4-25 shows a structure where most segment sequences were short. Exceptions are the list of patients on level $x - 1$ and the sequence of visits of a hypochondriac on level $x - 2$.

The number of blocks to be accessed on one level depends on the number and size of sibling segments and on the size of the blocks used. In order to use little core storage,

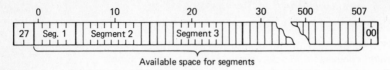

Figure **4-26** A block in MUMPS.

the implementers of MUMPS choose fairly small block sizes, from 128 to 512 characters in length. Figure 4-26 shows such a block. We will assume for our example a system with 512 bytes per block.

Two fields in each block are used for block management. One indicates the number of characters used in the block, and the other one contains the successor-block pointer. Binary integers are often used as pointers so that fields of two bytes in length can contain positive integer values up to 65 535. This value is not adequate for all blocks on a large disk unit, so that this block number is specific to one user. To each user, a number of cylinders are assigned, within which all the global variables are allocated, so that all the files of one user are limited to 65 535 blocks total.

Segment Formats A segment consists of a type identification, the key, and as goal either or both pointer and data fields. Figure 4-27 shows some possible segments.

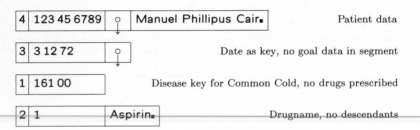

Figure **4-27** Segments in MUMPS files.

The *type identification* indicates what type of fields this segment contains. Two bits are required to encode the four possibilities:

{ 1: key only; 2: key, data; 3: key, pointer; 4: key, data, pointer; }.

The *key* field extends from the identification field and requires up to 9 digit positions. In binary form the value could be encoded in 33 bits.

A *pointer*, when present, occupies two character positions. Its presence indicates that this segment has a descendant subtree.

Data when present are of variable length, up to 255 characters, and are terminated with a special end-of-string marker.

Evaluation of the Hierarchical Data Structure We now will evaluate the drug file level by level using the assumptions made earlier. We will assume segment sizes based on the values in Table 4-3. The average length of the data strings (15 characters) includes the end-of-string marker. Computation of the segment size

$$R' = Pid + V_{key} + V_G + P \qquad\qquad 4\text{-}14$$

has to consider if a data or pointer value exists at the level. The example contains data at only two levels {1, 5} and pointer are needed on all levels but the bottom one $\{1\}$. Denoting the size of a segment of a record at level i as R'_i, we find that the number of segments per block

$$Bfs_i = dens \left\lfloor \frac{B - 2P}{R'_i} \right\rfloor \qquad \langle\text{hierarchical file}\rangle \; 4\text{-}15$$

The density for a B-tree data file implementation can again be estimated with Eq. 3-47 as $dens = 0.69\%$. Large segment sizes can lower the density further if spanning of blocks by single segments is avoided.

Since segments sequences can span blocks, a number of block accesses may be required to find a specific segment at one level. The expected number of blocks to be fetched for a segment sequence of fanout y is

$$b_i(y_i) = \lceil \tfrac{1}{2} + y_i/Bfs_i \rceil$$

The extra $\tfrac{1}{2}$ block appears because a segment sequence may start at an arbitrary position in the first block.

If $b_i \gg 1$, the fanout y_i is too high at level i because the number of block accesses will be large on one level. There will also be fewer segments in the last block of the sequence, so that for arbitrary sequences the number of accesses can be precisely estimated using the procedure leading to Eq. 4-12, assuming an equal frequency of access to all segments of the sequence. The number of expected block accesses are the sum of accesses to the first block, accesses to reach intermediate blocks, if any, and accesses to reach the remaining segments in the final block, all divided by the number of segments in the sequence.

$$b_G = \frac{1}{y_i}\left(\tfrac{1}{2}Bfs_i + \sum_{j=2}^{b_i-1} j\, Bfs_i + b_i\left(y_i - \tfrac{1}{2}Bfs_i - \sum_{j=2}^{b_i-1} Bfs_i \right) \right) \approx \left\lceil \frac{b_i + 1}{2} \right\rceil \qquad 4\text{-}16$$

The approximation applies when $y_i \gg Bfs_i$ so that the lesser number of segments in the first and last blocks does not affect the result greatly.

In MUMPS we find on level x the directory of file names or globals for a user. At this level the name strings are limited to 8 characters and no other key is needed. If the average global-variable name is 5 characters, the segment size $R'_x = 9$ and $y_x = \lfloor (512-4)/9 \rfloor = 56$. When there are many global files, including unsubscripted globals, it is likely that more than one block is required for the directory level of the user.

The initial segment for the **drug** file will be created when the first patient is stored by a statement as

     SET ↑drug(patno)='Manuel P. Cair'

The segment in level x will consist only of the key **drug** and a pointer, and a block on level $x - 1$ will be allocated to store the key value from **patno** and the string with **Cair**'s name and the end-of-string mark. We assume for **patno** a 9 digit or five character encoding. The above patient segment will require $R'_{x-1} = 1+5+15 = 21$ characters, but as soon as lower-level segments are entered, a pointer field will be inserted, so that the level $x - 1$ segments will actually become 23 characters in length. This will make $Bfs_{x-1} = \lfloor \frac{512-4}{23} \rfloor = 22$ so that there can be this many patient segments in a block. For the 450 patients seen in the clinic, the segment sequence will occupy 21 blocks. These have to be searched sequentially for every reference, requiring an average of 11 block accesses on this level. An approach to avoid this high cost is given at the end of this section.

We will summarize the remaining levels of the example rapidly since we find that all further segment sequences will fit into a block. On level $x - 2$ the visit dates are stored as keys. This means that no SET statements with only two subscripts will be executed. This level will be filled indirectly when the dateno is used as a subscript to lower levels. On level $x - 3$, we find the problem treated during the visit. Again, the problem is encoded as the key, 'Asthma'$\rightarrow$ icd=493.9 $\rightarrow$ icdno = 49390, and the key is set implicitly. If no drugs are prescribed for the problem the hierarchy terminates here with a segment of type 1.

Level $x - 4$ provides pointers to the drug description. An alternative design could store the drug name as a data field on this level. It again contains segments having only a key and a pointer. Level $x - 5$ contains the actual drug data as a sequence of three segments. This level would be loaded by statements such as

```
SET ↑drug(patno,dateno,icdno,dno,1)='Decadron'
SET ↑drug(patno,dateno,icdno,dno,2)=15
SET ↑drug(patno,dateno,icdno,dno,3)=3
```

Naked Variables To simplify and speed execution of such sequences, an option is available that will allow reuse of a previously reached node, so that redundant searches down the tree can be eliminated. The absence of a variable name implies the reuse of the previous global variable and all but the last one of the subscripts. Further subscripts leading to lower levels can be appended. Using the *naked* variable notation, the last two statements become

```
SET ↑(2)=15
SET ↑(3)=3
```

The number of blocks accesses to reach this level $(x - 5)$, assuming one block access for the directory level, is $T_F \approx (1 + 11 + 1 + 1 + 1 + 1)(s + r + btt) = 16(s + r + btt)$. Some seeks may be avoided, especially on level $x - 1$, if locality is maintained. Further naked accesses to the same segment sequence are free if the buffers are retained, at least until the end of a block is encountered.

Optimization by Change of the Hierarchy Optimal fanout would avoid sibling overflow blocks. When the fanout $y \gg Bfs$, the hierarchy becomes a poor match for the file, as seen on the patient level $x - 1$. A solution is to change the hierarchy originally envisaged for the file. We will apply this notion to the patient level of our example.

In order to obtain better performance, this level might be split into two levels, perhaps by using half of the patient number as the three-character key for each level. The name will appear only on the lower level $(x - 2)$. Now $R'_{x-1} = 1 + 3 + 2 = 6$, $Bfs_{x-1} = 84$ and $R'_{x-2} = 1 + 3 + 15 + 2 = 21$, $Bfs_{x-2} = 24$ (Eq. 4-14). The original fanout $y = 450$ is distributed over two levels, so that $y_{x-1}, y_{x-2} = \sqrt{y} \approx 22$. Both $y_{x-1} < Bfs_{x-1}$ and $y_{x-2} < Bfs_{x-2}$, so that most segment sequences will fit into one block. The block fetches for the patient data have been reduced from 11 to slightly over 2. This file will have 6 levels, and $Tf \approx 6(s + r + btt)$.

If the file would have to hold information for all patients seen during a long period, say a year, then at least two and probably more patient levels will be needed to provide adequate performance.

4-5-4 Storage Allocation

Occasionally long chains of sibling data create long segment sequence, and the optimization process described above on the patient name. The search for children down the hierarchical tree also follows pointers. Optimization of locality for the serial blocks according to both dimensions is hence important. Most MUMPS implementations, therefore, attempt to allocate the next block in a series within the next accessible sector. A *sector* is defined to consist of all the blocks which can be read on one cylinder at the same rotational position.

Figure 4-28 shows a series chained on an unwrapped cylinder surface. Optimal placement has been achieved for the first four of the five blocks of chain C shown.

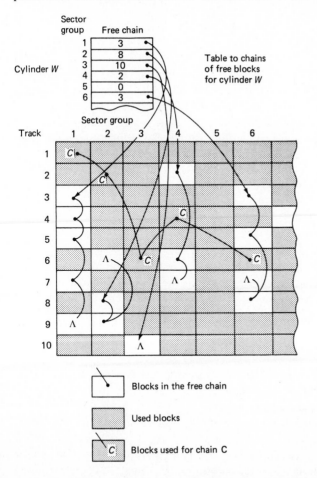

Figure 4-28 Storage for a MUMPS cylinder.

Accessing blocks of C avoids latency r and seek time s. The example assumes that the next sequential sector can be read. On computer systems where buffering constraints prevent this, alternate block referencing is preferred (see Fig. 2-15).

In order to locate the best free block, a table entry for each sector is maintained which points to the first block of a chain of free blocks within the sector. If there is a free block in the sector, it is assigned to the chain which requested it, and the table is updated with the link value from this newly obtained block. If all of a cylinder is filled, so that the new block has to be placed on another cylinder, no rotational optimization is attempted. In fact, an extra sequence of file accesses may be required to store the old free space table and fetch one for the new cylinder.

When storage is released by the delete statement KILL, such as

    KILL ↑drug(patno)

all descendants of the deleted segment are also released. A lower-priority task collects all freed blocks and attaches them to the appropriate free space chains. These blocks can then be reused. Alternate methods for free space management are discussed in Sec. 6-5.

4-5-5 Conclusion

The fact that the method used by programs to reference data in hierarchical systems, such as MUMPS, is so closely interwoven with the file structure is both an advantage and a liability. In Chap. 7 we will discuss methods that try to maximize program and file structure independence. The interdependence of data and file structure could also be perceived earlier, in Sec. 3-6, When discussing ring-structured files, which also implement a hierarchical design.

When a hierarchical file structure is called for, careful data analysis and data dimensioning has to precede a file design. Intermediate indexes or direct accessed lists may be interspersed to provide adequate performance over the expected range of quantities of data on each level.

Hierarchical views of data may also be provided by more general database systems which can provide a data-independent system design. When the range of data and applications cannot be adequately assessed initially, the higher overhead costs of these more formal systems will be less than the cost of frequent rewriting of the database and database programs in order to match the data structure.

4-6   METHODS BASED ON DIRECT ACCESS

The direct-access method is often the fastest means to access records, but three features make the basic method often unsuitable:

- Its dependence on fixed-length records
- The fetch arguments that are limited to one key attribute
- The lack of serial access

Simple adaptations of direct access can be used to overcome these three limitations for many applications. A number of these will be illustrated in corresponding sections below. A fourth section will deal with partial-match retrieval.

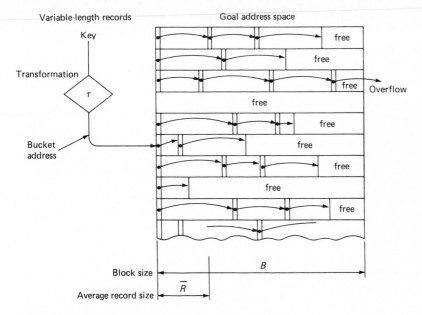

Figure 4-29 Bucket accessing to a direct file.

4-6-1 Variable-Length Records

The record length for directly accessed files is fixed because of the mapping from a record key to a slot number in the file area. If a direct-file organization is desired for its other features, either of two constructs will add variable-length record capability.

Bucket Accessing When buckets are used, variable-length records can be accommodated in the buckets. The search within a bucket becomes more complex.

The use of a record mark as shown in Fig. 2-11 enables serial searches through the bucket. Some disk hardware allows the channel or controller to locate a specific record on a track; this can cost considerable gap space but reduces the software needed to read through blocks in order to identify the marks. If the bucket search time cix is a problem, one of the schemes used to structure index blocks (Sec. 4-2-2) may help.

If an overflow from the bucket occurs because of the insertion of many records that were longer than the expected average, the existing-collision management mechanism can be invoked. On the other hand, when the records in a block are shorter than average, overflow resulting from collisions due to hashing will be deferred. The use of buckets for variable-length records works best if $R \ll B$.

When pointers are used to mark records, as shown in Fig. 4-29, overflow chains can be maintained using these same pointers. In Sec. 3-5 overflow chains were used to manage clusters occurring because of insertion and deletion. Deletion of variable-length records is best accompanied by a rearrangement of the records remaining within the block to avoid space fragmentation.

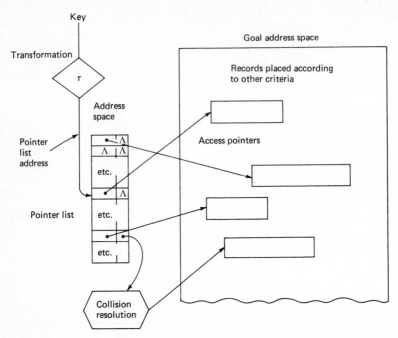

Figure 4-30 Indirect accessing to a direct file.

Indirect Accessing In this method, a small file containing a list of pointers is accessed directly; the selected entry in this list indicates the location of the actual record. The organization of the goal data file may be a pile or another organization type chosen according to other requirements placed on the file.

The *pointer-list* resembles the lowest level of an index, but the position of the entries is determined by the key-to-address transformation algorithm, so that the list is not suitable for serial searching. The benefit of the direct file, that only one block has to be fetched to locate a record, is lost, but two accesses will provide access to any record which is not in an overflow area.

The simple pointer-list can have a high fanout ratio, because no key is required if collisions are handled after accessing the main data records. The main file will use linkages to chain colliding records.

The alternative is to place the data keys also into the pointer-list entries. Now access efficiency is improved for colliding and missing records. The keys of overflow entries due to collisions will then also be placed in the pointer-list using open-addressing techniques. The associated record is itself placed in the main file as before.

If the pointer-list is kept using bucket techniques, a copy of the key is required in the pointer-list to identify the entry. These buckets will have many entries, so that techniques to increase the speed of searching through the bucket are desirable. A binary tree seems ideal for this purpose; its pointers can be used for locating child entries or goal records.

In each of these approaches, the collision rate is determined by the ratio of m/n of the address space. The means that only the pointer-list has to be given extra space and the main file can be kept dense. A high space ratio m/n and the many entries which fit into an index block Bfr will keep the occurrence of collisions minimal.

If some part of the goal record is required more frequently than the whole record, a mixed approach is feasible. A fixed-length record segment is constructed containing the most useful portions and placed so that it can be directly accessed. The variable segment which remains is retrieved when needed via a pointer from the fixed segment.

4-6-2 Multiattribute Direct Access

If the fetch requests are not restricted to one key attribute, the simple direct-access method fails. For each different attribute and its value in a goal record the particular transformation will produce its specific record address. If there is to be only one stored copy of each goal record, indirection via a pointer-list is again needed.

The pointer-list provides only pointers to the actual goal record; the goal is found at the cost of an additional access. Multiple pointer-lists will be used, similar to the multiplicity of indexes described for a multi-indexed file. Records can be found according to any attribute for which a transform and a pointer-list is provided. The pointer-lists are similar to the pointer-lists used above when provision for variable record length is made and the rate of collisions should again be low.

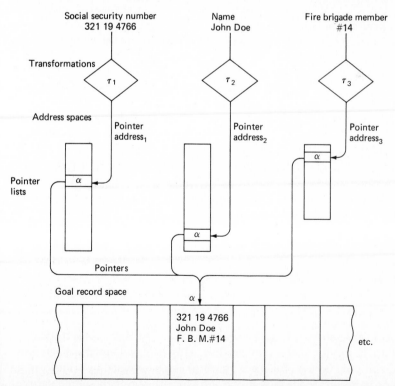

Figure 4-31 Three-way access to a direct file.

The records may still be located directly for the *primary* attribute and indirection employed for *secondary* keys. However, for symmetry, the system sketched in Fig. 4-31 uses indirect referencing throughout. Not all attributes need to have address spaces of equal length. The goal file itself may have a pile or a sequential organization. An insertion into a file using multiple pointer-lists will require changes to all pointer-lists in addition to the operation on the main file.

All entries for the same transformed value will have the same pointer-list address. This increases the collision rate for attributes which are not unique. When we dealt with simple direct files, whose records are stored by key values, we expected uniqueness. Many other attributes in records will not have unique values. The example of Fig. 4-31 is hence atypical; you may wish to consider the pointer-list for `sex = 'male'`. Identical data attributes must lead to identical addresses in the the pointer-list space. This problem can also be dealt with through the collision-handling mechanism, but obviously attributes with poor partitioning power can overwhelm the mechanics of many solutions. The result of the key-to-address transformation can no longer be uniform. The use of overflow buckets rather than open addressing is now called for.

A popular database management system, ADABAS, uses the types of access presented here. The pointer-lists may be predefined and maintained, or created dynamically in response to transaction requests.

Shared Pointer-List It also is possible to share a single pointer address space for several attributes by making this space appropriately larger and including the name, or another suitable identifier of the attribute itself, in the input to the address transformation function. Figure 4-32 sketches this design using the symbols (I_1, I_2, I_3) for attribute-type identification.

This method becomes especially interesting if the records have an irregular number of attributes, so that the individual pointer address spaces are of different sizes and possibly have dynamically varying length requirements. The fact that no individual pointer-list areas have to be dimensioned and allocated reduces the amount of unused space while keeping the probability of exceeding the pointer space low. A larger shared space can also reduce collisions due to clustering.

To verify that in case of a collision the correct pointer is picked, it is necessary that the pointer entry can be matched to its attribute name. If this check is not made, problems will arise if two key values of different attributes are both identical and produce the same result from the address transformation. An example would be a case where the `health_record_number` for John and the `employee_number` assigned to Peter are identical and both happen to transform to the same address by different algorithms. The author has come across a system where this case was not considered, but no access failure had ever been reported. Transformations could be designed to avoid this possibility, but this restricts the choices available and limits the adaptability of this approach.

A Common Transformation Procedure for Multiple Attributes A file using many attributes for access may need as many independent transformation routines. The definition and use of distinct routines can be avoided by transforming both the attribute name and value into an the address within a single shared pointer-list. The sketch in Fig. 4-33 explains the catenation of the name and value strings prior to hashing.

A disadvantage of the simple scheme is that the pointer entry has to carry a long identifier for verification purposes. The attribute name is better carried in abbreviated form. The abbreviation might be a sequence number $I, I = 1 \rightarrow a$ in a dictionary or schema for possible attributes, and this solution is illustrated. The abbreviation has only to add enough information to the hashing algorithm to compensate for the increase in address space size. The combined input to the hashing algorithm has to be kept as a key to test for collisions.

Another solution to the collision problem is to defer the recognition of collisions to the goal records. The exact implementation will vary depending on the form of the goal records.

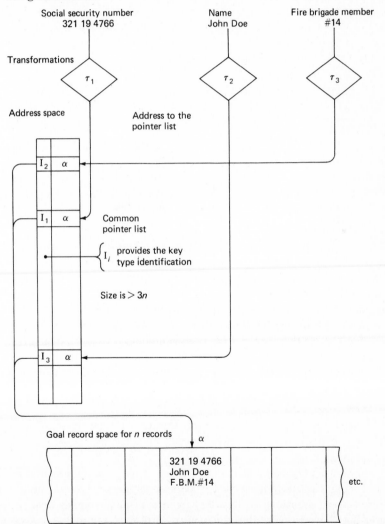

Figure 4-32 A shared pointer-list for a direct file.

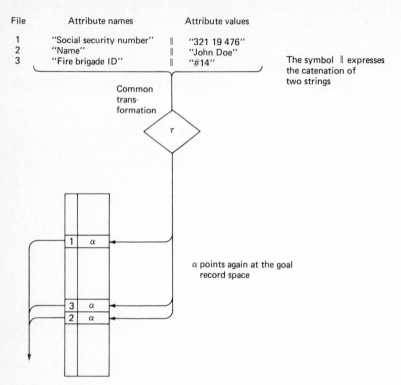

File	Attribute names		Attribute values
1	"Social security number"	‖	"321 19 476"
2	"Name"	‖	"John Doe"
3	"Fire brigade ID"	‖	"#14"

The symbol ‖ expresses the catenation of two strings

Common trans-formation

τ

α points again at the goal record space

1 α

3 α
2 α

Figure 4-33 A common key transformation for a direct file.

A Common Key-to-Address Transformation for Multiple Files We considered in the previous subsections very large goal files, accessed using multiple attributes. approach As part of most databases many small files have to be maintained as well. Examples of such files are the lexicons which translate from a numeric code to a string for output, for instance, a disease code to a disease name. In some applications there may be several dozens of such lexicons.

These many small files are effectively accessed directly. A technique using a common access mechanism, as sketched in Fig. 4-34, can be used to provide a single access mechanism for multiple files.

The goal data are in separate files. They may be maintained simply as sequential files and periodically reorganized. A batch update of the direct pointer file can be combined with a purge of the previous pointers pertaining to a given goal file.

Replicated Pointer-Lists to Distributed Data Another form of this technique can be used in *distributed* systems. It may be effective to partition a single large file into fragments which will reside on the processor of a site where the data is used the most or where updates are executed. An example is the **employees** file of a company having multiple locations. A pointer-list to all records of the file can be replicated at all locations so that any record in any fragment can be fetched. All pointer-lists have to be updated when an employee is added or leaves, but remain unchanged when a pay or work status attribute is updated.

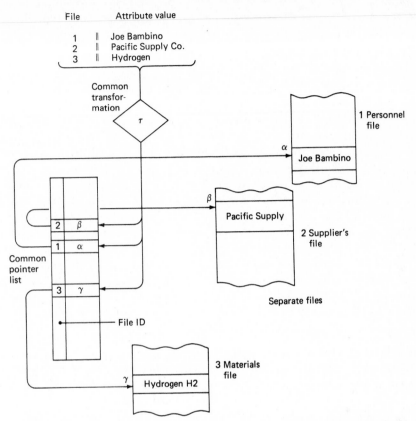

Figure 4-34 A common key transformation for multiple files.

Here we have cases where the definition of a file has been violated. It now is difficult to tell whether we are dealing with one, three, four, or even six files. The determination of number of files in these examples is left to the taste of the reader.

4-6-3 Serial File Access

Methods which use indirection by hashing to pointer-lists allow placing the data records sequentially according to one attribute. Serial processing of such a file by one attribute is now possible. Insertion, however, is now difficult, so that much of the flexibility of a direct-access file is lost. The use of a B-tree structured data file can keep updates convenient and provide seriality in one dimension.

In order to provide serial access according to multiple dimensions, the goal-record file may be organized as a ring structure. Flexibility of retrieval has been regained at some cost in complexity.

This combination of direct access and rings is found only in database systems, since procedural management of the complex structure is beyond the ambition of most programmers. Without pointer-lists direct access is provided for only one attribute, and this is a restriction of many CODASYL systems. If more general direct access is provided, the update process has to maintain simultaneously pointer-lists and change the ring pointers. The awkwardness of update may make the batch reorganization technique presented in Sec. 3-5, Eq. 3-89 appropriate here.

4-6-4 Partial-Match Retrieval with Direct Access

In basic direct files, access capability is restricted to one attribute. If intermediate pointer-lists are used, as described in Sec. 4-6-2, then access becomes possible by any of a variety of attributes. These pointer-lists can become the source for partial-match query processing.

The buckets that are created in the pointer-lists will contain TIDs for specific attribute-name and value combinations. If collision chains are maintained all identical entries will be on one chain; some irrelevant ones may be chained in as well and have to be removed based on their key value. The sets of TIDs obtained can be merged for partial-match retrieval, so that selection can be accomplished prior to accessing the goal file. The procedure can be visualized using Fig. 4-35 and compared with Fig. 4-12, where indexes were used.

We note that ranges of values are not supported unless the complications of additional serial access structures (Sec. 4-6-3) are accepted. The attribute values are hence made discrete; the `Price`, for instance, is given here as two distinct truncated values $\{31\,000, 32\,000\}$ rather than as $\{31\,000 \rightarrow 33\,000\}$ in the indexed case of Sec. 4-2-5. The information loss from truncation increases the number of collisions.

Partial-Match Hashing The accessing and merging of many buckets can still be costly. An obvious approach to rapid direct partial-match access is to develop hash functions and pointer-lists which permit immediate retrieval of records in response to queries which specify multiple attributes in their search argument. Any or all combinations of more than one attribute, as were considered for indexes in Sec. 4-2-5, may be defined and added to the a pointer-lists for the single attributes.

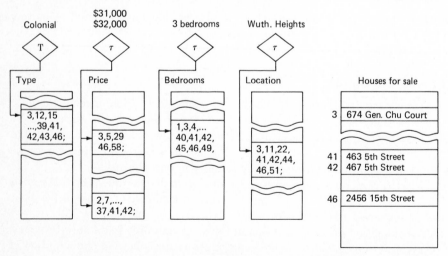

Figure 4-35 Multiattribute direct access lists for partial-match retrieval.

Providing for all possible $(2^a - 1)$ or even many partial-match attribute combinations increases the number and hence the redundancy in the access lists greatly. The reduction in number of indexes made possible by the sorted ordering within indexes does not apply here.

When multiattribute hashing techniques are being considered, the design decision has to balance redundancy in the files, leading to high update and storage costs versus the effort saved at retrieval time. This choice is actually equivalent to the familiar problem of binding-time selection, and we will abstract the alternatives using the binding paradigm.

Early Binding If fast access is paramount, all possible partial-match attribute combinations for each record can be hashed. At each hash address a set of pointers or TIDs will direct the fetch immediately to the goal records.

All these TIDs must be set when a record is inserted. If an average record has a' attributes of interest for retrieval, there will be $2^{a'} - 1$ entries per record.

The entries for the four **houses** retrieved for the query in example of Fig. 4-35 are shown in Fig. 4-36. These four **houses** have $4(2^a - 1) = 60$ TIDs distributed over the $2^a + 2^{a-1} - 1 = 23$ buckets for the $a = 4$ attributes and the fifth value for the extra **price**.

Entries for all records needed in response to a query will be found in the bucket; all records with identical key combinations cluster in the bucket. The bucket may contain further entries because of collisions from the randomization. Since the clustering of popular and few-attribute combinations leads to dense usage of some bucket addresses, a chained overflow to external buckets rather than open addressing is called for. Combinations which do not correspond to records in the file will not generate entries in the pointer-lists; there may be, for instance, no "Condominiums" in "Wuth.Heights".

Key combinations to be provided for in order to locate houses 3, 41, 42, 46

Figure 4-36 Hashed entries for all partial-match queries.

Late Binding The alternative design option presented uses a structured pointer table address. Here the *hash address* is constructed by catenating the hash addresses for all attributes a. The size of the hash address is based on the number of buckets. If the bucket size is one, an appropriate length for the hash address is $\log_2 n$ and to each of the a attributes $\log_2 n/a$ bits can be allocated.

For a file with a million records and 10 attributes,
the $\log_2(10^6) = 20$-bit address would allow $20/10 = 2$ bits per attribute.

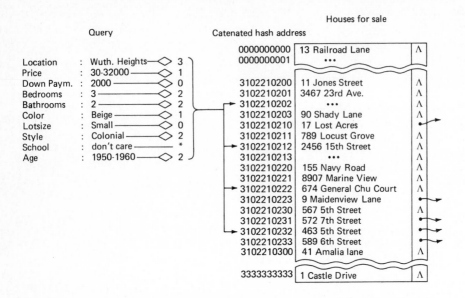

Figure 4-37 Multiattribute hashed partial-match retrieval.

Using this scheme, the attributes partition the search space only grossly. A retrieval based on only one argument will specify $1/a$ or two bits out of the twenty, and one could expect that one-fourth of the file is to be retrieved. The situation improves quickly as more attributes are specified in the query. When all attributes are specified, the expectation becomes close to one. Figure 4-37 illustrates the case for a nine-attribute query.

Applicability of Multiattribute Schemes for Partial-Match Retrieval
The partial-match indexing and hashing schemes presented are not very effective at extreme ranges. We can take advantage of these conditions and modify these schemes, so that the update effort is greatly reduced while much of the benefit is retained.

Small Number of Arguments There seems to be little point in supporting rapid access for queries which lead to retrieval of a large fraction of the file. A heuristic which states: *Search sequentially when looking for more than 20% of the records* remains a valid guideline.

In the early binding cases with many access lists (Fig. 4-36) or combined indexes (Fig. 4-12), update time and storage space can be saved by only entering combinations of several, say, > 3 attributes into the access lists.

In the late binding case illustrated in Fig. 4-37 the retrieval algorithm might as well search sequentially when near exhaustive requests are made. In an interactive environment it is well to have the system respond to a poorly partitioned query with a counter question as: *"Do you really want **13117** references on the topic:* **system?"**.

Large Number of Arguments The probability that a partial-match query will specify all attributes is slim. It is furthermore expected that, if many search arguments are specified, only a few or no records will respond to a query. There exists hence a further opportunity for reduction of file cost. Certain attribute keys can be placed in a *don't care* category, and not entered in combined lists. When queries are made, the retrieval from the file will fetch some unwanted records. The excess can then be pared down on the basis of the actual key values.

When early binding is used, this again reduces the number of entries in the pointer list; when late binding is used, it provides an opportunity for better use of the pointer list. Fewer combinations of attributes need be stored if for some queries a merge of two or more distinct TID lists is permissible. Then the attributes can be partitioned into these sets so that frequent queries require only one set. Some will need two or more, and an odd partial-match query may need one attribute from each set. The number of stored combinations reduces drastically, as was shown in Eq. 4-9.

Superimposed coding is another traditional technique used to reduce the number of distinct attribute fields. capplications where there are typically many attributes of binary (have or have-not) value, one column may be assigned to more than one attribute. It is hoped that the number of attributes will be such that a retrieval with many arguments will include few unwanted records (false drops). The percentage of *false drops* can, in fact, be statistically predicted, given data on attribute patterns in goal records and queries.

The schemes discussed above bring early and late binding multiattribute hashing schemes closer together. The handling of false drops is obviously a late-binding procedure; selection of attributes which can be omitted or superimposed is an early-binding process. There is still active research in this area where a rapid response to complex queries has to balanced with limits of update capability and storage.

4-7 OPTIONS OF THE COMPLEX RING ORGANIZATION

In Sec. 3-6 we presented the basic ring-structure organization. Implementations of file systems based on this structure offer a number of options which allow better performance at some increase in complexity. Such options can be selected to apply to those rings which play a crucial role in the performance of the file. We will find language specifications for such options in Chaps. 8 and 9 when the CODASYL database schema language is presented.

4-7-1 Prior Pointers

In the serial chain and ring structures, pointers may be kept that refer to the preceding record. The availability of such a *prior pointer* simplifies certain search and update operations considerably. Prior pointers allow spacing backward through a ring, so that the predecessor record is found using one access rather than using $y-1$ accesses through the ring. If an open-chain structure is used, access to predecessors is impossible unless prior pointers or equivalent mechanisms are available.

An example of a query requiring such a predecessor search could be in a factory where the goal is a list of five machines adequate at a lower level of production for the task now assigned to machine **B**. The search finds machine **B** according to the **task** chain, and a predecessor search is needed now since the **machine** chain is sorted in order of increasing capability.

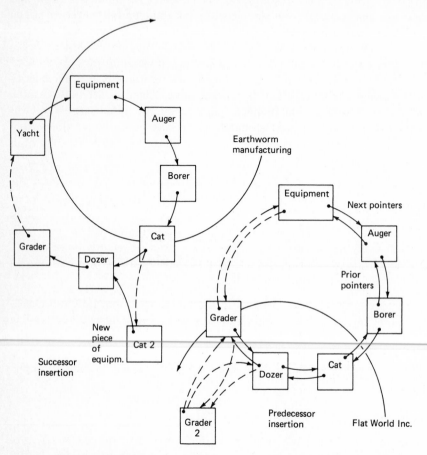

Figure 4-38 Updating a ring file.

Update is greatly affected by the existence of prior pointers. Figure 4-38 shows a part of a ring structure ("**Equipment**") which has been entered from another ring sequence ("**Supplier=Earthworm**") at record **Cat**. At this point a successor record is to be inserted. In order to add the successor record **Cat2** into the ring, the pointer address to record **Dozer** from the original record **Cat** is inserted into **Cat2**, and subsequently a pointer to **Cat2** is inserted into **Cat**. No other record accesses are required in this case.

If, however, a new record **Grader2** is to be inserted in the *preceding* position (**Grader2** is to be put in service before **Grader**) and no prior pointer exists, the update becomes costly. All the records of the ring will have to be read, since record **Dozer** will have to be modified to point to the record being inserted. The availability of prior pointers speeds this update process but adds some complexity to all update processes. General use of prior pointers can also impact storage requirements and reduce locality.

4-7-2 Pointers to the Master Record

Not all the needed data for a query may be found in a record of a ring structure. It may be neccessary to determine to which specific ring this record belongs, and then locate its header or master record for data pertaining to all members of the ring.

An example could be a case where a specific **personnel** record was found during a search for a certain **skill**. This record can be interpreted by establishing its category, but to determine in which **department** the **employee** belongs, the chain has to be followed to its header.

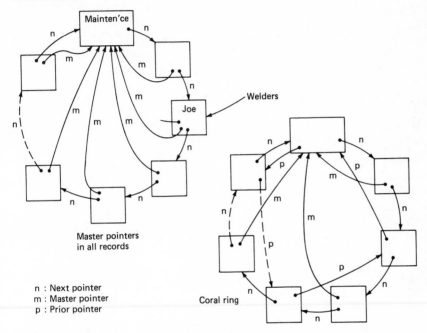

Figure 4-39 Rings with master pointers.

In order to accelerate such searches, pointers may be kept in the member records which refer back to the master record. When a record of a ring has been accessed, first the record category is determined in order to be able to interpret the data and pointer types stored in the record. This is achieved by identifying each record with a category code. All rings of the same type (e.g., **personnel** at various **locations**) will have records of the same record category.

If a master pointer exists, the master record can be quickly accessed. Use of master pointers allows efficient use of storage, since all master-dependent information can be stored only in the master record. The maintenance of master pointers is relatively easy, since both predecessor and successor records in the ring contain the same information. There is, of course, again an additional space requirement.

Typical master-record types seen are **Department**, **Supplier**, **Equipment**. If totals are maintained on a departmental level, relevant changes in a member **employee** record, such as a **salary** increase, can be reflected easily in the departmental total **payroll** field.

Some implementers let master pointers share space with prior pointers. The result has been called a *coral ring* and is illustrated also in Fig. 4-39. Alternate records have prior and master pointers. Locating the predecessor record now requires one or two accesses, and locating the header record also requires an average of 1.5 accesses.

4-7-3 Master Records with Indexes

If the need exists to quickly find individual member records in specific rings, indexes may be associated with master records. The resulting substructures have been discussed in the preceding sections. Since records of a a ring tend to be similar, and since rings are optimal if they are not very long, simple index structures will suffice. The relative benefits of indexes increases if individual rings have poor locality. Indexes become more interesting if they are not restricted to the ring hierarchy. In the personnel file example, good use could be made of an index by employee name to permit access to employee records without using department rings.

4-7-4 Rings and Direct Access

It is possible to combine a direct-access mechanism with a complex ring structure, since the ring structure makes no demands on the location (value of its own address)

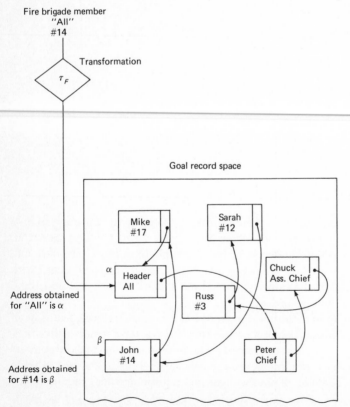

Figure 4-40 A ring with direct access to the header and to member records.

of a member record, whereas the direct-access methods are heavily dependent on them. The combination allows rapid fetching of a record and subsequent collection of multiple records which satisfy a request for a data subset by following the chain for this specific response.

In order to reach the header record of a ring, a standard identifying term can be used. Figure 4-40 shows such an access. Instead of name of the individual, the standard term "ALL" is given and combined with the class description "Fire Brigade". The pointer for this combination will lead to the header record for the Fire Brigade, so that the whole ring is available for processing.

Since the transformation controls the placement of the record, only one direct-access path can be provided per record. For instance, in Fig. 4-40 "John" can be found directly as Fire Brigade member #14, but he cannot also be accessed directly using his social security number. The ability to control placement of ring members to increase locality has also been lost.

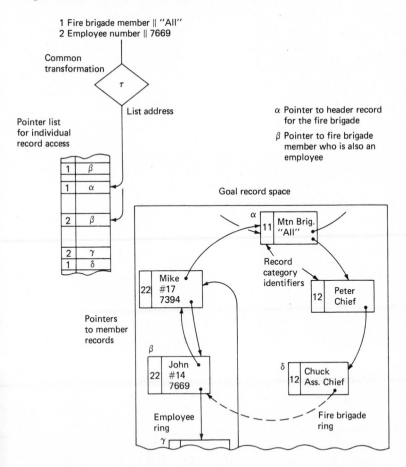

Figure 4-41 A ring file with direct access to multiple rings via a common pointer-list.

Rings with a Pointer-List and Direct Access The addition of indirection via pointers, as introduced in Sec. 4-6-2, can remove the record placement restrictions at additional access cost. The use of a pointer-list, as sketched in Fig. 4-33, is applied to the previous problem as shown in Fig. 4-41. Now multiple indirect paths to the goal records are possible.

There now also is freedom in record placement, which can be exploited to improve the locality of rings, so that retrieval of members will be fast.

The collision-handling mechanism can take several forms. Open addressing was preferred when records were not linked. In the ring structure, additional pointer chains can be considered but may require much maintenance.

A compromise using open addressing is to use the pointer-list for file-type verification and the goal record for record category and key identification. No key field is provided in the pointer-list. This becomes feasible when the pointer-list is shared by many rings. Most collisions will be recognized in the list, and can be resolved there. A collision which is detected when the goal record is accessed will require a continuation of the open addressing search through the pointer-list. The structures defined in such a system lend themselves well to some of the more formal information-retrieval methodologies. We will present a generalized view of such access in the next section.

4-7-5 Multiattribute Ring Access

In a ring structure with intersecting rings, as symbolically presented in Fig. 4-42, the records of the ring category "`Available_skills`" represent the *association* of "`Employees`" and "`Skills`". Let the number of `Employees` be ne and the total number of distinct `Skills` be ns. The associative level can be viewed either as ns rings, one for every skill, with ring sizes according to the number of employees which have that skill, $ne(\mathsf{s})$; or as ne rings, one for every employee with ring sizes according to the number of skills which an employee has $ns(\mathsf{e})$. The number of records in the association `Available_skills` na is then

$$na = \sum^{ns} ns(\mathsf{e}) = \sum^{ne} ne(\mathsf{s}) \qquad\qquad 4\text{-}17$$

If rapid access to the individual members of the association is desired, direct access can be provided using as key the catenation of the two parent values.

There can be multiple associations between two parent types; in the figure a second association is called `Training`. In general, there can be any number of associations between two sets of data elements. In order to generalize this aspect, a third parent, say `Expertise_Level`, can be considered to be the header of the set {`Training, Available_Skill, Craftsman, Teacher, ...`}, that is, all the associations made between `Employees` and `Skills`. The three-way symmetric concept is indicated in Fig. 4-43. The rings for which this parent provides the header records will link all records for `Training, Available_Skill, Craftsman, Teacher`, etc.

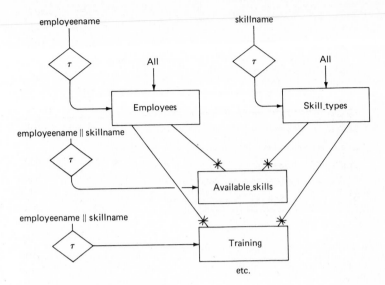

Figure 4-42 Association.

Implementation of a Fundamental Data Structure The associative structure of three elements represents the basic unit to carry information. It also forms a minimal record as defined in Sec. 3-1. To identify a record in such an association, three arguments are required; in a programming language implementation of such associations (LEAP-type data structures) these three are called

Table 4-4   General Associations in LEAP

Name	or	Sym	Function	Example
Object	or	O	Key	Employee
Attribute	or	A	Goal-attribute name	Skill_Type
Value	or	V	Goal-attribute value	Expertise_Level, Training, etc.

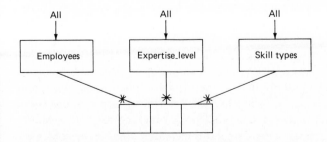

Figure 4-43 Generalized associative structure.

Given this structure, seven type of questions can be asked as in Table 4-5.

Table 4-5   Fundamental Queries in Data Triplets

#	Format	Example based on Fig. 4-42
1	A(O)=V	Does Jones have Welding as an Available_skill?
2	A(?)=V	Which Employees have Welding as an Available_skill?
3	A(?)=?	Which Employees relate to Welding and how expertly?
4	A(O)=?	Does Jones relate to Welding and how expertly?
5	?(?)=V	What Employees have which Skills Available?
6	?(O)=V	Jones has which Skills Available?
7	?(O)=?	To which Skills is Jones related and how expertly?

The first query can have only the response **true** or **false**. Multiple responses will be given, in general, for the other queries; for instance, the last query (**7**) may have as response three triplets:

```
Welding(Jones)   = Available_skill
Machining(Jones) = Training
Painting(Jones)  = Available_skill
```

If semantic considerations are disregarded, it can be seen that any of the three fields can take on any of the three roles.

These structures are used in applications where complex relationships have to be accessed rapidly, for instance, in graphics and in robot operation. When rings have to be followed in order to retrieve a subset, there is the possibility that the rings will cross many block boundaries, so that the objective of rapid access is not achieved. Good locality can be achieved, as presented in Sec. 3-6, for all rings relative to one parent by placing all member records of a ring within a block. If this is done in respect to "Skill_type", then queries of type **1**, **2**, **3**, and **4** can be answered rapidly. Direct access can identify the block for a specific argument value of A, and then the position within the block can be obtained by in-core direct accessing for O or V to find headers for these subrings, or by direct in-core accessing using the catenation of O∥V to locate individual records.

Implementations of LEAP-type structures have used redundancy in order to provide equivalent access for queries with unknown values of A; a copy of the file is organized based on O or V. The hash for query type **1** does not have to be supported in the second file. These structures have not had goal attributes appended to their records, but this is, of course, possible. The goal parts may be best kept remote, so that the locality of the primary access structure remains high. Collisions also have to be resolved appropriately; this is achieved by use of additional chains from header and member records.

4-8 FILES USING VIRTUAL STORAGE

Most modern computers permit the use of *virtual addressing*, an address space that is much larger than the actual primary or core storage available. A mechanism consisting of both hardware and software components is provided to allow references to be made throughout the entire space.

This approach is referred to as a demand paging environment or a *virtual-storage* system. We presented the choices of operating systems in Sec. 1-7.

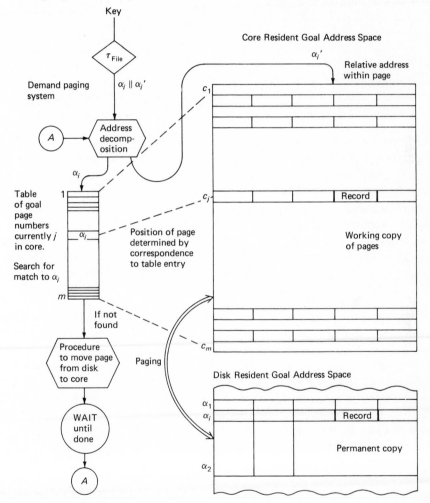

Figure 4-44 Accessing a virtual storage file.

There will be a division of the address space into working units called pages. A *page* is identified by the high-order digits of the address and will be a few thousand characters in length. A hardware table, possibly with a software extension, will record which pages from the entire address space are actually represented in core storage at any given moment. A page-not-present interrupt occurs when a referenced address falls into a page not currently in core memory. When this happens, a system software mechanism is invoked to find or to create free space in core memory, fetch the required page from drum or disk, update the page table, and resume execution of the interrupted task, as shown in Fig. 4-44. The page size of a virtual system will, in general, define the effective block size of the file system.

If enough address space exists to handle the size of expected data files, virtual addressing provides a very convenient mechanism for handling files. Systems have been written that perform key-to-address transformations into this data space, and use these system facilities for all further page transfers in and out of core memory. A collision-resolution mechanism remains necessary.

Two types of virtual systems can be found: those which have a single address space, and those which employ multiple named address spaces, called *segments*. The use of a single address space erases any formal distinction between the area used for programs, the area used for program data, and the area used for files. Boundaries between these areas are set up by convention. Such a convention could be that a file will consist of the space between two address values of α_1 and α_2. Reliability can be compromised if the conventions are difficult to enforce.

More sophisticated virtual systems will provide the capability for several separately named address spaces, called segments. Figure 4-45 sketches this approach, but details of the paging mechanism are omitted here.

A sequence of high-order bits of the hardware virtual address is used to pick up an entry from a segment table. One or more segments can be viewed as files, and the segment entry may have associated with it information regarding protection and sharing of such a file. The allocation of segment pages to disk storage and their movement to core when needed is again an operating-system function. Such a file still presents only a linear address blocked into pages, and no assistance is provided by the operating system to map records into this space. In order to better manage the virtual-address system, some operating systems, such as TENEX and TOPS-20 for the DEC-10/20 series of computers map only those file pages that have been referenced into the address space. Multiple processes can share an available file page. when the process using the files terminates, the file pages will be rewritten, if they were modified, and then released.

The use pattern associated with files may not have been considered by the designers of the virtual-memory system, who were concerned mainly with the manipulation of program sections and data referenced directly by these programs. Paging systems are especially effective if memory references, during time intervals commensurate with the time required to move a page to core, cluster within a limited number of pages.

To use a virtual-access mechanism effectively, it remains desirable to be aware of the page size and page boundaries and utilize pages densely. Blocks will be aligned to page boundaries to avoid accessing two pages for a single block request. The storage density can be very low if the file is not carefully allocated to the virtual address space. No matter how little is stored in a page, the entire page will be kept in the backup storage on the disk. Completely empty pages may or may not occupy file space, depending on the sophistication of the support system. The techniques used for blocking remain valid, since the same density considerations apply.

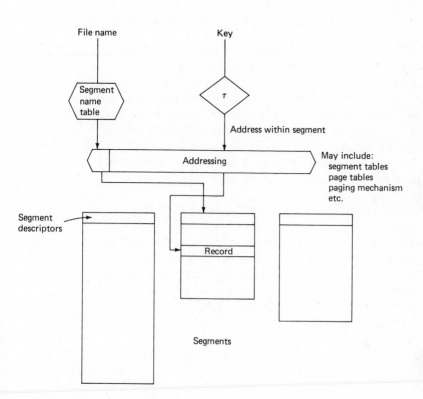

Figure 4-45 Segmented virtual addressing.

Sequential files, with fixed records, are easily mapped densely to a virtual address space, since we do not expect dynamic update. The performance of files using explicit block read access and virtual direct access will be similar, except that there will be no buffering to overlap computation with block reading in virtual systems. Paging facilities do provide good buffering when writing blocks, so that rewrite delays can be neglected except in terms of total system load.

Indexing is very desirable when using virtual memories, since it reduces the number of pages that have to be read. The pointer obtained from an index entry is an address in the virtual space. Only the high-order bits are kept and extended for reference by catenating $\log_2 pagesize$ zeros.

The use of direct-file approaches is simplified by the large address space, although effective space utilization has to be considered. The file storage density can be very low if the file is not carefully allocated to the virtual address space. The performance will be identical for similar values of m and Bfr. Open addressing with linear searching can make good use of any pages which have been brought in due to prefetching in systems which attempt high-performance page scheduling for program usage.

In systems with a single address space, shared use of the space by multiple files using a common transformation simplifies control of storage allocation. A marking convention using computable positions is required to indicate empty versus assigned record spaces. With ring structures locality remains a concern if excessive paging load is to be avoided when rings are being traversed.

We find then that the use of virtual storage does not change the approach to file design greatly, except that it does provide an alternative for the lowest level of file management. A trivial file system, as described in Sec. 4-1-1, is completely replaceable by virtual-storage access. Some database systems have been built directly on top of such virtual storage system, but these systems have incorporated within themselves one or more of the file-organization techniques presented in order to control locality while paging. A number of database systems for demonstration and educational purposes have not considered how to use the paging mechanisms effectively, since the implementers did not expect to operate in a production environment.

An evaluation of the performance of files based on paging can be obtained by combining data on file behavior in terms of block reads and writes with measurements regarding paging-system performance and available workspace size. Some paging algorithms assign priorities according to computer time to paging rate ratios. Whether this will penalize or benefit file-oriented programs depends on the objectives of the system administrators who set the parameters.

4-9 PHANTOM FILES

The key information in an index duplicates information in the file records. If this information is not needed as goal data when the record is accessed via other paths, the indexed attributes do not have to be kept in the goal records themselves. This data may still be stored on an inactive backup file so that it remains available for periodic regeneration of the index. If many fields are handled in this manner, a large portion of the goal file will not exist in active storage. We will refer to data which is used only for accessing, but is not available for result generation as *phantom* data.

Requests for goal data using multiple attributes can be resolved completely within the indexes by matching addresses of the goal records. Such an application is shown in Fig. 4-46, which is an example taken from a file system designed for a casting agency selecting models for TV advertisements.

If all goal data are kept only in indexed form, the entire file has become a phantom file. Files approaching this design have been called fully inverted files in the literature.

Another case of a phantom file can be found in bibliographic indexing. Searches through indexes are made using logical combinations of request parameters which in the end produce a set of call numbers for books. The call numbers are equivalent to the TIDs of the goal data. The goals are the books on the shelves of the library. A library which would always be accessed in this manner could store its books according to considerations other than the sequentiality of subject codes. If, instead of call numbers, the system would provide the actual shelf number and position, then books could be stored according to size, to minimize space used, or according to frequency of access, to minimize retrieval time. Browsing in such a library would be less productive but more surprising. Currently such optimizations are, in practice, restricted to computer files.

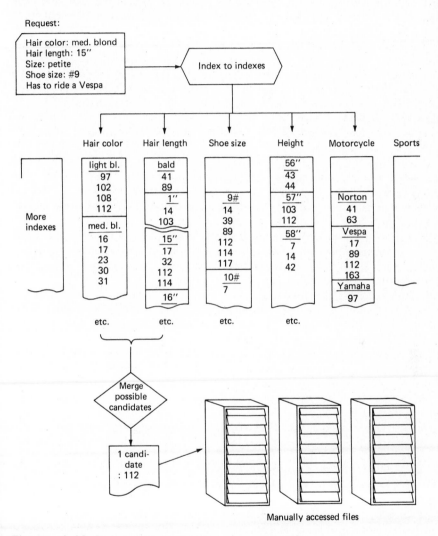

Figure 4-46 Indexes to a phantom or manual file.

BACKGROUND AND REFERENCES

Ingenious combinations of basic file methods have been part of most file-oriented applications. Descriptions of the techniques used can often be found in user-oriented system descriptions. The lack of a taxonomy of file organization methods has made analysis and comparison of complex approaches difficult. Techniques have been used, forgotten, reinvented, and sometimes applied in inappropriate environments, so that it becomes very difficult to trace the history of this subject area. A multi-index file system would be a useful tool for someone attempting such a review.

The simple file systems presented in Sec. 4-1 are commonly provided in systems not oriented toward data-processing as FORTRAN (Brainerd[78]), minicomputer, and small timeshared systems. Their inflexibility is sometimes hidden in footnotes: "Records are of variable-length, from 1 to 2048 characters (* Users are always charged for 2048 characters per record)". The reason for the surprising charging rate is that the system uses one block per record.

Descriptions of simple systems are not often found in the regular literature, but user manuals often provide enough detail that the structure and hence their performance in various situations becomes obvious. Access to textfiles is described in Reitman[69], Frey[71], and Lefkowitz[69] presents a variety of index-organization techniques. Index abbreviation is analyzed by Hu[71] and Wagner[73]. Transposed files are used by Easton[69], Selbman[74], Weyl[75] and analyzed by Batory[79].

Tries were described by Fredking[60]. Burkhard in Kerr[75] and Litwin[81T] look at tries and direct access. The tradeoffs in blocking factors are analyzed by March[77]. Yao[77] and Whang[81] evaluated formulas to estimate block accesses and found most wanting; they are important for optimizers in database systems. Combinations of operations are estimated by Demolombe[80].

An early system using multiple indexes, TDMS, is described by Bleier[68]; Bobrow in Rustin[72] develops this approach. O'Connell[71] describes use of multiple indexes. Optimization and selection of multiple indexes is considered by Lum[71], Stonebraker[74], Shneiderman[74], Schkolnick[75], Yao[77], Anderson[77], Comer[78], Hammer[79], and Whang[81].

Multiattribute access via indexes is evaluated by Lum[70], Mullin[71], and Schkolnick in Kerr[75]. Ray-Chaudhuri[68], Bose[69], Shneiderman[77], and Chang[81] develop strategies of combinatorial index organization. Ghosh[76] includes construction of optimal record sequences for known queries.

Detailed specifications regarding VSAM can be found in various IBM manuals. A description of its design is given by Wagner[73], and its storage allocation is discussed by Chin in Kerr[75] and optimized by Schkolnick[77]. Reorganization intervals are estimated by Maruyama[76]. This file system is becoming the basis for much database development where IBM equipment is used.

Landauer[63] and Sussengut[63] describe trees for file systems. Many B-tree papers cited in Chap. 3 describe their use for data files. McCreight[77] includes the blocking of variable length records.

Binary trees were described by Hibbard[62] and analyzed by Arora[69], and Overholt[73]. Bentley[75] extends a binary tree to deal with multiple attributes. The balancing of binary trees has had much attention. Adel'son-Vel'skiĭ and Landis presented a basic algorithm (AVL-trees) in 1962. An extensive analysis is in Knuth[73]. Baer[75], Nievergelt[74], and Bayer[76] consider access frequency. The SPIRES system is presented by Martin in Nance[74] and by Schroeder in Kerr[75].

Hierarchical structures are found in many applications. Examples are found in Connors[66] and Benner[67], include Davis[70] and Booth[60], and many more are cited in Senko[77].

Descriptions of MUMPS can be found in Allen[66] and in Greenes[69]. The MUMPS system was developed at Massachusetts General Hospital to support computing applications in medicine. The general system design was based on one of the earliest and best timesharing systems: JOSS. The file system was designed to match specifically the hierarchical organization of data perceived in the area of medical record keeping, as seen by the developers at MGH and General Electric in their FILECOMP system which preceded the MUMPS implementation. Modern implementations use B-trees. The standard (O'Neill[76]) is now available on many computers.

New hashing techniques are analyzed by Scholl[81]. Mullin[72] applies hashing to indexed sequential overflow. Chains were proposed and analyzed by Johnson[61] to provide multiattribute access to a direct file. Dimsdale[73] presents details of a system using direct access to pointer lists. Wong[71], Files[69], Burkhard[76,79], Chang[82], and Rivest[76] present multi-attribute hashing schemes from early to late binding. Before proposed techniques can be adopted, it is necessary to verify that they are applicable to the scale of the intended application. Some interesting techniques require exponentially increasing resources as the file size becomes greater.

Systems developed by Bachman[66], Dodd[66], and Kaiman[73] provided direct access to rings for various applications. Inglis[74] investigates maintenance of indexes using rings. Härder[78] uses both indexes and chains for a DBMS. The LEAP system is described in Feldman[69,72]. This system has spawned further interest (Ash[68], Symonds[68]).

Daley[65] presents the virtual systems approach to files; its application is described by Rothnie[74]. Denning[71] compares the objectives of storage and memory systems. Hatfield in Freiberger[72] evaluates locality in paged systems. Bibliographic systems as described by Lancaster[79] have phantom goal data.

EXERCISES

1 Determine the optimal bucket size for a text file structured as described in Sec. 4-1-3. The file is to be used for storing text lines of 70 characters and has a block size of 256 characters. Do not consider more than four blocks per key group. The lines are numbered sequentially 1, 2, 3, ...

   a   In terms of minimal file size.

   b   In terms of lowest block-access cost for the sum of 10 exhaustive reads of the file and 1000 random accesses of one line each. Assume a file of 1000 lines. Do not consider more than 4 blocks per bucket.

2 For the transposed file in Fig. 4-4 write a program to find the average man and compute the program's expected performance.

3 Apply the various techniques of key abbreviation discussed in Sec. 4-2-2 on all the blocks of Fig. 4-6.

4 Devise a method for implicit high-order key-segment deletion. Illustrate the effect on the example given in Fig. 4-6.

5 Write a program to produce full keys given the abbreviated text of Fig. 4-7, starting at the beginning of an index block.

6 Write a similar program, but allow it to start at any attribute pair of Example 4-3.

7 Estimate the average search time for a record in a multi-indexed file according to one search key using:

   a   Conventional multi-indexed organization

  b Abbreviated keys

  c Tree-structured files

Parameters for the evaluation are :

```
Block size       B  2000 characters    Full key size   V  20 characters
Record size      R   200  "            Pointer size    P   8  "
Number of records            n   100 000
Abbreviation factor for keys     50%
Time to seek and read one block T_B   50 milliseconds
```

Assume a uniform key distribution. Document all other assumptions.

  8 Describe the difference between an indexed and a tree-structured file.

  9 Which file structure provides the best description for the following structures found in our environment? Justify the decision in one or two sentences.

  a Genealogical chart

  b Telephone book, white pages (people)

  c Telephone book, yellow pages (services)

  d Telephone book, green pages (synonyms of service names)

  e Organization chart

  f Manual medical records

  g Railroad classification yard

  h Airline terminal

  i Social security office central files

  10 Samuel Blockdrawer has been assigned to a group which is designing a regional database application for health records. The known requirements are the following:

  • A large population (3.5 million).

  • Records of variable length.

  • Retrieval of patient records by name as well as by medical registration number. The medical registration number can be assigned at the first patient contact.

Occasionally, the database will be used for research purposes; however, most of its function is the individual health record.

A patient identification record will occupy at least 150 bytes, at most 280 bytes, with an average of 220 bytes. It contains information such as name, age, patient registration number, and so on. The average person has about three contacts with the health care delivery system per year, distributed as follows:

  • Two visits to a pharmacy, for an average of 1.2 drugs; each drug record is 20 bytes long.

  • 0.72 visits to a physician, each for a single complaint; the average visit generates 50 bytes.

  • 0.1 hospitalization which generates an average of 500 bytes.

  • 0.01 major hospitalization which is summarized to 2000 bytes.

The proposed computer system will use five byte pointers, four bytes each for data attribute descriptions and for the data values (names will be compressed to this length).

Blocks are 7000 bytes long and the interblock gaps are equivalent to 500 bytes. The average seek time is 30 ms. The rotational latency is 20 ms. The advertised data-transfer rate is 1 million bytes per second. There are six blocks per track and 50 tracks per cylinder.

Sam proposes a design as shown in Fig. 4-47.

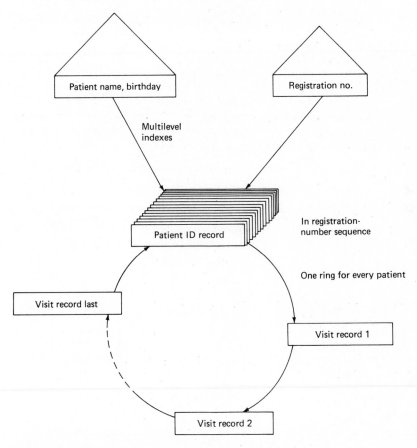

Figure 4-47 Regional health record system

Questions:

Provide the appropriate formula and its values at the end of the first year, second year, and fifth year for each of the seven aspects of the file design which are listed below. State any assumption which you have to make in order to obtain the results.

a The average record size in the system as well as for the total file size.

b The time required to locate one specific patient visit by name and date.

c Time to find the next visit of that patient.

d The time required to add a visit record.

e The time to change a data value in a patient's record, if the registration number is given.

f The time required to collect the entire patient's record.

g The time required to collect all usage data for one specific drug.

Give three suggestions how this design can be improved and mention for each suggestion both the benefit and the cost considerations. How can we handle people that move out of the region or die?

11 Develop an algorithm to generate the minimum number of combinatorial indexes in the general case (see Fig. 4-13). The author is not aware of such an algorithm and would appreciate communications regarding a solution.

12 A supplier's manual of MUMPS provides the following design example:

We wish to store patients' identifications, each of 60 characters, for 10 000 patients numbered from 1 to 10 000. The blocks have a net capacity of 762 characters. Each combination of segment-type identification and key requires three character spaces, a pointer also requires three, and the end-of-string character one space. Due to the design of the machine, segments have to be multiples of three characters.

    a How many segments fit into one block if all segments are on one level?

    b What is the number of blocks used?

    c What is the expected search time exclusive of the directory search?

13 We can get faster access in the above case by using segments consisting of a pointer only on level 1 and keeping the patient identification on level 2.

    a How many segments will be in one block on level 1?

    b How many segments will be in one block on level 2?

    c How many blocks are being used?

    d What is the expected search time?

14 Do you see any problem if the segment length would not always be 60 characters, but rather 60 characters on the average? (This problem will be refined and solved in Example 6-2.)

15 Design a file and evaluate it for questions as are posed in the epigraph from Vonnegut for Chap. 12.

16 Prove the statement in Sec. 4-2-2, that the number of empty pointer fields in binary index trees is $y + 1$ (Fig. 4-8).

17 To reduce the number of entries in a multi-attribute direct-access procedure only queries which catenate at least three of the four key attributes are accepted. How many entries will be required in the pointer-list?

18 How many search arguments should you have before using direct access to the file of Fig. 4-39?

19 Programming lore advises that input should be sorted in the descending order when doing batch updates of files which keep overflows in ascending ordered chains. Why? Quantify the effect.

20 Compare a MUMPS segment with a LEAP record.

Chapter 5

Overall File-System Evaluation

The purpose of computing is insight, not numbers

Richard Hamming

The number of computations without purpose is out of sight

Author's corollary

We have, up to this point, analyzed the technical performance of file systems. The parameters developed in the previous chapters have yet to be translated into financial costs and economic benefits before we can provide management with data which will allow them to judge the appropriateness of a database which uses computer-based file systems.

We have to assume now that the decision to install a database system is made on rational grounds. Other considerations that have led to the use of computer systems have been based on the expectation that rapid access to information would eliminate existing operational problems. This is unlikely to happen. Decisions have also been made in imitation of leaders in the same segment of industry. Frequently substantial pressures have been exerted by the sellers of computing equipment.

In the scope of this book we cannot evaluate all intangible elements which are part and parcel of decisions to install computers, but will rather present a model of a functional evaluation. A number of decisions of a nontechnical nature remain, specifically in the area of attributing financial or social benefits to system performance.

The Process of Evaluation Most benefit factors can only be estimated, but the fact that they are *estimates* does not at all diminish the importance of assigning quantitative values to all important parameters in a system design. The use of specific, documented, and consistent values for these quantities allows analysis of the decision and the comparison of system and nonsystem alternatives. When design decisions are made which are based on unrecorded assumptions, the probability of design errors is high, and correction of assumptions to improve the design is impossible.

If we have to make very many assumptions, then our conclusions will be mainly of a relative rather than absolute nature. This state will become obvious during the estimation process. Figure 5-1 provides an overview of the analysis process.

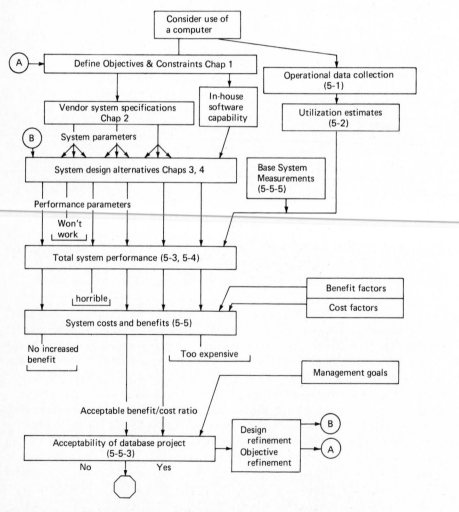

Figure 5-1 The system-analysis process.

Section 5-1 of this chapter deals with the estimation of system use, whereas the three sections following will deal respectively with system benefits, storage costs, and production costs. Section 5-4 includes considerations of multiprogramming, use of multiple processors, and data distribution. Section 5-5 presents the problems of integrating these factors and ensuring the robustness of the final results.

We will frequently relate the analysis to the seven performance parameters obtained in Chap. 3 and listed on the inside covers. These parameters describe the following:

1 The required data storage: $n_{total}R$
2 The expected search times: T_F, T_N, T_X
3 The expected update times: T_I, T_U
4 The time required for reorganizations: T_Y

5-1 THE ESTIMATION OF SYSTEM USAGE

In order to extract benefits out of a database, it has to be used. The benefits which may be obtained, the effectiveness with which they are obtained, and the cost of the database operation are all related to the load placed on the system. The load consists of demands on data storage and on operations requested by the transactions.

Data Volume A primary aspect of the load is the volume of stored data required for an effective operation. In many environments the volume of data is expected to increase steadily. The estimation of the load placed on the file system in terms of volume is controlled on the number of records n, the total number of attributes a, and the average number of attributes in a record a'. The lengths of the value fields V and the attribute description fields A also play a role.

The various file designs will combine these common parameters in different ways, so that at this point we are not prepared to evaluate the file size, since the design decision is yet to be made. If we cannot contain our anxiousness, we may quickly check the magnitude of the storage demand presented by a pile organization of the proposed data.

Data-Retrieval Load The retrieval of data elements is the central objective of a file system. A transaction may require data from more than one file. We stated earlier that a collection of related data forms a database. If it is made accessible to a set of transactions, we can speak of a database system. The primary objective of database systems is the synthesis of data and, hence, the creation of information. Some measure of what this means in terms of the utilization of the file system is required. We consider first the load on systems by data requests for services for operational purposes.

The operational load is provided by an estimate of the number of service requests to a file made by the transactions in a given period. The distribution of these requests over a daily or monthly cycle should also be estimated to determine periods of high demand. The load and time of busy intervals are used to verify that the proposed system is adequate at those times.

Example 5-1   Load for an airline reservation system

We wish to design a booking system for a small airline. We have studied the operation
and can summarize the result as follows:

> The number of salable items we have is determined by the number of flights
> between two adjacent points and the number of available seats. With 3
> aircraft of 70 seats each, which complete 20 flight segments per day, nearly
> 30 000 units are for sale each week. The average ticket sale represents 2.7
> units because people fly more than one segment and use return flights. The
> average number of people flying and booking together is 1.61. A survey shows
> that 20% of all reservations are subsequently changed. During the process
> of selling a ticket, typically three possible flight schedules are explored.

The load L on the system is stated in terms of fetch and get-next accesses for ticket sales

$$L_F = \frac{30\,000}{2.7 \times 1.61}\, 1.20 \times 3 = 25\,000$$

$$L_N = 30\,000 \times 1.20 \times 3 - L_F = 83\,000$$

We have to note for the subsequent file-design phases that additional segments of a flight
schedule and additional people on a flight are accommodated through get-next searches.

The estimates used in the example may be rough, but it is important that they
have been made and have been written down. A change in projected system usage
can be accommodated only if the original assumptions are known. In addition, it
is desirable to redo the complete evaluation for both high and low usage estimates
in order to be assured that the effects of misestimation are neither fatal in terms of
cost nor disastrous in terms of performance.

Load for Information Retrieval For a database system which is to produce
primarily *information*, rather than produce data to control sales of services or
equipment, the estimation of the load is considerably more difficult. The extent
of its use is mainly dependent on user satisfaction. Satisfaction in turn depends on
human factors, utility, and performance.

A retrospective health-status report on a patient loses its value quickly if the effort to
obtain it is greater than the desire of the physician to have the past record available
during the encounter with the patient. Such a health report only occasionally contains
information which is not obvious to the physician at the time of the visit. The average
benefit may be quite low.

For information systems the estimation of load may require investigations of
similar systems. If no similar situations exist, the operation of a *pilot model* can
provide data for load projections. In a pilot model, different technology can be
employed, since it is allowable to operate at much higher unit cost per query in
order to minimize the initial investment, while obtaining performance parameters
which match the intended final form of the proposed system.

A prediction based on a pilot model requires reflection and insight when the
pilot model was operated with a limited database. The designer can only conjecture
how system benefits, and hence usage patterns, are related to file size. A careful
analysis of the information-producing potential and the power this information
provides for the users may be required. Usage patterns also change over time. A
flexible design is needed to allow the system to grow and adapt.

The outcome of the above considerations should be the frequency of all types of retrieval:

Fetch requests L_F

Requests for *next* records L_N

Exhaustive searches L_X

both in terms of averages over long periods (days, weeks, or months), as well as the maximum rates for short, high-intensity periods that may be expected.

Update Load The frequency of updates of the system also will be considered in the estimation of system volume. We wish at this point to break down the update frequencies into types of tasks that represent:

Addition of a new record L_I

Change of a field in a record L_U

Extension of a record L_Z

Deletion of a record L_D

In the airline example introduced above, each unit of the flight inventory has to be updated for every successful sale and two updates are needed for a change.

$$L_U = 30\,000(1.00 + 2 \times 0.20) = 42\,000$$

In order to keep track of the passengers, a separate file P may be maintained. A new record is inserted for every new passenger (36%), and this record is extended with every additional purchase or change made.

$$L_I(\text{P}) = 0.36 \times 30\,000/2.7 = 4\,000$$

$$L_Z(\text{P}) = 0.64 \times 30\,000 \times 1.2/2.7 = 8\,540$$

All these values are weekly rates; a busy time to check separately may be Friday afternoon.

Eventually the load parameters have to be estimated for all files, all operations, and several activity periods.

Depending on the type of file organization, we will associate each of these load frequencies with the appropriate performance parameters.

If we consider only our six basic file methods, we find the relationships shown in Table 5-1. We note that the load parameters $\{L_I, L_U, L_Z, \ldots\}$ do not map directly into the file performance parameters $\{T_I, T_U, \ldots\}$, since not all actions are directly supported by all file organizations. The assignment may also depend on the expected response time. We have learned enough about the various file organizations to know that some file types are not suitable for certain on-line operations.

Table 5-1   Parameters Appropriate for Update Evaluation

	Pile	Seq.	Index Seq.	Index	Direct	Ring
L_I	T_I	T_I	T_I	T_I	T_I	T_I
L_U	T_U	T_I	T_U	T_U	T_U	T_U
L_Z	T_U			T_U		T_U
L_D	$T_U - T_I$	T_I	T_U	T_U	T_U	T_U

File Maintenance The frequency of reorganization is largely a function of system design and file dynamics. Reorganization may be combined with periodic exhaustive processing so that

$$L_Y = L_X$$

In other cases, reorganization can be specified as a function of the past update activity. Section 6-4-3 presents an analytic procedure to determine reorganization frequency.

The small airline of our example may clean up its passenger list once a week as part of a market summary but reorganize its inventory file as needed to keep access rapid. After 20% update activity, access to the weekly inventory file is measurably slowed down.

$$L_Y(\mathtt{P}) = L_X = 1$$
$$L_Y(\mathtt{I}) = (L_I + L_U + L_Z + L_D)/(0.20 \times 30\,000)$$

We will apply these load parameters to a file system in Sec. 5-4 but will first discuss the benefits to be obtained from the transactions which give rise to these load factors.

5-2 ANALYSIS OF SYSTEM BENEFITS

The first performance parameter (nR), which specifies the quantity of data to be stored, is not directly associated with any system benefits. This remark is meant to reinforce the realization that, except for some historians, the mere collection of data is not an end in itself. The benefits of having data arise from the use of data. The use of data may be vague and distant, but its probability needs to be evaluated and measured. The availability of stored data is, of course, a prerequisite for use of a database system.

5-2-1 Benefit Quantification

The value of a completed transaction is best quantified in financial terms. In the case that the use of the system is associated with sales, this value can simply be a fraction of the profit expected from sales.

In other cases, the benefit may be established by questioning the potential users to determine what they would be willing to pay for the service. If the situation is one where money does not provide a basis of measurement, a comparison of the desirability between this service and other services whose cost is known can be used to provide measures of service value.

An example is from the physician's office, where the availability of a past medical record may be compared in terms of diagnostic power with another laboratory test.

We can only get into trouble if we accept in this context a statement that the service is essential, so that its value seems infinite.

Frequently benefits are expected from lower personnel costs. Here we have to assure ourselves that these benefits are realizable, and even if they are, that they are socially desirable. Realization of personnel economies is difficult to achieve if fractions of the effort of a number of individuals are being saved. If new jobs have to be created out of portions of partially eliminated positions, we have to ensure that the new position is viable. Replacement of untrained personnel by fewer but more expensive trained people is also questionable. Problems can occur if the computer handles routine services but not some task which is to be done during a short time interval.

If a computer in a banking office allows two people to handle the customers previously served by four people but does not assist in the reconciliation of funds done daily between 3 and 5 P.M., then changes in the daily procedures will be needed.

The cost of readjustment of operations also has to be included before summing up the benefits.

Expectations of future benefits are often based on cost containment. This implies that while there is no net saving now, the new system will allow growth at a smaller increase in cost than can be foreseen otherwise. It is obvious that such reasoning requires an even more careful benefit analysis, since the rate of expected growth is always uncertain and affects, when achieved, many aspects of an organization beyond the area of computing systems.

Frequently the benefit of database operations diminishes gradually with increased response time. Figure 5-2 shows the estimated loss of benefit at a city airline counter where the customer has a choice of airlines and much of the business is on a walk-up basis. The logarithmic scale on the abscissa is used in these sketches because we are dealing with such a wide range of time values.

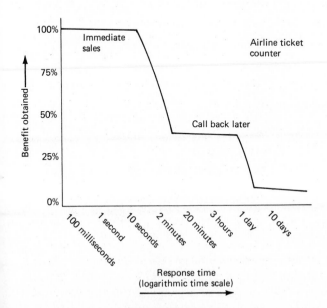

Figure 5-2 Benefit realization.

Real-Time Operation If the response time of the system is poor, the data may arrive too late to have the desired effect. This presents us with the *real-time* constraint. The value of this constraint depends on the application and can vary from milliseconds to months.

Table 5-2 lists some estimates of real-time constraints in various areas where computer systems with databases have been employed. The validity of some of the limits may be debatable, but for each of these categories, there are instances of systems which provided a longer response time and had problems in operational acceptance. The total response time includes the entry of the request, the computer system activity, and the presentation of the response. Only a fraction of the times shown is available for file operations. We also have listed in Table 5-2 the typical quantity of data expected corresponding to one request in these areas.

The need to keep within real-time constraints may mean that we will not be able to consider in some decisions all the possible information, since the time to fetch the data would be excessive. Decisions taken under operational real-time constraints hence may be less than optimal, but yet better than decisions taken without any data. It is possible that there are data elements which, although they are conceptually useful, do not actually contribute to the decision-making process of the user.

Table 5-2   Real-Time Constraints and Data Volume

Area	Value of constraint	Reason for size of constraint	Search volume/ request(bytes)
Annual accounting	Month	Annual report cycle	10^4
Full auditing report	Week	Audits are preannounced	10^3
Inventory report	2 days	Ordering cycle is a week	10^3
Payroll	2 or 3 days	Accepted by employees	10^3
Stock trade	1 day	SEC requirement	10^3 to 10^4
Bank account update	Overnight	Expectation by customers, early detection of problems	10^5
Audit inquiry	Few hours	Request has to be handled via employees of firm	10^2
Casting agency	10 min	Multiple contacts have to be made in an hour	10^2
Airline-ticket sales	1 to 5 min	Patience of passengers	10
Real-estate sales index	$\frac{1}{2}$ to 2 min	Salesperson does not want to lose continuity	1 to 20
Grocery counter credit check	3 to 20 s	Goodwill	1
Item from medical file	2 to 10 s	Operational cycle of MD	50 to 10
Positioning of a mass spectrometer	100 μs	Vaporization of sample	2

Effectiveness versus Benefits Systems are not always placed into operation with clear or measurable expectations of benefit. When, for instance, a certain service is mandated by law, only the effectiveness of the implementation can be determined; the benefits of the law have presumably been established already.

If no reasonable measure of benefit can be found, the base benefit is set to zero. It is still possible to proceed through the arguments which follow. Many considerations will reduce the expected benefits. Those reductions will have to be estimated in absolute terms, and by the end of this section, only negative benefits will be left. This still will allow the integrated system comparisons in Sec. 5-5 to be made, but the conclusions will have to be presented to management in a relative sense. This approach, termed cost-effectiveness analysis rather than cost-benefit analysis, is common in government operations.

Cost-benefit analysis attempts to obtain quantitative data so that *go/no-go* decisions can be made.

Cost-effectiveness analysis permits evaluation to select one of several system alternatives which will achieve a desirable goal.

Any system has to achieve a certain level of quality of performance in order to become effective. The benefits of the transactions can be fully realized only if the database system performs ideally. The topics following will discuss these effectiveness factors in terms of the performance parameters to be obtained.

5-2-2 System Utilization

The operator effort required to use a system diminishes its benefits. If there is a full-time operator the basic costs are easy to determine. A slow or awkward system will increase the basic cost per transaction. If the system is operated by people who have additional and perhaps more important tasks, the operability of the system will be an essential component of its usage cost.

Measures other than response time are not easily quantified. Counting of keystrokes, as done when comparing computer editors, seems futile. The effort required from the user is easy to underestimate, and predictions by system designers have to be substantiated during pilot operation with the intended users.

Direct time measures of the effort to use the system include

1 The time required to formulate queries

2 The time spent in order to describe the format of desired outputs

3 The time needed to enter the search parameters into the system

4 The time required for the actual processing of the request

5 The delay incurred for display or printing of the result

Comparison of these times with existing manual systems can provide some idea of the relative demands made on the users. Our performance parameters help mainly to establish the delay in item **4**, and some of that time can be overlapped with entry **3** and presentation **5**.

Consideration of the effort required to use the system is particularly significant where there is direct use of computers by professional users such as managers, lawyers, physicians, scientists, and researchers. Here one has to avoid a diminution of the time a professional has available for work of primary interest.

In a number of instances database systems intended for direct use by professionals have had to be augmented after installation with clerical personnel at the terminals. The costs and delays related to the use of intermediaries to operate the terminals seriously affect system economics.

Another component of the personnel effort is the amount of training required to use the system. The cost of training will be relatively low for frequent users, but if we expect occasional users to benefit from the system, the amount of requisite training should be minimized. The additional effort of designing database systems so that the user needs little indoctrination can be well justified in terms of overall system cost.

Personnel Cost   The effect of a system on personnel costs is an important part of proper system design. It is not unusual that the cost of terminal operators and time spent by people preparing and receiving data exceeds the cost of the hardware used by a system.

Various approaches can be followed to determine the relationships between performance and response time. Industrial engineers have measured user response time at the terminal. It has been found that different work habits will evolve depending on the interface that the system provides.

As an example, we will use the financial collection office of a hospital where unpaid accounts are reviewed for follow-up. The computer system is used to provide an up-to-date status report so that all payments, credits, adjustments, and so forth, will be known before a collection effort is made.

A system which responds instantaneously relative to the reaction time of the clerk will allow a continuous performance of the collection task as shown in Fig. 5-3.

If the system does not respond quickly, some waste of the operator's time will occur. The operator delay is generally greater than the system delay which caused it, because the operator's flow of consciousness is disturbed. If the delays become significant, they provide reasons for trips to the coffee machine, checkbook balancing, and such.

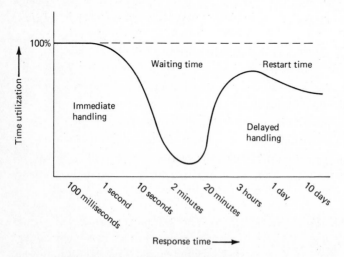

Figure 5-3 Personnel-time utilization.

At some point, the operators will adopt a different mode of operation; they will make a number of requests simultaneously, and during the time the system needs to produce the records, the clerk will process the previous batch. Now the wasted time is much less, since it consists only of an initial starting time and an increased frequency of attention switching. If the delays exceed 8 hours, yet other work procedures will be used. If the delays exceed a week, it is probably not worthwhile to use the system at all.

5-2-3 Data-Content Maintenance

Updating of the database is often the costliest component of the aggregate system. In some cases the data, or a portion of it, can be gathered automatically. Point-of-sale recording devices can provide the input to control an inventory when the sale occurs, and similar devices are becoming available for other areas. A large portion of the information in databases still is entered manually, either directly via computer terminals or indirectly via cards, tapes, or optically read documents.

In the evaluation of data-entry costs, we cannot consider only how much it costs to enter a data element. The proper question is how much it costs to enter a data element correctly. The cost of detection and correction of an element entered incorrectly, as well as the cost of the havoc the erroneous value might have wrought while it was part of the database, has to be added to the data-entry cost.

Errors on data entry can be classified into errors occurring before, during, or after the entry of the data into the computer.

Before Entry   The reduction of errors made prior to transcription into a computer is a problem largely outside of the scope of this book. If the transcription is close to the source of data, the frequency of such errors will be less. A proper overall system design can contribute greatly to minimization of errors. Coding methods appropriate to a given task are discussed in Chap. 14.

During Entry   The reduction of data entry errors is strongly related to the quality of the transcription device and its operation. The quality, i.e., the delay time and its consistency, of the system response to an update has an effect similar to the effect discussed earlier when searching for data. Here poor system performance actually can cause negative productivity, as shown in Fig. 5-4.

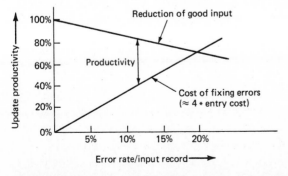

Figure 5-4 Error rate versus productivity during data entry.

This figure still excludes indirect costs due to erroneous data which entered the database. If, because of wrong information caused by a data-entry error, undesirable actions are performed, the cost of the error may cancel all benefits obtained from the system over a long period.

Through an erroneous inquiry, we could, for example, have committed our company to the delivery of stock which was already sold. Replacement stock to fulfill the obligation has to be obtained at a premium.

Feedback   The most important principle to reduce errors on data entry is the use of *feedback*. Feedback loops can be provided to the operators during data entry. to the data collectors by regular reports and summaries, and to higher level personnel by reducing data to trends and graphs. It is best if the feedback does not appear in the exact form that the data were entered, and that the output includes some additional information.

Entry errors due to mistyping of terms can, for instance, be reduced drastically through the use of input devices providing selection capability. Display screens on a CRT terminal that are formatted like a menu or a form with a number of listed choices require only an indication or a check mark for the entry of a data element. Feedback of the selected value is provided on the screen by listing the name of the data element in full, so that mis-hits will be recognizable. Selection is sketched in Fig. 10-5.

When codes or identification numbers are used to enter data, the feedback on the display, in the form of plain language, of the meaning of the entered code can aid significantly in error control. Feedback of numeric values which have been entered in a well-formatted and legible display is also helpful. Where the customer is present, the feedback can be shown to the customer for verification. In many cases a second display terminal is employed for this purpose.

Use of feedback reduces the error rate per data element; what the effect is per unit time is not well known. The problem of correct entry of arbitrary alphabetic text or large numbers is not solved by this approach. Numeric data entry correctness can be verified by using control totals. A batch total, prepared when the source data are collected, is compared with the sum of the entries, and any discrepancy is reported.

After Entry   Database systems may include automated input format verification procedures, as well as comparisons with previous data recorded or recently entered. Ranges of value linits of attributes may be kept with the database. In many instances, even for attributes whose data values can have a great range, incremental changes, say, month-to-month values for a particular item, will not change more than a few percent.

If an error can be detected while the source of the data still is available, the cost of correction may be only a few times the cost of the original data entry. If errors are found much later, considerable time may be wasted in the retrieval of a source document or by having to refer back to the supplier of the data.

When response messages are designed, the various message texts should have significant differences in the initial words of the message, so that less frequent, and hence important error messages are immediately distinguished from repetitive confirmations. An audible error signal (see Fig. 14-1) can be very helpful when visual-display terminals are used to enter large quantities of data.

An additional measure to catch errors is to report to the originator of the data the data values entered. If, for instance, an order has been received by telephone or mail, the system can print a confirmation, in plain language, for inspection by the customer. The purchaser then may realize that you are planning to deliver next week 501 adders instead of 50 ladders.

In many instances data are not entered directly into computer systems. A common indirect entry method is the sequence of keypunching and verification (by rekeying and comparing), followed later by entry of a batch of data into the system. Indirect data entry is often less costly and reduces dependence of system performance during data entry. On the other hand, the detection of errors and feedback to the operators is deferred so that the cost of correction can be very high and repair of data frequently is omitted, knowingly or accidentally.

The decoupling of entry personnel from the computer system does avoid waste and frustration due to poor reliability and inconsistency of performance found in many systems. Checking of data for consistency may be done only during periodic report generation. Systems which do not provide feedback and incentives for error correction are doomed to eventual disuse. Bad experiences by users, who attempt to obtain information from a database and receive obviously incorrect data, can easily cause rejection of positive aspects of automation as well.

Auditability In some situations the problem of improper action caused by poor data may be so serious that one should not allow an error correction to be made by an update of the record containing the error. Instead a correction will be entered as a new record whose value will replace the previous value for a normal inquiry.

If a problem develops, we want to be able to go backward in time with a query of the form

"What was the value for x that the system would have provided
at a time t and date d?"

and retrieve the erroneous value then in use.

An example of this requirement can be found in the maintenance of medical records where errors in actions resulting from poor data can cause great harm and invite legal claims of malpractice.

A general solution to this problem is to routinely identify *all* data elements with a *timestamp*. While this would in principle double the required storage space, the use of abbreviation techniques can reduce this factor. The availability of a time identifier with every data element can also help in the processing and management of data. Older data can be conveniently archived now, so that demands on high-performance storage devices may actually diminish.

Once correct data are entered into the system, we assume from the point of view of this chapter that they are safe. The chapters on data security (11 to 13) will deal with this problem on a technical level.

5-3 DATABASE STORAGE REQUIREMENTS

The operation of a computer requires personnel and hardware. We will concentrate in this chapter on the elements which relate to the load and performance factors that were developed in Sec. 5-1. Broader issues are discussed in Chap. 15.

In order to simplify the procedure, we will use methods which can provide rough initial estimates of load on a given system. These values can be refined later when the system being designed has taken a more definite form. This section will concentrate on the storage-related equipment, whereas Sec. 5-4 will discuss the processing-related system components.

5-3-1 Storage Utilization

When files undergo frequent and dynamic changes, not all the available file capacity can be utilized. Depending on the file system used, considerably more space may be needed. The density factor u_D is used to adjust the expected storage cost throughout the design process. The author has seen values for u_D ranging from 90% (stable files in an environment which provided good space-allocation capability) to 25% (dynamic files in a structurally limited environment).

A low value of u_D does not necessarily imply an undesirable file design. In files using direct access, for instance, available space will considerably enhance operational performance. In addition, there will be wasted space W because of unspanned packing of records into blocks, which reduces the number of blocks needed for some records.

The total storage capacity required for the files making up a database is

$$D = \sum_{all\,files} n\frac{R+W}{u_D} \qquad\qquad 5\text{-}1$$

Some additional storage capacity is needed for operating systems and programs. The parameters n, R, W, u_D are probably different for each file, but in this chapter we consider storage as if it were a single file to keep the notation simpler. The value D provides the initial estimate of the storage needs for a system.

5-3-2 Components

The primary hardware components of a system to provide storage of data are of course the storage devices, typically disks, themselves. We will in this section also consider the devices required to attach disks to the processors, *controllers* and *channels*. The performance and cost of a complete storage system are affected by the performance and costs of controllers and channels as well as the performance and costs of the disks.

Databases often require multiple disks and somtimes multiple controllers and channels as well. If the quantity D exceeds the capacity of one of the available disk units, multiple units will be employed. The value of the storage parameter $D_{available}$ is rounded to an integer multiple of the capacity of the devices to be used, unless we can convince others to purchase the remnant.

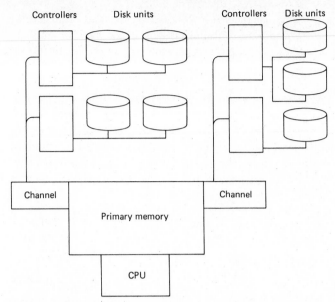

Figure 5-5 Storage-system components.

If the entire computer system is to be selected for a specific database, there may be much freedom in equipment selection. In general it is desirable to select storage devices so that one or few disks will satisfy the storage needs without the complexity of many units. Backup and archiving capacity is also needed now.

In most computers, disks are not directly coupled to the processors but require a *controller*. A controller may be able to handle 2, 4, 8, or 16 disk units. If many disks are to be used, there will be more than one controller. On the larger computers, controllers are connected to the processor by channels, which provide the data path into the processor memory.

Multiple *channels* may also be used, not so much in order to provide the connection capability, but rather to provide multiple simultaneous data access paths, giving a greater bandwidth into the computer. Figure 5-5 sketches the organization of the hardware components for a storage system.

5-3-3 Distribution and Replication of Data

Multiple processors are found in an increasing number of computer systems. When the processors are *closely coupled*, the storage can be shared, so that the data can be distributed. The benefits of having multiple processors, from the database point of view, are increased computational capability and backup in case of processor failures. If protection is required for storage-device failures, storage needs to be replicated. Replication is common when processors are not closely coupled.

When the processors are *remote* from each other, the storage facilities are not shared in the same manner. Access to remote sites is indirect, via communication lines and the remote processor. We do not find direct connections to remote storage devices useful, unless the storage device is used for remote input or output, and this situation is not appropriate for databases.

Distributed operations distinguish local and remote access, and transactions may be decomposed into subtransactions containing requests for distinct sites. A local request is processed as before, but a request to access remote data has to be communicated first to a remote processor. That processor obtains the result and returns it to the originator.

The capability of remote lines is an order of magnitude less than that of disk devices, i.e., $btt_{comm} \gg btt_{disks}$, so that the balance of a system design changes considerably when it is distributed. In order to overcome slow access to remote sites, some of the data may be *replicated*. Replication increases the cost of update but improves retrieval dramatically. Data that are frequenty read and infrequently updated are prime candidates for replication at the sites where the queries originate. If replication is used, the storage demands D increase.

With these considerations, we can estimate the types and number of components needed to satisfy the storage requirements for the database. Since the actual design parameters are not yet known, one can obtain a range of devices needed by establishing a range of the storage capacity needed, estimating the requirements at a low level of waste, free space, and redundancy (say $W = 0, u_D = 80\%) \rightarrow D_{low}$, and at a high level (maybe $W = R, u_D = 25\%) \rightarrow D_{high}$ of these conditions.

5-3-4 System Choice

Once the range of storage requirements is defined, we can limit the evaluation of alternative systems to an appropriate range. Since a similar range of disk devices is available from many manufacturers, we can concentrate initially on types of storage units, and avoid selection of a specific vendor. We will select from the alternatives a file configuration which promises minimum cost. Figure 5-6 shows cost estimates for three storage-system hardware combinations related to capacity.

Discontinuities exist in these cost functions because of disk type alternatives, controller increments, and choice of reasonable channel assignments. Since an approximate range for the storage requirements has been established, only a segment of the curve is of interest. Three outcomes are possible:

1   The actual storage cost does not change at all within the range of capacities being considered. The high limit should be reasonable and adequate for the foreseeable future. A specific file design can be chosen on the basis of other parameters.

2   There is a significant *jump* of the cost function in the range of interest. One can attempt to design the file system to remain at the low side of the jump. Careful evaluation is needed to assure that in the worst case the storage D_{high} will never exceed the capacity at the jump. The selection of file-design choices will be constrained. The alternative is to play it safe, acquire the higher-capacity device, and use the excess capacity to increase performance. Many file-organization methods, as B-trees and direct files, respond well to increased space.

3   Many jumps appear within the range being considered. This situation is frequently true for a large database system. This means that file cost is incremental, and that there is only an economic storage constraint in choosing a file method in addition to the performance requirements. We will discuss in Sec. 5-4-6 the estimation of the incremental cost of entire systems.

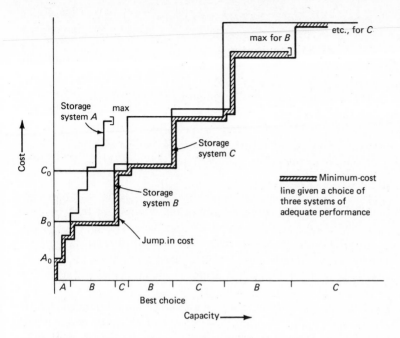

Figure 5-6 Cost versus storage capacity.

Costs are also incremental if the database operation is added to an existing computer system. The cost per increment of file storage is then known, but not controllable. The cost function starts at some point and curve of Fig. 5-6.

The method used to select the storage required may not be as mechanical as outlined above. Long-term growth expectations may make the eventual quantity D_{high}, and hence the cost range, impractically large. The rapid development of new hardware may make a design based on current storage device information impractical. If projections of future capabilties are being used, the delay between the inroduction of new technology and its availability with full software support has to be considered; three years has been a typical interval.

If one of the design objectives is a good understanding of a number of system-design alternatives, a fixed-storage-cost assumption (**1** or **2**) is misleading. In most instances, approximate methods provide adequate initial results. A reverification is always in order before a final commitment is made.

5-4 ACCESS LOAD AND CAPABILITY OF A FILE SYSTEM

Based on the known load and the file performance parameters we wish to select a system of adequate capability at a reasonable cost. We can estimate the file performance for any design, but the number of design choices is overwhelming.

One approach is to build a model of all possible file designs, and select an optimum. There is ongoing research based on this approach and methods are available which, for a constrained set of choices, will compute the optimum solution.

For instance, if indexed files are to be used, we can determine which attributes should be indexed. We can also optimize space-time trade-offs for direct files. Given a number of assumptions, we can show that in a database a global optimum can by achieved while optimizing the individual files separately, one by one. In distributed systems the optimal assignment of files or parts of files can also be determined. References to a number of such models can be found at the end of this chapter.

Unfortunately, all these methods have to make many assumptions about the available alternatives, so that their model tends to be simpler than the real world. Many of them are also mathematically complex. Their use will provide an excellent starting point for further determinations and will provide insight into complex design choices.

The second approach to select files follows conventional engineering practice. We assume here either that the choices are practically limited or that a prior modeling analysis has narrowed down the set of alternatives. The process begins with the selection of candidate hardware systems which can deal with the storage requirements estimated earlier. These are then compared and scaled up or down according to the degree of over- or underutilization which we perceive during the analysis.

It is not unusual in database work that the smallest computer adequate to store the data quantity and support the file programs is adequate to perform the remaining tasks. On the other hand, it does happen that there is no single computer capable of dealing with the data flow between core storage and disk which might be required in an active database environment. Then the tasks will have to be distributed over multiple processors.

After an approximate system is selected, a file design is chosen which matches the expected utilization pattern and can be supported using vendor and in-house resources. The procedure to establish the adequacy of the selected computer system is iterative:

1 The demand on the system is estimated.
2 The available resources of the system are similarly estimated.
3 The two are compared to see if a *satisfactory match* is obtained. A match is satisfactory when the demand is less than the capability of the resources by a ratio which is a function of the precision used to make the estimates.
4 If the demand is not comfortably within the capability of the resources, then both the demand and the resources are reestimated more precisely, and a new comparison (3) is made.
5 If there is a major mismatch, the equipment selected, the design of the files, or the tasks to be performed are changed and the design process is restarted at 2 or 1.

In order to simplify the exposition, we will begin with the assumption that the application using the file system will be the only use of the computer. Consideration of the effect of multiprogramming will appear in Sec. 5-4-3.

The measurement used to appraise the demand and the capability of the system is *time*. We will not worry in the presentation about the unit to be employed; in practice, it seems reasonable to scale all values for on-line systems to minutes.

5-4-1 Aggregate System Demand

The performance parameters, which were derived from the file design, provide estimates of the time required to complete the various transactions. These are multiplied by the estimates of the transaction loads to obtain the gross aggregate demand. Table 5-1 provided the rules for matching load parameters to systems. The performance parameters used here assume that this has been done.

We will perform the initial demand calculation for a period of high demand. If the daytime activities consist of searches and updates, and insertion of new data and exhaustive searches are delegated to evening operation, then the desired production during the daytime hours is computable as the sum of the activity times for all transactions to be carried out.

$$q_{total} = L_F T_F + L_N T_N + L_U T_U + L_Z T_Z \qquad 5\text{-}2$$

The appropriate equivalence for T_Z is found in Table 5-1.

The total available resource Q is, at this level of analysis, simply the available time during this period, perhaps 8 hours.

To compare the values of demand and resources, we will define a utilization ratio,

$$u_{overall} = \frac{q_{total}}{Q} \qquad 5\text{-}3$$

If this value is very low ($u < 0.05$), representing perhaps only a fraction of 1 hour during the day on a dedicated computer system, then we can expect few problems, and the analysis provided in Secs. 5-4-2, 5-4-3, and 5-4-4 can be omitted.

Other, highly intensive periods and the effect of other tasks should still be investigated.

In a bank the lunch hour and the time before closing may still give problems; in a hospital a busy time occurs when the physicians make their rounds prior to opening their offices. The expected evening load should also be estimated and compared.

If the value of the overall u is low, but not negligible during some periods (maybe as high as 0.2), scheduling of the load can be considered to reduce the peak utilization.

For instance, routine processing of banking work received by mail can be halted during the lunch hour. If scheduling does not reduce the utilization significantly, the analysis of Sec. 5-4-2 should be carried out for the busy periods.

5-4-2 Aggregate System Capability

A computer system actually can support in a given period a number of transactions whose weighted sum q_{total} is greater than the available time. The reason is that some operations can be performed in parallel in all but the simplest computer system. Figure 5-7 sketches a simple, but busy system to demonstrate this.

Two types of overlap are possible and will be discussed. We find that at the same time different component types will be *simultaneously* active, for instance, a disk and its channels during data transfer; and some identical component types will be active in *parallel*, for instance, two disks.

In Sec. 5-4-3 we will analyze the simultaneous operation of different component types. To analyze *simultaneity*, we have to consider overlap between dissimilar constituents of the transaction demand: seeks, rotational latencies, and block-transfer times, since the various component types participate in only some of these constituents. Overlap of computing cycles with disk operations was introduced in Sec. 2-3-2.

In Sec. 5-4-4 we will analyze the effect of *parallelism* in the operation of multiple hardware components of the same type. Having multiple components permits multiple seeks, latencies, block transfers, and computations to be carried out in parallel, and this permits increased system performance.

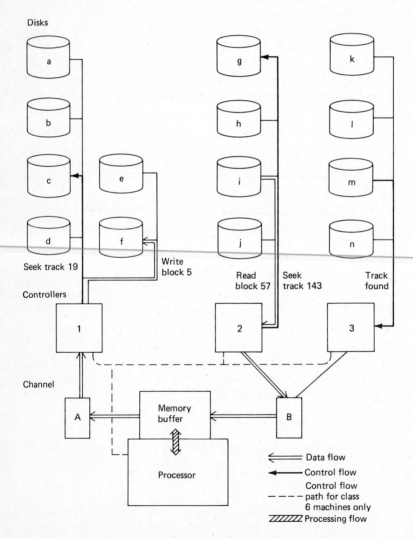

Figure 5-7 Opportunities for parallelism.

In order to overlap operation of either type, it is necessary that the system can handle multiple processes, since individual processes are made up of sections specified to occur in sequential order. In the typical on-line database application there will be one computation associated with every active terminal, so that even if the computations are so simple that they cannot be decomposed into multiple processes, one can expect a considerable amount of parallel demand. When complex information analysis is done, it becomes important that retrieval computations are decomposed into parallel processes, so that the capabilities of the equipment can be exploited.

In Fig. 5-7 data transfers are active between core memory and two disk units f and i using both channels and two controllers. At the same time seeks are taking place on disk units c and g and disk m is reporting the completion of a seek. Which combinations of operations are possible in parallel depends on the *architecture* of the storage system. Data transfer and control lines are bidirectional, so that it does not matter if the transfer activity is read or write, or if the control activity is demand or response.

Figure 5-8 defines a number of architectural classes to help analyze the activity of various types of storage-system components during the execution of constituents of disk operations.

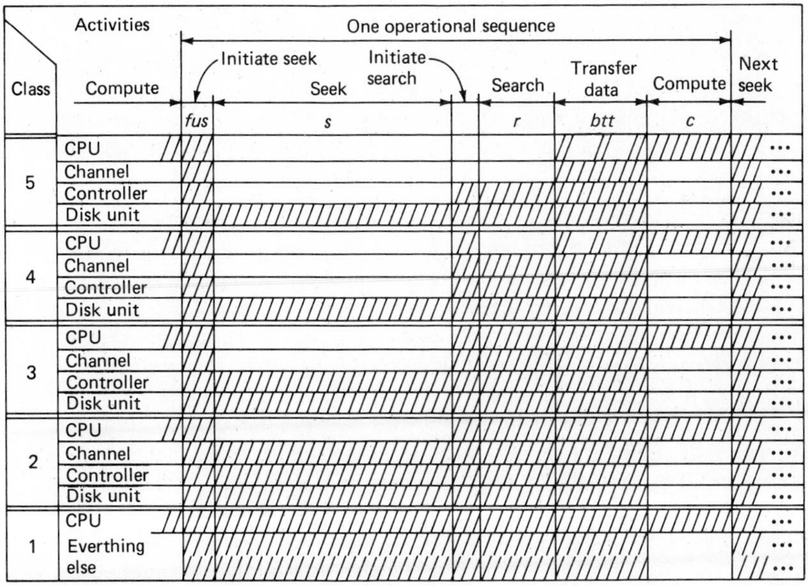

Class	Activities (Compute)	Initiate seek / Seek (fus, s)	Initiate search	Search (r)	Transfer data (btt)	Compute (c)	Next seek
5	CPU						···
	Channel						···
	Controller						···
	Disk unit						···
4	CPU						···
	Channel						···
	Controller						···
	Disk unit						···
3	CPU						···
	Channel						···
	Controller						···
	Disk unit						···
2	CPU						···
	Channel						···
	Controller						···
	Disk unit						···
1	CPU						···
	Everthing else						···

Definitions: Class 5: direct seek to block
Class 4: seek to track, controller search for block
Class 3: seek to track, CPU reads to find block
Class 2: channel searches for track, CPU reads to find block
Class 1: processor searches for track and block

Figure 5-8 System components active during storage operations.

Hardware Architecture, Simultaneity, and Parallelism We consider for simultaneous operation:

1 The processor and its primary memory, characterized by the value of c.

2 The channel connecting the disks or their controllers and the processor. A channel is busy during the period of data transfer btt as well as during initiation of the seeks (s).

3 The controller which transfers data and control signals to the disks. A controller can often signal to multiple disks as it receives control requests from the processor via the channel. We also find dedicated controllers, where one controller operates exactly one disk.

4 The actual disk drive which is busy during all of s, r, and btt.

A system is apt to have multiple disk units, so that this type of device, which is used most intensely, also is the device which can most often provide parallel operation. The capability to use multiple disks in parallel is limited, however, by the type and the number of controllers and channels available and the demands placed on them for simultaneous operation. For instance, in Fig. 5-7 no other disk can be active in parallel, since a typical channel (as **A,B**) is active simultaneously with its attached disk (as **f,i**) while data is being transferred.

In order to determine the amount of simultaneity and hence parallelism possible in a disk-system design, we recognize six possible architectures of storage systems, assigning increasing performance characteristics from class 1 to class 6. Other intermediate combinations are possible and can be analyzed similarly. Figure 5-8 sketches these architectural options. The architecture class determines the hardware components active during the several constituents (seek, block search, data transfer, and computation) of an operational sequence.

In the least powerful systems (*class 1*) the processor itself, the channel (if any), the controller (if any), and the disk are fully occupied during any disk operation from the beginning of the seek until the last byte has been transmitted. The processor may be less than fully involved in slightly more sophisticated machines, but its functions may be restricted by frequent control or data-transfer demands. Most microprocessors fall into this class, although microprocessor systems may employ multiple processors and dedicate some to the tasks identified with controllers and channels. Such a system may then be assigned to one of the higher classes.

If the processor only initiates the seek, and the channel, with the controller, executes the seek, then opportunities for simultaneous operation of more than one channel become possible. In such a *class 2* system, however, the processor is required to locate the appropriate block, and hence is tied up during the rotational latency time. If the file system designed for some application often reads blocks sequentially, without seeks, the computer time available will be small, which in turn limits the benefits of multiple channels.

If the channel is not required during the seek (*class 3*), control messages can be transmitted between the CPU and the controller, so that multiple controllers can be started and seek simultaneously.

In a *class 4* system, the channel, after being instructed by the CPU, can search for the proper block and then transmit data to memory. During data transfer the CPU is slowed only somewhat by memory-access interference. In this type of system, the channel, however, is fully tied up during the rotational latency and transfer time.

If the controller accepts combined track and block addresses (*class 5*), then the use of the channel takes place only at the initiation of the combined seek and block search sequence and during transmission of data. We assume that systems of this complexity use *cache memories* for active computations so that memory access interference is negligible.

We reserve *class 6* for systems having direct communication between controllers and CPU, which will allow seek operations to be initiated even when the channel is busy. The importance of this alternative will be discussed later.

In multiprocessor systems each of the machines may fall into one of these classes. Only one active processor will carry out the CPU tasks for one request. Memory interference may occur if memory is shared among processors. Other aspects of computer system architecture also affect performance but are not captured by this classification.

5-4-3 Estimating Demand by Constituent

In order to evaluate the effect of simultaneity, we have to make an evaluation separately for each constituent: seek s, latency r, block transfer btt, and computation c in each of the terms T_F, T_N, etc. This will provide a measure of the demand for each component type. In the previous derivations of the performance measures we have actually been careful to express the parameters T correctly in terms of their constituents, so that we now can safely dissect the earlier results. We will use here the symbols s, r, btt, and c also as subscripts to distinguish the various aspects of the demand parameter q.

For the seek load

$$q_s = L_F s(T_F) + L_N s(T_N) + L_U s(T_U) + \cdots \qquad \text{5-4}$$

or in a more general notation

$$q_s = \sum_{h1} L_{h1} s(T_{h1}) \qquad \text{for} \qquad h1 = F, N, U, Z, \text{ etc.} \qquad \text{5-5}$$

where $s(T_{h1})$ denotes the seek component of the performance parameter.

Similarly, we can evaluate the total time spent for the rotational delay constituent, for the data transfer constituent, and for the processing constituent, so that for any constituent

$$q_{h2} = \sum_{h1} L_{h1} h2(T_{h1}) \qquad \begin{array}{l} \text{for} \qquad h1 = F, N, U, Z, \text{etc.} \\ \text{and} \qquad h2 = s, r, btt, c \end{array} \qquad \text{5-6}$$

Here $h2(T_{h1})$ denotes the constituent $h2$ of the operation T_{h1}. The values q_{h2} give the demand on the system for the constituent due to the load imposed in a given period.

We have not evaluated the processor component c throughout, but it is useful to carry it here in symbolic form to verify the assumptions made in Sec. 2-3-2 relative to buffering and the bulk transfer rate t'. If the final system requires multiple components to satisfy the load, the demand on c grows proportionally, so that faster or multiple processors will be needed.

In Sec. 5-4-4 we will investigate opportunities of parallel operations of various system components, in order to determine the quantity of basic operations that a computer system can deliver.

Utilization of System Components The constituents of production demand q will have to be distributed onto the components of the system in order to obtain estimates of the utilization u for the various types of components. We refer to Fig. 5-8 to obtain the conditions for the assignment of q, appropriate for the storage-system architecture. We will assume now that we have a class 5 or 6 machine. These machines provide the greatest capability for overlap of constituents. The average utilization for a disk includes all but the computation time so that

$$u_{disks} = \frac{(1 + fus)q_s + q_r + q_{btt}}{Q} \qquad\qquad 5\text{-}7$$

where fus denotes the fraction of time in terms of s, $\ll 1$ (shown in Fig. 5-8), needed to get the seek mechanism started. We will discuss this term in the next paragraph. The controller and channel can be evaluated similarly: the controller is free while the disk unit is seeking; the channel is active only during command and data transfer

$$u_{controllers} = \frac{fus\, q_s + q_r + q_{btt}}{Q}$$

$$\qquad\qquad 5\text{-}8$$

$$u_{channels} = \frac{fus'\, q_s + q_{btt}}{Q}$$

If $s \gg r$, the controller can control multiple disks simultaneously without creating a bottleneck. If $s + r \gg btt$, the channel can control multiple controllers with active disks simultaneously without creating a bottleneck. The term fus' will take into account the control traffic when $s + r \ggg btt$. For the processors

$$u_{processors} = \frac{q_c + fus\, q_s}{Q} \qquad\qquad \langle\text{computational load}\rangle\ 5\text{-}9$$

If we do not have accurate data on processor usage, we go back to our assumptions about buffering, where we stated that we expect that $c\,Bfr < btt$ (Eq. 2-22), so that we can state initially

$$u_{processors} < \frac{q_{btt}}{Q} \qquad\qquad \langle\text{buffering constraint}\rangle\ 5\text{-}10$$

Effect of Interference between Control-Information Transfer and Data Transfer The factor fus above accounts for the time it takes to transfer the control information from the processor via the channel to the disk unit. Control information is required to initiate a seek, notify the processor, or perform address or key verification on cylinders and blocks.

In a class 6 machine, there is a data-independent path for such control information via each channel to the controllers. The dotted line in Fig. 5-7 indicates this control flow path. All that is required here is the transfer of a few, (pc), pointers of size P, and if the same transfer rate applies to such control information as applies to data, then for each seek

$$fus' = fus\frac{pc\,P}{t} = btt\frac{pc\,P}{B} \ll btt \approx 0 \qquad\qquad \langle\text{class 6}\rangle\ 5\text{-}11$$

In the other architectural classes, control information has to share the path used to transfer data, and hence the seek requests will be blocked when the channel is busy with data transfers. We consider that

1 The seek frequency is q_s/s.

2 The channels are busy with data transfer q_{btt}/Q of the available time.

3 The average delay when encountering a data transfer activity is $\frac{1}{2}btt$.

Then, in a period Q, the sum of the delays encountered when attempting to move seek commands to a controller or disk is the product of these three factors. To obtain fus' in terms of the seek load q_s, as fus is used in Eq. 5-8, the delays and the base load from Eq. 5-11 give a factor

$$fus' = \frac{q_s}{s}\frac{q_{btt}}{Q}\frac{1}{2}btt\frac{1}{q_s} + fus = \frac{btt}{2s}\frac{q_{btt}}{Q} + pc\frac{P}{t} \qquad \text{5-12}$$

With large values of btt, i.e., large blocks, fast seeks, and active channels, this factor becomes quite large, perhaps adding 25% or more to the seek delays. We find that large block sizes can have significant detrimental effects on the total channel capacity in class 3, 4, or 5 machines. This secondary demand on channel capacity is frequently unjustifiably neglected, and has surprised people who expected better file performance from their systems.

An extreme case is the IBM implementation of ISAM on a 360-type computer. The entire process of following the overflow chain is carried out by a loop in the channel-control program. This reduces the load on the CPU but makes any shared access to other devices on the same channel during this period impossible. Multiplexing capability has been introduced into the channel on the 370 series machines to mitigate this effect.

In this section we have distributed the constituents of the demand over the appropriate hardware-component categories: disks, controllers, channels, and processors. We still can expect to find that the disk component is as heavily loaded as the estimate on the entire system originally indicated, since the disk units are required for all constituents of file activity. We have not yet determined the extent of the beneficial effect of multiple disks, channels, or processors.

5-4-4 Load Distribution among Parallel Components

Having *parallel components*, that is, multiple units of the same type, permits sharing of the load assigned to the type of device. For instance, if there are two channels, each channel can be used to transmit data up to its own capacity, and it appears that the system's data-transmission capability could be doubled. If there are four disk units, some of them can be seeking and others transmitting data, again greatly increasing the aggregate capability of the system.

Two factors have to be considered when an evaluation of the increase of system performance due to parallel components is to be made

1 The design of the applications has to distribute the service demands equally over the parallel components.

2 The interference between simultaneous requests has to be assessed.

We will deal with both issues. The problem of interference is the one which can be formally addressed. The initial application load distribution requires much judgment.

Application Load Distribution The distribution of the load over parallel storage components has to balance the data quantity and the access rates to the data. Load balancing takes place at several levels.

Parallel user activity Users who work during the same time period can have their private files assigned to distinct devices.

Parallel file activity Files used simultaneously by one application can be assigned to distinct devices. This technique is common in sort programs.

Distribution of file fragments Fragments of a file, for instance, multiple indexes or pointer lists, can be placed on distinct devices, and the computation which accesses these subfiles can initiate multiple processes to permit parallel utilization.

The discussion which follows will treat the assignment problem in the aggregate sense, and the result can be applied to any level above.

If there is no access load problem, the data files may simply be distributed so that the storage space is well utilized. If we have *dev* parallel devices, the objective will be to

$$ud_i \approx ud_j \qquad \text{and} \qquad D = \sum_i ud_i \qquad \text{for} \qquad i,j = 1,\ldots,dev \qquad\qquad \text{5-13}$$

where ud_k is the data storage volume assigned to component number k of the component type being considered. The total storage requirement D is estimated as shown in Eq. 5-1.

If the access utilization u_{comp} of any system component of type $comp = \{disks, controllers, channels, processors\}$ is high, the designer will have to consider first of all the distribution of the access load. If the *dev* parallel devices $comp_i$, $i = 1,\ldots,dev$ are of equal performance, the distribution will attempt to make uc_i equal.

$$uc_i \approx uc_j \qquad \text{and} \qquad u_{comp} = \sum_i uc_i \qquad \text{for} \qquad i,j = 1,\ldots,dev \qquad\qquad \text{5-14}$$

To achieve this objective in practice, the files which receive a higher access load are placed on distinct components, and files which are less critical are distributed subsequently according to the storage capability left on the devices. Optimal placement of files within a disk unit is considered in Sec. 6-3-2.

In systems having parallel components of dissimilar performance (perhaps there are some fast disks and some are larger but slower), the rule of Eq. 5-14 is modified to consider a differential performance factor pf, now

$$uc_i/pf_i \approx uc_j/pf_j \qquad\qquad \text{5-15}$$

since the faster device $(pf_i > pf_{average})$ can handle a larger fraction of the load. This rule could be further refined to consider the actual constituent $h2$ (see Eq. 5-6) leading to the difference in performance among parallel components.

In practice, application loads are not known precisely in advance. The optimal distribution during one period will be different from the optimum a few hours or a few minutes later, and uncertainty about the time patterns can further upset the design of a system. Assignment of loads for optimal usage may hence be deferred to a time when the operation of a database has achieved a level of demand and stability so that measurements can be made to relate the load, demand, and utilization factors L_{h1}, q_{h2}, and u_{comp}.

Increased loads may also lead to the acquisition of additional disks, channels, and processors. It might even be desirable to get more disk units than are needed for data storage in order to spread the load among more devices.

The most dramatic solution to inadequate performance is an increase of the number of processors in the system. The change from one to multiple processors may involve major changes in the operating system, and its evaluation requires a separate assessment. Once several processors are being used in parallel, further increments of processors should have no deep repercussions and can be considered as any increase in component count.

When more devices are added to a system a redistribution of the utilization is always in order. It is important that file and database systems provide the flexibility to carry out the reassignments required to keep a database operation at a near optimal level.

If no satisfactory balance of utilization can be found, *replication* of files or file fragments may be called for. This will of course increase the storage demand and the update requirements, since now multiple copies have to be kept up to date. With the increase of storage devices come typically additional controllers, channels, and possibly processors. As indicated earlier, there is a strong interaction between replication and having multiple processors. Replication becomes easier but is also often needed to keep the demand on communication among processors within bounds.

The extent of benefits from load distribution is not easy to predict. There may also be many other constraints on channel assignments, storage assignments of file-organization components, separation of indexes, and so forth, which work against optimal distribution.

Interference of Parallel Loads   Even after the utilization over similar components has been explicitly balanced, we find that at any instant of time the distribution of demand is such that on some components $comp_i$ multiple requests are queued, while other components remain idle.

The extent of parallel utilization is limited by the number of simultaneous processes pr which request services from the components. In the worst active case $pr = 1$ and only one of the parallel components will actually be active. No parallel operations are enabled, even though parallel components are available.

When a large number of processes generates requests, the probability of simultaneous usage of parallel components increases, but even here no even distribution will be obtained, since the requests from the processes for the device will interfere with each other.

The actual operational sequences on this level of detail are difficult to analyze. Very simple models have, however, produced results which match the observed performance of simultaneous access to parallel components very well.

We assume that the processes request services from one of the *dev* components at random. All components have an identical performance ($pf_i = 1$). The request intervals are regular. Let us consider initially $pr = 2$ processes (P,Q) and $dev = 2$ devices (A,B). Four (dev^{pr}) combinations are possible and each of the 4 cases is equally likely

a: (P→A,Q→A), b: (P→A,Q→B), c: (P→B,Q→A), d: (P→B,Q→B).

We do not have to consider here which device receives the most requests. We are concerned with the delays occurring because a request cannot be satisfied while a parallel request needs the same device, and with a complementary issue: a device remains idle whenever none of the requests addresses it.

We find in the example above that in 2 out of the 4 cases (b,c) the distribution is good (both devices are being used) and in 2 cases (a,d) there is interference. During interference no parallelism occurs, and 1 of the 2 devices will be idle. The fraction of idle devices in these 4 cases is $fr_{idle} = (2 \times 1)/(4 \times 2) = 25\%$.

This interference reduces the productivity of the two disks by $fr_{idle} = 25\%$ to $Pc = 75\%$. The productivity of a single disk A would have been 100% since it would have been in continuous use. The parallel operation of the second disk B only increased the system capacity from $1 \times 100\%$ to $2 \times 75\% = 150\%$, i.e., by 50%.

If the number of processes P, Q, S,... is increased the utilization of the devices will increase. However, each process which cannot receive service will be delayed. In the example above two processes were delayed in the four cases. The average number of delayed processes is $pr_{del} = pr - Pc \times dev$. These delayed processes have to enter a queue. The relationship of queuing and delay is given in Eq. 6-28.

If the number of devices is large relative to the number of processes, interference will be reduced, but the devices will remain idle more often.

To estimate the productivity Pc of a system with parallel components a number of assumptions have to be made, and different models will affect the result. We assume here that a process, after it has had its turn, will immediately make another request and that new request is independent from the previous request. These conditions lead to a stable request pattern. More complex patterns have been explored for similar problems [Baskett76] or may be approached by simulation.

The values for the productivity Pc in Table 5-3 were derived by case analysis for the small parameters and by binomial approximations for the larger values. The values for the expected number of delayed processes pr_{del} were computed as above, $= pr - Pc \times dev$.

Table 5-3   Productivity of Systems Having *dev* Parallel Components

	Number of active processes pr												
	1		2		3		4		6		8		∞
dev	P_c	pr_{del}	P_c	pr_{del}	P_c	pr_{del}	P_c	pr_{del}	P_c	pr_{del}	P_c	pr_{del}	P_c pr_{del}
1	1.00	0	1.00	1.00	1.00	2.00	1.00	3.00	1.00	5.00	1.00	7.00	1.00 ∞
2	0.50	0	0.75	0.50	0.87	1.26	0.94	2.12	0.98	4.04	0.99	6.02	1.00 ∞
3	0.33	0	0.56	0.32	0.70	0.90	0.80	1.60	0.91	3.27	0.96	5.12	1.00 ∞
4	0.25	0	0.44	0.24	0.58	0.68	0.71	1.16	0.85	2.60	0.91	4.36	1.00 ∞
8	0.12	0	0.22	0.22	0.29	0.66	0.37	1.04	0.55	1.60	0.63	2.96	1.00 ∞
∞	0	0	0	0	0	0	0	0	0	0	0	0	0.5 ∞

We see in the table that the number of active processes pr should exceed the number of devices dev if systems with parallel components are to be more than 75% productive, but also that the number of delayed processes becomes significant. A high productivity becomes feasible only if the delays are tolerable, and for most on-line database operations they will not be.

To increase the productivity when $pr \approx dev$, queuing and buffers can be used to distribute poor short term request patterns over a longer time. However, when reading records from files randomly only one buffer can be effectively used by one read process. When writing blocks, multiple buffers can be employed and a good load distribution can be achieved. If some transactions can tolerate larger delays, a priority scheme may help.

Expected Distribution of Load   We have given above estimates for the productivity of of similar components when they are used in parallel. The model used here assumed a uniform demand pattern of the processes to the devices.

If the load per device LpD has not been explicitly balanced, the components will not receive an equal load from the processes. It is possible to analyze the expected load distribution based on a random behavior. Of interest is here the short term load distribution; the long term distribution, given uniform random behavior, will be equal for all devices.

Some values for $LpD(i/dev)$ for two and three devices are presented in Fig. 5-9, with $i = 1$ denoting the active device at any instant. The values appear to stabilize around (0.58, 0.42) and (0.50, 0.33, 0.16). The ideal values would of course have been $1/dev$ or (0.5, 0.5) and (0.33, 0.33, 0.33). These values can in turn be used to estimate a maximum utilization factor $umax(dev)$, which will limit the eventual productivity. Since the progress of transactions computation is limited by the busiest device, we find, for the limiting cases in Fig. 5-9 ($dev = 2$ and 3 parallel devices), that

$$umax(2) = \frac{1/dev}{\lim_{pr \to \infty} LpD(1/2)} = \frac{0.50}{0.58} = 0.86$$

$$\text{and} \quad umax(3) = \frac{1/dev}{\lim_{pr \to \infty} LpD(1/3)} = \frac{0.33}{0.50} = 0.66$$

5-16

It is better to measure the imbalance of a system to find $umax$ rather than use Eq. 5-16, since the statistical assumptions necessary for this or other analytical results can be quite unrealistic. File-access counts may be obtained by installing utilization-monitoring devices on the computer hardware. Other measurements can be obtained as part of operational statistics of the computer accounting system.

For a new system measurements cannot be taken and the estimates given above may be used as an initial design point. When hardware or its usage is unusual, simulation of the system may be required. If a reasonable facsimile of the system exists, some simple measurement programs can be used to obtain values of the maximum activity. These techniques are particularly important in a multiprogrammed environment.

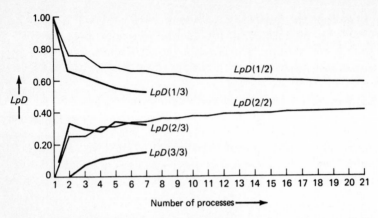

Figure 5-9 Random load distribution.

Load distributions seen in practice match approximately the pattern of LpD shown above if known and obvious imbalances are accounted for. It may, for instance, be wise to exclude logging or archival devices, and their assigned load. Figure 5-10 shows a long-term measurement of a file system which had actually been balanced. The test was designed so that $c \ll r, s$, so that the condition that the processes have high request rates was true. The imperfect long-term distribution may not affect the short-time distribution greatly since it is likely that at busy periods the files were used in a randomly balanced pattern. The fact that a component does not carry its "fair" share all the time cannot be helped unless the system can be scheduled in a rigorous lockstep fashion.

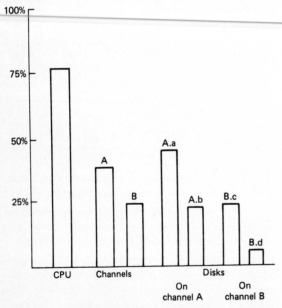

Figure 5-10 System measurement: utilization of components (data from an IBM VS evaluation).

Knowledge of disk, channel, and processor utilization based on machines using similar hardware and software architecture can provide further guidelines for prediction of realizable exploitation levels. If load imbalance, interference, or generally low productivity of a system is an issue of concern, operational data should be obtained for analysis.

It is obvious that adding more devices to a system does not increase the system capability in a linear fashion. it is, however, desirable to be able to have many processes available in order to utilize the available devices effectively.

We indicated earlier that queuing does increase the response time to requests. Techniques to evaluate the effect of queuing and also the effect of more complex service request distributions on file systems are presented in Chap. 6.

Application of Interference Effects The productivity factors from interference can be used to correct the utilization of the multiple disks, controller, channel, and processor components *comp* initially estimated in Eq. 5-14. We first apply the productivity factor to all component types having multiple ($dev(comp)$) units.

$$up_{comp(i)} = \frac{uc_i}{Pc(pr, dev(comp))} \qquad \text{for} \qquad i = 1, \ldots, dev(comp) \qquad \text{5-17}$$

Given the prediction of the imbalance of the load as distributed to the components, it is now possible to state conditions for each device type which are requisite for the system to operate satisfactorily,

$$up_{disk} < umax(dev_{disk})$$
$$up_{channel} < umax(dev_{channel}) \qquad \qquad \text{5-18}$$
$$up_{processor} < umax(dev_{processor})$$

Here much smaller margins apply than were needed in Eq. 5-3, since now inequalities of load distribution and the observed productivity is taken into account. If these conditions are not adequately met, a change to the hardware or to the file-system design has to be made and another iteration of the analysis is required.

The critical periods evaluated above occurred during daytime processing of transactions. It is still necessary to verify that other operations can be carried out when scheduled. It would be a pity if a user cannot inquire into a system in the morning because the reorganization, scheduled for the night, did not complete in time. The performance parameter for reorganization, T_Y, can be used without further modification. If the reorganization time is excessive, alternate file designs will have to be considered. In very large systems techniques which allow incremental reorganization may have to be used.

5-4-5 Sharing of Facilities

We have assumed, in the analyses to this point, that the database operation was the only user of the hardware facilities. This is rarely the case, although there are many instances where database operations dominate. In an environment where the major use is related to the database, and especially in systems where the database transactions have priority, the effect of the other tasks will be minor. It can be quite profitable to share the processing capability of a system with other users which have lower priority, but who still will receive many computational cycles, since the typical on-line database operation has to have an excess of computational capability in order to be responsive. If the data-storage units are shared, some interference may result.

If the database function is not the major part of system operation, several assumptions made previously are not valid.

Processor Competition In a heavily shared environment, the condition that $c < btt$ for the file operations will not guarantee that the file system will process sequential data without losing rotational latency because of other computational demands on the processor. Processor usage by tasks which are active at the same time will reduce the share of the processor available to the database computation, so that conditions for continuous data transfer may not be met. This will double or triple the response time when using files as shown in Eqs. 2-22 to 2-24.

Disk Competition If there is active use of the same disk units by different computations, the probability of having to precede every read sequence with a seek s will be high. In this case, a conservative estimate would associate every block fetch with a seek operation, greatly decreasing the expected performance due to decreased locality. In particular, Get-next operations and exhaustive searches may be affected. The advantages of certain file designs cannot be obtained under these conditions. Where separate disk units and channels are reserved for the database function, the interference may be small. It may be profitable to reduce the degree of multiprogramming in order to achieve better utilization on specific tasks. This might actually increase the overall throughput.

Measurement A pilot system which models the various file transactions within the existing computing environment can provide at a modest effort useful performance estimates. The performance data obtained will be compared with those expected in an isolated operation, which are derived theoretically. The ratio provides us with multiprogramming factors, M_h,

$$M_h = \frac{\text{measured performance of } h}{\text{computed performance of } h} \qquad\qquad 5\text{-}19$$

for each of the basic processes h which are part of the database computations. These factors may range in practice from 1 to 0.1.

Such tests do not require the existence of the entire, or even any, database. The pilot study consists of the execution of a proper sequence of random or sequential read or write operations, together with a comparable amount of CPU usage. A program to mimic the proposed operation can often be written and executed, on the actual system to be used, at the cost of a few days of effort. The availability of the system is, of course, crucial, and the test has to be made during typical and high-usage periods of the system functions with which the database will be sharing the resources.

Such a test is not equivalent to a full simulation study, where all computations, as well as the hardware, have to be parameterized and simulated.

Multiprogramming Alternatives The use of the database may itself require multiprogramming in order to serve multiple concurrent computations. This is, for instance, the case if a number of terminals are used for update or retrieval. The operation of one terminal can affect all the others.

Transaction-oriented systems are organized to minimize multiprogramming losses. The strategy is to attempt to finish current transactions before initiating new, possibly conflicting, ones. A transaction in progress may have the privilege of reserving a disk device until the task is completed or until the task frees the disk voluntarily. A transaction computation performing an extensive search has to be programmed by a responsible rather than by a competitive programmer and yield the device at regular intervals.

In multiprogramming and timesharing systems designed to support only scientific or engineering computations, no facilities may have been provided to hold disks to task completion, since their system objective is a fair distribution of capabilities rather than an overall system optimization. Here measurement or a worst case evaluation is needed to establish the multiprogramming factor.

The initial system-design choices made in Sec. 5-3 have to be adjusted in order to bring the utilization parameters into acceptable ranges, so that:

$$up_h < M_h umax(dev_h) \qquad\qquad 5\text{-}20$$

holds for all system components h.

5-4-6 Cost versus Capacity

At some point an adequate system configuration for the expected load and performance has been found. The file organization is also defined. This process will typically take several iterations.

It is now necessary to verify the validity of the design for a low and high level of load to be expected in the future. This can reveal problems as shown in Fig. 5-11. For application S the system design A is optimal; for application T, B is appropriate. At the average value of application U, design A is optimal, but it becomes prohibitive at the high point of the load range.

If we choose for application U system A, we will do well if the estimates of load are accurate or high. If the load grows, or the initial estimates were low, the conversion to another design has to be made. If this possibility is not foreseen, its occurrence will be embarrassing. If system B is chosen, the system operates at excessive cost until the load reaches the crossover point. The best alternative is to redesign the system so that effects of miscalculation or poor forecasting of the load will be neither fatal nor costly. The desired relationship had been achieved for applications S and T. The combinations of basic file methods and the selection of alternative hardware should make it possible to design a file system C equally appropriate for application U. The curves shown for file systems A and B are smooth representations of more realistic cost curves as presented in Fig. 5-6 which described storage system costs alone. This allows the cost of the system to be expressed in terms of the load placed on the system without getting bogged down in detailed discussion of hardware or implementation choices. Many of those

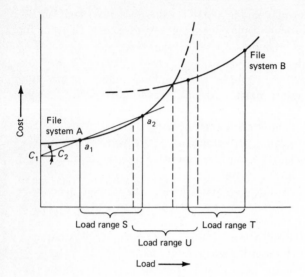

Figure 5-11 Cost versus load curves.

choices are in fact best deferred until operational experience has been gathered. The presentation of a cost versus load curve will make observers aware of incremental costs and limits, and hence is more satisfactory than such a statement as, "Another million dollars will solve our problems".

It is desirable to express incremental cost within the range of the load. Figure 5-11 shows this being done for application S by drawing a line through points a_1 and a_2. The angle at C_2 provides the rate as cost per unit load. Now the costs can be presented as

$$cost = C_1 + C_2 \times load \qquad \text{between } \min(L_S) \text{ and } \max(L_S) \qquad 5\text{-}21$$

While this final performance summary is not directly relevant to the system design, it is essential to provide to management the cost-to-load ratio which enables computer-acquisition decisions to be made in a manner analogous to the making of decisions in other business areas.

We have employed some greatly simplifying transformations and assumptions. Some experience is required to judge their effects in specific cases. Simplifications, however, are in common use in any situation where the need exists to provide understandable models of complex, *real-world*, relationships.

5-5 COST-BENEFIT COMPARISON

In the preceding sections, we have shown a general approach to the estimation of benefits, evaluated the storage costs, and verified that the computer system, or at least its file components, were adequate in terms of capability to handle the expected load. The latter analysis may have to be carried out repeatedly in order to achieve an acceptable solution.

We now combine the results of these sections and present them in a fashion which is related to basic business-economic terms.

5-5-1 Revenue versus Cost

A business which sells consumer goods places a price on its goods and expects to receive an income directly proportional to the amount of sales. Such a revenue curve is shown in Fig. 5-12a. Only a business in a monopolistic position will not be able to increase revenues by increasing sales and will have to resort to other tactics in order to boost income.

At the same time costs increase as production increases from a fixed basis at a zero production level. Some of this cost increase may be linear, that is, directly associated with quantity, as would be the cost incurred for supplies consumed in manufacturing. Other costs will increase less in proportion to quantity owing to efficiencies of mass production. The cost associated with sales will tend to increase somewhat faster with quantity since, after an initial demand is satisfied, more effort is required to convince additional customers. A sample of cost curves is sketched in Fig. 5-12b, and their total is presented in Fig. 5-12c.

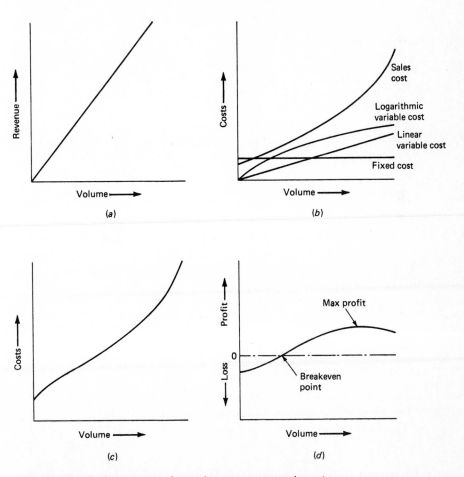

Figure 5-12 Basic manufacturing revenue and costs.

From the revenue and cost curves, a profit and loss can be derived which shows the break-even quantity, and the volume where the maximum profit as obtained (Fig. 5-12d).

In the information-selling business, the projection of costs and revenues is based on system capability and utilization. While the cost figures will be similar, the evaluation of benefits of an information system is more complex. An understanding of relevant factors is necessary when we wish to appraise the viability of a database system.

Benefits of Information We discussed the benefits earlier in some of the factors which control the realization from a database system. In order to relate benefits to costs, we can consider as factors the quantity of data available and the intensity of the use of the database. Figure 5-13 sketches some of these general considerations.

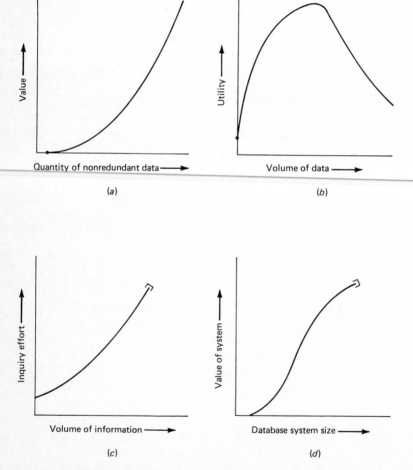

Figure 5-13 Benefits of information.

Information theory states that the information content of a nonredundant set of data increases exponentially with the quantity of data (Fig. 5-13a). In practice, redundancy will also increase with volume in order to maintain accessibility and this will reduce the rate of increase. The curve shown also takes into account that users have some prior knowledge, so that small data quantities have negligible information value. On the other hand, we find that as information increases, our ability to improve decisions does not keep pace. Most of the decisions made in enterprises are based on incomplete knowledge and yet appropriate to the general situation. Frequently statistics of relatively small samples can provide adequate answers with high reliability. This decrease in practical utility may have an effect as sketched in Fig. 5-13b.

In order to extract any information out of the database, it has to be queried and processed. Extracting more from the database requires more frequent or more complex inquiries. The effort to retrieve information will increase more steeply than the amount of applicable information obtained, as shown in Fig. 5-13c. The cost to process data is often proportional to $n \log n$, where n indicates the data quantity. When the value which is returned to the users diminishes to the point that it is no longer an effective application of their effort and funds, they cease to inquire further.

When all these factors are combined and displayed, relative to database-system size, the *revenue* curve may be of the form shown in Fig. 5-13d. The actual shape and the values will differ from application to application, but we notice the disparity between benefits from the sale of information and the sale of goods shown as Fig. 5-12a.

5-5-2 Costs

The cost of the storage facilities is a major component of file-system cost. There are many instances where the potential value of data is less than the minimal cost of storage. Consequently, one will want to verify that we can afford to store the data that we wish to process. In data storage there are often some economies of scale as was seen in Fig. 5-6. The marginal costs of additional storage can be obtained as Cm in Fig. 5-14, which presents the same data in smoothed form.

Charging for Storage When marginal costs are used to justify expansion or new projects, the fact that a low charge based on marginal cost hides a large basic storage expense Cd must not be forgotten. If earlier projects are charged at a higher marginal cost for data storage, unhappiness is sure to arise. If the unhappiness causes earlier projects to stop or atrophy, then the marginal cost of the later projects increases so that charges have to be increased. Now everybody is unhappy. A charging rate Cp based on strictly proportionate rates has the problems that does not reflect marginal costs well and leads to losses until the load exceeds capacity CP and to excessive profits thereafter. A desirable compromise can be a charging rate Cb which matches costs over a large fraction of the operating range. This will leave an amount Ce uncovered by storage charges, which will have to be obtained as a surcharge on database processing or data entry.

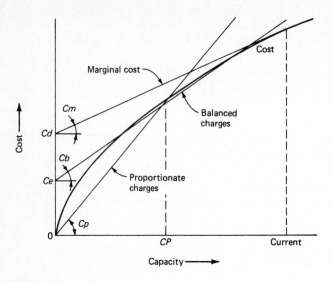

Figure 5-14 Marginal storage costs.

Companies which provide database services tend to use a balanced charging approach, since this encourages users to store data on their systems, which in turn will encourage data analysis. Companies which sell computer services tend to use the proportionate charging method, since they view file storage as an auxiliary service to the user which must pay its own way. Large databases are rarely found on such systems, although some companies have invested in database programs for their users.

Cost of Processing The processing costs for a given computer system have to be viewed in terms of performance. The addition of devices, such as channels and disks, increases the processing capability of a system, but the increase in capability is less than proportional. Increased interference, inability to distribute the load evenly, and dependence on specific critical components all combine to decrease performance beyond a certain usage volume.

Different systems may have different performance curves, but their shape will remain similar, as shown in Fig. 5-15. Systems **B** and **C** may have equal costs but differing processing and storage-arrangement algorithms, so that **B** is better at a relatively low load, but **C** outperforms **B** at a high load. System **A** would be attractive only if the cost is sufficiently less so that the performance difference does not matter.

The difference in these systems leads to different productivity. Productivity is a measure of benefits obtained taking into account that the performance must be realizable (Sec. 5-2). The result is shown in Fig. 5-15b, which combines the effect of increased productivity in terms of requests processed, and the negative effects of poor system performance.

Since there are just about infinitely many systems of equal cost, as **B** and **C** in the figures, then for every load a system could be chosen which would optimize

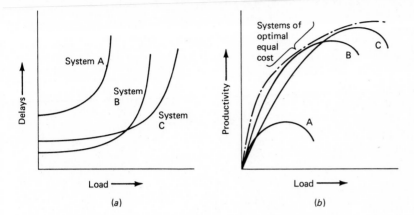

Figure 5-15 System performance versus load.

productivity. The dashed line indicates the envelope describing the set of these optimal systems.

This information can also be presented on the basis of system cost for a given load. Cost-performance curves have been presented by measuring existing, rather than optimum, systems. It has been shown that the raw hardware (mainly CPU) performance increases steeply with cost. A rule of thumb, referred to as Grosch's law, has been that,

$$\text{Computer performance} = C_G \text{ cost}^2 \qquad \text{where } C_G \text{ is some constant} \qquad 5\text{-}22$$

and this rule has been verified on IBM equipment of the early 360 type using a variety of scientific problems [Solomon[66] and Knight[68]]. There is, of course, the possibility that IBM used Grosch's law to determine its equipment prices, since it must be nearly impossible to relate prices to costs for a large integrated company. For data-processing operations, however, the same machines showed

$$\text{Data-processing performance} = C_G \text{ cost}^{1.5} \qquad 5\text{-}23$$

which still indicates advantages of scale, but to a lesser extent than seen in scientific computation.

The rule is less applicable to file-oriented and interactive systems, since it does not account for interference or for loss of productivity due to poor performance at the user terminal. While it is easy to concentrate on a single aspect when analyzing computers, it is obvious that in the more modern systems, raw processing power only indirectly increases throughput. Since file capability is governed more by design decisions than by computer equipment performance alone, software and its implementation become increasingly important. Interference among multiple computations is another area not solved by more powerful hardware. No satisfactory rules are available to decide how many functions a designer should provide within one system.

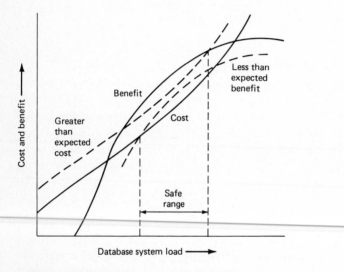

Figure 5-16 Total costs and benefits.

5-5-3 Summary

If we now combine the three elements: benefits, storage costs, and processing costs, and plot them only over the limited range of interest, we may generate cost-benefit lines as shown in Fig. 5-16.

When benefit and cost curves are similar in shape, the lines are relatively parallel. Parallel lines indicate that small errors in cost or benefit estimation will have a great effect on the range within which the system is profitable or effective. This example presents an undesirable but not unusual operation. Good documentation of the design effort and its parameters is essential, in order to be effective in manipulating the outcomes represented by these curves.

In practice, the cost picture gets even more complex because of discounts, special deals, and peculiar amortization methods. From a technical point of view, these anomalies are best disregarded and left to the financial staff to be dealt with independently of the system design. It is rare that the benefit of *good deals* exceeds the long-range cost of suboptimal system design. In order to make such issues clear, processing personnel have to be able to produce sensible and understandable numbers when they wish to present their views.

People outside of the computing clique often perceive correctly that many justifications for computer systems are only technical mumbo jumbo.

BACKGROUND AND REFERENCES

The process of system design, evaluation, and acquisition brings together people with technical, financial, and managerial orientation. In such a mixed environment clarity of expression, and measures which seem objective, are important communication tools. Graphical presentation can often help to present expectations, but can also be used to hide simplified assumptions. Brooks[75] presents much insight and data regarding the design process. A basic reference on the economics of computers is Sharpe[69]. Davis[74] and DeMarco[79] present a management-oriented approach. Davis[82] introduces a number of papers oriented toward requirement analysis of enterprises.

Wiking[71] and Lucas[73] prescribe the evaluation of information systems and Lucas[75] considers the feedback in between user benefit, usage, and performance. Alford[77] considers real-time constraints. Sevcik[81] presents a layered technique of load modelling. Robey[82] defines the stages of system development. A language for expressing requirements is presented by Ross[77].

Human factors are cataloged by Martin[73]; an important study is Reisner[77]. The subject has its own journal (*Human Factors*), published by the Human Factors Society in Santa Monica, CA. Important background in this area is provided by Sterling[74,75]. A conference on the subject was sponsored by the National Bureau of Standards (Schneider[82]). The cost of errors is discussed by Stover[73]. Morey[82] considers those errors that are due to delays. Arden[75] contains a number of papers on operating-system aspects of interaction and provides a useful bibliography.

Cost estimates used for projections change rapidly with time. At times projections are incomplete, for instance, reductions in mass-storage costs are projected (Copeland[82]) but the studies do not consider what is happening to processing and software costs. The spread of small computers has confused the picture greatly.

Most implementation descriptions consider benefits and costs, but the data are often difficult to compare. Some references are cited in Chapters 1, 9, and 10. Batteke[74] has details of a benefit evaluation in water management. Boyd[63] analyzes benefits in a manufacturing system, and Loo[71] describes the real-time needs for airlines. King[78] provides a survey of development tradeoffs.

The structure of file-system hardware is presented by Hellerman[73] and analyzed by Madnick[69]. Teorey[78] analyzes parallelism of disimilar components. Distributed systems designs were looked at by Peebles in Kerr[75] and Morgan[77]. Streeter[73] found few reasons for distribution.

Formal procedures to select file structures have been developed by Schneider in King[75], Hammer in Rothnie[76], Katz in Chen[80], Yao[77], and Whang[82]. File-method selection can be aided by FOREM (Senko[73]). Waters[74] describes the decision points. Cardenas[79] surveys file design, access structures and analyzes multi-attribute use and selection for partial-match queries. Gambino[77] presents a model for multiring file design. Lowe[68] and Long[71] analyze text files.

Ramamoorthy[70], Arora[71], Parkin[74], Lum[75], and Trivedi[81] evaluate distribution over a hierarchy of components of differing performance, and Major[81] derives the complexity measure. Chu[69], Hoffer in Kerr[75], and Du[82] evaluate the optimal allocation of files to multiple components. Lin[82] considers disk allocation in a local network. Chen[73] and Piepmeier[75] provide optimization policies to balance the load distribution over multiple devices. Dearnley[74M,O], Stocker[77], and Kollias[77], as well as Hammer[77], have done work on automatic optimization of file allocation. Marron[67] trades processing cost versus storage cost.

Interference problems are presented by Atwood[72] and analyzed by Omahen in Kerr[75]. Berelian in Merten[77] considers the effects of paging in a multifile database. Siler[76] and Baskett[76] provide results of straightforward evaluation models which show the limitations of benefits obtained by distributing files over multiple devices. Measurement of database operations is described by Krinos[73], Huang[74], Sreenivasan[74], and Heacox in Kerr[75].

Miller[70] has developed decision procedures for the acquisition of large computer systems. Applications of decision-analysis techniques are presented by Easton[73]; Keith in Cuadra[70], Langefors[73], and Miyamoto in Kerr[75] have models for evaluation of information systems. King[81] addresses general evaluation issues. Grosch's law has been tested by Solomon[66] and Knight[68]. McFadden[78] summarizes cost and benefit issues.

EXERCISES

1 a Write a proposal to install a data base system in some application area you know. Do a good *selling job*.

b Write a critique of such a proposal from the point of view of someone who will be negatively affected in some sense by the system.

c Now prepare an evaluation to management that lists the arguments for and against as fairly as possible, and then summarizes in management terms the decisions which have to be made by management in order to evaluate the value of the proposal. Assume that you are a private consultant.

2 Describe some of the costs and benefits of the *least* useful file system, including manual data collections, that you have encountered.

3 Using the manufacturers' description of a hardware file system, determine which class (Sec. 5-4-2) of file architecture it belongs to. Then evaluate the software system provided and see whether all the potential of the architecture is available.

4 An inquiry system has 3000 daily requests into a direct file of 50 000 records, each of 250 bytes. When a record is brought into core storage it has to be available for an average of 5 seconds. The system is used 8 hours per day, 300 days per year. A 2314 type disk is used for the file. Determine the minimum-cost file design. Included are the hardware cost ($200/day), the disk storage, and the buffer memory.

Chapter 6

Techniques

But then chiefly do they disdain the unhallowed crowd, as often with their triangles, quadrangles, circles, and the like mathematical devices, more confounded than a labyrinth, and letters disposed one against the other, as it were in battle-array, they cast a mist before the eyes of the ignorant. Nor is there wanting of this kind some that pretend to foretell things by the stars, and make promises of miracles beyond all things of soothsaying, and are so fortunate as to meet people that believe them.

Desiderius Erasmus (1509)
  on philosophers, from "The Praise of Folly"

Chapters 1 through 5 have shown the process of file system design. In order to be able to proceed with a minimum of interference, techniques used for their analysis have been ignored, and some of these will now be presented in a brief fashion.

In the design of database systems, the analytical techniques to be applied are derived from work in areas beyond the prime subject of this book. Many important tools are available from the field of statistics. In order to apply statistical techniques, the distribution patterns of the events which are to be analyzed have to be understood. A typical collection of events is the service demand placed on the file system. The lengths of fields in variable-length records will also show a certain distribution pattern. Section 6-1 discusses types of distributions which are frequently encountered and applies basic statistical tools to some file problems. Section 6-2 introduces simulation as a means to obtain performance estimates. A high level of demand for service leads to delays and generates waiting lines or queues which are discussed in Sec. 6-3. Some aspects of queuing theory and other disciplines from the area of operations research are touched upon in Sec. 6-4.

As the subject of file systems is brought to a close, the area of databases using multiple files begins to be of interest. A resource which is shared among files is the storage space in the computer systems, and the techniques used to allocate free space to files are the subject of Sec. 6-5.

The objective of this chapter is to demonstrate the availability of well developed tools which should be in the satchel of a serious database designer. Many relationships are presented already in programmed form, to make the techniques easy to use.

The casual reader may skim over the topics in this chapter and proceed to the second half of this book, which will introduce concepts beyond the file-structure level.

6-1 STATISTICAL TECHNIQUES

The process of analysis and design often can make use of information collected from the observation of the operation of related systems. Statistics provides a means to summarize and simplify the detailed data. The results which are obtained allow transfer of the experience to improved or new systems.

In order to apply statistical techniques, a number of sequential activities are required:

1 The process being analyzed has to be understood.
2 Parameters which affect the operation will be listed.
3 Data about the operation will be collected, displayed with the relevant parameters, and the cause of variations in the data values explained in terms of the parameters used.
4 Transfer functions will be developed to permit the application of the collected information to new systems.
5 The validity of the transfer will be tested in the new setting.

We will touch lightly on these points in the process using examples from database applications. The actual knowledge of statistics should be obtained from a course or textbooks in this area. The section is kept simple so that a background in statistics is not needed to follow the arguments.

Model and Parameters In the preceding chapters the use of basic parameters and their function in the operation of file systems have been explained. If the system being observed is described in the terms used throughout this book, then this description provides an adequate model. The basic operational parameters are often difficult to measure, and performance measurements taken often represent the combined effects of many parameters. The power of the use of statistical techniques is that observations of complex and random phenomena can be analyzed if the underlying model is understood. The results obtained can be used for further system development.

6-1-1 Typical Demand Distributions

In the preceding chapters many problems were analyzed in terms of averages. There is an inherent danger in these evaluations, unless we realize that average records and average files are as rare as average people. In most instances where averages were used, the measures obtained were reasonably robust, that is, not greatly affected by a certain amount of variation from the mean or average value. Unless rigidly constrained, however, the observed values of items such as record length, field length, and inquiry frequency will deviate from the mean.

Measurements of varying data taken are often profitably presented by graphical techniques suitable for data exploration. Data presented as a histogram can show the frequencies of occurrence of events, classified by value type. We say that the histogram presents a *distribution* of occurrences. For this short summary all values on the ordinate are considered to be frequencies and values along the abscissa to be categorized values of events. If there is no variation, all events will fall into the same column of the histogram, and we have a *constant* distribution.

A number of possible distributions are sketched in Fig. 6-1. We will describe conditions which lead to these distributions and then describe their behavior.

Data from file system operations can be sampled and plotted for data exploration. When frequencies of events are finely categorized, the graph will often have the shape of one of the popular distributions. Rarely will the match be exact, but if events show consistent patterns, the rules associated with the matching distribution type can be used to develop appropriate analysis tactics.

How Distributions Happen   *Uniform distributions* in which all the events considered are equally likely to occur are obtained when simple independent events are categorized. Uniformity may be obtained through truncation of high-order effects. The latency time when accessing a drum, given that the time between references to the drum c is many times greater than the revolution time for the drum $2r$, is apt to be uniformly distributed.

Uniformity of record distribution into a direct file minimizes interference and collisions. Truncation of high-order effects is the idea behind many of the key-to-address transformations discussed in Sec. 3-5. The remainder-of-division method typifies this approach.

Normal distributions occur naturally when the events being measured are the sums and products of many independent actions, and the events have a constant probability p of occurrence. The normal distribution is, in fact, the limit of the binomial distribution, used to calculate the probabilities of discrete events, which is reached as the number of samples f tends to infinity. If the product $fp > 15$, the normal curve becomes an adequate approximation.

Let a file consist of blocks with a fixed number f of records of two different sizes which occur with equal probability ($p = 0.5$). If $f > 30$, the expected total space used for the f records will be normally distributed. If the distribution of the record length varies uniformly, the normal distribution is an adequate approximation with even fewer records per block. Records whose lengths are distributed according to other symmetric distributions will also appear to be normally distributed when taken together.

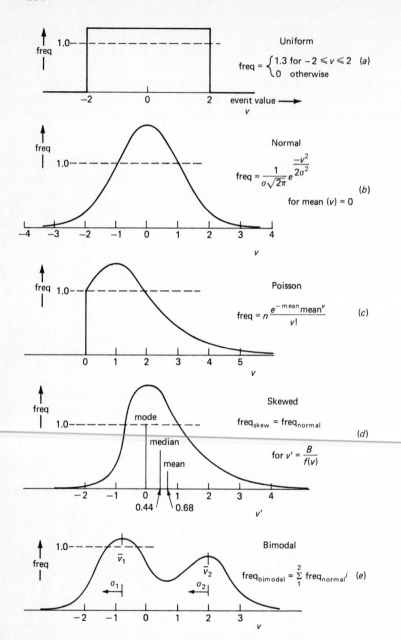

Figure 6-1 Popular distributions.

To visualize what happens, we can use a record type which can be 30, 40, or 50 bytes long, with equal probability, and then construct a sequence from three of these records. The sequence can be from 90 to 150 bytes long as shown in Fig. 6-2a, where each of the 27 possible record arrangements has been drawn. Each sequence has equal probability. Figure 6-2b presents the distribution of record lengths ($p = \frac{1}{3}, \frac{1}{3}, \frac{1}{3}$) and of the total lengths ($p = \frac{1}{27}, \frac{3}{27}, \frac{6}{27}, \frac{7}{27}, \frac{6}{27}, \frac{3}{27}, \frac{1}{27}$),

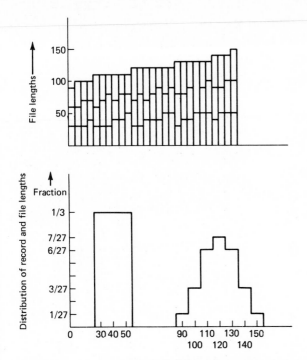

Figure 6-2 How normal distributions come about.

and it can be seen that even with this small aggregation of values from a discrete uniform distribution, the total begins to look like a normal distribution.

If the record lengths are already normally distributed, the sequence lengths will be normally distributed for any number of records.

Exponential distributions occur when the probability of values of a series of event types increases or decreases rapidly as the event values increase. Increasing exponentials are difficult to manage in models and in reality. An example of such disconcerting behavior in databases is the number of interconnection possibilities among its elements, and hence the time required for thorough checking of a complex database; the time required for sorting also goes up more than linearly with file size.

Negative exponentials decay initially quite rapidly, but then reach their asymptotic value of zero slowly. An example is seen in Fig. 6-3. Distributions of a similar shape arise when measurements of terminal requests and of access frequencies to records of files are made. These are best described by the Erlang and Zipf distributions noted in Sec. 6-1-6.

Figure 6-3 shows the distribution by date of charges for hospital services which have not yet been settled. Bills older than 18 months (August a year past) are either turned over to a collection agency or written off. A total of 94 048 bills were outstanding. The distribution has the form of a negative exponential, as shown by the curve fitted to the data using visual comparison on a display screen. The long tail of this distribution is handled through the imposition of an arbitrary cutoff date.

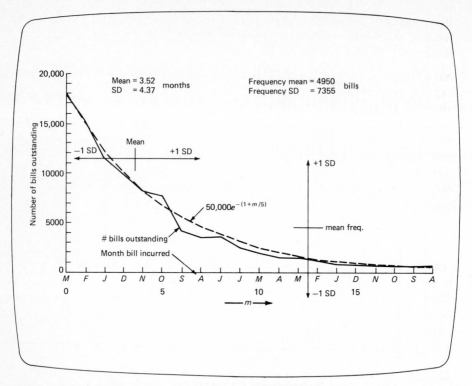

Figure 6-3 Distribution of outstanding bills by date.

A negative exponential distribution is typically generated by a succession of mutually dependent events of the same probability. In Figure 6-3 it appears that the probability of a customer paying an outstanding bill is about 20% every month. Negative exponential distributions are also found when the times between random arrivals of service requests are displayed. Exponential and Erlang distributions are important when queues of service requests are analyzed.

Poisson distributions occur when important contributing events have a small probability. This distribution is the limit of the binomial distribution for the case where the likelihood of a particular event is small. The Poisson distribution become a valid approximation when $f > 25$ while $fp = mean < 5$. When the mean becomes large ($fp > 30$), the peak is sufficiently away from the left boundary that a normal distribution can be used to approximate the Poisson distribution. It should be noted that Poisson distributions which have a mean value of less than one do not show the initial rise shown in Fig. 6-1 but decline immediately and hence look similar to exponential distributions. For a moderate sample size, the Poisson distribution diminishes more rapidly than the exponential to the asymptotic value of zero. A Poisson distribution is typically caused by independent events, whereas an exponential distribution occurs more often where successive events are related.

As an example of a Poisson distribution we take the overflow file from an indexed-sequential file organization. The expected number of overflows per block is 1.33 insertions (ranging from 0 to 6) for a file of 400 blocks, as shown in Fig. 6-1c. The probability of a block being updated is only 1/400 per insertion, and fp is 1.33.

It can be shown that for events which have an exponential interarrival-time distribution, the number of expected arrivals in a given time period has a Poisson distribution.

Skewed distributions occur whenever nonlinear transformations affect the outcome of events. A distribution as shown in Fig. 6-1d can represent the number of records *Bfr* in a block. Since the operation $Bfr = B/R$ is not linear for R, the normal distribution of record sizes R is distorted. Skewed distributions are characterized by the fact that their mean occurs at a different point than their median; the median is the value with equal number of observations to either side; in Fig. 6-1d the mean is at 0.63, but the median is 0.44. Yet another measure of *central tendency* is the mode, the position of the most frequent value, here at zero. For moderately skewed distributions,

$$(mean - mode) \approx 3(mean - median) \qquad\qquad 6\text{-}1$$

This can provide a quick estimate of the median from the mode and the mean, which are easier to compute.

Bimodal distributions occur when the events being measured are due to two separate underlying phenomena. An example is the response time for queries, where some can be answered by using an index and others require an exhaustive reading of the file or of a subset of the file.

Cumulative Distribution Function　Often a frequency distribution is used to obtain an estimate of the fraction of cases exceeding a certain limit. For each distribution shown a *cumulative distribution function (c.d.f.)* can be obtained by summing or integrating the frequency distribution from the left. The height of the curve is directly proportional to the number of events occurring with values less than the corresponding value. A few c.d.f.s are shown with their source functions in Fig. 6-4. Table 6-1 and Fig. 6-15 use c.d.f.s to predict the fraction of desirable or undesirable events.

These cumulative distributions may also appear in the system measurements, since often only the aggregate effect is observed. Differencing or differentiation of these functions can be used to re-create frequency distributions. Skew, multiple modes, etc., are more difficult to recognize when they occur in c.d.f.s instead of in frequency distributions.

6-1-2 Describing Distributions

When the result of a measurement generates a distribution, a similarity to one of the distribution types shown will provide some clues about the process causing this distribution. As a next step, some quantitative measures can be obtained. Two basic parameters useful with nearly any observed distribution are: the *mean* **xbar** and the standard deviation *sigma* σ of the observations, given f samples **x(1),x(2),...,x(f)**. In order to have an unbiased estimate these sample observations should be a random sample of the events. For the standard deviation we will use the symbol σ in equations, but **sd** in program examples.

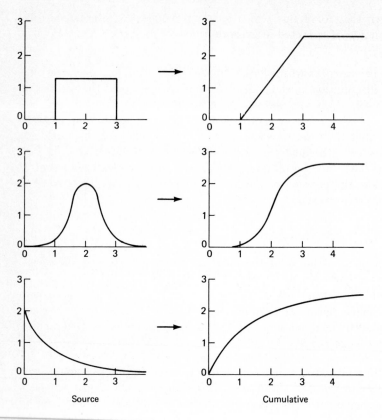

Source   Cumulative

Figure 6-4 Cumulative distributions.

For any collection of observed events we can compute the *mean* and σ parameters:

```
/* Mean (xbar) and Standard Deviation (sd) of array x */ /* 6-1 */
     xsum,xsqsum = 0;
     DO i = 1 TO f;
         xsum = xsum+x(i);
         xsqsum = xsqsum+x(i)**2;
     END;
     xbar = xsum/f;
     sd = SQRT((xsqsum-xsum**2/f)/(f-1));
     ...
```

The number of samples f should be large enough that we can have confidence that
the sample set used is representative of the events occurring within the system. Any
of the statistics texts referenced can be consulted for tests which provide measures
of confidence. A *chi-square test* will be used in an example in Sec. 6-1-5.

6-1-3 Uniform Distribution

If a distribution looks flat or uniform over a range of values, many estimation tasks
are simplified. A uniform distribution of events has often been assumed in examples
in the earlier chapters, since the uniform distribution often gives a relatively poor,

and therefore conservative result. A uniform distribution of addresses of seek requests to a disk will cause a higher average seek time than all but a bimodal distribution. The probability that a next record is not available in the current block is greater for a uniform distribution of requests than for any other. The average cost, however, of following overflow chains is lower when update insertions were distributed uniformly and greater for nonuniform update distributions.

A uniform distribution is described by its height, that is, the frequency of occurrence of categorized events, and by its range, which has to be finite for a finite number of events as shown in program segment 6-2 below

```
/* Parameters of the uniform distribution */              /* 6-2 */
     height = f/number_of_categories;
     range = MAX(x) - MIN(x);
```

The size and the value for each category icn = 1, ..., number_of_categories can be computed as

```
/* Create histogram categories for the frequency distribution 6-3 */
     size_of_category = CEIL(range/(number_of_categories-1));
     base = FLOOR(MIN(x));
     category_low_value = base + (icn-1)*size_of_category;
```

The CEIL and FLOOR functions are used to improve the presentation of the data in a histogram.

If an investigation is made to determine the amount of cylinder overflow for a direct or indexed-sequential file, then f may be the number of records, and the number_of_categories may be the number of cylinders allocated to the file. The expected mean and standard deviation of samples which present a perfectly uniform distribution are

```
/* mean and sd of a uniform distribution */               /* 6-4 */
     xbar_uniform = range/2;
     sd_uniform = SQRT(range**2/12);
```

If the observed xbar and sd from program segment 6-1 do not match these values well, other distributions should be considered.

Even if the parameters match well, the observed frequencies will vary about the expected height, so that it may be desirable to analyze how good the fit is. In the example, variations can cause the capacity of some cylinders to be exceeded. The frequency distribution can be plotted from an array fx, filled from the observed values x as follows:

```
/* Compute the frequency histogram of observed values */   /* 6-5 */
       DECLARE fx(number_of_categories);
       fx = 0;
       DO i = 1 TO f;
           ifr = CEIL((x(i)-base)/size_of_category);
           fx(ifr) = fx(ifr) + 1;
       END;
```

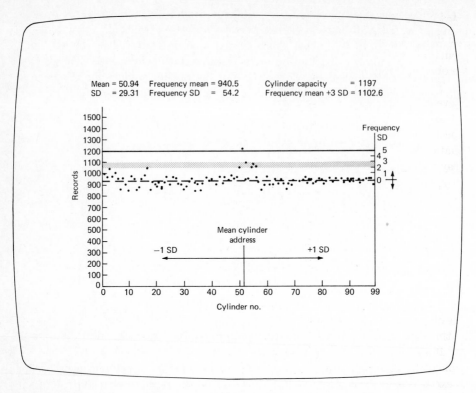

Figure 6-5 Test of uniformity of an algorithmic key-to-address transform.

Computing the standard deviation of the frequencies, `sdfreq`, and obtaining a value which is small relatively to the height or mean frequency indicates a satisfactory degree of uniformity. Sample values will be based on a file to store the billing data shown in Fig. 6-3.

Example 6-1   Creating a Uniform Distribution for Direct Access

In order to use fast direct access to the billing file for the numerous inquiries, while keeping the file in chronological order, a sequentiality-maintaining, exponential key-to-address transformation, based on the inverse of the cumulative distribution function, was investigated. The file was to be stored on 100 cylinders, each with a capacity of 1197 records, so that $m = 119\,700$, for $n = 94\,048$. The key-to-address algorithm computes a cylinder address for a given date, taking into account the weekends, which have lower billing rates. The name of the person billed provides the record address within the area allocated to the date. Figure 6-5 shows the distribution of records over cylinders.

The expected frequency is 940.5 per cylinder. The resulting distribution is quite uniform, with some irregularities due to the fact that the low-order cylinders are affected by the many recent bills generated on single days and also by irregular billings from some holidays. Only one cylinder overflow occurs with this sample. Further analysis is needed to determine the rate of block overflow, given the distribution of names and buckets of 63 records using blocks of 14\,000 bytes. The results are shown in Fig. 6-5.

6-1-4 Normal Distribution

The difference of observed and expected frequencies can often be expected to be a normally distributed variable, since it is based on many independent samples from the observed events.

To describe a normal looking distribution found in array **fx**, the mean value of events **xbar** and the standard deviation **sd**, as computed in program fragment 6-1 are the descriptors. Using these two parameters from the observed values an expected normal distribution can be generated for comparision purposes. Using the equation for the normal curve, programmed for **f** observations we obtain values in array **xnf** which should match the values **fx**, if the distribution was indeed normal.

```
/* Expected Normal Frequency Distribution Function  xnf      6-6 */
    scalefactor = f/(sd*2.5066283);   /* 2.5066283 = sqrt(2*pi) */
    shapefactor = -0.5/sd**2;
    DO i = 1 TO number_of_categories;
        category_center_value = base + (icn-0.5)*size_of_category;
        xnf(icn) = scalefactor*EXP(shapefactor*
                (category_center_value-xbar) **2);
    END;
```

The observed frequencies at **x(i)** can be compared with the values **exp(i)** generated by this function.

If a distribution is approximately normal, many useful estimation rules can be applied. In file design, it is often desirable to estimate how often a certain limit will be exceeded; for a distribution which is approximately normal, the cumulative area of the normal curve beyond the limit provides the desired estimate. Table 6-1 lists some of these values in terms of t, the difference between the mean and the limit in terms of the standard deviation σ.

Table 6-1   Normal One-Tail Probabilities

t	p(*value* > *limit*)	
0	0.500	$limit = mean + t\sigma$
0.25	0.401	
0.50	0.309	
0.75	0.227	
1.00	0.159	
1.25	0.106	
1.50	0.067	
1.75	0.040	
2.00	0.023	
2.25	0.012	
2.50	0.006	
2.75	0.003	
3.00	0.0013	
4.00	0.00003	
5.00	0.0000007	

It can be seen that events of value greater than the $mean + 3\sigma$ are quite rare.

In Example 6-1 the frequencies can be tabulated, and this provides a mean of 940.5 records per cylinder with an σ of 54.2. It takes $+4.73\sigma$ to exceed the cylinder capacity of 1197. For a normal distribution this is expected to happen less than once in a million cases, but the distribution of bills per cylinder is not quite normal, and one overflow was found in 100 cylinders, as shown in Fig. 6-5.

Even when data are truly normally distributed, rare events can, of course, still happen; in fact, the high activity rates in data-processing systems can cause rare events to occur with annoying regularity.

Block Overflow Due to Record Variability When the normal distribution was introduced, the statement was made that distributions, when summed, become more normal. This phenomenon is known as the *the central limit theorem*. In the example which follows that rule will be applied to the problem of packing records into blocks for the tree-structured file evaluated in Example 4-8(**1b**).

In order to pack fixed length records effectively into one block, the capability of a block in terms of record segments was computed.

$$n_{block} = y - 1 = \left\lfloor \frac{B - P}{R + P} \right\rfloor \qquad\qquad 6\text{-}2$$

In Example 4-5 $B = 1000, R = 180, P = 4$, so that $n_{block} = 5$. A certain number of characters per block remained unused. We will name this excess G' and find that

$$G' = B - P - n_{block}(R + P) \qquad\qquad 6\text{-}3$$

Here $G' = 76 \approx R/2$.

These files are designed to always place n_{block} entries into a block, so that $G' < R$. The file-space usage for fixed-length records is most efficient if $G' = 0$.

If the records are actually of variable length, the distribution of R has to be described. A normal distribution may be a reasonable assumption if the average length is sufficiently greater than the standard deviation; otherwise, record-length distributions tend to be of the Poisson type. To make a choice its best to look at a histogram. When assuming normality the distribution is determined by the value of the mean record length *Rbar* and the standard deviation σ.

Example 6-2 Fixed Space Allocation per Record

Given that the average record is still 180 characters long, with a small standard deviation σ of 20 characters. We allocate all the space in the block to the records ($G = 0$), providing $(B-P)/n_{block} - P = 195.2$ characters of space for each record. The parameter t of Table 6-1 defines the space between mean and limit in terms of the σ:

$$t = \frac{195.2 - 180}{20} = 0.75$$

Table 6-1 shows that 22.7% of the records will not fit into their allotted space.

Sums of Normally Distributed Values In practice variable-length records will be packed together within a block, so that space not used by one record will be usable by other records. The relative variability of a sum is less than the variability of individual items, so that we can expect that the possibility of overflow will be less. For a fixed number n_{block} records per block, the parameters for the entire sequence of records in a block are

$$mean_{block} = n_{block}\,mean_{record} \qquad\qquad 6\text{-}4$$

$$\sigma_{block} = \sqrt{n_{block}}\,\sigma_{record} \qquad\qquad 6\text{-}5$$

Because of these relationships, if the ratio of extra space is the same, the overflow probability is less

$$t_{block} = \sqrt{n_{block}}\,t_{record} \qquad\qquad 6\text{-}6$$

Example 6-3 shows the effect of having $n_{block} = 5$ and 11 records per block.

Optimization of Allocation for Variable-Length Records It is sometimes wise to use a value of n_{block} which is less than the value computed based on the average, in order to reduce the probability of overflows further. In dense files overflows can be costly and using some additional space can provide a good trade-off. Example 6-3 shows this effect too, using small variable-length records.

Example 6-3 Allocation of Variable Length Records to a Block

If 5 records with the same behavior as those of Example 6-2 share a block, then

$$t_{block} = \sqrt{n_{block}}\,t_{record} = \sqrt{5} \times 0.75 = 1.68$$

From Table 6-1 we find that the overflow probability is less than 6.7% (actually 4.7%) versus the 22.7% for single record slots.

To demonstrate the space versus overflow tradeoff we will use the same standard deviation $\sigma = 20$ used in Example 6-2, but with smaller records ($R = 66$ vs. 180) so that the effect will be even more pronounced. The values used are based on Exercise 4-12.

Given that $n = 10\,000$, $B = 762$, the average record length $R = 66$, then an initial value of $n_{block} = \lfloor 762/66 \rfloor = 11$, and the number of unused characters per block $G' = 762 - 66 \times 11 = 36$. The total file will occupy $b = \lceil 10\,000/11 \rceil = 910$ blocks.

Given the σ of 20 per record the σ_{block} for the sequence of 11 records is $20\sqrt{11} = 66.33$ and the $mean_{block}$ is $11 \times 66 = 726$ characters. Now $t = 36/66.33 = 0.54$ and Table 6-1 indicates that the probability of overflow is about 29.5% per block. If we allocate and link an overflow block to each overflowing primary block $910 \times 0.295 = 269$ additional blocks will be required. The total used for this file is 1179 blocks.

If only $n_{block} = 10$ entries are placed in every block, then 1000 primary blocks are needed instead of 910, but 102 characters are available to cope with the variability of the length of the entries. This makes $t = 1.54$ and reduces the overflow to 6.2% or 62 blocks. The net saving in this case is $1179 - (1000 + 62) = 117$ blocks. There will also be a proportional savings in expected access time.

A further reduction to nine entries reduces the overflow probability to 0.61% but requires a total of 1118 blocks instead of 1062. The expected access time will still be slightly reduced.

6-1-5 The Poisson Distribution

Poisson distributions occur due to independent events. The shape of the Poisson distribution is fully described by the value of the mean of the observations, since in this distribution the mean and the variance are equal. The variance is the standard deviation squared σ^2. To avoid introducing another symbol for the variance, we will use σ^2 or sd**2 as appropriate. To compare an observed distribution with the curve describing a Poisson distribution, the corresponding values can again be computed. Program segment 6-7 computes expected values for event counts from 0 to 20 following a Poisson distribution.

```
/* Poisson Distribution for 21 Categories  */          /* 6-7 */
        DECLARE expfr(0:20);
        expfr(0) = n*EXP(-mean);
        DO ov = 1 BY 1 TO 20;
            expfr(ov) = expfr(ov-1)*mean/ov;
        END;
```

A sample problem is tabulated in Example 6-4, which shows the observed distribution of insertions and the equivalent Poisson probability computed by program segment 6-7 given above. When the two columns are compared, a Poisson distribution appears likely.

Example 6-4   Poisson Distribution of Insertions for an Indexed-sequential File

There were 550 insertions into a dense indexed-sequential file of 400 blocks. These insertions caused $0, 1, 2, \ldots$ overflow records to be written for each of the blocks. The mean number of insertions per block is mean $= 550/400 = 1.38$. The expected frequency is computed for n=400.

No. of overflows ov	Observations		Expectations
	Frequency fr(ov)	Records ov×fr(ov)	Frequency expfr(ov)
0	101		101.4
1	138	138	139.1
2	98	196	95.6
3	45	135	43.8
4	11	44	15.1
5	5	25	4.1
6	2	12	0.9
7	0	0	0.2
...	0	0	...
	400	550	400

The events which lead to this distribution are such that a Poisson curve is indeed likely: the distribution is the sum of many events, each with a low probability, and the probability for events in high-numbered categories tends to zero.

Testing for Goodness of Fit A more formal test to determine if a distribution fits the data can be made using the *chi-square* function. The *chi-square*, or χ^2, test compares categories of observations and their expectations, but each category should contain at least one expected sample. To avoid invalid categories, the Poisson values of less than 1 can be grouped with the last good category as follows:

```
/* Poisson Distribution with Grouping of Low Frequencies    6-8 */
    DECLARE expfr(0:20);
    expfr(0) = n*EXP(-mean);
    left = n-expfr(0);      /* number of blocks for assignment */
    prod = expfr(0)*mean;
    DO ov = 1 BY 1 WHILE(prod<ov);     /* ok if next expfr > 1 */
       expfr(ov) = prod/ov;
       left = left-expfr(ov);
       prod = expfr(ov)*mean;
    END;
    last_category = ov; /* used in program fragment 6-9 below */
    expfr(last_category) = left;
```

The observed values are summarized in a histogram **fx**, as done in program segment 6-5. The cells of low expected value are combined into the last category. Then the chi-square values are computed. The results are seen in Example 6-5.

```
/* Combine tail values of observed frequency histogram    6-9 */
    DO i = last_category+1 TO number_of_categories;
       fx(last_category) = fx(last_category) + fx(i);
    END;
```

```
/* Computation of Chi-Square Value for Goodness of Fit    6-10 */
    chisquare = 0;
    DO ov = 0 TO last_category;
       dif = fx(ov)- expfr(ov);
       chisqterm = dif**2 / expfr(ov);
       chisquare = chisquare + chisqterm;
       PUT DATA( ov, fx(ov), expfr(ov), dif, chisqterm);
    END;
    PUT DATA( SUM(fx), SUM(expfr), chisquare);
```

Example 6-5   Testing a Poisson Distribution

ov	fx(ov)	expfr	dif	χ^2term
0	101	101.1	0.1	0.001
1	138	139.1	1.1	0.009
2	98	95.6	2.4	0.060
3	45	43.8	1.2	0.033
4	11	15.1	4.1	1.113
last	7	5.3	1.7	0.545
$n =$	400	400		$\chi^2 = 1.761$

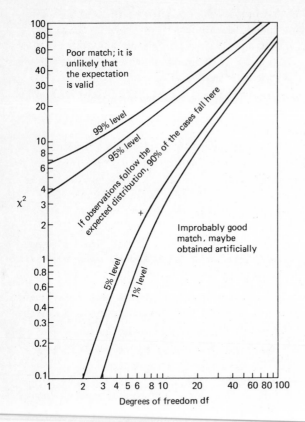

Figure 6-6 Standard chi-square distribution.

Values obtained for χ^2 can be compared with standard values, which are based on the assumption that the difference of distributions was caused by random events. These standard values for χ^2 can be computed as needed using approximations of binomial distributions or can be found in statistical tables and graphs.

Figure 6-6 presents the standard χ^2 distribution in graphical form. In order to use the χ^2 distribution, the number of degrees of freedom df has to be known. Where we distribute our samples over a specific number of categories c, df will be equal to $c - 1$.

The value for χ^2, 1.761 at a $df = 5$ for the indexed-sequential file observations shown in Examples 6-4 and 6-5 falls within the area of Fig. 6-6 appropriate for most cases which match an expected distribution. The point is close enough to the good side that it seems likely that the changes are not quite random, but somewhat uniform. Perhaps many of the insertions are due to some regular customer activity.

A very high value of χ^2 makes it unlikely that the frequencies are related; a very low value could cause suspicion that the data are arranged to show a beautiful fit. The chi-square test is useful when distributions are being compared. Other tests, as the *t-test* and *F-test*, can be used to compare means and standard deviations obtained from samples with their expected values, if the distribution is known or assumed to be known.

Collision Probability   To derive Eq. 3-72 in Sec. 3-5, use was made of a relationship which gave the probability of occurrence of collisions in direct access slots given n entries into m slots. This result will now be derived using the tools developed.

Each record has a probability of $1/m$ of being assigned to any one slot. The probability for one slot to receive q records is given by the binomial distribution

$$P_b(q) = \frac{n!}{q!(n-q)!}\left(\frac{1}{m}\right)^q\left(1-\frac{1}{m}\right)^{n-q} \qquad \text{6-7}$$

For the case that $n \gg 1, m \gg 1, q \ll n$, we can approximate this expression by the Poisson distribution for the mean density n/m:

$$P_b(q) = e^{-(n/m)}\frac{(n/m)^q}{q!} \qquad \text{6-8}$$

$P_b(0)$ is the probability of the slot remaining empty, and $P_b(n)$ is the (very small) probability of this slot receiving all n records (see again Fig. 3-19). If q records appear in one slot, causing $q-1$ overflows, then the number of accesses to fetch all these records, which form one sequential chain, will be

$$0 + 1 + 2 + \ldots + q - 1 = \tfrac{1}{2}q(q-1) \qquad \text{6-9}$$

Taking the sum of all the $P_b(j), j = 1 \ldots n$, multiplied by their cost in terms of disk accesses, gives for any one slot the expected access load AL

$$AL_{slot} = \sum_{j=0}^{n}\frac{j(j-1)}{2}P_b(j) \qquad \text{6-10}$$

The successive terms of the Poisson distribution are related to each other by the iteration

$$P(j) = P(j-1)\frac{mean}{j} \qquad \text{6-11}$$

The mean is here n/m, so that using the Poisson distribution for P_b

$$AL_{slot} = \frac{1}{2}\frac{n}{m}\sum_{j=0}^{n}(j-1)P(j-1) \qquad \text{6-12}$$

Since at $j = 0:\quad P(j-1) = 0 \qquad$ and at $j = 1:\quad j - 1 = 0$

$$\sum_{j=0}^{n}(j-1)P(j-1) = \sum_{j=2}^{n}(j-1)P(j-1) = \sum_{k=1}^{n}k\,P_b(k) \qquad \text{6-13}$$

where $k = j - 1$. The expected record load RL per slot is the mean which in turn is equal to the cumulative frequency distribution, specifically the sum of the products of the number of records per slot i and the probability of the occurrence of the event $P(i)$

$$RL_{slot} = \frac{n}{m} = \sum_{i=1}^{m}i\,P(i) \qquad \text{6-14}$$

and when $m \approx n$ the series terms are equal, so that the expected increase of accesses for overflows due to collisions per record p is

$$p = \frac{AL}{RL} = \frac{1}{2}\frac{n}{m}$$ 6-15

If multiple records ($Bfr = B/R$) can be kept in a *bucket*, the probability of another record entering a slot can be predicted using $P_b(q)$ as derived above. The number of buckets will be m/Bfr and the number of collisions per bucket will be higher. There will be no overflows, however, until Bfr records have entered the bucket, so that the cost of accessing overflows AL becomes less. For this case Johnson[61] derives similarly,

$$p = \frac{1}{2}\frac{n}{m/Bfr}\sum_{k=Bfr-1}^{n}(k-Bfr)(k-Bfr-1)P(k)$$ 6-16

Of course, the processor's computing effort cix to search within one bucket increases now. An evaluation of this effect in indexed files is given in Sec. 4-2-4.

Collision Expectations for Direct Files The results obtained above can be further developed to give the expected overflow space requirement or the average overflow chain length LC due to collisions. These can then be compared with observations from the operational file.

The probability of a slot being empty was approximated by the zero term of the Poisson distribution so that

$$P_b(0) = e^{-n/m}$$ 6-17

The probability of a slot of the primary file being used is then

$$P1u = 1 - e^{-n/m}$$ 6-18

and the number of records in the primary file is then $m\,P1u$, and in the overflow file is

$$o' = n - m\,P1u$$ 6-19

The overflow area contains the tails of all the Poisson-distributed record sequences. Using Eq. 6-5 for the σ of a sequence and the fact that σ^2 of a Poisson distribution is equal to the mean n/m, we expect a standard deviation of o' of

$$\sigma = \frac{n}{m}\sqrt{m}$$ 6-20

and this σ applies of course to the entire file. If an observed standard deviation is less, we can deduce that the keys are more uniform than a Poisson-distribution-based model expects and that a smaller prime or overflow area may suffice. If the observations are worse, the key-to-address transformation is not doing its job.

For a file as used in Example 3-10 (Sec. 3-5-3) $n = 1000, m = 1500$, we find $P1u = 0.49$, and expect $o' = 265$ with a σ of 25.8. This value can be compared with observed values from operational measurements.

When the buckets contain more than one record ($Bfr > 1$), the above computation can be carried out using the cumulative Poisson probability for the records 1 to Bfr being in the buckets and the records from $Bfr + 1$ to n overflowing.

Tables of the values of the mean total accesses $1 + LC_I$ are used in Knuth[73S] (page 535) to compute the length for an unsuccessful fetch leading to an insertion. The value of

$$P1u = n/m - LC_I \qquad\qquad 6\text{-}21$$

so that the same case corresponds to $LC_I = 0.18$.

6-1-6 Other Distributions

When a distribution does not seem uniform, normal, exponential, or Poisson-like to an acceptable extent, the behavior may follow one of many other functions which are available to describe distributions. An important reciprocal distribution, similar in shape to a negative exponential, is presented by Zipf's law (Eq. 14-5). This distribution is used to describe activity ratios of records and type/token ratios of words in text. Zipf's law can be viewed as a generalization of *Heising's rule*:

80 percent of accesses to a file address 20 percent of its records.

An example of its use is given in Sec. 14-3-2.

When requests arrive from users at terminals queues can form due to conflicting requests of independent users. The requests from each single user are mutually dependent, so that the total set of requests is more complex than a Poisson distribution. This behaviour is modelled well by Erlang distributions; they are presented in Sec. 6-4-1.

Some cases where the distributions are not simple can be solved by algebraic transformations of the observations until some fit to a known distribution is obtained. Reciprocal, logarithmic, and hyperbolic functions are used frequently. Observations may also be broken down by differencing or decomposed into sums or products of functions. Differentiation or taking successive differences helps to remove the effect of aggregation if the observations are some form of c.d.f. A visual display of the transformed data is helpful to rapidly establish the benefit of a transformation.

Any transformation are best based on an understanding of the underlying phenomena, so that we have some model of what is happening. In the examples shown earlier we tried to find a causal mechanism; for instance, utility customers pay in regular cycles and the hospital patients in Fig. 6-3 pay according to individual pressures. If such an empirical model fits the observations well, it can be used with some confidence for extrapolations and the design of databases that work in general and over a long term. The algebraic transformations of the observations based on the simple patient-payment model were adequate to exploit the distribution for effective direct access.

If transformations make observed data tractable, but the underlying model which generates the observations is still not understood, then much care has to be taken in applying the results. The use of many variables or of complex transformations to describe observations is apt to generate very misleading results when the values obtained after the fit for these variables are used to *extrapolate* the behavior of new systems. Empirical functions based on a few reasonable variables can be used for *interpolation*, since this procedure is less risky. Since there is a degree of arbitrariness in assigning a transformation function, subsequent testing for validity should be done with fewer degrees of freedom *df*.

Skewed Distribution   If a distribution appears lopsided or skewed, it is wise to analyze the relationships being considered for nonlinearities. It may be that the parameter being measured is some function which distorts the behavior of parameters of the model at a more basic level.

The skewed distribution in Fig. 6-1 occurred because the blocking factor *Bfr* was described for a fixed number of variable-length records per block. The underlying measure, the distribution of record lengths or the inverse $1/Bfr$, had a normal distribution.

Bimodal Distribution   A bimodal distribution as shown in Fig. 6-1 can best be decomposed by fitting two normal distributions to the data. Four parameters have to be determined: $mean_1$, σ_1, $mean_2$, σ_2. If the modes are well separated, the means can be estimated at each node and fitting of two normal curves will be simple. It helps if the σ's are equal or have a predetermined relationship. Sometimes the position of the means can be determined by alternative reasoning.

Unrecognizable Distributions   Even when the shape of the distribution does not match any known distribution, there is still a conservative statistical tool available, *Chebyshev's inequality theorem*, to describe the behavior of the variables.

Given the mean and the standard deviation, which are always computable for a set of observations, Chebyshev's inequality provides directly the probability of values from the set of observations $x_i, i = 1,\ldots,n$ falling outside of a range. The range *rg* is defined in terms of a number *c* of standard deviations σ to either side of the mean of *x*. The mean and standard deviation are computed from the observation without any assumptions regarding the behavior of the distribution. If the sample observations are not biased, then for some k

$$p(x_k \text{ not in } rg) \leq \frac{1}{c^2} \qquad \text{where} \qquad mean - c\sigma < rg < mean + c\sigma \qquad \text{6-22}$$

This relationship can, for instance, be used to state that given any observed distribution, 90% of the values will be within $\sqrt{10}\,\sigma = 3.162\sigma$ to either side of its mean. If the distribution is approximately symmetrical, we can assume that only 5% of the values exceed the $mean + 3.162\sigma$. The worst case is that all 10% of the values exceed the $mean + 3.162\sigma$.

If the distribution has a single mode and is symmetric, then

$$p(x \text{ not in } rg) \leq \frac{2}{3c^2} \qquad \text{6-23}$$

and correspondingly the probability that a value x_k of the observations exceeds the *mean* by $c\,\sigma$ is

$$p(x_k > mean + c\sigma) \leq \frac{1}{3c^2} \qquad \text{6-24}$$

For the direct file used to illustrate Eq. 6-20, the Chebyshev inequality can be used to evaluate the chance of exceeding a primary overflow area of a given size. The distribution of overflows is not symmetric, so that the worst case approximation should be used. Given was $o' = 265$, $\sigma = 25.8$, and we wish to guarantee that in all but 1% of the cases the records fit into the primary overflow area. Here

$$c = \sqrt{100} = 10 \qquad \text{and the required space} \qquad o = o' + 10\sigma = 523$$

This value is based on the sample observations. Multiple samples should be used to verify stability of the result.

6-1-7 Other Statistics

At times an observed response is a function of multiple variables. With assumption of independence among these variables we can separate the effects given a sufficiently large number of observations. Two types of analysis methods are in use for this work: multiple regression and analysis of variance. Regression analysis determines a line describing a linear relationship between the individual variables and the resulting dependent variable. Many relationships in computer systems are not linear. Analysis of variance relates causes and effects by discrete groupings and has been used to analyze the performance of paging operating systems based on the variables: memory size, program size, loading sequence, and paging algorithms. Both regression and analysis of variance assume linear relationships of the combination of independent variables on the dependent variable.

6-1-8 Help with Statistics

Many statistical packages exist to help perform the calculations. The use of graphical output can make the models being used accessible to people who are not comfortable with the numerical aspects of statistics. The understanding and modeling of the system being evaluated remains as important as the application of analytical techniques. This also means that assistance of statistical experts is of much more value when there is also expertise available about the computer system being evaluated and its applications. The actual design process cannot be delegated to specialists in a single narrow area, and neither programmers nor statisticians can be expected to provide acceptable system evaluations by themselves.

6-2 SIMULATION

When no source of data is available which can be used to predict the behavior of a new system, it may be necessary to build a scale model to generate predictive data. Such a simulation model will be based on the process and hardware to be used in reality and will be fed with a sequence of descriptions of the desired computations. The output of a simulation will not be the results of the computation, but rather measurements of parameters collected in the simulation process.

The principal components of a discrete, event-driven simulation are shown in Fig. 6-7. The input to the simulation itself is an event queue, which contains entries of events that are created external of the system being simulated, say, a request to retrieve a record, and internal events, say, a completion of a seek. The output is a log of events with their times, which can be further analyzed.

The external event entries may be generated by a program. It will use the expected distribution of external requests to make up request types and their times.

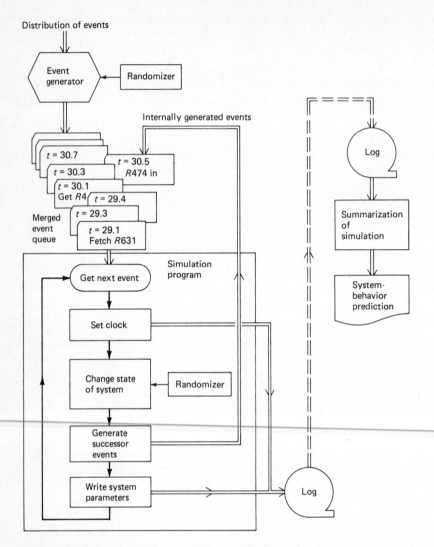

Figure 6-7 Components of a simulation.

Another source for external events may be a log file from an existing system or a synthetic program which generates event requests during its execution. Logs or programs have the advantage that they provide a standard for system testing.

The Process of Simulation A simulation has its own timing mechanism. To determine how long the simulated computation will take in real life, the simulation uses a variable `clock` to keep the simulated time. The `clock` is incremented to the next event to be simulated. An external event may specify:

"At time $= 29.1$: `Fetch Record for employee 631 ('Jones')`"

After setting the clock to 29.1 and logging the receipt of this event, the steps of the process are simulated to the extent required.

If a direct-access file is being simulated, the following steps are appropriate:

1 A block address is computed for record with key 631 using the key-to-address transform being considered. A constant value c for this operation will have been obtained earlier by a separate test.

2 The desired cylinder position is determined.

3 The amount of seek cyl from the current position is calculated.

4 The required seek time s_{cyl} is found.

5 A random latency r is generated.

6 The block transfer time btt is calculated from the transfer rate r and the block size B. It will be constant for a given system.

7 A random function based on m/n is used to determine if there is a collision, if yes go to step **2** to compute the incremental times, else

8 The completion time is computed as $29.1 + c + s + r + btt$, say, 29.4.

9 The status of the disk unit used is set to "busy".

Now an internal event is generated which states that

"At time 29.4: Record 631 ('Jones') is in core, and disk D is free"

The internal events are merged with the external events, and the simulation continues until the event list is exhausted.

When a device is found busy, the requests are put into a device queue. A "device is free" signal from the internal queue directs the simulation to look at the device queue, select a request to be processed, and simulate it. Queuing will be the subject of Sec. 6-3. Because of the existence of queues, requests may not be processed when they arrive.

A problem with simulations driven by external events lists is that there is no feedback from the system to the generator. This is fine if the process requesting services is indeed independent of the system.

An independent request function would be the distribution of flight inquiries by phone from potential passengers. If the requests are issued by airline reservation agents, however, then a poor response rate by the system response will reduce their actual rate of entering inquiries.

These nonindependent requests are best modeled internally within the simulation. A response function based on data as shown in Fig. 5-3 can be used to describe the effects of the man-machine interaction. When randomly generated events are used, multiple tests or partitioned long tests are needed to verify the stability of the simulation results.

The parameters of interest are either processed incrementally or written on a log file for later summarization. Typical parameters of interest are the total time to process all the events, the time required to process individual events, and the activity ratios of the devices used. The data obtained are again conveniently presented as histograms or described as distributions. Then predictions can be made as, "The response time to an inquiry is less than 10 seconds 90% of the time."

Writing a Simulation   The use of simulation techniques to investigate file system behavior is simplified by the large gap between processor and file speeds. Adequate results can often be obtained from a simulation which concentrates on file delays and models the computation only in a gross fashion.

In one area computational delays, other than those affecting bulk transfer, have to be considered. A large fraction of the computational overhead in file operations is due to the overhead in operating systems. Frequently several milliseconds can elapse between the execution of a CALL for service and the emitting of a command to actually move the disk arm. Mean overhead times for these operations can sometimes be obtained from manuals and are otherwise obtained by executing a large number (n) of a disk operation. The known disk processing times can be subtracted from the elapsed time, or the CPU time measurement may be available from the system. Dividing by n gives the mean service CPU time for the operation. If no paging of code occurs, this value is apt to have a very low standard deviation.

A number of simulation languages are available and have been used extensively for system simulation. The author has found that simple simulations can be written rapidly on an interactive system in any higher-level language. The simulation languages now commonly available use batch processing techniques. When a simulation becomes large, the computing time required can become a significant item in the design budget, and the simulations have to be planned carefully so that they will return an adequate benefit for the expended effort.

A simulation model which includes many variables will first be tested by changing the variables one by one to select those which have a major effect on the outcomes. Then these important variables can be evaluated by having the randomizer generate test values throughout their range, while keeping the variables which had less importance constant. When a desirable model has been found, the minor variables will be tested again in order to verify that the perceived lack of effect is also true at the final setting of the model variables.

Another approach to handle simulations of large systems is to attack the simulation hierarchically. First the cost of primitive operations is simulated, and the results are fitted to a simple mathematical formulation. These formulations are then used by simulations of more complex tasks. Several simulation levels may be used until the needed results are obtained. At each level a verification is done that the parameters used do not exceed the range simulated at the lower level, since extrapolations based on fitted functions are risky. This scheme requires some sophistication so that the mathematical abstractions from each level are viable.

6-3 QUEUES AND SCHEDULING TECHNIQUES

When a computation requests service from a device which is busy, the computation will be delayed. Since the computation should not be abandoned, the request will be noted as an entry in a queue for the device. A single process of a computation (by definition) is delayed when it requests a file operation until it gets permission to use the file. The user's requests may be issued directly by the user's programs, or indirectly by systems programs. The elements that make up a queue for a device are sketched in Fig. 6-8.

The parameters listed are vital when systems are monitored for augmentation and improvement. If the queue is being simulated, then not only these, but many other variables will be collected, so that the entire usage distribution can be reconstructed.

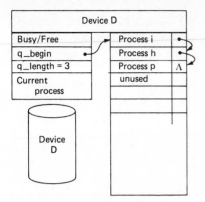

Summary parameters collected during system operation:

Number of requests for the device

Number of requests which found
    the queue empty

Maximum and average queue size when
    a request was made

Fraction of time that the device
    was busy

Figure 6-8 Elements of a queue.

Queues and Processes One computation may initiate multiple processes which will independently go to the file system to request services. The entire computation cannot proceed beyond certain joining (P) points until outstanding processes have been completed. Figure 6-9 shows the progress of a small computation, which spawns processes for each file operation. Processes which have to read data frequently require delay of computations. Processes which write data may only prevent the final termination of a computation.

Each service request in a queue is due to a request by one individual process. The sum of all the queue lengths in the system is limited by the number of possible processes in the system. This number may be quite large.

Processes, unless specifically constrained, operate asynchronously. This means it is not wise to generate a bunch of individual processes to write a sequence of blocks into a file: the blocks may not be written in the desired order. If, however, the blocks have individual addresses, a smart queue-management system will be able

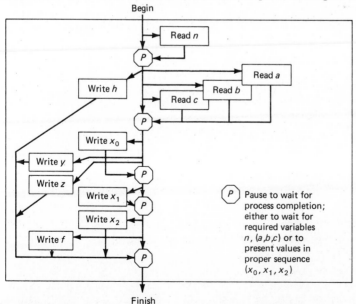

Figure 6-9 A Computation with file processes.

to write the blocks onto the file in an order which minimizes hardware delays. Every write or read process will be associated with one or more buffers to hold the data. The number of buffer lists possible limits the number of active file processes and hence the degree of parallel operation possible. The number of buffers permissible in a list limits the maximum queue length. The total number of buffers that can be assigned to all lists is limited by memory availability and in turn keeps the number and size of queues manageable.

6-3-1 Queue Management

The activities which are part of the queue management for files are sketched in Fig. 6-10. There will be at least one queue for every file device and there may be also a number of queues for other device types, all scheduled by the same *queue-management program* (QMP). The QMP is invoked either by a user, who wishes access to a device being managed by the QMP, or by the operating system, when it has analyzed that a signal for service involves the QMP.

The typical reason for the operating system to invoke the QMP is that a device has been released by the process that was holding it. Such a release is often initiated by a hardware signal which indicates the completion of the actual data transfer for device D. This will be followed by a verification procedure, after which the device D is no longer needed by the process. It can now be assigned to another process.

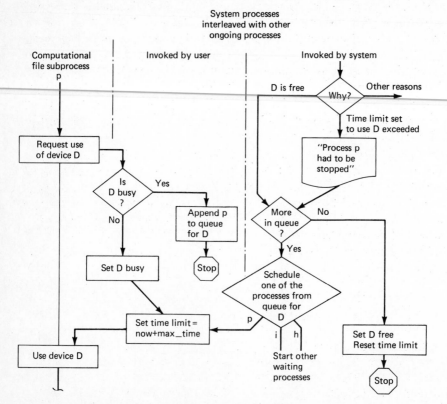

Figure 6-10 Queue management.

Occasionally, because of a failure of the hardware or of a program, a process does not release, or maybe does not even begin to use device D. If a time limit or *time-out* is set, the faulty process can be canceled when the allowed time is exceeded, and the device given to another process. In systems where no time limits are set, all computations requesting D will come to a halt, and eventually all activity of a system will cease.

Some simple transaction systems attempt to prevent time-out errors by having all file-access processes use code sections which are provided as part of the transaction operating system. This, of course, increases the complexity of the operating system itself. Excessive restrictions imposed by a system on the user for the sake of protection are indicative of an excessively weak operating system.

In order to provide space for infrequent large queues, a QMP may share the space for all queues active in the system, using linked-list structures. In interacting systems the queues for a few devices are often long, while other queues are empty. The monitoring of queues is important when systems are to be tuned for best performance. Queues may be created dynamically when a new resource is added to the system.

When more than one process is waiting in the queue for the device, one of these processes has to be selected. The selection or *scheduling* of service requests from a queue is the topic of the remainder of this section.

6-3-2 Scheduling from a Queue

The scheduler selects one of multiple candidate processes, which are waiting for service, for execution. The scheduler is the big diamond-shaped box in Fig. 6-10. It is invoked by the queue-management programs but should be a distinct module. Queue management concerns itself with the correct operation of the devices. The scheduler implements management policy, and is frequently subject to change. Many operating systems are built so that correct operation may be compromised when a scheduling policy is changed.

The choice of policy to select request elements from a queue is wide. The intuitively fairest policy is to select the process which has been waiting the longest, that is, use *first in first out* (FIFO) as the scheduling policy. Table 6-2 list scheduling policies that have been used, using the abbreviation which is most common in the queuing literature. Most of these policies have also been given computer-oriented names; several of these abbreviations are provided in Appendix A. The reason for alternate scheduling policies is the diversity of objectives to be achieved. Objectives in file and database scheduling can be: minimal user delay, minimal variability of user delay, maximum utilization of the processor, maximum utilization of the transfer capability from the device, or maximization of locality for a currently active process so that a single process at a time is flushed through the system as fast as possible. Objectives may also be combined; a typical combination is the maximal utilization of the device, constrained by a requirement to provide an adequate response time for any user.

The scheduling choice is important to system performance only when the queues are filled; when there is no, or only one, process to be served, all algorithms behave equally well.

Scheduling Policies for a Drum When using a FIFO policy, an average of one rotation will be lost between successive block accesses to a drum. Since other blocks may pass under the reading heads during this time, it is desirable to arrange that any requested blocks are read when they appear, rather than read strictly in the order in which they were requested. Such an approach is called *shortest service time first*, or SSTF. Control units for drums and disks are available which allow the maintenance of multiple requests, one per sector, and these requests will be processed in sector sequence. Examples are the Burroughs B6375 and the IBM 2835.

When block lengths are fixed and track-switching time is predictable, an SSTF schedule can be implemented through software arrangement of requests. Sector-specific queues are shown in Fig. 6-11, with an example of the selection path for the next sector of a fixed head disk. The gap between sectors provides the time needed for switching tracks. If all sector queues $Q1, \ldots, Qb_{track}$ are filled, then b_{track} blocks can be accessed during one track revolution, giving the maximal *utilization factor* uf, defined as #(user blocks accessed)/#(disk blocks passed), of one.

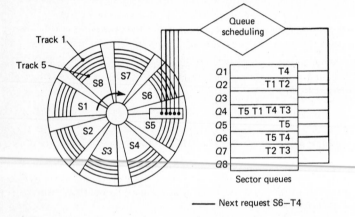

Figure 6-11 Queue optimization for a drumlike device.

Even if b_{track} or more blocks are waiting to be processed, there will usually be empty queues. In Fig. 6-11 there are 12 requests for the 5 tracks in the 8 sector queues, but Q8 for sector S8 is still empty, and unless a request arrives for this queue during the next two sector times S6,7 the time for passing sector S8 will be unutilized. The probability of having an empty queue will be less for the sectors about to be accessed (S6, 7, ...) than for the sectors which have just been processed (S5, 4, ...). If the arrival of requests to the drum has a certain distribution, the arrival of requests to a sector queue (if they are independent of each other) will have the same distribution.

Long queues increase productivity, so that SSTF scheduling promotes a stable equilibrium as long as

$$uf = \frac{\lambda 2r}{b_{track}} < 1 \qquad\qquad 6\text{-}25$$

where $\lambda 2r$ is the number of arrivals during one revolution.

A *uf* of 0.75 corresponds, for a drum with $b_{track} = 8$ sectors and a rotation time of $2r = 50$ ms, to an arrival rate λ of 120 requests per second.

Unfortunately, a high utilization is associated with long queues, and hence long delays to processing requests. The mean delay for waiting in a sector queue w, which has to be added to $r + btt$, has been derived for a Poisson-type distribution of arrival times by Coffman[69]. For a moderately large number of sectors ($b_{track} > 3$) the effects of the discrete sector boundaries can be disregarded; then

$$w = \frac{uf}{1 - uf} \, r \qquad\qquad \langle\text{Poisson arrivals}\rangle \text{ 6-26}$$

giving a total average processing time for a request of

$$T_F = w + r + btt \qquad\qquad \langle\text{drum queue}\rangle \text{ 6-27}$$

While a high utilization rate does increase the productivity of a drum, the waiting times, and hence the queue lengths, increase rapidly with heavy utilization.

At a utilization $uf = 0.75$ the waiting time w becomes $3r$, or the equivalent of one and a half revolutions. At $uf = 0.9$ it is up to $9r$, and as $uf \to 1$ the queues get longer and will never be worked off if the arrivals don't cease.

A result of queuing theory, *Little's formula* [Jewell[67]], states that at equilibrium the total number of requests queued Rq depends on their delays w'

$$Rq = \lambda w' \qquad\qquad \text{6-28}$$

For the case above, Rq includes requests delayed in the queue owing to the sum $w + r \to w'$, so that with $r = 0.025$ s $Rq = (120 \text{ requests/s})(3 + 1) \times 0.025 = 12\text{s}$

Denning[72] has analyzed the case of uniform distribution of arrivals in the sector queue, taking into account the changing density before and after access. Uniform arrivals is a reasonable assumption if drum requests are due to sequential processing or due to direct-access algorithms. Here, the utilization

$$uf = \frac{1}{\frac{1}{2}b_{track}/Rq \; + 1} \qquad\qquad \langle\text{uniform arrivals}\rangle \text{ 6-29}$$

Under extreme conditions ($Rq > 10, \lambda 2r > 10$ or $Rq < 1, \lambda 2r < 1$) the models behave similarly under either arrival distribution.

For drums the other scheduling algorithms listed in Table 6-2 are of interest only when variable-length blocks are collected. Since such usage is uncommon, we will proceed to consider disk units.

Scheduling Policies for Disks All considerations in regard to drum scheduling apply equally well to the cylinders of a disk. A disk will have typically fewer tracks (2, 6, 10, 19, or 20) per cylinder than a drum has tracks (32, 64, 128, 200), and at the same time, with the greater aggregate storage volume, the intensity of use per block will tend to be less for disk blocks. Because of these factors, the expected length of the sector queue often becomes less than 1 and the cost of scheduling by sector does not provide commensurate benefits.

The optimization of seek times, however, can cause significant performance improvements for disklike devices. This requires again the use of scheduling policies other than FIFO.

The minimization of seek time is completely independent of the minimization of rotational latency within a cylinder so that two different schedulers may be operative within one file system at the same time. Each of the policies listed in Table 6-2 will now be considered.

The use of LIFO is intended to optimize the use of the disk by minimizing disk distances. The idea here is that, by giving the device to the most recent user, no or little arm movement will be required for sequential reading of the file. LIFO can also minimize congestion and queue lengths, since jobs, as long as they can actively use the file system, are processed as fast as possible.

Table 6-2   Scheduling Algorithms

Name	Description	Remarks
Selection according to requestor:		
FIFO	First in first out	Fairest of them all
PRI	Priority by process	Control outside of QMP
LIFO	Last in first out	May maximize locality
RSS	Random scheduling	Used in analysis and simulation only
Selection according to requested item:		
SSTF	Shortest service time first	High utilization, small queues
SCAN	Back and forth over disk	Better service distribution
CSCAN	One-way with fast return	Lower service variability
N-step-SCAN	SCAN, of N records at a time	Service guarantee
FSCAN	N-step SCAN with N based on the queue length at the begin of a SCAN cycle	Load sensitive

The use of *PRIority*, frequently given to small computations, also has the effect of flushing selected computations through the system. If the number of computations having equally high priority becomes large, the disk usage efficiencies diminish. Users with large computations and low priorities often wait exceedingly long. Priority-driven systems will have a high rate of completed computations and have small queues. Statistics from these systems are used by computer center directors to demonstrate the effectiveness of their operations, while the users split their computations into small pieces in order to share in the benefits. This type of operation tends to be poor for databases.

If the current cylinder position of the disk-access mechanism is known, scheduling can be based on the requested item rather than based on attributes of the queue or the requestor.

The SSTF algorithm for disks is equivalent to highest locality first. All requests on the current cylinder will be processed, and then requests on the nearest cylinder. A random tie-breaking algorithm may be used to resolve the case of equal distances. Since the center tracks are apt to be favored, an alternate tie-breaking rule is to choose the direction of the nearest extremity. This means that if the current position is 115 out of $j = 200$ tracks and requests are waiting at 110 and 120, then 120 will be chosen.

It is obvious that all previous methods except FIFO can leave some request unfulfilled until the entire queue is emptied. It is hence necessary to modify these techniques in order to reintroduce some minimum service level into the system. One augmentation is the addition of a dynamic priority structure which is based on the length of time that a process has been delayed. The rate of priority increase has to be chosen to satisfy response time constraints while not losing advantage of improved locality.

The SCAN algorithm adds regularity of control to a SSTF method. When all requests on a cylinder have been served, it proceeds to one specific side, and this direction is maintained until the extreme cylinder is reached. The service direction changes whenever the inner or outer cylinder is reached. A modification of SCAN (LOOK) reverses direction as soon as there are no more requests in that direction. A SCAN policy will operate similarly to SSTF unless the request pattern is particularly poor, since the probability of requests in SSTF is biased against the area most recently processed.

The CSCAN method reduces the maximum delay times of the scan by restricting the SCAN to one direction. If the expected time for a SCAN to go from inner to outer track is $t(\text{SCAN})$, the expected service interval for blocks at the periphery is $2t(\text{SCAN})$ using SCAN and less than $t(\text{SCAN})+s_{max}$ for CSCAN, since in the shorter time interval fewer requests will enter the queue.

The relative productivity of SCAN and CSCAN depends on the ratio of incremental seek times to cylinder processing times, and on the maximum seek time. For SCAN this ratio varies with cylinder position, since the most recently processed area is processed first.

Figure 6-12 sketches the queue behavior for the case of perfect processing equilibrium. The arrival rate is uniform (1.5 per unit of time). The top boundary of the queue area B→C→ ... indicates the aggregate arrivals, during the period to point F their volume is proportionate to the area A,B,C. The lower boundary of the queue area D→E→ ... indicates the requests that have been served and have departed from the queue. The areas (A,B,C)=(D,E,F) and the areas (A′,B′,C′)= (D′,E′,F′) since under long term equilibrium conditions the arrivals and the departures have to be equal in each cycle. SCAN encounters increasing numbers of requests per track as it goes back and forth. CSCAN encounters a steady load but is idle during the seek to the beginning of the cycle.

The simplifying assumption made here, that processing time is linearly related to track position and does not depend on the number of requests per cylinder, is valid only when the average number of requests per cylinder during a scan is ≤ 1,

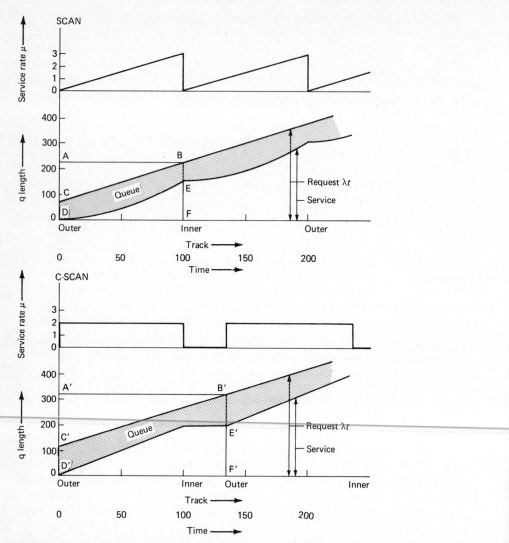

Figure 6-12 Queue behavior for SCAN and CSCAN.

or at least much less than the number of blocks or sectors on a track, so that no additional rotational latency accrues. The seek time from inner to outer track s_{max} is taken to be one-third of the sum of single track seek times $(j\,s_1)$. It can be observed that the average queue length is slightly greater under CSCAN than under SCAN (about 100 versus 90), since during the time s_{max} no requests are serviced.

SSTF, SCAN, and CSCAN may still fail to move the access arm for a long time. If, for instance, two processes have high access rates to one cylinder, they can monopolize the entire device by interleaving. High-density multisurface disks are more likely to be affected by this characteristic than disks with a low capacity per cylinder. To avoid forgetting requests for long periods, the request queues may be segmented, and one segment processed completely before any requests from the next segment are taken. This approach is refined in the N-step-SCAN and the FSCAN policies.

The N-step-SCAN schedules requests using queues segmented into subqueues of length N. Within a subqueue requests are processed using the SCAN policy. If fewer than N requests are in the queue at the end of a cycle, these are processed during a cycle. The larger the value of N, the more the performance of the N-step-SCAN approaches the performance of SCAN. If $N = 1$, the service is equal to FIFO. The scan has only to cover the range required for the N requests. If at the beginning of cycle the access mechanism is not wholly on one side of the range of cylinders for which service is requested, then again a tie-breaking decision is required to determine the initial direction. In devices with complex seek patterns, the optimum strategy to process the N requests may be difficult to determine, but in general moving first to the nearest extreme point of the range, and then scanning in one direction uses the disk near optimally. User response time within a group of N requests might be best if SSTF were used within a cycle. Policies which leave the arm at the end of a cycle in an extreme position will contribute to the performance of the next cycle.

FSCAN is an implementation of an N-step-SCAN which uses as N the total length of the queue when a cycle commences, and defers all arrivals, during the cycle to the next cycle. FSCAN shows improved efficiency as the load increases over CSCAN. The maximum queue length, however, increases to the number of arrivals per cycle. For the values used in Fig. 6-12 the average queue length becomes $1.5j/2 = 1.5 \times 200/2 = 150$ entries.

An *Eschenbach scan* extends the optimization used for a drum or a cylinder of a disk to the entire disk area. This is done by limiting the time to be spent at each cylinder position. A cylinder with a queue may be allotted between $1 \rightarrow k$ rotations, where k is number of tracks on the cylinder. A parameter E is used to indicate the order of the Eschenbach scan. An order $E = k$ scan will obtain all the blocks from a cylinder position and is hence similar to a CSCAN, except that incremental requests requiring more than k revolutions will not be serviced in the current cycle. A small parameter of E $(1, 2, \ldots)$ will obtain blocks while the queue for the cylinder is still relatively long and will hence deal with higher average sector densities.

Example 6-6 shows the effect of the Eschenbach scheme applied to the single cylinder shown in Fig. 6-11.

Example 6-6   Utilization Factors Using Eschenbach Scans

E	Blocks accessed	*uf*
1	6 out of 8	0.75
2	+4 out of the next 8	0.625
3	+1 out of the next 8	0.457
4	+1 out of the next 8	0.375
5	skip since track is empty	0.375

This table does not account for small probability of new arrivals for this cylinder during its processing. It is obvious that the Eschenbach scheme trades longer queues and greater waiting times for the capability to provide a very high utilization rate. It is clear that a high device-utilization rate will provide, at an equal request rate, better aggregate service to the user. For an Eschenbach scheme to be effective, the request rates will be high. This method has been used more in message switching and in the collection of transactions for subsequent batch processing than in the area of standard file services.

The Eschenbach scheme does not provide a service guarantee, but since the scanning cycle time t_{cycle} is guaranteed

$$t_{cycle} \leq j(s_1 + 2\,E\,r) + s_j \qquad\qquad\qquad 6\text{-}30$$

where j is the number of cylinders allotted to the file, a service guarantee for priority messages can be provided. The required augmentation is the rearrangement of the sector queues to place priority requests at the head of the line. Unless a cylinder has for one sector more than E priority messages, t_{cycle} will be the maximum queue delay.

6-3-3 Use of Scheduling

Other techniques to optimize disk usage include the placement of frequently used blocks in the central cylinders of a disk. A SCAN policy will then access these cylinders most effectively; and even FIFO will show lower average seektimes. FIFO and PRIority policies are frequently used because of their simplicity and the fact that the more complex scheduling policies excel at utilization rates not often reached in practice.

The lack of scheduling, however, is one of the reasons for poor performance of some systems which collect transactions from many terminals for later batch processing of a database [Winick[69]]. If we represent data from a transaction coming from terminal $T, (1, \ldots, t)$ during time interval $I, (1, \ldots, i)$ as (T, I), the file containing data from these transactions will be approximately arranged in the sequence, $\{(1,1), (2,1), \ldots, (t,1), (1,2), (2,2), \ldots, (t,2), \ldots, (1,i), (2,i), \ldots, (t,i)\}$

When this file has to be processed, the data from one source terminal will be needed serially, requiring access in the order $\{(1,1), (1,2), \ldots, (i,1)\}$, followed by $\{(2,1), \ldots, \}$ etc. This places extremely heavy loads on the file services supporting these systems, loads which can be considerably ameliorated by effective queue scheduling policies.

In many operating systems the scheduler is integrated with other functions, so that implemented scheduling policies are difficult to discern and nearly impossible to change. Since the scheduler, after making the scheduling decision, allocates not only resources but also access privileges to the users, as described in Chaps. 12 and 13, the interaction can be complex. Some concepts, for instance the notion of a monitor to protect critical sections of programs [BrinchHansen[73]], encourage such integration. The lack of modularity which exists in those systems can make it difficult to implement effective scheduling techniques.

6-4 OPERATIONS RESEARCH IN DATABASE DESIGN

Operations Research is an area of applied mathematics which addresses problems faced by the management of enterprises in the scheduling, operations, and development of facilities. In this context Operations Research (OR) is closely identified with *management science*, although it is obvious that there is more to the science of management than the application of OR techniques.

Tools of OR include:

Queuing theory
Inventory theory
Linear and integer programming
Decision theory

Each of these fields is now a discipline in its own right.

6-4-1 Queuing Distributions and Their Application

Because of the importance of queues in manufacturing and communications, the subject of queues has been intensively studied. The parameters required for the mathematical treatment of queues include:

Description of the source of the requests for service
Number of requests
Arrival rate distribution
Description of the queue waiting for service
Queue capacity
Scheduling policy
Description of the service
Number of servers
Service time distribution

The previous section has described queues as they are managed in file systems. A convention used to classify queuing models for analysis, *Kendall's notation*, specifies

arrival process/service process/number of servers

using the symbols for the distributions of arrival or service processes below.

M : exponential
D : constant or otherwise determined
$E(m)$: Erlang
I : general and independent
G : general

Of interest to problems in file analysis are primarily queuing models of the type $M/G/1$ and $E/G/1$.

Events in queuing are described by their average arrival rate (λ). An alternative to the arrival rate is the distribution of interarrival times, $t = 1/\lambda$. In Fig. 6-12 requests arrive uniformly distributed, the arrival rate λ was 1.5 per time unit, and the interarrival time t was a constant 0.66.

We have encountered exponential and constant distributions in Sec. 6-1 and associate exponential rates with independence of successive events and constant rates with complete dependence of the arrival time on the time of the preceding event. The important case where the distribution of arrivals are neither completely random nor constant is described by distributions of the Erlang type.

The servers are characterized by the potential service (μ) rates they represent. The service types in the systems we describe are dominated by seeks and latencies which can be determined using hardware parameters. Requests will depart from the system at a throughput rate $\rho = uf\,\mu$. During equilibrium λ and ρ are equal. The number of departures is limited by the number of arrivals ($\int \lambda\,dt \geq \int \rho\,dt$); unprocessed arrivals are collected in queues.

When a service request addresses a specific file, the applicable number of servers is one; only in communication networks between processors, access to fully redundant files, or when writing without specifying the disk address can the case of multiple servers occur.

Erlang Distributions When the demands for service to file and communications systems are measured, it is often found that the times between services requests are distributed in a pattern which is due neither to completely random nor to constant behavior. The behavior may be explained by the fact that after a service request has been granted, the time for the service and analysis of the obtained data is not at all random, so that one computation will emit service requests in a cyclical pattern. Similar, but randomly interleaving, patterns are presented by other, independent computations being processed.

To capture the range between random and constant interarrival times a parameterized distribution, Erlang(m), can be used. Figure 6-13 shows some Erlang distributions for an average arrival rate $\lambda = 1$. Figure 6-13 and the accompanying Eq. 6-31 show that the Erlang distribution for $m = 1$ is equal to the

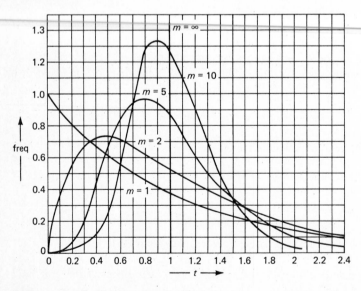

Figure 6-13 Erlang distributions.

$$freq(t) = \frac{\lambda(\lambda t)^{m-1}}{(m-1)!}e^{-\lambda t} \quad \text{for } t \geq 0 \qquad 6\text{-}31$$

exponential distribution, while as $m \to \infty$ the distribution becomes constant. The parameters for the Erlang distribution are

$$mean(t) = \frac{1}{\lambda} \qquad \text{(of course) and} \qquad \sigma(t) = \frac{1}{\sqrt{m}\,\lambda} \qquad \qquad 6\text{-}32$$

The appropriate Erlang parameter m for an observed Erlang-like distribution can hence be found from the computed mean and standard deviation, as shown in program segment 6-11. High values of `m_erlang` (> 10) indicate little variability in interarrival times.

```
/* Computation of Erlang Parameter */                    /* 6-11 */
       m_erlang = (mean/sd)**2   ;
```

The Effect of Variability   The fact that random service times or service requests have a detrimental effect on service performance can be demonstrated with the simple example of Fig. 6-14.

There are two disks which provide service at mean intervals of 30 ms. The expected delay for a request arriving in the interval $(0, 120)$ to receive service from disk **D1** is 15 ms, but the delay for a randomly arriving service request for disk **D2** is

$$\tfrac{15}{120}\tfrac{1}{2}(15) + \tfrac{15}{120}\tfrac{1}{2}(15) + \tfrac{60}{120}\tfrac{1}{2}(60) + \tfrac{30}{120}\tfrac{1}{2}(30) = 20.6\text{ms}$$

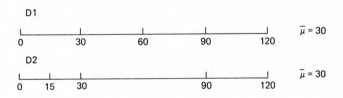

Figure 6-14 Disk service times.

Queue Length and Delays for Erlang Distributions   When the order m_erlang of the Erlang distribution for requests, and the utilization factor `uf` of the service facility are known, the queuing behavior is defined. Formulas and graphs are given in [IBM F20-7[71]]. The computations required are

```
/* Computation of Expected Queue Length */               /* 6-12 */
    idlef = 1 - uf;              ufsq = uf**2;
    factor1 = 1 - 1/m_erlang;    factor2 = 1 - uf/2*factor1;
/* Queue Length */
    queue_bar = uf * factor2/idlef;
    queue_sd = SQRT(uf * (1 - uf/2*(3
                       - (10*uf-ufsq)/6 - (3*idlef + ufsq)/m_erlang
                       - (8*uf-5*ufsq)/(6*m_erlang**2)) ) ) / idlef;
/* Waiting Time before Begin of Service */               /* 6-13 */
    w_bar = (s+r+btt) * factor2/idlef;
    w_sd = (s+r+btt) * SQRT((1-(4*uf-ufsq)/6*factor1)*(1+1/m_erlang)
                       - factor2**2)/idlef;
```

The availability of computers is appreciated when Erlang distributions are used.

The factor `idlef=1-uf` had already been encountered in the analysis of drum scheduling. It accounts for the rapid decline of performance when a high utilization is achieved while arrival or service times show random or stochastic variation.

Example 6-7   Sample Calculation of a Queue Length

The times needed to fetch a large number of records from a file system have been collected. The mean time was 90 ms, and the standard deviation 40 ms. A histogram of the distribution makes an Erlang distribution likely. The appropriate Erlang parameter, following program segment 6-11, is

$$\texttt{m\_erlang} \; = \; \texttt{(90/40)**2} \; \approx \; \texttt{5.0}$$

The disk unit was busy during the test 40% of the time, so that `uf = 0.4`. The queue length expected is computed, using program segment 6-12 as

$$\texttt{queue\_bar = 0.56}$$
$$\texttt{queue\_sd \; = 0.84}$$

Given that the mean service time `s+r+btt` is 50 ms we find from program segment 6-13 the mean delay and its standard deviation

$$\texttt{w\_bar = 70.0 milliseconds}$$
$$\texttt{w\_sd \; = 42.8 milliseconds}$$

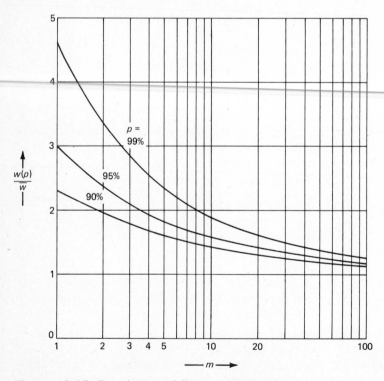

Figure 6-15 Percentiles of Erlang distributions.

Use of Percentiles to Define Performance The type of distribution with its mean and standard deviation defines the distribution of events in a system precisely. The result has to be translated into terms useful for operational decisions. The use of fractions or percentiles of occurrence of certain events is a well-understood approach. Figure 6-15 provides this information for Erlang and hence exponential distributions.

It provides the values of t where the areas of the Erlang distribution from $0 \rightarrow t$ are 90%, 95%, and 99% of the total area. Events that fall into the tail for $t \rightarrow$ inf will have longer delays. The result is that the waiting time is less than $w(p)/\overline{w}$ times the average waiting time $\overline{w}$ in $p\%$ of the cases.

Let us provide the waiting-time limit for 90% of the record fetches in the example above. For `m_erlang` = 5 the 90th percentile in Fig. 6-15 gives a ratio of 1.6, or a delay of $1.6 \times 70 = 112$ ms.

A Chebyshev inequality can only promise for the 90th percentile a delay of less than $70 + \sqrt{10}\,42.8 = 205$ s, and this is the value to be used if the distribution does not match the Erlang curve for `m_erlang` = 5.

Mix of Distributions When the behavior of a mixture of different services is needed, the joint distribution and the mean will be the sum of the scaled distributions. The expected mean and standard deviation in the mix will be

$$mean_{mix} = \sum_h pc_h mean_h \qquad\qquad 6\text{-}33$$

$$\sigma_{mix} = \sqrt{\sum_h pc_h^2(\sigma_h^2 + (mean_h - mean_{mix})^2)} \qquad\qquad 6\text{-}34$$

where pc_h is the proportion of the computation h in the mix [IBM F20-7[71]].

6-4-2 Transients in Service Demands

Up to this point we have discussed queuing models which are in equilibrium, so that within all intervals considered, the service rate was adequate to provide the requested services. In many systems, however, there will be certain periods where the rate of arrival of requests for service λ exceeds the service capacity μ. Such a period is called a *transient*, since it can only be a temporary situation; a situation where the average rate of arrivals $\overline{\lambda}$ remains greater than μ is of course intolerable.

Examples in Sec. 6-3 have demonstrated how rapidly the expected queue length and the wait time w can rise as the utilization factor $uf = \overline{\lambda}/\mu$ approaches one. If later $\overline{\lambda} \rightarrow\!\!\ll \mu$, the queues will empty and $w \rightarrow 0$. Unused computing capacity is a very perishable commodity; it cannot be put into a bank to provide later benefits.

Transients are fairly difficult to analyze using the probabilistic techniques used earlier, so that graphic constructions based on flow concepts will be used here. We will consider now only the part of a queue due to overload and not the part of the queue which is generated because of the delays caused by seek and rotational latency.

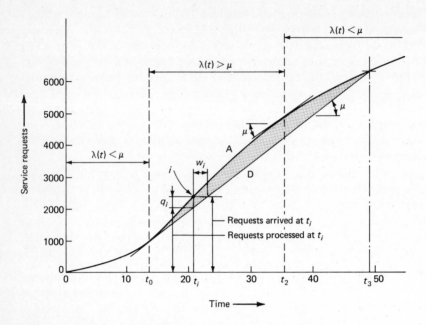

Figure 6-16 Transient arrivals.

$$\lambda(t) = \bar{\lambda} + (\lambda_{max} - \bar{\lambda}) \sin(t \frac{2\pi}{t_c})$$

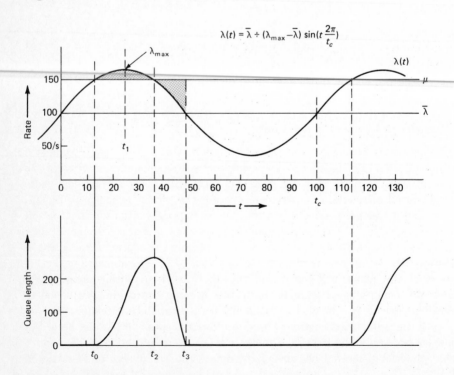

Figure 6-17 Transient queue.

Figure 6-16 shows the cumulative arrivals as line **A** and the cumulative service requests which are being processed as line **D**. Processing of requests (**D**) is limited both by the slope μ giving the service rate capacity and by the arrival of requests **A**. The space between **A** and **D** depicts the queue which is generated. The queue begins forming at $t = t_0$ where for the first time the instantaneous arrival rate $\lambda(t) > \mu$. At t_2 the arrival rate has subdued and $\lambda(t) = \mu$, but the queue has yet to be worked off. The queue will not be reduced to zero until time t_3, where **D**, continued at angle μ from t_0, intersects **A**. The average rate of arrivals λ during the total transient between t_0 and t_3 is equal to μ, but the overall $\overline{\lambda}$ in the cycle of t_c is less than the available service rate μ. The values are given below.

If the shape of the arrival distribution **A** is known, a graphical construction can provide the desired values of queue lengths. This graph can easily be interpreted, for instance, for a FIFO scheduling discipline the waiting time for an arrival at t_i, when the queue length is q_i, is indicated by line w_i.

In order to treat a transient analytically, an assumption regarding its shape has to be made. The simplest relationship which can describe a cyclic transient of $\lambda(t)$ is a sine curve, as sketched in Fig. 6-17. The curve is defined by three parameters. For the example we assign values to these and to the service rate.

Cycle time t_c	cycle	100 s
Average arrival rate $\overline{\lambda}$	lambdabar	100/s
Maximum arrival rate λ_{max}	lambdamax	165/s
Service rate μ	mu	150/s

The queue begins to form at t_0, where $\lambda(t) = \mu$ and and substitution of this value in the sine-wave equation for $\lambda(t)$ allows computation of this point. The arrival rate is maximal at $t_1 = t_c/4$. Symmetry about t_1 determines t_2.

```
/* Compute Queue Times for Transient */              /* 6-14 */
        two_pi = 2 * 3.14159;
        sine_t0 = (mu-lambdabar)/(lambdamax-lambdabar);
        t0 = cycle * ARCSIN(sine_t0)/two_pi;
        t1 = cycle/4;
        t2 = t1 + (t1-t0);
```

Program fragment **6-14** gives for the example values

```
        t0 = 13.6 s
        t1 = 25.0 s
        t2 = 36.4 s
```

The queue length at **t2** can be computed by analytical integration between **t0** and **t2** or by finite, stepwise integration. The time when the queue vanishes, **t3**, is tedious to derive analytically, so that a simple stepwise computation will be used which simulates the queue behavior. This computation will step through time and estimate arrivals λ using the assumed *sine* function superimposed on $\overline{\lambda}$. When λ exceeds the possible service rate μ, the excess arrivals are added to a queue. If there is a queue, it is decreased by any excess $\mu - \lambda$. When the queue length becomes zero, the time **t3** is computed and printed. At each second of the cycle the queue length is reported.

```
/* Queue Length and Times for Transient */                    /* 6-15 */
        radius = lambdamax - lambdabar;
        queue = 0;
        lastlambda = lambdabar;
 DO second = 1 TO cycle;                  angle = second/cycle*two_pi;
            lambda = radius*SIN(angle) + lambdabar;
            IF lambda>mu THEN
                /* Approximate Arrivals by Average in Interval */
                queue = queue + (lastlambda+lambda)/2 - mu;
            ELSE DO;
                IF queue > 0 THEN DO;
                    /* Work off Queue */
                    decrease = mu - (lastlambda+lambda)/2;
                    IF decrease < queue THEN queue = queue - decrease;
                      ELSE DO;
                        /* queue is gone, interpolate between seconds */
                            t3 = second - 1 + queue/decrease;
                            queue = 0;
                            PUT DATA(t3,queue);
                        END;
                END;
              END;
            lastlambda=lambda;
            PUT DATA(second, queue);
        END period;
```

Applying program segment 6-15 to our example computes a value of t3 = 48.2 s, so that there are here three similar intervals,

> Increasing rate of queue growth: t1-t0 = 11.4 s
> Decreasing rate of queue growth: t2-t1 = 11.4 s
> Queue collapse   :   t3-t2 = 11.8 s

Behavior of Transients The pattern of equal thirds observed in the example can also be analytically deduced. The time to work off the queue depends on the ratio of $\overline{\lambda}$ to μ. If there is a reasonable margin between $\overline{\lambda}$ and μ, the transient takes less than half of the total cycle t_c. If now $t_3 \approx \frac{1}{2}t_c$ we find four phases in a cycle as shown in Fig. 6-17: no queue from 0 to t_0 and the three phases of queue growth increase, growth decrease, and collapse to t_3. In the last phase t_2, t_3 the steepness of the arrival rate λ is about twice as great for cyclic functions as the steepness of λ during growth in t_0, t_1 and t_1, t_2. Because of this difference the queue will collapse in about half the time it took to grow. The two phases of growth are equal because of the symmetry we assumed for the cycle. The reasoning of double steepness and symmetry continues to hold for transients with $t_3 < \frac{1}{2}t_c$ or transient lengths $t_3 - t_0 < \frac{3}{8}t_c$. This pattern of equal thirds is typical and has also been concluded for other second-order assumptions.

When transients increase in length, the time to work off the queue increases relatively to the transient length. At the limit for long-term operation, $\overline{\lambda} = \mu$, $t_2 - t_0 = t_3 - t_2$ and the time for the queue to grow is equal to the time needed for the queue to disappear. This can be easily visualized in Fig. 6-17 by reducing μ to 100; then t_3 occurs at the end of the cycle, namely, at $t_c = 100$ s.

When the transients are not due to cyclic phenomena, the same analysis method can still be used by fitting the sine curve according to observed values of any two of the time points { t0,t1,t2,t3 } in addition to using the service and arrival rates as before.

The expected queue length, as computed here, is entirely due to the transient, and additional queue capacity is required for random variations of arrivals and service, and for hardware-caused delays.

6-4-3 An Application of Inventory Theory

In classical inventory theory, there is a collection of goods which are gradually consumed. Before the inventory is exhausted, an order is to be placed, so that the supply is replenished. A cost is associated with placing an order, with storing the inventory, and with having run out of the goods. A large variety of models is available to solve inventory problems.

A file or database tends to become less efficient over time until an order to reorganize is placed. so that its behavior presents a similar cost function as shown in Fig. 6-18. The cost functions depend on the overflow parameter o seen in Chapter 3. In direct files the cost is related to the degree of clustering and to the file density.

After reorganization at a cost $C_Y = f(T_Y)$ the file will be more efficient. The original efficiency should be regained unless the file has grown. If statistics about record activity are available, reorganization can be used to improve the file efficiency. While the method and its effect depend on the file organization, usage costs will be lower if records of highest activity are reloaded first. In a direct file, for instance, the frequently accessed records will be found at the initial address.

We will consider only the case of a static file because the principle of the analysis remains the same. The reorganization cost is equivalent to the cost of placing an order, and the time required between the placing of the order and the receipt of the goods can be ignored.

The cost of operating the file system can be split into the component for the static portion $n\,C_n$ and for the overflow portion $o\,C_o$, where $C_{n,o}$ are the costs per record of the file fragments. To simplify matters further, a linear growth of overflow o over time t is assumed, so that $o = c_o t, t = 0 \rightarrow t_Y$. The cost of overflows at a given instant can be written as $t\,c_o C_o = t\,C'_o$. Reorganizations are performed after an interval t_Y, and the cost of operating the system during such an interval can be estimated from the two areas shown in Fig. 6-17 and the cost of reorganization

$$C_{op}(t_Y) = t_Y n\,C_n + \frac{1}{2}t_Y^2 C'_o + C_Y \qquad\qquad 6\text{-}35$$

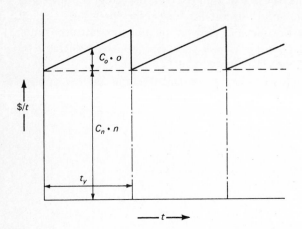

Figure 6-18 Cost function of a file which is being updated.

During a long period Per there will be Per/t_Y reorganizations and the cost over Per will be

$$C_{op}(Per) = Per\, n\, C_n + \frac{1}{2} Per\, t_Y C'_o + Per\, \frac{C_Y}{t_Y} \qquad 6\text{-}36$$

The lowest cost as a function of the reorganization interval can be found by taking the derivative with respect to t_Y and setting it to zero.

$$\frac{1}{2} Per C'_o - Per\, \frac{C_Y}{t_Y^2} = 0 \qquad giving \qquad t_Y(optimal) = \sqrt{2\,\frac{C_Y}{C'_o}} \qquad 6\text{-}37$$

This rule will be applied to the indexed-sequential file presented in Sec. 3-3.

Example 6-8   Calculation of Reorganization Period

Given are load quantites of

$$L_F = 20\,000/\text{day fetch requests}$$

$$L_I = 300/\text{day new records, causing overflow } o$$

The file has $n = 40000$ records of length $R = 500$ on blocks of size $B = 2000$, the index has a fanout $y = 100$. We derive $Bfr = B/R = 4$, $x = \log_{100}(n/Bfr) = 2$. We assume that that the index level x is in core, also that level $1(x-1)$ is on the same cylinder as the data and that $n/o \gg Bfr$, so that we can use Eq. 3-39. We simplify the overflow term $o'/(n+o')$ to o/n, since we use o here to denote the current overflow and $o \ll n$.

$$T_F = c + s + 2(r + btt) + \frac{o}{n}(r + btt)$$

$$T_Y = 2n\frac{R}{t'}\frac{SI}{t}$$

The low ratio of insertions to fetch operations $L_I/L_F = 300/20\,000 = 1.5\%$ permits T_I to be ignored.

For an indexed-sequential file the relationship for $C_o = f(T_F)$ is, given the assumptions in Example 6-8, linear in respect to o and T_Y is independent, as required by the assumptions made in the model used to optimize the reorganization time. Then

$$C_o = \frac{r + btt}{n} \qquad\qquad 6\text{-}38$$

and with one overflow per insertion L_I

$$C'_o = L_F L_I (r + btt)\frac{cost}{n} \qquad\qquad 6\text{-}39$$

where $cost$ is the processing cost per second. The reorganization will be scheduled for lower cost time, so that $0.5\,cost$ will be used below to compute C_Y.

Continuing Example 6-8, it is assumed that the index SI requires 5% space over the rest of the file and hence a proportionate effect to rewrite. Then

$$C_Y = 2.05\,n\,\frac{R}{t'}\,0.5\,cost$$

For a 2314-type disk unit the parameters for this file will be

$r = 0.025$ s
$t' = 120\,000$ bytes/s
$btt = 0.005$ s

and for simplicity, we set the processor cost at

$$cost = \$0.10/\text{s}$$

The actual absolute values of these parameters are not very critical since they tend to cancel each other out. With this $cost$

$$C_Y = \$17.10 \qquad \text{and} \qquad C'_o = \$0.45/day^2$$

so that

$$t_Y(\text{optimum}) = 8.7 \text{ days}$$

6-5 STORAGE ALLOCATION

A computer system has to be able to support a variety of files of different types. A function of an operating system is the allocation of storage space to the separate files. There is an interaction between file structure and allocation policy: file systems which do not use indexes or pointers to locate blocks require contiguous space; other files can receive space incrementally. Two methods to keep track of the portions allocated to files and of the space which remains free have already been encountered in Secs. 4-3 (VSAM) and 4-5 (MUMPS). In this section we will review this subject more completely.

In the beginning the system establishes the area required for its operation and then defines the areas available for users. The user's area is without form and void. The first task for the system is the creation of a directory to all the available storage units. During operation the system has to identify removable diskpacks, tapes, etc., which are currently mounted. The storage-device directory is re-created whenever the system is initialized, and directory entries are updated upon receipt of a "ready" signal from a device on which a diskpack or such has been mounted. When this has been done, the users can come forth and demand their share of the resources. We note that the allocation of space is a function carried out at a level which is more basic than the level on which the file systems operates. When multiple file systems share one computer system, the operating system may have to support more than one space-allocation strategy. Good space management is essential to keep the system's ecology in balance.

6-5-1 Portions, Size versus Number

Space will be allocated to users in response to their requests. The shape, number, and size of the portions of the system storage space given to users is a compromise between the requirements for efficiency by the individual files and overall system efficiency.

If contiguous space is to be allocated, large portions are needed to make the contiguity effective. To prevent waste of storage space for small files, the portions will be of various sizes. Allocations may be restricted to a small number of portions; this number is, for instance, limited to 16 in IBM's OS. The tables used to keep track of allocated storage in OS are relatively small.

In systems with a high degree of multiprogramming it is not very beneficial to provide contiguous space for the users, so that allocation can be based on blocks (CDC SIS) or trains of blocks (IBM VSAM). The user's request will be rounded to the next larger unit. Some file systems may be able to utilize the extra space given, and will request less space the next time. Figure 6-19 sketches a storage space layout after an identical space request and release sequence for variable and block allocation.

Allocation by variable portion leaves more total free space, but in less usable form, than allocation by block or train. The storage efficiency of block allocation improves with smaller block or train sizes. When allocating blocks or small multiples of blocks, the storage allocation tables will be larger. Since secondary storage is typically allocated over long periods of time, the storage-control tables reside on disk.

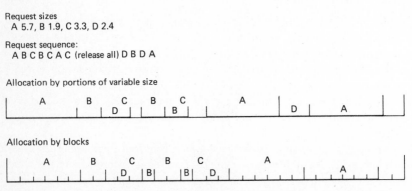

Request sizes
  A 5.7, B 1.9, C 3.3, D 2.4

Request sequence:
  A B C B C A C (release all) D B D A

Allocation by portions of variable size

Allocation by blocks

Figure 6-19 Storage-allocation alternatives.

Management of Portion Allocation to Files When portions are to be allocated to files, the waste of space and lack of contiguity have to balanced. To achieve contiguity, the VSAM approach was to prespecify the eventual file size and allocate large portions, which may remain unused. Many other systems abandon contiguity and allocate blocks as needed. This strategy also requires large tables to find the portions of a file and can, for instance, seriously affect the performance of a direct file.

A scheme to avoid the problem of preallocation versus waste or lack of contiguity is to allocate portions of increasing size as the file grows. If the next portion is always doubled, the size of the portion table for the file is limited to $\log_2(n/Bfr)$ entries. Less than half the allocated file space is unused at any time.

This scheme can be improved by allocating fractional portions, say, 4 portions of 25% of the previous allocation, before doubling the allocation size. Now the portion table is four times as large, but a file of 10^6 blocks still requires only 80 entries. Less than 25% of the allocated file space is unused at any point.

Allocation of Free Storage The storage-control table also contains, explicitly or implicitly, the information regarding which secondary storage areas are not yet allocated and hence are free to be given away. To assign from free space, a section of the storage-control table is fetched from disk to determine which space to give to the requesting user. When variable portions are used, decisions have to be made whether to allocate according to *first fit* (done above), *best fit*, or closest to the previous allocation for the file to increase locality. It is not clear which strategy is best.

Before giving any portion to a user, it is wise to rewrite the storage-control table into permanent storage to reflect the fact that the portion is no longer free. If this is not done immediately, an intervening system failure could cause loss of this information from core storage. When the system is restarted later, the same portion could again be given away, causing serious problems for two users. The cost of keeping storage secure in this manner can triple the cost of writing a new block. To avoid this overhead, a batch of entries denoting free portions can be kept in a working area in core storage. To keep the storage allocation secure, the computation should follow the sequence below:

Batch Storage Allocation

1 Obtain batch of free portions from the storage-control table on file for allocation into a work area.

2 Mark these portions in the work area as `'in use'`.

3 Rewrite the work area to the storage-control table on the file.

4 Allocate portions from the work area to the users as requests are received, and identify the portions allocated.

5 When the batch is used up, rewrite the work area again to the storage-control table area on file.

6 Return to step **1**.

After a failure there will be entries for portions marked "owned by user X", entries for portions marked "free", and entries for portions marked only "in use". The latter portions will not be reallocated. If the allocated portions themselves are identified with their owner, date and time of most recent write operation, it is possible to check the portions whose entries are marked "in use" when they are again retrieved by the user and correct the storage-control table eventually. Other techniques may be possible, depending on the file system's protocol. These housekeeping tasks may be deferred and combined with file-reorganization tasks, since the storage-control table remains usable. Chapter 13 discusses more aspects of file maintenance.

6-5-2 Storage-Control Tables

The structure of the storage-control table is affected by the allocation procedure it has to support. Three methods are in common use to define the available storage space and its allocation.

Table of Contents A file, maintained by the system on every unit may be used to describe the space allocation, using one or several records per file. A file may have an extensive description. Typically included are such items as the owner's identification, the file name, the date of creation, the date of most recent use, the date of most recent updating, and for every portion the position and size. This technique is typically used for systems which allocate large portions. Such a *table of contents* is kept on every disk in the system and is found from a fixed position on every unit.

Free portions could be located by searching the table and finding unallocated space, but this is apt to be costly. To avoid this cost, a dummy file with owner SYSTEM and name FREE_SPACE is kept in the table of contents. Since the number of portions of free space can be larger than the limit of portions per single file, the free portions may be chained to each other and found from a single or a few entries.

Chaining of Portions The free portions may be chained together through the free-space portions themselves. This method is also applicable when portions are smaller, for instance, in block-based allocation. It has negligible space overhead since it uses free space for storage of the free storage-control data. Only one, or a few, header entries are kept in a pseudo-file entry. When space is needed, the headers from the portions are fetched one by one to determine the next suitable free portion in the chain. Then the portion is removed from the chain and the chain is rewritten, taking care again not to leave the free storage control data vulnerable to system failure.

Multiple chains may be kept to group cylinders or sectors in order to create efficient user files. MUMPS used free chains in that manner (Fig. 4-28). If variable-length portions are being allocated, there may be multiple chains to implement a best-fit algorithm. Files will obtain portions from the chain appropriate for the size of portions required, and large portions are preserved until needed.

Chained free-storage management does not keep track of data allocated to the user's file. It is desirable for the operating system to be cognizant of all allocations made. When there is no table of contents, this can be achieved by an extension of the chaining method. The allocated portions are chained together for each file using a header similar to the header used for free storage management. The relative space overhead to do this depends on the size of the portions allocated but will be bearable unless portions are of a size much less than a thousand bytes.

Bit Tables A third approach to manage free space is to keep a *bit table*. This method uses an array containing one bit per portion in the system. It is used only when all portion sizes are the same, generally equal to one block. Each entry of a "0" indicates a corresponding free portion, and a "1" indicates a portion which is in use. The list of portions allocated to a specific file is kept as part of the file mechanism. A bit table has the advantage that large sections of the table can be kept in core memory and that the allocation and deallocation cost is minimal. This advantage is of importance in highly dynamic environments. The tables, on the other hand, are quite vulnerable to errors, so that they tend to be practical only where the file system keeps track of its allocation in a manner which can be used by the operating system. It is then possible to reconstruct or verify the bit table by checking through all the individual file tables.

File systems themselves can also use bit tables to locate their member portions. The use of bit tables is especially effective where the portion-allocation data do not have to be kept in serial order. Bit tables for a specific file tend to be very sparse, but their efficiency can be increased by a technique of packing. The packing of a sparse bit table is achieved by indexing groups of the bit array. A group which has only zero entries is indexed by a zero, and not actually represented. The index itself can be recursively grouped and indexed. Figure 6-20 illustrates this technique for File B.

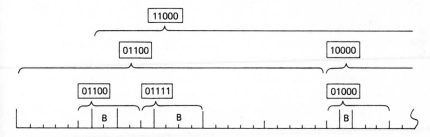

Figure 6-20 A packed bit array.

Bit arrays have also been used where portions, or records, are being shared by multiple files. Since no space is required within the portion, there is no limit to the number of owners that such a portion can have.

We see that there are a number of possibly conflicting objectives in the design of a free-storage-management algorithm. The primary conflict is again speed versus space. To increase file performance, it is desirable to provide large portions, and also to locate new portions close to the predecessor portions. To decrease the cost of space management, one may also wish to allocate large portions, which reduces the frequency of allocation as well as the size of the required tables and lists. To use storage space well, it is desirable to allocate variable or small portions.

6-5-3 Summary

Table 6-3 summarizes these free-space-management methods. The basic methods can, of course, be improved at some cost in complexity, time, and core requirements.

Table 6-3   Evaluation of Three Free Space Management Techniques

Methods Criteria	Contents directory	Chained free portions	Bit tables
Portion size	Large	Large or small	Small
Portion variability	Variable	Variable or fixed	Fixed
Allocation frequency	Low	Low to high	High
Time to allocate space	Medium	Long	Short
Free space control	Poor	Medium	High
Basic crash security	Medium	Medium	Low
Core space required	Moderate	Low	Moderate

An operating system which does not provide good management of storage space imposes a greater load on the file system. Some file systems allocate separately for files within a larger space assigned to a user (MUMPS), or allocate from a very large space allocated by the operating system for all files in its purview, as seen in VSAM in Sec. 4-3.

6-5-4 Reliability in Allocation

An important aspect of free-space management is file reliability. The assignment of permanent file resources to a user is even more critical than the assignment of core memory to the user's processes. While there are routine hardware-protection features which require a storage key to be matched for every data reference to core storage, equivalent facilities have to be implemented through software in the file-system area, except in those systems where files are considered extensions of virtual core storage segments. In Chapter 11 we will discuss some file-protection structures. It is the free-space-allocation routine and hence the operating system, however, which controls ownership and has to set the privilege codes and keys which enable file protection schemes to perform their work.

Because of the great risk inherent in the reassignment of space, computer systems have been designed which would never have to reuse an address. This is achieved by providing an extremely large virtual address space ($\gg 10^{20}$). The MULTICS system achieves this goal for all data at a given point in time. In more commonly available hardware some of this protection can be achieved by assigning portions for reuse that have been free for the longest period. Then there is increased recovery capability when portions have been released to free space in error, either by the system due to a program error, or by the user due to a mistake. Unfortunately, many systems assign free space on a LIFO basis rather than according to the safer FIFO rule, since the "last in first out" method is much easier to implement when free-space portions are maintained in chains. A ringlike structure could be used to hold free portions of storage for FIFO allocation.

BACKGROUND AND REFERENCES

Out of the many available statistics texts, Dixon[69], Freund[62], and Snedecor[67] provided the required background. Feller[68] presents a comprehensive foundation of probability theory. Moroney[56] is a very readable introduction, and Huff[54] warns of many pitfalls in the use of statistics.

Useful mathematical techniques can be found in Knuth[69,73S] and in Acton[70]. Agarwala[70] addresses the problems of recognizing distributions, and Bhattacharya[67] separates bimodal mixtures of normal distributions. Statistically based analysis of file systems has concentrated on direct access methods: Peterson[57], Johnson[61], and Buchholz[63]. Measurements of access patterns are provided by Lum[71K,73], and Deutscher[75].

The application of a variety of techniques to computer-system behavior analysis is demonstrated in Freiberger[72]. There is not much incentive to publish the routine application of statistical techniques to system design, and because of this void, it is difficult to judge how much these techniques are used and how powerful they have shown themselves to be.

Simulation as a tool has been used for planning of a large variety of technical and social projects and is often associated with database efforts in order to provide the required input to the simulation model. A journal, *Simulation*, is devoted to this field. A very readable introduction to simulation is given by MacDougall[70], and Teichrow[66] presents an extensive survey and categorization of simulation types and languages with many references. A textbook in this area is Gordon[69], who is the designer of GPSS, a simulation program often used for computer-system modeling. Kiviat[69] describes SIMSCRIPT and some applications. Computer systems have been simulated to evaluate interacting processes (Nielsen[67] and Skinner[69] are examples), but the relative importance of file operations has been low in these studies. Seaman[69] includes input-output processes applicable to files. Glinka[67] sketches a simulation of an information-retrieval design. Reiter in Kerr[75] presents the development of a simulator to handle a variety of files. Cheng[69] describes the use of logging files to drive simulations. Buchholz[69] presents a synthetic file-updating program, and Sreenivasan[74] uses this program to derive a workload for testing. Fishman[67] analyzes the problem of the validity of simulation results generated from random inputs.

Any computer managing more than one process at a time will need queue management as part of required operating system services. Methods to obtain effective scheduling of queues were initially tried in the teleprocessing environment, where message queuing was a familiar concept. Seaman[66] mentions scanning to improve disk access, and Weingarten[66] presents the case for drum queuing by sector, the Eschenbach scheme and in Weingarten[68] extends this method to disk. Denning[67] give a simple analysis of practical queue scheduling policies. These and other early papers take into account track-switching delays, which are no longer important.

Coffman[69] gives results for queue optimization with SSTF. Burge[71] and Denning[72] resolve the problem of drum performance for random arrivals of requests which access sectors uniformly, using Markov processes.

Frank[69] analyzed SCAN and N-step-SCAN for uniform requests and complex disk devices using discrete probabilities and simulation. Teorey[72] analyzes and simulates a number of scheduling algorithms, and proposes CSCAN as well as switching of scheduling policies. The assumptions made in these analyses have to be considered very carefully before the results can be used. Coffman[72] analyses FSCAN; it is the technique used in the CII SIRIS operating system which supports the database system SOCRATE. Stone[73] compares SSTF with other scheduling disciplines for drums with variable-length blocks. Wilhelm[76] presents the case where FIFO outperforms SSTF on disk and Goldberg[79] presents a problem in paging. Fuller[75] summarizes queuing policies and their analyses; included are confirmations of results in earlier reports.

Operations Research has emerged as an applied science mainly because of the problems faced by the industrial mobilization of World War II. Much of the mathematical background was already available. Queuing theory had been developed and applied to telephone systems by A. K. Erlang in 1909. A basic and easily read textbook describing methods used in OR is Wagner[75]; Hillier[67] or Hertz[69] provide fundamentals. Feller[68] includes some examples of queuing in his treatment of probability theory, and Kleinrock[75] covers the theory and practice of queuing systems.

Hellerman[75] and Stone[75] consider queuing problems in computer systems; Graham[78] and Denning[78] provide surveys. Kobayashi[78] aproaches performance issues formally. BrinchHansen[73] analyzes queuing in time-shared processing, but many of the assumptions do not hold for file systems. Allen[75] and IBM F20-7[71] summarize queuing theory for message-processing systems, and Martin[72] includes some approximations to queuing results. Newell[71] applies queuing to rush-hour transients, using a parabolic approximation; the sine-based approach presented here is original and appears simpler. Many of the analyses of scheduling disciplines in the previous section use results from queuing theory.

Morgan[74] describes replacement algorithms for files on mountable diskpacks and uses linear programming (LP) for some solutions. Benner[67] uses LP to optimize record allocation in an IMS-like hierarchical structure, and Stanfel[70] uses LP to optimize fetch time in trees. Chu[69] and Severance[72] apply LP to file design. A CODASYL database is optimized by De[78]. Ramamoorthy[79], Chen[80], and Ceri[82] use OR to design distributed databases. Levin[78] uses a branch-and-bound method. Pelegatti in Bernstein[79] and Ceri[82] minimize the communication costs.

The use of techniques developed for inventory control to determine the time interval for file reorganization is due to Shneiderman[73]. Arora[71], Vold[73], Yao[76], Tuel[78], and Batory[82] address the same problem. Sockut[78] models concurrent reorganization and provides a survey (Sockut[79]). Young[74] and Lohman[77] use a similar technique to obtain the required interval for checkpointing.

The specific procedures for storage allocation are found in the internal documentation of operating systems. Brinch Hansen[73] reviews some of the techniques used. Frey[71] provides an evaluation of a file system with block allocation and many reliability considerations. The algorithm for dynamically increasing file allocations is provided by Litwin[80]. Fragmentation as it occurs in core memory has been analyzed, and some of the results are transferable to files. Knuth[73F], for instance, shows that "first-fit" storage allocation performs better than expected.

EXERCISES

1 Redo Exercise 4-1 given that the text lines are of length 70 with a standard deviation of 30 characters.

2 Redo Exercise 2-8 given that the request rate for tracks has a Poisson distribution over the track numbers with a mean of 0.5.

3 a Sketch a distribution of the access times between blocks on tape.

  b Calculate the standard deviation.

4 Do Exercise 3 for a disk or other direct-access unit.

5 What queue-scheduling policy is used by the file system that you have been using? Do you find the policy reasonable? Which users are being favored and which are being discriminated against? Prepare an argument to management for changing the policy.

6 In Example 6-2, used to demonstrate the normal distribution, space was saved by placing fewer records into a block. When is the technique apt to be effective in an indexed or in a direct file?

7 Reevaluate the same example for the case that the distribution was not normal, but symmetric and unimodal.

8 Section 6-1-6 stresses understanding of the model when applying transformations. What was the model used for the billing data? Does it make sense? Using this model, what is the expectation of outstanding bills if the hospital doubles size and billings? What can cause failure of the model?

9 Specify the simulation steps for
" 29.4: Record 'Jones' is in core and disk D is free."

10 Read a scheduling algorithm other than FIFO used for processor scheduling and apply it to a file system. Compare the effectiveness and the validity of the analysis in the file environment.

11 During lunch hour a large number of orders for stock purchases are placed at a brokerage, creating a queue within the processor which updates the order file. Estimate the earliest time when the entire order file can be tabulated.

12 Write a program to simulate the queue management problem, and apply it to two selection algorithms. Compare the processing of two identical workloads. Explain the differences in behavior.

13 Describe the free-space-allocation procedure of the system you have available. Is it safe? Is it efficient? If you want a bunch of contiguous space, how do you get it?

14 Describe how a random-number-generating routine generates a uniform distribution. Describe how a normal random-distribution routine generates values which are normally distributed, using a uniform-distribution-generating routine. The listings of the programs used can be found in the documentation of your computer service.

15 Using the Poisson distribution of Sec. 6-1-5 as an example, compute the median and the mode, and use Eq. 6-1 to estimate the median from the mean and the mode. Apply these to some moderately skewed distributions.

16 Recalculate the expected update cost for an indexed file (Sec. 3-4) given that it has been determined that data changes are distributed normally around the current data value.

Files and Databases

We have now completed Part 1 of this book, the discussion of file organizations and their design. Part 1 provides the basis for Part 2 of this book, the design of database structures. A database contains a diversity of related data so that typically several files are used to hold the data. Other files may be needed to hold descriptive information about the data and their relationships.

The analysis of files is characterized by an emphasis on performance issues. The analysis of databases concentrates on logical structures. The result of this analysis is a precise specification of the contents and the required manipulations of the database. Files and support programs that are chosen for implementation of a database have to satisfy the database specification and provide adequate performance for the users of the database.

An integrated collection of support programs and file structures to support a database, its logical requirements, and an interface to users and user programs is called a database system. We will first deal with databases in an abstract fashion.

Chapter 7

Database Structure

An abstract term is like a valise with a false bottom, you may put in it what ideas you please, and take them out again, without being observed.

Alexis de Tocqueville
Democracy in America (1835)

We now consider the organization of a database. After some initial discussion of models we introduce some formal aspects of database semantics. In our model files are abstracted as relations and the interaction between files as connections. Section 7-3 presents six relation types and three connection types which become the building blocks for our database models. Section 7-4 defines the operations to manipulate these building blocks, and in Sec. 7-5 we discuss building an integrated database with these tools.

A *database system* is the combination of programs and files which are used together. An integrated collection of programs to support databases can form a *database management system*. A database system has to provide facilities at the level of individual data elements so that our models will consider the semantics of individual attribute types. Chapter 8 will concern itself with the description of data elements and file structures for implementation.

7-0 STRUCTURE DEFINITION

Data values derive their meaning from their relationship to other data elements. The grouping of data elements into the linear structure of a record has been the principal means to define relationships seen so far. A record typically contains data values related to one instance of some real-world entity or concept. Another linear relationship used has been the concept of seriality of records, exemplified by the *get-next* operation. More complex relationships have been encountered in the discussion of the ring-structured file, the hierarchical files, and in some of the examples of hybrid file structures. In order to be able to discuss the structure of a database consisting of many files we will need to define a number of concepts which can describe relationships among records and sets of records.

Structure in Data Processing In conventional data processing the relationship between records for a computation is implied by the processing action of programs. A program will fetch records from several files, associate the values found, and produce information for the user. The processing programs are written with knowledge of the contents of the files.

Example 7-1   Related files
_____

For example, a vendor of goods will have
> A file containing data on invoices sent for which payment is to be received
> A file containing data on payments received during the day
> A file giving a credit rating code to the firm's customers

The three files are structurally related. The **Payments** received are related to the **Invoices** issued through an **invoice_number** and the **Invoices** are related to the **Credit_rating** file via a **customer_number**. A computational procedure updates the credit rating based on all the invoices sent to a customer which are not marked **paid**, so that there is also a less obvious procedural relationship. Figure 7-1 illustrates the relationships recognized by an **Enter payments** application for a particular set of records.
_____

The programmer will select records with matching values for related attributes for processing. Errors in the structure will lead to errors in the programs.

A payment without an **invoice_number** cannot be posted.

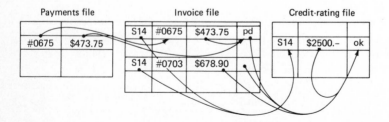

Figure 7-1 File structure to enter payments.

Introduction to Models The major method for database design is the construction of models which represent the database structure in a manner which allows the manipulation of the conceptual building blocks for the database. Only when the structure is well understood can a suitable file design be chosen. A model is hence the prime tool for the database designer. The objective of the modeling approach presented in this book is to provide a basis for the design of effective and usable databases.

The material in this chapter includes results of researchers and practitioners. While the more practical aspects of current work have been selected, many of the approaches in the literature have not been widely verified through application in the implementation of large systems. The structural model presented here has been used in a variety of situations, but any application has to be combined with *common sense* and *insight*.

This chapter will also make current research in database design more accessible. We have tried to use established terminology as much as possible. Reference to Appendix A is recommended to provide linkages to terms used in work of some authors. In the background section for this chapter a number of alternative modeling approaches are summarized in the terms developed here. Chapter 9 provides examples of the implementations of some modelling approaches.

We stated that, in conventional processing, the transaction program selects and combines records based on relationships defined by the programmer. These relationships are, however, independent of the processing programs. Relationships among the data within a file and among multiple files form a structure which establishes the meaning of the data. The objective of this chapter is to develop a means for recognizing and describing this structure in a way that guidance is provided for the design of databases and the selection of database management systems.

The tool used to describe databases is the *structural model*. It is based on a well-known formal model, the relational model, which defines single files or relations and operations applied to them. The relational model has been augmented with a formal definition of relationships between files, called *connections*. Three types of connections are used to classify relations into five types, which have distinct structural features (see Sec. 7-3-9 for a summary). When all the definitions for the database have been collected, we have a structural model of the database, or a *database model*.

The model captures some of the meaning or *semantics* of the data, so that less is left to the imagination of the programmers who write application procedures. Only the semantics that affect the structure of a database are captured in this model; finer semantic distinctions are ignored. If the information contained in a database model can be automatically interpreted by a database management program, some data-processing functions can be automated. Requests (queries and updates) to such a system can now be expressed in a higher-level language than a programming language. A language which lets us state the problem rather than the procedure to follow to get a solution, is called a *nonprocedural language*.

Our task is now to understand the basic concepts used to describe data and their relationships.

The fact that attribute values are relatable may be implied by observing that they are selected from a common domain of values (`customer_number`, `invoice_number`, or `dollars`), although relationships (say `credit_rating_code` to `dollars`) can also exist between domains that are not explicitly the same. We will concentrate on the simpler cases where domains are identical. A function could be defined to create a derived attribute `dollar_limit` of type domain `dollars` for the `Credit_rating` in order to define procedural relationships in a structural manner.

Multiple Files and the Database   In modern enterprises many functions are performed by computers. This means that many files will be in use. Many relationships will exist among these files. We defined database to be a collection of related files. In order to have a database system, the usage of these files must be integrated and coordinated. When we speak of a structure for the database, we consider all relationships among all files.

The management of available data is a major problem in many large businesses where files have been established as the need for data arose. The `Personnel` file will contain data on employee history and pay scales. When this file is processed at the end of a pay period, an output is generated which provides financial input data to an accounting system. Other financial data may come from manufacturing and sales applications. For the writing of a proposal for a new contract, data may be required from personnel and manufacturing files. For a cash-flow projection sales data will be needed together with financial data. Without a database system each time that data are jointly processed they will be selectively copied from source files and merged to construct new files appropriate for the application. The number of files in an enterprise can easily exceed several hundred, so that a major effort is required to manage the data and avoid errors.

The maintenance of a complex set of interrelated files can become a major bottleneck in a complex enterprise. When this problem is recognized, an integration of the files will be seen as desirable and a system to manage all the files as a database will be considered. Throughout the remainder of this chapter the assumption is made that the necessity for an integrated database does indeed exist.

Multiple Views   If we want to consider the semantics of data in a model, we face an immediate problem. A database which is used for two different purposes may have two distinct models when viewed by the two users. While multiple views of a database may be implemented using multiple distinct file arrangements, the resulting multiplicity of files and the duplicated data in them create severe problems in updating and maintaining consistency of data.

A case of three views of the same database can occur in the `Patient-Drug` file presented in Sec. 4-5. One purpose for a drug database is to keep track of drugs prescribed for a specific problem of the patient, and the file was structured to make the drugs subordinate to the patient's problems. Certain drugs, however, will interfere with other drugs given. For a drug-interaction analysis it is preferable if all the drugs used by one patient are kept together. For a study of the effectiveness of dangerous drugs, researchers may see a hierarchy which begins with the drug type. A patient using many drugs appears in many records according to the drug researchers' view.

Dealing with several views simultaneously can make the construction of a valid database model nearly impossible. The views may conflict, although they are each correct. The more uses a database serves, the more conflicts arise between the

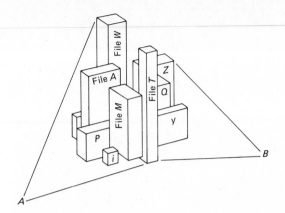

Figure 7-2 Two views of a database.

different views. In order to cope with this problem, we will define a database initially from one point of view only. Eventually the same database may be defined similarly from other points of view. The structural model provides the means to *integrate* two or more distinct views.

In the next four sections we define means to describe models for a single view. Integration of views is discussed in Sec. 7-5.

7-1 VIEW MODELS

One single view of the database can be described by one model. A view model represents a small subset of reality, appropriate to one application of the database contents. Most databases will require several view models for their specification. The parochial view-by-view approach to understand the structure of a database has the advantage that the complexities of relationships seen in real-world databases may be conquered.

Most modeling concepts apply equally well to database models as to view models. We will stress the term *view* only where the emphasis is warranted. Many models in the literature do not deal with the multiple-view problem directly, so that the term database model is often applied to what is actually a view model.

7-1-1 Relations and Their Domains

A view model is constructed from data elements and their relationships. Data elements represent values of attributes of entities. The most basic expression of a relationship is the binary relationship (Fig. 7-3a). The three elements of a binary relation (object, attribute, value) were recognized in the LEAP structures (Sec. 4-7).

Multiple relationships are found when data are collected and organized for processing. The steps in Fig. 7-3a,b,c,d provide examples of the initial building blocks of view models. First a number, say n, of simply related data elements may be placed into a list or *n-tuple*. One *n*-tuple represents multiple attributes of some object. This grouping simplifies the management but makes the original relationships less obvious.

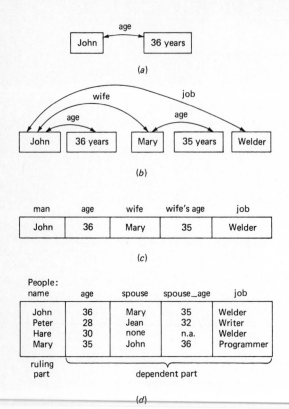

Figure 7-3 Relationships, tuples, and relations. *(a)* A binary relationship. *(b)* Multiple binary relationships. *(c)* Tuple. *(d)* Relation.

Sets of similar tuples are assembled into *relations*. Each tuple in a relation represents some distinct object and expresses similar relationships among its attributes. The choice of values for any of the attributes, the *domain*, is also specified.

Each relationship in a record is defined by the name labelling the tuple columns: the *attribute*. A column of a relation now contains similar data elements. The specific relationships among attributes is not represented in the relation but is implied by the heading line of attributes, the *relation-schema*. The ordering of attributes is immaterial as long as the tuple layout matches the relation-schema. The database structure will be defined so that the original relationships can be properly recovered.

Each tuple exists in order to describe a specific object O. We can consider one or some of the attribute columns to name or define the object. These attributes form the *ruling part*. The remaining attributes (V) are the *dependent part*. This distinction provides the essence of the original relationships among the attributes and will be vital when models are manipulated. We will make sure that the relation-schema of a view model contains only attributes which can be properly assigned to the ruling or to the dependent part.

In Fig. 7-3 the decision to include the `spouse_age` into the tuple has led to redundancy in the `People` relation. Another model for the given relationships will be less troublesome, but more than one relation will be needed.

We can summarize the important definitions given as follows:

> A *tuple* is a collection of related heterogeneous atomic data elements.
>
> A *relation* is a set of homogeneous tuples. Within one relation the data elements in a specific position of any tuple belong to the same attribute.
>
> A *relation-schema* describes the attributes in terms of their *domain* of values and their participation in the ruling or the dependent part.

Table 7-1 compares the terminology for the four levels of abstraction which we encounter in file and database design. We now formalize these definitions.

Domains The form and content of a tuple are governed by rules derived from its membership in a relation. With each attribute a specific *domain* is defined from which values can be selected. The number of values in a domain can be extremely large or can be quite limited. We consider domain semantics formally in Sec. 7-2.

The domain of an attribute for an invoice amount can range from millions of dollars to an equally large credit. The domain D_t of an attribute `temperature` in a tuple describing people may be {`97.0`, `97.1`, `...`, `105.0`} and the domain D_c `color`{`black`, `brown`, `white`, `yellow`, `ruddy`, `red`, `purple`}. The sizes of the two sample domains D_t, D_c are $\#D_t = 71$ and $\#D_c = 7$.

Relations Tuples are formed by taking one value for each attribute out of the domain corresponding to this attribute. Representing the domains of the data element values by sets D_j, where a D_j is known for each of the attributes A_i for each position, allows the definition of a relation R with attributes A in its relation schema to be a subset of the cartesian product of the underlying domains $D(A_i)$

$$R\{A_1, A_2, \ldots, A_a\} \subseteq D(A_1) \times D(A_2) \times \ldots \times D(A_a) \qquad 7\text{-}1$$

and a tuple is one *row* of such a relation. The possible range of values of an attribute A_j is the domain D_j. Attributes of relations must have distinct names; in the model the order of the columns will be of no formal concern. More than one attribute of a relation can have the same domain.

Two identical domains in one tuple could occur in a relation describing an inventory of automobiles, where each car has two attribute columns listed with the domain `color`, one for the exterior and one for the interior of the vehicle. This permits a computation to match the interior color to the color of the exterior.

These identical domains have two different *roles*. Each role of a domain in a tuple implies a relationship and a distinct column. An attribute name within a relation identifies both domain and role and is unique. We do not define a formal syntax to relate domains and attribute names In the earlier example `age` and `spouse_age` are distinct attributes which have identical domains. We will always

Table 7-1   Terminology

Hardware	Software	Model	Semantics
Disk	File	Relation	Entity set
Documentation	Schema (see Chap. 8)	Relation-schema	Description
Block	Record	Tuple	Object
Address	Key	Ruling part	Object name
Content	Goal	Dependent part	Attributes
Byte number	Attribute name	Attribute	Attribute
Data format	Data type	Domain	Value range
Byte or word	Attribute value	Data element	Value

give unique names to attributes in a relation, so that any column in the model is identified by giving `Relation.attribute`. For each attribute of any relation R_p in the model the domain D_d will be known

$$R_p . A_i \rightarrow D_d \quad \text{where } i = 1, \ldots, a_p \qquad\qquad 7\text{-}2$$

Domains of attributes have to be identical for comparison or merging of attributes. We call such attributes *compatible*.

Domains for some attributes may appear to be identical when they are actually not. An example is an employee's home and business phone numbers. Not only are the two value sets distinct, but they also obey different rules for updating. The office phone number, possibly shared with many employees, changes when the employee moves to another office. The home phone number remains valid, since it is dependent on the individual employee only. This distinction may be best expressed through the use of distinct domains, rather than through different roles on the same domain.

The simple but formal definition of a relation permits the manipulation of the model. In the construction of view models we place further restrictions on the structure of the relations. These restrictions will assure that the intent of the views is preserved. In Secs. 7-1-2 to 7-3-6 we develop these restrictions. We will require that the number of attributes is fixed, that there are no duplicated tuples, that no attributes are themselves relations, and that there is no redundancy caused by awkward assignment of attributes to relations.

7-1-2 First Normal Form

When we manipulate the relations of a the view model we treat them as mathematical sets of tuples. This requires among other things that the attributes within each tuple are ordered and complete, and that the domains permit only simple values. *Simple values* cannot be decomposed into multiple values, and cannot themselves be sets or relations.

A feature of records in programs which therefore cannot be modeled in a single relation is a nested repeating data element or a nested repeating group of elements such as a subarray for `children` in Fig. 7-4. If a nested group is of bounded size, and preferably small (here 10), such a subset can be represented by a fixed number of attributes assigned to different roles over the same domain. Since groups may be smaller than the fixed maximum number, the domain has to include the value `null` or `undefined`.

More often we remove the nested group to another relation. In Fig. 7-4 this is done with the nests of supervised employees, the **no_of_supervisees** can range from 0 for the janitor to $n - 1$ for the company president. A new relation **Supervision** is used to capture all the nested **supervisees** lists for all employees. The repetition of the supervising employee's name in the **super** field provides the linkage from the tuples in the new **Employee_1** relation, so that the information about who supervises whom is not lost.

The process of removing nested groups is called *normalization*, and the resulting relations are designated to be in *first normal form*. When relationships are expressed through common domains in separate relations rather than by being in the same tuples of one relation, the structure is less tightly bound. Searching the databases for a relationship takes more effort when binding is weaker, but flexibility increases. Some binding can be provided in the relation-schema. The schema of the **Employee_1** relation indicates that there exists a connected relation **Supervision**. Relations throughout the remainder of this chapter are in first normal form. Schemas are the subject of Chap. 8.

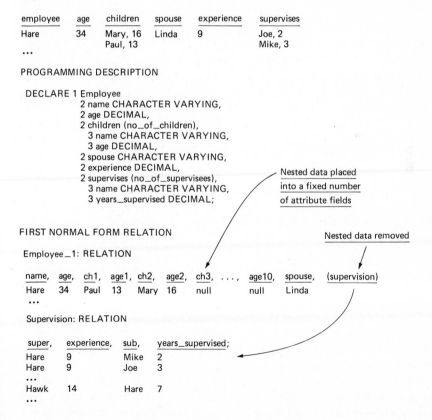

DATA

employee	age	children	spouse	experience	supervises
Hare	34	Mary, 16	Linda	9	Joe, 2
		Paul, 13			Mike, 3
...					

PROGRAMMING DESCRIPTION

```
DECLARE 1 Employee
         2 name CHARACTER VARYING,
         2 age DECIMAL,
         2 children (no_of_children),
            3 name CHARACTER VARYING,
            3 age DECIMAL,
         2 spouse CHARACTER VARYING,
         2 experience DECIMAL,
         2 supervises (no_of_supervisees),
            3 name CHARACTER VARYING,
            3 years_supervised DECIMAL;
```

Nested data placed into a fixed number of attribute fields

FIRST NORMAL FORM RELATION

Nested data removed

Employee_1: RELATION

name,	age,	ch1,	age1,	ch2,	age2,	ch3,	...,	age10,	spouse,	(supervision)
Hare	34	Paul	13	Mary	16	null		null	Linda	
...										

Supervision: RELATION

super,	experience,	sub,	years_supervised;
Hare	9	Mike	2
Hare	9	Joe	3
...			
Hawk	14	Hare	7
...			

Figure 7-4 Relation in first normal form.

7-2 SEMANTICS OF RELATIONS

In order to build a model we have to define the internal structure of the relations and the relationships between the relations. In this section we present the underlying formalisms and in Sec. 7-3 we will employ them to create building blocks for database design.

7-2-1 Ruling and Dependent Parts

A tuple of a relation can be considered to be a partial description of an entity or a real-world object. Entities used in earlier examples were people, invoices, payments, and creditors.

Within one relation we distinguish the set of attributes which define the object described by the tuples - *the ruling part* - and those which provide data regarding the object - the *dependent part*.

In most our view models relations should have ruling parts which are unique, since we wish to have only one descriptive tuple per object. This immediately makes the tuples themselves unique. The ruling part should not contain redundant attributes; that is, it should not contain attributes, which when removed, would still leave a ruling part with the property of uniqueness. When an employee number is in the ruling part of a relation, the employee name is not also in the ruling part, since employee numbers are assigned uniquely. As a notational convenience in the examples that follow, we will in relation-schemas place the ruling part before the dependent part and separate them with the symbol " :⟩ ".

Example 7-2   Relation-schema for a automobile registry

```
Automobile: RELATION
     state, license_number :) make, model, year_manufactured, owner;
```

Since first-normal-form relations are also mathematical sets, the tuples of a relation *must* be unique. Given this constraint it is always possible to find a unique ruling part; in the worst case, it includes all the attributes and the dependent part is null.

Structure versus Meaning   Finer distinctions among relationships can be made. A single concept, *dependent attribute*, is used to convey all the shades of meaning available through expressions such as "belongs to", "being", "married to", "possessed by", "purchased by", and "having". A model connection to another relation can describe the employees with whom a person works, the department, the position held, or the product produced. Knowledge of the semantic structure supplements in an essential manner the contents of the database itself. We treat the semantics in a simplified manner, discussing meaning only to the extent that the semantic relationships affect the structure of a view or database model.

Dependent part attributes of a relation depend on the ruling part of the relation for their definition and existence. Similarily we find that attributes in one, secondary relation may depend on attributes in another, primary relation. If the dependent attributes are in the ruling part of the secondary relation, the existence of tuples in that relation becomes dependent on attributes of the primary relation.

We will now consider some formal definitions and axioms about these dependencies. In many practical database design problems an intuitive understanding of dependencies is sufficient. This section may be skipped or skimmed lightly by readers who want to proceed to the building blocks for the structural model presented in Sec. 7-3.

7-2-2 Functional Dependencies

If the value of some attributes B is always determined by the value of other attributes A, then we say that B is functionally dependent on A. In our model the dependent part of a relation is functionally dependent on the ruling part.

A dependency is derived from reasoning about the data; it is not deducible from any given collection of data, although it can be disproved by testing a database which is factually correct.

The ruling part of example 7-2 has two attributes A_1, A_2. The concept of dependencies is the basis for establishing correctness in the models and the databases we design. A functional dependency FD is defined as follows:

Attributes B are functionally dependent on attributes A, or

$$FD(A_1, A_2, \ldots, A_h, \ldots, A_j) = B_1, B_2, \ldots, B_i, \ldots, B_k \qquad 7\text{-}3$$

if the value B_i in any tuple is always fully determined by the set of values $A_1, A_2, \ldots, A_h, \ldots, A_j$.

A_h, B_i are simple attributes as defined in Sec. 7-1-2.

To avoid redundancy in the ruling part, we require that no subset of the ruling part can be found which would also be an adequate ruling part:

If both $\quad FD(A_p, A_q, \ldots, A_r) = B_i \quad$ and $\quad FD(A_1, A_2, \ldots, A_j) = B_i$

$\qquad$ where $(A_p, A_q, \ldots, A_r) \subseteq (A_1, A_2, \ldots, A_j)$ $\qquad\qquad$ 7-4

$\qquad$ then use $\quad FD(A_p, A_q, \ldots, A_r) = B_i$

There may be more than one candidate ruling part, for an `Employee` perhaps an `employee_number` and {`employee_name`,`employee_address`}. Both alternatives satisfy Eqs. 7-3 and 7-4. The choice depends on the view model.

Example 7-3   Redundancy in Dependencies

An example of a redundancy in ruling-part attributes can be found in a relation describing departments of a store. The ruling part contains both the name of the manager and the title of the department.

```
Departments: RELATION
    manager_name, department_name :) budget, no_of_personnel;
```

If we know that a department always has one manager even though one manager may direct more than one department, then FD_1(`department_name`) = `manager_name`.

The manager's name is functionally dependent on the department name, as are the other attributes (`budget`, `no_of_personnel`), and the `manager`'s name should be removed to the dependent part. In an `Employee` relation the name may be the ruling part. For the manager the `job` = `'Manager'` may appear in the dependent part.

7-2-3 Dependencies and View Models

When we construct a model, we may find functional dependencies which are redundant. A simple case of a redundant set of functional dependencies is given below:

$$FD_2(\texttt{employee}) = \texttt{spouse}$$
$$FD_3(\texttt{employee}) = \texttt{home\_address}$$
$$FD_4(\texttt{spouse}) = \texttt{home\_address}$$

This simple case can be resolved by striking out FD_3 or FD_4; the choice will be determined by the desire to have the most realistic view model for the user. A view model has to be kept small if functional dependencies are to be verified by comparision with real-world practice. The view model for the company psychiatrist may reject FD_3, but the payroll department will ignore FD_4.

We will add one more constraint to our definitions of functional dependencies in major view relations: *no reverse functional dependencies*. This rule holds only for any single view model but not for lexicons (Sec. 7-3-3) and may be violated in an integrated database model:

There exists no FD, say FD_q,

such that $FD_q(B_i) = \{A_p, \ldots, A_r\}$ where $i \in \{1, \ldots, k\}$ 7-5

and A, B are defined as in Eqs. 7-3 and 7-4.

This means we do not recognize any dependencies from the dependent part on the ruling part within a view model. This rule also helps to avoid cases of circularity. A well-known but dull example of circularity is the set of dependencies

$$FD_5(\texttt{zip\_code}) = \texttt{city}$$
$$FD_6(\texttt{city, address}) = \texttt{zip\_code}$$

We resolve this issue in structural modeling again by having two view models, one for the mail delivery service (FD_5) and one for the senders of mail (FD_6).

The database model has to resolve differences among the view models; correct view models can always be integrated. Keeping view models simple helps attain correctness. Complex redundant functional dependencies occur when a composite attribute provides the ruling part of the relationship. Further normalization of relations, discussed below, will assist in the recognition of functional dependencies and avoidance of awkward structures.

7-2-4 Multivalued Dependencies

A *multivalued dependency* occurs when an attribute value determines a set of multiple values. Examples seen earlier were the sets of **children** and **supervisees** of an **employee** in Fig. 7-4(a). We can state for such sets of dependent attributes

If each set $\{B_{l,1}, \ldots, B_{l,s_l}\}$ is fully determined by the values $A_1, \ldots, A_j$

then $MVD(A_1, \ldots, A_j) = \{B_{1,1}, B_{1,2}, \ldots, B_{1,s_1}\}, \{B_{2,1}, B_{2,2}, \ldots, B_{2,s_2}\}, \ldots$ 7-6

The set $\{B_{1,1}, B_{1,2}, \ldots, B_{1,s_1}\}$, say, the **children** of the **employee** object defined by $A_1, \ldots, A_j$, is independent of the $\{B_{2,1}, B_{2,2}, \ldots, B_{2,s_2}\}$, the **supervisees**, just as the **employee**'s **home_address** is independent of the **birthdate**.

In a model which includes any MVD, say $MVD(\textbf{employee}) =$**child**, all children should be represented for the **employee** whenever any **child** is, so that the data are complete. This will satisfy the MVD. If any **supervisee**s, or other $B_{l,r}$ are being represented the same rule of completeness holds.

Completeness is being further defined in dependency theory and is related to the universal instance assumption. This work is outside of the scope of this text.

If always only one entry exists in a set $(s_l = 1)$, then $B_{l,1}$ or B_l is functionally dependent on the $(A_1, \ldots, A_j)$. Functional dependency is hence a special case of multivalued dependency.

$$\text{If} \qquad FD(A) = B_l \qquad \text{then} \qquad MVD(A) = B_l \qquad \qquad 7\text{-}7$$

Since a FD is more restrictive, it is more powerful in database design than a MVD.

Dependencies within a tuple of a fully normalized relation should be FDs. We are concerned only with MVDs when there is no FD between the attributes. The attributes $B_{h,p}$ in multivalued dependencies may also be themselves composed of multiple values or groups. The **employee**'s **salary_history** will consist of subtuples with attributes **date_given, salary**.

Multivalued dependencies cannot be represented within a model using only normalized relations; a relation can only include any nested sets $B_{h,\ldots,s_h}$ by enumeration. Such a relation has to contain each legal combination. For i included sets this requires $s_1 \times s_2 \times \ldots \times s_i$ tuples. For the **Employee** with 3 **children**, 5 **supervisee**s, and 4 entries in the **salary_history** 60 tuples are implied. This representation contains obviously much redundancy and is not in first normal form. This representation is not at all clear since the dependencies leading to this representation are not explicit.

The structural model, and other models dealing with this issue, represent multivalued dependencies by an ownership connection between a main relation and nest relations for each multivalued dependency. A operation, the *natural join*, which combines the two relations, is described in Sec. 7-4-4 and permits creation of the enumerated format when it is needed.

Example 7-4   Organizing data with multivalued dependencies

As example we use the case where an employee **Joe** has multiple supervisors. Which supervisor is in charge depends on the job being worked on. Supervisor **Peter** may supervise **Joe** when doing **Maintenance** and supervisor **Paul** when **Joe** does **Development**. We have a relation-schema with the attributes {**supervisor, job, employee;**}. Neither **supervisor** nor **job** is a correct ruling part here; they are not neccessarily unique over the tuples. We want to state

$$\textbf{employee} \;\; :\rangle \;\; \{\textbf{supervisor, job}\};$$

Alternative single relation-schemas to store the data are

Supervision_job_list: RELATION	Supervision_employee_list:RELATION
supervisor, job :⟩ employee;	supervisor, employee :⟩ job;

but these two views do not express the underlying MVD.

The set of dependent values need not be a nested group but may be any set of multiple values which are not independently functionally dependent on the ruling attribute. The problems of representation are illustrated in Example 7-4.

7-2-5 Rules for the Transformation of Relation Schemas

Given that we have been able to express all required functional and multivalued dependencies from a real world view in terms of simple and composite attributes, the relation-schemas can be manipulated. The first three transformations are known as *Armstrong's axioms*, and others are derived from these [Ullman[82]]. They represent formal rules of transformations which will, in general, be intuitively obvious during the design process.

Reflexivity Subsets of a set of attributes are functionally dependent on their full set. In terms of our definitions, there is

$$FD(A_1, A_2, \ldots, A_j) = A_k, A_m, \ldots, A_o \quad \text{for } k, m, \ldots, o \in \{1, 2, \ldots, j\} \qquad \text{7-8}$$

This axiom defines the *trivial dependencies* which exist since in any relation tuples which agree in the values for $A_1, \ldots, A_j$ also agree in the values for any $A_k \mid k \in \{1, \ldots, j\}$.

Reflexivity also applies to *MVD*s as defined in Eq. 7-6. Reflexivity of *FD*s also implies an *MVD* as demonstrated by Eq. 7-7.

Augmentation Ruling and dependent parts can be augmented with the same attributes.

If $\qquad FD(A_1, A_2, \ldots, A_j) = B_1, B_2, \ldots, B_k$

then $\qquad FD(A_1, A_2, \ldots, A_j, C) = B_1, B_2, \ldots, B_k, C$ $\qquad$ 7-9

Augmentation also applies to *MVD*s.

Transitivity Dependencies are transitive, so that a chain of dependencies can be merged.

If $\qquad FD(A_1, A_2, \ldots, A_j) = B_1, B_2, \ldots, B_k$

and $\qquad FD(B_1, B_2, \ldots, B_k) = C_1, C_2, \ldots, C_m$ $\qquad$ 7-10

then $\qquad FD(A_1, A_2, \ldots, A_j) = C_1, C_2, \ldots, C_m$

Transitivity as defined above applies also to *MVD*s but is actually more restrictive, because sets of attributes $B_{l,1} \ldots, B_{l,s_l}$ are not acceptable as ruling parts.

Union Dependent parts can be merged, so that we can combine relations that have the same ruling part.

If $\qquad FD(A_1, A_2, \ldots, A_j) = B_1, B_2, \ldots, B_k$

and $\qquad FD(A_1, A_2, \ldots, A_j) = C_1, C_2, \ldots, C_m$ $\qquad$ 7-11

then $\qquad FD(A_1, A_2, \ldots, A_j) = B_1, B_2, \ldots, B_k, C_1, C_2, \ldots, C_m$

Dependent parts of *MVD*s cannot be merged, since the dependent attributes $B_{i,r}$ of an *MVD* exist independently of other *MVD*s.

We will in the view model always merge FDs having the same ruling part, so that only one relation will be needed to describe all simple facts about an entity. We applied this rule already when constructing tuples out of dependencies in Fig. 7-4.

The only time when we will have more than one relation with the same apparent ruling part $A_1, A_2, \ldots, A_j$ occurs when the domains $D(A_i)$ differ in some sense.

Example 7-5   Relations with differing ruling part domains

Consider the two relations

```
Employee: RELATION
   employee_number :) jobtitle, date_of_birth, ...;

Managers: RELATION
   employee_number :) jobtitle, date_of_birth, ..., stock_options;
```

In the `Managers` relation the domain for `employee_number` is restricted, but such restrictions are awkward to express in terms of domain rules. A better way of expressing the restrictions is to state that `jobtitle = 'Manager'`.

To keep our examples clear we will always use identical attribute names A_i to imply identical domains, so that $D(A_i) = D(R_y.A_i) = D(R_z.A_i)$. The notation $D(R_x.A_i)$ to determine some D_d is based on Eq. 7-2.

> **Decomposition** Dependent parts can be split, so that one relation can be transformed to several relations having the same ruling part.
>
> If $\qquad FD(A_1, A_2, \ldots, A_j) = B_1, B_2, \ldots, B_k$
>
> then $\qquad FD(A_1, A_2, \ldots, A_j) = B_1, B_2, \ldots, B_i$ $\qquad$ 7-12
>
> and $\qquad FD(A_1, A_2, \ldots, A_j) = B_{i+1}, B_{i+2}, \ldots, B_k$
>
> The selection of a dependent attribute B_d to become a member of the first, the second, or both relations is of course arbitrary.
>
> View models are decomposed mainly to form building blocks for new relations. We also decompose relations to separate MVDs and FDs.

Some secondary axioms can be derived from these by straightforward processes. The union axiom (Eq. 7-11) is in fact derived using Eqs. 7-9 and 7-10 by augmenting both FDs, one with the A's and the other with the B's and applying the transitivity axiom to the results. The decomposition axiom (Eq. 7-12) is derived by selecting a subset of the B's, recognizing the FD of this subset due to reflexivity (Eq. 7-8) and applying transitivity (Eq. 7-10) to this FD and the original $FD(A) = B$.

These axioms can be used to rearrange the view models and to create the database model from the view models. They are sufficient to obtain a complete set of functional dependencies FD^+. This set is obtained by initializing FD^+ with the known set of FDs, and applying the three Armstrong axioms (Eqs. 7-8, 7-9, 7-10) in turn to FD^+ to create more entries into FD^+ for the next phase.

The process of obtaining all FD's may be costly, since the set FD^+ becomes rapidly large, but could be useful to understand a view model.

A nonredundant model in terms of functional dependencies can be obtained from a set of relation-schemas by

1 Decomposing all dependent parts to single attributes in order to create binary relation-schemas

2 Ordering the simplified relation-schemas by their ruling part

3 Removing all redundant FDs in this list by retaining only one, and only the simplest ruling part for any dependent attribute

4 Composing new relations where ruling parts match

We frequently use these axioms when trying to arrive at a semantically clear and effective model. The transformations required for this purpose are typically easy to prove correct using these axioms, and if they cannot be shown correct are likely to have an error.

Functional dependencies continue to exist among relations that have been decomposed during normalization, and may also be defined among relations that have been established separately. Multivalued dependencies will always be between distinct relations in a structural model.

7-2-6 Value and Reference Attributes

When we analyze the attributes for a model, we find two types of domains being used. Figure 7-5 provides examples of both types. Some attributes describe characteristic properties of an entity directly by assigning a value to the data element. A permanent domain definition, kept with the relation-schema, permits verification of values for new entries.

Examples of *value* attributes are the `height`, `weight`, and `age` of the employee. If the employee is dismissed and the employee's data tuple is deleted from the relation, the values will also disappear. No instance of `age = 34` may exist if `Hare` leaves the company.

Other attributes describe characteristics of an entity indirectly by reference to another entity. The domain used here is termed *reference domain* and the allowable values in the domain are defined by the existence of tuples in another relation. The domain definition can be changed by an update to the referenced relation. The referencing attribute and the referenced relation establish a *reference connection* in the model.

The employee tuple, for example, has an attribute which contains the name of the employee's department. The department will continue to exist when the employee leaves, and will even continue to exist, barring other action, even if all employees leave the department. We will in our models find distinct relations for the department, so that its existence is recorded in the database independently of assignments of employees.

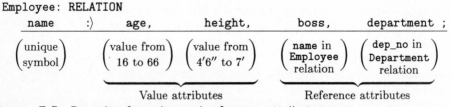

Figure 7-5 Domains for value and reference attributes.

7-3 BUILDING BLOCKS FOR MODELS

We now define relation types to be used in building view and database models. We will describe these informally, so that the function of the different types can be appreciated without reference to the formalisms presented in Sec. 7-2. We also describe conditions and normalizations which assure that all types of relations support a consistent update and deletion behavior. The relation types being introduced are summarized in Sec. 7-3-9.

7-3-1 Entity Relations

A relation which defines a set of independent objects or entities is termed an *entity relation*. The choice of entity types is a fundamental aspect of the design of a view model. Relations which define objects that are not entities (nest relations, lexicons, and associations) will be presented below and their usage will clarify the issues. Entities are typically objects that can be touched, counted, moved, purchased, or sold and that do not lose their identity during such manipulations. A change due to an update to a tuple of another relation will not require a change in an entity relation. An entity relation itself, when updated, may require further changes in subsidiary relations.

In Fig. 7-5 the referenced department was considered an entity. Even without any employees a specific department entity object will exist and be described by a tuple in the entity relation **Departments**. The tuples for the nested **children** of an **employee** will be removed when the employee quits. A new employee may require new entries to be made in the **Children** relation. We observe that from the point of view of the view model for company personnel, the children are not entities. The relation **Supervision** is not an entity relation either.

```
Employee: RELATION
  name :)  birthdate, height,  weight,  job,              dep_no,  health_no ;
  Gerbil   1938       5'3"     173      Welder             38       854
  Hare     1947       5'5"     160      Asst.welder        38       2650
  Hawk     1921       5'6"     153      Manager            38       12
  Hound    1956       6'2"     155      Trainee            38       1366
  Havic    1938       5'4"     193      Welder             32       855
```
Figure 7-6 An entity relation.

The attributes may be basic values or references to tuples in other relations, as shown for the **Employee** of Fig. 7-6.

7-3-2 Nest Relations

First-normal form excludes repeating nests of attributes or of groups of attributes. During normalization we remove these nests to separate relations which we call *nest relations*. Tuples of nest relations have a ruling part which is the composite of the ruling part of the owning relation and an attribute value which is unique within the nest. This constraint permits recovery of the semantic linkage implied by the multivalued dependency from the owner tuples to the nest tuples. The structural model notes the dependency as an *ownership connection*. A nest relation derived from the example in Fig. 7-4 is shown in Fig. 7-7.

```
Children: RELATION
  father,  child :) age_c;
  Gerbil   Phillip   5
  Hare     Paul     13
  Hare     Mary     16
  Hart     Bea       1
```
(*a*) Nest relation

(*b*) Example showing pointers

(*c*) Symbolic notation; Bachman arrow
denotes the ownership connection

Figure 7-7   Nest relation.

The tuples of these nest relations are dependent on the owner tuples for their
continued existence. This means that tuples can be inserted in a nest relation only
if there is a matching owner tuple and that tuples in a nest relation have to be
removed when the owner tuple is removed. This constraint will be formalized as
the *ownership rules* in Sec. 7-3-6.

These rules derive from the $MVD(owner) = nest$, and assure that the actions
are consistent with the actions taken if no normalization would have taken place or
if the nest was expanded to a fixed set within the relation, as shown in Fig. 7-3.

The dependent part of a nest relation is ruled properly by the catenation of
the parent's ruling part and the tuple-specific ruling attribute, for instance, in Fig.
7-7: `father,child`. Nest relations may, of course, be the parents of other nest
relations, as shown in Fig. 7-8. This hierarchy also shows the transitivity of *MVDs*
(Eq. 7-10).

Many levels of nesting can be encountered. The models may also require
multiple nest relations at the same level. The `Employee` relation in Fig. 7-3 had
two potential nest relations, `Children` and `Supervision`. The tuples from these
two nests should not be merged (Eq. 7-11).

```
Education: RELATION
  father,  child,  schooltype :)  school_name,     subject       ;
  Hare     Paul    High school    St.  Mary         Science
  Hare     Mary    High school    St.  Mary         Social science
  Hare     Mary    College        U.C. Berkeley     Political science
  Hawk     Buzzy   ...
  ...      ...
```
Figure 7-8   Second-level nest relation.

7-3-3 Lexicons

In any relation the ruling and dependent parts should be clearly identified. We do often encounter relations which have more than one *candidate ruling part*, for instance

```
Department_detail: RELATION
    dep_no ∨ dep_name :⟩ manager, location, budget, ...   ;
```

To resolve the ambiguities in the dependencies when there are multiple candidate ruling parts we remove redundant ruling parts of a relation R into a very specific type of a relation, the *lexicon L*.

After this process, for R,

$$FD(B_i) \neq (A_1, A_2, \ldots, A_j) \qquad\qquad 7\text{-}13$$

where B_i and A_i are defined as in Eq. 7-3. Now Eq. 7-5 is satisfied, except for the lexicon relation L itself.

A lexicon defines a one-to-one correspondence between two sets A and B by the binary relation $L : A \leftrightarrow B$. Here the dependent part is functionally dependent on the ruling part and the ruling part is functionally dependent on the dependent part, i.e., $FD(A) = B$ and $FD(B) = A$. In simple terms we can say that a lexicon implements equivalency.

Each tuple in a lexicon should reference a corresponding tuple in the entity relation and vice versa. We note in the view model this structural dependency using *reference connections* between the relations.

A lexicon relation, giving a listing of department names versus department numbers, is shown in Fig. 7-9. Since the ruling and the dependent part are symmetric, either attribute can be used as the ruling part in an implementation and the other part can then be uniquely determined.

The final entity relation which describes departments in detail (`Dep_detail`) has as its ruling part the `dep_name`, and the `dep_no` would be the key for the related lexicon. To get data about a department known by number, one would use the lexicon to obtain the `dep_name`, and then proceed to `Dep_detail`.

```
Departments: RELATION
   dep_no ⟨:⟩  dep_name     ;
   23          Bookkeeping
   27          Auditing
   31          Foundry
   32          Forge
   34          Stamping
   38          Finishing
   38          Assembly
   50          Test
   33          Quality control
   24          Inside sales
   25          Outside sales
```

Figure 7-9 A lexicon.

Lexicons occur frequently in operational databases, and recognition of lexicons during the view analysis simplifies the design process since ruling-part conflicts are avoided. Such conflicts also occur when distinct view models are integrated, and lexicons are often created during that process.

Another case for a lexicon appears in the `Employee` relation of Fig. 7-6. The relation has another candidate for the ruling part, namely, the `health_no`. In a view model for employee health care, this number may be the ruling part. A lexicon will connect the two view models.

Lexicons can be treated conceptually as a single attribute while designing a database model, and this approach can greatly reduce the number of possible alternatives of the model. This pseudo-attribute could be named `department_id`, deferring the decision on how the department is actually identified. Once a lexical pseudo-attribute is defined, the lexicon does not take part in the model manipulations until the file implementation is considered.

7-3-4 Second and Third Normal Form

In Fig. 7-4 we placed the years of experience of the employee in the `Supervision` relation, since this provided a meaningful separation of personal and professional data. The ruling part for this relation, using the earlier definitions, is the two attributes `super` and `sub`. The `years_supervised` are functionally dependent on this ruling part, but the `experience` is functionally dependent only on a subset of the ruling part, `super`. We note that the `experience` is hence redundantly recorded in every tuple beyond the first one for each supervising employee. To avoid this redundancy the attributes which depend on subsets of the ruling part are moved to a separate relation or added to another, appropriate relation.

In this case the `experience` attribute will be assigned to the `Employee` relation rather than to the `Supervision` to in order to achieve a nonredundant form as shown in Fig. 7-10. At other times a new relation may have to be defined, as shown in Example 7-5.

```
Employee_2: RELATION
  name :)  age,   ch1,   age1,  ...    spouse,   experience, (Supervision) ;
  Hare     34     Mary   16     ...    Wendy     9
  ...      ...

Supervision: RELATION
  super,  sub :)  years_supervised,    (Employee_2.experience) ;
  Hare    Mike    2
  Hare    Joe     3
  ...     ...     ...
  Hawk    Hare    7
  ...     ...     ...
```

Figure 7-10 Second normal form relations based on Fig. 7-4.

Example 7-6　　Creating a referenced entity relation

Given a relation-schema

```
Job_performance: RELATION
    employee_name, duty :⟩ hours_worked, bonus_pay, ...  ;
```

we may find that the `bonus_pay` is a factor which depends on the `duty` only, i.e., there is a $FD(\text{duty}) = \text{bonus\_pay}$. A new relation will be established and the old relation will be transformed:

```
Job_performance_2: RELATION
    employee_name, duty :⟩ hours_worked, ...  ;
```

$$\longrightarrow \text{Duty\_description: RELATION}$$
$$\text{duty :⟩ bonus\_pay;}$$

The relation `Duty_description` collects this factor and any other information about the duties. This information is now retained even if no employee currently performs some `duty`. Without the `Duty_description` relation the `bonus_pay` must be entered with every change of `duty`.

The removal of functional dependencies on attributes which are subsets of the ruling part is called *normalization to second normal form*. It does not apply when the ruling part has only a single attribute. The dependent part of a relation in second normal form now contains only attributes that are functionally dependent on the entire ruling part. Relations in second normal form obey the rule stated as Eq. 7-4 for all subsets of the dependent part B.

New *referenced entity* relations may be established during this process; for instance, the relation `Duty_description` in Example 7-5. This type of relation also obeys all rules established for relations: since it is a set, redundant tuples will be eliminated and the number of tuples in it will be equal or less, often much less than the number of tuples in the primary or referencing relation. The referencing attribute will appear in both relations, and becomes the ruling part of the referenced relation.

Tuples which are being referenced by a tuple in a primary relation should not be deleted; otherwise processing errors may occur. The reference attribute will have a value suitable for accessing the referenced relation. Since the relation-schemas shown in our examples do not indicate the domain types, we do not know if `job` or `dep_no` reference other entity relations.

We may not be able to compute an employee's pay if the `duty` performed does not exist in the `Duty_description`.

A further transformation, to *third-normal-form*, removes any dependencies found among attributes within the dependent part. The dependent part of a relation may still contain attributes which are mutually dependent; or, formally, there may exist an $FD(B_q) = B_p$ or a $MVD(B_q) = B_p$, where B_i is defined as in Eqs. 7-3 and 7-4. New *referenced relations* are defined for such dependencies. The structural model will again note the relationship between the referencing and the referenced relation using a *reference connection*.

```
Auto_section_a: RELATION
 assembly,  type :⟩   color,   colorcode,  ...  ;
 750381    Body      Red      93471
 750381    Fender    Red      93471
 750381    Engine    Red      93471
 750381    Seatframe White    93474
 750382    Body      White    93474
 750382    Fender    White    93474
 ...       ...
```

(a) Relation with $FD(B_1) = B_2$

```
Auto_section_b: RELATION
 assembly,  type :⟩   color,  ...  ;
 750381    Body      Red
 750381    Fender    Red
 750381    Engine    Red
 730381    Seatframe White
 730382    Body      White
 730382    Fender    White
 ...       ...
```

```
Colors: RELATION
 color    :⟩   colorcode;
 Red          93471
 White        93474
 Blue         93476
```

(b) Third-normal-form relations

Figure 7-11 Transformation to third-normal form.

In Fig. 7-11 the dependent part of a relation describes the colors of automobile subassemblies. Each **color** has a **colorcode** assigned. This redundancy can be removed by assigning a lexicon for **Colors**. In the final structure (b) only the **colors** relation has to be changed if the decision is made to change the **colorcode** of the color **red** for parts in the inventory. Such an update is correct and safe if the color code because functionally dependent on the color name.

If this functional dependency would not have been extracted and the model changed accordingly to Fig. 7-11b, this update would have to change many tuples in Fig. 7-11a. During the update transaction the file will be inconsistent. If the functional dependency were not recognized by the update transaction, some needed changes could be missed.

Redundancies in the dependent part are not restricted to one-to-one attribute relationships. An employee's job specification may contain many subsidiary attributes. Among these will be values which are functionally dependent on the job title. In order to remove this redundancy, a new referenced entity relation will be created which describes the properties of the job as shown in Fig. 7-12. A single reference attribute in the employee entity relation will then refer to the job relation by using the ruling part of the job tuples.

In the initial **People** relation (Fig. 7-3d), both **spouse** and **spouse_age** were included within the dependent part of the relation, but Fig. 7-3b indicated a relationship between these attributes: $FD(\text{spouse}) = \text{spouse\_age}$, just as $FD(\text{name}) = \text{age}$. This leads to a redundancy when a **spouse**, say **Mary**, is also entered in the **People** relation. Transformation to third normal form will eliminate this redundancy.

```
Job_description: RELATION
 job               :⟩ Education_required,   Experience_required;
 Assistant welder    Bachelor's degree        2 years
 Manager             High school diploma     12 years
 Trainee             Bachelor's degree        None
 Welder              Bachelor's degree        8 years
 ...
```

Figure 7-12 An entity relation for reference.

7-3-5 Boyce-Codd-Normal Form

Normalization provided us with relations in *third normal form*. Because of the constraints we impose on our view models (Eqs. 7-4, 7-5, 7-12), we find that the view relations obtained also satisfy the conditions for *Boyce-Codd-normal form* (BCNF).

> **Boyce-Codd-normal form** A relation is in Boyce-Codd-normal form if the only nontrivial dependencies are functional dependencies from the entire ruling part to each of the attributes in the dependent part.

The trivial dependencies to be ignored are due to reflexivity as defined in Eq. 7-8.

In the first normalization (Sec. 7-3-2) nests of attributes were removed, then lexicons (Sec. 7-3-3) were used to remove redundant candidate keys, and in the second and third normalization (Sec. 7-3-4) dependent attributes that did not depend only on all the ruling-part attributes were removed. Since Eq. 7-5 prohibits circularity in views we can now deal with BCNF relations. A sketch of dependencies within a relation reveals rapidly that a relation is in BCNF. The BCNF constraint is sufficient for all transformations we make in defining database models.

By transforming relations in a view model to relations in Boyce-Codd-normal form and establishing a number of connections between the relations we have described the structural features of a view of a database using simple building blocks. The normalized model reduces redundancy and makes explicit those functional dependencies which otherwise remain within the semantics of the tuple attribute description. The connections make the dependencies betwenn relations explicit. Both of these building blocks: BCNF relations and connections, are well defined and can be used for integration of the database and for implementing a database.

The referenced entity relations, nest relations, or lexicons created by the normalizations are constrained by their connections to the primary relation. These constraints will now be discussed.

Establishing Views The new `Employee_2` relation in Fig. 7-10, after normalization, contains data about the personal and the professional history of the employee. If it is desired to keep semantically distinct areas separate, we may employ two view models. Three relations are used for the data:

```
Personal_view:       Employee_personal: RELATION; .
Professional_view:   Employee_professional: RELATION;
                     Supervision: RELATION; .
```

The view models should avoid conflict and preserve meaning and understandability. Relations which contain data unrelated to each other except by common dependency on a ruling part reduce clarity; on the other hand, an excessive number of view models will make the eventual database model equally incomprehensible.

7-3-6 Connections

During the normalization process we encountered two types of connections. When entities are described independently within a view but are found to be related, further connections will be defined among the relations within a view. We will also describe now a third type of connection and review the functions of all of them.

Table 7-2   Connection Types in the Structural Model

Ownership connection	⟶∗	from single to multiple owned tuples
Reference connection	⟶	from multiple to single referenced tuples
Subset connection	⟹	from single general to single subset tuples

Ownership connections   We created ownership connections in Sec. 7-3-2, when describing the dependency of nest relations on the owner relations, and will encounter them again when describing associations between relations in Sec. 7-3-7. They are used to define a specific type of MVD (Eq. 7-6), namely, the case where the dependent attributes of each tuple themselves form similar sets or relations, rather than arbitrary sets. We refer to these sets as the owned set; a specific form was called a nest. The owned relation will have one owned set for each tuple of the owning relation. Ownership requires a match

$$OWNER.A_i = OWNED.A_i \text{ for } i = 1, \ldots, j \qquad\qquad 7\text{-}14$$

The owned relation will have one or more additional ruling part attributes $A_{j+1}, \ldots$ to identify individual members $r \in 0, \ldots, s$ of the owned sets. The size s of these owned sets ranges from $0 \to \#D(A_{j+1}) \times \ldots$; $\#D$ is the cardinality of a domain as shown in Sec. 7-1-1. We can now state the rules for ownership connections:

> **Ownership rules**   The ruling part of the owned relation is the catenation of the ruling part of the owner relation and an attribute to distinguish individuals in the owned sets. A new tuple can be inserted into the owned relation only if there is a matching owner tuple in the owning relation. Deletion of an owner tuple implies deletion of its owned set.

Reference connections   In the models we identified primary entity relations and referenced entity relations. Other relation types may also include references; we will use the term *primary relations* for all referencing relations. Primary relations contain attributes whose values reference tuples of the referenced relation. A tuple of the referenced entity relation provides a more detailed description for the entity or abstraction named by the referencing attribute of the primary relation. We expect to find tuples in a referenced relation to match any value assumed by the referencing attribute; absence of a referenced tuple constitutes an error. A referenced relation hence defines the domain for the referencing attribute. Referencing alternatives are sketched in Fig. 7-13.

> **Reference Rules:**   The ruling part of a referenced relation matches the referencing attribute of the primary or referencing relation. Tuples in referenced relations may not be removed while any reference exists. The removal of referencing tuples from the primary relation does not imply removal of the corresponding referenced tuple.

If these rules are not obeyed, vital information may not be available during processing, causing transactions to fail.

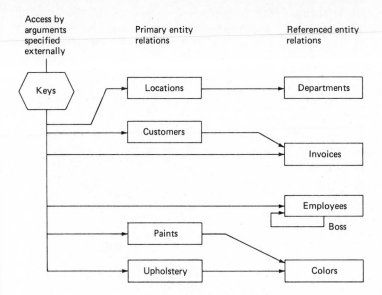

Figure 7-13   Referenced relations.

Referenced relations have to be maintained distinctly but cooperatively with the primary relations. A reference connection is based on an attribute of the primary relation, Data values being entered for that attribute must an be restricted by the domain defined by the tuples of the referenced relation. In Fig. 7-11*b* no **Mauve** fender is permitted in **Auto_section_b**.

Errors in the maintenance of referenced relations can also occur when files belonging to one database are due to different views and maintained by separate departments in an enterprise. An example where referenced relations are augmented without full consideration of the meaning of the relationship is shown in Fig. 7-14.

To avoid redundancy of **color** specifications in Fig. 7-11 a relation was created for the three colors in use at the factory. When it became desirable to specify also the paint type used, this relation was extended, but now an inappropriate type of paint is specified for the engine.

Auto_section_c: RELATION

assembly,	type	:)	color;
750381	Body		Red
750381	Fender		Red
750381	Engine		Red
750381	Seatframe		White

Color_b: RELATION

color	:)	colorcode,	painttype;
Red		93471	Acrylic
White		93474	Lacquer
Blue		93476	Acrylic

Figure 7-14   Improper extension of a referenced relation.

A lexicon is a special type of referenced relation. Because of the restriction of a one-to-one correspondence between ruling parts and dependent parts, either part of a lexicon can fulfill the ruling part function required in referenced relations.

Artificial Reference Tuples The existence of a value in the referencing attribute requires the existence of a corresponding referenced tuple. When a `null` value is permitted in the referencing domain, this fact has to be noted in the referenced relation.

This can happen if the color for a new automobile part is yet unknown or if a part, say a drive shaft, does not have a color.

To satisfy the model rules in a consistent manner, we allow the referenced relation to have a tuple with the value `null` in its ruling part, and appropriate values in the dependent domains. There are other conditions which may make the use of *artificial reference tuples* desirable. Some frequent types of key values for artificial reference tuples are shown below.

Table 7-3   Artificial Reference Tuples

Key	Condition	Function	Action
*	null	unknown	`'check_with_supervisor'`
Λ	none	not applicable	ignore
?	any	placeholder	to be computed

The last type of tuple (`any`) is useful when constructing query relations; the symbol "?" is to be replaced with appropriate matching entry for "any" color.

The effect of the use of the artificial reference tuple `null` is to defer error messages or inconsistency reports to a later stage, so that major database updates are not made impossible or delayed because of minor omissions in the input data. The extent to which this deferred binding of reference values is desirable depends on the operational and management philosophy of the database user.

Subset connections A subset connection is needed when we find relations with formally identical ruling parts, but differing attributes or domains.

Example 7-7   Decomposition to subset relations

In Fig. 7-3 we had a first-normal form relation

```
People: RELATION
   name :) age, spouse, spouse_age, job;
```

and had to remove the `spouse_age` to obtain a relation in Boyce-Codd-normal form. Those spouses who are not employees are entered into a general relation, and attributes specific to employees form a subrelation. The subrelation is constructed by decomposition and the general relation by decomposition and a union where $D(\text{name}) = D(\text{spouse})$ and $D(\text{age}) = D(\text{spouse\_age})$ so that

```
All_people:RELATION          ⟹          Employees:RELATION
   name :) age;                             name :) spouse, job;
```

A subset connection identifies the `Employee` tuples to belong to tuples of `All_people`. A change of `spouse` now no longer requires an update of `spouse_age`.

Subset relations occur frequently. We may want to collect attributes for managers or sales staff that are not needed for other employees, as was shown in Example
7-5. We may collect data on classes of vehicles such as cars, buses, and trucks.
which have many commonalities and some differences.

> **Subset rules** The ruling part of a subrelation matches the ruling part
> of its connected general relation. Every subset tuple depends on
> one general tuple. A general tuple may have no or one tuple in any
> connected subset relation.

The *generalization* of subclasses to larger classes is essential to data-processing;
the recognition of individual subclasses and the collection of detailed data is important to give depth to the database and is often needed in specific views. The
integrated database model has typically a much higher fraction of subrelations than
the individual view models. During integration in Sec. 7-5 we will see how such
subrelations are created.

7-3-7 Associative Relations

Finally we will consider relationships which contain data which depend on the interaction or association of entity relations. These relations will be termed *associative
relations*. An associative relation has a ruling part composed of two or more
attributes. The attributes relate each tuple in the associative relation to tuples
in two or more owner relations. Figure 7-15 presents an associative relation. The
connections from the owner relations to the association are ownership connections,
and all the stated rules apply.

The attribute or attributes $A_{j+1}, \ldots$ which distinguish individuals r in the
owned subsets (see Eq. 7-14) are now taken from the other owner relations. Any
other ruling part attributes will be redundant and removed during normalization.
The number of owners is arbitrary, although during normalization we often find
dependent attributes on associations owned by two relations. Associations of have
as ruling part the union of the ruling part of their owners.

In general for an association

$$A_{association} = \bigcup_{owners} A_{owners} \qquad\qquad 7\text{-}15$$

where the sets A are the ruling part attributes as originally defined in Eq. 7-4 and
used throughout.

There may again be $0 \rightarrow s$ tuples corresponding to one tuple in any of the
owner relations. A classical example is the relationship between parts used by a
manufacturing company and the suppliers of these parts, as shown in Fig. 7-16.

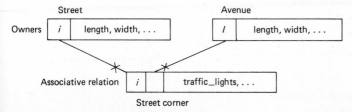

Figure 7-15 Associative relation.

Suppliers: RELATION

s_id :)	name ,	etc. ;
S1	Acme Screw Co.	...
S2	Bay Bolt Co.	
S3	Consolidated Nuts	
S4	Dzus Fasteners	
S5	Ilium Works	

Parts: RELATION

p_id :)	name,	size,	weight,	etc. ;
P2	Machine bolt	11x4	0.31	...
P3	Nut	4	0.07	
P4	Lock washer	4	0.04	
P5	Washer	4	0.02	

Supply: RELATION

s_id,	p_id :)	quantity ;
S1	P1	160
S1	P3	60
S2	P2	140
S2	P3	50
S2	P4	90
S4	P4	100

Figure 7-16 Associative relation with its two owners.

It is possible for associative relations to have no dependent part. This would be appropriate for a relation which describes the capability of a specific **Supplier** to deliver certain **Parts**. This relationship contains information, and must be explicitly modeled by a relation and two connections. Such a relation which associates suppliers which may be called upon to supply specific parts with the **Parts** relation is shown in Fig. 7-17.

The semantic difference between these two relations is not obvious from the connection structure and has to be described by attaching a definition to the relation. An association can also associate tuples within the same relation.

Possible_supplier: RELATION

s_id,	p_id :) ;
S1	P1
S1	P2
S1	P3
S2	P2
S2	P3
S2	P4
S3	P3
S4	P3
S4	P4
S5	P3

Figure 7-17 Associative relation without a dependent part.

A simple case of an association within a relation is created if we were to keep both **streets** and **avenues** of Fig. 7-15 in one relation **Roads**. Another case occurs when an employee can have multiple supervisors. An association **Supervision_matrix** between **Employee** and supervisors in the **Employee** relation will permit description of this many-to-many relationship. We see that the ownership rules apply here too. An entry in the **Supervision_matrix** requires existence of the employee and the supervisor.

7-3-8 The View Model

We have considered up to now the relations and their connections one by one. The view model will of course have many relations and connections; values on the order of a dozen are seen in practice.

Any relation can participate in multiple connections, and hence have multiple constraining rules imposed on it. For instance, referenced relations are often shared by multiple primary relations, and the primary relations may in turn be entitity relations, nests, lexicons, associations, or other referenced entity relations.

A single-view model should, however, be clear to the participants in the design process. If it is not, it is unlikely that semantic errors will be recognized. Use of a graphic representation, with the connection symbols given in Sec. 7-3-6, reveals the structure of the model.

If a view model avoids redundancy, the only attributes that appear in more than one relation are those that define connections. The owner, the reference, and the general attribute(s) are repeated, respectively, in the owned, the referenced, and the subset relation. The number of attributes $\#a_H$ found in all *nrel* relations is the number of all distinct attributes in all relations plus the number of attributes in connections.

$$\#a_H = \sum_{h=1}^{nrel} \#R_h.C = \#\left(\bigcup_{h=1}^{nrel} R_h.C\right) + \#a(\text{connections}) \qquad 7\text{-}16$$

where the set of attributes $C = A\|B$ is particular to each relation R_h.

We note also that all replicated attributes are ruling parts on one of the sides of the connections.

The definition of functional dependencies is useful to verify view models which have been intuitively constructed. The functional dependencies may in turn be verified by using available data. Although it is not possible to use data to *prove* the correctness of a functional dependency or of the view model, it is possible to find errors from existing data. Any inconsistencies that are found will be due either to errors in the data, say, different **ages** for the same employee; or to an incorrect perception of the real world: there is indeed a department with two managers, although we stated $FD(\text{department}) = \text{manager}$. In the latter case the decision has to be made whether the real world should be adjusted (the old department can be split into two departments, each with one manager) or the view model be changed (a new associative relation can be created with a ruling part composed of manager and department jointly).

It is tempting to normalize relations based on an analysis of the values of their attributes. It should be realized, however, that values in the database at a given moment in time may show relationships which are accidental and not based on true functional dependencies.

An observation made from Fig. 7-6, "All employees born in **1938** are **'Welders'**", should not be taken to be a functional dependency.

On the other hand, the main reason for the existence of databases is to support the search for new dependencies. If we find that all or many welders develop a certain type of disease, and we can eventually prevent this dependency, then the effort to develop and collect data for this database will have been very worthwhile. Such an analysis is the concern of information-retrieval processes and not part of the view model.

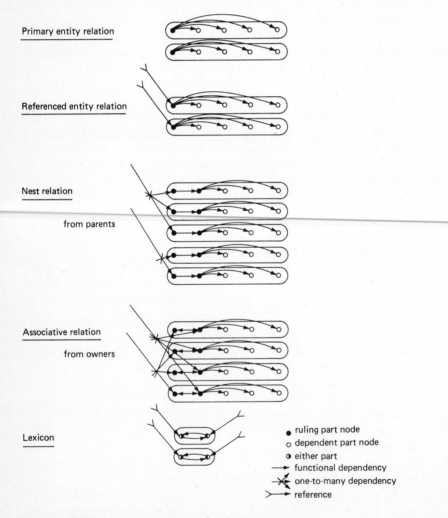

Figure 7-18   An erector set of relation types.

7-3-9 Summary

We have in this section discussed how semantic concepts regarding one particular view model or eventual database model can be described in terms of five relatively simple relation types and their subrelations:

> Entity relations
> Referenced entity relations
> Nest relations
> Associative relations
> Lexicons

and three connection types

> Reference connections
> Ownership connections
> Subset connections

The two concepts are duals of each other; a relation type defines the connections it participates in and a connection type defines the relation types it connects. Both concepts are useful, however, in dealing with models and their implementation, and both are found instantiated in database systems. Constraints between relations are more easily described using connections. Data elements and their semantics are better described using relations. A data-processing transaction is defined on both.

Figure 7-18 provides a graphical image of these types using the Bachman arrows for ownership connections, arrows with tails for reference connections, and plain arrows for functional dependencies within the tuples themselves. Use of these graphic symbols is extremely useful in presenting view models for review to the participants in a database design process. No tables or lists will illustrate the dependencies and hence the semantics of the view model as well.

When the view is approved, automatic processing of the information in the view models to arrive at a database model becomes feasible.

We will review the sematics of the relation types below, using the rules defined with the connections.

A *A primary entity relation:*
    1 Not referenced within the view model.
    2 The ruling part defines the entity.
    3 The existence of tuples is determined externally, i.e., by the user.

B *A referenced entity relation:*
    1 Referenced from within the view model.
    2 The ruling part defines the entity and establishes domains for referencing attributes. A ruling part typically has a single attribute.
    3 Existence of tuples is determined externally, but deletion is constrained by existing references.

C *A nest relation:*
    1 Each tuple must have an owner tuple within the view model.
    2 The ruling part defines one specific owner and the tuple within the owned set.
    3 An owned nest can have zero or more tuples.

D *An associative relation of order n:*

    1 Each tuple has *n* owners within the view model.

    2 The ruling part defines each of *n* specific owners only.

    3 One combination of owners can have 0 or 1 tuple in the association.

E *A lexicon:*

    1 Referenced within the view model.

    2 Either part can be the ruling part.

    3 The existence of tuples is determined externally but deletion is constrained by existing references.

    4 Its existence is transparent to the model.

F *Subrelations:*

    1 Referenced from any general relation.

    2 The ruling part matches the ruling part of the general relation.

    3 The dependent part contains attributes which do not apply to non–matching tuples within the general relation.

    4 Insertion requires existence of a matching tuple in the general relation.

The construction of each of these relation types obeys certain rules so that we can also describe these types using a Backus-Naur notation. Since such a description is essentially syntactic, some semantic constraints are added to the rules in quotes.

Table 7-4   Backus-Naur Description of Relation Types

```
DEFINITIONS:
  <value attribute>           ::= "a collection of data elements of one domain"
  <reference attribute>       ::= "a collection of references to one relation "
  <value attributes>          ::= <value attribute>
                                | <value attributes>,<value attribute>
  <attributes>                ::= <value attributes> | <reference attribute>
  <value key>                 ::= <value attributes>          "unique instances"
  <reference key>             ::= <reference attribute>       "unique instances"
  <primary entity key>        ::= <value key>                 "not referenced"
  <referenced entity key>     ::= <reference attribute>           "referenced"
  <nest key>                  ::= <attributes>   "unique within each owned set"
  <dependent part>            ::= null | <attributes>

RULING PARTS:
  <entity ruling part>        ::= <primary entity key>
  <referenced ruling part>    ::= <referenced entity key>
  <qualification>             ::= <general ruling part>      "in owner relation"
  <nest ruling part>          ::= <qualification>,<nest key>
  <assoc. ruling part>        ::= <entity ruling part>,<entity ruling part>
                                | <assoc. ruling part>,<entity ruling part>
  <general ruling part>       ::= <entity ruling part> | <referenced ruling part>
                                | <nest ruling part> | <assoc. ruling part>

RELATIONS:
  <entity>                    ::= <entity ruling part> :) <dependent part>
  <referenced entity>         ::= <referenced ruling part> :) <dependent part>
  <nest>                      ::= <nest ruling part> :) <dependent part>
  <association>               ::= <assoc. ruling part> :) <dependent part>
  <lexicon>                   ::= <key> <:) <key>
  <subrelation>               ::= <general ruling part> :) <dependent part>
```

It is possible to create from these basic semantic types other forms of relations which satisfy special conditions. A synthesis of published material indicates that these five types, plus the concepts of subrelations, cover the semantic possibilities controlling the structure of databases in an economic and conceptually convenient manner. Combinations of ownership and reference connections, for instance, lead to four types of $n \times m$ relationships among two relations. Each of the four cases has distinctive semantics.

If we have constructed and normalized a view model in an economic fashion, that is, have kept no redundant attributes, then only attributes which implement reference, ownership, or subset linkages will be duplicated. Further minimization of redundancy can be achieved by minimizing the number of relations. The extent to which this is desirable depends on the further use of the view model. If the view model is to become a basis for extended applications using the database it may by transformed to a *database submodel*.

7-4 OPERATIONS ON RELATIONS

Procedures which derive new relations by selecting from or by merging other relations can be applied to the model to formulate alternate view models. Multiple view models can be combined into database models using such procedures. Derived relations introduce redundancies when added to the view model. When a view model has been manipulated, the result has to be reevaluated and renormalized to achieve the desired degree of redundancy.

Once a database model has been defined, database submodels can be extracted which define the portion of the database which can be accessed by some group of users. This might be a user group which has provided a view but now wishes to use elements not in its original view, or it can be a user group which is new to the database. A database submodel may include *derived relations*, which are defined by transformations of the database relations and its attributes.

Derived relations are also created when a database is manipulated to provide answers to queries. Examples are found in Sec. 9-2. Of the four conventional operations between sets:

Union	$\cup$	set of elements of 2 or more (s) sets
Intersection	$\cap$	set of matching elements from s sets
Set difference	$-$	remove elements that match another set
Cartesian product	$\times$	catenate all elements from s sets

the first three ($\cup$, $\cap$, $-$) are easily applied when the relations involved have identical scope, that is have compatible relation-schemas as defined in Eq. 7-17. A fourth operation ($\times$) creates a set of all combinations of arbitrary relations. These operations are defined in Sec. 7-4-1.

Operations which are specifically defined to deal with relations are:

Projection	Π	reduce the number of attributes
Selection	$\supseteq$	select specific tuples
Join	$\bowtie$	combine attributes from two relations

These operations are defined in Secs. 7-4-2 to 7-4-5.

Transformations using these operations on relations are applicable in two situations: during the design phase we apply these operations to the relation-schema in order to transform the models of the database; after implementation we apply them the relations representing the database itself in order to compute results. When relation-schemas are transformed, we wish to make sure that any defined FD and MVDs are maintained by considering Eqs. 7-4 to 7-12.

We define the operations on relations $R(S, T)$, where S specifies the relation schema and hence the attributes and their domains, and T specifies the collection of tuples in the instantiation of the relation. We let n be the number of tuples or the *cardinality* of a relation and a be the number of attribute columns, so that we have n tuples of degree a in $R(S, T)$. The range of the number of tuples n for the results is indicated for each of the operations. For clarity we define the operations in the context of two relations; their generalization to an arbitrary number of relations is obvious where applicable.

7-4-1 Union, Intersection, Difference, and Cartesian Product

Basic are the three operations which combine relations with compatible relation-schemas, as illustrated in Fig. 7-19. Relation schemas of two relations R_1, R_2, both having a attributes, are compatible when their domains are identical

$$D(R_1.A_i) = D(R_2.A_i) \quad \text{for } i = 1, \ldots, a \qquad \qquad 7\text{-}17$$

Domains were defined in Eq. 7-2. Figure 7-20 depicts the union, intersection, and difference operations.

Taking the union of two relations which have compatible relation-schemas combines the two relations. This will increase the number of tuples, unless the two relations were identical.

$$R_3(S, T_3) = R_1(S, T_1) \cup R_2(S, T_2)$$
$$\text{so that each tuple} \quad t \in T_3 = \text{ some } t \in T_1 \text{ or } t \in T_2 \qquad \qquad 7\text{-}18$$
$$\text{Then} \qquad \max(n_1, n_2) \leq n_3 \leq n_1 + n_2$$

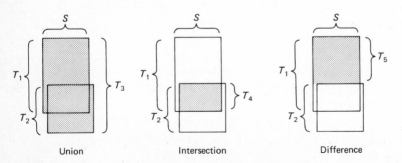

Union   Intersection   Difference

Figure 7-19   Set operations on tuples.

```
Colors: RELATION                 Fashion: RELATION
  color,    colorcode;             color,    colorcode;
  Red       93471                  Red       93471
  White     93474                  Magenta   93479
  Blue      93476                  Blue      93477

     Colors ∪ Fashion                 Colors ∩ Fashion
  color,    colorcode;             color,    colorcode;
  Red       93471                  Red       93471
  White     93474
  Blue      93476                     Colors — Fashion
  Magenta   93479                  color     colorcode;
  Blue      93477                  White     93474
                                   Blue      93476
```

Figure 7-20   Relational set operations.

The **intersection** of two relations will select all the identical tuples appearing in both relations

$$R_4(S, T_4) = R_1(S, T_1) \cap R_2(S, T_2)$$

so that each tuple $t \in T_4 = ($ some $t \in T_1 = $ some $t \in T_2)$

Then $0 \leq n_4 \leq \min(n_1, n_2)$

also $n_4 = n_1 + n_2 - n_3$

7-19

The **difference** of two relations removes from the first relation all those tuples which exist also in the second relation.

$$R_5(S, T_5) = R_1(S, T_1) - R_2(S, T_2)$$

so that each tuple $t \in T_5 = $ some $t \in T_1$ but $t \notin T_2$

Then $0 \leq n_5 \leq n_1$

also $n_5 = n_3 - n_2 = n_1 - n_4$

7-20

Another definition of the difference operation (used in PRTV) does not require both relation-schemas to be the same. The tuples which have equivalent entries on the corresponding attributes are removed from relation R_1.

The **cartesian product** of two relations creates a set of all combinations of the tuples of the relations. Here a new relation-schema is created during the process.

$$R_6(S_6, T_6) = R_1(S_1, T_1) \times R_2(S_2, T_2)$$

giving $S_6 = S_1 \parallel S_2$

so that each tuple $t \in T_6 = t_1 \parallel t_2$ for all $t_1 \in T_1$ and $t_2 \in T_2$

Then $n_6 = n_1 n_2$

and $a_6 = a_1 + a_2$

7-21

It is obvious that the product will be very large for all but the smallest R_1, R_2. We use this operation mainly as a basis for some further definitions.

A cartesian product of 15 **Streets** and 10 **Avenues** will provide the list of the 150 possible **Road_intersections** that could have traffic lights.

7-4-2 Projection

Projection reduces a relation $R(T, S)$ by limiting the attributes. The *projection* operation Π requires a list K containing the names $k_1, \ldots, k_l$ of the m attribute columns to be extracted. We recall that the attribute names uniquely identify the columns of the relations. We will first define an extract operation π which obtains a single value v from a single tuple t; v is the value corresponding to attribute A_p.

$$v = v_p = \pi\, t.k \mid t = v_1 \| \ldots \| v_p \| \ldots \| v_a\,, \quad k = A_p \in S \qquad\qquad 7\text{-}22$$

Then, performing this extraction repeatedly, for l values on n tuples of a given relation with a attributes, we obtain the projected relation. It will have k attributes and $l \le n$ tuples. The number of tuples is reduced if we have to strike out duplicate entries from the result relation; it will remain equal ($l = n$) if all attributes within the ruling part were included in the list K. In general,

$$R_7(S_7, T_7) = \Pi\, R_1(S_1, T_1).K \mid K = \{k_1, \ldots, k_l\}$$

so that the schema $S_7 = S_1 \cap K$

and each tuple $t \in T_7 = \pi t'.k_1 \| \ldots \| \pi t'.k_l\,, \quad t' \in T_1$ 7-23

Then $a_7 = l \le a_1,\ n_7 \le n_1$

Projection is used during the decomposition of a relation-schema. For instance, to create referenced entity relation the source relation is projected on the reference attribute and attributes dependent on it instead of on the ruling part. The source relation is then projected to obtain a primary relation by removing these internally dependent attributes. We can now describe the transformations applied in Fig. 7-11 from (*a*) to (*b*) as Π **R.K**, for example,

```
Colors = ∏ Auto_section_a.(color,colorcode)
Auto_section_b = ∏ Auto_section_a.(assembly,type,color)
```

The `Colors` relation in Fig. 7-11 shows how the number of tuples is reduced in order to satisfy set constraints once columns with ruling parts are excluded.

If tuples of a relation represent instances or tokens of entities, the projection by one attribute represents the categories or types for these entities. If a relation is a text, with each word being a tuple, a projection over this single attribute is the list of unique words. This concept is applied in Fig. 7-21 to the sample of the Chanson de Roland of Fig. 3-14.

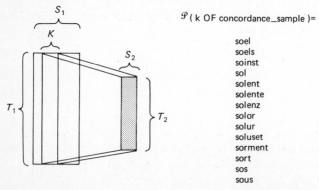

$\mathscr{P}$ (k OF concordance_sample)=

```
soel
soels
soinst
sol
solent
solente
solenz
solor
solur
soluset
sorment
sort
sos
sous
```

Figure 7-21   Projection.

7-4-3 Selection of Tuples

For the set and the projection operations the actions were expressed in terms of the relation-schemas S; the same action is performed for all tuples T of the relation $R(S,T)$. The selection operation $\subseteq$ permits the creation of a relation having the same relation-schema containing a subset of the tuples based on the values of their attributes.

For selection the tuples t are selected one by one, according to an expression list L containing l selection expressions of the form $(A \ominus constant)$, where the *constant* is some value from the domain of A. Values matching A are extracted as defined in Eq. 7-22. In general a tuple will be selected if any expression in L is true, so that the expressions are combined combined using *or*. The definition of selection is now

$$R_8(S, T_8) = \underset{L}{\subseteq} R_1(S, T_1) \mid L = \{(A_p \ominus_1 c_1) \vee \ldots \vee (A_r \ominus_l c_l)\}$$

so that $\quad t \in T_8 = \{(\pi t'.A_p \ominus_1 c_1) \vee \ldots \vee (\pi t'.A_r \ominus_l c_l)\},\ t' \in T_1$ 7-24

$$\text{with}\quad c_1 \in D(S.A_p), \ldots, c_l \in D(S.A_r)$$

Then $\qquad n_8 \leq n_1$

The selection expressions in L may also be combined using other boolean functions than $\vee$; $\wedge$ and $\neg$ are common. The most common form of test in a selection expression is of course equality ($\ominus$ ='='').

In the construction of view models selection is required when the model is partioned in new ways; for instance, the tuples for `job = 'Manager'` are selected to form the **Manager** subrelation.

This operation has its most important function in transactions. The retrieval of specific information from a database is best formulated in terms of projection of a list K of attributes to be retrieved and the list L of attributes and matching values which specify the conditions for selection of tuples, as shown in Table 9-1.

Selection can produce relations with none, one, or a set of tuples.

In program examples we write a request in the form

    `Selection_result =` $\subseteq$ `R.L`

Example 7-8 Selection of an employee category

To obtain the names and birthdates of the welders of Fig. 7-6 we create a result relation containing three tuples as follows:

```
Retrieve: RELATION
    = ⊆ Employee.(job = 'Welder' ∨ job = 'Asst.welder')
```

name :)	birthdate,	height,	weight,	job,		dep_no,	health_no ;
Gerbil	1938	5'3"	173	Welder		38	854
Hare	1947	5'5"	160	Asst.welder		38	2650
Havic	1938	5'4"	193	Welder		32	855

Selection and projection can reduce the number of tuples. If in Example 7-8 only the **birthdate** for the welders was wanted and the ruling part, here **name**, is omitted from the result, then the redundant tuple with 1938 would not show, leaving the impression that only two welders are available.

7-4-4 Join

The *join* operation ⋈ composes a new relation which combines the data elements from two relations. A join can be defined as a cartesian product of two relations followed by a selection creating a subset (Eqs. 7-21 and 7-24). The subset consists of those tuples which have identical or matching values for the *join attribute*.

A join is sufficiently important and frequent that it warrants its own definition. Each relation R_1, R_2 being joined will have a join attribute J. To permit the comparison $\ominus$ the attributes $R_i.J$ have to be compatible, just as the entire relation-schemas had to be compatible for the set operations (Eq. 7-17).

$$R_9(S_9, T_9) = R_1(S_1, T_1) \underset{J_1 \ominus J_2}{\bowtie} R_2(S_2, T_2)$$

giving $\qquad S_9 = S_1 \parallel S_2$

so that each tuple $\quad t \in T_9 = t_1 \in T_1 \parallel t_2 \in T_2, \ \pi t_1.J_1 \ominus \pi t_2.J_2$

$$\text{Then} \quad 0 \le n_9 \le n_1 n_2 \text{ and } a_9 = a_1 + a_2$$

7-25

The extract function π used is as defined in Eq. 7-22, but may be extended to include cases where J consists of multiple attributes. In our program examples we specify a join based on an equal comparison ($\ominus = \texttt{'='}$) as follows:

```
Pilots: RELATION                    Join_result = R_1.J_1 ⋈ R_2.J_2
  name, lic,  duty;
  Abe    727    on
  Bob    737    on
  Co     707    ret
  Dee    727    on
  Gay    767    tr.
  Fil    737    on
  Hap    727    off

Planes: RELATION
  no,   type,  status;
  101   727    ready
  102   727    hold
  103   737    ready
  104   737    maint.
  105   737    ready
  106   767    order
```

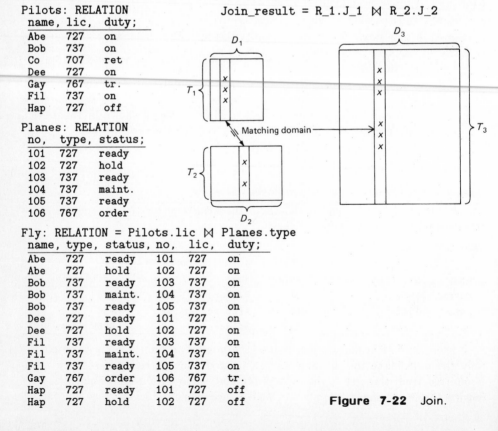

```
Fly: RELATION = Pilots.lic ⋈ Planes.type
  name, type, status, no,   lic,   duty;
  Abe    727   ready   101   727    on
  Abe    727   hold    102   727    on
  Bob    737   ready   103   737    on
  Bob    737   maint.  104   737    on
  Bob    737   ready   105   737    on
  Dee    727   ready   101   727    on
  Dee    727   hold    102   727    on
  Fil    737   ready   103   737    on
  Fil    737   maint.  104   737    on
  Fil    737   ready   105   737    on
  Gay    767   order   106   767    tr.
  Hap    727   ready   101   727    off
  Hap    727   hold    102   727    off
```

Figure 7-22 Join.

All attributes of the two relations are included in the resulting tuples. We note that if a tuple matches multiple entries in the other relation, multiple tuples are placed into the result, and if several entries in both relations match each other, their cartesian product appears in the join.

The join comes in various flavors. The most common join is the *equi-join* shown, with $\ominus$ = '='. Here all result tuples are formed by combining input tuples which have identical values in the attribute columns identified by J. The columns from the two relations involved in the equi-join are equal and one set can be omitted from the result relation, making this a *natural join*. If the number of attributes in J is j, the relation-schema for a natural join $R_9 = R_1 \underset{J_1=J_2}{\bowtie} R_2$ will be

$$S_9 = S_1 \, \| S_2 - J$$
$$a_9 = a_1 + a_2 - j$$

7-26

The equi-join is the join intended when no further specifications are given. A symbolic presentation of a join is shown in Fig. 7-22.

Joins are also implemented which use for $\ominus$ $r_1.j \neq, >, < r_2.j$. Conceptually arbitrary functions might be used for $\ominus$, so that the constraint of compatible domains for J might be relaxed. Such extensions have not been explored.

The implementation of a join rarely follows the steps implied by the definition. Generation of the cartesion product is avoided. A simple scheme is the *inner-outer-loop join*. For each tuple in R_1 all tuples of R_2 are inspected and if the condition $R_1.J \ominus R_2.J$ is true an output tuple is constructed. Other and better methods will be found in Sec. 9-3-3.

Parts_skill_required: RELATION

assembly,	type,	p_id :⟩	no_req,	skill_req ;
750381	Body	P1	10	Machinist
750381	Body	P2	12	Machinist
750381	Body	P4	22	Welder
750381	Fender	P1	26	Machinist
750381	Fender	P3	26	Welder

Supply: RELATION

s_id,	p_id :⟩	quantity ;
see Fig. 7-16		

Parts_assembly: RELATION = Parts_skill_required.p_id $\bowtie$ Supply.p_id

assembly,	type,	p_id,	s_id:⟩	no_req,	skill_req,	quantity;
750381	Body	P1	S1	10	Machinist	160
750381	Body	P2	S2	12	Machinist	140
750381	Body	P4	S2	22	Welder	90
750381	Body	P4	S4	22	Welder	100
750381	Fender	P1	S1	26	Machinist	160
750381	Fender	P3	S1	26	Welder	60
750381	Fender	P3	S2	26	Welder	50

Figure 7-23 Natural join.

A natural join is shown in Fig. 7-23. The join attribute is called `p_id` in both relations and the domain is obviously identical. While deleting the redundant join attribute we will rearrange the attributes in accordance with our ruling :) dependent part conventions.

Computed Join In Eq. 7-25 we defined the join for an arbitrary computation $\ominus$. A join operation based on a complex comparison which uses the same relations is shown in Fig. 7-24. The objective is to obtain a list of production combinations for which the part `Supply.p_id` in stock is less than ten times the `assembly,type` requirement.

Supply: RELATION see Fig. 7-16

Parts_skill_required: RELATION see Fig. 7-23

Low_stock: RELATION = Parts_skill_required ⋈ Supply
               | Parts_skill_required.p_id = Supply.p_id,
                   Parts_skill_required.no_req * 10 > Supply.quantity;

assembly,	type,	p_id,	no_req,	skill_req,	s_id,	p_id',	quantity ;
750381	Body	P4	22	Welder	S2	P4	90
750381	Body	P4	22	Welder	S4	P4	100
750381	Fender	P1	26	Machinist	S1	P1	160
750381	Fender	P3	26	Welder	S1	P3	60
750381	Fender	P3	26	Welder	S2	P3	50

Figure 7-24 Computed join.

To avoid an excess of meaningless attributes in the result of a join, it is often desirable to carry out projections on the relations before joining them. It is also desirable to eliminate common attributes of the two relations which are not useful to the join. Such attributes do not exist if the relations of the database do not contain redundant attributes, as defined in Sec. 7-3-8. The joining of relations with redundant common attributes can at best reveal an inconsistency in the data (see Exercise 7-8).

7-4-5 Transforming the Database

The operations we described in Secs. 7-4-1 to 7-4-4 apply to any relation. We will now consider how these operations affect the relation types and connections of a database described by a structural model. Connections represents knowledge about dependencies among relations. If two relations are to be joined, and there is only one connection between the relations, the default condition is an equi-join along the connection. Now the required arguments for a structural equi-join operation are only the two relations.

The join of Example 7-9 is furthermore a join where no information has been lost, since all tuples from the original two relations are represented. This is true if the projections on the corresponding attributes in both relations are equal.

Example 7-9   Join along a connection

Given from Fig. 7-11 the relations and connection

Auto_section_b: RELATION   Colors: RELATION
  assembly, type :) color;   color :) colorcode;

Color_specification: CONNECTION
  Auto_section_b.color ⟶   Colors.color;

the join operation on the relations

    Auto_section_a = Auto_section_b ⋈ Colors;

will re-create the original unnormalized relation.

In Fig. 7-16 we had an association Supply of Suppliers and Parts. Joining

    Suppliers ⋈ Supply   or   Parts ⋈ Supply

along the ownership connections of the association does not retain all the original information of the owners, since suppliers S3 and S5 and parts P5 are not represented in the tuples of resulting relation. A crossproduct of Suppliers and Parts would keep data from all tuples; the association Supply contains the information about the current subset of the cartesian product represented in the Supply inventory.

A join does not introduce new, external information into the result. Data fields which are now replicated in multiple tuples are redundant. In Fig. 7-23 we created Parts_assembly by joining Parts-skill-required and Supply, on p-id giving information on the state of the inventory for required parts. There was no connection. Note that the result is not in second-normal form, and further, that the meaning of the data in the dependent part is not obvious. Joins along connections will in general have obvious results.

The useful information in Fig. 7-23 is the combination of (assembly,type), p_id, and s_id, which informs us for each part which Suppliers are represented in the inventory, for each assembly and type. In bills-of-material processing a join of this type is called a *parts-explosion* because of the volume of detail it produces.

Joining Structural Relation Types We consider now how a join applies to the six relation types established in Sec. 7-3-9, since the semantic features of these relation types determine the semantics of the result relation. Since joins depend on correspondence of attributes which are defined in the view model, the results have predictable characteristics.

An *entity relation* when joined with another entity relation becomes an association, as seen with the street intersections of Fig. 7-15. The join only produces a list of all possible intersections; actual road crossings or crossings having traffic lights are a subset of the join result. If such a subset is specified, the membership in the subset association carries real information and cannot be omitted from the model. If a user's original data specification lists all actual Road_crossings, this set may be much smaller than the result of the join, but we can obtain a list of Streets and Avenues by projection of the attributes street and avenue in Road_crossings.

Lossless Joins   When we manipulate a view model we may use projections to decompose relations, but do not wish to lose information. Loss occurs when subsequent joins cannot restore the original relation. The first requirement is of course that all attributes are represented in the result, i.e., the relation-schemas of the projections include all attributes from the original relation-schema. We also collect information to establish connections among the result relations. If the original relation includes attributes dependent on all of the ruling part, one of the projected relations will require this ruling part and have the same cardinality as the original relation. Then, a join along the connection will recover all the original data; such a join is defined to be a *lossless join*. Tuples subsequently added to the separate relations, say a new `color` not yet used, will not appear in the result. For a lossless join

$$(\Pi\, R(S,T).(K \cup J)) \underset{J}{\bowtie} (\Pi\, R(S,T).((S-K) \cup J)) = R(S,T) \qquad \text{7-27}$$

A lossless join is guaranteed if both projections are in Boyce-Codd-normal form and J specifies the connection.

If these constraints are not followed when relations are obtained by projection and later joined again, data may be lost. When a data model is being manipulated, we are concerned that any join used to reconstruct the source specifications is loss-free; if it is, the source relations can be deleted to avoid redundancy.

When join operations are used on the database during information retrieval any compatible attributes can be used as the join attributes J. In the general case not all tuples from both relations appear in the result. In most cases this set of data presents the desired information, as shown in Example 7-10.

Example 7-10   Information loss in a join

We wish to find which `Employee` from Fig. 7-6 has the skills (`Mechanic, Welder`) to work on the assemblies given in `Parts_skill_required` of Fig. 7-23. The result is projected to retain only the attributes wanted.

```
Print_out:RELATION = Π
        ( Parts_skill_required.skill_req ⋈ Employee.job ).(name, job)
```
Two employees (`Gerbil Welder` and `Havic Welder`) will appear in the result. The fact that no `Mechanic` is available is shown only implicitly.

To deal with the problem of losing information an extension of the join, the *outer-join*, has been defined [Codd[79]]. In the result will be at least one instance of each participating tuple. In the tuples that are not matched by J the missing attributes fields are filled with `null`.

Example 7-11   Outer-join

```
Print_out_all: RELATION = Π
        ( Parts_skill_required.skill_req ⋈ Employee.job ).(name, job)
```

name,	job ;
Gerbil	Welder
Havic	Welder
null	Machinist

Joins along Connections In the beginning of this section we considered joining structurally independent relations. We now review the effect of joins along connections in the structural model. While all relations in the model are in Boyce-Codd-normal form, the relations which result from joins will rarely be in Boyce-Codd-normal form.

When an entity relation is joined with its owned relation, the result will be the size of the owned relation. Tuples from the owning relation are represented only if their owned set ≥ 1.

A join with a referenced relation will increase the number of attributes, but the result has as many tuples as the entity relation. If the referenced relation is a *lexicon* the result will have one more attribute than the referenced relation. Lexicons can also be used to substitute attributes with no loss of information.

Joins between *nest relations* belonging to the same owner relation generate new nest relations which are not in second normal form, since they share at least one of the ruling-part attributes.

Joins between *associative relations* or between associative and other entity relations will generate new associative relations.

Joins between subrelations and their general relations will merely increase the number of attributes for the tuples in the subrelations. The difference of the general relation and the new relation can be used to provide an alternate view.

```
Hierarchical_view: Employees: RELATION  ⟶⊃  Managers: RELATION;
Partitioned_view:  Non_managers: RELATION ∪  Managers: RELATION;
```

7-4-6 Sequences

In many view models the tuples in the relations are considered to be ordered. Such an order implies restrictions on the structure and operations but can also provide some benefits. We define a relation to be a *sequence* if it is ordered according to its ruling part. For numeric domains we assume ascending numerical order. Otherwise the collating sequence of the character representation provides an ordering; see, for instance, the ASCII table (14-1).

A sequential lexicon can provide sequential access to a general relation, or to a sequence which has the ruling part sequenced differently because of another attribute ordering, i.e., `child,father :⟩` versus `father,child :⟩`.

A number of new operations are applicable to sequences and other operations require new definitions. For instance, adding a tuple to a sequence implies insertion between specific tuples rather than the simple union which is adequate for relations.

For selection we can now specify the

`FIRST, LAST, and TUPLE(i)`

The discussions which follows are based on relations in their general form. If a sequence is required in the model, a lexicon can be used to describe the ordering requirements without invalidating the construction of the core of the model. Ordered attributes implemented through a lexicon have been termed *synthetic keys*.

7-4-7 Queries

The operations presented in Sec. 7-4 are combined to query the database content. A wide range of implementation approaches is possible for query processing. For actual data retrieval issues of ease of use and generality become important. These topics occupy most of Chap. 9.

Queries as Relations Projection and selection expressions can be combined and executed similar to a join when formulating a query. A query with selections and projection can be expressed in the form of a relation where the relation-schema is based on the list K and the tuples represent the selection list L. An artificial domain entry "?" is now used to represent the notion **any** to indicate that a data element value or set of values is to be obtained.

Example 7-12   Query in relation format

Selection is performed now using joins and projections applied to the query and data relations. A query for **name, birthdate** on **Employee** who can weld becomes

```
Age_of_welders: QUERY  Employee
  name,      birthdate,    job ;
    ?           ?          Welder
    ?           ?          Asst.welder
```

For general retrieval from a database selection expressions can include attributes from multiple relations.

Programmed Queries When the programming language used does not handle general sets of records, sequences become important. The information obtained from the databases has to be handled one record at a time, using the operations described in Sec. 7-4-6. It may be possible to specify that we wish to loop through all the tuples in sequence. Within the context of a current position within the sequence we can also reference the

   PRIOR, CURRENT, and NEXT tuple.

The concept of *currency* allows the specification of tuple-by-tuple algebraic procedures which would not be applicable to sets in general.

Some algebraic operations for tuple-by-tuple functions can also be applied to unsequenced relations, but the required generalization is not always obvious. In many situations encountered in practice, the conceptual view model is based on *natural* sequences, and users tend to formulate queries oriented toward these sequential models.

An example of sequential processing is the computation of group subtotals within a relation which has as the ruling part a group attribute and a detail attribute, for instance, **s_id** and **p_id** in **Supply** of Fig. 7-16. To determine the quantity of all parts supplied by one supplier we naturally add the quantities in sequence until the value of **s_id** changes. Then a new subtotal can be computed for the next supplier group.

To obtain such subtotals in unsequenced relations is a function of the **Group by** clauses shown in Sec. 9-2. A query-processing program can use the structural or a similar model to help the user in the formulation of queries by translating from the user's conceptual view model to the implemented database model.

7-5 THE DESIGN OF A DATABASE MODEL

When a comprehensive set of view models has been established, the construction of a model for the entire database can be established. Relations from separate view models may be combined based on the attributes which they have in common. If view models have no attributes in common, there is no benefit in joining these data into a single database model. Figure 7-25 sketches the concept.

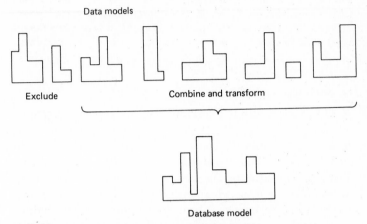

Figure 7-25 Construction of the database model.

Even when there are common attributes there may be no connections. A lack of connections indicates that the views or groups of views can be maintained independently of each other. We will call a database created from views which do not connect to other databases an *independent database*. An independent database is best maintained in a distributed manner, even if computer equipment is shared. As we discussed in Sec. 2-4-4, there are benefits to distribution, and if databases can be left smaller and managed autonomously, total costs will probably be lower.

Forcing independent databases into one integrated database is sometimes done to permit retrieval queries to access the data from multiple independent databases. Only a few database management systems today permit queries to be processed which access more than one database. The cost of combining independent databases is increased database system overhead cost in order to provide the required view model independence and protection for update transactions. Management costs, incurred to bring communality about in areas where there is little natural incentive to cooperate, may also be high.

Not even all connected view models should be integrated. The linkage between some sets of views may be relatively weak and will not warrant the integration of a view model into the database. A weak linkage may be due to a shared, but unchanging attribute. In those cases we will also design independent databases, with a procedure to keep the shared attribute synchronized.

If, for instance, employees are identified with a department, and production of goods with a department, then the list of departments may provide such a relatively constant link. Only if employees are to be related to production will there be a sufficiently strong coupling between the two areas to justify the combination of the view models.

The existence of a shared attribute which is frequently updated in two otherwise independent models provides another incentive to combine the models in order to avoid redundant update effort, even if the linkage is otherwise weak.

An example of a centralized database is found in the airlines reservations systems. The basic relations giving seat availability and flight schedules have to be shared by all users and are accessed frequently.

In manufacturing companies distributed databases are often desirable. There is much activity within a single factory which is not of interest to the company as a whole. Overall input and output data, in terms of materials, dollars, and products, describe the factory adequately from an external point of view.

Decisions regarding distribution are mainly based on experience and intuition.

7-5-1 Distributed Databases

If we have independent databases, multiple databases may be kept which are organizationally and physically distributed. Databases which are not fully independent may be made independent by replacing connection constraints with synchronization procedures. This can provide considerable advantages in terms of management and flexibility. The management of smaller, homogeneous information areas is effectively carried out within a department where expertise in the area is available.

The extent to which distribution versus centralization is desirable depends on the cost of management, operations, communications, and processing. In order to reduce operational and communications cost of distributed databases, the actual computer equipment may be shared. A distributed database does not imply physical distribution, but rather a distribution of responsibilities over multiple databases.

If the users of the separate databases are located far apart, the increased management cost for remote operation and the increased communication cost for data entry and output to the user may make separate facilities desirable. A multiple site system can be strongly integrated or distributed. The cost of the required communications for an integrated system spread over physically remote sites will make a distributed approach likely.

The constraints among connected but distributed databases implied by the connections have to be maintained. Messages will be transmitted between distributed databases to cause subsidiary transactions which maintain the databases according to the connection constraint rules described in Sec. 7-3-6.

Each database in the distributed set will have its internal connections and some connections to the other sites. The relations and connections made available at one site can be described by one *database submodel*. A database submodel may represent a single view or be augmented and modified to take into account information and data from other views included in the database. A site could also have a global, integrated model of all the data in the distributed databases.

If a database which operates at one site has the right to access data from databases at other sites, it may be wise to have a copy of the *global database model* available at each site, although only data for the local database submodel will be stored on site. The ability to change even the local part of a database model locally will now be constrained, since remote models will be affected, even if their databases are not affected by the model change.

Since communication of voluminous data between distinct databases will be more difficult than within a database, we find two features related to the implementation of database models in a distributed system. We find messages being used to communicate among subsystems, and we find *replication* of relations.

When a relation is replicated in two databases, the databases are synchronized by keeping those relations identical. We can now speak of an *identity* connection between the copies of the replicated relations in the distributed databases. If the only constraints between independent databases are formulated as identity connections, the management rules for distributed databases are simplified. All other connections now are maintained within a database. Most work (see Sec. 13-2) on integrity of distributed databases is based on replication of relations. Retrieval operations on replicated data can be performed locally, permitting rapid query processing.

If at all possible one database should be designated as the primary database; all updates are performed there and subsequently update messages are sent to the databases having identity connections. If update responsibility cannot be assigned to one database, the message traffic required to maintain integrity increases greatly. In some cases periodic switching of the primary responsibility is possible.

An example occurs in a bank, where during business hours the primary databases are in the branch office. After daily closing the correspondence of the local data with the central office data is verified, and primary responsibilty is given to the central site. Overnight the central database can be rapidly updated with transactions which arrive from other banks at the central office. Update messages are communicated to the branch offices. In the morning responsibility is switched to the branches after an integrity verification.

We note that the creation of database submodels implies the existence of an integrated database model, even though the data may not be integrated. In a distributed database there may be a global schema based on the integrated database model to aid global queries. The next section will apply to distributed as well as to centralized databases.

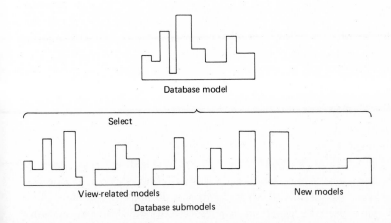

Database model

Select

View-related models   New models

Database submodels

Figure 7-26   Establishing database submodels.

7-5-2 The Integrated Database

Once the decisions have been made on which view models are to be included in a single database model, the integrated model can be constructed. The database model will consist of relations of various types, and the connections between the relations. The combination may look like a tree, like a number of trees (a *forest*), or like a network when displayed.

Objectives When the integrated database is being constructed, a number of objectives can be considered.

    1 Obtain relations with the greatest degree of semantic clarity.
    2 Retain view independence to simplify subsequent distribution.
    3 Have the smallest number of relations.
    4 Have the smallest number of tuples.
    5 Let the number of data elements stored will be minimal.
    6 Let the number of connections between relations and shared attributes be minimal.
    7 Let the total activity along all connections between relations be minimal.

Rules to establish optimality according to the last four criteria have been studied using functional dependencies between attributes as the basic elements for decision making. In many practical instances the database designs based on any of the six criteria will not differ greatly.

Semantic clarity is enhanced when strongly related attributes are grouped together, and this may be accomplished with a limited number of relations and interrelation connections. Normalization will often have increased the number of tuples and reduced the number of data elements. Integration can reduce the number of total tuples by combining them, but typically increases the total number of relations and their connections.

Transformation for Integration To integrate view models into a database model the following steps are required:

    1 Identification of identical or subset domains.
    2 Identification of compatible entities using these domain definitions.
    3 Merging of relation schemas for compatible entities.
    4 Generalization of entities.
    5 Adaptation of generalizable relations.
    6 Integration of differing dependent parts.
    7 Definition of derivable attributes.
    8 Identification of differences in view connections.
    9 Database model extensions to satisfy connection differences.

We will not treat these topics formally, but indicate for each of these steps the requirements and objectives. Simple examples will be used to clarify the process.

Integration of distinct views will often take considerable design time, since conflicts between the views will arise and require resolution. While all apparent conflicts can be solved on a technical level when using the structural model, all technical transformations should include consideration of the user's intent.

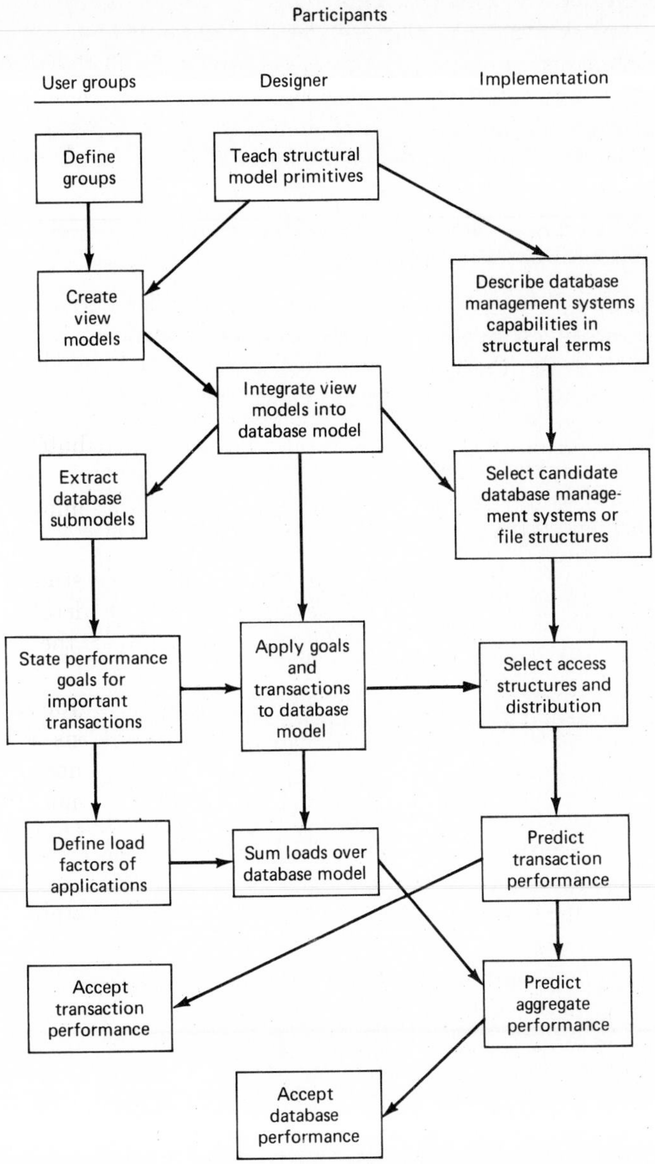

Participants

Figure 7-27 Functions during the design process.

Figure 7-27 brings together the design phases considered in this chapter and some of the issues discussed earlier. Such a diagram is of course simplified and ignores all the feedback and iterations which go on during a real design process. the time required for such a design ranges from a couple of weeks for a well-understood application which does not pose performance problems to more than a year for systems where major distinct applications are integrated and performance demands are stringent.

Identification of Domains All definitions of *FD*s and *MVD*s which lead to the entire model structure are based on the definition of attributes and their domains. In practice most domains are easy to recognize, but often difficult to define exactly. Where the domains define real entities: people, parts, planes, etc., the domains are defined by their use in the view. Where domains define abstractions: color, departments, schedules, etc., the domains may be formally defined. Domains coming from views which were obtained independently will often partially overlap.

The `colors` in cars had two roles, which might be associated with two views. The interior colors may not include metallic hues available for the exterior.

Identification of compatible entities We will first consider entities to be defined by the ruling part of view relations. Precise domain definitions applied to the ruling part attributes define the entity to be collected into the database precisely. Domain differences may reveal that different views keep data on differing subsets of an entity class.

The `Employee` relations are a prime example. If the enterprise hires consultants, the view of the personnel department may not include them, but the payroll department will, since they will have to be paid, and taxes have to be withheld on their pay and reported to the government.

Two solutions to resolve view conflicts are feasible: one is to change one or both views until they are compatible, the other is to include both views in the model. The first solution keeps database models simpler but may do violence to the user intent and make the resulting database unacceptable. Some compromises are easy; others quite impossible. The second solution is technical, and we will concentrate on that approach throughout.

Using the structural model we create subrelations and general relations in the database model to resolve conflicts. Specific cases are reviewed below.

The assignment of attributes to ruling and dependent parts was based on the concept of functional dependencies. We note that the term *always* was used in the definition of a functional dependency. A model describes a stable situation. We cannot base the design or the integration on the current contents of a database which may exhibit additional, but temporary relationships. Functional dependencies have to remain valid although data values change.

However, a functional dependency can be disproved by facts found in the database, as shown in Example 7-13.

Example 7-13   Relation-schema for a telephone book

A telephone book might be set up as

```
Telephone_book: RELATION
    name :) address, telephone_number;
```
but later shown not to represent a correct functional dependency if for one **name** combination multiple telephone numbers are found. A change is

```
Telephone_book: RELATION
    name, address :) telephone_number;
```

Merging of relations which have compatible entities   Consider R_1 to come from view model $V1$ and R_2 to come from $V2$. If the ruling part attributes A have completely identical domains $D(R.A)$ the relation-schemas can be merged and a single relation R_{db} will appear in the database model. The dependent part may have more attributes; we will consider that aspect further.

$$D(R_1.A) = D(R_2.A) \;\Rightarrow\; R_1(S_1, T) \cup R_2(S_2, T) \;\text{ so that }\; R_{db}(S_1 \cup S_2, T) \qquad \text{7-28}$$

If a ruling part attribute A has $D(R_1.A)$ which is a proper subset of $D(R_2.A)$ the relation R_1 becomes a subrelation R_1' in the model, with a connection

$$D(R_1.A) \subseteq D(R_2.A) \;\Rightarrow\; R_2 \longrightarrow R_1' \qquad \text{7-29}$$

The dependent part of R_1' will not include attributes already available in R_2. The use of a subset can be avoided by taking the union as in Eq. 7-28 and permitting `null` values to appear in the attributes $R_2(S_2 - S_1)$ for which no tuples R_1 appear. The introduction of `nulls` for the sake of reducing the number of relations in the model hides, however, some of the semantics.

Generalization of entities   Often entities are not subsets of each other, but are generalizable.

The personnel department above may not consider consultants but may keep data on retired people, who are paid by an outside pension plan. Now the payroll view is no longer a proper subset of the personnel view, although their overlap is great.

If two key domains overlap, a new general relation R_g will be created

$$\begin{aligned} D(R_1.A) \cup D(R_2.A) \to D(R_g.A) \;\Rightarrow\; R_g &\longrightarrow R_1' \\ R_g &\longrightarrow R_2' \end{aligned} \qquad \text{7-30}$$

The general relation contains all common data. Subrelations will be retained to hold instances and data particular to the subgroups. The general relation is the one to be used for general queries, where presence of special categories, here `consultants` and `retirees`, could bias the results.

Adaptation of generalizable relations   Even when ruling-part domains do not overlap, the entities may be generalizable. These cases are recognized by finding relation-schemas that are similar.

Trucks, vans, and cars are generalizable to vehicles, and this generalization is useful because similar data are kept on all of them. They also share as ruling part the attribute `license_number`.

Integration of differing dependent parts   We merged in the earlier steps relations based on compatibility of entities. Often this required the creation of subrelations. Now all the relations have been established. We now assign dependent attributes to the most general relation possible. If the original relations have dependent-part attributes that do not correspond to attributes within the general relation, these attributes have to be managed distinctly. The two approaches used earlier are feasible: changing the domains obtained from the views by augmenting the domains values so that the domains can range over all attributes is the first approach; creating subrelations is the second approach.

In the first approach an adaptation is made to the domain, the relation with fewer dependent attributes is augmented, and then the integrated relation is created. augmented with the dependent attributes on that domain. A typical augmentation is performed by taking the cartesian product of the relation with the constant **none**. Equivalently a join of relation and constant with the condition $\ominus = $ **true** may be used.

If, for instance, the attribute `cargo_capacity` is missing from `Cars`, a value "`Passengers only`" is added to the domain for `cargo_capacity` and the relation-schema and the tuples for `Cars` are augmented with this attribute prior to the merger into `Vehicles`.

Sometimes both relations need to be augmented before integration, as shown in Example 7-14.

Populating the database with many data elements of little value not only wastes space but can also confuse the user. The value **null** leads to particular problems, for instance an average of an attribute column should not include **null** values in the count. Also a join on an attribute which includes **null** in its domain will return unexpected tuples in the result. Section 8-1-3 discusses this issue. The first approach, defining special values within the domain, is often easy but should be used with care.

Example 7-14   Generalizing two relation
___
The integrated database is to have a single **Education** relation, created from the similar **Highschool_record** and **College_record** relations. Since the attribute **minor** does not exist in the high school record, the constant attribute **null** is added to the relation. Given the relations

```
Highschool_record: RELATION
    child, schoolname :⟩ subject;
```
and

```
College_record: RELATION
    child, schoolname :⟩ major, minor;
```
the relation **Education** can be generated as follows

```
Education: RELATION =
    ( Highschool_record × (schooltype='high school',minor='null') )
  ∪ ( College_record × (schooltype='college') );
    child, schooltype, schoolname :⟩ major, minor;
```

The new attribute **schooltype** distinguishes the tuples obtained from the two views when needed. Since we do not know whether **schoolname** is unique in the combined domain, **schooltype** has to appear in the ruling part.
___

The second, technical solution is again to create subrelations. The subrelations contain all those dependent attributes which are not appropriate to the general relation.

We find subrelations of the Employees for Managers with their stock_options, for Salesmen with their sales_quotas and territories, and for Retirees with the attribute last_day_worked. We note that having subrelations in the database model does not imply having corresponding files. There may well be one EMPLOYEE file with a number of variant records.

Derivable Attributes We may find in some views attributes which are derivable from other attributes. These embody strong connections which are easy to miss. Only the enumeration of a more general category, *computational functional dependencies*, of the *FD*s treated earlier will show such redundancy. Analysis of the data does not show conflicts in a model containing derived values, since the attributes are not comparable with the source attributes. Such attributes may have existed within view models or arisen after integration.

Example 7-15   Derived attribute

Perhaps a field price appeared on bills, but not within the same view as the detailed invoice, which was always recomputed. After integration we note the computation explicitly, as seen in the price field of the Invoice below.

Invoice: RELATION
    date, customer, item :⟩ value, number, price = number * value;

Derived attributes are redundant, but not always obviously so, so that inclusion of the derivation in the relation-schema can prevent later problems. Queries can now automatically incorporate the computation when a derivable attribute is requested.

Identification of differences in view connections The connections in the view models imply the constraints that update transactions must obey in order to keep the database according to the semantics specified by the user. The connections can also be exploited at retrieval time to simplify the formulation of queries (see Sec. 10-2-3). All the known connections are mapped into the integrated model and identified with their original view.

Conflicts may be found among relation pairs that now have more than one connection among them. Again two choices are available: adaptation to a single connection type and a change of one users semantics view, or the use of subrelations to represent the differing original views.

Satisfy connection differences We may find that relations to be merged have differences in connections. While there are many combinations, the essential conflict is the ownership constraint versus the reference constraint. The subset connection can be taken as a special case of an ownership. Subrelations permit again a technical solution. An illustration follows.

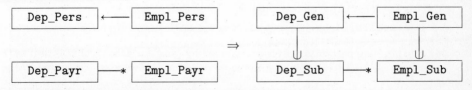

Figure 7-28 Resolving a connection conflict.

The personnel department views employees as primary entities, and includes a reference attribute to the department relation in their dependent part. The payroll department takes a narrower view; it considers only employees whose pay can be charged to a department. Here the department relation owns the employees. The transformation is shown in Fig. 7-28.

Now employees can be deleted from the payroll, but remain available to personnel. The general department relation may have a department `Limbo` as a reference for personnel not currently associated with a department.

We will illustrate some of the transformations occurring during integration. In this example ruling parts are being transformed to compatible entities. To permit a view access using the original ruling part, a lexicon is created.

Example 7-16   Integration

A paternalistic corporation provides a school for the employees' and other children in the area. For budget analysis purposes it is desirable to combine the employee view model and the school view model, so that school benefits can be credited to the employee's account.

The school view model contains the relation for the entity `schoolchildren`:

```
Schoolchildren: RELATION
    school_child_id :⟩ guardian, child_first_name, age, ...;
```
We had earlier the nest relation `Children` in the model containing `Employees`.

```
Children: RELATION
    father, child :⟩ age_c, ...;
```
The following steps are carried out in order to create the database model shown in Fig. 7-29.

1 The two attributes, father's name and child's name which constituted the ruling part of `Children` will be combined into one attribute, called `child_id_emp`. This attribute becomes the ruling part of a `Children'` relation.

2 An associative relation is constructed from the two attributes `father` and `child_id_emp` using the projection,
```
Employee_child = Π Children'.(father,child_id_emp)
```

3 The data on the children in both relations is merged by the outer-join:
```
Children'.(father, child, age_c)
    ⋈ schoolchildren.(guardian,child_first_name,age)
```

4 A final ruling part `child_id` is constructed by using for `school_child_id` if `null` the value from `child_id_emp`, for any employee children who were not registered in the school.

Many such processes can be applied when a database model is to be formed.

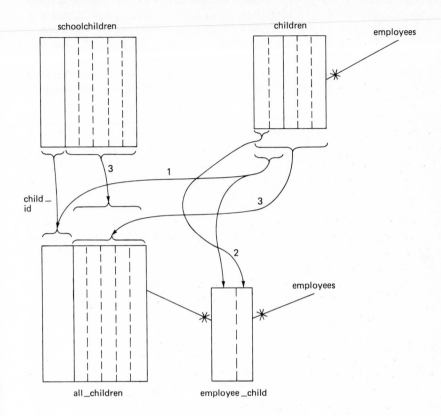

Figure 7-29 A transformation during creation of the database model.

The Datamodel after Integration The integrated database model may be complex but presents an accurate description of the user requirements. Non trivial databases in use have included from two to a few hundred relations, and from a few dozen to nearly a thousand attributes. Because of the size of integrated database models a tabular representation is preferred. Software packages have been developed to maintain much of the type of information we used in modeling, and greater automation of the databases design process is foreseen. The integrated model can be used by programmers developing a database or as the skeleton for a database to be supported by a database management system. Chapter 8 will present ways to specify the desired model and its implementation to various database-management systems.

Database designs often become unwieldly if they are forced too early into the straitjacket of a specific database-management system. The ability to design a database model without concerns for specifics of physical implementation is considered critical for the successful development of databases which are to serve multiple objectives. This does not mean that we no longer care about performance. The model provides a basis for the design of a well-performing system.

Many alternatives are available for the implementation of a high performance database. Only when the logical specifications of the database are well defined can an implementation designer evaluate what alternatives are acceptable and what alternatives will lead to errors.

When the database is eventually implemented, some compromises may be made, and these can be noted with the model documentation. Compromises may be due to limitations of a database-management system or may be neccessary to meet performance objectives.

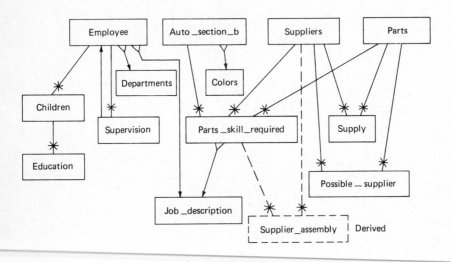

Figure 7-30 Semantic relationships in a database model.

Some observations can be made about the relation types found in integrated database models:

Former entity relations may now be referenced by relations from other views, constraining the freedom of deletion that existed previously, unless subrelations are used to resolve the view differences. Referenced entity relations which expand an attribute of an entity relation in detail, often used originally in a specialized view, are now widely available.

Two relations which share a dependent attribute domain may now both reference a new referenced entity relation to show this relation more explicitly. The use of a shared entity relation assures continued domain compatibility.

Associations appear among relations which now share owned relations. The number of pure nest relations, frequent in the hierarchical models which dominate individual views, is reduced.

We observe that integrated models contain many subrelations. Multiple subrelations and their general relation are often implemented within a single file.

Figure 7-30 depicts a connection graph based on the relations used earlier in this chapter.

Database Submodels When the view models have been transformed as indicated to accommodate the database model, the views presented by the original applications have been broadened and perhaps altered. It is desirable to maintain a description of the database in terms of the original view models, since that provides the documentation for the design.

In order to accommodate access to the database after integration, we define further database submodels. Database submodels permit an application to access the integrated database, taking advantage of new relations to which access has been made available, and at the same time presenting the structure and attributes largely in terms of its original model.

Sometimes it is better to adapt the database submodel to be a proper subset of the integrated database, since this may provide a more realistic view of the actual operation and its constraints. When database submodels are subsets in the database model, such a transformation from database model to database submodel only requires selection and can be easily achieved.

When substantial transformations have taken place, automatic transformation of queries phrased according to different submodels is difficult to achieve. We see little of that concept in practice. An approach to this problem is presented in Sec. 9-6, in an example of a database-system implementation.

Means to describe the relationships in the database are shown in the next chapter.

BACKGROUND AND REFERENCES

In order to develop the conceptual basis for database planning we have used relations as the basic units and classified five types of relations in order to describe the required choices. Many other models to aid database design have been developed and have influenced the concepts presented here.

The *relational model* which provides the basis for the conceptual view presented in this chapter allows a great deal of formal analysis. Several early papers (Langefors[63], Levien[67], and Childs[68]) suggested the use of a model based on set theory to describe file and database structures. Most of the current activity was kicked off by E.F. Codd, who, in a series of papers (Codd[70,74], and in Rustin[72]), presented the relational model in terms of its relevance to database design and implementation. In a second paper in Rustin[72], Codd describes the required operations and their power. Associated early contributions are Heath and Date in Codd[71], Delobel[73], Armstrong[74], Wang[75], and Forsyth in King[75], which provided mathematically oriented criteria for the optimization, manipulation, and demonstration of the correctness of the manipulations in relational models.

Fagin[77] defined multivalued dependencies and a fourth normal form. Up to seven normalizations have been proposed (Beeri[78]). Issues of relational decomposition are summarized by Maier[80]. The mathematical theory of dependencies in databases is now a subfield of its own, with a rapidly exploding literature. The set of axioms defining transformations is due to Armstrong[74]. A basic text is Ullman[82] and recent results may be found in journals, see for instance, Sadri[82] and in the proceedings of the ACM-PODS conferences (Aho[82]).

A tool in the developmemt of dependency theory is the *universal relation*. All data is placed into a single abstract unnormalized relation representing all entities and all their attributes. Many cells will be null. The formal knowledge to manipulate the universal relation consists of a collection of various dependencies which relate the attributes.

In our structural model we avoid many of these issues by concentrating on the simpler view models. The practical importance and sufficiency of Boyce-Codd-normal form was presented by LeDoux[82]. Date in Tou[74] expresses strongly the distinction between the database submodel and the database model. Several related papers appear in King[75].

Integration of databases is presented by ElMasri[79], Hubbard[81], and Navathe[82]. It also appears as phase in Schkolnick[78] and Lum[79]. Generalization of entities is addressed by Smith[77]. The concept of multiple linked databases is due to Litwin[81L] and tested within the POLYPHEME project. Languages to describe the semantics have been defined by Mylopoulos[80] and Hammer[81]. Work by Earley[71,73] is oriented toward language aspects of relational structures.

In order to construct relevant database models, the semantics of the interrrelational structure have played an important part in this chapter. Work by Schmid in King[75] and Manacher in Kerr[75] was especially influential. ElMasri[80] compares the how the structural concepts are modeled in alternative schemes. Questions of semantic relevance of the structure of databases were analyzed in Langefors[73], Deheneffe[74], Hainaut[74], Robinson in Douque[76], and Roussopoulos in Kerr[75]. Kent[78] reports on experience with a conceptual modeling tool.

Integration of relations can lead to null entries. Vassiliou[80], Goldstein[81], Lipski[79], and Zaniolo[82] consider the problem of nulls, Imielinski[81] extends the relational operations to deal with nulls.

Later work by Codd[79] and Date[82] extends the semantics of the original relational model. The new model, RM/T, includes 5 referenced relation types and 8 integrity rules, which can be mappped into the structural model. An exhaustive review is in Date[82]. Some of this work is influenced by the concepts of semantic nets; a comprehensive reference is Schank[73]. Joins are extended by LaCroix[76].

Other types of models can be easily related to the concepts presented here. Some of the models which are attracting attention are summarized here.

Entity models use the concept of the entity as their basic unit. Data structures are composed of entities defined by information requirements. Entities have properties, which were in our model decomposed into attributes, subsets, or data elements. Extending entities with the notion of relationships, as done by Chen[76], extends the descriptive capability, and this work has also spawned much interest, collections are found in Chen[80] and successor proceedings. Relationships may be simple $(1 : n)$, as our ownership and reference connections, or $m : n$, as modelled by associations and other multiple connections. Such relationships are *essential*, since the information is stored within them. The guidance given by these models tends to be less formal than the rules based on relations.

Functional models formalize the relationships among entities. Shipman[81] provides a language to express them and Buneman[82] provides a query language based on the functional concept.

An *access-path model* defines the database as collections of sequential transformation sequences, required to obtain a physically coded entity in response to a logical query. A rigorous hierarchy of the transformations allows the prediction of information loss and access cost at the various levels. Entity and access-path models (DIAM) have been developed by Senko[73] and compared with alternate approaches in Bachman[75] and by Hall in Neuhold[76]. A level to model hardware functions is also available. DIAM is shown to be capable of modeling many current concepts (Senko in Rustin[72], in Benci[75], in Kerr[75], in Douque[76], and in Neuhold[76]). The flexibility of the model may diminish its didactic power.

A *hierarchical model* uses the nest concept as its basic unit. Trees are created by nesting nests of nests, and forests are created by collecting trees. The view model and the database model are identical. This model has been used to develop access and update strategies. Hierarchical and network models have been influenced by early applied work as Hsiao[71] and Bachman in Jardine[74].

A *network model* uses the association as its basic unit. An integrated model is created by defining independent entities, their nests, and the possible or actual binding between them through the associations. In the traditional network model, abstracted from the CODASYL specification, all joins of interest were predefined so that the operations stress navigation between bound data elements. Recent developmemts are separating the logical and implementation design phases, as shown in this book.

The commonality of the various models is becoming obvious. Their strength tend to be relative.

In Rustin[74] network and relational approaches were presented. A lively discussion between camps committed to various approaches has appeared in the Proceedings of the ACM-SIGFIDET and -SIGMOD conferences. Misunderstandings developed because of the difference in origin; the relational approach was initially conceived as a modelling tool and the network approach began as a generalization of descriptions of actual databases. Sometimes the alternatives were used as strawmen to defend philosophies. A special issue of ACM COMPUTING SURVEYS (Sibley[76]) provided a forum for several approaches.

Data models which integrate these and information structure concepts are presented in Sundgren[75] and Kobayashi[75], those notions are further developed by Cook in King[75], and Chen[76]. The transformations of databases between models of the relational and network type has been defined by Adiba in Nijssen[76], De[78], Zaniolo in Bernstein[79], and Lien[82]. Lien[81] considers hierarchies in relational darabases. Date[80] presents a unified language to deal with access communality. Many issues in modeling of databases are summarized in Tsichritzis[81].

The proceedings of several conferences, two sponsored by the SHARE organization (Jardine[74,77]), one by the Institut de l'Informatique in Namur (Benci[75]), and a series organized by IFIP technical committees (Klimbie[75], Douque[76], Neuhold[76], Nijssen[77], Schneider[79], and Bracchi[79]), contain papers which discuss many aspects of database design. Abstract issues of modelling were the topic in Brodie[81]. Another source of current material on database modelling are the proceedings of the annual VLDB conferences. Selected papers appear in ACM's Transactions on Database Systems, a number of them have been cited above.

EXERCISES

1 Why is the **state** attribute in the ruling part in the **Automobile** relation of Example 7-2?

2 Sketch two view models for student grades.

3 Give the maximal size of a relation following Eq. 7-1.

4 What is the projection Π (**(birthdate,job) OF employee**), given Fig. 7-6?

5 What is the join of relations **employee** and **job-description**?

6 Show why the number of tuples in the difference of two relations is as shown in Section 7-4-1.

7 What is the expected number of tuples from a join? The limits were given in Section 7-4-3.

8 Why would one be interested in predicting the number of tuples?

9 Carry out a join of the relations `Employee_2` and `employee`. Which attributes control the join? Describe the cause for any inconsistencies you find. How could they have been avoided?

10 Construct two relations which, when joined, reveal an inconsistency. What would you do if such a problem occurred in the execution of a program?

11 Using Figs. 7-6 and 7-7, construct a relation

```
PTA: RELATION
   father, age, child, age_c, schooltype, schoolname;
```

Define the reverse process. Show that there is no information loss when applying both transformations in sequence. Is this realistic?

What additional information is needed in reality?

12 Take a paper describing a database example and define the files, sets, or relations used in terms of entity relations, lexicons, etc.

13 Is it necessary for proper execution of a join that the relations are in any particular normal form?

14 Flowchart or write in a high-level language the elemental steps required to carry out the set difference $(-)$ operation on two relations and two sequences.

15 Assume that the database shown in Fig. 7-29 is too large to manage and should be distributed. How could it be split in two parts, and what would be the problems in the distributed operation?

16 Read one of the papers on database models from the references given and compare the exposition with this chapter. Consider particularly which concepts described here are lacking in the paper and vice versa. Prepare a cross-reference dictionary for the defined terms.

17 If it turns out to be very difficult to integrate view models into a database model, what does that indicate?

Chapter 8

Schemas

The best laid schemes o' mice and men
Gang aft a-gley

Robert Burns
To a Mouse, 1787

The previous chapter described models of databases. The structure of the database was modeled by relations and connections. The relations were defined by their relation-schemas. In order to translate a model into an operational system, the model has to be described in a form which lends itself to implementation.

Such a description is called a *schema*, and the language used to describe it will be called the *schema language*. The schemas will have to include some practical detail which could be ignored in the models. Using the model concepts of domains, relations, and connections, the schema language has to be able to specify the types of the data elements, their organization into files, and the manner in which files are related.

A schema defines initially the structure of the database and makes the description available to the users of the database. If a database management system is used to manage the database, the schema will be used to automatically control the execution of the transaction programs which operate on the database.

An objective of a database system is to systematize the access to data elements. File systems have provided the means to fetch specific records according to defined keys or according to sequentiality. In order to fetch individual data elements the names of the data attributes, as known by the schema, are used to locate the data elements within the records. The data type information stored in the schema can be used by the processing transactions to direct the computation. Queries can use the connection specifications in the schema to locate successor data.

Predecessors of schemas are called *data dictionaries* and *database directories*. These systems collect information about the data and perhaps the database model, but do not make it directly available to a database management system.

In this chapter we present the construction and use of schemas to describe data elements and their relationships. Section 8-1 will look at the data elements to be described; Sec. 8-2 presents the schema for single files and gives some examples. The description of connecting structures is given in Sec. 8-3. In contrast with Chap. 7 we will present the material using mostly examples from available database management systems. This approach enhances the realism, but reduces the consistency of the material.

There is no universal schema language today. To apply the earlier concepts we have to use a variety of schema languages. Schema languages in the examples have been selected for specific features or because of widespread use. We do not go into detail to the extent that this chapter can replace system manuals, but relating the concepts developed here to actual examples should help greatly in the use of system documentation. For actual database specification a manual of the chosen language will be needed.

8-1 DEFINING THE ELEMENTS FOR A DATABASE

We need a description of the view requirements if we wish to design a database system. If an operational database is available, perhaps using a conventional file system, then we can begin by reviewing the usage of the file system by the programs that operate on the data to be integrated. A set of files used together may already contain multiple views, but if no conflicts have been experienced, the analysis can begin treating the existing database as a unit.

8-1-1 Analysis of Existing Data

Database problems are generally not recognizable until a certain volume of data has been collected. When a database system is to be installed, there are often already many programs which operate on the data to be incorporated in the database. The schema definition begins then with the collection of the information used to generate the processing programs that deal with the database. Information about the domains of the data elements and their dependencies can be used for the modeling processes described in Chap. 7.

Since the transactions will also be included in the eventual design, the processing steps applied to the information are also documented. For instance, results and intermediate derived data are defined in terms of their source variables. Many existing procedures must be studied in order to obtain a composite picture of the actions that are carried out. Documentation of data sources and destinations is collected. The frequency of use, the desired response time, and even the accuracy requirements are captured if feasible.

Similar information is obtained for new procedures and the data elements required for their operation. Here estimates may be needed, but documentation of assumptions made is at least as important to the design process as the documentation of established processes.

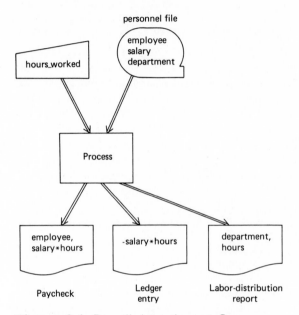

Figure 8-1 Payroll data element flow.

Figure 8-1 sketches an example of a very simple data flow. In practice, tabular descriptions for each variable are more convenient than a flowchart. The equivalent flow would be described as as follows:

Example 8-1   Table of Data Elements

Variable	Source	Destination
hours_worked	time recorder	payroll program
employee_salary	supervisor	personnel file
employee_department	personnel office	personnel file
employee_salary_item	personnel file	payroll program
employee_dept_item	personnel file	payroll program
. . .	. . .	. . .

Elements may, of course, also have multiple destinations.

The analysis of current procedures has to be carried out with due regard to the actual information flow. The fact that certain reports produced contain a specific data element is not necessarily an indication that the element is being used, or if it is used, that it is the best means of presenting the desired information. On the other hand, there often are informal methods of data distribution which are not obvious during a system analysis which depends wholly on existing documents. Talking is an important, unformalized, and flexible form of communication.

For example, the fact that an engineering department manager warns an inventory clerk that he expects new employees so that necessary tools will be available when they arrive is an information function easily overlooked when automating a personnel system.

8-1-2 Characteristics of Data

We begin by describing the *characteristics* of data elements. The most important description of a data element are its name and its domain. These are familiar concepts to any programmer.

Programming languages have always provided facilities to name and characterize data elements. The domain of a data element, needed for computation, is mostly given as the *type* and perhaps the *length*. Some modern languages permit further specifications.

Other characteristics, for instance, the largest and smallest value expected, are defined implicitly or in the program documentation. For the database complete and explicit descriptions are advantageous.

We will present the quantitative characteristics of data elements – type or domain, length, conditionals, count – in this subsection. Qualitative specifications of data element characteristics are presented in Sec. 8-1-3. The number of attributes used to describe each type of data element is sufficiently large that we may keep the schema itself as a relation.

Name   Names have been used throughout to define attributes in records and relations. The name given to a data element by a programming language is restricted by fairly simple rules. These rules generally allow a short, variable–length string of alphabetic and numeric characters; the first character has to be alphabetic. This string is easily parsed or separated from other elements that make up the statements accepted by the schema language. Compatibility between the programming language and the schema language is desirable. If multiple languages are used, the sum of compatibilities can restrict names unduly.

Names used in files and databases are global; i.e., they are bound to their meaning over all programs while the files or database is open. The schema will be used by many programs over a long time. In programming languages a name can have a different definition as the process changes scope. In a database the scope of a name of a data element is affected only by structural scope, the name is defined within the database or relation that contains the data element.

To locate the values, the position or byte number within the record is kept associated with the names in the schema. If the field allocation is flexible, an approach as seen in a *pile file* may be used. A coded name is kept with each element in the record. The schema keeps the codes with the names to allow translation from name to code and vice versa.

Most schema language translators will assign positions only according to their own data allocation methods. Some languages permit the users to specify the position explicitly so that the schema can be applied to previously existing files.

Type It is common to associate a specific data type with each data element name. The type specification has several functions:

1 It limits the values to be associated with the data element names to a specific domain.

2 It simplifies processing by implying the category of legal operations to be used in the transformation of the data.

3 It provides specifications for encoding of the data values. (Encoding methods and associated semantics are summarized in Chap. 14.)

Most programming languages provide a small number of data types. Schema languages should handle at least the types that are used in the programmed transactions:

CHARACTER: variable or fixed-length string of arbitrary characters;

DECIMAL: fixed-length string of decimal digits;

BINARY INTEGER: fixed-length string of binary digits;

DECIMAL FIXED POINT: scaled decimal number;

BINARY FIXED POINT: scaled binary number;

FLOATING POINT: approximation to a real number;

and   REFERENCE.

The types defining computational values need little elaboration. Decimal fixed point is often scaled by two to represent dollars and cents. Binary fixed point is mainly used for representing real-time sensor acquired data in the range $\{0.00.....1.00..\}$.

A reference variable in a program language, for instance, a record pointer in PASCAL or a base variable in PL/1, is however quite distinct from a reference in a database. One difference is their lifetime. References in databases have lifetimes that greatly exceed the execution time of a program. The other difference is the action taken when the referenced object is moved or deleted. Garbage collection methods are used in programs to retrieve or change invalid pointers; this approach is not feasible in a large database.

A *database reference* is a data element that refers to some object in the database. Three types of references are employed in database systems: pointers, symbolic references, and indirect pointers, as sketched in Fig. 8-2.

A *pointer reference* has the value of an address in the database space. If the number and location of all references to an object are known, specific pointers affected by the move of an object can be changed. In the general case pointers cannot be changed if the referenced data element is moved or deleted without a database reorganization. Until that time the old object spaces are marked with tombstones.

A *symbolic reference* contains the key of the referenced object. A procedure using key-based fetching has to be invoked in order to locate the referenced object in the database. The objects can be moved freely, as long as the access structures (indexes, etc.) are maintained. A symbolic reference will simply fail to find an object which has been deleted.

An *indirect reference* attempts to combine the benefits of symbolic references with the speed of pointer references. Here simple keys, perhaps organized as shown in Sec. 4-1, are used to access a table of pointer references. Now, when the object is moved, only the pointer value in the table has to be changed, and this takes care of all instances where this record has been referenced. If an object is deleted, the entry in the pointer table is set to a universal entry indicating DELETED. The look-up table is organized to be faster than a fetch using the symbolic reference key. If sufficient memory is available, the look-up may not require a file access.

Figure 8-2 Reference types.

Domain The type of a variable has a strong connotation of its representation. We prefer to define a set of permissible values; this is closer to the concept of a *domain* as used in the database model. Statements to define a data domain are available in some modern programming languages as an adjunct to *type* declarations.

A DEFINE statement describes a new data type by associating a type name with a *domain* specification. The use of data elements outside of the domain during processing is detected and reported in a manner similar to the type conflicts occurring when, for instance, numbers and character strings are mixed up. Domain definitions are available in the language PASCAL. Example 8-2 shows such statements using a PL/1 style syntax.

Example 8-2   Data Domain Definitions

```
      DEFINE color AS('Red','Blue','Green','Mauve');
      DEFINE year AS(FROM 1961 BY 1 TO 1976);
```
A declaration is used to create data elements of the type defined.
```
      DECLARE (model) year;
      DECLARE (body,fender,hood) color;
```
These elements can be used in statements for processing:
```
      IF body = fender THEN CALL assemble_body;
                       ELSE GO TO get_next_fender;
```
The above statements will prevent the assembly of
multicolored cars.
Such a rigorous type of definition will allow detection of erroneous
statements such as:
```
      body = 'CHEVROLET';
      body = model;
```
since in the context defined, body can only be set to
a value of type color.

Domain definitions and their use to restrict assignment can play an important role in keeping improper elements out of a database. Furthermore, since the set of values is limited, an efficient encoding can be derived to cover the domain. We will try to incorporate such facilities in the schema languages for our database element definition even where the programming languages do not have such provisions.

Length   The length of a data element can be fixed or variable. If the length is fixed, it can be specified as a number of bits or characters with the element description. If the element length is variable, the marking method which is used to determine the length for a given instance of the element can be indicated. The available methods are those discussed for marking records (see Sec. 2-2-4).

The use of variable length data elements leads to a need for variable-length records. An example of a variable-length record specified in PL/1 is shown in Example 8-3. The variable (**address**) could also be decomposed into multiple lower–level elements.

Example 8-3   Variable-Length Record

```
DECLARE 1  employer_record,    2   name CHAR VARYING(40),
                               2   sex CHAR(6),
                               2   birthdate INTEGER,
                               2   address CHAR VARYING(80);
```

As we have indicated earlier, the record written on the file is a direct image of the declared specification. The fact that the character strings are specified to be **VARYING** is ignored by most compilers, and the maximum specified is always allocated when the **employer_record** is written to a file. This practice leads to a considerable waste of space if long records occur infrequently. The record cannot be processed without the associated declaration.

The stored record can be composed as shown in Fig. 8-3.

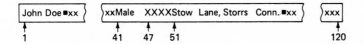

        ■   represents an end-of-string character

        x   is unspecified garbage
        X   is a character position which contains two decimal digits

Figure 8-3 PL/1 record with variable-length entries.

Conditional Data Elements   When a relation and its subrelations are implemented in one file we may have alternate data elements in different record subtypes. Some programming languages support this concept.

Records in PASCAL allow variants in their structure; a record can have alternate elements. Given a variable with two choices,

```
sex = (male,female);
```

then the record of Example 8-3 can be expanded as shown in Example 8-4.

Example 8-4   Conditional Data Elements

```
RECORD      name        : PACKED ARRAY(1..†40) OF CHAR;
            sex         : (Male,Female);
            day         : 1..31;
            month       : 1..12;
            year        : 1800..2000;
            address     : PACKED ARRAY(1..80) OF CHAR;
    CASE sex OF
        Male    : (years_military: 0..50);
        Female  : (pregnancies, children: 0..20)
END;
```

---

†PASCAL uses `..` to indicate TO in the sense of up-to-and-including.

Here the record has two possible variants, and we should know the value of **sex** before processing the conditional elements of the record.

Count Within a single record it may be desirable to repeat a data element to account for multiple instances of one subsidiary item. This option enables us to implement simple nest concepts from the model within one record. An example was the list of children of an employee and their ages in Fig. 7-3. Identifying keys were used to distinguish the elements. To determine the number of elements in a specific record, mark techniques can also be used. If the count and size of such repeating elements is large, the manipulation of these records may become difficult. The general solution to this problem is the creation of a nest file for these elements. Nest structures are widely supported within database management systems and are described in Sec. 8-3.

8-1-3 Data Element Descriptions

In Sec. 8-1-2 we listed traditional and essential characteristics of the attributes describing the data elements. Schema entries which complement these essential but programming–
oriented characteristics will be listed in this section. These schema entries provide information beyond the programs' needs. Recording the characteristics shown here can greatly improve the automatic and manual aspects of the database interface presented to the users.

Title A descriptive sentence or title may be desired which allows a more detailed identification of the data elements than the program language name permits. Sometimes the title can also include abbreviations, synonyms, antonyms, or aliases. Specialist in a subject area often use abbreviations unique to their field of discourse when specifying a data element for entry or retrieval. When data are shared among a larger audience, a full identification or title is required.

For example, the variable **bp_dst** will have the title:

```
'Diastolic bloodpressure, measured with patient sitting'
```

Unit Specification A code or identification of the units of measurement for numeric data elements is often important. It might be essential to know whether a pressure is stated in pounds force per square inch, atmospheric fractions, millibars, millimeters or inches of mercury, kilograms per square centimeter, pascals, or football players per quarterback. The unit specification might be used only for reporting or verification of domain matching when files are joined, but could also be used to convert values automatically if the system has the necessary conversion factors available.

Essential Data An indication of whether this data element is essential or optional in the record may have to be maintained. We may wish to prevent the creation of records which have critical elements missing. An employee file needs to have a social security number and a departmental assignment for every employee. Other fields, such as a spouse name or a health certification, may be optional.

Undefined Values If data can be missing or left undefined, it becomes necessary that programs which operate on the database recognize this fact. Undefined values are due to several causes.

`Missing data` Some data values may not have been available or known when the remainder of the record was entered.

`Not applicable` Some attributes may not be relevant in some records, especially when subrelations are combined into a file.

`Not collected` Some past data may be unavailable in areas where the scope of the database has expanded over time. In the design of a new system or the change of an existing one there is an opportunity to add new capabilities. This means that new data elements have to be described and their structural relationships charted. The new database will then have attributes for which no past values are available.

To manage these cases of undefined a notation in the database is needed. The schema must assign a value representation which does not conflict with legal values in the domain of the attribute. It is not clear if distinct values are needed for the three cases above, although the difference between "not applicable" and "missing" can lead to different actions.

Very few programming systems make appropriate provisions to handle any kind of undefined values in a manner distinct from zero values. The programmers are then forced to use codes as `-1, -0, 999999, 'undefined'`, and the like. These codes invariably find their way into computations and lead to major errors. Some statistical systems have provisions for missing data, and the database can provide the required input format automatically. For programming systems which do not handle undefined values the databases system should trigger an exception procedure when an undefined value is accessed, so that the processing programs will not compute nonsense.

Nonsense can be created for instance if a join operation creates result tuples for `null = null`. This type of problem can be avoided by never equating a `null` value with another `null` value, i.e., by treating each `null` value as distinct. In counting operations `null` values should be ignored, so that they do not distort computed averages or deviations. Not all problems are solved by these rules, and more sophisticated schemes have been proposed but have never been used in practice.

Transformations There may be a need to transform data between the outside world and the database. Typical of such a transformation is the internal storage of dates in integer or Julian form (year.day) for computational convenience, while output of these dates is presented in **dd/mon/yy** form, so that the values make sense to humans. Using letters for the month removes the ambiguity of English and European notations.

Such a transformation may be carried out by encoding and decoding procedures appropriate for the domain of values. These routines will reside in a database library, and the schema can indicate which routine to use. If the transformation program can be handled similar to a domain definition, new and composite data types can be created and used.

The domain definitions in PASCAL are not adequate to permit

```
DECLARE birthdate DATE
```

but transformation programs can de defined which will take input as **12FEB82** and convert it to 29 993 (days since **1JAN00**) and vice versa. The input transformation can report errors, and interval computations can be performed on the internal value.

Database Submodels and Access Privilege The schema will also identify elements as belonging to specific database submodels, if this concept is supported by the database system and the database has been integrated. Within each submodel there will be elements for which a user has update responsibilities and privileges, and others which the user may only read but not modify. The schema is the obvious repository of access privilege information, that is, the specification of the users who have permission to access these data elements. Chapter 12 will deal with this aspect in detail.

File Management A schema may also be the repository for file management information. Data to control indexing, transposition, control of integrity, archiving, and erasure cycles can be placed in the schema. We will encounter such aspects incrementally as we proceed.

8-2 THE SCHEMA AND ITS USE

The collection of information that describes the database, when organized in a formal manner, is called the *schema*. Data element descriptions are an important part of the schema. Before discussing the definitions of the structural aspects of a database within the schema, we will illustrate its use. When the use of a schema is clear, it will be easier to deal with other requirements placed on the schema, since there is still no consensus on how schemas can satisfy those requirements.

A set of documents that is used by a programming staff to generate programs is an informal and often inconsistent form of a schema. Programmers will perform an analysis of the tasks and consider the available data elements. Subsequently they can code the required programs. Many statistical systems have provided directory facilities with their data files, so that the collected observations will always be properly identified and titled.

In the following sections we will discuss stronger, more automated approaches to the use of the schema information. The schema will be coded so that it can be read by the database system and used by generalized programs to control the flow of data to the files which contain the database. It will be stored within the system to be accessible when needed. The formal schema description also provides a means for the database users, database designers, and programming staff to communicate and to define their concepts.

The definition of the database using the schema precedes use of the database. In order to create a schema, we will need schema language services separate from the language services which are used when the database is manipulated. Often the processors for the schema language and the data-manipulation language are distinct. Sometimes they even have a completely different vocabulary and syntax.

Figure 8-4 places the idea of a schema in perspective. During computation the schema is used both to place incoming data properly into the files, and to locate requested data at a later time. The dictionaries in the schema aid the users in describing their requests, and perform a filtering function to improve data quality within the database. The database users do not modify the schema during database operations.

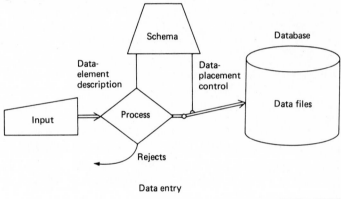

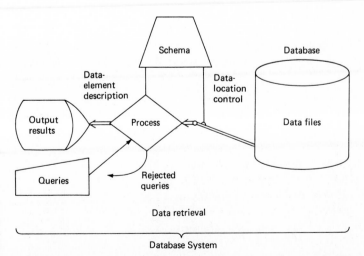

Figure 8-4 The place of a schema in input and output.

8-2-1 An Example of a Simple Schema-Driven System

Schemas may be employed with very simple file systems. The resulting database system will also be simple, and yet may provide a useful service. A schema for a database which uses only a single sequential file is shown here. This example shows operations using the TYMSHARE RETRIEVE system. The system operates interactively on a terminal. Figure 8-5 is an example of the initial definition of a schema. At this point no data exist in the data file.

-RETRIEVE ⊃

PLEASE NAME YOUR DATABASE: EMPLOYEE ⊃

I NEED TO KNOW THE STRUCTURE OF YOUR DATABASE.
PLEASE DESCRIBE EACH ITEM

ITEM   NAME SIZE TYPE

1   EMPLOYEE, 20,C ⊃
2   JOB, 5,C ⊃
3   SALARY, 6,N ⊃
4   ADDRESS, 20,C ⊃
5   CITY, 20,C ⊃
6   ⊃   *Carriage Return terminates structure description.*

EMPLOYEE CURRENTLY CONTAINS 0 72-CHARACTER RECORDS.
EMPLOYEE'STR.D'NOW CONTAINS BASE STRUCTURE.

Figure 8-5 Schema creation.

The schema, however, has been saved on a separate file so that it can be used by subsequent processes. The name of the schema file is obtained by suffixing the database name with some unusual characters; here ""STR.D"" is used. The system is now ready to receive data, and Fig. 8-6 demonstrates this phase.

The information from the schema is used to place each field properly into the file. These data may now be manipulated using computational instructions and selection statements. Table 8-1 lists the commands available to the user.

A complete session, which involves retrieval of the schema, addition of records, changing of data fields, selective computation of result fields, and a final printout, is shown in Fig. 8-7.

. APPEND ⊃

EMPLOYEE   JOB   SALARY ADDRESS   CITY

MEIER ARTHUR, MS-2,245.00,14971 BROOK DR, FAIRFAX VA ⊃
HARKER RICHARD, MS-3,307.00,91 RICHMOND RD, ARLINGTON VA ⊃
BAIN GORDON, SR-1,188.00, TWIN OAKS, FALLS CHURCH VA ⊃
COPPER SARA, SC-2,165.00,1300 6TH ST SW #715, WASHINGTON DC ⊃
⊃
                                    The APPEND command is terminated
4 RECORDS PROCESSED   *with a Carriage Return.*

Figure 8-6 Entering data into the database.

Table 8-1   RETRIEVE **Commands**

Database manipulation commands:

```
APPEND
CHANGE attribute [ FOR conditions ]
COUNT [ FOR conditions ]
DELETE [ FOR conditions ]
LIST [ FOR conditions ]
PRINT ( attributes ) [ FOR conditions ]
REPLACE attribute WITH expression [ FOR conditions ]
REPORT [ FOR conditions ]
SAVE file
SORT BY key attribute [ FOR conditions ]
SUM expression [ FOR conditions ]
```

Clauses as   [FOR conditions]   are optional.

In order to explain the nature of such a database system, a possible implementation of the APPEND command is shown in Example 8-5. The following steps take place:

1 The schema is fetched from its file

2 Storage is allocated for a data record

3 A header line is created from the schema and put on the terminal as a prompt

4 The data file is opened

5 The data lines provided by the user are obtained

6 The values are extracted and placed into the data record

7 Each record is appended to the data file

8 A blank input line causes the data file to be closed and a message to be placed on the terminal.

The entire schema is assumed to be small enough to fit in core. The actual code is considerably longer, since checks are provided throughout to prevent program failures if the schema and the data do not match.

The PL/1 function SUBSTR(string, begin [,length]), used extensively in this model program, takes a number of characters, up to the value length, out of astring of characters, beginning at position begin.

A system such as RETRIEVE is not adequate to support a general database. No means exist to cross-reference multiple files, and the data elements are limited to two simple types. The fact that the files are strictly sequential can cause long delays on large files. On the other hand, the facilities are easy to comprehend by the types of users the system designers envisaged, the possibilities for processing errors are reduced, and results of processing are well identified.

The facilities shown here are similar to those for manipulating a single file or relation of a larger system.

RETRIEVE ⊃

PLEASE NAME YOUR DATABASE: PERSONNEL ⊃   *The database was created in a previous session of RETRIEVE.*

PERSONNEL CURRENTLY CONTAINS 8 48-CHARACTER RECORDS.

• STRUCTURE ⊃   *The structure defined previously is displayed.*

ITEM TYPE WIDTH NAME

    1   C   20   EMPLOYEE
    2   C   11   SOC.SEC
    3   N   6   SALARY
    4   N   3   HRS
    5   N   7   PAY

• APPEND ⊃   *Two records are added to the database.*

EMPLOYEE   SOC.SEC   SALARY HRS   PAY

MARSHALL MICHAEL, 347-72-6528,283.00,40,0 ⊃
COLLINS WILLIAM, 462-99-3369,6.70,40,0 ⊃
⊃

2 RECORDS PROCESSED

• SORT BY EMPLOYEE ⊃   *The database is sorted alphabetically by EMPLOYEE.*

PERSONNEL'OLD'CONTAINS YOUR UNSORTED DATABASE.
PERSONNEL IS NOW SORTED.
SHALL WE RETAIN PERSONNEL'OLD'? NO ⊃

• LIST ⊃   *The entire database is displayed.*

RECNO	EMPLOYEE	SOC.SEC	SALARY	HRS	PAY
1	ANDREWS KARL	469-20-9531	2.35	40	0
2	BRADFORD SUSAN	202-46-9277	4.90	40	0
3	COLLINS WILLIAM	462-99-3369	6.70	40	0
4	FRENCH MARK	519-45-6218	7.20	40	0
5	MARSHALL MICHAEL	347-72-6528	283.00	40	0
6	NELSON DONALD	311-61-2629	5.10	40	0
7	PALMER DAVID	357-48-3158	410.00	40	0
8	PARKER MARY	351-04-8260	4.10	40	0
9	RODRIGUES MARIA	373-75-7302	198.70	40	0
10	WINTON JOAN	421-98-7244	4.25	40	0

10 RECORDS PROCESSED

(a)

Figure 8-7 A database session.

• <u>IN 1,6 CHANGE HRS</u> ⊃   *The item HRS is modified in records 1 and 6.*

HRS

```
 40
 48 ⊃
 40
 44 ⊃
```

2 RECORDS PROCESSED

• <u>IN 10 CHANGE SALARY</u> ⊃   *The item SALARY is modified in record 10.*

SALARY

```
 4.25
 4.70 ⊃
```

1 RECORDS PROCESSED

• <u>REPLACE PAY WITH (SALARY*40) + (SALARY*2*(HRS−40)) FOR SALARY < 20</u> ⊃

A new value of PAY is calculated for hourly employees using the REPLACE command.

7 RECORDS PROCESSED

• <u>REPLACE PAY WITH SALARY FOR SALARY > 20</u> ⊃   *The REPLACE command is used again to obtain PAY for salaried employees.*

3 RECORDS PROCESSED

• <u>PRINT EMPLOYEE, PAY</u> ⊃   *PRINT is used to list only the items EMPLOYEE and PAY. Note that headings are printed.*

EMPLOYEE	PAY
ANDREWS KARL	131.6
BRADFORD SUSAN	196
COLLINS WILLIAM	268
FRENCH MARK	288
MARSHALL MICHAEL	283
NELSON DONALD	244.8
PALMER DAVID	410
PARKER MARY	164
RODRIGUES MARIA	198.7
WINTON JOAN	188

10 RECORDS PROCESSED

• <u>SUM PAY</u> ⊃   *The SUM command computes the total value of PAY for the database.*

SUM IS 2372.1

10 RECORDS PROCESSED

• <u>QUIT</u>   *The QUIT command returns control to the EXECUTIVE.*

—

(b)

Figure 8-7 A database session (continued).

Example 8-5   Example of Schema Usage: Implementation of APPEND

```
append: PROCEDURE(data_file_name);     /* Schema driven file append */
   DECLARE data_file_name CHAR(*), schema_file_name CHAR(50);
   DECLARE 1 schema(50),   /* No more than 50 attributes per record */
              2 type CHAR(1),
              2 width BINARY FIXED,
              2 name CHAR(40) VARYING;
   DECLARE headng CHAR(200) INITIAL(''),        /* empty */
           blanks CHAR(200) INITIAL((200)' '),  /* full */
           line CHAR(200) VARYING,
           datarecord CHAR(*) CONTROLLED;
/* Fetch schema */
        schema_file_name=data_file_name||'"STR.D"';
        type,name=''; width=0;       /* Initialize all schema lines */
        OPEN FILE(schema_file) INPUT TITLE(schema_file_name);
        READ FILE(schema_file) INTO(schema);
        CLOSE FILE(schema_file);
/* Set up data_record */
        tot_width=SUM(width); ALLOCATE datarecord CHAR(tot_width);
/* Make a heading out of the names, extend each to the width       */
        DO item=1 BY 1 WHILE(name(item) ¬= '');
           headng=headng||SUBSTR((name(item)||blanks),1,width(item));
        END;           PUT SKIP EDIT(headng)(A(200));
/* Prepare to write additional records onto the data file */
        OPEN FILE(data_file) OUTPUT TITLE(data_file_name);
        records=0;
/* Get a line from the user, if it's not empty, process it as the */
 more: DO records = 0 BY 1;                      /* schema requires */
        datarecord=''; PUT SKIP;
        GET EDIT(line)(A(200));   IF line='' THEN GO TO done;
  extract: DO item=1 BY 1 WHILE(name(item) ¬='');
           commapos=INDEX(line,',');               /* locate a value */
           IF commapos>0 THEN cp=commapos-1; ELSE cp=LENGTH(line);
/* Take out characters from line, adjust right or left, set width */
        IF type(item) = 'N'                    /* and put away */
           THEN datarecord=datarecord || SUBSTR(
                (blanks||SUBSTR(line,1,cp)), 200-width, width );
           ELSE datarecord=datarecord|| SUBSTR(
                     (SUBSTR(line,1,cp)||blanks), 1, width );
        line=SUBSTR(line,cp+2); /* Chop processed input and  */
        END extract;            /* Go to pick up next element */
        WRITE FILE(data_file) FROM(datarecord);
      END more;           /* Loop terminated by blank input line */
 done: PUT EDIT(records,' RECORDS PROCESSED')(I(4),A(18));
        CLOSE FILE(data_file);   RETURN;
END append;           /* End of transaction, return for next command */
```

8-3 DEFINING THE STRUCTURE OF A DATABASE

We have concentrated above on the description of data elements and then demonstrated a schema for a database with a minimal structure. The database management system only had to support the access of a record based on an attribute name and argument value.

An important aspect of a database is its structure. The relationships expressed by the structure allow the retrieval of related data elements and support the get-next type of operation. Structure can be found at three levels: within data elements, within records, and among records. Different database systems approach questions of structure in very diverse ways.

8-3-1 Structure within Data Elements

Some data elements are composed of smaller, simple elements. A few computer languages, notably COBOL and PL/1, have provisions to define such structures by assigning level numbers. An example of such a substructure can be shown by expanding the **address** shown in Example 8-3 into its component fields.

```
2 address,    3  street CHAR VARYING(80),
              3  city   CHAR VARYING(80),
              3  zip    DECIMAL(9);
```

Most database systems consider attributes only as simple elements. Any internal structure of a data field as **address** is the responsibility of the programs and their compilers. When modeling we also treat attributes only as having domains with simple values and ignore composite values. A technique to resolve these variables defines a domain having some transformation functions.

Several data elements may be grouped within a record, so that a single retrieval command may retrieve multiple elements. Such a group is typically composed of elements normally used together, perhaps belonging to one database submodel, or elements which are assigned to the same access privilege.

The smallest unit which a database can physically manipulate, be it a single element, a group of several data elements, or an entire record, will be called a *segment*. If the concept of database submodels is supported by a database management system, a segment should never contain attributes from more than one submodel. A read request will always obtain an entire segment.

A segment may have its own name in the schema or may be implied by referencing an attribute within it. If a segment is a single attribute or an entire record no segment name is expected. The attributes within a segment may be named in the schema, so that application programs can refer to individual data elements. We encountered single-attribute segments in MUMPS files. Those segments were named using a subscript notation.

8-3-2 Connections Placed within a Record

We have described the structure among elements within a record. The schema should state which data elements compose the ruling part and the dependent part. If a lexicon has been combined into the file, a secondary ruling part may appear in the record, and such information may be important to the processing programs.

How a data element is related to the file and hence to the entire database is critical but is difficult to describe in a manner which can be automatically interpreted by processing programs. The fact that an element is placed within a record implies a strong relationship with other elements in this record, but an analysis of a typical record (for example, Table 3-1) reveals a variety of relationships between the elements. The database model contains this information.

That an attribute belongs to the ruling part is often only implied in schema languages. An example is the specification of sequentiality and uniqueness (SEQ,U) in the key attribute description of a **Person** record segment defined using IBM's schema language DL/1. This field and key fields of any ancestor segments make up the ruling part.

        FIELD NAME=(social_security_number,SEQ,U),BYTES=11, ...

Attributes in the dependent part may not be normalized in file structures. Denormalization may have been done explicitly, to achieve certain performance goals, or implicitly, when no normalized model was defined during the design process. We will show some more examples from DL/1.

Segments themselves may repeat within a record in order to implement a nest relationship within a record. The ownership connection is then implemented using physical sequentiality. This works only for one owner per owned record and does not support an *association* instance within a record. A **PARENT** specification in a segment relates nested segments to their owner, so that multiple-level nests can be described. This can make records very large indeed, at times spanning many blocks.

The DL/1 schema first specifies the relation and its file (**DBD** and **DATASET**), and then each segment in turn. Since in this example a direct file organization (**HDAM**)

Example 8-6 DL/1 **Record Specification**

```
* filename
    DBD      NAME=Employee,ACCESS=HDAM,RMNAME=hashprogram
* device specification
    DATASET DD1=empty,DEVICE=2314,BLOCK=2000,SCAN=5
* Record name, length, position, and maximum frequency
    SEGM     NAME=employee,BYTES=143,PARENT=0,FREQ=200
* attribute specifications
    FIELD   NAME=name,BYTES=30,START=1,TYPE=0
    FIELD   NAME=age,BYTES=4,START=31,TYPE=P
    FIELD   NAME=sex,BYTES=1,START=140,TYPE=C
    FIELD   NAME=years_military,BYTES=1,START=141,TYPE=P
    FIELD   NAME=pregnancies,BYTES=1,START=142,TYPE=P
    FIELD   NAME=children,BYTES=1,START=143,TYPE=P
* nest record specification
    SEGM     NAME=skills,PARENT=employee,BYTES=26,FREQ=20
    FIELD   NAME=(type,SEQ,U),BYTES=25,START=1,TYPE=C
    FIELD   NAME=years_experience,BYTES=1,START=26,TYPE=P
* instruct assembler to generate the tables
    DBDGEN
    FINISH
```

is specified, there is no opportunity in the schema to specify the ruling part of the employee relation. The key used is a secret of the **hashprogram** which provides the key-to-address translation.

A frequency field in the schema (here **FREQ**) for a nest segment provides a count parameter to aid in the estimation of storage requirements.

The **TYPE** specification is limited to:

O	none
C	character
P	packed decimal

The DL/1 language is mainly concerned about segments, and only FIELDs containing keys for sorting or referencing have to be specified. The record in the example shows in fact a large gap between **age** and **sex** containing unnamed fields. Use of DL/1 will be investigated when the IMS database management system is described in Sec. 9-6. Schema tables set up by DL/1 can also be used by a number of other IBM and independent data manipulation and query systems.

8-3-3 Connections between Records

An ownership connection is best described by defining separate records for the nest or association records and providing references from owner to owned records. Pointer references can also implement reference and subset connections between records of entity, referenced entity, and lexicon relations.

When symbolic references are used, the database system need not be concerned with the relationship, since the reference attribute will contain a key value which can be used in a fetch operation. Constraints on deletion and insertion cannot be enforced if the relationship is not described.

When pointer references are to be used, the schema has to provide a description of the connection. The database system has to be able to place the reference value in the referencing attribute field. In DL/1 such specifications are explicit; an association, for instance, is denoted by specifying a pair of owners:

```
SEGM NAME=supply,,PARENT((supplier,SNGL)(parts,PHYSICAL))
```

The fact that the first **PARENT** is **SNGL** reflects only on the fact that there are only next and no prior pointers to the **supplier** owner. The indication that the other **PARENT** (**parts**) is **PHYSICAL** means that this owner is in the primary hierarchy, so that the owned record might also be found sequentially, selecting segments using the key attribute. Many other coupling arrangements are available in DL/1.

In the CII SOCRATE database management system, the specifications for nests and their linkages are implicit, so that the decision to use large records or multiple records for a nest implementation is independent of the schema description provided by the user. The term **SET** defines a nest with the tuple attributes delimited by a **BEGIN ... END** pair. Example 8-6 shows also the specification of the data element characteristics, with character type (**WORD**), domain definitions (**FROM ... TO ...** or as listed), unit (**IN ...**), and use of a conditional structure (**IF ... THEN store_one ELSE store_another**). The characteristic **LIKE** allows a domain specification to be copied.

In Example 8-7 we find a nest of skills within each record. If skills is extensive, it becomes desirable to use a referenced entity relation which allows the tuples to be shared. This alternative is shown in Example 8-8. The pointer reference to this relation (here SET) remains in a nest structure, so that again multiple skills can be entered for one employee. The years_experience can in this case only be implied from the requirements in the referenced Skills relation.

Example 8-7   SOCRATE **Record Description**

```
BEGIN
   SET  Employee
      BEGIN
         name  WORD
         age FROM 16 TO 66 IN Years
         address WORD
         eye_color(Brown,Black,Blue)
         hair_color(Black,Brown,Blond,Red,Gray)
         sex(Male,Female)
         IF sex = 'Male'
            THEN  years_military FROM 0 TO 25 IN Years
            ELSE
              BEGIN
                 pregnancies FROM 0 TO 20
                 children    LIKE pregnancies
              END
         SET skills
          BEGIN
             type  WORD
             years_experience FROM 0 TO 50 IN Years
          END
      END
END
```

Example 8-8   Cross-Referenced Relations

```
BEGIN
   SET Employee
      BEGIN
         name WORD
         ...
         SET skills
           BEGIN
                 skill REFERENCE Skill_description
           END
      END
   SET Skill_description
      BEGIN
         skill_type WORD
         years_of_school_req FROM 0 TO 20 IN Years
         years_of_experience_req LIKE years_of_school_req
         ...
      END
END
```

Sometimes references may be to other tuples of the same relation:

```
supervisor REFERENCE employee
```

An explicit reference may be bound by a join to be performed when the CURRENT employee_record is defined for insertion into the database.

```
back_up_person REFERENCE employee
HAVING skill = FIRST skill OF CURRENT employee
```

The schema implemented by SOCRATE describes a concept from a user's view rather than the structure of relations or files. We will discuss the subschema structure to support multiple user views in Sec. 8-4.

8-3-4 Derived Data

Processing derives new data, using source data found in the database. Processing implies having source data and an algorithm to process the data. We have described knowledge about the data in the model and encode this knowledge in the schema which implements the model. The schema makes the data description available to all users of the database.

If we have knowledge about processing which is useful to multiple users we should also store this information with the database schema. Knowledge about processing algorithms is encoded in the programs used to derive data. To make such algorithms available within the framework of a schema we associate programs with a new class of data elements: *derived data*. The use of derived data defined in the schema automatically invokes the processing programs and accesses the appropriate source data.

The effort to derive data can be such that it becomes desirable to store derived intermediate or final data also within the database, in addition to the algorithms or programs used to derive them. While the programs are still attached to the databases schema, actual stored derived data will appear in the database itself. If data are defined as derived they will not be available for conventional update.

A Warning   In some instances removal of computational responsibility from the users to the database-management system can increase the potential for serious errors. As an example, we take the automatic calculation of an **area** as the product of **width** and **length**. Some day a user will add an object to the database which is not rectangular and assume that the system-produced value for derived **area** is correct. A schema with a good descriptive capability, perhaps defining the computation in the title for the attribute, can help avoid such errors.

The user expects that derived data are as current as the source data available to the system. We distinguish two approaches to achieve this objective when supporting the generation of derived data:

On Entry   Derived data is computed and the result stored whenever a source value is entered into the database, updated, or changed during processing.

On Access   Derived data is computed from the current source elements only when a retrieval request to the result element is made.

Both alternatives are presented next, and then a mixed strategy will be suggested.

Results Derived on Entry   With each source data element a process is identified which is automatically invoked when the data element is updated. The execution of the process causes the automatic updating of derived elements. Derived values kept in the file are actual results of entered data. All results derived on entry are always up to date relative to available source data elements.

Example 8-9   Derivation on Entry of Actual Results

A part of a database is used for budgeting expenses on a yearly basis. The element for salary could be defined as

```
1 Employee;
      ...
   2 salary, PICTURE IS 9999.99, ON MODIFY CALL pay_proc.
      ...
```

pay_proc is a procedure which is invoked whenever a salary is changed. This procedure may include statements as follows:

```
pay_proc: PROCEDURE;
      raise = Employee.salary(NEW)-Employee.salary(OLD);
      expense = raise*(12-current_month+1)
      ...
      Department.salaries = Department.salaries + expense;
      Department.profit = Department.profit - expense;
      ...
      END pay_proc;
```

The summary fields in the Department relation reflect all changes introduced into the Employee.salary fields.

Use of this concept can lead to costly data entry. A chain of procedure calls may be generated during entry of a single value. The change of **salary** here leads to changes in the derived values in the **Department** record, and this in turn could affect a **Company** record.

The statement in Example 8-9, used to recompute the **Department.profit**, could also be generalized and be defined as a derived value to be invoked whenever a departmental budget amount is modified for whatever reason. Now no explicit profit calculation will be included in **pay_proc**, but when the **Department.salaries**, **Department.office_rent**, or a similar expense or income element changes, the procedure deriving **profit** will be executed.

These procedures assure that the derived results are immediately available when requested. An update to the file may, however, initiate a costly sequence of events, and a batch of updates (for a cost-of-living increase, for instance) may lead to a truly horrifying level of activity.

Results Derived on Access   The other method of accommodating changes in source data avoids the actual storage of derived data. Derived data to be computed on access are also described by means of a program which allows them to be automatically computed at the time of a retrieval request. Using the same situation shown above, the schema coding could read as shown in Example 8-10.

Example 8-10   Derivation on Access of Potential Results

In the schema we find

```
DECLARE Department.profit  ...   GET_FROM(sum_budget_elements)
DECLARE Department.salaries  ... GET_FROM(sum_empl_salary)
```

and the processes would include two database procedures:

```
    sum_budget_elements: PROCEDURE;
        result = department_sales -
                 department_salaries -
                 department_overhead;
        RETURN(result); END sum_budget_elements;
    sum_empl_salary: PROCEDURE;
        result = 0;
        DO WHILE DEFINED(employee);
        IF employee_department=department
           THEN result = result + Employee.salary;
        END;
        RETURN(result);  END sum_empl_salary;
```

Here the chain of processes to be executed occurs at retrieval time. The results are never stored; the capability to generate them, however, is maintained. The cost of obtaining answers is high, and the same result will be computed many times if it requested frequently. If, for instance, `Product.profits` are compared with the overall `Department.profit`, the latter value will be recomputed from the source data once for each product comparision.

There are instances where an attribute value should certainly be defined to be derived on access; an `age` should always be derived from `birthdate` and today's date, a `shipping_cost` is best derived from `weight` and `shipping_rate`, and so forth.

On-Entry versus On-Access Derivation of Results Both of these methods lead to high costs when a usage pattern causes excessive recomputation. On-entry derivations require much effort when source-data are being entered, and on-access definitions cost when result-data are being generated. For each derived element the relative frequencies of access have to evaluted and the cost of the alternatives compared.   On-entry derivation also increases storage and data transfer costs. Schema specifications for either choice are found in Sec. 8-3-5.

Where data do not need to be of ultimate currency, the problem of excessive cost can be resolved by not computing derived data at entry or at query time, but rather according to some regular processing cycle, using nightly or weekend processing resources. It is now well worthwhile to keep an additional data element with a *time-stamp* "`last_update_time`". The time-stamp is always set to the date and time of the last update of the derived data. One time-stamp may be used per record segment if the derivation process will update all derived elements in a segment as one transaction. This value can be used to check that expected derivations have indeed been recently computed.

Time-Triggered Derivation A combination of the two approaches is possible. We suggest that both dated *derived data* is kept as well as references to regeneration procedures to be used on access. A query can check if the derived data are adequately up to date, and if they are not, the query can trigger a regeneration.

Given this choice only time-critical queries have to cause a regeneration of the derived data element. The decision is made according to the time-stamp associated with the element and the need of this query, rather than according to some predefined schedule. There are several benefits:

No generation is triggered by data entry.

Casual queries can avoid any regeneration.

Multiple regeneration processes associated with repetitive accesses are avoided.

At query time the first access to a data segment with derived data will trigger a regeneration only if the `acceptable_time > last_update_time` for some data

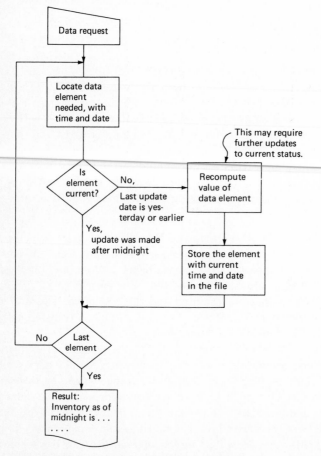

Figure 8-8 Time-triggered data derivation.

segment. Since the regeneration sets the time-stamp to the current time, no segment will be regenerated more than once during one query transaction. A default decision can be to set the `acceptable_time` to the time the transaction began. Now the first reference will initiate a derivation on access, and any further refernces to the same element will use the stored value, as if the data were derived on entry.

The general flow of such an implementation is sketched in Fig. 8-8. A technique of this type is now employed within DEC PDP-10 programming systems: if the binary output code derived from some source code by a compiler is dated later than the last source code modification, a recompilation is triggered.

8-3-5 Summary: The DBTG Schemas

Figures 8-9 and 8-10 present the essentials of the specifications for a schema language developed by Data Description Language Committees of CODASYL (Conference on Data System Languages), an organization devoted to the development and standardization of business programming, which illustrates many of the points made above.

There are two distinct sections to the schema, one to contain the more conceptual definitions, as determined during establishment of the database model, using a Data Description Language (*DDL*), and the other, the *storage schema*, to contain the results of the mapping decisions to physical storage, which define the file structure to be eemployed, using a Data Storage Description Language (*DSDL*). The purpose of the separation is to permit changes of the storage structure to be made for efficiency reasons, without affecting the user's programs, which are solely derived from the database model. Any database model change has to be supported, of course, by a corresponding storage schema change. Changes of a user's external database submodel alone should not affect the model schema or the storage schema. In earlier versions of the DBTG proposals both schema sections were combined, and in the implementation a combination of the two sections is still permitted.

The specifications shown are abstracted from the third major revision, issued in 1978. Most existing systems are based on 1969 and 1974 specifications. Many of them have not implemented all the clauses and have changed some of them.

The Model Schema - DDL   A schema contains all the definitions for the integrated database. A database may be divided into areas with distinct access and management responsibilities. The principal unit defined in the DDL schema is the *record-type*, roughly equivalent to one relation. Keys define ruling parts as needed to represent entity relations, nests, or associations.

Each record-type has one RECORD-NAME and within the record name the data elements can be specified. A data element is identified by a `data_name`; Data elements may be hierarchically arranged within a record by means of the `level_no`. An OCCURS clause with a `variable_count` can be given to indicate repetition of a data element within the record. Most of the options for data elements were discussed in Sec. 8-2.

The SOURCE and RESULT clauses specify derived attributes. Derivations are restricted to copying of values from the owner records and summarization of values in member records.

```
SCHEMA NAME IS model_schema_name.
    /* Within a SCHEMA several areas can be defined */
AREA NAME IS area_name.
    /* and several record types may live within an AREA. */
RECORD NAME IS record_type_name        /* implements a relation table */
      WITHIN  ⎧ ANY AREA                                          ⎫
              ⎨ area_name                                         ⎬
              ⎩ AREA OF OWNER OF set_name                         ⎭
      ⎡ KEY key_name IS [{ASCENDING / DESCENDING}] data_in_key [, ...] ⎤
      ⎢   DUPLICATES ARE{FIRST / LAST / NOT ALLOWED / SYSTEM DEFAULT}   ⎥
      ⎣   FREQUENCY OF  [DIRECT][SEQUENTIAL]  RETRIEVAL IS HIGH         ⎦ .

    /* and then the attributes or data elements are specified  */

level_no   data_name
           [PICTURE ... /* a COBOL style format specification  */ ]
      ⎡ TYPE    ⎧ ⎛BINARY ⎞ ⎛FIXED⎞ ⎛REAL   ⎞                        ⎫ ⎤
      ⎢    IS   ⎨ ⎝DECIMAL⎠ ⎝FLOAT⎠ ⎝COMPLEX⎠ number_size [,frac_size] ⎬ ⎥
      ⎢         ⎪ {BIT / CHARACTER} [size [DEPENDING ON variable]  ]  ⎪ ⎥
      ⎣         ⎩ implementor_name  /*  for special types        */   ⎭ ⎦
           [OCCURS{integer_count / variable_count} TIMES]
           [CONVERSION IS NOT ALLOWED]
           ⎡ CHECK IS [ NONULL                                      ]
           ⎢          [ PROCEDURE procedure_name                    ]
           ⎣          [ VALUE [NOT] literal_1 [THRU literal_2] ]  ⎤   .
    /* Derived data */
           [SOURCE IS some_data_identifier OF OWNER of set_name_1]
           ⎡ RESULT OF PROCEDURE derive_procedure ON CHANGE TO          ⎤
           ⎢ ⎧ALL DATA              ⎫ ⎧OF THIS RECORD         ⎫         ⎥
           ⎢ ⎨DATA identifier [,...] ⎬ ⎨OF ALL MEMBERS         ⎬ OF set_⎥
           ⎣ ⎩TENANCY               ⎭ ⎩OF MEMBER record_name_m ⎭ _name_m⎦ .
         /* CHANGE OF TENANCY means change of link-set membership or ownership */

    /* The connections to be implemented in a schema are defined as follows */

SET NAME IS link_set_name          /* implements a connection */
    OWNER IS{record_name_o / SYSTEM }
    ORDER ⎧PERMANENT⎫ INSERTION ⎧FIRST / LAST / NEXT / PRIOR / SYSTEM DEFAULT⎫
      IS  ⎩TEMPORARY⎭     IS    ⎨SORTED ⎧WITHIN RECORD-TYPE             ⎫    ⎬  .
                                ⎩       ⎩BY DEFINED KEYS [ ... ]        ⎭    ⎭
    MEMBER IS record_name_m
      [DUPLICATES ARE NOT ALLOWED FOR attribute_k1 [, ...] ]
      [ STRUCTURAL CONSTRAINT IS variable_a EQUAL TO variable_b [, ...]] .
```

/* Omitted is detail of RESULT and SET. Also omitted are some size parameters, access procedures, locks, escape calls, as well as some FREQUENCY clauses for optimization advice. SET features relevant to data manipulation are shown in Fig. 9-12. */

Figure 8-9 Data Description Language defined by the CODASYL DDL Committee (1978). Clauses in [ ] are optional, in { ... / ... } are alternatives, with [,...] are repeatable.

Procedures, written by the user community, to carry out actions beyond the capability of the database system may be specified. They can be used to protect data items, or to carry out special conversions or derivations. We encountered such procedures as escape procedures in VSAM, Sec. 4-3-5. They will be CALLed when the SCHEMA, or a specific AREA, RECORD or data_name is accessed. These routines can be designated to be entered BEFORE, ON ERROR, or AFTER access, and can also be limited to specific actions as ALTER, COPY, DISPLAY, OPEN, CLOSE, GET, MODIFY, STORE.

ACCESS CONTROL LOCKs are available at every level to force entry of a keyword or cause some verification procedure, as shown in Fig. 12-5. The specifications for the connections "SET NAME IS link_set_name" are strongly related to database manipulation and are covered in more detail in Figs. 9-13 and 9-14.

The Storage Schema - DSDL The storage (DSDL) schema as being defined by a CODASYL commitee has to provide the physical facilities for all the records and connections defined in the model DDL schema. Figure 8-10 summarizes the proposal for the DDLC storage schema.

Optionally more than one storage schema may be used to serve a model schema, and then each storage schema has to state which model records and link_sets it REPRESENTs. A specific record type used in the model schema can also be supported by multiple storage record types. The mapping rules from model record names to storage record names permit a conditional expression, so that, for instance, records having certain values, say sales_location = 'France' may be selected for the record type European_sales. This record type can then be assigned a certain access protection distinct from, say, Canadian_sales. A subschema notion is hence possible, and if the storage schemas are distinct, a distributed system can be supported. The connections can not be mapped.

To support link_sets for connection either direct or indirect pointers, or indexes may be used. If no physical structure to provide link_sets is provided, the connections have to be established using sequential scanning.

Several alternatives and hybrids for placing storage records into the storage areas are available. PLACEMENT can be determined by a hashing function (CALC), so that all members of a nest occupy the same blocks if possible (CLUSTERED VIA SET link_set), perhaps sharing the pages WITH another nest, and optionally sharing the blocks with the owner record (NEAR OWNER) according to this ownership connection. Placement may also be sequential according to a key attribute. Indexes to the nests may be placed by CALC or NEAR OWNER. An area contains a specified, but extendible number of blocks (pages).

The representation of the data elements is also defined in the storage schema in the FORMAT clause. The format alternatives are intended to cover any representation chosen in the schema. If no format is specified, the implementor can choose any representation consistent with the TYPE given in the schema.

Derived data are also defined here, and an option is provided to permit storage of data derived on access. The actual derivation procedure is given in the RESULT clause in the main schema. Schema clauses related to processing and the statements used to manipulate the CODASYL database are shown in Sec. 9-5. In the next section we now will present some typical alternatives for schema implementation.

```
STORAGE SCHEMA NAME IS storage_schema_name
   FOR schema_name SCHEMA
   ⎡ REPRESENT  ⎧ ALL [EXCEPT] ⎫ schema_record_name RECORDS  ⎤
   ⎢            ⎩ ONLY         ⎭                              ⎥
   ⎢ AND        ⎧ ALL [EXCEPT] ⎫ schema_linkset_name SETS     ⎥
   ⎣            ⎩ ONLY         ⎭                              ⎦
   ⎡ MAPPING FOR schema_record_name_y                          ⎤
   ⎢      [ If condition ] STORAGE RECORD IS storage_record_name_x ⎥ .
   ⎣                                                           ⎦

   STORAGE AREA NAME IS storage_area_name
      INITIAL SIZE IS integer_1 PAGES
      [EXPANDABLE [BY integer_2 PAGES] [TO integer_3 PAGES]]
      PAGE SIZE IS integer_4 { CHARACTERS / WORDS }.
```

/ The clauses below are repeated for each storage record type */*

```
STORAGE RECORD NAME IS storage_record_name_1
   ⎡LINK TO storage_record_name_2 ⎡ IS ⎧ DIRECT   ⎫ ⎤⎤ [ , ... [...] ]
   ⎢                              ⎣    ⎩ INDIRECT ⎭ ⎦⎥
   ⎣[RESERVE integer_5 POINTERS]                     ⎦
   [ [ If condition ] DENSITY IS n_block STORAGE RECORDS PER b_train PAGES]
   PLACEMENT IS
      ⎧ CALC [hash_procedure_name] USING identifier_1, ...      ⎫
      ⎪ CLUSTERED VIA SET schema_set_name                       ⎪
      ⎨              [NEAR OWNER storage_record_name_0]          ⎬
      ⎪              [WITH storage_record_name_3]                ⎪
      ⎩ SEQUENTIAL { ASCENDING / DESCENDING } identifier_2, ... ⎭
         WITHIN storage_area_name [FROM PAGE int_8 THRU int_9].
```

/ And now come the actual field definitions */*

```
level_no data_name
            [ALIGNMENT IS integer_10 {BITS / CHARACTER / WORDS}]
            [EVALUATION IS ON ⎧ ACCESS [STORAGE [NOT] REQUIRED] ⎫
                              ⎩ UPDATE                          ⎭
            [FORMAT IS /*  a variety of standard or implementor defined types */]
            [NULL IS {literal_value / COMPACTED}]
            [SIZE IS integer_size {BITS / CHARACTER / WORDS}].
```

/ The clauses below are repeated for each link_set connection in the schema */*

```
SET schema_set    [ALLOCATION IS {STATIC / DYNAMIC }]
    POINTER ⎧ INDEX index_name                                    ⎫
        FOR ⎨ ... RECORD schema_record IS ... TO storage_record ...⎬ .
            ⎩                                                      ⎭
```

These clauses relate the model CODASYL *definition of Fig. 8-9 to implementation concepts presented in Chaps. 2 to 5; the use of many of these clauses is described in Sec. 9-5-4. Omitted are* ACCESS CONTROL, *details of If* CONDITION, DENSITY, *and data alignment. Details of* SET ... POINTER *are given in Fig. 9-15.*

Figure 8-10 The 1978 CODASYL Data Storage Description Language proposal.
Clauses in [ ] are optional, in { .../... } are alternatives, with [, ...] are repeatable.

8-4 MANIPULATION OF THE SCHEMA

The data in the schema contains the information to be used to control a database. The information can be used to generate a database system and its processing functions, or its use can be deferred to the execution time of the processes that manipulate the database. This choice is related to the concept of a binding time introduced in Sec. 1-4.

The schema, as written by the organizer of the database, has to be translated for use by a database-management system. The binding choices are the familiar alternative of compiling versus interpretation.

In the environment of the database, compiling is equivalent to using all the information in the schema when the application programs are created; the schema can then be discarded. Interpreting, on the other hand, is equivalent to the use of a general program that, when called upon to carry out database manipulations, looks at the schema to find data items and determine their relationships.

8-4-1 Examples of Schema Translation

In order to clarify the alternatives, will sketch some examples of schema translation and schema use. In Sec. 8-4-2 we will summarize the relative advatages and disadvantages.

The schema in the RETRIEVE example (Fig. 8-5) used in Sec. 8-2-1 is simply stored in the form of an array on the schema file. The translation process consisted only of formatting the three fields of each schema entry. The schema subsequently was used interpretively. Figure 8-11 shows a similar process for a more complete schema language. Here, however, the source schema is analyzed and its elements are used to build tables and dictionaries for the interpreter shown in Fig. 8-14. The dictionaries are used for recognizing the terms which appear in the user's commands, and the tables direct a set of interpreting routines to the contents of the database.

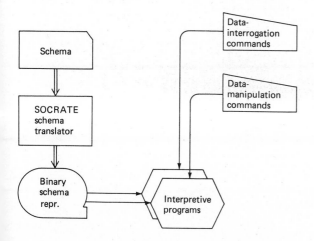

Figure 8-11 SOCRATE interpretive sequence.

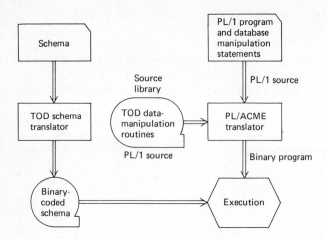

Figure 8-12 TOD schema compilation for execution interpretation.

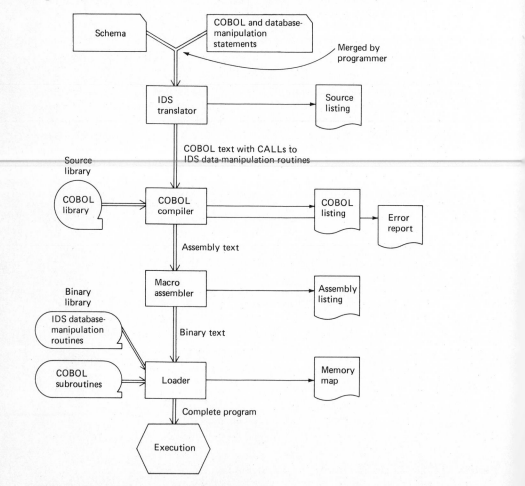

Figure 8-13 IDS compilation sequence.

Figure 8-12 sketches the process in the Time-Oriented Database System (TOD). In order to support extensive data analysis in a research environment, a set of functions to manipulate the database is available in a TOD routine library. The users write programs using these functions. The database is kept in transposed form for rapid attribute access (see Sec. 4-1-4), but the users have a traditional tabular view.

The source schema is translated by a separate compiler into an encoded tabular form, essentially a relation, for interpretation. The library routines, invoked by the user's programs, fetch at execution time the required schema tables for request interpetation and data access.

Interpretation of the schema is avoided in the process used in many commercial database systems. We show the specifics of the Honeywell IDS system in Fig. 8-13. Here a user's COBOL program, with special database reference statements, is combined with the schema and processed by the IDS compiler. The result of the IDS translator is a clean COBOL program text which contains statement sequences and declarations to carry out the IDS functions as well as the user's own COBOL data processing specifications. This

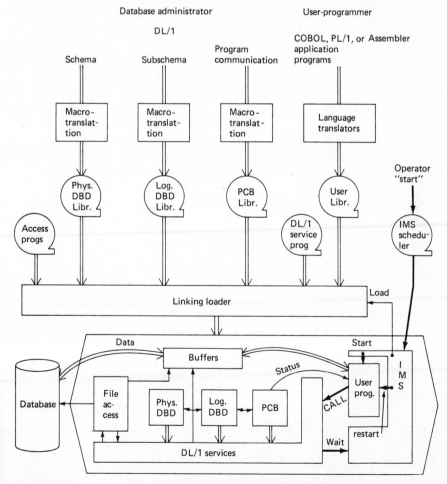

Figure 8-14 IMS translation and operation sequence.

text is compiled by a COBOL compiler to produce assembly text, which in turn, is assembled into a binary program. Basic IDS file-manipulation routines, as well as COBOL subroutines, are added by the loader, and execution can commence without any further reference to the schema.

In the approach taken by the IBM IMS system, the schema and program components which become part of the final execution package are generated at different times, stored on separate libraries, and scheduled for execution by the scheduler component of the IMS system. The components and their integration are sketched in Fig. 8-14. The schema language, DL/1, concentrates on the structure of the file and leaves usage specification largely to the users' programs. No separate translator is provided for the schema language DL/1; all statements are assembly language macros. The assembler generates table entries from these macros, and these are linked by IMS to the user programs when IMS starts a user process.

Out of the DL/1 file, description subschemas, which omit unnecessary detail, can be extracted to be used by the programs. Some additional macro-statements in the schema provide a cross-referencing capability so that referenced relation types can be defined. We will discuss the use of DL/1 schemas in Sec. 9-6 when the IMS data-management system is discussed.

Many more implementation alternatives are possible. Which alternative is chosen will have a major effect on the structure permitted by the schema. The user and system developer perceive the data organization through the schema presented to them. The use of the database will depend on the concepts supported by the schema, since these concepts are needed for the user to manipulate the database. The debate which concepts are best will continue forever. Tabular models have served models of reasonable size well. When the models become large a schema which supports a hierarchical decomposition of the model space becomes desirable. An integrated database will probably require a schema which can support more than one hierachical view.

8-4-2 Evaluating the Alterntives for Translation of the Schema

The approach shown for IDS is typical of compilation methods, while the approach shown for SOCRATE is typical for interpretation. We will discuss the arguments for and against these two approaches, keeping in mind that compromises between the two methods exist as well.

Compilation   The benefits of compiling the schema information are the following:

1 High process time efficiency due to use of actual machine code. It is generally conceded that interpretation of simple arithmetic statements is anywhere from 10 to 200 times slower than the execution of compiled code, and this experience may lead us to reject the interpretive approach.

2 Special programs can be written and compiled to deal with special situations. The entire processing repertory of the computer is available, including multiple compiler language and their libraries.

3 No explicit space is required at process time to hold the schema.

4 Facilities exist within programming languages to support this approach. One of these is the capability to include source modules from a schema file, and another is the tailoring of programs provided by the use of macro expansion capabilities.

The disadvantages of the compiled approach are the following:

1 All programs have to be regenerated when the schema changes, and new programs have to be written when new data and relationships have been specified.

2 It is difficult to control whether all programs use the schema completely and are not dependent on specific internal knowledge of the data organization. This can leead to unpleasant suprises when changes to the schema are made.

3 The apparent benefit of not requiring storage for the schema at processing time is largely illusory, since all the required information is stored somehow within the processing programs and might well appear multiple times in independent programs.

4 Most compilers and higher level languages do not have the capability of defining database structures as complex as we would like to be able to handle. Conditional, composite, and iterative fields, for example, are rarely available on the language level.

5 It can be difficult to adapt an existing compiler to generate code for some new hardware features which are being developed to aid databases.

Interpretation The benefits of the interpretive methods are related, of course, to the disadvantages of compiling. We can emphasize the following:

1 Data-oriented changes need to be introduced in the schema only, and do not need programming effort.

2 Better control exists over the contents of, and access to, the database.

3 Programming can be carried out before the exact data specifications are known.

4 Synchronization of accesses to a shared file is easier to maintain in a multi-programmed environment because more process information is available.

5 Greater independence between processes and files exists. This feature will protect the system from hardware changes.

6 It may be possible to implement frequently used and well-established functions in hardware or in micro-coded procedures.

6 The source-language statements may require less storage space than the machine instructions needed for file access.

Disadvantages of the interpretive method include the following:

1 The general interpreter has less flexibility when special considerations have to be taken care of. Recompiling of programs is not costly compared with the file reorganization effort involved when the schema is changed.

2 There is a high central processor cost to interpreting. Although, in terms of the total time to complete a job, this cost may be minimal because of the lengthy file accesses, less CPU time will be available to other processes.

3 Good general programs are difficult to construct and debug.

4 The single generalized interpreting program may occupy more space than the separate processing programs which are brought in on demand only. In a paging system, the demands on primary memory space for either approach may be substantially equal.

Compromises include compiled references to programs which can adapt to changes in the database schema. The actual choice of approach will be determined largely by available facilities and expertise, although the wrong choice can be costly.

8-4-3 Internal Representation of a Schema

The internal representation of a complex schema may itself require a linked structure to describe the structural dependencies of the data elements. In SOCRATE this is achieved through a number of interlinked tables as shown in Fig. 8-15, which is based on the schema in Example 8-6.

The dictionary table includes both attribute names and the data values permitted in domain controlled by lists of choices. The *next-pointers* provide rings within a nest and the *detail-pointers* provide access to nests when required.

Structure table

s#	source	Type	Next	Detail	Dict.
1	file	block*	0	2 s‡	1 d
2	employee	set	1 sP†	3 s	2 d
3	employee	block	2 sP	4 s	2 d
4	name	word	5 sS	0	3 d
5	age	num.	6 sS	1 n	4 d
6	address	text	7 sS	0	6 d
7	eyecolor	list, 3	8 sS	5 n	7 d
8	haircolor	list, 5	9 sS	8 n	11 d
9	sex	list, 2	10 sS	13 n	15 d
10	if sex	cond.	16 sS	11 s	15 d
11	then	block'	13 sS	12 s	16 d
12	years_mil.	num.	11 sP	15 n	18 d
13	else	block'	10 sP	14 s	0
14	preg.	num.	15 sP	19 n	19 d
15	children	num.	13 sP	19 n	20 d
16	skills	set	3 sP	17 s	21 d
17	skills	block	16 sS	18 s	21 d
18	type	word	19 sS	0	22 d
19	years_exp.	num.	17 sP	23 n	23 d

Dictionary

d#	Entry
1	FILE
2	employee
3	name
4	age
5	Years
6	address
7	eye_color
8	Brown
9	Black
10	Blue
11	hair_color
12	Blond
13	Red
14	Gray
15	sex
16	Male
17	Female
18	years_mil. . .
19	pregnancies
20	children
21	skills
22	type
23	years_exp. . .

Number table

n#	Entry	source
1	16	age
2	66	
3	0 §	
4	5 d¶	
5	8 d	eye_c.
6	9 d	
7	10 d	
8	9 d	hair_c.
9	8 d	
10	12 d	
11	13 d	
12	14 d	
13	16 d	sex
14	17 d	
15	0	y._mil.
16	25	
17	0	
18	5 d	
19	0	preg.
20	20	
21	0	
22	0	y._exp.
23	0	
24	50	
25	0	
26	5 d	

Notes;
* The Type field is actually coded.
† The Next pointer refers to a
   Parent entry if next$_i < i$, and to a
   Sibling entry if next$_i > i$.
‡ The Detail entry refers to the structure table for
   entries of type(block, set, condition) and otherwise
   to the number table.
§ The third entry for numeric ranges specifies a scale factor.
¶ The fourth entry for numeric ranges and the entries for lists
   refer to the dictionary.

Figure 8-15 SOCRATE internal schema representation.

8-5   SUBSCHEMAS

In a large database, the schema itself may be of massive proportions. Since not all the information in the schema is required by every user or program, the data in the schema may be categorized and selected according to several dimensions. These dimensions include:

Functional level of the schema user	Host-language adaptations
Responsibility and ownership of data	Location of stored database fragments
Processing function	

All these dimensions can be used to divide schemas into subschemas which restrict the user or the database to a subset of data and function, depending on responsibility, *need-to-know*, and location.

The diversity and complexities of schemas are in part caused by the differences in objectives seen by schema designers.

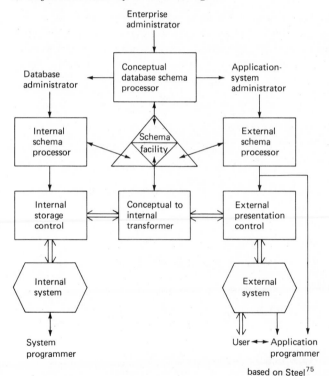

Figure 8-16

based on Steel[75]   Schemas and interfaces.

8-5-1 Subschemas Based on View and Function

As a part of preparations for a possible standardization effort, a committee of the American National Standards Institute (ANSI), X3-SPARC, defined in detail the schema function–user function correspondences and some of the many interfaces among people and system modules to be considered. The terminolgy used here and the interfaces shown in Fig. 8-16 are based on this work. The ANSI-SPARC descriptions are based on a three-part schema: the conceptual schema implements the database model, the internal schema implements the storage definitions, and external schemas implement the concept of a database submodel.

External Schema A user who is interested in obtaining information from the database may need only an *external* description of the content of the database. The user can obtain a list of the entities, their attributes, and the type characteristics of these attributes from the system. The user can request the data in interesting combinations and specify data reduction processes.

The external schema for a user of the database may be closely related to the view model which was used to construct this portion of the database model. Many external schemas are composed of subsets of the database relations and subsets of the attributes of the selected relations. Where the database submodel differs structurally from the implemented database, substantial transformations may be required, including joins and sorts. Simple transformations include the specification of record segments. Substantial delays may be encountered if the transformations are major. A user who uses the database frequently will, of course, form concepts about the system by learning what the system does poorly and what it does well and willadapt to the database, ignoring the original view. External schemas may be changed to adapt to the needs of the user without impacting other schemas.

An example of simple subschema definition is shown in Example 8-11. A VIEW on the relations or TABLEs in IBM SQL/DS permits projection and rearranging of attribute columns, selection of rows, and specification of derived variables. The VIEWs in SQL/DS never create relations; all mapping is performed at the time when the view is used. The SQL language is summarized in Sec. 9-2.

Example 8-11   An SQL External Subschema Definition

Given a relation Children with data in traditional measurements:

```
Children: RELATION
   child_id, guardian, class, rank, age_c, height, weight, year_entered;
```
we define a view for the modern metric-thinking school nurse
```
   CREATE VIEW School_nurse
              ( child,    age,    height_cm,    weight_kg    )
      AS SELECT child_id, age_c, height * 2.54, weight * 0.4536
         FROM Children;
```

A database will be accessed via multiple external schemas. One external schema contains the entries required for the data processing of one area of interest. External schemas may overlap to reflect overlapping data models. The use of multiple schemas also aids in the maintenance of the integrity of the database, since fewer of the relations are exposed to processes which may contain errors.

This concept of an external schema to constrain access provides control at little additional cost. If access programs are not constrained, a database system, in order to protect data from unauthorizee access, will have to verify of every record and field address submitted as being appropriate for the user. In SQL the original database TABLE creator can define VIEWS and assign them to specific users with certain privileges to provide access control.

Multiple active processes may use the same external schema. Distinct external schemas may overlap. If any overlapping schemas are used at the same time, it is desirable that the processes share the schema entries at some level. This provides a linkage which the system can use to avoid problems of access interference. Only privilege information, tied to the users rather than to the database elements, must remain separate.

Conceptual Schema   The external view is derived from the overall *conceptual* schema which represents the entire database model. Here all relationships are described. The conceptual model covers the information-processing needs of an enterprise or a large portion of the enterprise. As the real world changes, the conceptual schema will have to be adjusted. It is desirable that derived external schemas using conceptual elements which are changed can be restated to provide a relatively constant user interface. Only the external schema which required a conceptual change due to a related change in its view model will require modification.

If all users access the database through external schemas, the conceptual model may not be physically present during database processing; its main function is design and schema generation.

Internal Schema   The operational management of the stored files requires further information to be placed in an *internal* schema. The internal schema defines where the database attribute values are placed and how they are accessed. The decisions encoded in the internal schema present the aggregate requirements of all the users. Here the notion of a *database administrator* appears. The load estimates or measurements, as defined in Sec. 5-4, are applied here and are balanced with response-time requirements for specific transactions. Figure 8-10 provided examples of the tools available to tune the performance of a database. The principal concept is always the addition of redundant access structures and the maintenance of locality. Control over actual and potential data derivations is part of the internal schema.

To provide input to performance control functions, the internal schema may also contain descriptive statistical data elements which are updated during operation. The TOD system, for instance, collects in its schema the access counts to attributes, to be used for periodic restructuring by the data administrator. If the database is distributed over multiple physical locations, corresponding multiple internal schemas can be used to implement the single conceptual schema.

8-5-2 Physical Organization of Schema Characteristics

A database schema may be organized by attribute or by characteristic: *names, domains, titles, control of access to data, etc.*

Certain database processes will not need all the characteristics that we have associated with each data element. Processing programs specifically may only need access to the type and length characteristics of the data elements. If data are only to be moved, only the length and count are needed. The descriptive information which contains titles, unit specifications, etc., can remain inaccessible. This physical organization reduces memory and paging requirements.

The TOD schema table, for instance, is transposed during translation to provide the schema tables in a compact form to the interpreter. This means that, for instance, all TITLE information is available as a single array to the output processor, and all TYPE information is placed into another array to be used by the computational processes.

8-5-3 Adaptation to a Host Language

Yet another aspect of a subschema is considered by CODASYL and SQL. The intention is that the schema and the schema description language can be utilized by programs written in a number of different computer languages. Variations of the subschema language are designed to fit the syntax, semantics, and power of the host language. Languages to be supported include COBOL, FORTRAN, and PL/1. Languages with flexible data structures, like LISP, are not easily supported by traditional schemas and have either used intermediate modules as interfaces, or treated databases as large virtual memory segments.

Even in procedural languages there are problems to be resolved due to representation and structure differences. An instance is the COBOL language capability to have a structure containing element types which OCCUR a variable number of times, as shown in Fig. 8-9, a notion not included in FORTRAN. In PL/1 a feature affecting schema power is the capability to handle variable-length character strings.

The problem is aggravated in a distributed system with heterogeneous processors, where, for instance, real values may have different representations. In a mixed language or computer environments users will have to agree to avoid incompatible data types.

8-5-4 Data Ownership

The database administrator has the responsibility for the successful operation of the database system. While the structural integrity and the adequacy of the interfaces between external, conceptual, and internal schemas require a central view, it may be necessary to delegate data content responsibility to those most closely associated with a particular database submodel. Other aspects of this function are discussed in Sec. 8-6-2.

The use of multiple external database schemas is related to the assignment of responsibilty for the maintenance of the stored data. Certain data elements may be collected and controlled for quality by one group. This group then may use an external schema to manage its data and assign permission for its use. A new concept pertaining to data emerges here, namely, *data ownership.* This is another candidate for an attribute to be specified in the schema language, or it may be a part of the access privilege specification. When attributes or relations are to be added, the maintenance responsibility over these data should be established. Private and public data may be distinguished, as well as source and derived data elements.

Feedback may be necessary to inform owners of the outside uses of the data, since not all functions of data elements and data relationships can be perceived from one external schema. The DBTG AREA specification allows the partitioning of the database into a number of areas. Areas can be individually protected. In several implementations this also means that the data can reside on physically distinct devices.

Derived data Ownership and data responsibility also extends to derived data. When on-entry and on-access database procedures are used, control can be well defined, but most derived data is placed into databases by explicit programming. These derived data, when stored within the database, become indistinguishable from data which entered the database from the outside. The responsibility for the validity of results derived by processing source input is assigned to the group which controls the processing programs. Errors in the source data may be the responsibility of another group. The chain of derived results can go through various levels and may have involved recursion, making checking and restoration difficult.

Protection by Database Procedures There may, for instance, be an **AREA** for medical data of employees which can only be updated and written by authorized staff, defined by a keyword variable check_MD.number. To disable access by nonauthorized staff to certain disease data, the database administrator can also specify a database procedure hush which disables retrieval of data based on values in the access path as shown in Example 8-12. Monitoring of access to data also may be necessary for confidential data items. The hush routine could achieve this by also reporting every approved use to a logging device.

Example 8-12 Subschema Protection

```
AREA_NAME IS medical.
  RECORD_NAME IS diseases WITHIN medical.
    ON GET   CALL hush  USING diseases;
    PRIVACY LOCK FOR STORE IS check_MD_number.
    1     patient_name    PICTURE 20(X); OCCURS 1 TIMES; CHECK IS NULL.
    1     social_sec      PICTURE 9(9); OCCURS 1 TIMES; CHECK IS NULL.
    1     sick_call_no    PICTURE 99.
    1     sick_call    OCCURS sick_call_no TIMES.
      2    disease       PICTURE 50(X).
      2    ICDA_code     PICTURE 9999V9.
      2    days          PICTURE 999.
```

Once a database is operational any changes to the schema can cause many programs to fail. The use of a database may not have been controlled so that all users who are potentially affected by a contemplated change can be identified and warned. A check_program attached to the record type to be changed or to an entire **AREA** can be used to report on usage which may conflict with contemplated changes.

8-6 STRUCTURE, SCHEMA, AND USAGE

The approaches associated with the different structures and schema formulations also imply differences in the approaches to the envisaged use of the database. These differences will be accentuated in the implementation of database systems as described in Chap. 9. A categorization into three conceptual approaches follows:

1 A schema which concentrates on the naming and the semantics of source attributes and domains will be associated with a *relational* approach to database systems. The entire database is a potential resource, where linkages, derivations, and associations are established when needed. Potential relationships are found through matching domains in the schema.

2 A schema which organizes the data elements and segments into record-like structures is associated most strongly with traditional *data-processing* technology. Reports, tables, and the like will be easy to generate and to process. Structural binding between files increases the efficiency of the common processes. Potential relationships are specified in the schema; corresponding attribute values in the database relate actual tuples.

3 If the relationships among data elements are irregular and complex, and the data records are also irregular, it may not be possible to place relationship information into a schema. Now data segments found along network paths which are dynamically selected by the user's programs and interaction. Examples of such approaches are found in some *artificial intelligence* systems. Such a system will support the *retrieval of information* in an intellectually complex mode. The volume of data is typically relatively small. The potential diversity of data and structure encountered may make traditional data processing difficult.

In practice the three categories are rarely pure. The DBTG approach, for instance, falls between **2** and **3**, and many statistics support systems are between categories **1** and **2**.

Important objectives of the use of databases are *data independence* and *control over the database*. The final sections of this chapter will comment on these issues.

8-6-1 Data Independence

An early impetus toward the use of schemas to describe content and structure of databases was the desire to move databases from one computer to another in order to support growth or to obtain the use of newer, more economical systems. The user of a large database is currently tied to the hardware that supports the files and programs for that database. Some of these anchors are due to low level constructs that are used in high-level programming. For instance, if pointer references have been used in one database system, it becomes very difficult to translate these references to another system directly, since we cannot expect that the new database structure will be mapped into the same relative positions on the files. More serious difficulties are caused when in one system, data is accessed via indexes and reside on sequential or random files, and on the other system the data is accessed through links as in a multiring structure.

The desired independence of applications from hardware and software systems has been called *data independence*. We can, however, distinguish three dependencies which have to be resolved:

Data Dependence   Program instructions depend on the encoding of data elements. Issues are the size of elemental fields (i.e., 32- versus 36- or 60-bit words, and 6-, 7-, or 8-bit characters), floating-point representations, and pointer values.

Structure Dependence   Program logic depends on facilities to segment records, manage nests, and provide and follow interfile linkages. Whether an employee's department is found by tracing through a ring, using a direct pointer, reading the file backward to obtain a master record, or reentering the file with a fetch argument can bind the employee-department relationship in specific ways, not foreseen in the original conceptual database model.

Program Dependence The dependency on assumptions made in the programs in regard to usage and data structure that are not reflected in the schemas. Aspects of data that are not essential to the information-storage and -manipulation problems but provide convenience and programming efficiency can bind data structures in unexpected ways. A programmer may *know* that an employee's personal data are in a record position which corresponds to the record position in the payroll file and make use of this knowledge, even though no direct relationship is defined.

A tool which helps to achieve data independence is the schema. In order to achieve structure independence the structure of the data has to be described in a standardized form. Programming independence will be achieved only if programs make full use of the capability for data and structural independence. It is not yet clear how much independence can be achieved while retaining maximal efficiency in large databases.

Database Translation The development of automatic or semiautomatic tools to move a database with its programs from one system to another has demonstrated the need for the schematic description of the database. Database translation, if successful, provides an alternative to complete data and structure independence, since it should allow the translation of the database from an efficient version on one system into an efficient version in another situation. In general, the process is carried out in two stages. An intermediate stage is the formal representation of the database, which is not concerned with efficiency but rather with generality. The description of the intermediate stage is related to the conceptual schema obtained from a database-model construction. Previously existing constraints add detail and complications to the data translation process. We will not discuss the subject of database translation further, but it should be clear that many of the rigorous approaches to database management are closely related to the problem of database translation.

8-6-2 Database Control

In an organization where many users and programmers share the database and use the facilities of the schema, or of subschemas, some joint control of the data organization will be required. This may be implemented through an automatic protection system, which prevents schema changes that could cause problems to others. In general, a human arbiter will be called upon to resolve conflicts. Typical conflicts occur when an overall system improvement causes severe inconveniences for a few users, or when new requirements by some users affect many others to a slight extent. We will refer to this set of control decisions as *database management*, and we consider both automatic and manual actions under this heading.

In order to carry out the database management functions, additional information may be appended to the schema. Required are parameters that control system performance and the assignment of access privileges as mentioned previously. Maintaining additional copies of data, linkages, indexes, maintenance of actual results, and so forth, improves the retrieval performance of systems but leads to redundancy in stored data. In order to evaluate how much redundancy is cost-effective, the database manager will continuously monitor the operation of the database system at various levels.

The person who has the responsibility for the database, the *database administrator*, has extraordinary privileges. Because of these privileges, the individual should have insights which are beyond the scope of most users and programmers. This role as seen in one system is indicated in Fig. 8-13. Database systems intentionally screen unnecessary information between the levels and compartments of the database. The benefits of controlled communication between levels were discussed in Chap. 1. The user works with a simplified model of the system and is not able to improve or defeat the system. Because of this lack of knowledge, the procedures that have been developed can continue to work effectively as the database changes.

The database administrator, on the other hand, does have knowledge of the current internal structure. To safeguard the concept of a well-structured communication between levels, a database administrator may be denied the privilege to write data-manipulating programs.

As databases become bigger and more complex, the concept of centralized control by a single database administrator for the entire database may no longer be acceptable. The knowledge required to carry out the function, and the cost of failure to properly control a very large database may make the position untenable. Whether a committee can do better is also questionable. An associated problem is the understandable reluctance of managers of enterprises to cede much of their power. These considerations may put a limit on the growth of databases and encourages distribution of database functions. Issues associated with very large databases will appear in Chap. 9, and their security problems will be touched on in Chaps. 11, 12, and 13. The role of the database adminstrator is further analyzed in Chap. 15.

BACKGROUND AND REFERENCES

The concepts which combined and evolved into the idea of a schema, as presented here, have had their origins from many relatively independent efforts. The users of statistical databases felt the need for tabular definition of the data elements they were using at a very early time, and many statistical systems support data dictionaries (Kidd[69], Ellis[72]). An outstanding example of such a system is OSIRIS (Rattenbury[74]).

Techniques to capture the required information are surveyed by Taggart[77]; a method is described by Teichroew[77]. Data dictionaries and their use are described by Uhrowczik[73] and Curtice[81]. Several systems available as independent software products are listed in Appendix B. The importance of data dictionaries to organize data, even if no DBMS is being used, has caused the National Bureau of Standards to issue proposals for standardization (NBS[80]).

COBOL and some of its predecessor commercial languages separate file-definition statements from procedural specifications (McGee[59]). An early database system using data descriptions to provide generalized retrieval capabilities was TDMS (Franks[66]). The term "schema" appeared about 1969. The SOCRATE system of CII has one of the nicest schema languages available.

Work by the CODASYL Development Committee produced a document on an information algebra (Bosak[62]) which considered a separation of the data and their description.

CODASYL's System Committee began to look at database concepts in 1966, influenced by IDS (Bachman[66,73]) and the "Associative Programming Language" (Dodd[66]). This effort generated two analyses of existing database systems (CODASYL[69S,71A], Olle[71]), and the CODASYL Data Base Task Group produced proposals for a schema-oriented system facility (CODASYL[69R,71R] and CODASYL[74]). The proposals for the COBOL augmentation are now part of the COBOL specifications (CODASYL[73,75,78]). A number of CODASYL committees are active in the database area: DDLC on the aggregate schema CODASYL[78L], DBLTG on the COBOL subschema, FDMLC on the FORTRAN subschema, and others on subjects as database translation, end-user interfaces, and database distribution (CODASYL[78D]). Palmer[75] gives a historical overview. A reference for CODASYL approaches is Olle[78].

The publication of the CODASYL proposal led to an evaluation of database requirements and standards. The SHARE-GUIDE group of IBM system users developed a set of database-system requirements, using mainly original terminology, which reflect on the need for a schema and the information it should contain and exclude. This work was reviewed by Everest in Codd[71].

These requirements led to the ANSI-SPARC report detailing three schemas levels (Steel[75]) which greatly influenced recent proposals. Papers in Jardine[77] review that work. Kent[80] proposes a further split of the conceptual schema. Issues of distribution have also been addressed (CODASYL[78D]). A method for representation of the external user view is considered by Navathe[78], how to update the database through views is the concern of Dayal[78] and Keller[82].

A standardization effort for relational systems is underway (Brodie[81]) and was accompanied by a survey of many current systems. External schemas for relational system have tended to be simple since no connections are specified. The availability of IBM's SQL system (see Sec. 9-2) is bound to influence this area.

Most database systems developed commercially or in academia do contain schemas of various flavors, i.e., Karpinski[71], Weyl[75] or Wiederhold[75], Chamberlin[76]. Others are listed in Appendix B. Data-domain definition is handled well in PASCAL (Wirth[72]). Claybrook in Rustin[74] and Nance[75] presents facilities to specify the file organization.

Katz[79] proposes query compilation for schemas while the cost of interpretation is evaluated by Baroody[82]. Compilation while retaining flexibility is achieved in SYSTEM R (Chamberlin[81A]).

External schemas and derived data are unified by Adiba[81] and management of derived data is considered by Cammarata[81].

The subject of database independence and translation has been an area of interest for many years, some contributions are Sibley[73], McGee in Klimbie[75], Shu[75], Navathe[76], and Shneiderman[82]. The SIGFIDET Proceedings contain many papers devoted to this topic.

Periodicals The activity in the database area has led to the publication of several *journals* devoted to database subjects. The rapid development in this field makes bibliographies and descriptive books rapidly obsolete. We will use this space to indicate sources for current material to complement the background sections of this and the earlier chapters.

Major journals in the database area are *Informations Systems* (Pargemon Press, since 1974) and *Transactions on Database Systems* (ACM TODS, since 1975). Other database-oriented publications include the *Database Journal* (A. P. Publications Ltd., 322 St.John Street, London UK, since 1975) and *Management Datamatics*, published by the IFIP Administrative Data Processing Group (Nordhoff Pub., Leyden Netherlands, since 1971).

Newsletters in the area are *Database Engineering*, produced since 1977 by the IEEE Computer Society technical committee of that name and the *ACM-SIGMOD Record* of the ACM Special Interest Group (SIG) on Management of Data. From 1968 to 1976 it was named *FDT*, for File Definition and Translation. The annual conferences (ACM-SIGFIDET 1969 to 1974 and ACM-SIGMOD since 1975) sponsored by this interest group contain many important papers (i.e., Codd[71], Dean[72], Rustin[74], King[75], Rothnie[76], Lowenthal[78], Bernstein[79], Chen[80]).

A series of conferences on *Very Large Data Bases* (VLDB) cover all database topics. The first, in 1975 (Kerr[75], ed.), was published by the ACM. VLDB 2, in 1976, Lockemann[77] and Neuhold(eds.), was published by North-Holland in 1977. VLDB 3, Merten[77](ed.), VLDB 4, Bubenko[78] and Yao(eds.), VLDB 5, Furtado[79] and Morgan(eds.), VLDB 6, Lochovsky[80] and Taylor(eds.), and VLDB 7, Zaniolo[81] and Delobel(eds.) were published by the IEEE Computer Society. The Proceedings of VLDB 8, McLeod[82] and Villasenor(eds.), are published by the VLDB Endowment, Saratoga CA.

In Chap. 11 we present some journals which are not specific to databases, but carry much relevant material as well.

EXERCISES

1 Discuss, based on statements given in Secs. 1-3 to 1-6, how a schema solves or fails to solve some of the requirements for large database systems.

2 Use a schema language to describe the file examples given in Sec. 3-0.

3 Use a schema language to describe the MUMPS example from Sec. 4-5.

4 Computer languages have rules for data-value transformations when more than one data type appears in an expression. Find such a specification and discuss its advantages and disadvantages. Relate to databases.

5 How could one specify transformations between programmer-defined data types?

6 Provide domain names and domain sizes for the example in Sec. 4-5.

7 Which units in Sec. 8-1-3 can be automatically converted to each other? (Not a real database question, but a valid database problem.)

8 Categorize SOCRATE according to the definitions given in Sec. 8-6. Explain your choice.

9 Write a schema suitable for description of the schema file itself.

Chapter 9

Database Implementation

Traveler, there is no path,
paths are made by walking.

Antonio Machado

Chapter 7 has presented models of databases; Chap. 8 discussed means to describe databases, and now we can finally look at actual database implementation problems. In this chapter we will proceed in a top-down fashion. We begin with methods derived from formal models and continue on to systems developed over time and regular use. The discussion in this chapter proceeds in the direction of increased binding, which causes loss of flexibility but increases the performance of systems. Such important implementation issues such as reliability, access protection, integrity, and data representation are not covered in this chapter; they are separately discussed in Chaps. 11, 12, 13, and 14.

We concentrate on concepts, and do not present complete system descriptions, although many actual systems will be referenced to allow further study. Appendix B can be consulted for references about the systems named in this chapter. The exact syntax of examples based on these systems has been modified at times in order to provide continuity. The fact that a certain system is cited here as a commendable example does not imply an endorsement of this implementation for a given application but only reflects on the values of the concepts being discussed.

Database Systems versus File Systems To review the necessity for a database system, its benefits and costs can be compared with the benefits and costs incurred when a file structure is superimposed on a hardware system.

A *file system* organizes the data-storage capability that is provided by the hardware. The hardware is partitioned into files, which are associated with a particular user. These users are now able to work in apparent isolation.

A *database system* organizes the file storage capability that is provided by the file systems. The relationships between the elements of the relations are made accessible. The data can be shared by cooperating users.

Figure 9-1 File and database system.

It is not essential that all secondary storage in a computer be managed through a file system. When multiple users share the computer, however, the more formal and complex approach has to be supported in order to enable these users to do productive work in isolation. The benefits of a well-organized file structure may already be a boon to a specific user; on the other hand, many respectable data files exist without any file-system support, specifically in small single-application computers.

It is not essential that storage of databases in a computer be controlled by means of a database system. When large amounts of interrelated data are stored that are of interest to diverse groups of users, a database system becomes necessary.

Objectives We have implied earlier a number of objectives for a database system design:

    1 The ability to refer to data items without having knowledge of record or file structure

and as a corollary:

    2 The ability to change record or file content and structure without affecting existing database programs

We also desire

    3 The ability to handle related files within one general framework, so that the data in separate files can remain consistent and so that excessive redundancy in updating and storage can be avoided

and

    4 A description of the database integrating diverse points of view, so that this description can become a communication medium between data generators and information seekers

In order to achieve these lofty goals, we will consider how to implement systems that use schemas to present high-level services while using file-based, record-oriented structures.

9-1 ISSUES IN DATABASE IMPLEMENTATION

In this introductory section we will introduce briefly some concepts that recur throughout this chapter.

9-1-1 Functionality and Generality

Database-management systems can be built with a wide range of generality. A categorization of these approaches into three levels distinguishes systems which support a single application, several applications of the same type, or multiple types of applications. Some systems have developed through these three levels; others have been designed consciously to attack problems at one specific level.

Single-Application Database Systems An organization establishes a database operation using available file system facilities, and designs application programs that interface to the database using a centrally maintained package which implements the required degree of data and structure description.

The original airline reservation system at American Airlines, SABRE, many large information systems, such as MEDLARS (a system to query the medical literature), and military command and control systems are examples of this approach.

Single-Application-Type Database Systems A group of users working in some type of application area recognizes the commonality of their needs. They or their vendor design a system to match their needs. User differences are incorporated into tables and schemas specific to the user. This step often follows success with a more single-minded system.

Examples of this approach are the generalized airline reservation systems (PARS), clinical information systems (TOD, GEMISCH), and bills-of-materials systems (BOMP).

Multiple-Application-Type Database Systems A vendor or academic group designs a system with the intent to serve the general database needs in a better fashion. An effort is made to provide a complete set of services. There will, of course, be a tendency to emphasize aspects relating to the experience of the designers, so that in practice a great deal of difference is found among the generalized systems. Another source for generalized systems is a continued evolution from single application or application-type services. An understanding of the history of generalized systems helps to explain features of their design.

The development of the CODASYL specification and of the relational model for databases has provided a basis for generalized systems that are relatively independent of past history. Generalized systems developed independently encountered so far in the text are PRTV, RETRIEVE, SOCRATE, and SQL/DS. The IDS and IMS systems owe much to the BOMP applications.

This chapter will consider mainly *generalized database management systems*. This is not intended to imply that more specific approaches are not valid. An orientation toward a specific application or type of application allows the recognition of semantic relationships which are difficult to exploit in a generalized system. A generalized system, however, presents a better balance of the problems of database system implementation. The term *database management system* (DBMS) is used here to refer to any of these approaches, and the adjective *generalized* is added only when the emphasis is required.

9-1-2 Models and Implementation Style

A database implementation carries a strong implication of the style of model the user is expected to have of the database. Since different classes of users will have different problems and different approaches to their use of the database, no single style of representation may be adequate for all users.

A major distinction can be made between information-retrieval usage and data-processing. Another, related, distinction is the predominant type of operational use of the system. We distinguish especially operations that retrieve simple items of data versus operations that require retrieval of data collections for further processing. We will present these issues in Chap. 10, but consider now styles of models and their effect on the implementation of the database.

The structural model defined in Sec. 7-3 used relations and connections. This model implies that data values can be obtainable by naming relations and attributes, and defining operations between them. Joins along connections have a predictable behavior.

We distinguish styles based on their stress on *relations versus connections*. We note first that a fully decomposed normalized model may contain many more relations than the user's personal model needs. The use of a submodel, which defines a specific and perhaps nonnormalized view, can present the database in a way that is more natural to some users.

A user's model which ignores the connections is called a *relational model*. The user will define explicitly all connections to be used in queries or updates.

To find a `child` of an `employee_name`, both the `Children` and the `Employee` relations have to be referenced, and the connection has to be defined in the query.

A *universal relation scheme* provides a view to the user of only a single relation. All the component attributes will have unique names. All connections are deduced from specification of the dependencies among attributes. The complexities of a normalized model are now hidden from the user, and the underlying database relations can be freely rearranged to support optimal processing strategies. Any processing that relates attributes by paths other than defined dependencies will still require explicit definitions, as the pure relational model does. If multiple paths between the attributes are possible, either user interaction or a set of predefined rules can be used to determine the best path.

The user's model can be simplified by exploiting the known connections, or relationships as defined in the structural model and in the general class of *entity-relationship* models. Now related attributes in connected relations can be found by following the connections. Intermediate relations can be ignored.

If the implementable or actual implemented connections are restricted to a tree, we can talk about a *hierarchical model*. These models tend to be easy to follow if they match the user's model, and the paths between attributes can be determined without ambiguity.

The parts in a subassembly (Fig. 4-23) were found via the connections defined by the hierarchy. A name with hierarchical qualifiers implies how the data element is accessed:

`machine.assembly.subassembly.part.`

Some problems remain for retrieval involving elements from more than two relations. We will present these with the hierarchical implementations in Sec. 9-4.

In a network with associations and multiply referenced entity relations in the model the connections become more complex. In those models the accessing style tends to require procedural descriptions. Two attributes in a network may be connected by more than one path. If there are multiple connections in a database model the appropriate path has to be found. The user can avoid ambiguity in a network by providing the full path definition in a query. An example of two paths based on Figs. 7-16 and 7-17 follows.

Example 9-1   Alternate Paths in a Network

We have the owner relations

```
Suppliers: RELATION              Parts : RELATION
   s_id :) name, etc.  ;            p_id :) name, size, weight, etc.  ;
```

and two associations owned by them

```
Supply: RELATION                 Possible_supplier : RELATION
   s_id, p_id :) quantity ;         s_id, p_id :)  ;
```

Two possible query fragments to "Locate Source of Heavy Parts" are:

```
   GET Parts.weight, Supplier.address    FOR Supply
   GET Parts.weight, Supplier.address    FOR Possible_supplier
```

The two paths will lead to different result tuples.

A number of alternative techniques to retrieve data from a database are feasible. We list them in order of increased sophistication.

1 No path selection is attempted, and the user will move explicitly from one relation to the next, generally using the familiar and defined connections.

2 A database submodel is predefined to provide the desired view for the user, and that submodel selects one connection, determining the path.

3 All possible pathways are computed and presented to the user for selection.

4 Rules for selecting the *best* from the set of all possible pathways are applied by the system.

An implementation often does not define all the known connections, so that implemented networks are often simpler than the database model indicated.

The dual problem also exists in networks, when one data item may be found by more than one name. The two queries below, using a different path, will locate the same data item.

```
   Location('Atlanta').dept('Assembly').job('Welder').name('Mike').age
   Healthrecordno(13436).age
```

Alternate names for the same item can lead to problems in integrity protection. This issue is addressed in Chap. 13.

9-1-3 Self-Contained versus Host Language Services

The obvious role of a database-management system is retrieval from and update of the database. In the implementation of a complete system it is also necessary to support analysis capability on the retrieved data. There are two basic approaches to the incorporation of analysis capability into database systems, as illustrated in Fig. 9-2, namely, *self-contained* and *host-based*.

Self-Contained Systems   The database system provides all the required services. There has to be at least some capability to execute computations on data retrieved from the database system. The RETRIEVE system (Figs. 8-5, 8-6, 8-7) and SOCRATE (Fig. 8-10) provided examples of self-contained systems.

Host-Based Systems   The database system carries out the retrieval and update functions only, and delivers the data on request to programs written in a *host system language*. The IDS system (Fig. 8-12) and the DBTG specifications (Fig. 8-9) shown in Chap. 8 provide examples of the host-based approach.

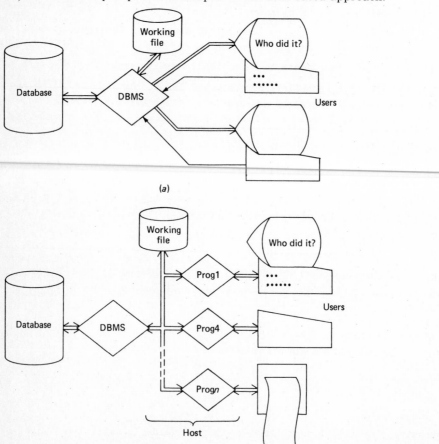

Figure 9-2 Database system alternatives.

It is possible to provide systems that combine approaches. In the TOD approach (Fig. 8-11) a host-based DBMS also provides programs which allow the use of preprogrammed search requests (i.e., **Prog1** in Fig. 9-2). The user is prompted for parameters. Functions such as file updating (**Prog**n), which require more general processing capabilities, are written by programmers in the PL/1 language.

Having a host available for processing does not remove all concerns about processing from the DBMS. In any database system it is desirable to retrieve data in a form that matches the user's view of the data. The selection algorithms for data may become quite complex if a user's requirements for a relation involve selection from multiple files. Selection requests addressed to the DBMS may retrieve many tuples, but few programming languages can deal with more than one record at a time. The DBMS serving a host language has to be able to provide a set of tuples, one record at a time, in a form the language can understand.

The interface of a host system and DBMS can lead to problems and inefficiency. If the DBMS cannot select tuples based on powerful selection criteria, the DBMS will deliver many tuples to the host programs that the programs will reject, so that retrieval and communication effort will be wasted. The host programs do not know the internal schema of the DBMS, so the requests will not be submitted in an optimal sequence. Effective sharing of capabilities requires a very complex interface between host system and DBMS.

In a self-contained DBMS closer interaction between processing and database is possible, this allows greater efficiency. Queries can be rearranged to take advantage of the relative accessing effectiveness of the query attributes. Indexes and other auxiliary information available in the system can be used beneficially. It is difficult, however, to provide in a self-contained DBMS all the processing facilities available through conventional computing systems, such as auxiliary files, statistical library programs, simulation systems, and communication facilities to other users and their computers.

The expectations which the users bring to generalized DBMSs are increasing, so that fewer pure self-contained systems are being implemented. The availability of a competent host system provides access to many processing facilities. The hybrid approach, where the DBMS provides some packages for self-contained operations as well as access for user programs to carry out operations that are not provided as part of the DBMS, is becoming prevalent.

9-1-4 Information Hiding and Secrecy

The database content will be easier to adapt to changing conditions if the user's external schema can remain unchanged. For that reason, it may seem desirable that the actual database structure remains hidden from the user. This implies that the internal database schema is to be kept secret from the user of the external schema. Elements of the internal schema that may be of interest to a user are the data representation and access path information. The data representation indicates the permissible range of domain values in those systems where domains are not explicit. Knowledge of access paths can affect the processing of transactions where more than one computational sequence is feasible. The assumption that favors hiding is that lack of knowledge will prevent users from taking advantage of coding or access structure in order to optimize their programs or retrieval operations, and that hiding will avoid problems when the internal structure has to be changed.

Some problems, however, will develop when there is excessive emphasis on keeping the structure of the database secret. The mere fact that information is being kept from users will make them suspicious and will have a negative effect on the relations between users and the service organization. Such secrecy then becomes very costly in terms of human productivity. Exceptions to secrecy become necessary when some applications do not receive adequate performance levels, and this can create further conflicts between users who are more and those who are less privileged.

Differences in response time also reveal to the user differences in the access paths, and any human will take advantage of alternatives which have shown themselves to be profitable.

A typical example is seen in a medical clinic where the search for the patient's record by number takes less than 3 seconds and a search by name requires nearly a minute. The clerks will demand the number from the patient and the system will be regarded as a typical example of dehumanization. The fact that the system designer told the users that the patient's name is just as good a retrieval key will be ignored.

A more comfortable solution is reached if the database system has a clean structure, provides means to extract any combination of data available in the system with an effort proportional to the result, and allows the users to determine if certain patterns of usage are advantageous or not. This implies some education about the systems, especially for frequent and intensive users of the services. The benefits of education are always two-sided, since the feedback from educated users provides the system designer with criteria for decision making. The effort expended by the user in the demystification process is probably less than the effort spent in ferreting secrets and half truths out of the black systems box. Information hiding remains a valid concept if it is used to design clean interfaces among system components. The approaches favored here use clean models, with understandable semantics and documented trade-offs in performance issues.

9-2 RELATIONAL CALCULUS IMPLEMENTATION

An elegant approach to manipulation of a database is to use the concepts of relations and transformations of relations presented when modeling databases in Chap. 7. In those implementations the relations are implemented by files, the schema is used to name the relations and their attributes, and the operations are specified implicitly by defining result relations.

A result relation is specified by a formula which expresses the desired result in terms of the relations in the database. A formula in the relational calculus has the general form

$$Result\ relation = \{\ tuple\ \ definition\ \mid\ conditions\ \}$$

The attributes used to define tuples and test conditions come from the database relations. We note that the process of arriving at a result is not specified. We have here a language that is not procedural, like a programming language, but is result- or problem-oriented.

9-2-1 A Relational Calculus System

We will begin by presenting aspects of a language, SQL, used by several implementations of the relational calculus, and will then discuss some features of similar systems as well as some implementation issues. We focus on retrieval and present the principal command in Table 9-1, followed by examples of its use.

The SELECT command presents a result table based on attributes from the database tables listed in the FROM clause. The WHERE clause restricts the result to rows meeting certain conditions. Aggregation during selection and other commands will be touched on later. The notation follows Fig. 8-10.

Table 9-1   The Retrieval Command of SQL/DS

```
                                                    /* * means all attributes */
SELECT {        *            }
       { attribute_ac [ ,... ] }

    FROM table_name [tuple_variable] [, ... [ ... ]]

    [ WHERE selection_expression ]

    [ GROUP BY attribute [HAVING selection_expression], ... ]
    [ ORDER BY attribute [DESCending], ...]
```

/* *The principal primitive component of the* Select *command is:* */
       attribute   /* *must be listed in the schema of some* FROM *table* */
       attribute_ac   /* *is a simple* attribute *or*
                          an arithmetic expression of attribute*s and constants.* */
       /* tuple_variable*s are presented in Sec. 9-2-2.* */

  Selection_expression ::=   /* *a boolean expression using* attribute_expression*s:* */
       [NOT] selection_expression [[NOT] { AND / OR } selection_expression]
       (selection_expression)
       attribute = USER   /* *user id, good for checking a* VIEW */
       attribute_expression

  Attribute_expression ::=   /* *a simple or a complex conditional expression:* */
       attribute_ac $\ominus$ constant
               /* $\ominus$ *is one of the set* { = ¬= > >= < <= } */
       attribute_ac $\ominus$ attribute_ac
       attribute_ac BETWEEN low_attribute_ac AND high_attribute_ac
       attribute_ac [NOT] IN (constant_1, ..., constant_n)
       attribute $\ominus$ {ANY / ALL} (constant_1, ..., constant_n)
       attribute IS [NOT] NULL
       attribute [NOT] LIKE 'search_string'   /* *See note in Table 9-3* */
/* Attribute_expression*s can include other* SELECT *substatements:* */
    /* *If the subquery leads to a single value:* */
       attribute_ac $\ominus$ (SELECT ... FROM ... ...)
    /* *If the subquery can lead to a set of values:* */
       attribute_ac [NOT] IN (SELECT ... FROM ... ...)
       attribute_ac $\ominus$ { ANY / ALL } (SELECT ... FROM ... ...)
    /* *If the result of the subquery is to be quantified (see Sec. 9-2-3):* */
       [NOT] EXISTS (SELECT ... FROM ... ...)

The expressions found in the formulas are translated into sequences of operations to be carried out on the database. The translator we refer to is the IBM SQL/DS system. A translator will rearrange the execution steps of the expression in order to minimize the total time required for CPU usage and disk accesses. Since block accesses are the principal cost factor, the optimization of the query will concentrate on this aspect. If indexes are available, these will be used whenever it seems profitable.

In the SQL documentation the term for a file is **table** and for a record is **row**. A table may contain duplicate identical rows, and is hence not a relation according to the stricter definition used in modeling. Example 9-3 clarifies this distinction. The available data types are two sizes of integers, decimal, floating point, and three types of strings: fixed, limited varying ($n < 255$), and long varying($< 32\,768$).

Any **attribute** used in a SQL expression must have been defined in the schema of a **FROM** table. If multiple rows of the same table appear in a statement, a *tuple variable* has to be specified. Tuple variables are presented in Sec. 9-2-2.

Example 9-2   Relational Calculus Statement

A simple example is a query for rows of one table based on one attribute value. Given

```
Employee: RELATION
    name  :) birthdate, height, weight, job, dep_no, health_no ;
```

the statement to create a table Welders with their names and birthdates
```
    SELECT name, birthdate  FROM Employee  WHERE job = 'Welder';
```
when applied to the relation instance shown in Fig. 7-6, defines the result table
```
Welders: RELATION
    name,  birthdate;
    Gerbil 1938
    Havic  1938
```

Joins in the relational calculus are implied. When more than one relation is specified in the **FROM table_name, ...** list, the attributes in the **SELECT** attribute list may come from any of the relations specified, requiring a join. A clause such as **WHERE one_table.attribute_1 = another_table.attribute_2** specifies the join condition; without such a condition a Cartesian product of the relations in the **attribute_r** list is implied. The "=" here implies execution of an equijoin during the processing of the query. Other joins are possible depending on $\ominus$. The subquery (**SELECT ...**) expression may have its own **WHERE** clauses, to restrict the rows which participate in the join.

Other commands for retrieval in SQL/DS are **PRINT** and **FORMAT** commands for report generation. A **GROUP** clause causes a result table to be broken into groups. For instance, **GROUP BY school_name** would list the **Children** school by school. In PRINTed reports **FORMAT** options can be used to generate a summary row with each group, and this row can contain **COUNT**s, **SUBTOTAL**s, and the like.

Tables versus Relations In the description of SQL we already found a number of instances where the basic concepts of a calculus have been extended to provide more suitable or effective facilities. An important feature is that SELECTed TABLEs are not treated as pure sets; they are permitted to include duplicate tuples. We follow SQL and use the term *table* to refer to such relations; sets of this type are also called *multi-sets* or *bags*. The alternatives, table versus relation, lead to the existence in SQL of two types of SELECT. The default version considers ALL the rows of a table independently and the other permits treatment of a table as a set of DISTINCT rows, with any identical rows removed.

Example 9-3   Tables versus Relations

A simple example is a query for rows applied to the stored table shown in Fig. 7-6, the WHERE clause is based on one attribute value:
Age_of_all_welders:
    SELECT birthdate, job FROM Employee WHERE job LIKE '%Welder%'

                /* Note: the % symbol stands for an arbitrary substring
                        to ensure that all kinds of 'Welders' will be found. */
                /* In a SQL search_string: a _ denotes any single character,
                                          a % denotes any substring.   */

This statement defines the table:

All_welders: RELATION
     birthdate, job ;
     1938   Welder
     1947   Asst. Welder
     1938   Welder

The alternative type of query states:
Age_of_welders:
    SELECT DISTINCT birthdate, job FROM Employee WHERE job LIKE '%Welder%'
and, when applied to the same data, defines a true relation with

Distinct_welders: RELATION
     birthdate, job ;
     1938   Welder
     1947   Asst. Welder

Aggregation Instead of producing a table to be displayed, it is also possible to apply functions to summarize the resulting table. The final result is a single row or several rows each representing a group.

In this form of a SELECT, if a GROUP BY clause is used, the functions will be applied group by group. A group is defined as the set of rows having the same value in the specified attribute column. For instance, GROUP BY school_name would apply the functions to the Children rows school by school. The HAVING clause can be used to eliminate summary rows and it can use the functions as well. Only functions and the grouping attributes, here school_name, can appear in the function lists of Table 9-2.

The SELECT command as used for summarization is shown in Table 9-2. This type of SELECT can also be used to define subqueries within another SELECT statement.

Table 9-2   Use of Aggregation Functions

```
SELECT function [, ...] FROM ...
          [GROUP BY ... ] [HAVING function ⊖ ... [, ...]  ]
          ...
```
available functions include:
COUNT (*)	/* count the table rows */
COUNT (DISTINCT attributes)	/* project and count the rows */
MAX (attribute)	
MIN (attribute)	
SUM (DISTINCT attribute)	/* SUM over projected result rows */
SUM (ALL attribute)	/* SUM over all result rows */
AVG (DISTINCT attribute)	/* AVeraGe over projected result rows */
AVG (ALL attribute)	/* AVeraGe over all result rows */

/* AVG *excludes* NULLs. *There is unfortunately no* Standard_Deviation */

To COUNT rows in SQL a table as All_welders has first to be defined in a WHERE SELECT clause. Then the count of all table instances or the distinct types can be obtained. For the All_welders table of Example 9-3 the two alternatives are:

```
COUNT (*)                  FROM All_welders   = 3
COUNT (DISTINCT birthdate) FROM All_welders   = 2
```

The alternative of tables versus relations supports the *token versus type* choice often required in data analysis, e.g. Sec. 14-3-2, and query design. The average number of token instances of a given type for some attribute Rel.att is

token_type_ratio = COUNT (*) FROM Rel / COUNT (Distinct Rel.att)...

A high token_type_ratio for an attribute indicates a poor partitioning effectiveness. The ratio is 1 for unique attributes.

Updating   The update commands are similar in syntax to the SELECT command, but affect the stored tables. More care is required here to assure that the database is correctly maintained. The update commands include: INSERT, UPDATE, DELETE.

An INSERT INTO table VALUES (list) command only inserts one row, with the listed attributes values, so that they match the position of the columns in the TABLE or VIEW definition given for the relation. Fields of the row missing from the list are set to NULL. Several clauses shown with the SELECT command are also available here.

An UPDATE table SET attribute = constant,... [WHERE ...] command affects all rows satisfying its WHERE clause; it reports the number of rows changed. A DELETE FROM table ... WHERE ... statement deletes all rows satisfying the WHERE clause.

All types of update have to be severely restricted on views (see Sec. 8-5-1). A view which was created with a join in its SELECT clause cannot be updated. The view definition does provide a convenient way to define transactions, since a view can incorporate an arbitrarily complex SELECT clause, exclusive of any ORDER or GROUP BY phrases. A privileged user, having DBA status, can GRANT or withdraw updating and other privileges to any user for any table, view, or specific attribute.

An EXTRACT statement permits the insertion of many rows from an existing DL/1 file, as defined in Sec. 8-3-2. The extracted data is redundant, however, and no identity connection (Sec. 7-5-1) is maintained. Tables created this way are typically only queried, but not updated.

9-2-2 Tuple Variables

The attributes used in the statements belong to a specific table named in the FROM clause. Specific data elements used, especially during comparisons within WHERE clauses, also belong to specific row instances. In many situations the proper instance in the proper table can be found without any ambiguity. There are cases, however, where a precise definition is needed, for instance, if a relation is joined with itself.

The use of *tuple variables* with the attributes provides an unambiguous notation for attributes and value instances. A tuple variable is a free variable with a domain which is the identification of the tuples of a relation. Some relational languages, for instance, INGRES' QUEL, consistently demand that all attributes be qualified with a tuple variable to designate a specific instance in a specific relation.

Example 9-4   Use of Tuple Variables to Distinguish Attributes

We wish to produce a result table with names and departments for all employees with school age children. Given tables based on the employees and their children from Figs. 7-6 and 7-7

```
Employee: RELATION              Children : RELATION
    name :) age, height, ... ;      father, child :) age;
```

but with an identical attribute name age. We let one tuple variable kid range over the Children relation and another one, emp, identify tuples in the Employee relation.

```
    SELECT emp.name, emp.age
        FROM  Children kid, Employee emp
        WHERE kid.father = emp.name  ∧  kid.age >= 6
```

For each emp.name all kid.father values will be investigated. When there is any match (here once for Gerbil, twice for Hare), the second condition, kid.age > 6 is tested. Only the tuple

    Hare 38

fulfills both requirements. Since two of Hare's children are older, the tuple will appear twice in an SQL result table.

In SQL the case shown in Example 9-4 does not actually require an explicit specification of tuple variables; the table_name can be used as the tuple variable so that Employee.age and Children.age can be used to distinguish between attributes having identical names.

In SQL the use of explicitly defined tuple variables is needed only to avoid ambiguity. This requirement often occurs with subqueries. For instance, when a SELECT subquery in a WHERE clause has to refer to the same row as another SELECT clause, the tuple_variables must be defined with their table names in the FROM ... clause; the syntax is indicated in Table 9-1. The attribute is then written as tuple_variable.attribute.

Queries with two or more distinct rows instances of one relation cannot be formulated without the use of tuple variables. Example 9-5 provides an example with a query where the boss and the subordinate are distinct entries in the same Employee_2 relation.

Example 9-5   Use of Tuple Variables to Distinguish Tuples

In order to form a table which contains all the employees who supervise other employees it is necessary to look at the Employee_2 row for the boss and the Employee_2 row for the subordinate at the same time.

The result table is to contain both names and the years of supervision. Two tuple variables range independently over the employee table (see Fig. 7-10 for the instance), so that given

Employee_2: RELATION   Supervision : RELATION
    name :) age, ..., experience;   super, sub :) years;

```
SELECT boss.name, subord.name, superv.years
        FROM  Employee_2 boss, Employee_2 subord, Supervision superv
        WHERE boss.name  = superv.super ∧
              superv.sub = subord.name;
```
In SQL the tuple variable superv is not required.

9-2-3 Quantification

In the examples up to now the WHERE clause contained an attribute_expression. The resulting boolean True or False value is used to control the result of SELECT expressions. The boolean for the WHERE clause can also be obtained by asking about the result of a subquery in a quantitative sense. We distinguish two types, referred to as *existential* and *universal quantification*.

Existential quantification is obtained through use of the EXISTS clause in SQL. The EXISTS (SELECT * ...) clause is satisfied whenever there is *any* match in the SELECT * ... subquery. Universal quantification is true only if *all* instances are true. Universal quantification is not directly available in SQL but in most cases can be obtained by using NOT EXISTS applied to the complement of the condition.

The use in both types of quantification is shown in Example 9-6. Note that use of EXISTS produces a True-or-False condition for a row identified with a tuple variable, while there was a join implied in Example 9-4.

Example 9-6   Use of Quantification

We use again the employees and their children from Figs. 7-6 and 7-7. We first find employees with at least one child of school age and then employees where all children are of school age.

```
Employee: RELATION                    Children : RELATION
    name :) age, height, ...  ;           father, child :) age ;

    SELECT emp.name FROM Employee emp
        WHERE EXISTS ( SELECT *  FROM Children kids
                        WHERE emp.name = kids.father AND kids.age >= 6 );
```

To find employees that do not have school age children use NOT EXISTS:

```
    SELECT emp.name FROM Employee emp
        WHERE NOT EXISTS ( SELECT *  FROM Children kids
                        WHERE emp.name = kids.father AND kids.age >= 6 );
```

To find employees where all the children are of school age, we transform the query from universal to existential quantification by using the complement:

```
    SELECT emp.name FROM Employee emp
        WHERE NOT EXISTS ( SELECT *  FROM Children kids
                        WHERE emp.name = kids.father AND kids.age < 6 );
```

There are queries involving universal quantification which cannot be reasonably transformed into existential form. Such cases occur when a condition has to hold for all members of a group, and that condition is to be computed within the group. An example is a query to locate suppliers capable of manufacturing subassemblies using only their own parts, formulated later using the relational algebra in Examples 9-12 and 9-13.

Requests of this form can generate a collection of tuples which describe subsets of a relation, and hence provide a link to the hierarchical presentation of data.

The composition of statements with quantification can become quite difficult, and expressions with universal quantification are avoided in most current systems. Some uses for universal quantification are satisfied by the GROUP BY statement. Programmed access may be used to collect the required information and perform further analysis on the retrieved data, including the checking for some condition over all instances in a subgroup.

9-2-4 Management of the Database

In order to use SQL, a database has to be designed and described in a schema, space for the database has to be acquired, and access structures have to be specified to satisfy performance demands. We only list some of the relevant commands. Usage of SQL/DS beyond simple on-line retrieval and update requires knowledge of these statements.

SQL includes, of course, the commands to define the schema: CREATE TABLE, DROP TABLE, and ALTER TABLE. You can CREATE INDEX or DROP INDEX. To manage external views use CREATE VIEW with subschema definition commands as shown in Example 8-11 or DROP VIEW. All these can be issued at any time, and SQL/DS will recompile or rebind any routines which have been invalidated.

Repeated use of a sequence of SQL statements is made possible by collecting the statements themselves into a TABLE for recall and reuse. To manage an interactive session, some additional commands are available; they are shown in Table 9-3.

Table 9-3   Controlling a Transaction

CONNECT	identify and assign the privileges available to the user; disconnects a prior user.
COMMIT WORK	indicate the end of a logical transaction
ROLLBACK WORK	remove all changes made since the last COMMIT or CONNECT

Programming Access   We have presented SQL in the preceding sections as seen by a user executing on-line requests. If more general computations are needed than single SQL commands conveniently provide, or if there is a large volume of updates, then access by a program is needed.

A type of computation not possible within the relational calculus is a transitive search through an undetermined number of relations. An example of such a query is 'Find the top-level manager for an employee'. Here the iteration of joins of the attributes Employee.name and Employee.manager terminates only when Employee.manager = null.

Five steps provide programmed access to relational calculus operations:

1 Variables to match the attributes used are declared in the programs.

2 SQL SELECT commands, augmented with INTO variable clauses, are inserted into the program.

3 A cursor is declared for every SELECT which might retrieve more than one row.

4 A parameter area is defined to receive condition and error codes; we encountered such areas with VSAM programming in Sec. 4-3-5.

5 The program is completed with computational and control statements.

A user program containing SQL declarations and INTO commands is processed through a preprocessor, which translates them into CALL statements to SQL routines kept on a library and declarations acceptable to the host language, similar to the sequence shown in Fig. 8-12. After compilation and loading, the programs can be executed and access the SQL database.

The programs in the SQL/DS library are associated with the version and status of the database. A program which tries to access a database whose access structure is changed, will be automatically recompiled. Since these programs are independent of access paths, no programmer intervention is needed.

The cursor used to identify individual rows from a SELECT table is manipulated by OPEN, FETCH, DELETE, UPDATE, and CLOSE commands. Cursors perform functions similar to tuple variables on the result table of the SELECT commands in the programs.

The OPEN statement initializes the execution of the SELECT command and identifies a cursor. A subsequent FETCH retrieves one row as specified, places the values into the designated variables, and sets the cursor. If no row is fetched a condition code is set; otherwise another FETCH can be executed to attempt to retrieve data from a row not yet fetched via the cursor. DELETE and UPDATE commands can use the same cursor in a WHERE clause. The CLOSE command makes the cursor unavailable.

9-2-5 Extensions of the Relational Calculus

We will present two facilities which can improve the usability of these systems. *Workspaces* provide the capability to use temporary relations for intermediate results and *integrity assertion statements* permit the definition of constraints.

Workspaces   A user of the relational calculus may find it easier to define intermediate relations using simple statements, and then define further conditions on relations previously defined. In order to allow manipulations to be specified as a number of steps, systems which support the relational calculus as a user language provide for the definition of intermediate relations. These relations are kept in *workspaces*. Workspaces have the following features:

1 They are not part of the database itself, so that there will be no inconsistency due to the creation of redundant data.

2 The workspaces belong to one individual user or process, so that the manipulations of data within such workspaces do not conflict with other users.

3 A naming scheme is employed to distinguish relations and their attributes within the workspace from the relations and attributes in the database.

4 Workspaces may also be used to collect input data prior to update of the database relations.

In order to illustrate the use of workspaces we will augment the SQL statement described with a statement from SEQUEL, a predecessor of SQL. The request for supervisors from Example 9-5 can now be written as shown in Example 9-7.

Since SQL permits dynamic definition and creation of tables, specific workspace statements are not part of the language. In a host-based DBMS general array and file facilties may serve as workspaces. In self-contained implementations of a relational calculus, for example, INGRES, workspaces are important to satisfy complex general processing needs. Workspaces may also be used to store derived attributes and tuples.

Example 9-7   Use of Workspaces

We use again the employee relations from Fig. 7-10:

```
Employee_2: RELATION              Supervision : RELATION
    name :) age, ..., experience;     super, sub :) years;

  Bosses(b_name, b_age)  <- SELECT  name, age FROM Employee_2, Supervision
                              WHERE name = super;
  Workers(w_super, w_age)<- SELECT  super, age FROM Employee_2, Supervision
                              WHERE  name = sub;
  SELECT b_name FROM Bosses, Workers
     WHERE b_name = w_super;
```

Example 9-8   Derived Values in Workspaces

An operation which can create a new attribute would be the calculation of the weight in stock for the various parts, given the Supply and Parts relations of Fig. 7-16. We have to use tuple variables to distinguish the attributes.

```
Parts: RELATION                        Supply : RELATION
    p_id :) name,size,weight,...;          s_id, p_id :) quantity ;

Stockweight(p_id, pounds) <- SELECT part.p_id, sup.quantity * part.weight
                             FROM  Parts part, Supply sup
                             WHERE part.p_id = sup.p_id;
```

The relation Stockweight contains as many tuples as the Supply relation (7) since the join implied here of Parts and Supply uses an ownership connection from Parts to Supply in the model. Some part numbers are repeated since they came from different Suppliers.

Workspaces are useful when the result relations are further processed. For instance, to obtain a commercial-looking output a "**Total**" tuple should be appended to the list created above. Example 9-9 uses a SEQUEL statement, since SQL does not permit the same table to be used as the destination and source of an INSERT.

Example 9-9   Inserting a SUM into the Workspace

We will augment this workspace with a single tuple for the total weight. Using the function SUM and the INSERT INTO operation from SEQUEL:

```
INSERT INTO Stockweight(p_id, pounds)
        : ('Total', SUM( SELECT pounds FROM Stockweight) );
```

Supplementary capabilities have been proposed for the relational sublanguage SQUARE. SQUARE as defined uses a two-dimensional notation to avoid workspaces and tuple variables. To demonstrate the features of SQUARE in the notation used here, a relation is created which contains the total weight of each part type.

Example 9-10   Inserting SUMs of Groups into the Workspace

```
Stockweight(p_id, pounds) <-
    SELECT DISTINCT part.p_id, SUM ( SELECT sup.quantity * part_grp.weight
                                 WHERE part.p_id = sup.p_id       )
        FROM  Parts as part, Supply as sup ;
```

Now only one tuple per p_id is left. We can still insert a total tuple; the result relation is shown in Fig. 9-3.

Stockweight: RELATION

p_id,	pounds;
P1	58.00
P2	7.70
P3	43.00
P4	7.60
Total	114.90

wsummary: RELATION

p_id :>	t_weight
P1	56.00
P3	7.70
P2	43.60
P4	7.60
Total	114.90

Figure 9-3 Subtotal relation.

Integrity Constraints In order to maintain a database correctly, the constraints implied by the connections defined in the database model still have to be imposed.

For instance, without the maintenance of the ownership connection among the relations we might not be sure that all `p_ids` in `Supply` were listed in `Parts`. If any `p_ids` are missing from `Parts`, the join caused by the `WHERE` clause of Example 9-8 will fail to include those parts in the result and in the final `pounds` calculations.

In most relational systems such constraints are the responsibility of the user; a basic relational schema does not provide for specification of update constraints. Two alternatives have to be considered, maintenance of integrity during update or consideration of lack of integrity during retrieval. Even if most update commands are executed with care, and include `WHERE` clauses to assure that constraints are obeyed, no guarantee can be given by the system that there are no inconsistencies. This means that queries have to formulated with great care. There is, for instance, no guarantee that attributes along a connection will match, and hence a chance that a join will fail to retrieve expected data.

In Example 9-3 we wrote the `WHERE` clause permitting arbitrary substrings:

    job LIKE '%Welder%'

to ensure that the query will also retrieve `Hare`, the `Asst. Welder`. We found that the prior query in Example 9-2, using `LIKE 'Welder'` for an exact match along the presumed reference connection, did not retrieve that record. In this case the reference connection to the table defining the domain of `jobs` was not maintained for this attribute.

Such maintenance constraints have to be added explicitly to update commands or queries have to be written to take care of approximate matches to reduce the chance of missing records that should be connected.

Integrity Constraint Assertions The INGRES system, from the University of California, Berkeley, allows constraints to be specified with the database description. Integrity constraints are provided as assertions and will be kept with the schema. They do not affect the structure of the database. At execution time the assertion statements are merged, if relevant, with the queries or update statements and interpreted as if they were additional `WHERE` clauses. Exploitation of the constraints to simplify queries may be done by a user who is sure that they have been applied throughout.

Some constraints applicable to Example 9-8 are shown in Example 9-11. For the `COUNT` functions introduced in Table 9-2 we use a token (`_ALL`) and type (`_DISTINCT`) notation which is symmetric and closer to INGRES.

Example 9-11   Integrity Constraint Statements

```
/* Field limit */
    INTEGRITY Parts.weight > 0;
/* Reference */
    INTEGRITY Employee.dept = Departments.name
/* Unique key: tokens = types */
    INTEGRITY COUNT_ALL(Parts.p_id) = COUNT_DISTINCT(Parts.pid);
/* Complete ownership: owned types = owner tokens */
    INTEGRITY COUNT_DISTINCT(Supply.p_id) = COUNT_ALL(Parts.p_id);
```

9-2-6 File Support

Many relational implementations use simple file structures. When the mapping of relational tables to files is one-to-one, the file records will have a fixed number of fields. If the fields are also restricted to be of fixed length, the records will also be of fixed length. If data values can be variable, or if more complex mapping from relations to files is permitted, the demands on the supporting files increase.

For instance, one SQL row is stored as one record, but SQL/DS does permit variable-length strings, up to 32 767 characters, and hence needs variable-length-record support. This support is provided by VSAM (Sec. 4-3), and the index structure of VSAM also provides the maintenance for indexed attributes.

Statistical descriptive information is maintained by SQL, so that a decision can be made whether to use indexes or sorting to perform the join. Estimates about the expected partitioning effectiveness of selection clauses on attributes, or *selectivity*, provide information used to reorder the primitive operations into which a complex query may be decomposed. We consider this aspect in Sec. 9-2-7.

To provide the capability for recovery of a transaction, log files may be specified to collect all inputs and affected records. These logs are also VSAM files. The principles and the use of logs are presented in Secs. 11-3 and 11-4. The existence of a log permits the **ROLLBACK** operation mentioned in Table 9-3.

The allocation and extension of space for an SQL database is handled by a set of commands which direct VSAM. Multiple tables can share a single file space. The information is itself collected in SQL TABLES and used during operation of the database, so that the user does not have to be concerned about the underlying file structure.

The INGRES implementation cited in Secs. 9-2-2 and 9-2-5 provides four alternative file types to the system implementor. All records are of fixed length. For each relation to be implemented the file type may be either a **HEAP** – similar to a pile, a **HEAPSORT** – similar to sequential file, **ISAM** – an indexed sequential file, or **HASH** – a direct file. The file implementation choice determines if the stored data is kept as a table (**HEAP**) or as a relation (**HEAPSORT, ISAM, HASH**), according to the definitions shown in Example 9-3.

The ORACLE system, which uses SEQUEL, the query language used in the development system which preceded SQL/DS, implements its files using a hierarchical organization, similar to DL/1 files.

9-2-7 The Execution of Calculus Statements

In order to execute the statements of the relational calculus, a transformation to a sequence of relational operations is required. The operations are essentially those described in Sec. 7-4, perhaps modified to deal with tables instead of relations. The parsing of the calculus statements is similar to the problem faced by compilers, with the additional consideration that reordering of clauses is possible and sometimes necessary. Reordering is also part of the compiling process for other nonprocedural languages which describe relationships, and is seen in simulation languages.

The execution of the statements requires a capable and sophisticated DBMS if adequate efficiency is to be obtained. A high degree of optimization is possible in the relational calculus by rearranging the clauses into an optimal sequence. The general rule is to first reduce the number of records to be accessed by exploiting indexes for attributes appearing in restricting **WHERE** clauses. When multiple *restriction* clauses are available and have indexes, the clause with the greatest expected partitioning effectiveness should be chosen first. The partitioning effectiveness of an attribute could be kept in a schema entry using a suitable encoding. A practical problem is that different values within one attribute have greatly differing power.

If, for instance, we wish to find personnel in a relation identified by **p** for a construction task in Alaska,

   (p.name,p.dep_no) WHERE (p.sex='Male' ∧ p.experience>10)

then the predicate **experience>10** should be evaluated first, since we can expect that this will leave a smaller intermediate relation than predicate **sex='Male'**.

In the case above, the value **Female** applied to construction workers will in all probability retrieve a much smaller intermediate result than the **WHERE** clause does now.

Intermediate results are often not materialized into intermediate relations. It is often more effective to process result tuples further, and so avoid repetitive storing and retrieval of intermediate values. Whenever possible the TIDs of the database records will be manipulated, since a large number of TIDs can be kept in memory.

When a record containing the tuple is located, all required attributes are projected to reduce the tuple size but avoid any further record access. Cross-product and join operations, which have the potential to generate large intermediate results, are typically scheduled last. If the number of tuples satisfying the join condition or *join selectivity* can be estimated, however, and appears low, joins may be performed earlier. Along a connection a join result will never be greater than the larger relation.

The eventual choice of execution sequence for a query is determined by minimization of the total cost of all operations required to carry out the query. In a transaction with multiple embedded queries yet better performance is possible by an overall optimization. Within a transaction the queries may refer to different aspects of a similar subset of data, so that a single retrieval from the database files can serve multiple queries.

An airline transaction may first retrieve the times of the flights between two points, and then, conditionally, the seat availability and the cost of the flight. A single retrieval can obtain all potentially relevant data at a low incremental cost and can greatly reduce the average transaction cost.

The overall effect of query optimization in a relational system will depend greatly on the variability of the access patterns. It is difficult to beat a system with defined connections along a query path, as we encountered in Sec. 8-3, when the query matches the defined physical structure and the database is reasonably large. For unexpected queries, however, the optimization will provide much better performance than a system designed to address a different pattern will provide.

The cost of the relational operations ($\bowtie$, Π, etc.) can vary a great deal from simplistic approaches to methods that exploit optimal algorithms and locality. We will discuss these in the next section with the relational algebras.

9-3 RELATIONAL ALGEBRA IMPLEMENTATION

We encountered in Sec. 7-4 the basic operations of the relational algebra:

Union, intersection, and difference of matching relations, $(\cup, \cap, -)$
Projection by domains (Π)
Selection of tuples $(\subseteq)$
Join of arbitrary relations $(\bowtie)$

These operations, together with the comparison and boolean operators used in the qualification statements of the relational calculus, provide the tools for systems based on the relational algebra.

These systems may be used to support a relational calculus or can be made directly available to users. Their nature is inherently procedural and these systems are comparable with systems using multiple unlinked nonhierarchical files and conventional data-processing operations. An important early implementation based on a relational algebra is the Prototype Relational Test Vehicle (PRTV). We encountered it in Sec. 7-4-1 when discussing the relational difference operation. The systems seen today range from small to large, from microcomputers to large systems for multiple users. An early APL implementation of a relational algebra was limited to numeric data values and had no schema; attributes were referenced using column indexes. Some systems based on the relational algebra, RDMS, which will be used for our first examples, are in routine data-processing use at MIT.

9-3-1 Relational Manipulations

In the relational algebraic systems the computations are specified and carried out statement by statement. There will be a greater use of workspaces and there is no need for tuple variables. Selection is generally made available through WHERE clauses, but these will apply only to attributes of the referenced relation.

The syntax differs greatly among these systems; the functions are nearly the same. Some systems implement relations only as sets with distinct tuples; others permit more general tables. Some of the more competent systems permit complex expressions of relational primitives, and then may try to minimize record accesses.

The query for employees of Example 9-4 to locate parents with children of school age can be presented to RDMS as follows:

```
Fathers(name) = PROJECT(Children WHERE age_c >= 6 BY father);
Output(name,dep_no) = COMPOSE(PROJECT(Employee BY(name,dep_no)),Fathers)
```

```
COMPOSE(r1,r2)is a natural join operation using matching attribute names
PROJECT(r BY a)specifies projection ∏ r.a
```

Additional relational and aggregation operators are available. The statements can be part of programs to be executed together or can be used as commands entered on a terminal and executed immediately. RDMS also provides facilities for self-contained use of the database through the use of inquiry packages and report generators.

Other operations seen in relational algebras are also provided. We need union, intersection, difference, and cartesian product:

```
Union_result          =  Rel_1 UNION Rel_2
Intersection_result   =  Rel_1 INTER Rel_2
Difference_result     =  Rel_1 DIFF  Rel_2
Cross_product_result  =  Rel_1 XPROD Rel_2
```

and a generalized join, of which the equi-join is one form,

```
Join_result = JOIN[(⊖)] Rel_1 ON attr_1 WITH Rel_2 ON attr_2
```

and also an operation, *divide*, to perform a function which in the relational calculus normally requires use of universal quantification. Division generates a quotient relation with one tuple for every group of tuples in the dividend which completely matches tuples of the divisor. We will write division

```
Quotient_result = DIVIDE Dividend ON attr_1 BY Divisor ON attr_2
```

where `attr_1` and `attr_2` define the matching attribute domains of dividend and divisor that control the division. The attributes in the quotient consist of the complement of the matching attributes of the divisor, so that

```
quot_attr = ¬ (Dividend.attr_1 )
```

Hence, this quotient is a projection of the dividend by `quot_attr`, containing only the tuple types whose associated tuple tokens have all instances in dividend and divisor matched for the controlling `attr_1` and `attr_2` domains. An example, effectively phrasing a problem requiring universal quantification, can demonstrate the use of a relational division:

Example 9-12   Use of DIVIDE

Given the Possible_supplier and Parts_skill required relations of Figs. 7-17 and 7-23, we wish to determine which Possible_supplier.s_id can deliver ALL parts for which (assembly, type). The relation schemas are:

```
Possible_supplier: RELATION        Parts_skill_required : RELATION
   s_id, p_id :) ;                     assembly, type, p_id :) no_req, ...;
```

We first select the tuples for each assembly,type:

```
Parts_req_for_body = SELECT(*) FROM Parts_skill_required
                   WHERE assembly = '750381' AND type = 'Body';
Parts_req_for_fender = SELECT(*) FROM Parts_skill_required
                   WHERE assembly = '750381' AND type = 'Fender';
```

and then divide

```
Good_guys_body =   DIVIDE Possible_supplier ON parts
                 BY Parts_req_for_body ON parts;
Good_guys_fender = DIVIDE Possible_supplier ON parts
                 BY Parts_req_for_fender ON parts;
```

The quotient relations can have only one attribute here.
Since Possible_supplier had only two attributes, s_id and p_id, and p_id controls the division, only s_id is left.

```
Good_guys_body: RELATION        Good_guys_fender: RELATION
   s_id;                           s_id;
   null                            s1
```

Division in Terms of Relational Primitives Division can be written using primitive functions. Given two relations composed of multiple attributes grouped for division,

```
Dividend: RELATION
    quot_attr, attr_1;

Divisor : RELATION
    any_attr, attr_2;
```

where `attr_1` and `attr_2` are sets of attributes have the same domains, but not the same attribute values, the operations defined above allow the rewriting of the division,

```
Quotient = DIVIDE Dividend ON attr_1 WITH Divisor ON attr_2
```

into an equivalent sequence,

```
Wanted_segm     = PROJ Dividend BY quot_attr;
Divisor_match   = PROJ Divisor BY attr_2;
Full_set        = Wanted_segm XPROD Divisor_match;
Remainder       = Full_set DIFF Dividend;
Remainder_segm  = PROJ Remainder BY quot_attr;
Quotient        = Wanted_segm DIFF Remainder_segm.
```

The cost of the cartesian product in the third statement of this definition makes a direct implementation of division desirable. Without division, sequences of boolean operations and counting operations are required to provide the power of universal quantifiers when sets of subsets are needed.

Group Summarization An industrial implementation, REGIS, solves the problem of constructing sets which summarize subsets with a special statement:

```
Sub_rel = SUMMARY Rel ONKEY quot_attr COUNT count_attr
```

Example 9-13   Use of SUMMARY

The query to determine which `Possible_supplier.s_id` can deliver all parts for which (assembly, type), applied to:

```
Possible_supplier: RELATION        Parts_skill_required : RELATION
    s_id, p_id :) ;                    assembly, type, p_id :) no_req, ...;
```

can now be constructed as follows:

To find the suppliers who can supply all the parts create a relation by joining

`Parts_skill_required` and `Possible_supplier` which contains all types to be supplied.

The natural join of the two summaries over two domains provides the result.

```
Supplier_explosion = JOIN (PROJECT Parts_skill_required BY type, p_id)
                                          ON p_id
                       WITH Possible_supplier ON p_id;
Supplier_capability = SUMMARY Supplier_explosion
                       ONKEY(type,s_id)  COUNT p_id;
Type_needs = SUMMARY (PROJECT Parts_skill_required BY type, p_id)
                       ONKEY type  COUNT p_id;
Result = JOIN Supplier_capability ON type WITH Type_needs ON type.
```

The relation `Sub_rel` will have one tuple for each value type in `quot_attr`. There will be as many domains in `Sub_rel` as there were in `Rel`, and all domains other than `quot_attr` will contain the totals of the matching source domains, except for one arbitrary domain specified by `count_attr`, which will be replaced with an attribute column containing the number of value-tokens for each type-token which defined a subset tuple in `Sub_rel`. In the example we will name the new domain with a prefix "#". This count can be used for testing or for the computation of averages, and for operations on subsets, as Example 9-13 shows.

Supplier_explosion:			Supplier_capability:			Type_needs:	
type,	p_id,	s_id;	type,	s_id,	#p_id;	type,	#p_id;
Body	P1	S1	Body	S1	2	Body	3
Body	P2	S1	Body	S2	2	Fender	2
Body	P2	S2	Body	S4	1		
Body	P4	S2	Fender	S1	2		
Body	P4	S4	Fender	S2	1		
Fender	P1	S1	Fender	S3	1		
Fender	P3	S1	Fender	S4	1		
Fender	P3	S2	Fender	S5	1		
Fender	P3	S3					
Fender	P3	S4				Result:		
Fender	P3	S5				type,	s_id,	#p_id;
						Fender	S1	2

Figure 9-4 Relation summarized to provide universal quantification.

It can be seen that the **SUMMARY** operation in a relational environment provides a facility similar to the subtotal capability used in conventional data processing. The domain-naming convention was added for clarity. REGIS supports about 40 operation types, including the capability to produce graphical output.

9-3-2 File Support

RDMS as well as several other systems built at MIT use the virtual storage facilities of the MULTICS system for file support. The sequential nature of the set operations used in systems which are based on relations increases the locality over random file access. In order to work with fixed-length records, which is important for dense utilization of a sequential file space, all string data in RDMS are coded, and only reference numbers are kept in the database records. All strings are hence retrieved indirectly. String arrays are assigned reference numbers which define the collating sequence. Data elements in the domain `DATE` (see Sec. 8-1-3) are also replaced by numbers allowing sequencing. The coding scheme will be described in Chap. 14.

The use of *indirection* to manage variable-length data is a feature of many systems, including TDMS and TOD. Indirect access to data elements is expensive, but coding can avoid excessive use of indirection. In many production systems arbitrary strings are not used in data-processing analysis so that the cost of indirection is incurred only when reports are generated. If the strings have limited domains, they are best not kept as strings, but coded via a lexicon. The codes are kept in directly accessible storage and can be used for comparison and similar data-processing purposes.

PRTV is based on an extension of PL/1. There is a user language which, when interpreted, manages the user variables and provides them as parameters to PL/1 subroutines. The basic relations are kept as compressed variable-length sequential files, with indexes for fast retrieval. They are updated only by periodic rewriting in off-line mode. Derived relations for the workspace are kept in *on-access* form: the operation sequences specified to create working relations are cataloged to be used for regeneration of the tuples as needed. This keeps the database free of redundancy and the apparent workspace fully current. A cataloged collection of potential derived relations provides also another view of the database. A cataloged sequence of operations is analyzed for optimal execution when the relation is regenerated.

Optimization of Relational Expressions Since PRTV can collect relational processing steps it has the same capability to optimize the execution of requests which exists in the relational calculus systems.

The following optimization steps are considered by PRTV:

1 Restriction due to selection is done as early as possible to reduce tuple volume.

2 Projections of projections are combined.

3 Projections by unsorted attributes are deferred.

4 Projections by sorted attributes are done early.

5 Expressions are rearranged according to the estimated partitioning efficiency of their terms.

6 Intermediate relations appearing in separate processing sequences are shared when this is profitable.

7 Attributes which control joins are presorted if this reduces execution effort.

8 Comparison or merging of files which are being presorted can be carried out as the tuples are being emitted in sorted order, so that sorted files do not have to be actually generated.

Relational systems which provide indexes will also treat indexed attributes early, similar to sorted attributes in PRTV.

9-3-3 The Execution Cost of Relational Operations

The simplicity of relational operations can hide potentially high execution costs. Effective use of access structures, as encountered in Chaps. 3 and 4, can reduce these costs greatly. A good database-management system hence has to match the operations to the available access structures and determine how to execute the operations. If the queries can be rearranged, as described for PRTV and relational calculus systems, there will be an interaction between the way operations can be processed and the optimal arrangement of the operations from a query. Here we consider only the basic operations, and specifically the join.

The brute force approach to obtain the result relation specified by statements using multiple relations is to compare each tuple of one with each tuple of each of the other relations. More specifically this is done by executing nested loops fetching tuples from the relations, one loop for each explicit or implicit tuple variable. This technique is called an *inner-outer loop join*. The number of steps $S(\bowtie)$ required for a join of two relations is the product of the relation sizes #(Rel_i):

$$S(\bowtie) = \#\texttt{(Rel\_1)} \times \#\texttt{(Rel\_2)} \qquad \langle\text{Inner-outer loop}\rangle \; 9\text{-}1$$

In each loop step a tuple has to be retrieved and analyzed. To excute Example 9-4, finding employees with older children, the number of operations would be on the order of #(Employee) $\times$ #(Children). Example 9-5, finding bosses, would require #(Employee_2)^2 $\times$ #(Supervision) operations.

If, in either or both files, the relations are already in some sequence for the join attribute, the attributes can be processed in order and no loop is required on that file. If both files are in sequence only a merge is required. A merge alone requires only

$$S(\bowtie) = \#\texttt{(Rel\_1)} + \#\texttt{(Rel\_2)} \qquad \langle\text{Merge for Join of Sequenced Files}\rangle \; 9\text{-}2$$

A file can only be in one sequence, and maintenance of sequentiality can be costly, but we need not limit this approach to files which are initially sequential on the join attribute. Previous operations within a relational expression may be able to leave a workspace in sorted order, or the files may be accessed to obtain tuples in join-attribute sequence.

In order to obtain tuples in sequence, if the files are not, two techniques are possible: sorting, or fetching the tuples via an index or by hashing. The cost of sorting was estimated in Eq. 3-11 and will involve on the order of

$$S(sort) = 2\,\#\texttt{(Rel)}/Bfr \times (1 + \log_2(\#\texttt{(Rel)}/Bfr)) \qquad 9\text{-}3$$

steps for each file. The initial factor 2 accounts for the need to read and rewrite tuples, and the factor Bfr accounts for the advantage obtained because sorting is performed on sequential blocks. Retrieval of #(Rel) tuples via an index has a cost of similar magnitude

$$S(indexed\ fetching) = \#\texttt{(Rel)} \times (\log_y +1)(\#\texttt{(Rel)}) \qquad 9\text{-}4$$

Of course, an index has to be available. Since many index accesses on the join attribute will be made, it can be profitable to attempt to keep much of the index in memory, effectively reducing the $\log_y$ term. If a file holding a relation provides direct access via the join attribute, #(Rel) tuples can be retrieved at a cost of

$$S(hashed\ fetching) = (1 + p) \times \#\texttt{(Rel)} \qquad 9\text{-}5$$

where the overflow cost p can be kept quite low and constant, as discussed with Eq. 3-71. The constraint is, of course, that only one hashed access attribute is possible per file; a database designer will allocate it to a known frequent join attribute, typically along an important connection.

Separability An aspect of designing databases is to determine access structures, i.e., assign indexes, clustering, and hashing to record attributes. It is important to note that the techniques based on merging (Eq. 9-2 with 9-3 and 9-4) have the property of *separability*; that is, the file implementation and access structures chosen for one relation do not affect the processing method of the other relation. The designer can hence choose the best implementation scheme on a relation-by-relation basis. The existence of indexes is assumed in the design phase. After the design is complete, no indexes need be assigned to attributes which do not use them for join or restriction purposes.

The exception to separability is when merging occurs with hashed access (Eq. 9-5). Hashed access can be used on only one relation and only one attribute. Here the join is carried out using the join attributes obtained from sequentially retrieved tuples from the other relation (`Rel_2`) to fetch matching tuples by hashing in the hashed relation (`Rel_1`). If the join attribute in `Rel_2` is unique, no sequencing at all is required in `Rel_2`, since any sequence will do for hashed access to `Rel_1`.

Any restriction is easily applied to the merging methods prior to the join. Only selected records need be submitted to a sort, and when indexes are used the TID list of records to be joined can be restricted based on matching TIDs from selection attributes, as shown in Sec. 4-2-3.

If the inner-outer-loop join method is chosen, the decision which file is to be assigned to the outer loop and which one to the inner loop can be deferred to query-processing time, so that some separability exists within this choice. If one of the relations will fit into memory, perhaps after restriction, this relation will be used for the inner loop. If restrictions will not reduce one of the relations sufficiently, the inner-outer-loop method will also be hampered by the inability to incorporate restrictions prior to looping without making a copy of the file.

A further design step is the decision on which attribute to select for clustering, so that sequentiality can be exploited. The ability to cluster exists for only one attribute for each relation. The attribute chosen will be the one involved in most retrievals and joins, with consideration of the update cost of clustered attributes. Chapter 3 provides the basis for optimization of database performance.

Projection Relational projection requires also that each tuple be compared with every other tuple in the relation to eliminate duplicates, a computation which takes about $\frac{1}{2}\#(\texttt{Rel})^2$ operations when implemented simply by looping. Some systems avoid this cost by generating tables with redundant entries unless explicitly instructed as shown in Example 9-3.

If the relation collapses materially in the process, because many tuples are identical, fewer steps will be used. A merge-sorting process, where the merge eliminates one of two identical tuples, allows the projection process to be done in $S(\Pi)$ steps, where

$$\#_b \log(\#_b) \geq S(\Pi) > \#_f \log(\#_f) \qquad\qquad 9\text{-}6$$

where $\#_b$ and $\#_f$ are the beginning and final sizes of the projected relation `Rel`. Projection is also often combined with selection; each accessed tuple is inspected for relevance and immediately discarded if not wanted.

9-4 HIERARCHICAL DATABASES

In the development of view models hierarchical concepts as nests play an important role. A model based on hierarchies can be directly implemented using nest-oriented file structures and appropriate schema facilities. Such a model is then restricted to one entity relation and its nest relations. In order to accommodate data that do not fit within a single tree, a hierarchical database system will allow the existence of multiple trees or a *forest*. The trees of the forest will have different heights; there are often many single-level trees, equivalent to entity relations in first normal form. These contain data structures which do not fit into the hierarchical structure. A small forest based on the example relations used in Chap. 7 is shown in Fig. 9-5, the structure is again visually simplified through the use of Bachman arrows.

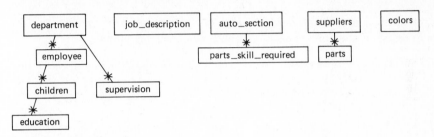

Figure 9-5 Our relations in a forest.

A database model which is bound to any predefined structure will lose considerably in flexibility. On the other hand, the definition of access paths, implied by the structure, means that these paths do not have to be created during query or update processing, but that they already exist when needed. The advantage of such early binding is often a considerable gain in processing speed and a simplification of query formulation when the data model relevant to the query is within the bound database structure. Database structures can be implemented to match almost *any* model but will never be able to match *all* models satisfactorily. One person's hierarchy is often another one's bureaucracy. The hierarchical model is relatively simple and satisfies the conceptual needs of database users in many cases.

9-4-1 Manipulating Trees

A *tree* is by definition not in first normal form. We are dealing therefore with a basic structure whose elements cannot be described by the triple: relation name, tuple name, attribute name. Relational operations, such as projection or join, are difficult to define and rarely implemented in these systems. It is, however, possible in most cases to reformulate relational queries into search strategies on trees, or to transform unambiguous hierarchical queries into equivalent relational queries.

Relations which will often participate in the equivalent of joins are best kept at the top level of the hierarchy; this includes primary and referenced entity relations as well as lexicons. Tuples in the lower-level nests of a tree provide only record segments, since ancestor data are a logical part of such tuples.

Brooms If a segment in a hierarchical structure has been selected, for instance, `employee='Hare'` in Fig. 9-6, we can identify with this segment the structural sequence of all segments which are its owners or ancestors, namely,

(`department='Assembly', file='Personnel'`),

as well as the subtrees for this segment, namely, nests of

(`children, education, and supervision`).

This construct has been named a *broom*, and the segments which make up the broom of `employee='Hare'` are indicated in the figure. A broom is often the unit to be manipulated here, rather than a single segment. Segments in hierarchical structures depend greatly on their ancestors and hence cannot be freely moved about.

The operations *union*, *intersection*, and *complement* of two brooms remain definable in terms of the operations $\vee$, $\wedge$, and $\neg$ on their members.

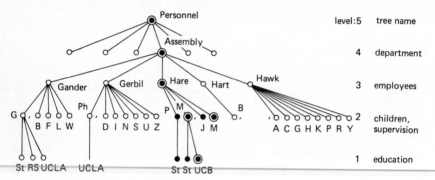

Figure 9-6 Personnel tree in a hierarchical database.

Operations with brooms require some care. The broom based on `'Hare'` includes `'Assembly'`, as does a broom based on `'Gander'`. The *union* of the two brooms includes all elements in both brooms. The *intersection* of the two brooms contains only `'Assembly'` and `'Personnel'`. The *complement* of the broom of `'Hare'` contains all employees except `'Hare'`, but not `'Assembly'` or `'Personnel'`.

The results of *intersection* and *complement* are hence incomplete brooms, and subsequent operations may not be obvious, as will be shown in Example 9-14.

Retrieval of records based on selected segments requires definition of the record based on a qualifying segment. To identify a segment in a nest qualifying terms as

FIRST, LAST, NUMBER = ns, ANY, ALL

can be used. To find now the current school for the oldest child, we can request

LAST.children.LAST.education

or to find who sent all his children to St. Mary's,

ALL.children.ANY.education = 'St. Mary'

An understanding of the structure plays an important role in these systems. A search for a specific record is constrained by the nesting structure.

In order to simplify the construction of queries, we introduce the operation BROOM which defines all segments of the broom for a segment. Membership of a segment in a BROOM is tested by the operator IN, analogous to the set membership operator $\in$. In order to constrain a search to a specific broom, say the assembly department, we can state

    `employees IN BROOM(department='Assembly')`

Brooms can also define segments based on selected segments lower in the hierarchy.

    `employees IN BROOM(education.schoolname='St. Mary')`

The use of broom in such a case implies `ANY.education`.

We will show some examples below. These are not based on any specific implementation but represent a generalization of available facilities in query languages and database-analysis programs, as well as some ideas from a proposal for a database retrieval language for tree-structured system, BOLTS [Hardgrave[80]]. Most hierarchical query languages do provide for correct expression of arbitrary queries, but their syntax may actually be awkward and not show the issue in an obvious manner.

Example 9-14   Use of BROOMS

Let us assume that there is a celebration at St. Mary's school on Thursday. To find which employees will be affected, we can ask

    `GET employees.name |`
       `employees.children.LAST.education.schoolname='St. Mary'`

Employees with more than one child at St. Mary's will be listed multiple times. We really want

    `GET employees.name |`
       `employee IN BROOM(LAST.education,schoolname='St. Mary')`

Now employees is the controlling variable and the descendants or ancestors can be tested for the validity of the predicate. When multiple predicates have to be combined, brooms can provide more flexibility, since the access path does not have to be specified segment by segment. We want to locate the employees who have children at St. Mary's and at UC Berkeley. The simple question

    `GET employees.name |`
       `LAST education.schoolname='St. Mary' ∧`
       `LAST education.schoolname='UC Berkeley'`

does not make sense; if one predicate is true, the other one is false, and the result of this query will always be NULL. Using a BROOM clause allows precision:

    `GET employees`
       `IN BROOM(LAST education.schoolname='St. Mary') ∧`
       `IN BROOM(LAST education.schoolname='UC Berkeley')`

using a simplified form of the query retrieval specifications to obtain complete segments.

The qualification is now brought to the level of the employee. Similar action is required if we are interested only in employees of the assembly department. The attribute `department.name` is not defined in the employees segments, so that we will ask

```
GET employees IN BROOM(department.name='Assembly') ∧
    IN BROOM(LAST education.schoolname='St. Mary') ∧
    IN BROOM(LAST education.schoolname='UC Berkeley').
```

The qualification can be at a different level than the object being retrieved. We can ask which employees have children who went to St. Mary's and reform school.

```
GET employees IN BROOM(children
    IN BROOM(education.schoolname='St. Mary') ∧
    IN BROOM(education.schoolname='Reform school') ).
```

Failing to specify children would also retrieve employees with one child in Reform school and another child in St. Mary's. These expressions may combine segments from different levels. The question above, "Which employee has children at UC Berkeley who are younger than 18 years old?" is stated as

```
GET employees IN BROOM(children ∧
    IN BROOM(LAST.education.schoolname='UC Berkeley') ∧
        children.age_c < 18 )
```

Only within the BROOM(children) are the predicates related; wrong answers would again be obtained if the data satisfying the predicates are aggregated for the employees broom.

In complex hierarchical structures, especially if some levels do not have a strong semantic identity, the formulation and analysis of queries requires care and insight. Levels will sometimes not be obvious if a hierarchical database is constructed out of hierarchical data models which differ in level. A financial model may view employees within departments, but an organizational model may consider employees to be within sections which are within departments.

Currency An interface with a conventional programming language which does not have capabilities to manipulate repeating segments or nests requires establishing a correspondence of one data segment or item per name. The programming interface will obtain a record with one segment instance for each type of segment.

In order to provide data in such a flat presentation from a hierarchical file, a *currency* indicator for each segment type identifies the segments of the total record which are to be used. This means that for the entity relation at the highest level, one segment is identified and one member is identified out of each nest below. An example of currency is given in Fig. 9-6.

```
Personnel_record: Department, Employee, Children, School,      Supervision.
                  Assembly    Hare      Mary      UC Berkeley  Mike
```

A record is a catenation of all current segments. When the result of a query identifies a segment, say **Mary**, all the ancestral owners, the handle of the broom, should also be presented, because the element by itself is not sufficiently identified. Records are well defined, but incomplete, if some lower-level segments have not been chosen, say **UC Berkeley** and **Mike**.

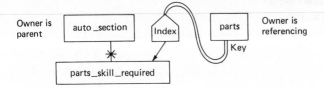

Figure 9-7 Association in a hierarchy.

Nonhierarchical Relations An associative relation, if required, has to be made a nest of either one of the owners as shown in Fig. 9-7. Access from outside of the implemented hierarchy requires a search, through an index if needed for speed, as it does in a relational implementation. Since the situation is not symmetric, the user has to be aware of the design decisions and their implementation. Efficiency considerations create the temptation to put the data which is functionally dependent on the nonhierarchical owner (here `Parts`) into the nest (`Parts_skill_required`). Two considerations prohibit this:

Orphans Members in a hierarchy cannot be kept around without their owner. If a part is not required at one point on the production cycle by any of the `auto_sections`, information about this part kept in the nest would be lost. The lack of a distinct `Part` relation also makes it impossible to store data about a new part not yet used by any `auto_section`.

Redundancy There will be multiple `Parts_skill_required` records for each `Parts` record. Inclusion of a part description with several dependent fields in each instance of the `Parts_skill_required` increases update efforts. If updating of the descriptions of one part is required, many records of `Parts_skill_required` have to be modified. Also, if the part description is at all voluminous, much space is wasted due to the redundancy.

The design problems shown here are common to all bound databases. In a system which is strictly hierarchical the binding of associations is not completed until the time that the query is being processed.

Example 9-15   SYSTEM 2000 **Schema Entries**

The schema entries specify
```
fieldnumber,fieldname (data_type, format(length) IN owner_segment)
```

```
       . . .
1*  name   (NAME X(16))
2*  birthdate (DATE)
3*  height (DECIMAL NUMBER 9.99)
4*  weight (NON-KEY INTEGER NUMBER 999)
5*  children (REPEATING GROUP)
6*  child (NAME X IN 5)
7*  age_c (INTEGER NUMBER 99 IN 5)
8*  education (REPEATING GROUP)
9*  school_type (NAME X(10) IN 8)
       . . .
```

9-4-2 Hierarchical Database Systems

A commercial system which provides a hierarchical structure and is available for many large computer systems is the INTEL/MRI SYSTEM 2000. It provides self-contained system services and also allows database access from COBOL, PL/1, FORTRAN, or assembly language programs. The database definition is independent of the processing programs.

The definition for the **Employee** entry in the schema for S2000 might be as shown in Example 9-15. Default values are assigned as needed. One database may have multiple entity relations plus their owned nest relations, up to 32 levels deep. A relation can be the owner of multiple nest relation types, as is required to implement in our example the **Children** and **Supervision** of **Employee**.

A subschema and data-manipulation statements are combined with host-language statements when programmed access is required. In order to process such a hybrid program a technique similar to the one illustrated for IDS in Fig. 8-13 is used. The subschema and data-manipulation statement translator is specific to the source language and computer type, but the SYSTEM 2000 statements are the same for any host language. The subschema for the personnel tree is shown in Example 9-16 as it would appear in a COBOL† environment. This host schema description has to be a proper subset of the schema used when the database was defined.

Example 9-16   SYSTEM 2000 **Subschema**

```
COMMBLOCK OF Personnel
  01  Personnel
    02  /*  Area to communicate system status, error, and control data */
  SCHEMA Employee OF Personnel
  01  Employee
    02  name         PICTURE IS X(16).
    02  birthdate    PICTURE IS X(8).
    02  height       PICTURE IS 9(6).
    02  weight       PICTURE IS 9(8).
  SCHEMA Children OF Employee
  01  Children
    02  child        PICTURE IS X(6).
    02  age_c        PICTURE IS 99.
  SCHEMA Education OF Children
  01  Education
    02  school_type  PICTURE IS X(10).
    02  school_name  PICTURE IS X(12).
    02  subject      PICTURE IS X(8).
  SCHEMA  Supervision OF Employee
  01  Supervision
    02  subordinate  PICTURE IS X(16).
    02  year         PICTURE IS 99.
  END SCHEMAS.
```

---

†Variable names are kept consistent with earlier usage, COBOL conventions use "–" for "_".

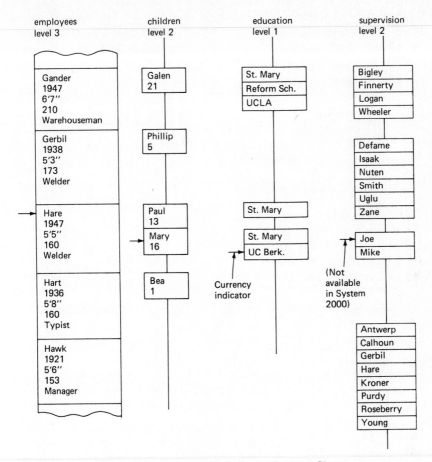

Figure 9-8 Hierarchy implemented through nest files.

Figure 9-8 shows the relationships of the four files comprising the single hierarchy. Each relation, entity or nest, is implemented with a separate file. The level 01 entries in the SCHEMA for each file provide space for the owner ruling part in the nest relations. All cross references between the files are maintained by the system, so that the user is not aware of any structure outside of the declared schema.

All attributes are indexed unless NON-KEY appears in the schema definitions. If a retrieval request involves an attribute which is not indexed, or requires an exhaustive scan of the database because of the form of the selection clause, i.e.

    GET employee WHERE weight > 150

then long processing times can be encountered.

One currency indicator for each level is maintained by SYSTEM 2000, as indicated in Fig. 9-8. The collection of current segments defines a record, which may be incomplete. A GET1 command with a key establishes a new currency indicator position for the matched segment, and also sets ancestor currency indicators, while descendant currency indicators are reset to NULL. GET1 NEXT commands which refer to a NULL level move the currency indicator to the first record while again resetting yet descendant currency indicators to NULL. From the first record onward GET1 NEXT will obtain the other records sequentially in the nest file, moving from nest to nest. Currency is redefined as the retrieval proceeds. GETA and GETD commands obtain ancestors and descendants.

If one nest at a time is to be obtained, it is necessary to recognize when the current owner is about to change. SYSTEM 2000 provides the combination LOCATE and GET NEXT for this purpose. An END_OF_DATA message is generated as a result when the NEXT entry is outside of the broom of the current ancestor. The ancestor is not restricted to the immediate owner. To obtain, for instance, the schools attended by the children of Hare, the sequence could be

Example 9-17   Navigating in a Hierarchy

```
LOCATE education WHERE name = 'Hare'
GET NEXT education -> 'St. Mary'
GET NEXT education -> 'St. Mary'
GET NEXT education -> 'UC Berkeley'
GET NEXT education -> END_OF_DATA
```

In addition the program will contain OPEN, GET, INSERT, MODIFY, REMOVE, and CLOSE statements of various flavors which will allow accessing the various files comprising the tree. A WHERE clause adds selection capability, and ORDER BY provides sequencing. A HAS clause allows specification of the descendants of a segment, so that a predicate can be restricted to that part of a broom. Aggregation operations available in the self-contained language are   SUM, COUNT, MINIMUM, MAXIMUM, AVERAGE, and the equally important SIGMA to obtain the standard deviation.

Completeness Earlier versions of SYSTEM 2000 as well as some other DBMSs will not permit retrieval requests to be executed which require exhaustive searches of the database. Such systems are therefore not *functionally complete* for retrieval. Most relational systems discussed earlier were functionally complete, since they implemented a mathematical approach which covers all possibilities. The fact that a system is complete does not imply that all retrievals are carried out with equal dispatch. The documentation for OASIS, a hierarchical database system for university administrative needs, provides detailed guidelines for programmers, so that they can formulate queries with optimal partitioning and indexing efficiency. The system still allows arbitrary queries, so that management can use the database completely, without regard to efficiency.

9-4-3 File Support

Database systems such as SYSTEM 2000 or ADABAS do not actually implement the database by distinct files for each relation. The segments of the hierarchical record are placed as they are entered into one data file. All hierarchical relationships in SYSTEM 2000 are expressed by a second file which contains pointer chains that are similar to ring structures, but all data fields are referenced by pointers to the data file. The pointer file has high locality because of its small size, but getting the next record requires file accesses. Indexes are kept in other files.

The ADABAS system permits these access structures to be created either at schema definition time or at access time. Selecting when and which connections are to be bound becomes partially a decision of the user. A good understanding of the underlying database structure can make much difference in performance.

A completely different approach is followed by OASIS. An instance of a tuple in an entity relation, together with all its descendants, is placed into a single compact variable-length record. The entries appear within the record in a compact and fixed order, beginning with the entity relation segments. Figure 9-9 sketches the record content where employees is the top level entity file.

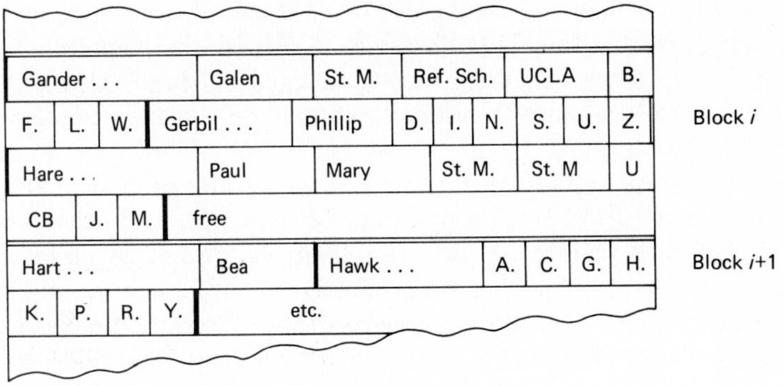

Figure 9-9 Compacted hierarchy.

A fetch of a record provides access to an entire broom at a time, but the design limits the size of a hierarchy, since a record cannot span blocks.

A block will contain several records, and since records can grow over time, the original space allocation, even if a low loading density was originally specified, may not be adequate. This problem is solved through the use of *indirect references*. A record number index is maintained which allows placement of a record into any block in the file having sufficient free space. All indexes based on attribute values in the records refer to the record number, so that indexes are not bound to relative block addresses.

Other alternatives used to implement hierarchical systems have included the use of ring structures. We will find samples of this design among systems with network capability.

9-5 DATABASES WITH NETWORK CAPABILITY

A *network* is created when structures more complex than hierarchies are bound. A hierarchy is as complex a structure as can be built within a single file using ordering conventions for the segments. Even then reference pointers are found in many implementations. In a network references are an inherent part of the structure. We will refer to these structural references as *links*.

Links can be implemented by any of the reference structures discussed in Sec. 8-1-2 (pointer, symbolic, indirect). Symbolic references are not of practical interest in this section since they defer the binding and hence the existence of a network to query processing time. Direct pointer references can be used only if records are not moved within the database during their lifetime, since otherwise the pointers lose validity. On the other hand, indirect pointers can be changed by simply changing the pointer index when records are moved. Indirect pointers are hence the common means to implement linkages.

Loss or invalidation of a link implies loss of information. Pointer or indirect references may describe the structure redundantly because of the continued existence of symbolic references. If such pointer or indirect references are not redundant, however, because the symbolic reference has been omitted, we call them *essential links*. Maintenance of files using essential links requires carefully worked out procedures to avoid invalidation of these links. In many network systems, links are essential, although an application designer may decide to maintain redundancy of links by keeping symbolic references within the data records as well.

9-5-1 A Simple Network Implementation

A DBMS available on many small and large computers is TOTAL. It provides a two-level network hierarchy. The top level contains entity relations, and the bottom level contains either nest or associative relations. Figure 9-10 shows the placement of relations in such a structure. The top-level relations are implemented as direct files, and the bottom-level relations as chains. These chains are rings without the final link back to the top-level record.

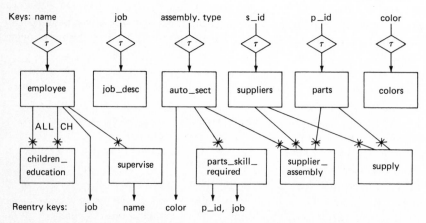

Figure 9-10 TOTAL network structure.

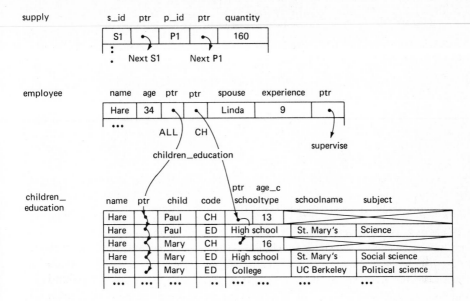

Figure 9-11 TOTAL network records.

A top-level entity record can start multiple chains. A bottom-level, owned record may be a member of multiple chains. At the bottom level we find then nest relations and associations of entity relations, as shown by the **supply** record in Fig. 9-11. There may be multiple chains from an entity record which link different record subtypes within one owned relation. Such connections allow an approximation of more complex structures, say, the required three-level hierarchy of **Employee**—*∗ **Children**—*∗ **Education** by **Employee**—*∗ **Children_education**.

Linkages are created and modified automatically when a record is inserted. The linkages are not *essential*: a complete ruling part is kept in all the bottom-level records. Since the chains do not return to the owner records, the key in the ruling part provides a symbolic reference argument, as the only means to locate the owner of a bottom-level record. This is indicated by reference arrows.

Deletion of an entity record is not permitted while it has chain members. In the example member records in **Children_education** must be deleted before the **Employee** record can be deleted. This implements a reference connection.

Referenced relations and lexicons are hence best placed with the entity relations at the top level. When they refer in turn to relations on the bottom level, they can use linkages. Linkages to implement additional connections have to be handled by the application programs, using symbolic references. Because of the use of direct file access the top-level relations cannot be processed serially; only unordered sequential access is possible. This may force some relations to the bottom level which otherwise would fit better on top.

All linkages maintained by TOTAL are defined in the schema. No new relations or new linkage types can be dynamically created. An associative relation, such as **supplier_assembly**, has to be created at the time the schema is defined and will be updated as its owners change.

9-5-2 The DBTG Access Specifications

Links and sets of links are an important aspect of the database architecture defined in the schema language of the Data Description Language Committee (DDLC) of CODASYL. Although the original Database Task Group (DBTG) reports provided only the language specifications and functional requirements, the specifications had so much detail that many implementation choices were implied. Ring structured files (Sec. 3-6) and hashing are common implementation techniques; we will review their use here in Sec. 9-5-4. Changes issued in 1978 by DDLC are directed toward increased implementation independence. The desire to obtain machine-independent software, achieved by CODASYL to a large extent with the COBOL language, is the reason for the degree of detail in the specification. We describe here the recent specifications. The examples shown also consider earlier implementations, since most available systems are based on the 1974 specifications.

Network Structure The CODASYL schema permits the construction of nearly arbitrary networks of connected relations. We encountered in the DDL schema specification shown in Fig. 8-9 the two principal components used to construct a CODASYL database:

RECORDs: Records implement the relation concept of tuples, and contain the data fields. A collection of records of the same name implements either a relation or a table, since there is a clause which indicates whether duplicate tuples are not or are allowed.

SETs: Records may be linked to each other, thereby implementing the concept of a connection. Each *link-set* specifies the owner and member record names. The owner of a linkage is often the owner relation in a hierarchy, or one of the owners in an associative relationship. Link-sets may also be maintained in such a way that they implement reference connections. Specifying that the SYSTEM is the owner provides an initial entry point to a collection of record.

To illustrate the use of some of the alternatives we will define in Example 9-18 a simple schema, similar to the hierarchical schema given in Example 9-16. To show the network capabilities, we implement the Department as an entity and add an association of Employees and Departments as a record type Worked_in. The ownership connections from Fig. 7-29 are implemented as link-sets.

Example 9-18   CODASYL **Schema**

```
SCHEMA NAME IS Personnel.
  AREA NAME IS personal_data.
  AREA NAME IS company_data.
    RECORD-NAME is Employee WITHIN personal_data
      KEY empl_key IS ASCENDING ssn  DUPLICATES ARE NOT ALLOWED.
        02  name            PICTURE IS X(16).
        02  ssn             PICTURE IS 9(6) CHECK IS NONULL.
        02  birthdate       PICTURE IS X(8) CHECK IS PROCEDURE date_verify.
        02  supervisor      PIC X(16). /* Reference to another Employee */
        02  job             PIC X(8).  /* Reference to a Job file */
```

```
RECORD-NAME IS Children WITHIN personal_data.
    02  child           PICTURE IS X(6).
    02  age_c           PICTURE IS 99.
RECORD-NAME is Education WITHIN personal_data.
    02  school_type     PICTURE IS X(10).
    02  school_year     PICTURE IS 9(4) CHECK IS VALUE 1900 THRU 2000.
    02  school_name     PICTURE IS X(12).
    02  subject         PICTURE IS X(8).
RECORD-NAME Supervision WITHIN company_data.
    02  subordinate     PICTURE IS X(16).
    02  year            PICTURE IS 99.
RECORD-NAME Department WITHIN company_data
    KEY department_key IS ASCENDING dep_name   DUPLICATES ARE NOT ALLOWED.
    02  dep_name        PICTURE IS X(10).
    02  year_established PICTURE IS 99.
    02  year_dismantled PICTURE IS 99.
RECORD-NAME Worked_in WITHIN company_data.
    02  w_emp_name      PICTURE IS X(16).
    02  w_dep_name      PICTURE IS X(10).
    02  w_year          PICTURE IS 99.

SET Our_employees.
    OWNER IS SYSTEM.
    ORDER IS PERMANENT     INSERTION IS SORTED BY DEFINED KEYS.
    MEMBER IS Employee
    INSERTION IS MANUAL    RETENTION IS OPTIONAL.
SET Parenthood.
    OWNER IS Employee.
    ORDER IS PERMANENT     INSERTION IS SORTED BY DEFINED KEYS.
    MEMBER IS Children
    INSERTION IS AUTOMATIC    RETENTION IS FIXED.
SET Children_education.
    OWNER IS Children.
    ORDER IS PERMANENT     INSERTION IS LAST.
    MEMBER IS Education
    INSERTION IS AUTOMATIC    RETENTION IS FIXED
    RANGE KEY edu_key IS ASCENDING school_year DUPLICATES LAST.
SET Employee_ties.        /* defines both ownership of supervisees   */
    OWNER IS Employee.    /*       and association with departments */
    ORDER IS PERMANENT
        INSERTION IS SORTED WITHIN RECORD-TYPE BY DEFINED KEYS.
    MEMBER IS Supervision  /* One record type owned by this set   */
    INSERTION IS MANUAL    RETENTION IS FIXED
    RANGE KEY IS ASCENDING year  DUPLICATES ARE LAST.
    MEMBER IS Worked_in    /* and another one owned by it    */
    INSERTION IS MANUAL    RETENTION IS MANDATORY
    RANGE KEY IS ASCENDING year  DUPLICATES ARE LAST.
SET Department_assignments.
    OWNER IS Department.
    ORDER IS PERMANENT  INSERTION IS LAST.
    MEMBER IS Worked_in  INSERTION IS MANUAL  RETENTION IS MANDATORY.
```

A single link-set, `Employee_ties`, is used for both the **Supervision** and the `Worked_in` connection, perhaps since for most **Employees** the total number of members will be small. A better reason for a link-set to have several types of members occurs if different record types have to be managed similarly, such as `Infants`, `School_age_children`, and `Other_dependents`. All members of a link-set must specify keys of the same format to allow an overall sorted sequence to be maintained.

To simplify the presentation we skip the COBOL subschema, which is the extenal schema actually made available to the data manipulation programs. We also leave out the header statements used by COBOL to separate sections of a program.

Not all connections specified in a conceptual schema as developed in Chap. 7 need to be implemented as link-sets. There is a cost to maintaining link-sets, and the benefits are obtained only when link-sets are used to retrieve information. Design decisions similar to those made for index selection in Sec. 9-3-3 are made for selecting link-sets, but accessing relations without link-sets is quite awkward in many CODASYL-based systems. To reach a connected record for which no link-set has been defined a program has to search through all the records which implement the destination relation.

In order to obtain a certain record an iterative process is performed:

1 Enter the database in one of two ways: either use a **SYSTEM** owned link-set and continue according to step **2**, or select a record by giving a record name and its key or position and continue according to step **3**.

2 Select a link-set; determine which entry to follow to a member record.

3 From the member record found continue either to successor members of this set and continue according to this step **3**, or select a link-set owned by this member record, if any, and continue with step **2**.

It is obvious that a programmer has many choices available in a schema which specifies extensive connections. The repeated process of moving from a current record to a goal record was termed *"navigation"* in a Turing award lecture given by the major contributor to this database approach [Bachman[73]]. At each embarkation point one record can be retrieved, modified, or stored. The manipulation of the single records obtained at each point is easily achieved using host programming statements. The map available during the voyages is the external schema allocated to the programmer. Figure 9-12 sketches the entire structure specified by the schema designed for one of the first applications of a system based on the DBTG report, with an indication of the external subschema used by one application group.

An important aspect of CODASYL databases is the ability to implement non-hierarchical connections. Associative relations can be implemented since a record may be a member of more than one link-set. The relation `Worked_in` is linked in Example 9-18 both to **Employee** and to **Department**. The traditional relation **Supply** would be owned both by **Suppliers** and by **Parts**. A network resembling the semantic connections shown in Fig. 7-29 can be constructed.

Reference connections are not as conveniently established with link-sets. To assure correct manipulation, an accessible key for the referenced relation must be defined. Then the connections can be maintained using **MANUAL INSERTION**, as shown in Example 9-24.

Networks are typical for "bills-of-materials" problems. We can access through the links all the parts needed for an **Auto_section**, and, if we have a shortage, go via the link-set to **Parts**, and obtain the list of other equipment using the same part. Then the other relevant **Auto_sections** can be consulted for their requirements and a possible surplus.

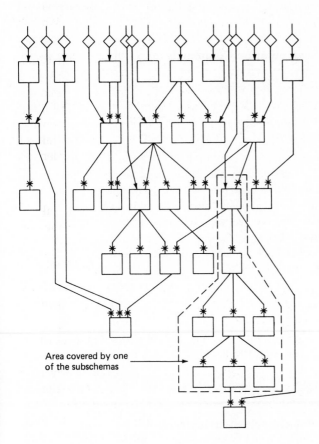

Area covered by one
of the subschemas

Figure 9-12 Sketch of a commercial database.

Currency Pointers Whenever a link-set entry or member record is reached a *currency* pointer is defined, so that it is always possible to return to an earlier link-set entry or member record. The **NEXT** and **PRIOR** options permit forward and backward tracking relative to these currency pointers. A large number of currency pointers can be active at any time: one for each link-set and each record type in the schema. Currency pointers are also available for the last reference in an **AREA**, and there is one procedure currency pointer which always identifies the last record referenced by the processing program. We use the symbol **db_cp** for a currency pointer reference; the actual variable name may be a `record_name`, a `link_set_name`, an `area_name` or the name of the current procedure.

Database Manipulation   The statement types to be available for manipulation of a 1978 CODASYL database are given in Table 9-4. Specific formats for the COBOL language are given in the documentation for COBOL of the CODASYL committee, and FORTRAN versions have also been specified.

Each executable statement has a numeric code. The number is used when the manipulation functions of a DBMS are invoked by one of the different host languages.

Table 9-4   Declarations and Manipulation Commands for a CODASYL **Database**

```
/* Obtain access to the relevant portions of a schema, its storage schema, and
   the contents of the database defined by it by invoking a subschema, using COBOL */
  DB sub_schema_name WITHIN schema_name [; ACCESS CONTROL KEY = xxxx].
  LD keep_list_name LIMIT IS integer.   /* to keep currency indicators */
```

`/* Transaction control */`

13	READY	lock areas as specified in the **AREA** clause of the schema.
01	COMMIT	release record locks and reset all currency indicators and `keep_lists`. The statements coded 02, 03, 04, 11, 12, 15, and 16 lock the records and link-set entries accessed.
06	FINISH	release locked areas.
09	IF ...	test database status and error condition codes.
14	ROLLBACK	remove all database changes since **READY** or **COMMIT**.

`/* Finding and manipulating records */`

05	FIND	locate a record.
08	GET	obtain specified data items or all of the current record.
15	STORE	insert a record according to the schema specifications.
11	MODIFY	update the current record.
04	ERASE	delete the current record.
10	KEEP db_cp	obtain a currency indicator and place it into a `keep_list`.

`/* Manipulation of link-sets */`

02	CONNECT	establish **MANUAL** link-set membership.
03	DISCONNECT	remove a record from link-set membership.
16	RECONNECT	move a record from one link-set to another link-set.

`/* Other */`

07	FREE db_cp	release currency indicator, including any entries kept for currency indicator db_cp in a `keep_list`.
12	ORDER	sort the members of the current set logically so that they can be retrieved in a certain order.
	USE ...	declaration to identify procedure to be executed when an exception or error condition occurs and to identify access control procedures.

Program Flow Control The standard COBOL statements that permit conditional expressions (IF, EVALUATE, PERFORM, SEARCH) can also refer to database conditions. The three condition codes which permit testing the database are named:

TENANCY Is the current record an owner or a member, or either (a tenant) of a specified link-set?

MEMBERS Is the specified link-set empty, i.e., are there any member records?

DB-KEY Is the currency indicator of a found record the same as a previously obtained currency indicator, or does it match one kept within a given keep_list?

There are five predefined registers to provide information when an error occurs: DB-STATUS gives a numeric code defining the error, as shown in Example 9-19; while DB-SET-NAME, DB-RECORD-NAME, DB-ACCESS-CONTROL-KEY, and DB-DATA-NAME contain character strings defining the current position in the database.

9-5-3 Finding Records

The FIND command is the principal means of *navigation* through the network. A FIND command does not cause the actual record to be put into the user's program area but does change relevant currency pointers. After a FIND command locates a record which contains desired data, some or all of its datafields may be retrieved by the execution of a GET command. The GET command specifies which data fields are required or if the entire record is to desired. The data is copied from the record indicated by the currency pointer into the program area associated with the GET data. To obtain another record a new FIND statement has to be executed.

COBOL statements to retrieve ages of the children for all employees are shown in Example 9-19. We assume a subschema corresponding to Example 9-18 has been invoked. The program finds all records by traversal in link-set order. For Employees without children, no link-set will be found and their name will be ignored.

Example 9-19   Finding Records with Link-Sets

```
READY personal_data.                    /* Start transaction, lock an AREA */
   FIND FIRST WITHIN Our_employees.     /* Use link-set order based on ssn */
next_parent.                            /* 02100   indicates end of link-set */
   IF DB-STATUS EQUALS 02100, THEN GO TO no_more_employees.
      GET name.                         /* of potential parent */
      MOVE name TO name_field IN print_line.
   next_child.                          /* 02300   indicates empty link-set */
      FIND NEXT Children WITHIN Parenthood.    /*  if any or if any left) */
      IF DB-STATUS EQUALS 02100 OR EQUALS 02300, THEN GO TO done_parent.
         GET age_c.                     /* There is one or another child */
         MOVE age_c TO age_field IN print_line.
         WRITE output FROM print_line AFTER ADVANCING LINE.
         GO TO next_child.
   done_parent.
      FIND NEXT WITHIN Our_employees.  /* Use link-set order based on ssn */
      GO TO next_parent.
 no_more_employees.
* End of parent, child age listing.
```

Navigation through a CODASYL structure can become much more complex than the simple hierarchical traversal shown in Example 9-19. There are in fact 10 conceptually distinct ways to locate a record, as shown in Table 9-5. Some of the choices have similar syntax, and given specific options may in fact carry out an identical process. Once programs use certain ways to retrieve records, it becomes difficult to change the database structure. It is hence very important to design the initial database with the utmost care.

Table 9-5   How to Find a Record

---

1 Locate a record using the link-set order. Requires KEY and ORDER:
```
     FIND { FIRST, NEXT } record.
```
2 Locate a record with a matching key using a search argument value. Requires KEY and ORDER. The search argument is placed into the declared record area. The NEXT record is the next record with a matching key. Next is based on the link-set order and relative to the currency pointer.
```
     MOVE value TO data_item IN record_name.
     FIND { FIRST, NEXT } record USING data_item.
```
3 Using access by a key with a prespecified search argument value. The storage schema typically indicates a direct storage (CALC) organization:
```
     MOVE value TO key_name IN record_name.
     FIND ANY record.              for the first of any duplicates and
     FIND DUPLICATE record.        for successors
```
4 Using a link-set of the current owner to find any, or a specific type, member record, NEXT may be the first member of the link-set:
```
     FIND { FIRST, NEXT, PRIOR, LAST, integer, variable } [record]
               WITHIN link_set.
```
5 Using an argument to locate a member of the current link-set by attribute value:
```
     FIND record WITHIN link_set CURRENT USING search_arg_value.
```
6 Using an argument to locate further link-set members having the same attribute value:
```
     FIND DUPLICATE WITHIN link_set USING search_argument_value.
```
7 Using a SET SELECTION clause from the schema to determine the link-set instance for the record type and an argument to locate the link-set member by attribute value (see Example 9-22):
```
     FIND record WITHIN link_set USING search_argument_value.
```
8 Using the pointer-value (TID) sequence for references within the storage area, for all or for specific record types:
```
     FIND { NEXT, PRIOR, FIRST, LAST, integer, variable } [record]
               WITHIN area_name.
```
9 Using a link-set to locate the owner of a current member record:
```
     FIND OWNER WITHIN link_set.
```
10 Using a currency pointer as defined in Sec. 9-5-2:
```
     FIND db_cp.
```

We will now illustrate some specific cases of navigation with the `FIND` command. Programs are written to access data according to the structure specified in the schema. The use of a database system as specified by the DDLC does not eliminate programming in this respect, although it greatly simplifies the task of dealing with the detailed complexity of network structures.

Using Keys If a key has been defined in the record definition of the schema, a record may be found by using a search argument to match the key. Precisely how the record is found depends on the available physical structure defined in the storage schema; the basic choices are sequential, indexed, or direct. Section 9-5-4 will deal with these implementation structures. To retrieve ages of the children for a particular `Employee`, the COBOL statements would be as shown in Example 9-20.

Example 9-20   Use of a Key

To find the age of the children of `Employee` having the key in `parent_ssn`:
```
find_employee.
    MOVE parent_ssn TO empl_key IN Employee.
    FIND Employee.              /* Find matching social security number */
    GET name.
```
*   *Continue to* `MOVE name`   *and* `next_child.`   *to* `FIND Children`   *as in Example 9-19.*

Link-Set Usage for Networks The various `FIND` operations using link-sets provide the capability to traverse the network defined in the schema. All link-sets can be used to find the the `FIRST` or `LAST` entries. If a specific entry of a link-set is frequently needed, say, the most recent `Department_assignment` of an `Employee`, the link-set may be ordered `INSERTION LAST`. Now the `LAST` entry will correspond to the current and most needed one. The corresponding storage schema (see Fig. 9-14) should provide a `POINTER FOR PRIOR` and a ring where the `POINTER FOR LAST` member links to the owner.

The order of link-set entries can also be used to limit the search to part of the ring, for example to all young `Children`. The option `RANGE KEY` provides a warning that retrieval may occur by range. This means that not only exact matches for a given key, but also `GREATER` or `LESS THAN` matches have to be supported by the links.

Any link-set can also be used to find an `OWNER` when given a `MEMBER`. One important application of this function is to find the other owner of a member in an association. One link-set is used to find the shared member, and then the other is used to find the other owner. In a relational approach the equivalent operation will use two joins. Both owner relations are joined with their association relation, on different attributes. If finding owners is done frequently, a `POINTER FOR OWNER` specification will maintain a direct pointer from each entry to the owner record (see Fig. 4-41). This pointer would be advantageous in moving from an arbitrary member to its owner but is of no benefit if the `LAST` member or an entire subset is processed.

Link-set features are illustrated in Example 9-21, where one key and four link-sets of the given schema are traversed in order to provide the required listing. The output includes fields from three of the record types touched during the traversal. You may want to sketch a diagram to help you find your way during the journey.

Example 9-21   Traversal of a Network

We wish to list Children younger than 19, who now attend 'Harvard', of Employees now working for the 'Foundry' Department.
Of the two potential search arguments: 'Harvard' and 'Foundry', only the second one can be used, since only the Department record has a KEY, so we enter the database there.

```
find_department.
    MOVE 'Foundry' TO department_key IN Department.
    FIND Department.                                        /* by KEY */
another_employee.
    FIND NEXT Worked_in WITHIN Department_assignments.
    IF DB-STATUS EQUALS 02100, THEN GO TO list_done.    /* No more workers */
*   Test if this is the last Worked_in entry for this Employee
    FIND NEXT Worked_in WITHIN Employee_ties.        /* Ignore if record not */
    IF DB-STATUS NOT EQUALS 02100, THEN GO TO another_employee.  /* LAST */
    FIND OWNER WITHIN Employee_ties.           /* Employee currently in dept. */
        GET name.                              /* and potential Harvard parent */
            MOVE name TO name_field IN print_line.
next_child.
    FIND NEXT Children WITHIN Parenthood.
    IF DB-STATUS EQUALS 02100 OR EQUALS 02300, THEN GO TO another_employee.
        GET age_c.                      /* Parenthood is SORTED BY edu_key */
        IF age_c GREATER THAN 18, THEN GO TO another_employee.
            GET child.                  /* a potential Harvard student */
            MOVE child TO child_field IN print_line.
        FIND LAST Education WITHIN Children_education.   /* look only at last */
        IF DB-STATUS EQUALS 02300, THEN GO TO next_child.  /* entry, if any */
        GET Education.                /* entire last Education record for child */
        IF school_name NOT EQUALS 'Harvard', THEN GO TO next_child.
*   found one!
            MOVE school_year TO year_field IN print_line.
            MOVE subject TO subject_field IN print_line.
            WRITE output FROM print_line AFTER ADVANCING LINE.
        GO TO next_child.
*
list_done.
```

Set Selection   When the CODASYL database schema language was summarized in Sec. 8-3-5; the SET SELECTION clause was not described since it relates to the database manipulation process rather than to the database structure. Access choices to records specified under this keyword and other clauses related to link-set manipulation are now shown in Fig. 9-13. The statement FIND can use the SELECTION path specified in the schema to locate a record without specification of the path within the program.

SET SELECTION permits predefinition of the initial link-set or record key, and can specify a path through multiple levels of the structure. Again, a subsequent GET is needed to read the record, once it is found, from the file into core storage. Set selection also permits a subschema to ignore some intermediate level.

/* *The connections to be implemented in a* CODASYL *schema are defined as follows* */
```
     SET NAME IS link_set_name.
        OWNER IS {record_name_o / SYSTEM }.
```

ORDER ⎧PERMANENT⎫ INSERTION ⎛FIRST / LAST / NEXT / PRIOR / SYSTEM DEFAULT⎞
```
   IS ⎨TEMPORARY⎬     IS   ⎨ SORTED ⎛WITHIN RECORD-TYPE
      ⎩          ⎭            ⎨ BY DEFINED KEYS
                               [RECORD-TYPE SEQUENCE
                                   IS record_name, ... ]
                               [DUPLICATES ARE  ... ]
```
          MEMBER IS record_name_m ... *as shown in Fig. 9-14.*

```
     SET       ⎛THRU set_name_owner OWNER IDENTIFIED BY
     SELECTION ⎨ ⎛SYSTEM / APPLICATION
        IS     ⎨ ⎨KEY owner_key_name [o_key EQUAL TO parameter_1[, ...]]
               ⎨ ⎨SELECTION DEFINED FOR record_name_1
               ⎨ ⎩  [ THEN THRU ... /*  other sets down the hierarchy  */ ]
               ⎨ BY PROCEDURE procedure_name_s
               ⎩ BY STRUCTURAL CONSTRAINT
```
/* *Omitted are access procedures and escape calls.* */

Figure 9-13 The DDL clauses related to data manipulation.

Use of set selection is especially useful if a member record is many hierarchical levels below the level of the owner of the link-set, since it allows members to be found without having to find intermediate-level records. Example 9-22 provides a simple case.

Currency variables of all implied records and link-sets are, however, defined as a result of set selection traversal, and this permits references to data along the selection path, as will be shown in Example 9-23.

Example 9-22   Use of Set Selection

If we had specified for the link-set Parenthood that the Children are to be found implicitly by stating in the schema with the Parenthood SET:

```
SELECTION IS THRU Employee OWNER IDENTIFIED BY KEY empl_key.
```

then the explicit FIND for the Employee in Example 9-20 is not necessary when searching for the Children.

```
what_age.
     MOVE parent_ssn TO Emp_key IN Employee.
  next_child.
     FIND NEXT Children RECORD OF Parenthood SET.
        IF DB-STATUS ...
        GET age_c.
        MOVE age_c TO age_field IN print_line.
* The print_line does not yet contain the parent's name; see Example 9-23.
        ...
```

Using Currency The use of the currency pointer associated with a database structural element db_cp implies a reference to a previously found position in storage. We continue Example 9-22 to illustrate a use of currency.

Example 9-23   Use of Currency Pointers

```
        . . .
*  A Children record was found, and the parent's name is needed.
      FIND Employee.    /* Uses the currency pointer defined earlier */
      GET name.
      MOVE name TO name_field IN print_line.
      WRITE output FROM print_line AFTER ADVANCING LINE.
      GO TO next_child.
```

The FIND statement will return the navigator to the record defined by the currency pointer Employee, so that the data items in the record become available for a subsequent GET operation.

In order to deal with more than one record of a given record type, a currency indicator may be placed into a keep_list by the KEEP statement and used later for comparison or to reset the actual currency indicator.

The representation format of such a currency indicator is not specified, and the currency indicators will lose their validity when the program COMMITs or terminates. During the execution of a transaction the currency pointers are to remain valid, even during update operations. A keep_list can be used to compare and manipulate TIDs as defined in Sec. 4-2-3.

Earlier versions of the CODASYL specifications defined a special, manipulable data type, called DB-KEY, to handle currency pointers. It was possible, but dangerous, to use these DB-KEYs to implement semipermanent reference lists for records.

Manipulation of Link-Sets In the description of the MEMBER clause of a link-set appear some parameters which specify the manner in which link-sets will be maintained. Figure 9-14 reiterates that clause; INSERTION of a MEMBER record may be AUTOMATIC or MANUAL, while deletion is constrained by a RETENTION clause to be either FIXED, MANDATORY, or OPTIONAL.

```
/* The connections to be implemented in a CODASYL schema are defined as follows */
  SET NAME IS link_set_name.
      . . .
  MEMBER IS record_name_m
    INSERTION IS{AUTOMATIC / MANUAL}
    RETENTION IS{FIXED / MANDATORY / OPTIONAL}
    [DUPLICATES ARE NOT ALLOWED FOR key_attribute [, ...] ]
   ⎡ [RANGE] KEY IS{ASCENDING / DESCENDING}{key_at / RECORD-TYPE[, ...]} ⎤
   ⎢         [DUPLICATES ARE{FIRST / LAST / NOT ALLOWED / SYSTEM DEFAULT}]⎢
   ⎣         [NULL IS [NOT] ALLOWED]                                      ⎦
    [ STRUCTURAL CONSTRAINT IS variable_a EQUAL TO variable_b [, ...]].
```

Figure 9-14 The DDL MEMBER clause of a link-set.

Automatic insertion means that when the member record is STOREd the currency pointer for the current OWNER will be used to create an entry into the link-set. For instance, the link-set **Parenthood** to the **Children** relation was specified AUTOMATIC. A sequence of FIND **Employee** and STORE **Children** will establish the linkage.

Manual means that the user transaction program will have to execute CONNECT or DISCONNECT statements to manage the entries. The schema specified MANUAL insertion for the **Supervision** records in the link-set **Employee_ties**. Example 9-24 presents the statements needed to add a supervisee to **Employee_ties**. A MANUAL connection is appropriate here to avoid possible confusion since both owner and member can have currency **Employee**. To link boss and subordinate the program stores the record for the subordinate, establishes a currency indicator for the boss in the **Employee** relation, and then connects the two by inserting an entry into the link-set. The ORDER of the link-set was defined in the schema to depend on the KEY **year**.

Example 9-24   Adding a Supervisee

Establish a linkage from supervisor identified by boss_ssn to subordinate having sub_name:
```
new_subordinate.
   MOVE sub_name TO subordinate IN Supervision.        /* Create record */
   MOVE 1982 TO year IN Supervision.            /* Determines ORDER KEY */
   STORE Supervision.                    /* Place the record into the file */
   MOVE boss_ssn TO emp_key IN Employee.
   FIND Employee.
   CONNECT Supervision TO Employee_ties.  /* OWNER determined by currency */
```

The RETENTION clause FIXED indicates an ownership dependence of the member record on the owner of this link-set. When an owner record is deleted, its link-set disappears and the link-set's members alsodisappear. This is the expected constraint for the **Children** of the **Employees** and their **Education**.

A DISCONNECT statement will also cause the FIXED record to disappear, say, if a child becomes independent. To avoid losing the member record if a member has to change owners, a RECONNECT statement may be used. In our schema this might be necessary if **Children** had to be switched to another **Employee** parent. A more frequent case would occur if the schema would include a link-set **Current_department** from **Department** to a FIXED **Employee** member. This link-set would require the RECONNECT statement whenever the **Employee** switches **Department**s.

The option MANDATORY indicates an ownership dependence on the union of the owners of all link-sets that this record is a member of. This means a record is not necessarily deleted when the owner of one link-set disappears, only when there are no more owners at all. This choice is like a reference connection with garbage collection. We made membership of the **Worked_in** records MANDATORY for both owners. Now, if an **Employee** record disappears, the name of such an **Employee** can still be found from the **Department** record and vice versa. A search from that record to find employee data will fail, however. The `Worked_in` records will be deleted if the `Employee` disappears and the `Department` is dismantled.

The choice `OPTIONAL RETENTION` means that the member records exist independently of their link-set owners. This clause is appropriate for entity and referenced entity relations. It is wise to have a `KEY` field in such a record to avoid making the record inaccessible while manipulating link-sets.

9-5-4 File Organization in a CODASYL system

The storage schema, following the definitions given in Fig. 8-10, specifies alternatives for the implementation of records and link-sets. It is not intended to be restrictive; other implementation techniques which provide identical functionality are permitted. The writer of a storage schema has to be very careful that the model schema is appropriately supported. We can expect that software tools will be developed to help create efficient storage schemas for model schemas and estimated file sizes and access frequencies.

There are quite a number of restrictions in the model schema definition to prevent requiring implementations which are awkward or inefficient. There are also some restrictions on data manipulation which are implicitly derived from the storage schema. The intent of the storage schema is to make the model schema user independent of physical placement considerations. The restrictions will make sense to a user who understands file storage alternatives, but will appear capricious to someone without such insight.

For the `PLACEMENT` of records five alternatives are specified in the storage schema: direct, close to link-set members, close to owner records, close to some other records, and sequential. The implementation of these methods was covered in Chap. 3, and only a quick summary is given here.

Direct (`CALC`) The records will be placed into the `AREA` for direct access according to a hashing algorithm operating on the `KEY` of the record. The `KEY` in the model schema lists the attribute fields. A lexicon typically uses direct access for the most frequent access path. If access according to either attribute is required, a redundant copy can be kept, or the other attribute of the lexicon can be accessed using a link-set. Here duplicates would not be allowed.

Direct access is common for the records at a top level of some hierarchy. For entity relations serial access is generally needed as well. If an `ASCENDING` or `DESCENDING` sequence is specified in the model, further records can be obtained serially. This may require the additional availability of a link-set with an `ORDER` clause, probably owned by the `SYSTEM`.

Clustered `VIA SET` The records that are members of the same link-set (`SET`) will be placed in the same or adjoining blocks. Finding the next member of a link-set will then be fast.

Clustered `NEAR OWNER` The records that are members of the same `SET` instance will be placed in the block or in blocks adjoining the block which contains the specified type `OWNER` record. This implies, of course, that the `OWNER` records themselves will have poor locality.

Clustered VIA SET ... WITH ... . The records that are members of the same link-set (SET ...) will be placed in the block or in blocks adjoining the block which contains the specified record type (WITH ...).

Placement is SEQUENTIAL The records of this type will be placed so that they can be efficiently retrieved for serial access. The ordering will be according to the named identifier.

The organization of the link-set structure is also specified in the storage schema; the ORDERing of the link-set members is specified in the model definition. The essentials of the 1978 storage schema definition for link-sets are given in Fig. 9-15. In earlier DDLC documents similar specifications appeared as the MODE of the link-set. In the 1978 schema the choices are basically limited to two alternatives:

Access members using an INDEX Use of an in a link-set index is appropriate if the number of member records for a link-set is large. It is used predominantly for SYSTEM-owned records.

Access members using a chain This choice defines the common ring structure. Options include either all or some of forward, backward, and owner pointers, as well as a choice of chains or rings. The POINTER FOR clause may be repeated as often as necessary.

Within each record the actual data fields and the required linkage fields have to be declared. The pointers in the linkage fields can be specified to be DIRECT or INDIRECT, implementing the two nonsymbolic alternatives shown in Fig. 8-2.

The SET clause describes a link_set connection in the storage schema:
```
SET SCHEMA_SET    [ALLOCATION IS {STATIC / DYNAMIC }]
     POINTER (   INDEX index_name
         FOR {   [NEXT] [PRIOR]   [OWNER]
                                                    [ RECORD
                 [LAST] [FIRST] /* connects to owner */
                 schema_record_name]  ( IS [DIRECT] [INDIRECT]
                                      {  TO storage_record_name_memb, ...} )  .
```
/* In each storage record type each member and owner pointer has to be defined */
```
STORAGE RECORD NAME IS storage_record_name_1
     [LINK TO storage_record_name_2 [ IS{DIRECT / INDIRECT}]]  [, ... [...] ]
     [RESERVE integer_5 POINTERS]       /* spares for later record expansion */
```

Figure 9-15 DDLC-DSDL linkage implementation specification.

9-5-5 Design Considerations

The many options available for CODASYL databases can make the design process complex. The opportunities for restructuring of a database are quite limited once a design is implemented and programs have been written to use the database.

One consideration in database design is whether linkages in the records should replace attributes from the conceptual tuples. If attributes are omitted, certain access choices are no longer available.

Structural linkages to the `Children` relation of Example 9-18 are *essential* since the `parent_name` is not kept in the record. Link-sets using `OWNER` or `NEXT` and `LAST` pointers are required to find the parent. If the reference value `parent_name` is also put into the `Children` record, retrieval of the parent can also be carried out by a fetch to `Employee`. The linkage is redundant with the value. To preserve integrity of the databases links and values must match. The maintenance of such integrity constraints is left to the user's update programs.

Major reorganizations of data relationships (e.g., reversal of an owner-member connection) will cause problems even when structure independence has been carefully considered. An example of such a reversal would be a decision to maintain lists of patients of a clinic according to the problems they have presented (maybe to improve medical management), whereas these patients were traditionally seen as individual entries in an entity relation, and their problems were handled as a nest relation.

It is possible within the CODASYL specification to design service programs and applications that maintain databases according to rigorous standards. This can be achieved if management is willing to support a well-defined conceptual model. This means setting and enforcing design and programming standards. Use of the access procedures can help provide some enforcement, although many DBMSs do not yet have complete implementations. Some storage and update costs will be incurred if increased redundancy is required.

The description of the DBTG proposal given above is intended only to convey the flavor of the proposal. The full set of specifications exceeds 400 pages but is easily read if the objectives, structure, and underlying fundamentals are understood, although some ambiguities remain. We will now discuss some of the actual implementation issues.

9-5-6 Current Implementations

Many CODASYL systems are now available, although no system has implemented all the features. The richness of the specification makes it difficult to provide a full system on a small computer, but implementations for large minicomputers are also in progress. As indicated earlier, most current CODASYL DBMSs are based on earlier specifications. They also may vary, as implementors became aware of problems with the initial specifications and devised their own solutions.

Using Subschemas   An external schema, to be included with the compilation of programs accessing the database, includes only the file-organization specifications required for data manipulation. A CODASYL subschema, for instance, does not include information from the storage schema. Optionally, further elements (data attributes, records, link-sets, and areas) may be omitted to force programs to be independent of certain information. Such programs will be less affected if a portion of the database is reorganized. In order to provide subschemas for the programmers to use, an `INVOKE` command is available for COBOL which will copy the selected subschema from a file maintained by the database administrator:

INVOKE SUBSCHEMA production_schedule OF SCHEMA order_entry.

A single program can use only one subschema, so that a large number of separate subschemas may be developed if access privileges are to be controlled using subschemas. Programs which are under direct management control can be given access to more features via a more comprehensive subschema.

Data-Manipulation Statements One system, Cullinane's IDMS, originally developed by B.F.Goodrich, implements the CODASYL architecture on a variety of computers. Table 9-6 summarizes the statements available to a COBOL user for manipulation of the database. We note with the statements variances with the 1978 specifications when the difference is confusing or critical.

Table 9-6   IDMS **Statements**

Control Operations:
```
    INVOKE SUBSCHEMA ...
    OPEN AREA realm_name USAGE MODE IS protection_clause.
    CLOSE ALL AREAS.
    IF link_set SET EMPTY GO TO label.           /* check DB-STATUS */
    IF RECORD MEMBER OF link_set SET GO TO label. /* compare db_cp */
    MOVE STATUS FOR ... TO variable.              /* keep currency */
    CALL data_base_procedure ON operation.
```
Operations on Records and Link Sets:
```
    STORE record_name RECORD.
    FIND ...        .                  /* as described in Table 9-5 */
    GET record_name RECORD.            /* always the entire record */
    OBTAIN ...      .                  /* combines FIND and GET */
    MODIFY record_name RECORD.
    DELETE record_name RECORD ...    .
    INSERT record_name INTO link_set.   /* CONNECT    */
    REMOVE record_name FROM link_set.   /* DISCONNECT */
```

For IDMS users who are programming in FORTRAN, BASIC, PL/1, or assembly language CALL statements are available to carry out the functions provided.

The Storage Schema IDMS is based on the 1972 DBTG specification, but it already defined a schema language augmented with statements which control the assignment of the database to the storage devices. IDMS translates all database keys, both the internal DBMS pointers and the users' DB-KEYs, into indirect references to the blocks of the direct access files. One file can contain multiple AREAs and each AREA provides blocks which are packed with multiple record types as shown in Fig. 4-33. To avoid block overflow, a new block will be assigned when a record does not fit. To provide the control mechanism for the physical storage assignment, a device and media control language (DMCL) is defined which interacts with the stored schema. The process of schema translation is as shown in Fig. 9-16, which may be compared with the processes described in Sec. 8-4-2 (Figs. 8-10 to 8-13).

During execution the database handler can be dedicated to one user or can be shared among multiple users. Users will have a copy of the subschema table relevant to them in their own section of core storage, as well as a copy of the IDMS modules which accept the CALL statements created during the process of translation of the database-manipulation statements to COBOL statements (A). UNIVAC has an implementation based on the earlier 1969 DBTG report, DMS1100, which adds two statements to make and break the subroutine linkages between the user's executing program and the database handler: IMPART and DEPART (B).

An example of statements used for storage assignment by IDMS is given in Table 9-7. The allocation of the physical devices is completed by using operating system control language statements referring to sys009, sys010, sys011. The defined ranges describe the high-order digits of the database pointers which will be used. The numbers assigned within the files are the relative block addresses to be used for each AREA. The size of a block is described in the PAGE statement.

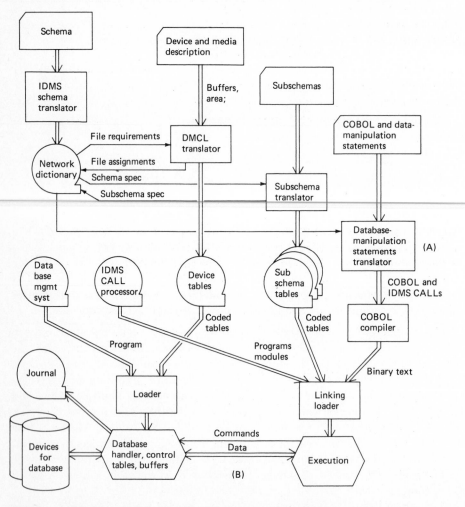

Figure 9-16 Translation sequence of IDMS statements.

Table 9-7   Storage Assignment Statements in IDMS

```
/*  In the Schema */
  FILE DESCRIPTION.
     FILE NAME IS IDMS_file_1 ASSIGN TO sys010 DEVICE TYPE 2314.
     FILE NAME IS IDMS_file-2 ASSIGN TO sys011 DEVICE TYPE 2314.
     FILE NAME IS journal ASSIGN TO sys009.
  AREA DESCRIPTION.
     AREA NAME IS customer_area    RANGE IS 1002 THRU 1100
                                   WITHIN FILE IDMS_file_1 FROM 1 TO 99.
     AREA NAME IS order_area       RANGE IS 1101 THRU 1300
                                   WITHIN FILE IDMS_file_1 FROM 100 THRU 199
                                   WITHIN FILE IDMS_file_2 FROM 111 thru 120.
     AREA NAME IS product_area     RANGE IS 301 THRU 1310
                                   WITHIN FILE IDMS_file_2 FROM 1 THRU 10.
/*  In the Device and Media Description */
  BUFFER SECTION.           BUFFER NAME IS IDMS_buffer
                            PAGE CONTAINS 1508 CHARACTERS
                            BUFFER CONTAINS 5 PAGES.
  AREA SECTION.             COPY customer-area AREA
                            COPY order_area AREA
                            COPY product_area AREA.
```

9-6 INTERLINKED HIERARCHIES

The final database implementation to be described is one of the earliest to be used for commercial or industrial use. IMS was originally conceived at North American Aviation in order to solve the bills-of-materials problem in a large company with strong central management. The system has been extensively developed by IBM, and IMS/360 and IMS/VS are now principal database products of that company. IMS includes also a scheduler and communication interface, so that it can be used on-line within batch-oriented systems. Database schema and manipulation support is mainly provided through the DL/1 subsystem.

The IMS system is relatively unique in its approach. In its storage representation it is strictly hierarchical, so that a database schema will again be composed of a forest of schema trees. Various storage alternatives are available for the entity and nest relations. The schema trees, however, can also be linked to each other, and alternate schema tree definitions can be formed using the stored segments. The aggregate conceptual structure can become more complex than DBTG networks.

The programmer, however, does not have direct access to these links. The links are used to construct alternate hierarchies. Access to an alternate external or *logical* hierarchy is made possible through the interposition of DBMS procedures which use the available links to obtain the appropriate segments. In order to obtain data the programmer specifies some hierarchical view and uses only hierarchical operations to navigate through the database. The actual database structure may remain hidden.

Internal schema

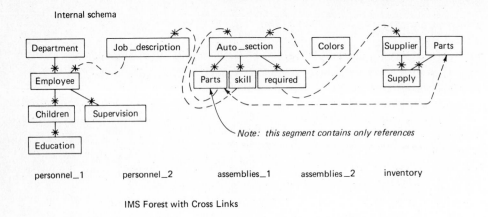

IMS Forest with Cross Links

External schemas which can be developed from the internal schema

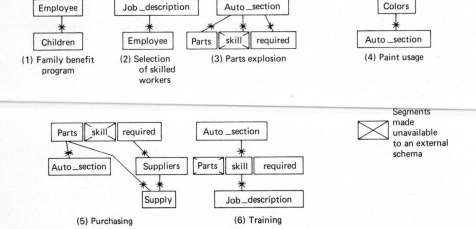

Figure 9-17 Derivation of IMS external schemas.

The hierarchy of the external schemas means that in IMS the accent is still on the retrieval of a composite record. A record consists of current segments at each level of the selected hierarchy. A database administrator is required to maintain the overall structural specifications and their implementation.

An organizational separation of application and database system staff categories is assumed. A third category consists of the users of the programs, who enter and retrieve data. The administrator has to be able to maintain an integrated database which allows concurrent existence of the various logical hierarchies. The complexity of this task is such that considerable programming and management resources are required when IMS is used.

9-6-1 The IMS Schema

The schema language for an IMS database is DL/1 as described in Sec. 8-2. DL/1 is used in another mode to provide external logical schemas for the users. Each external schema can depict a hierarchical structure appropriate to the user's data model, subject to the existence of relations and linkages in the internal database schema. Procedures within IMS use the linkages in the schema to transform the data from the database relations into the data presentation specified by a DL/1 subschema. Numerous structural restrictions exist in regard to the permissible transformation, but as IMS developed these restrictions have become less severe. The *logical* view of the database, described by the user's external schema, is neither a conceptual view of the database or a database subset, nor a view of physical reality, but rather an imitation of a physical view of a database subset.

In the joint schema all structures depicted form a forest of entity and nest relations. A hierarchical structure for the database used earlier (see Figs. 7-27, 9-5, and 9-10), suitable for a DL/1 internal schema is shown in Fig. 9-17, together with some possibilities for external schemas.

Each external subschema is in itself logically hierarchical. The choices of subschema structures are limited by the predefined linkages in the internal schema. Linkages between trees can implement *owner, member, or sibling* relationships, and can be specified to be *next*, or *next and prior*. In addition, pointers are used to link nests into rings or to link overflow areas to records as required by the file organization chosen. All the linkages to be implemented require, of course, specifications in the DL/1 internal schema, storage space in the files, and updating effort during database use. The trade-off between linkage availability and excess redundancy has to be made carefully. When frequency of usage does not warrant the maintenance of linkages, symbolic references can still provide access to other files.

An external schema is defined using the same DL/1 mechanism used for the internal schema. SEGMENT definitions obtain position and size information from the database and the segment names of the internal schema. FIELD definitions are completely ignored here. For the `parts_explosion` external schema the definition might read as shown in Example 9-25.

Example 9-25   DL/1 **Logical Hierarchy for the External Schema**

```
DBD       NAME=explosion,ACCESS=LOGICAL
DATASET   LOGICAL
SEGM      NAME=section,SOURCE=((auto_section,,assemblies_1))
SEGM      NAME=all_about_parts,PARENT=section,
          SOURCE=((parts_skill_required,,assemblies_1),(parts,,inventory))
DBDGEN
FINISH
```

The segment `all_about_parts` consists of the catenation of two source segments, so that this associative relation is formed without actual duplication of entries from the `parts` owner. This is possible because of the existence of *logical sibling* pointers in the `parts_skill_required` segments.

A lexicon can also be composed of two logical sibling segments, so that access to the relation can use either of the two attributes, but the access is not symmetric in performance. Access procedures, however, using either one of the two attributes, given that the lexicon is properly specified in two external schemas, can use the same operation formats.

9-6-2 Operations on the Logical Hierarchy

IMS procedures are initiated by executing CALL statements. The argument of a CALL is a communication area containing the specifications for the operation. Three operands are specified:

1 The type of *operation* to be performed

2 The *object* of the manipulation

3 The user's *data area* for the retrieval results or update values

Operations The permissible operations are given in Table 9-8.

Table 9-8 IMS **Data Manipulation operations**

Get_Unique	for a fetch according to a key adequate to identify segments up to the desired level in the hierarchy
Get_Next	for a sequential read to a successor segment or segment sequence
Get_Next_with_same_Parent	for a read within a nest
InSeRT	to add a segment
DeLETe	to delete a segment
REPLace	to replace a segment

Locking options for these statements are discussed in Sec. 13-1-1.

Objects The objects to be manipulated are described by reference to another DL/1 construct, the *program communication block* or PCB. This table, generated also through an assembly process, specifies the segments from the program point of view, references the logical hierarchical structure given in the external schema, and controls the access privileges. A PCB which uses the external schema **Training** (see Fig. 9-19) could read as shown in Example 9-26. The parameter PROCOPT specifies that segments may be retrieved (G), inserted (I), replaced (R), or deleted (D).

Example 9-26   DL/1 **Schema Selection**

```
PCB     TYPE=DB,DBDNAME=Training,KEYLEN=34
SENSEG  NAME=section,PROCOPT=G
SENSEG  NAME=job_descr,PROCOPT=GR
```

It is also possible for the program's PCB to refer to the internal schema directly if no (or no appropriate), external schema was defined. Since not all segments of the external schema have to be included in a PCB, the PCB provides a further subsetting capability for the database: in Fig. 9-19 skill data are omitted from the Parts_explosion. A program may use multiple PCBs if it wishes to use more than one external schema simultaneously. This allows the use of multiple records, since each external schema defines one record, constructed of current segments in a hierarchy. A currency indicator is associated with every PCB in use. The individual data fields are not subject to DL/1 control; the units *retrieved, inserted, deleted, or replaced* are single segments or a string of multiple segments, each segment at a different hierarchical level. We will call the segment at the highest level the *root segment.*

In order to reference a lower-level segment in a hierarchical structure, a sequence of keys is required. A key for a segment to be fetched is the catenation of the keys of all ancestor segments beginning with the root segment and ending with the key of the goal segment. The maximum total key length is given as KEYLEN in the PCB. To get data regarding the supervised employee Mike, the fully qualified search key would be

    (dep='Assembly').(employee='Hare').(supervision='Mike')

These keys are presented to DL/1 in a compact form. When the computation retrieves a successor segment using the GET-NEXT operation, DL/1 provides the key.

Data Areas The data input or output area for the program is a conventional PL/1, COBOL, or assembly language data structure, and the names given to the fields by the programmer are the actual data element names used in computational manipulations. The type, unit, length, etc. of the elements remain fully under control of the program which has access to the segments containing the data. Segments not included in the PCBs, however, do not appear to exist at all. The programmer has hence to construct data areas where the size of the segments is determined by the internal schema, but which segments will appear in the data area is determined by the external schema and by the entries in the PCB. The order of the segments is determined by the external schema. The programmer ignores the linkages; these will not appear in the program data area. The size and content of key fields must be calculated in a similar manner from the field specifications. If alternate segments are possible, such as children.education or supervision, the record and key fields have to be dimensioned according to the maximum length, and overlapping data structures will be used using the REDEFINES clause in COBOL and BASED variables in PL/1.

9-6-3 Storage and Linkage

In order to support the hierarchical structures, IMS uses a mapping procedure, so that all data for an entity relation and all its nests appear in a single file. There are hence as many files as there are trees in the IMS forest. Each top-level entry in a file, for instance, each department of Personnel_1 in Fig. 9-17, is the root segment for a *tree instance*. Each tree instance, with all its subsidiary segments, is treated as if it were a long and complex record. Such IMS trees can span many blocks.

The file structures used by IMS are extensions of standard file organization methods. Extensions were needed in order to serve the hierarchical nature and potentially large size of the tree instances. The four file choices for IMS are

HSAM	Sequential
HISAM	Indexed sequential
HDAM	Direct access
HIDAM	Indexed direct access

We will first present how entire trees instances are placed into blocks, and then see how segments and blocks are manipulated within these files.

Mapping of the Hierarchy The mapping of the segments comprising the hierarchical tree is

top-to-bottom, then left-to-right

or *preorder* using the terminology used by Knuth[73F]. This order was also used by OASIS; see Fig. 9-9. One tree instance, when completed, will be followed by the next tree instance, until all entity tuples and their nest members are stored. For the `Personnel_1` tree of Fig. 9-19, using the same data as the SYSTEM 2000 files of Fig. 9-8, the sequence would be as given in Example 9-27.

Example 9-27   Segment Storage for One DL/1 Record

```
department(1),employee(1,1),child(1,1,1),education(1,1,
1,1),education(1,1,1,2),education(1,1,1,3),supervision(
1,1,1),supervision(1,1,2),supervision(1,1,3),supervisio
n(1,1,4),employee(1,2),child(1,2,1),supervision(1,2,1),
supervision(1,2,2),...,supervision(1,2,6),employee(1,3)
,child(1,3,1),education(1,3,1,1),child(1,3,2),education
(1,3,2,1),education(1,3,2,2),supervision(1,3,1),supervi
sion(1,3,2),employee(1,4),...,supervision(1,5,8)
```

A new record begins with the next root segment: `department(2), ... .`

In Example 9-27 the first sequence of four segments provides one complete flat record. A successor record according to the lowest level hierarchy will use `education(1,1,1,2)` instead of `education(1,1,1,1)`. An alternate successor record can be built from `dep(1)`, `employee(1,1)`, `supervision(1,1,1)`. Successor records are constructed by replacing low-order segments with their successors, using an algorithm reminiscent of reconstitution of an index key after rear compression (Sec. 4-2-2). Sequential processing allows any complete record to be available without ever backing up.

Linkages The links which provide the capability for the derivation of sub-schemas do not come free. Every nested segment which can logically exist in some secondary external schema requires in the corresponding actual file an entry at its apparent position containing the reference pointers to the real segment. A segment which implements an association will contain the dependent data and links to the logical second owner.

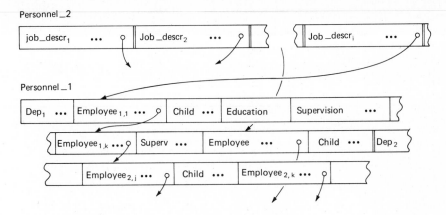

Figure 9-18 Logical pointers between segments.

For the personnel trees in Fig. 9-17 the files will contain segments with pointers as shown in Fig. 9-18 given that `employees(1,1),(1,k),(2,j),...` all have `job_descr(i)`.

Files with many logical linkages will hence be in practice much larger than they appear to one user. The requirements for linkages are specified in the DL/1 internal schema through segment entries for logical members (`LCHILD`) and segment options for siblings (`LTWIN`), owners (`LPARNT`), and catenations of two segments only (`PAIRED`) for associative relations. It is also possible to specify prior linkages allowing, for instance, owners to be found from members segments.

It should be noted that these linkages allow the reversal of hierarchical relationships in different internal schemas for the same database. This is a facility not commonly available in database systems.

File Structures The file structures used by IMS are not identical to the standard methods provided by IBM for the 360 systems, since these were insufficient. This is only one of many instances where inadequate file facilities have added considerably to the cost, complexity, and inadequate structuring of database systems. Figure 9-19 sketches the four approaches used by IMS. The storage linkages shown in the sketches are supplementary to the linkages used for the data models.

The basic unit to be stored, a DL/1 *record*, is a tree instance with one root segment and all its nested segments in *preorder* sequence. Such a tree instance can be very large and may span many blocks. Segments are not spanned. The entire tree instance does not have to be read into core storage at one time but is accessed segment by segment, as was shown above. Since access is based on the key of the root it is often wise to shorten the hierarchy by decaptation. This creates more and smaller trees. In the database laid out in Example 9-27 we may move the **department** level to a referenced relation, and use **employee** as the root.

HSAM The sequential file organization is available in IMS to allow tape or disk storage for files where mainly sequential access is expected. The fetch of a tree instance based on an arbitrary search key will be very time-consuming. The only

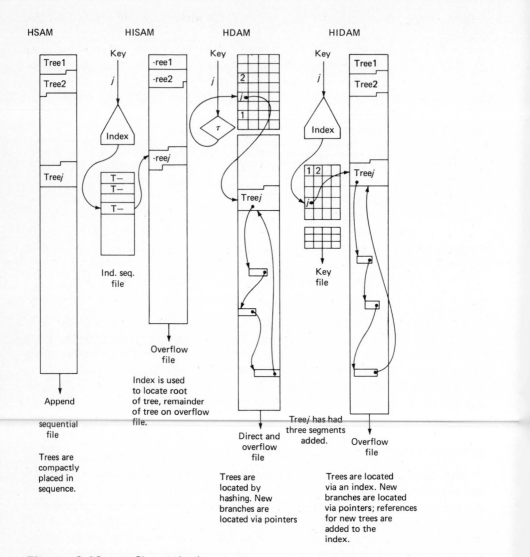

Figure 9-19 IMS file methods.

dynamic updating possible is the addition of trees to the end. All other updating is to be performed by batch programs which copy the file.

HISAM   The indexed-sequential ISAM or VSAM have been extended with an overflow file to permit the management of the large and variable-length tree instances. The HISAM method is suitable when sequential access, indexed access, and some updating are required. The initial loading is done by a batch process, using an input file which contains the segments in the desired *preorder* sequence.

Only the initial block of a tree instance is kept on the indexed-sequential file. Successor blocks for a big tree are placed on an overflow file. This overflow file is a disk-resident sequential file, augmented so that blocks can be appended, marked deleted, or replaced. In IMS VS another VSAM file without an index is used for this purpose.

In IMS/360 the insertion of a new tree instance is accommodated by use of an IMS-provided link chain to the overflow file, ignoring the ISAM overflow mechanism. Insertion of new segments is accomplished by placing the segment in its proper physical position and moving the successor segments of this tree instance out of the way. Overflow blocks will be acquired at the end of the overflow file, to accommodate any final segments of a tree that do not fit within the old blocks.

HDAM The direct-access organization has also been extended with an overflow file. The HDAM method is useful if sequentiality is not required and updates are frequent. Collisions are resolved by chaining in key sequence within a bucket.

Only the key of a root segment and a pointer to the remainder of the tree instance is stored in the direct-access file; the remainder of the root segment and all other segments of the tree are kept on the overflow file. The direct file and the overflow file are actually separate areas of the same operating system file. New segments are placed in any free area of the overflow file. The segments of a tree instance are related to each other using pointers and will not be physically moved during updating. Segments belonging to different tree instances may share blocks. Two linkage choices for segments of a tree are available:

1 A chain which links the segments in the *preorder* sequence

2 A hierarchical ring structure using member and sibling pointers

The first choice is sketched in Fig. 9-19.

The insertion algorithm attempts to place the segment according to best locality and minimal space fragmentation. A bit map which indicates blocks that have free space adequate for segments and a free space list within each block are used by this algorithm to achieve efficient placement and allow recovery of space from deleted segments.

HIDAM A combination of indexed-sequential access to those tree segments which are loaded initially and linked access to new segments placed into the file allows sequential processing, indexed access, and frequent updating. Only the key fields of the top segment of a tree instance are kept in the indexed-sequential file; the complete tree instances are kept in the overflow file. A separate indexed-overflow file is used to hold keys for new tree instances. The initial generation of the file is again a batch process, receiving segments in the desired *preorder* sequence. Updating will disturb this sequence. Sequential processing will be slow if updating has scattered the segments of a tree instance over many blocks, or if many new tree instances have been inserted at the end of the file. These are also retrieved via the key file, unless two trees have identical keys.

Other Options When tree instances become excessively large, collections of subtree instances can be kept on a different file using as root segments only copies of the keys of the original root segments. IMS provides this option for HISAM using schema specifications without requiring programmer intervention.

If any indexing, outside of the primary index to the tree instances, is required, lexicons have to be defined by the user. These can be kept using HDAM or HISAM file organization. As a dependent part they will use *logical* segments, which are connected by next and prior pointers to the real segment instances to be indexed.

A plethora of additional options to control storage and linkage is available. Traditional database education does little to prepare a programmer to make decisions which deal with systems of this complexity while attempting to provide reliable, responsive, and cost-effective service to the folks who require the information hidden in the database. The database administrator may need some automatic design tools.

9-7 ADVANCES IN IMPLEMENTATION

The systems we presented in this chapter have a long history. Many of their design concepts were developed in the late 1960s or early 1970s. They are important now because of their maturity. They can handle nontrivial databases, have the backup and reliability mechanisms necessary in a multiuser environment, and are known to a wide range of data-processing professionals. At the same time they tend to lack features we would like to see in more advanced systems. We will discuss such features now without citing specific systems. It is hard to predict commercial success of any new system; much depends on marketing and financing. No new system we investigated includes all or even most of these features.

9-7-1 Distribution of Databases

If data are distributed, schemas at each site have to carry information about remote as well as about local data. A local subschema has only to keep track of remote elements which may be requested by queries originating at the site of the subschema. Such subschemas will contain definitional entries for the data elements at other sites, but only the names and sites of attributes at remote sites have to be kept in the storage schema section. Even then the distributed schemas may become large and difficult to maintain, since schema information is replicated over multiple sites.

Some of the data may be replicated onto more than one site. A retrieval request needs only to be directed to the site which is easiest to reach or has the lowest load. An update has to be directed to all copies of the data. To execute a transaction which involves multiple sites, those portions of the transaction which cannot be executed locally will be transformed into subtransactions to be transmitted over the communication links for execution at the remote sites.

For optimization of transactions on distributed databases the following points need to be considered:

Sources Which sites contain the requested data elements?

Data-segment sizes What is the expected partial result or data-segment size for the subtransaction? This question is repeated after each processing step.

Retrieval capability What are the speed and cost for retrieval at those sites?

Communication capability What are the data transmission capabilities, i.e., the available data transfer rates, between the sites?

Processing capability What is the capability of various sites to carry out any required processing? Especially joins or partial joins (see Sec. 9-3-5) are important.

Result site Is the final output required at the site of the request, at another site, or anywhere in the net? The last case applies to subtransactions creating data segments for further processing.

If one node has all this information, the query can be preplanned at one site, and all the subtransactions can be generated and scheduled there. Linear programming algorithms have been used to solve such problems, at least for the case without replicated data.

It can, however, be impractical to provide all other nodes with procedures for estimation of remote data-segment sizes, since the data volume and key distribution at a site will fluctuate. The global performance of these schemes is unfortunately critically dependent on data-segment sizes, since the transfer rates across communication links tend to be an order of magnitude slower than those of storage devices. In that case only primitive retrieval subtransactions will be spawned, and optimization will proceed step by step, as the data-segment sizes become known. Current systems tend to rely on programmer decision to handle such problems.

9-7-2 Multimodel Capability

We find instances where programmed, navigational access appears to be appropriate to look for specific instances in a database. For a single user a hierarchical view is often clear and adequate. Relational queries provide the most generality and manipulability. Relational formulations may also be appropriate as an intermediate interface for queries stated in a natural language such as English or in an interactive manner on on-line terminals, perhaps with graphics. Translation of navigational queries on a relational implementation is equally feasible, but efficient execution may be difficult. We discuss such issues in Chap. 10.

9-7-3 Choice of Access Structures

A database system should be able to support a wide variety of query types and the corresponding updates. Most relational systems will process a query using indexes if indexes are available for the search arguments. Similarly other access constructs which use locality, pointers, etc., can be used to permit general and efficient retrieval capability on any database structure. We are aware that locality is central to good retrieval performance.

In order to increase locality for critical data, it is often desirable to replicate data elements. *Replication* does increase update and storage costs, but its benefits can outweigh these costs, especially for data which are read much more frequently than updated. The database systems should deal formally with replicated data, so that updates will be correctly and completely executed. Some experiments have been made on relational systems; the process was called *denormalization*, and demonstrated its feasibility. In current systems this technique is used only in an ad hoc fashion during database design, and the correctness of updates has to be assured by user programs.

9-7-4 Binding Alternatives

There are query situations and data collections where efficiency is important, and

situations where flexibility is paramount. The alternatives of compiled and interpretive access are appropriate for some and not for other cases. It is hence desirable
to be able to provide a mix of translation schemes.

In a system which provides a range of binding choices it may become feasible
to add relations to the model, add attributes to existing relations, and define and
implement new connections. Then it may become possible to change the database
model without an extensive reorganization.

In current systems a reorganization tends to be traumatic. It takes many hours,
and a failure of the process will also require many hours of restoration to the earlier
state.

Very Large Databases To allow growth of the database, the 1978 DSDL storage
schema can specify an initial loading **DENSITY** of fewer records than fit into a block.
Equivalent facilities were actually provided in earlier implementations; for instance,
the UNIVAC DBMS-1100 provides an **INTERVAL** statement for this function.

When extra space is exhausted, a database reorganization may be required.
Reorganization of a database is apt to be a major effort. Data for TOTAL indicates,
for instance, that on a large IBM 360 computer, it takes about 1 minute to reload
1000 records. Reorganization of the database at Equitable Life Assurance takes 72
hours of computer time [Gosden in Jardine[74]]. This leads to the following definition
of a *very large database*.

A very large database is a database whose reorganization by reloading takes a
longer time than the users can afford to have the database unavailable.

Problems of very large databases are now being addressed prior to standardization
efforts [Steel[75]]. To avoid frequent reorganizations, the records of the database may
be extended with spare fields, so that attributes can be added later. A sophisticated
method to cope with database reorganization will be presented in Sec. 11-4-3.

9-7-5 Tools for the Design and Testing of a Database

The complexity of databases is such that it is difficult for a single individual to
maintain control. The structural model provides conceptual assistance. Database
dictionary systems provide the capability to create catalogs of the data in the
database, and many can be used for automatic schema generation. They will
typically support only one type of DBMS, however.

Testing has its own risks. The danger of a misprogrammed transaction destroying the corporate database is real. Keeping a test copy of the database is expensive
in storage costs and maintenance.

It should be possible to run transactions during checkout on the real database
for read accesses and on test blocks when writing or reading data created during
the test.

9-7-6 Schemas with High Level Definitions of Connections

Recent developments in query languages do recognize relationships among entities.
They need to be supported by data-definition facilities of equivalent power. An
important issue in schema management is integrity and constraint specifications. In

most systems today such specifications are closely linked to implementation techniques. It is desirable that logical constraints be specified first, and the implementation choice be left to something akin to a storage schema.

Rigorous domain definitions can do much to increase the integrity of databases.
Just stating the computer representation (i.e., `integer`, `floating point`, `char`,
...) does not indicate the constraints appropriate to connections and joins in a
database. Character type variables are appropriate for connections or joins only if
defined by a common referenced entity relation or lexicon; otherwise many matches
will be missed. Real values are rarely appropriate for connections or equijoins.
Joins with integer-type attributes can easily attempt to match domains which are
inappropriate, say, `age` and `number-of-children`.

9-7-7 Modularity

The requirements listed above could imply that a future DBMS will be even more
massive than the current ones. To avoid this trap we look forward to having
database systems composed out of manageable modules. Candidate modules are:

File Systems Current file systems are often awkward for database system use
because of lack of symmetry and formal interfaces. Most DBMSs today build their
own file support out of primitive facilities. Our understanding of file alternatives is
such that this should not be necessary.

Schema Management Translation and manipulation of the tables for a data
definition language is a general function which can be handled separately.

Query Interface The translation of queries from a user-friendly language is a
major and specialized task. Use of well-defined schema tables and a general data
manipulation language will provide interfaces to isolate this function into a module.

Backup and Recovery Protection of the content of a database, presented in
Secs. 11-3 and 11-4, is an important task in many but not all database applications.
The level of protection required may be specified in the schema, and actions which
may require protection can be triggered when the database is manipulated. In a
transaction oriented database system the tasks are well-defined (see Sec. 11-3-1)
but exceed often the services provided by the operating system. The module can
provide a consistent interface while size of this module will depend on the capability
of the operating system.

BACKGROUND AND REFERENCES

Descriptions about the the implementation of databases tend to be scattered through user
manuals, company reports, academic research reports, and internal documents. Manufacturers' manuals describe only what the system will do and not what it will not do; a
number of systems are referenced in Appendix B. Manuals do, of course, provide much
more detail than can be found in scholarly publications. The reference material on IMS
alone exceeds by far the size of this book. The terminology used is often specific to the
system and may even differ from the terminology used to describe other systems of the
same manufacturer. Appendix A is intended to be helpful here. Descriptions of new
systems are found in the popular computing magazines.

A number of textbooks as Cardenas[79], Kroenke[78], and Tsichritzis[77] stress description and comparison of database-management systems. Specialized database systems are typically described in application-oriented publications; see the references in Chap. 1.

Early descriptions in the computer literature included Bachman[64], Dodd[66], Bleier[68], and Hsiao[71]. Specialized systems include PARS (Siwiec[77]) and TOD (Weyl[75]).

Improvement of binding choices is considered by Stemple[76]. Nunamaker[73] considers the database system as a unit in a larger user support system.

Some early work in set-oriented databases (Childs[68]) led to RDMS (Steuert in Rustin[74]), and related systems as MACAIMS (Strnad[71]), SAM (Symonds[68]), and DAMAS (Rothnie in Rustin[74]). Papers by E.F. Codd (in Codd[71], Rustin[72], and Klimbie[75]) and his colleagues (Boyce[75]) have provided impetus for relational implementations. After initial experimentation using APL (Palermo[75]) came several developmental systems, as IS/1 or PRTV (Todd in Kerr[75]), MORIS (Bracchi in Klimbie[75]), INGRES (Held[75], Stonebraker[76]), and SYSTEM-R (Chamberlin[76], King[80]). Some systems try to integrate the programming language with database manipulation (Schmidt[77], Shopiro[79], and vandeRiet[81])

Some of these systems are now moving into commerce (Chamberlin[81G]). King[80] assesses their status. Brodie[82] surveys the large number of relational systems are now on the market; Appendix B lists many. Not all systems going by the name "relational" provide the same range of functions and their performance differs greatly. Some systems appear even to be limited to handling one relation at a time.

The process of translation of relational calculus languages is detailed by Codd in Rustin[72] and has received much attention. Gotlieb in King[75] analyzed the cost of joins. Merrett[81] tries to reduce their costs. Problems of operational efficiency are being attacked by Rothnie in Rustin[74], Wong[76], Härder[78], Selinger in Bernstein[79], Yao[79], Aho[79S], and Katz in Chen[80]. Sequences of queries are optimized by Finkelstein[82]. Hall[76] and Smith[75] consider relational algebras.

Major joint efforts by users and manufacturers produced the first large commercial database systems, IDS (Bachman[66]) and IMS (Lutz[71], McGee[77]).

Techniques for optimal design, considering both retrieval and update, are due to Yao[77,79] and Whang[81] Design of CODASYL databases was considered by Gambino[77], and Whang[82] provides separability rules.

Methods to aid database design decisions has been published (Mehl in Rustin[74], Smith in King[75]). Lusk in Chen[80], Hubbard[81], and Gerritsen in Yao[82] They all tend to apply to specific system styles.

At the same time a number of relatively simple but clean implementations of databases have become available commercially: SYSTEM 2000, ADABAS, TOTAL. Commercially available systems have been compared in CODASYL[71A] (see Olle[71]), Cohen[75], and Palmer[75]. Many comparisons describe features and suffer from lack of an underlying model. Comparisons of systems are often part of a company's software selection process and, if they can be obtained will provide good study material. Problems faced in hierarchical query design are described by Hardgrave[80]. Lefkovitz[74] describes implementation issues in a general sense.

The work of the CODASYL group has become the basis for the implementation or augmentation of a number of commercial database systems: DBMS-1100 (Emerson in Jardine[74]), IDMS and Boeing IPAD (Swanson[80]).

Issues of CODASYL implementation (Olle[78], Douque[76], and Parsons[74]) and appropriate usage (Stacey[74], Taylor in Rustin[74] and in Douque[76]) have been presented. Buneman[82] implemented a functional query language within a CODASYL structure.

Some worked-out example programs have become available to aid in the evaluation of the DBTG design: Frank[73] (Codd in Rustin[74] uses the same example), and Robinson in Douque[76]. In Sibley[76] a sample database about U.S. presidents is used for three approaches. The work of CODASYL is continuing and changes in syntax and semantics continue to be made. These changes are published regularily as *change pages* to the Journal of Development (CODASYL[73,...]).

The relational approach is compared with the implementation of IMS and the specification of CODASYL by Bachman[75], Martin[77], Date[81], Olle in Benci[75], and Nijssen in Neuhold[76]. The significance of the relational approach is stated by Codd[82]. Analyses of the effects of implementation choices are given by Bachman in Jardine[74], Stonebraker[80], Kay in Douque[76], and Engles in Neuhold[76].

The issues of optimal distribution of data and queries in a network have been analyzed by Eswaran[74], Chu[79], Baldissera[79], Hevner[79], and Ceri[81]. When replication of fragments of the database is permitted the optimal allocation problem becomes very hard, although designers have been able to deal in an ad hoc manner with practical cases. Morgan[77] considers the constraints due to the dependencies between programs and data. Bernstein[81] analyzes a method to minimize join costs between sites. The topics have been surveyed by Epstein[80] and Hevner in Wiederhold[82].

Recent developments in implementation include Tandem's ENFORM system. At CCA investigations were based on the design of SDD-1 (Rothnie[80]). Proposals for distribution have made by Stonebraker[79] and several systems in development are presented in Wiederhold[82].

EXERCISES

1 What are the result relations from the examples in Sec. 9-1-2 given the data in the relations from Chap. 7?

2 How would the query for employees supervised by younger empoyees shown in Example 9-3 be formulated if there were no necessity to specify the relation names?

3 Write the statements required in the relational calculus to obtain the names of departments which have employees with the skill to assemble a given `Assembly` from the `Automobile_section_b` relation using the examples summarized in Fig. 7-29.

4 Work out the division in Example 9-4, using the definition of division given below the example.

5 Formulate for the hierarchy of Fig. 9-8 the query, "Who has children at UC Berkeley and UCLA?"

6 Estimate the retrieval time of the query in Exercise 5 in terms of `fetch` and `get-next` for a hierarchical and a relational database structure.

7 Determine the answer for the query: "Which department has employees with children at UC Berkeley who supervise more than two people?" which is formulated as follows:

```
GET department | schoolname='UC Berkeley' ∧ COUNT(supervision) > 2
```
Then fix the query to represent the stated intent.

8 For which attributes would you expect to find the specification KEY or NON-KEY in SYSTEM 2000? Who in an organization using such a database should know about the existence of the specification, and who should not?

9 Sketch the layout of the relations
auto_section, suppliers, parts, supply, possible_supplier and
parts_skill_required in a hierarchical and in a network-type database.

10 Program at a high level the process of locating the suppliers of any part in an auto_section in a relational algebra database, a hierarchy, and a network.

11 Estimate the retrieval times of each of the above processes. State all assumptions, and use the same assumptions in all three cases.

12 Compare the above process given the SYSTEM 2000 file structure and the OASIS file structure.

13 What attributes are stored redundantly in the TOTAL network database design given in Fig. 9-10?

14 Sketch the TOTAL records for supplier and supplier_assembly of Fig. 9-10.

15 What is the difference between KEY in SYSTEM 2000 and LOCATION MODE EQUALS CALC in CODASYL.

16 What CODASYL access choice would you use to locate an employee given his name? Why?

17 To avoid problems with reference pointers, an implementor decides to use symbolic references. What will happen to each of the seven performance parameters used in Chap. 3 for such a system?

18 Could a programmer effectively navigate through a DBTG structure for the relations shown in Fig. 9-19? What about a manager?

19 What is the difference in the implementation of multiple member types in a TOTAL nest relation and multiple member types of a DBTG link set?

20 Compare the storage of IMS tree instances with the storage of MUMPS tree instances in terms of storage density, and fetch and get-next speed.

21 Find an example of a database system other than the ones mentioned in the text which incorporates features belonging more properly to a file system. Explain why the database system was designed in this manner. Suggest an alternate approach.

Chapter 10

Information Retrieval

The value of knowledge lies not in its accumulation, but in its utilization.

E. Green

Information retrieval is carried out by application of queries to databases where the result is expected to increase the users' knowledge. Database applications which are not considered information retrieval are systems which provide regular operational service, for instance, systems which schedule activities, manage inventories, or prepare bills or payrolls. Applications of databases in areas such as airline reservations and skill registries are close to information-retrieval applications. These and many other operational systems overlap with information-retrieval systems to an extent that much material in this chapter will also be relevant in the context of operational systems. In information retrieval the ability of systems to cope with a wide variety of ad hoc queries is stressed.

The intent of this chapter is not to cover the field of information retrieval in a comprehensive manner; more has already been written about information retrieval than about the subject of database itself, and several excellent books on this subject exist. It is, however, necessary to relate the concepts found in information retrieval to the objectives found in database design. When issues in the area of information retrieval are discussed, there is often an implied understanding regarding the data-organization concepts which are valid for the information-retrieval problem. While the data organization chosen for an application may be quite appropriate, it can be puzzling to the uninitiated why one data-organization method was favored over the others. An explicit evaluation of the approach selected becomes important when an information-retrieval system is being considered in an application which is not a mirror image of the task foreseen during the original implementation of the information-retrieval programs. In order to develop a basis for comparison of information-retrieval objectives, we will categorize information retrieval into three areas:

1 Fact finding

2 Statistical inference

3 Deductive inference

In Sec. 10-2 these approaches will be discussed in detail. It should be understood, however, that a single system may have to support all three areas to some extent. Section 10-1 will abstract the data requirements for information retrieval in terms of the database system choices presented earlier. The formulation of queries to actually retrieve information is the subject of Sec. 10-3.

When information retrieval is discussed, the updating of the files is not considered to present a major problem. This greatly simplifies the comparison of the approaches. In practice, however, the updating problem is of concern for any information-retrieval system. If the information content is entirely static, dissemination of the material in printed form or on microfilm could very well provide a better alternative than the use of computers.

10-1 DATA CONSTELLATIONS

In order to obtain information from a system, a constellation of related data elements has to be extracted from a database and presented to the user in a meaningful form. The data may consist of a list of homogeneous values, relating to different entities; they may consist of a list of heterogeneous values describing a single entity, or a matrix of both.

One list could present the fuel consumption of various automobiles and another one the weight, horsepower, load capacity, etc., of one specific car. A single attribute may also record changing values over time, say, the temperature of a patient.

Whenever the data become voluminous, data-reduction algorithms become desirable.

The average fuel consumption, the trend of the temperature, and such provide information abstracted from a set of basic data in a compact form. These abstractions have always to be viewed critically. With an average value the standard deviation should be presented, with a trend the linearity.

A database system should permit rapid access to abstractions and summarizations, often supporting multiple views, while still permitting access to the underlying source data, so that questions can be resolved by *zooming in* to less abstract levels.

We will review how appropriate *constellations* of data can be obtained from the database structures presented in the preceding chapters. Three types of database structure suffice to distinguish databases from the point of view of information retrieval.

- Relational data structures
- Hierarchical data structures
- Network data structures

Each of the model structures may be implemented in various ways. In fact, the same software system might be configured to provide any of the three types.

In a *relational structure* the data are stored in tabular form. Operations combine and select from tuples, using fetch arguments selected from the query and from intermediate tuples. All binding occurs at query-processing time. The result is presented as a relation in the user's workspace.

In a *hierarchical structure* the search arguments define currency indicators. Fetch arguments define entry points into the database. Get-next operations are confined to the hierarchical structure. The result presented is a broom or a record composed of one segment of each segment type. Frequently network database structures are used to present hierarchically structured results.

In a *network structure* there are nearly arbitrary connections which bind data records to successor and predecessor records. The retrieval process enters the structure using a fetch argument and then navigates through the structure using get-next, get-owner, or get-member operations, collecting data values on the way. These data values are delivered incrementally to the query-processing process, and are used to control the progress of the query. The result is not made available as a unit, since its structure is not predictable. Figure 10-1 sketches the alternatives.

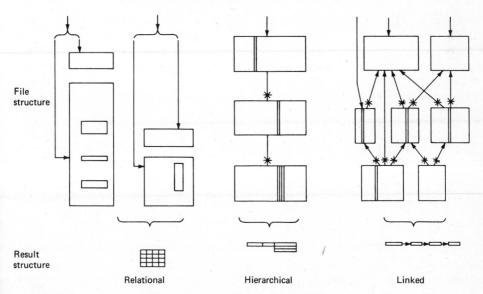

Figure 10-1 Database structure and data retrieval.

The manner in which the database systems present the results will obviously influence how the user perceives the information-retrieval process. It is still possible to interpose programs between the user and the primary database-manipulation facilities which put a different facade on the database structure.

Bibliographic Data A short note on a class of information-retrieval systems which do not involve data-processing is in order. These are the bibliographic systems which maintain data about collections of publications. They typically have records composed of authors, keywords, abstract, and a reference. Figure 4-21 presented the internal structure of such a system. The data stored in such a system is preprocessed and will have information value, if appropriately retrieved, without further processing. The records may be complex: each element can contain multiple entries and require multiple indexes or linkages for access. The content of such a data bank is abstracted material and references to more detailed data. The search arguments are also often complex; otherwise the use of a computer system may not be warranted.

These systems are frequently and correctly called *information-storage systems*, since what they contain is already potential information. The contents is selected, prepared, and classified with the expectation of eventual retrieval and use. The entities stored are complete and independent.

Example 10-1   Use of a Bibliographic Information-retrieval System

---

A query to the SPIRES I system, (Parker[67]) may be
 FIND TITLE 'Model' AND TITLE 'Quark' NOT AUTHOR 'Gupta'
                AND DATE BETWEEN 'Jul.67 & Nov.67'
The response to this query was
   count = 2
   Exchange Current and Decays of Decuplet Baryons in the Quark Model
   Kobayashi, Tsunehior   Konno, Kimiaki
   Waseda U.   Nihon U., Tokyo
   Preprint 67-2194 14 pages
   Quark-Diquark Model of Baryons and SU(6)
   Lichtenberg, D.B. Tassie, L.J.   Kelemen, P.J.
   Tel-Aviv U.   Australian Nat. U.   Indiana U.
   Preprint 67-2172 31 pages

When documents are prepared for data entry into bibliographic information-retrieval systems, it is necessary to assign index terms as keys for later retrieval. Within the field of bibliographic processing, this process is referred to as indexing; to avoid confusion with the creation of file indexes, we will use the term *classifying* in this chapter.

The classification of documents is the major challenge in bibliographic information-retrieval systems. Both manual and automatic classification methods are used. The terms used for classification will form the classification vocabulary and be the basis for the index to the database. Most operational systems rely on manual classification by reference to a *controlled vocabulary*. Computer interaction can be of assistance in the classification process; all terms chosen can be rapidly checked during preparation of the classification. All terms actually used to classify a document should be within the vocabulary, but terms missed are collected for analysis. A review of terms tried by classifiers and users, but not found in the vocabulary, can be used to update the vocabulary or a list of synonyms. The frequency of use of terms, singly or in combination, can provide further input to vocabulary control.

10-2 CATEGORIES OF INFORMATION RETRIEVAL

In this section we will present the alternatives in information-retrieval requirements which the users may bring to a database system. We use the three categories: *fact retrieval, statistical inference*, and *deductive inference*.

10-2-1 Fact Retrieval

Fact retrieval is the traditional and popular view of an information-retrieval operation. The query is entered into the computer system, and the computer system looks through its data collection and selects an answer. In essence, the answer is stored somewhere in the data bank, and the problem is to find the answer. The task of the system is to find a data constellation identified by a set of keys. Fact retrieval is the primary use of bibliographic data banks or data banks containing material in textual form.

Many business inquiry systems also fall into the fact-retrieval category. A credit verification system will respond **yes** or **no**, or maybe turn on a green or red light in response to the query about the customer's creditworthiness. This answer, the actual information, is prestored in the database. It is not expected that at this point significant computational efforts will be carried out to determine if the customer is indeed capable of settling debts.

Demands on the Database   A fact retrieval-system is characterized by extensive use of the fetch operation and by the use of indexed or direct access. One or few relations will participate in a query. Since the answers are already bound to a particular query type, it is also possible to bind the database structure to match the queries so that rapid responses are obtained.

10-2-2 Statistical Inference

When the size of a response to a query is so large that the user cannot comprehend it, techniques of data reduction must be employed. The techniques required may range from simple cross-tabulations to extensive statistical processing in order to provide meaningful data. The process of obtaining these results is more complex than the simple request-response sequence. Many intermediate data elements are obtained from the database to be incorporated into the result.

Frequently requests are made iteratively until it is possible to obtain a satisfactory formulation for the query. When cross tabulations are generated, many of the possible combinations may not produce results of interest. When statistical approaches are used for the selection of relevant factors, finding an appropriate analysis technique may require several trials. It is often desirable to produce results in an intermediary form in order to help the user formulate the data relationships and analysis concepts. Examples of outputs to aid in concept formation are graphical outputs of trendlines, histograms of different subsets of the data variables of interest, and presentation of the data in scattergrams to get impressions of possible correlations between variables.

Example 10-2   Query to Present a Data Relationship

A query to help formulate the question,
"Can aspirin treatment in patients with arthritis affect uric acid ?"
can be entered into a system which supports statistical data analysis (TOD)
as follows:

```
PROGRAM?    scatterplot
ELEMENT FOR HORIZONTAL AXIS = Ur_Acid
ELEMENT FOR VERTICAL AXIS   = ASA
SUBSET?     5          /* A subfile from a previously defined catalog is chosen */
Rheumatoid Arthritis   249 Patients
```

The response is shown in Fig. 10-2. This initial query shows some correlation
and helps a user conceptualize a relationship. The researcher may now look at
the same data for all records in the file, or for more specific patient groups.

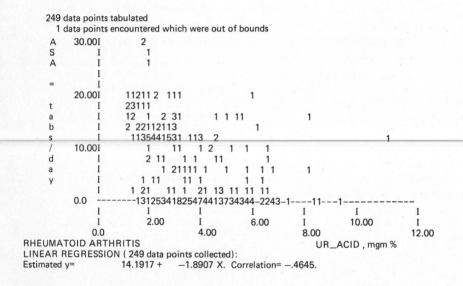

Figure 10-2 Graphical query output.

Retrieval of a few attributes of a large subset of tuples is not all restricted to the
scientific environment. In management-oriented database systems, the selection of
data describing a part of the enterprise and comparing the performance of these
parts with averages based on the entire enterprise, or on industrial standards, is the
preferred mode of operation. Graphical output can again aid in concept formation,
and simple statistics can provide baseline data so that unusual events or trends can
be recognized. This type of processing may produce exception reports that trigger
action to determine and correct, if necessary, unexpected patterns. In this manner
data can become information.

Demands on the Database Statistical inference implies the retrieval of large quantities of well-structured data. Use of the get-next operation becomes predominant. Since processing programs can only understand files in tabular form, the output presentation of the database system must make the data constellations available in an array or as linear structures. Subset selection and retrieval has to be effective in order to process subsets proportionally faster than the entire data collection. The use of transposed files can be very beneficial.

It is difficult to present with common technology more than three-dimensional situations. This increases the processing requirements on the system: data constellations have to be presented in various combinations in order to develop an understanding of relationships among the data.

To avoid reprocessing large volumes of data, it may be desirable to collect intermediate results in workspaces. When a ring structure is used, the header records provide an opportunity to collect totals and counts for the detail values which are kept in the members of the ring. The availability of actual summary data can significantly reduce reprocessing effort.

In many of these applications, it is desirable that the database is *not* updated during analysis in order to avoid inconsistencies. A subset of the database can be copied into a temporary workspace to escape interference. Data structures in a user workspace can be bound increasingly tight as the analysis progresses.

10-2-3 Deductive Inference

In the previous two approaches to information retrieval, the results were directly related to the query; in the case of fact retrieval and in the case of statistical inference multiple entities are selected based on search arguments. A question of the type: **Why does aspirin reduce uric acid concentrations?** cannot be answered within such databases. There is no single tuple in the system which has the answer, although a relationship may exist between the two search arguments, via many intermediate facts and relationships stored in the database. The construction of systems which contain statements describing basic logical relationships and which will process queries about complex relationships is one of the most interesting applications involving database technology.

The problem can be seen as the building of a bridge between search arguments and the goal. When the database containing possible relationships becomes moderately large, the number of possible combinations becomes immense. Techniques of artificial intelligence have to be applied to reduce the search possibilities to a manageable number.

Data Structures to Express Relationships A database used for deductive inference requires a finer semantic categorization of relationships than was used when database models were constructed. An example of such a refinement is the categorization of the relationship represented by an ownership connection. The particular meaning of the relationship of a person entity to children, jobs, skills, or diseases can be made specific. The same relationships in the opposite direction would be named: parent, employee, expert, or patient. A deductive query-processing program has to be aware of the meaning of the relationship in order to follow the appropriate path. If the database is unbound, the search algorithm will collect tuples with keys matching the query and then select further tuples based on values found in those tuples. When the database is bound, the query will find successors by following pointers.

In order to organize relationships for deductive inference, the relations are often decomposed into binary form. Now the implied relationships kept otherwise within a multiattribute tuple can be treated identically to relationships between tuples. The binary relations form triads of relationship name (or pathname), key, and goal. An example of such a structure was shown as LEAP in Sec. 4-7-5. The query will also be composed into binary relations.

An example of a network database for deductive inference is shown in Fig. 10-3, using a partial model of glaucoma. The records represent elements of the disease, and the relationships given are cause and effect, and similarity. The records are generated from a disease description provided by physicians. Only a part of the model and only one of the weights which can be applied to the relationships is shown in Fig. 10-3

Searches begin at the entry points corresponding to known data about a patient. More data can be requested; the analysis program has information about the cost of the tests which have to be administered to obtain data and can optimize the diagnostic effectiveness. The records are written by a SNOBOL program; the information retrieval is performed by a FORTRAN program.

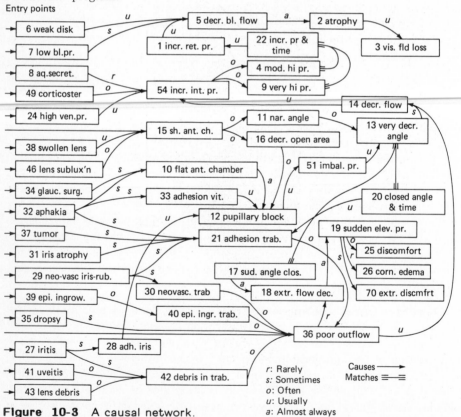

Figure 10-3 A causal network.

Demands on the Database The query process, possibly aided by information from a schema, has to evaluate the probability of success in following a particular path. The database may be constructed using *rules*, representing functions, or *frames*, representing entities, or a combination of both. It may also be profitable to provide a weight or strength measure between the frames so that concepts of being **a little bit happy**, being **very sick**, etc., can be expressed.

There is typically a preprocessing pass where the symbolically specified relationships are converted into a bound structure with chains or links. During execution the branches of the network can be rapidly traversed.

Many experimental systems have used relatively small databases. For these support of virtual memory systems has been adequate. Efficient tracing of linkages is possible if sufficient pages can be kept available so that the workspace can be maintained without heavy paging requirements. It is not yet clear how database systems can support the requirements posed by deductive inference systems using more than several thousand tuples.

10-2-4 Summary

The categories of database services available can now be evaluated relative to their effectiveness in information retrieval. When desirable features occur in different database approaches, combinations of database methods can be considered to yield a compromise solution.

The relational approach, by deferring binding to the time of query execution, is the most flexible. However, the amount of processing required may be excessive for on-line operation with large databases. When statistical inference over many tuples is part of the query process, the retrieval costs may be high in any case. For deductive inference semantic rules are required to reduce the number of relationships to be explored. These rules are in effect a form of early binding. Without such rules an unbound database will be very costly to explore.

Hierarchical structures lend themselves to rapid fact finding. For statistical processing data elements will be taken only from one level at a time, so that only structures with good access to siblings support this type of information retrieval well. Since a hierarchy is well defined and bound, deductive techniques are not required or supported by this approach.

Networks provide fact-finding capability using complex but bound structures. Statistical processing will be limited to hierarchical single level data subsets. Deductive goal seeking can be carried out by navigation in a network structure. The navigator may be a combination of an intelligent program which interacts with a knowledgeable user.

10-3 QUERY FORMULATION

Query formulation is the process performed by the user in order to communicate through the information-retrieval system with the database. The design of a query-formulation language will be affected by these three components:

- The users' needs and background
- The information-retrieval system
- The database

Users may range from casual users wishing to retrieve simple facts (weather predictions, automobile traffic, etc.) to specialists who spend many hours with the system and understand its capabilities and contents. For the former group convenience and clarity are important; for the latter group, efficiency and availability of tools to manipulate retrieved data are of consequence. There may also be intermediaries between the end users and the system: assistants who formulate queries to obtain data for decision makers, programmers who write programs to carry out more complex analyses of database contents than have been provided within the information retrieval system, people who collect data and maintain the database contents, and, finally, a database administrator, the only one who can *make the trees* on which the data are placed. In order to support this variety of users, a variety of approaches to query formulation can be considered.

The availability of a schema is an important aid in the process of query formulation, as sketched in Fig. 10-4. The definition of the attributes, availability of indexes or search paths, and the partitioning effectiveness of query arguments is best resolved before the database itself is accessed. In a hierarchical structure, aggregate values in header records can also provide data to aid in the optimization of processing during query execution.

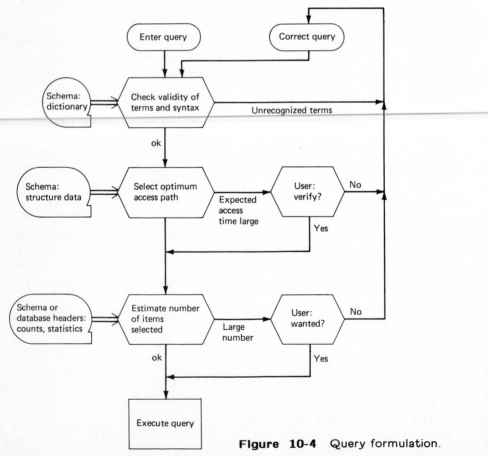

Figure 10-4 Query formulation.

10-3-1 Interrogative Query Formulation

Interrogative systems presuppose the least knowledge. The ability to pick up a telephone may be the only requirement posed. Successive questions posed by the computer are answered in simple yes-no or multiple-choice mode, or by the entry of commonly known identifying terms or names of objects. A HELP function is provided in case the user fails to understand the terms presented by the system. This approach can be relatively slow but is satisfactory if not carried out for extensive periods.

Examples of such devices are credit inquiry system, using special telephones, and serve-yourself banking terminals.

When a higher rate of data flow is required, display terminals can interrogate a user effectively by permitting several choices in one interaction. The user may indicate the chosen item by means of a lightpen or a touchscreen. One selection can lead to presentation of a more specific set of choices. The hierarchical nature of this query process is supported well by hierarchical file systems.

Given a patient file as illustrated in Fig. 4-25, the choices would be presented in the sequence: Select drug, laboratory, other data? Patient name? Date? Problem? Drug type? Frequency? .... . Figure 10-5 shows some sample screens.

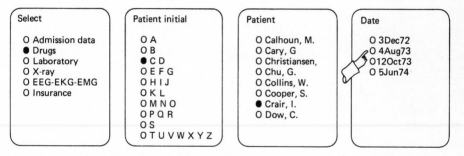

Figure 10-5   Screen selection.

The fanout on a display screen can provide a few dozen choices, so that when following a hierarchy after a few screen selections a great deal of data can be accessed. A high rate of communication capability is required to support this type of query formulation, since screen selection can be accomplished in a fraction of a second.

10-3-2 Tabular Queries

When access to the system is limited, preparation of the query using a printed questionnaire is another alternative. Directions are provided specifying the choice of parameters to be entered to describe the query. If the user has adequate knowledge about the database, a query can be formulated in a short time and then be presented to the system. Many report generators work very effectively in this mode. The

Query request

Title   Check excess salaries
Date   5 June 75

Attribute name (see schema)	Selection		Print		Sort	Format	Total at attribute
	Op	Value	Col	Cond.			
salary	>	10000	20				department
manager	=	"J. Nerous"					
employee			1		2		
age			30				
year_hired			35				
skill			40				
department			1	total	1		

Check excess salaries

Andrews, Karl	12444	45	1963	Machinist
Calhoun, Mike	26900	37	1974	Welder
Hare, Leo	11700	28	1972	Asst. Welder
Lusch, Rosemary	23450	21	1974	Secretary
Palmer, David	15000	34	1969	Sheetmetal Worker
Foundry	89494			
Cooper, Sara	13120	25	1972	Secretary
Gordon, Richard	15600	24	1974	Asst. Welder
•••				

Figure 10-6 Tabular query formulation.

form of a query is often matched by database systems which provide tabular representations of their content.

A tabular query form will contain attribute names as well as space to indicate conditionals and simple result expressions. Typically several levels of subtotals and totals can be produced in the result. Modifiers are available to indicate ordering and grouping. Generalized computation tends to be awkward; an example is shown as Fig. 10-6.

When more complex computations or selection criteria are needed, the rigid tabular structure becomes inadequate. To overcome such problems statements and expressions as seen in computer languages are introduced. The formulation of queries then requires increased expertise.

To avoid the need for knowledge of the schema contents, a technique of specifying queries by example has been developed [Zloof[77]]. The same query as above formulated by example is shown in Fig. 10-7. Associated with the example entries are notations indicating selection and printing.

Personnel

employee	department	manager	salary	spouse	age	year_hired
P. Calhoun	P. Foundry	J. Nerous	P.TOTAL;>1000	0	P. 37	P. 1944

Figure 10-7 Query by example.

Interaction is used to construct queries by example. First the database or file name is requested. This permits the system to list the schema elements on the display terminal. Those schema elements which are not desired as part of the query or the responses are ignored.

Here the **spouse** is ignored, and this heading can be deleted. Empty columns of the table can also be requested and named. Into the columns values for the query constants can be placed. Here **J.Nerous** and **>10000** provide constants. Underlining indicates that the values are samples, and the **P** prefix indicates that the column is to be printed. An extra underline indicates grouping for the generation of **TOTAL**s.

Several relations can be included in a query. A join is generated when the same underlined sample term appears in both relations. If the supervised employees are also to be listed in the evaluation, **Calhoun** would be placed in the **supervisor** column of **supervision**; such a use is equivalent to defining a tuple variable. The system is oriented toward a relational database but has been explored for other environments.

This query approach has been shown to have surprising power. Database schemas can also be specified by use of examples. Specifications by example are an effective means to describe output formats to computer systems. When conditions become complex, the coding rules required may diminish the initial simplicity.

10-3-3 Interactive Query Statements

For general query processing interactive methods provide the greatest flexibility. The user formulates a query using a query language, and the query statement is parsed and executed. The response to one query often leads the user to formulate further queries.

Many languages to state queries have been developed. They range from very formal, calculus-oriented languages to relatively simple languages which provide statements similar to those found in procedural languages. These languages are always influenced by the underlying database structure, by the degree of on-line interaction supported, and by the communication devices used. While techniques from procedural languages are used to parse and execute query statements, no common, system-independent query language has yet been accepted.

A similar query is specified in a display-oriented language (ASI-INQUIRY) as in Example 10-3.

Example 10-3   Query to Produce a Table on a Display Terminal

```
FIND ALL PUT employee, salary TOTAL, age, year_hired, skill
          WHEN salary > 10,000
          AND manager = 'J.Nerous'
          AND department = foundry
```

This statement will fill the display screen for inspection by the user. Entering **CONTINUE** will present another screen full of data, until the query result is completed. Entering **SHOWTOTAL** will present the total for the attributes indicated. A new query can then be entered for the next department.

This, and similar, languages can interface with hierarchical structures. The problems in formulating queries appropriately when data and selection elements appear on different levels have been discussed in Sec. 9-4.

In order to perform complex operations without repeated extensive accesses to the database, some query languages allow the creation of subset files, which can then be sorted and used as input to statistical processes.

In GIS the same query as Example 10-3, without the totals, can be written as in Example 10-4, using `Work` as an intermediate file.

Example 10-4   Query Using a Work File

```
SAVEX   excess_salary;
QUERY   Personnel;        /* file */
LOCATE  departments;      higher hierarchical level */
WHEN    salary > 10000;
AND     manager = 'J.Nerous';
HOLD    Work←employee, salary, age, year_hired, skill, department;
SORT    Work←department,employee;
LIST    employee, salary, age, year_hired, skill;
```

The query is filed under the name **excess_salary** and can be retrieved later.

Query Language Operators Most query languages provide the capability to combine search arguments with boolean operators: **AND** and **OR**. A request which includes a **NOT** operator has a very low partitioning power for files, and hence its use is often limited. Comparative operators other than =, namely, $\{<, \leq, \neq, \geq, >\}$, also have low partitioning power. When comparative operators appear in expressions, a restricted subset of the file is defined. Complex expressions should not be executed piecemeal but should be analyzed to consider the available access facilities to determine how the file can be best partitioned. It is, for example, obviously desirable to combine the two subexpressions in the query

$$\text{salary} > 10000 \wedge \text{salary} < 12000$$

before applying either expression by itself to the file. The use of comparative operators favors indexing over direct access, since serial searches are required.

When the database is in text form, the conditionals in query expressions may become more complex. The query processor has to define words as character sequences between delimiters as blanks, and symbols as $\{.\quad , \quad ; \quad " \quad '\}$. The words which appear in text have many variants. Capabilities for obtaining synonyms of words may be needed; it is also desirable to recognize words which have the same stem. Boolean combinations of words which are related may be limited to appear in the same sentence or same paragraph.

An example of a search through a file containing the "What's New" columns from the Wall Street Journal using a **TEXT** option of GIS is shown in Fig. 10-8. The symbol ($) indicates truncation and the symbols (+1), etc., indicate the permissible word distance. The labels **L1**, **L2**, and **L3** provide references to query expressions. The figure shows also one of the articles obtained.

```
        SEARCH WHATSNEW, TEXT;
        OPTION WHATSNEW, TEXT, STAT;
L1      PRODUCTION, DEMAND, SHIPMENT;
L2      DECLIN($), DOWN, DECREAS($), SLIP($);
L3      STEEL&L1(+1)&L2(+3);
        LIST TEXT, PRNTDATE;
        END;
```

```
243              L3

PRNTDATE: OCTOBER 24, 1966

TEXT:

STEEL DEMAND AS A WHOLE SLIPPED LAST WEEK
FROM THE MONTH-EARLIER LEVEL DESPITE NEW
INDICATIONS THAT AUTO COMPANIES ARE STEPPING UP
THEIR BUYING OF THE METAL. STEEL SHIPMENTS
FROM MAJOR MILLS ARE MAINTAINING THE SEPTEMBER
PACE ALMOST WITHOUT EXCEPTION.
```

Figure 10-8 Free text query in GIS. *From Semple*[67]

Term Weights If, in addition to STEEL, other products which contain combinations of metals to are of interest, the terms in the expression can be assigned *weights* to indicate relevance. A formulation which will retrieve a variety of references is shown in Example 10-5.

Example 10-5   Specification of Term Weights

Terms of interest in the query are assigned measures of importance:
WEIGHT: Steel(5),Aluminum(3),Copper(3),Tin(3),Metal(2),ferrous(2)
and the query can include the conditional expression
TOTAL_WEIGHT $\geq$ 5 ?

The notion of a weight as a measure of interest can also be used in queries applied to formatted data; the query into excess salaries might be formulated as in Example 10-6 to select cases for further investigation. The TOTAL_WEIGHT is computed as $\sum$ sign(value + basis)/scale. Using the data from Fig. 10-6 the search expression IF TOTAL_WEIGHT > 0 THEN PRINT employee will select employees Calhoun and Lusch.

Example 10-6   Attribute Weight Computation Table

attribute	basis	scale	sign
salary	-10000	/1000	+
age	-20	/10	-
year_hired	-1975		-

The user of statement-oriented languages is typically an intermediary between the requester of the information and the system. Some training is required to use the available facilities and the system. The relations and connections which comprise the database and the binding implemented among them have to be understood to allow this approach to be effective. There are often minor syntax and keyword differences between query languages and similar programming languages. These differences lead to errors and frustrations.

10-3-4 Natural Language

The specification of queries with many parameters tends to be awkward when not supported by forms or formatted display screens. It seems then much more desirable to allow free-form English-like input. This can also provide the ability to have expressions of much greater complexity than can be obtained using formatted queries. We cannot yet expect that computers will understand English, or any other language which is natural to humans, in a general sense. The problem of using natural language in queries in a database environment is happily much less difficult than the problem of understanding English in general. In a formatted database which relates to some enterprise or problem area the user will operate in a well-defined context. A limited area of discourse makes it possible to parse queries without confusion due to the ambiguities of natural English. If natural language queries are being supported a parsing scheme which recognizes the functions of verbs, nouns, adverbs, etc. has to be present.

The schema defines the data names which are known to the system. In general, computer systems distinguish rigorously between attribute names and attribute values, even though both may have overlapping vocabularies. The structure of the internal schema representation used in SOCRATE as illustrated in Fig. 8-7 shows a dictionary which encompasses both attribute names and values from defined domains. Here it is possible to decide which query terms are values and which ones are attribute names. The database dictionary, in addition to the terms used in the schema, should include the words for the basic actions to be performed: `FIND`, `GET`, etc., as well as those words that describe common operations: `IS, HAS, EQUALS`.

Within limited fields success has been achieved in English-like communication without parsing the query according to grammatical rules. The query is tested only for word matches. If the general parsing problem is avoided, it is not fair to talk about a natural-language or English query capability. The actual effectiveness of pseudo-natural-language systems has to be carefully evaluated, since the examples presented in the literature provided by the supplier are obviously chosen to convey the strength rather than the weakness of the given approach. Pseudo-English can lead to expectations which are eventually frustrated.

Statements in pseudo-English have to be translated into a form which matches the structure of the database. Where the database has a hierarchical structure, one can expect that the query will be decomposed according to rules which generate a hierarchical subtree. When a full or partial match is found, the broom of the node found provides data elements which are relevant to the query. In network data structures interaction is required. Pseudo-English can cope well with the limited path choices, but screen selection will provide faster interaction.

Most systems today which support natural English translate the statements to a relational query format. Relational queries have a high degree of independence from the underlying database structure, unless there are many relations in the database. In that case a universal relation view, as defined in Sec. 9-1-2, can provide another intermediary step. The relational query is subsequently analyzed to permit efficient execution as described in Secs. 9-2-7 and 9-3-2, or it may be mapped into a hierarchical or network system. If the semantics of a databases network structure can be exploited for query processing, the apparent intelligence of the natural-language understanding processes can be greatly enhanced.

Example 10-7 shows the capability of a powerful translator from English to a formal propositional language [Kellogg[71]].

Example 10-7   Processing a Natural-Language Query

```
Are all large western cities smoggy?
```
is transformed to
```
RETURN(TOTAL(IMPLICATION(IS large,(IS western,city)),smoggy))
```
for database processing. The evaluation of the expression begins by finding a relationship of type IS and selecting tuples with attribute value western for objects of domain city. A subsequent IS operation can be applied to this result relation, etc. We have encountered relational queries in Sec. 9-2 and will not show further examples here.

The relational approach provides the sharpest definition of queries. Not all users will be comfortable with the mathematical formalism implied. If we wish to allow queries to a relational database in either interactive, tabular, or English form, a query translator will translate from those forms to the relational form. It may be instructive as part of the learning process to present the result of the translation from the original statements. The formal form will define the query more thoroughly. The user may eventually want to use or modify the statements in this rigorous form.

10-3-5 Summary

Much work remains to be done in the area of query processing. It is necessary to understand the needs of the user and the human factors in information search in order to find the proper balance between flexibility and expressiveness, ease of use and tedium. There are few examples where operational databases containing important information have been combined with fast-access techniques, adequate interaction capability, and good query languages. The pseudo-English used in query systems has often been more unnatural than computer languages. In hierarchical systems the need to specify accurately the level for the conditional and for the response attributes has been obscured by attempts at query-language simplification. In network approaches the path-choice problem may need interaction during the query processing for information retrieval.

The existence of valuable data in the database is of paramount importance. The best conceivable system will remain a toy if it does not warrant usage, and some primitive systems have seen intensive use because the data they contained was valuable to the community of users.

10-4 DYNAMICS OF INFORMATION-RETRIEVAL SYSTEMS

The design of information retrieval using databases has to match three components. For each of those components a number of choices have been presented.

Some of the choices are strongly associated with the data contents and the tools applicable to manage such data. The interface choice may be made on the basis of both technical suitability and their appropriateness in regard to users' involvement with the system and their sophistication. The underlying *database system* choices determine the the manner in which the data structure is presented to the interface, but also the performance for classes of usage.

Table 10-1 presents a summary. At any specific time, for one specific user, the choice from each column of the menu may be clear. The system designer cannot select just one item from each of three courses on the menu; there are often multiple types of users, and even one category of users may need to move from one approach to another as their objectives change over time.

Table 10-1   Components of an Information-retrieval System

Retrieval methodology	User interfaces	Database organization
	Interrogative	
Fact retrieval	Interactive	Relational
Statistical inference	Tabular	Hierarchical
Deductive inference	Procedural	Linked
	Pseudo English	
	Natural English	

Example 10-8   Phases of Database Usage

Data exploration The initial task is the acquisition of simple facts of immediate interest, i.e., how much oil reserves exist here or there, how much oil is consumed in summer or winter. The correctness of data elements is individually verified and provides a basis for further development of the database. Subsequently a researcher wants to develop an understanding regarding the distribution mechanism and the balance of available resources. Aggregations of resources and consumers are derived and presented to aid in concept formation. Interesting relationships lead to hypotheses which can be verified using statistical techniques on the data.

Evaluation of Hypotheses When a quantitative understanding of the problems has been achieved, alternate solutions can be evaluated. Now relationships between supply and demand, preferences, psychological habits, capital spending, etc., may have to be explored using techniques of deductive inference. Throughout this process the users will have changed in their understanding and expectations of the database and its capabilities.

Planning and Execution In the end there will be a proposal for action and the collected data have to be presented for financial analysis. Here tabulation and graphics to present projections will be useful.

10-4-1 User Dynamics

The change of users' needs over time is illustrated in Example 10-8 using a case of current interest, analysis of energy problems. The example demonstrates how user needs will shift over time in a single application. Other, parallel applications will show differing patterns at differing time frames.

It may be impossible to build single systems that will satisfy the full range of requirements. It is desirable, however, to be able to specify at a conceptual level which choices were made in the design and implementation of the information-retrieval system. The definition of choices at a high architectural level will considerably simplify the lower-level implementation decisions regarding file system support processes, update capability, and cost versus performance trade-offs.

10-4-2 System Dynamics

By definition one specific data value can provide information to a user only once, unless the user has forgotten data received earlier. An information-retrieval system hence remains valuable only if there is continuing change in data contents, data-analysis capability, or users. In order to operate an adequate information-retrieval system, the adequacy of the output in terms of providing useful information has to be monitored, and a mechanism has to be established to enhance both data organization and content as required.

Utilization statistics are one measure of database usage. Attributes which are frequently accessed can be provided with indexes to increase access speeds. Relationships which are frequently investigated can be bound as stored relations or can be materialized through pointer connections. Users who interact with the database system will adapt faster to the system than the systems will adapt to them, and hence exclusive reliance on utilization statistics is not adequate.

The fact that a certain type of retrieval has been used only once in the last year may be due to the fact that the system took more than 24 hours to generate the response, discouraging the user from any further attempts.

Figure 10-9 illustrates the monitoring process for the information-retrieval system. Automatic adaptation of systems to changes in usage has been considered. The potential damage if an infrequent query, asked in an emergency, cannot be answered within an acceptable interval, makes automation risky. Aggregate performance should only be optimized subject to constraints in response time for important queries and update transactions.

In practice the database system will not be judged only by its intrinsic quality but also by its response to the needs of users. Inadequate, unreliable communications systems connected to a good database-management system frustrate users. Existence of inadequate, erroneous data in the database will be equally frustrating. There exists the chicken-and-egg problem that a database system will not produce information without a large volume of high-quality data, and at the same time, it is difficult to convince users of the importance of collecting and verifying large amounts of data unless the system provides useful information in a responsive manner.

Over the lifetime of a database system, the costs of data acquisition and maintenance, will greatly exceed the cost of the database system itself. Procedures to test the content of the database for correctness, integrity, and logical completeness are all part of an effective continuing operation. Their development is part of the system design process and their quality will determine the effectiveness of the system over the long haul. The chapters which follow will discuss these aspects of database systems.

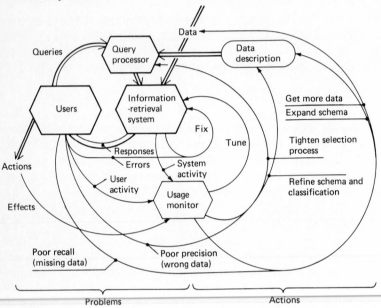

Figure 10-9 Monitoring of an information retrieval system.

BACKGROUND AND REFERENCES

The area of information retrieval is nearly as old as the field of computing itself. As soon as reasonably large external memories were available, people used these memories to store data for data retrieval. An issue of the *Communications of the ACM* (vol.5 no.1, *Jan.* 1962) surveyed the state of the field at that time. The field has been followed for the American Society for Information Systems (ASIS) in Cuadra[66:75] and Williams[76-81]. The literature on information retrieval, although the application of its concepts is critically dependent on database technology, does not provide a comprehensive view of database issues. An early comprehensive view is by Langefors[61]. Nearly every *Proceedings of the National Computer Conferences*, published by AFIPS, contains several papers describing information-retrieval systems. The ACM special interest group on information retrieval (ACM-SIGIR) has published *Proceedings of the Symposia on Information Storage and Retrieval* in 1969 and 1971. Another ACM publication is the *Proceedings of the SIGPLAN-SIGIR Interface meeting on Programming Languages and Information Retrieval* in 1973 (Nance[75]). A source of related material is the *Journal of the Association for Computational Linguistics*.

Much information retrieval work has been oriented toward the management of bibliographic data and textual material. Examples of bibliographic systems are SMART (Salton[75]), LEADER (Kasarda[72]), and SPIRES (Martin in Walker[71]). A state-of-the-art summary from a workshop in Palo Alto (Jan. 1971) has been edited by Walker[71], and an AFIPS seminar oriented toward "computer types" at the 1972 FJCC is presented by Clifton[73]. A comprehensive reference is Lancaster[79]; the subject has also been covered by Kent[71] and Meadow[73]. Kochen[74] describes many societal issues of information retrieval.

Some systems TRAMP(Ash[68]), CONVERSE32 (Kellogg[71]) used LEAP-type relations while RDF (Levien[67]) is based on a complex network of relationships. Salton[62] considers queries in tree structures, and Schroeder in Kerr[75] describes an information-retrieval system using trees. Craig[67] describes DEACON, a system using ring structures. Reisner[75] and Rothnie[75] compare relational query alternatives. Several retrieval systems based on the relational calculus are found in Appendix B. Procedural versus nonprocedural queries are evaluated by Welty[81].

Statistical inference is supported by systems described by Rattenbury[74] (OSIRIS), Weyl[75] and Wiederhold[75] (TOD), Joyce[76] (REGIS), and Chan[81] (SUBJECT). Automation of statistical inference is explored by Blum[80] (RX).

Important work in the area of deductive inference processing has been published by Levien[67], Green[68], and Kellogg[71]. Simmons[70] surveyed the state of the art in intelligent query systems. Biss[71] and Minker[78] present later developments. Related papers appear in Gallaire[78,81]. Representations of data in such systems is the topic of papers in Findler[79]. A recent experiment by Dahl[82] uses PROLOG.

Senko[73] and Ghosh[74] treat the problem of finding the access path to data, beginning from the schema entries, in a formal model. Chang[78] uses a schema describing the connections among relations for query processing. The structural connections are exploited by ElMasri[81] to simplify queries. Davidson[80] uses lexical database relations to help parse the queries.

King in Nance[75] proposes an interaction protocol for casual users in business. Dana[72] presents a report generator. Query by example has been developed by Zloof[77]; evaluations have been made by Thomas[75] and by Reisner[77]. Semple[67] and Yu[82] discuss access using weights. Access to a database via a graphic color-display interface is demonstrated by Herot[80].

Cheatham[62] presented a formal approach to English queries, while Zadeh[72] and Chang[78] consider the handling of *fuzzy* queries. How interaction can make pseudo-English effective is shown by Rubinoff[68]. Hammer[80K] and King[81Q] use additional semantic knowledge to help with query processing.

Codd in Shneiderman[78] presents a methodology for interactive natural language query handling. English in a limited context is used by Woods[73] on moonrock data, and by Shortliffe[73] for antibiotic selection. Cooper[76] presents a detailed example of an algorithm to parse English-language queries. Work on an adaptable processor (REL) is described by The use of English as a query language is questioned by Montgomery[72]. Recent progress is due to Harris[77], Sagalowicz[77], Waltz[78], and Hendrix[78]. We see natural language systems now becoming commercially available; some entries are listed in Appendix B.

User expectations are described by Nichols and by Sibley in Jardine[74]. Sibley[74] and Ghosh in Furtado[79] describe experience with very large national systems, and Lancaster[69] evaluates MEDLARS.

EXERCISES

1 Locate a description of an information retrieval system, and

   a Describe its objective

   b Describe the data structure used

   c Describe the database structure used

   d Describe the query method

   e Discuss the appropriateness of the choices made

   f Give suggestion for improvements.

2 Which category of information retrieval can benefit fron the use of deriving data on entry or on query, as described in Sec. 8-3-4?

3 Formulate a query based on the **TEXT** option of GIS to specify the result shown in Examples 10-1 and 10-4. Comment on the suitability of weights.

4 Devise a DBTG-type structure for the data of Example 10-2.

Chapter 11

Methods to Gain
Reliability

As far as we know, our computer has never had an undetected error.

Conrad H. Weisert

Union Carbide Corporation

This, and the two chapters which follow, discuss the areas that, in combination, are concerned with the security of database systems. The term *security* is used here to describe the protection of systems and their contents from destruction. The term security has often been used in a more narrow sense, but with a scope that varies from discussion to discussion. We will not cover the aspects of security which concern themselves with issues of building and personnel security, although it is obvious that without physical security most computer-system oriented efforts can be brought to naught.

If we wish to secure a database, we will need to achieve a reliable and predictable mode of operation; we also have to provide a protection mechanism to achieve the desired control of access to the data. Finally, we have to assure that there will be no destructive interference as multiple users share access to the database.

These three issues of security are presented in Chaps. 11, 12, and 13:

> *Reliability:* improving the probability that the system does what it is instructed to do.
>
> *Protection:* understanding, organizing, and controlling access to data in accordance with specified rights.
>
> *Integrity:* maintenance of security in a system where multiple users are permitted to access the system and share the database.

There is clearly a strong interrelation among these areas. The partitioning is chosen to simplify the presentation. Some general issues on cost and benefits related to security problems will be discussed in Chap. 12 on the protection of data.

11-1 RELIABILITY

Reliability is achieved when a computer system, both hardware and software, always produces correct results. One obvious problem is the determination of correctness. We use the term *fault* to denote the cause, and the word *error* for the manifestation of a fault. Lack of correctness is demonstrated by the occurrence of an error.

Hardware, database design, programs, and data input mechanisms all contain faults. Program faults or *bugs* are familiar to us all.

Current methods of program debugging by testing are clearly inadequate, since they are typically limited to the verification of a few sample computations. Analysis of the program structure can create a test plan which assures that each program section is executed once, but testing of every possible execution sequence is rarely feasible, since the number of combinations is nearly always too large. Extreme values of input data can often induce errors and are useful in testing.

The application of structured programming techniques should lead to a reduction and better identification of *bugs* but will still not eliminate them. Formal verification of programs attempts to eliminate faults. These techniques depend on a detailed specification of the data transforms, and here a comprehensive database model is essential.

We will not discuss the important specific issue of program faults further but will concentrate on methods to deal with all kinds of faults found in databases. Procedures of integrity monitoring (Sec. 13-3) can also help in the maintenance of database reliability.

In order to produce correct results, we need correct data and correct algorithms, and the system has to carry out the algorithms correctly. In each of these areas the problem reduces to two subproblems:

1 The existence of a fault has to be detected, or the absence of faults has to be proved.

2 When an error is detected, a means of correcting and recovering from the error has to be available.

Frequently, a single technique may provide both detection and also some restoration capability. We will discuss some common techniques in the light of these two aspects and then evaluate how these methods may be combined into a system that will have desirable characteristics.

Failure Probabilities Computer systems are composed of many parts that are prone to failure, so that success in a given time period is achieved only if none of the parts fails. For q parts having each a failure probability of p_f the probability of successful operation is

$$p_{success} = (1 - p_f)^q \qquad\qquad 11\text{-}1$$

We will look at the effects of failures using some simple examples.

If 10 parts, each with a probability of failure of 1% for a given operation, are used in a logically serial arrangement, the probability of achieving the correct result is

$$p_{success} = 0.99^{10} = 0.904$$

which amounts to a failure probability of nearly 10%.

For 100 such parts, the probability of system operation decreases to

$$p_{success} = 0.99^{100} = 37\%$$

It should be noted that parallel electric circuits still have serial failure characteristics. If one bit out of a 16-bit word is not transmitted correctly between storage and a device controller, the entire result is wrong.

MTBF Computer-system components have very high reliability probabilities. The failure rate of modern electronics is not greatly affected by the number of operations carried out, and hence is specified in terms of operational time. A typical *mean time between failures* (MTBF) for a highly loaded digital switching transistor is 40 000 hours. This time is equivalent to an error probability of only 0.000 025 per hour. A moderately large system containing and using 10 000 such components would, however, have a probability of only 0.78 of avoiding an error in an hour's span or a MTBF of 1.3 hours. The error rate of components is significantly reduced by conservative usage and a controlled environment. In practice, not all component errors will have a detectable effect in terms of the computer's results, since not all components are contributing to the operation of the computer at any one time, and hence are not actually in use. On highly loaded systems failure rates do increase.

Storage-System Failures Mechanical parts of computer systems have higher error rates than electronics. Magnetic storage devices, communication lines, and data entry and output devices are quite prone to errors. Human beings are essential elements of computer systems and show even higher error rates.

We can make, however, one important observation about modern disk drives. *A block will be written either completely or not at all.* The electrical and mechanical inertia in these systems is typically sufficient to allow a write operation, once started, to complete completely and correctly. This means that, if blocks are properly managed, a high level of system reliability can be achieved.

Failure Control It is important to realize the continued existence of faults and to provide resources to cope with errors as well as to prevent errors. Early detection is needed to stop propagation of errors. For types of errors which occur frequently, automatic correction or recovery is required. Since the same error can be due to more than one fault, the proper recovery procedure may not be obvious. Halting the entire system whenever errors occur can have a very high cost not only in terms of system unavailability but also in terms of confusion generated if the cause for a halt is not clear to everyone affected. In a chaotic environment, fixes and temporary patches are apt to endanger the database more than a reasonable and consistent error recovery algorithm. The formalization of error recovery also enables the application of lessons learned during failure situations, so that the fraction of cases for which the error recovery procedure is correct increases over time.

MTTR The time required to get a system going again is referred to as the *mean time to repair* (MTTR). In this context repair can range from complete fault identification and correction to merely logging of the error occurrence and restarting of the system. The MTTR can be reduced by having a duplicated computer system. This means that more than twice the number of components have to be maintained, since additional components will be needed to connect the two systems. The trade-off between decreased MTBF due to system complexity and increased MTTR has to be carefully evaluated in any system where a high availability of the database is desired.

Use of Replicated Systems A duplicate computer facility can be used fully in parallel, or it can be used to provide backup only, and process less critical work up to the time a failure occurs. In the first case, the MTTR can be as small as the time that it takes to detect the error condition and disconnect the faulty computer.

In the second case, programs running in the backup computer will have to be discontinued, and the processing programs from the failing machine will have to be initiated at a proper point. Here a larger MTTR can be expected; the MTTR in fact may be greater than the time it takes to reinitiate processing on the primary machine if the failures detected were transient. A failure type analysis will be required to decide which of these two alternatives will be best. Making the decision itself may add to the MTTR.

With two machines which operate in parallel, recognition of a discrepancy of results detects the error but does not allow the system to determine automatically which of the duplicated units caused the error. Replication of systems or subsystems in triplicate, *triple modular redundancy* (TMR), has been used in unusually critical applications. This approach allows two computers to annul the output of the failing computer.

The space shuttle system uses four computers, so that TMR can be maintained even after a computer has failed. A fifth one is available as a spare.

Since the cost of processors is dropping rapidly, replication of processing units is becoming more common, and some "*non-stop*" transaction systems are now being delivered with a minimum of 2 and up to 16 processors.

In practice many computer circuit failures are transient and will not repeat for a long time. Such errors may be due to a rare combination of the state of the system, power fluctuations, electrical noise, or accumulation of static electricity. Hence a *retry* capability, replication of a process along the time axis, can provide many of the same benefits.

In the remainder of this chapter, we will avoid the discussion of complete system replication, since this is a problem which involves the architecture of the entire computer hardware and operating systems. Selective replication, however, can be employed in various ways by file and database systems. Typical hardware replication is the provision of extra disk units, tape drives, or controllers.

Availability The effect of dealing with faults as seen by the user is often measured as the *availability*, namely the fraction of time that the system is capable of production.

$$\text{Availability} = 1 - \frac{\text{time for scheduled maintenance}}{\text{scheduled maintenance interval}} - \frac{\text{MTTR}}{\text{MTBF}} \qquad \text{11-2}$$

The availability measure does not include the aftereffects of failures to the user. Whenever a failure occurs, the current transaction is lost. In an environment with long transactions the cost of recovery increases substantially with a poor MTBF. If the users depend greatly on the system for running their business, a poor MTTR will be unacceptable.

Recovery Components Those components which are used only to provide recovery capability should be isolated so that their failures do not affect the productive operation of the entire system. Isolation will increase the net MTBF. Errors in recovery components should, however, generate a warning signal, so that repair action can be undertaken. The repair response should be carefully and formally specified, taking into account the possible effects due to insufficient backup during the repair period. Where file integrity is more important than system availability, an immediate controlled shutdown may be in order. There is a tendency by computer operations staff to continue the provision of services, which they view as their major task, rather than initiate repair procedures to eliminate faults that seem not to affect current system operations.

11-2 REDUNDANCY

Redundancy is obtained when data units (bytes, words, blocks, etc.) are expanded to provide more information than is strictly necessary. The data units can be checked for internal consistency. If they are found to be in error they may be corrected.

11-2-1 Parity

A simple form of redundancy is obtained by adding a parity bit to elemental data units. Characters on tape or in computer memory frequently have a parity bit added when they are initially generated. The count of the number of bits of value 1 in the character representation is termed the *Hamming weight*. If the character is represented by 8 bits, the parity bit in the ninth position will be set so that the Hamming weight of the combination is odd (odd parity encoding) or even (even parity encoding). Odd parity is the preferred code, since it avoids any occurrences of all 0 or all blank sections on the recording medium, which is useful to assure

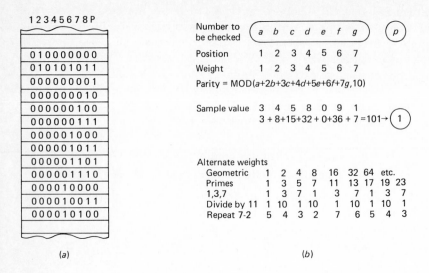

1 2 3 4 5 6 7 8 P
0 1 0 0 0 0 0 0 0
0 1 0 1 0 1 0 1 1
0 0 0 0 0 0 0 0 1
0 0 0 0 0 0 0 1 0
0 0 0 0 0 0 1 0 0
0 0 0 0 0 0 1 1 1
0 0 0 0 0 1 0 0 0
0 0 0 0 0 1 0 1 1
0 0 0 0 0 1 1 0 1
0 0 0 0 0 1 1 1 0
0 0 0 0 1 0 0 0 0
0 0 0 0 1 0 0 1 1
0 0 0 0 1 0 1 0 0

Number to be checked a b c d e f g p

Position	1	2	3	4	5	6	7
Weight	1	2	3	4	5	6	7

Parity = MOD$(a+2b+3c+4d+5e+6f+7g,10)$

Sample value   3   4   5   8   0   9   1
$3 + 8 + 15 + 32 + 0 + 36 + 7 = 101 \rightarrow (1)$

Alternate weights
Geometric	1	2	4	8	16	32	64	etc.
Primes	1	3	5	7	11	13	17	19 23
1,3,7	1	3	7	1	3	7	1	3 7
Divide by 11	1	10	1	10	1	10	1	10 1
Repeat 7-2	5	4	3	2	7	6	5	4 3

(a)   (b)

Figure 11-1 Parity.(a) Section of tape with odd parity. (b) Check-digit computation.

detection of the existence of a character, especially on tapes. Figure 11-1a shows odd-parity encoding for some 8-bit characters on a 9-track tape.

Odd parity produces a code with a minimum Hamming weight of 1. The counting of bits is done easily by computer hardware, and some machines have specific instructions for bit counting. Most machines perform the encoding and checking processes, until an error occurs, without user intervention.

The addition of the one parity bit doubles the number of possible symbols that a code can transmit. Half of these codes are not valid characters and should not occur in the received input. Their appearance hence signals an error condition. The number of bits which are different between the intended and actual code received is termed the *Hamming distance* of the two codes. The Hamming distance is, of course, equal to the difference in the Hamming weights of the two codes.

Simple parity coding is well suited to the communication-oriented processes in computing. Parity coding is independent of the content of the data. This is both an advantage, in that it can be universally applied, and a disadvantage, since it cannot detect errors related to the content of the data. Techniques similar to parity encoding are also used for numbers which are transmitted outside of computer systems. Decimal identification numbers may have check digits appended which are verifiable. Since accidental transposition of digits is a frequent error, the check digit is best computed not as a simple sum but as a sum of products as shown in Fig. 11-1b. Only a one-digit remainder of the sum is retained for checking. An interchange of 3 and 4 in the sample will generate a check digit $p = 0$ instead of $p = 1$. Many systems invert the check digit to simplify checking, so that $p = 1$ becomes 9.

Modulo 10, as used in Fig. 11-1b, will not detect certain transposition errors between alternate columns; in the sample a transposition of 5 and 0 will not be detected. Because of the high frequency of transposition errors, use of modulo 9 or 11 ($p = 10 \rightarrow 0$) is preferred even though it reduces the power of the check digit. Digits in the position equal to the modulus are not checked at all using the simple successive arithmetic weights scheme. Alternate weight assignments which have been used are also shown in Fig. 11-1b; the series $(1, 10, 1, \ldots)$ is obtained in effect by division of the number by 11.

Only detection is provided by parity encoding, and even the detection capability is limited. Whereas with simple parity all one-bit errors will be detected, reversals of an even number of bits within a single character will not be noted. In situations where errors are apt to occur in batches or bursts, the detection probability remains high since a number of sequential characters will be affected, many of which will have a detectable parity error.

11-2-2 Duplication

Duplication of data is another simple form of achieving redundancy. It is used during input, in some tape systems, and in the storage of critical data. If the data are processed through different channels and then matched, the error-detection probability will be quite high. To decide which copy to use for correction requires another indicator, for instance, a parity error. This approach is hence mainly effective for hardware faults, program faults will create the same error in both paths. The cost of duplicate entry and maintenance of data is, of course, quite high. Keypunching with subsequent verification of the punched cards by retyping and matching is an example of duplication of data during one small interval of the information-processing cycle. The original document must remain available to arbitrate when an error is found.

When information is copied or transmitted, a duplicate will exist for some length of time. It can be useful to design the system so that this duplicate remains available until correctness of the copy has been verified. The detection of an error can be used to initiate recopying of the data. This technique is prevalent in the transmission of data over transmission lines. Not only is the vulnerability of data during transmission high, but the size of the damaged areas is frequently large. A reason for errors to occur in bursts is that the data are transmitted serially, using separate clocks, one on each end, which are used to define the individual bit positions. A relatively long time will be required to resynchronize these clocks after a timing error. Burst errors are also caused by transients induced when lines are being switched in the dial-telephone network.

Maintenance of completely duplicate files on disks is rarely feasible on general-purpose computers. The cost of completely duplicated storage and of extra channel capacity may also be excessive if one considers the current high reliability of computer storage devices. Complete data redundancy also increases the time required for file update. The computer systems designed for *non-stop* operation have fully duplicated channels and controllers to avoid delays in writing to duplicated or mirrored disk units.

To achieve much of the reliability that a duplicated system can provide, a small amount of selected critical information may be replicated. In a file system, this may be the index information or the linkage between records. The damage due to loss of a data element can be expected to be minor compared with the effect of the loss of a pointer which causes all data beyond a certain point to become unavailable. Selective replication will be combined with other error-detection mechanisms, perhaps parity, so that it can be determined which copy is the correct one. Then the erroneous file may be restored. In case of doubt the data file contents, rather than pointer information, will be used for correction.

In order to avoid some of the overhead that would be caused by writing indexes or pointer values into duplicate blocks, a copy of the information required to build the linkages may be written as a preface to the data records themselves. This practice avoids additional seek and rotational overhead times and only adds to the record transmission time and storage cost. Restoration of damaged indexes is now more expensive, since it involves analysis of the bulk of the data files. It is hoped that such a recovery action is an infrequent occurrence.

11-2-3 Error-Correcting Codes

Error-correcting codes provide a high degree of the benefits obtained by replication of data without all the costs. Here a certain number of bits are added to each data element. These check bits are produced similarly to the parity bits, but each check bit represents different groupings of the information bits. These groups are organized in such a fashion that on error an indication of which bit is in error will result. The principle is shown in Fig. 11-2.

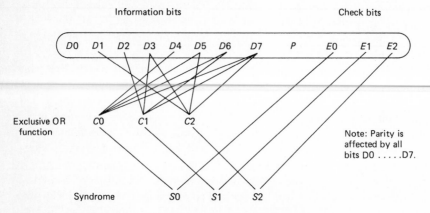

Figure 11-2 The idea behind error correction.

If the parity bit P indicates that there is an error, the three error-code bits C0, C1, C2 can be generated from the data bits and compared with the checkbits E0, E1, E2 that were carried along. A difference in these bits is obtained in the syndrome S, and this will indicate (in binary) the number of the bit in error. For example, an error in D5 will cause a *syndrome* of 101, implicating data bit 5.

This example is incomplete, since it does not provide error control for the parity and the error-correction bits themselves. The number of check bits r required for codes which can correct ec bits and can definitely detect errors of up to ed bits is determined by a minimum Hamming weight of

$$Hw_{min} = 2ec + ed + 1 \qquad\qquad \text{11-3}$$

for the complete error-correcting data codes.

If a frame of coded information has a total of n bits it can represent of 2^n codes. For the byte with 8 data bits in Fig. 11-2 the value of $n = d + r = 12$. We can now consider that out of the 2^n codes are received, only 2^d codes are correct. Out of the remainder $(2^n - 2^d)$ those codes which have a low $(ec = 1, 2, \ldots)$ Hamming distance to any of the correct codes are used for correction by being converted to their neighbors. The correct codes have to be seperated by a Hamming distance of at least $2ec$. The remainder of the codes is undecodable, and hence will detect, but not correct an error.

Procedures are available to select a code transform matrix. which will generate the least number of check bits r, from the information bits d, given ec, ed. From the transformation matrix, a check matrix can be obtained which will generate a 0 if the code received was correct (or possibly had more than ed errors) and which generates on error a bit-string which can be used to correct an incorrect code, if there were not more than ec errors. An example for $n = 7, d = 4, r = 3, ed = 3, ec = 1$ is shown in Fig. 11-3.

Assuring that all errors involving a limited number of bits are checked is appropriate when errors occur independently. For $ec = 1$ and $ed = 2$, it has been shown that the minimum number of check bits required is determined by

$$2^{r-1} \geq r + d > 2^{r-2} \qquad\qquad 11\text{-}4$$

We see that for $d = 8$ this capability is obtained with $r = 5$ check bits.

Position	1	2	3	4	5	6	7
Data pos.			$D0$		$D1$	$D2$	$D3$
Sample value			1		1	0	0
Hamming codes							
Pos. 1	$H0 = \text{ODD}($		$D0$	$+$	$D1$	$+$	$D3) \to 1$
Pos. 2	$H1 = \text{ODD}($	$D0$			$+$	$D2 +$	$D3) \to 0$
Pos. 3			$H2{=}\text{ODD}(D1 +$		$D2$	$+$	$D3) \to 0$
Stored	1	0	1	0	1	0	0
Fault					*		
Read	1	0	1	0	0	0	0
Check 1	$C0 = \text{ODD}($		$D0$	$+$	$D1$	$+$	$D3) \cdot 0, S0 = 1$
Check 2	$C1 = \text{ODD}($	$D0$			$+$	$D2 +$	$D3) \cdot 0, S1 = 0$
Check 3			$C2{=}\text{ODD}(D1 +$		$D2$	$+$	$D3) \cdot 1, S2 = 1$
Syndrome is 5							
Correct position 5					X		
Corrected data	1		1		1	0	0

Figure 11-3 Hamming-code error correction.

The number of check bits required is a logarithmic function of the length of the data unit. This fact makes the cost in terms of bits relatively low when the units are long $(d \gg 8)$, although the circuitry becomes more complex.

Other error-correcting codes, such as Bose-Chaudhuri and Fire codes, provide similar capabilities but are more advantageous for variable-length blocks, since they are cyclic and can correct errors occurring in a data stream rather than only by transformation of a complete block. They also can be designed to cope better with burst-type, that is, dependent bit-errors.

The correction of the error by hardware will delay transmission by the length of the error-correcting cycle. However, since a longer cycle uses relatively fewer check bits, an increase in net transmission rate will occur. Advertised data-transmission rates generally include only the net information bits, so that the actual disk-to-controller bit transfer occurs at a higher rate. The difference between the data and the real transfer rate can be great; the 6250-bpi tapes and mass-storage units described in Sec. 2-1-1 have actual bit densities of approximately 9000 bpi.

Occasional but large bursts of errors found in communication lines make the use of error-correcting codes in data transmission less profitable. Here detection and retransmit techniques are prevalent. Files, however, are maintained on closely coupled devices with controllers which have the logical capability to generate error codes as well as to check and correct errors. Error correction here permits a drastic increase in storage density.

11-2-4 Batch Checking

Where data are manually processed before submission to an input transaction or where additional software checking is desired, *checksums* or *batch totals* may be employed. A checksum is the sum of all values in a critical column. Checksums are typically computed before data entry and within the transaction, and these sums are compared. This method is conceptually identical to parity checking, but since the result is a large number rather than a single bit, the error-detection probability is quite high. For a large batch the added data quantity remains relatively low.

The method cannot be used for correction, except for some transpositions. Transposition of adjacent digits is a common error in manual entry and can easily be spotted in checksum comparisons, since transposition causes a checksum with errors in two adjacent digits, with a digit error sum of 9; an example is given in Fig. 11-4.

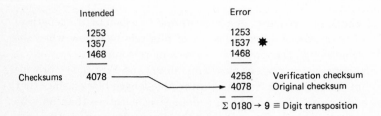

Figure 11-4 Example of checksum.

Another technique to avoid errors in manually prepared data is the use of *transaction sequence numbers.* Each batch of input documents for one transaction is assigned a sequential identifier and this number is also entered. The data-entry program can check that all transactions have been received. If it is important that transactions are processed in the same sequence, the check can simply verify that transaction numbers increase by one. Many such systems check transactions in this manner, but the sequentiality constraint may place unnecessary constraints on operations. If one batch is late, all processing ceases.

11-2-5 Natural Redundancy

Even without explicit addition of redundant information, we find that much data coding is highly redundant. A prime example is information coded in English or any other natural language. If the data processed is English text, a dictionary look-up can be used to detect errors, and with intelligent processing, as done by human beings when reading text with typographical errors, a large fraction of single-character errors might corrected.

Frequently the number of choices in coded data are much more limited than the whole of the English language, and simple searches, possibly to lexicons accessed directly or via indexes, can determine whether an entry is valid. Such look-ups are performed routinely to verify items entered such as employee names, identification codes, and similar data elements in many processing systems.

There frequently is a considerable amount of redundancy within the character encoding itself; and this too can be used for error detection. An 8-bit code, for instance, allows 256 characters, but frequently the data are restricted to uppercase letters (26) or alphanumeric (36) characters (see Sec. 14-2). Filtering to detect erroneous characters can be done at little incremental effort during other text-processing operations and can prevent serious problems which may be caused when wrong characters enter communications channels. A bad character may have unexpected control functions such as mode shifts, disconnect, or screen erase on displays.

11-2-6 Error Compensation

Careful system design can reduce the effect of some errors. As an example we will cite a case where data is acquired periodically.

The electric meter on a house is read every month. If a transcription error occurs, there may be an overbilling in one month, but next month, if the reading is entered correctly, there will be a compensating underbilling. There is, in fact, a duplicate memory here; one is the meter and the other is the computer file.

If the meter were reset after each reading, a transcription error would not be compensated.

Wherever errors are not compensated the database can diverge from the real world. If an inventory is maintained using counts of items sold and items purchased, periodic verification is essential.

11-2-7 Buffer Protection

File data are most vulnerable while they are in primary memory, especially where computer systems are used for many parallel tasks or undergo frequent change.

    Checksums taken of a buffer contents may be used to verify that data have not been changed by other than approved procedure. The maintenance and frequent recalculation of checksums can be quite costly.

    Another alternative to protect buffers is the use of *barriers*. These consist of a pair of codes which are apt to occur infrequently. The buffer contents itself is not verified, but the barriers are matched at critical times. Such checks will prevent the use of buffers which have been damaged by overruns or overflows from other areas due to loop or limit code failures. Since a great fraction of programming errors are due to limit failures, and since these errors are not easily detected by their perpetrators, the use of check barriers can provide a fair amount of protection at low cost. No correction capability is provided.

    A barrier value which is not a defined character code, not a normalized floating-point number, a very large negative integer, and not a computer instruction is depicted in Fig. 11-5.

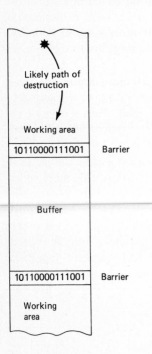

Figure 11-5 Buffer barriers.

11-2-8 Feedback

We discussed in Sec. 5-2 how human error detection can be aided by interactive selection and playback. It cannot be emphasized too much that the best quality control consists of frequent generation of useful output to the various levels of personnel involved in data collection, preparation, and entry. Neither mechanical means nor constant exhortations will keep the contents of a database at an acceptable level when the data are not used regularly.

    It is especially important to assure correctness of data which will be stored for long periods of time. A failure in a file of historic data is frequently not correctable, since the source material will have turned to some functional equivalent of dust.

11-3 TRANSACTION RELIABILITY

In the previous sections we have treated general aspects of file-system reliability, and we can now consider issues specific to databases. We relate issues of database reliability with the successful completion of transactions. As presented in Sec. 1-7-5 we define a transaction as a program which changes the state of the database so that, if the initial state of the database was correct and the transaction does not introduce an error due to a fault or bad input data, the state of the database is again correct after the transaction has successfully terminated. If the transaction does not terminate properly, none of its effects should be visible in the database.

The issue of input errors is often ignored in papers discussing transaction control. We do consider input errors in the approaches that will be presented.

We now analyze transactions and in Sec. 11-3-2 techniques to deal with errors.

11-3-1 Two-Phase Transactions

A transaction can fail for a number of reasons. It can find that the input data is not correct or does not match the database. The input data can be poorly formatted or incomplete, it can be outside of schema limits, or it can require computations with data values which do not exist in the database.

The transaction can also find that it cannot proceed because of a lack of resources. Perhaps some needed blocks are currently held by another user, as discussed in Sec. 13-2. Finally the computer itself may fail or *crash* during a transaction.

In order to minimize the effect of a failure, the actions in a transaction are best separated into two phases. During the first phase the transaction acquires all the resources needed for its execution, including any blocks it needs to update. It also carries out any specified computations. Any blocks which do not destroy the prior state of the database can be written during the first phase. During the second phase all remaining changes are placed into the database, and eventually the resources held by the transaction are released.

During the first phase the transaction can terminate without having affected the database in a meaningful way. At worst some blocks have been allocated and not put into use.

Upon entering phase two, the transaction is committed to complete. A failure during the second phase, by an internal fault in the transaction or caused externally, by the system, can have affected the database. Dealing with failures in phase two requires a mechanism to complete the transaction so that a consistent state is again obtained. Phase-two failures will be avoided as much as possible, however, in a real world, they cannot be eliminated.

We can now define the point where a transaction can be aborted without a restart operation as the *commit point*. This definition leads to two cases for error recovery within a transaction:

> **Transaction abort:** An error is recognized during the processing of a transaction, prior to the commit point. An abort command is executed and the affected state of the database is rolled back to the state prior to the begin of the transaction.

Transaction restart: An error is recognized during the processing of a transaction, after the commit point. A restart command is executed and the database actions required by the transaction are completed.

At times a third type of action is required:

Transaction undo: An error is found in the database. The cause is traced to a fault in some completed transaction or to an error in the input data for that transaction. An undo transaction command is executed to correct all effects.

Some of the same techniques can be used for either restart or undo, but both cases are much more complex than transaction abort.

In some transactions it can be awkward to define a single commit point. Long and complex transactions may have been *nested* into a hierarchy.

An example can be a travel agent's trip reservation. Each subtransaction, obtaining the airline ticket, the car rental, the hotel booking, etc., can have a definite commit point. An eventual failure, say the unavailability of hotel space, can force an undo of previously committed subtransactions. Delaying the commit of the separate subtransactions can cause a loss of airline reservations while hotel space is being explored.

The complexities of commit protocols increase where the database is distributed over multiple processing nodes. The decision to commit has to be made jointly by the affected nodes. A commit-managing node may give the final go-ahead to commit to all the participating nodes when notifications of being ready-to-commit have been received from every node. Any node which has indicated a readiness to commit has to remain in a state which permits it to abort or complete the transaction until the go-ahead or an abort message has been received from the commit manager. A centralization of commit management is in conflict with the notions leading to distribution. Alternate techniques have been explored but seem to lead either to a relaxation of update consistency over the nodes or to higher management cost in terms of message transmission [GarciaMolina[81]].

We continue now with the case of simple two-phase transactions.

11-3-2 Transaction Management

In order to deal with the management of transactions we expect the operating system to include a program module called the *transaction manager*. If the operating system does not include adequate transaction services such a module may have to be supplied by the database management system. The transaction manager will receive the following control messages during the execution of a transaction:

```
Transaction begin
Transaction commit  or  Transaction abort
Transaction done
```

Each message will be acknowledged by the transaction manager. The transaction manager will also receive data from the transaction to aid in recovery, if needed.

Abort The transaction program can initiate an abort upon finding an error. The only requirement is to inform the user and the system. The system should be notified, since it may hold resources for the transaction, which should now be released. A system may also maintain logging information to aid a later recovery, and this logging information should be marked `invalid` to avoid a later restart of an erroneous transaction.

The system may also be forced to cancel a transaction if it finds errors, or the user may decide to interrupt a transaction which does not behave correctly. In either case, if the commit point has not been reached, an orderly shutdown presents no serious problem.

Completion After a crash, any transaction which had issued a commit should be completed. This means that the transaction manager needs to have sufficient information to complete the transaction. The transaction may be restarted from its beginning, or completed from its commit point. In order to complete a transaction from the commit point, any data to be written into the database must be kept securely available. In any case some secure storage is needed. We present three alternatives for achieving completion; the first one has two options.

• The *transaction log*, presented in more detail in Sec. 11-3-4, is a separate file which provides secure storage for the data blocks created in phase one and to be written in phase two. Any blocks to be written in phase two are placed on the transaction log before the commit request is granted; these blocks are called *after-images*. Any blocks that do not overwrite prior data in the database are best written directly into the database before commit; the blocks written in phase two will contain references to these blocks so that they too become part of the database during phase two.

When a restart completion is required, the transaction manager copies the after-images into the database. Any blocks already written by the interrupted transaction during its phase two are rewritten by identical blocks, and when the transaction manager's restart action is completed the database is in the desired state. The user should be notified of the successful completion.

An option of the transaction-log approach is to let the transaction manager always write the blocks. At the commit point the transaction turns the resposibility for completion of phase two of the transaction over to the transaction manager. Since the transaction manager already receives the data on the log and has the capability to complete the effect of the transaction, little incremental effort is needed. The transaction itself can terminate earlier and release its resources. The transaction manager will still have to secure the after-images prior to writing into the database. The transaction program and its submitter can be informed of the expected successful completion right after the after-images are safely stored.

• Transactions may maintain their own after-images. Then the transaction manager simply executes a *transaction restart* when completion is required. At the commit point a transaction provides a restart address. When restarted by the transaction manager it carries out its own completion. *Self-completion* is quite feasible if a transaction has some nonvolatile storage available. Some modern semiconductor memories will retain their contents so that such write blocks are retained and restart is feasible without having copied the after-images. This technique requires very careful verification of the transaction's correctness and its capability to restart. It is rarely done in commercial data-processing but is useful in some scientific environments, where data are acquired rapidly from experiments and cannot be reentered.

- The third alternative for completion is the *reexecution* of the entire transaction. Here the transaction manager obtains the name of the transaction and the input data and places it on the transaction log for safekeeping. By waiting to the commit point the transaction has already performed any checking that could have caused an internal abort, so that no erroneous transactions will be restarted.

If a committed transaction cannot be completed, the transaction must be *undone* to avoid leaving the database in an inconsistent state. The submitter of the transaction should be informed that the transaction has not been carried out. The information required to resubmit a very recent transaction which failed is typically still available at the submitter's site. A transaction manager should always inform the user when a transaction has been successfully completed, since the user at the terminal may have sensed the failure of the system and will be tempted to reenter a transaction submitted prior to a failure.

Undo   In order to undo a transaction the prior state of the database must have been preserved. Two techniques are feasible to support undo transactions:

> **Version creation**   All new or updated data to be written is placed into previously unused storage. No older data are destroyed. A pointer to the most recent valid data, the *high-water mark*, is updated only after the new data has been successfully written.
>
> **Logging and backup**   All old data are saved on a transaction-log file. When an error requires an undo, the older data are located and the files are restored to a state which eliminates the effect of the transaction. The old blocks saved are referred to as *before-images*. They should be written before the commit point.

We will deal with version creation in Sec. 11-3-3 and with logging and backup in the remainder of this chapter. Problems caused by intermingling of versions or logs from concurrent transactions are addressed in Sec. 13-2-5.

In any case it is important to reduce the probability of failure after a commit is declared. This reduction can be achieved by reducing the number of blocks which have to be written to file after the commit point.

As described when discussing completion, any blocks that can be written without destroying older data are best written before the commit point. After the commitment one or more blocks will be written which make reference to the blocks written prior to the commit point, so that now all blocks become part of the new database state. The transaction will be excellently protected from hardware failures if only one block has to be written in order to link all changed blocks into the active database, since a single block is generally written completely or not at all. This technique already mimics the notions from the versioning concept.

11-3-3 Version Creation

Any time that new data are added or old data are updated we can create a new version of the database. If we save the prior version of a database we obtain a good basis for restoration in case of errors. Periodic copies of database versions are called *backup copies* or *dumps*. They are discussed in Sec. 11-4-3.

If prior data are not overwrittten, previous versions may be kept available without copying the old data to some other device or area, Creation of an entire new version of a database is feasible if the new database consists requires rewriting much of the old data. We see this being done where small databases are created by periodic abstraction of some other database, for instance the list of invalid credit cards of some financial institution. Typically, however, a new version consists of both old and new units of data. Candidate units are areas, files, blocks, and records.

We will consider blocks to be the unit of data. A version of a database is defined as the collection of all the most up to date versions of each relative to some point in time. The current version of the database is composed of all the most block recent versions of the data blocks it covers. New blocks can be simply appended to the file storage. The address of the last block written is the *high-water mark*. A previous version can be recovered by resetting the high-water mark to an earlier state.

The notion of having versions is simple but it is obvious that the storage demands due to keeping data for all past versions can be high. Older data is kept on storage devices with the same cost and performance as current data. Maintenance of efficient access to the set of current blocks requires careful support. The use of versions is becoming feasible and necessary with the appearance of large-capacity storage devices which can write the data only once. Optical disks are the prime candidate for such techniques.

The complexity of dealing with versions relates to our demands for access performance. If a pile-file organization (Sec. 3-1) satisfies our access needs, versioning is simple. A reverse search from the high-water mark can recover any desired block of the database. Such modest requirements are rare; most files require some access organization and each data rewrite will in fact require the update of some index or access information. Issues of access management when using versions have not yet been thoroughly studied.

It appears that three schemes for access management to versions are feasible:

> **Access and data are mixed** The rewritten blocks contain the relevant access information themselves. This information will have to include the equivalent of the root index block, and the paths to the new data block.
>
> **Access indirection** The volume of block references is reduced by using indirection. The rewritten block includes only replacement information for indirect referencing, as described in Sec. 8-1-2.
>
> **Backup maintenance for access information** Only data blocks are versioned; any index or other access information is maintained in core buffers and rewritable storage. When an error occurs, index information is recreated from backup data, including the versioned data.

Support for the last scheme is provided through the same logging mechanisms used for recovery in nonversioned databases, which are introduced in Sec. 11-3-4, but versioning of the primary data will greatly reduce the logging volume.

Resetting of the database to a prior version does not solve all recovery problems. An effect of a transaction which was carried out after the transaction to be undone will also be lost if the later transaction updated the same block. More information is required if this case is to be handled correctly. Even more problematic is dealing with the effects of concurrent transactions. The activity-logging techniques described in Sec. 11-4 address these issues.

11-3-4 Transaction Execution

Transactions may be update requests with new data or may be queries. Queries do not have a second phase. The execution of update transaction is now accompanied by logging of sufficient information to guarantee abort or completion. The transaction manager, after receiving the commit request, verifies that all data required for completion have been secured and grants the transaction the permit to go ahead. In a distributed database this verification may require communication with multiple or even all nodes.

Saving of the prior database state by logging also makes the undoing of a specific transaction possible. Transaction logging is often incorporated into a larger scheme for database protection, *activity logging*, which will be covered in Sec. 11-4. The specific data elements being logged are described there. Activity logging also considers correction of erroneous output for query transactions.

The data elements logged for a transaction must be identified. The *transaction identifier* must be unique and should be serial if the effect of one transaction upon other transactions is to be evaluated. For this purpose we may assign a sequential identification number to every transaction. A time stamp with a sufficiently small time increment can also provide a sequence number. The date and time of transaction arrival is always useful.

Execution Sequence   It is in general important that the sequence in which the transactions were executed matches the sequence in which they may be restored.

If transactions A and B include update operations to the same data, say

    A: X = X + 100
    B: X = X * 2

reversing their execution sequence during recovery will create new errors.

Many operations found in commercial processing are *compatible*; i.e., their execution order does not matter. Addition and subtraction are compatible, and these dominate in financial and inventory transactions.

Transactions having operations on multiple shared data items still have to be constrained in general and keep the same execution and restart order:

If transactions C and D include apparently *compatible updates* to shared data, say

    C: X = Y + 100
    D: Y = X + 50

reversing their execution sequence during recovery will also create errors.

Still, in commercial processing many transactions are found which are not affected by changes of their execution sequence. Banking deposits and withdrawals, but not transfers between accounts, remain insensitive to the execution sequence, as do inventory updates and withdrawals, if they are not accompanied by more complex financial operations. The definition of *sequence-insensitive transactions* becomes a matter of transaction design, and this feature must be indicated to the transaction manager if advantage is to be taken of the insensitivity.

In the absence of information about sequence-insensitivity the transaction execution and reexecution will be controlled rigidly by the sequence numbers and proceed serially.

Execution Control of Distributed Transactions In a distributed system the transaction identifier should include a site number. This will make a locally unique number globally unique. Since not all subtransactions will appear at each node the number of last prior request may be shipped along to permit checking for lost subtransactions between node pairs.

Sequence numbers generated at distinct sites will not have a meaningful global ordering, but a time-stamp from a remote node may not be completely synchronized with the local time. Only in very remote sites should this difference be measurable, and users at such sites will rarely sense the effect. We had best assume in any case that users at distinct sites operate in independent time frames. This notion can be generalized to state that transactions submitted at distinct nodes will always be relatively *sequence-insensitive* to each other.

An adequate global identifier can be obtained by catenating local time and the site number. The execution and recovery sequence will be determined by this identifier. The execution sequence may then differ from the submission sequence by the difference in local and remote clocks used for the time stamps.

The identification numbers which have been created in a distributed system will move with the subtransactions through the network, and excution must occur in the same ascending order at all nodes. To assure a complete global ordering the transaction manager should grant commits only in order of transaction identifier. One node or its communication link may be tardy in submitting commit requests. The transaction manager should check that no logically prior requests from any other node are waiting. This requires sending and waiting for messages from all nodes. A tardy node may still not respond, so that the potential arrival of a logically earlier request is not known and it is not feasible to delay requests from other nodes which have arrived. A majority of responses can be used to let the transaction manager go ahead.

The transaction manager now has to deny delayed commit requests and demand an abort of the transaction. If the transaction manager receives detailed information about all activities required for completion, namely the block identifications of all blocks to be written at each node, the potential for conflict can be analyzed. If no conflict exists, a commit can be granted, even when the remote transaction request was delayed.

Another alternative is that a node wishing to commit requests a sequence number from centralized resource. Even though this scheme identifies all potential requests, it is still possible to have a subsequent failure of the requestor, so that the central transaction manager still needs the ability to skip an assigned sequence number.

11-4 ACTIVITY LOGGING

For proper restoration of a damaged database, it is necessary to reestablish the database files without the effects of an error. In Secs. 11-3-3 and 11-3-4 we have shown two methods, versioning and logging, for obtaining the database state prior to some single transaction failure. A version of the database prior to an error can be obtained by resetting a database with past versions to an earlier state or by the application of all saved *before-images* to the current state. A third alternative to reset the state is the use of a backup file, described in Sec. 11-4-3. We will now also deal with secondary transaction failures and with device failures.

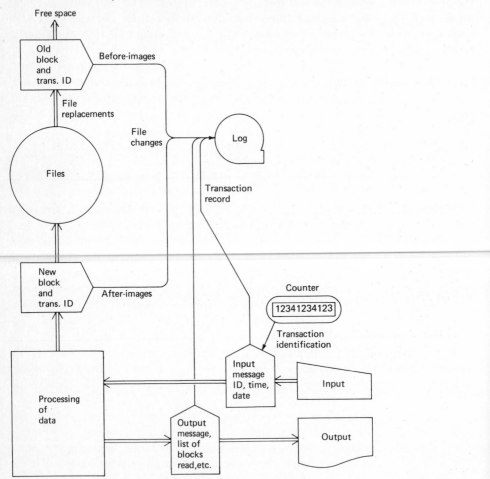

Figure 11-6 Data flow with activity logging.

Restoration of the state to a time before the error occurred will erase the effect of other transactions which caused concurrent or later changes to the database files. Subsequent transactions may, however, have used erroneous data placed into the database from a primary error and can now generate secondary errors.

If a new employee was assigned to the wrong department, any subsequent payroll and budget calculations will be wrong. If these calculations also update the database, the error can spread.

If there was a hardware failure causing actual disk damage, there may not be a current version to apply before-images to.

In order to enable complete restoration, a more extensive log can be kept of all the activities which affect the database. Data are only appended to the log; it cannot be updated. Such a log is often written onto magnetic tape, since on such a tape one can collect economically a sequential record of activities. Tapes also provide mechanically reliable storage, particularly for blocks which are already on the part of the tape which is wound on the receiving reel. Disks are finding increasing use for logs, and can reduce the labor costs. Figure 11-6 illustrates the functions which will be discussed.

11-4-1 Recovery Methods

The purpose of these logs is to allow the recreation of files. Depending on the type of error, database recovery can be performed by

Restoration: combining earlier, correct versions of the file with updates due to correct input received later. Restoration proceeds forward from a past version to the proper current state. Even when versioning is not used throughout, a version or backup copy may be created periodically.

Rollback: undoing effects of errors from the current state until an error-free state is restored. After rollback some restoration may be done.

In either case considerable information must be placed on the transaction log.

11-4-2 Elements to Be Logged

For the protection of individual transactions (Sec. 11-3-1) we required the *transaction identification*, some *after-images* for completion, and if transaction undo is also supported, corresponding *before-images*. For transaction protection the before- and after-images need not be kept longer than required to confirm successful completion of the transaction.

In order to support general restoration or rollback these elements are kept much longer, at least to a point where a complete *database backup*, as discussed in Sec. 11-4-3, is available. Also all after-images have to be logged to assure recovery from storage errors. Additional elements to be logged are the *transaction input*, the *transaction output*, and a *transaction progress thread*. Transaction progress is documented by keeping a list of records or blocks touched by the transaction. All these elements will be labeled with the transaction identifier. A transaction message, all images, and the activity thread due to one transaction are shown in Fig. 11-7.

Transaction input In order to select faulty transactions or find poor input data, the transaction request itself should be logged. The full message text entered, or a code identifying the transaction type and its input, will be copied onto the transaction log.

Replaying of all transactions inputs since the original creation of the database should enable the restoration of any subsequent database state. Any input messages of transaction that caused errors are of course eliminated from the replay. In this manner a recent and proper file status can be established. In practice the cost of such a recovery might be enormous. This technique is useful after a recovery to an earlier state by rollback or may be applied to a backup copy of the database.

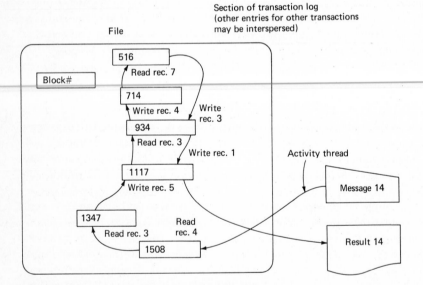

```
3/11/72   13:14:07   14   message text;
3/11/72   13:14:15   14   before-image 1117
                          after-image 1117
3/11/72   13:14:21   14   before-image 714
                          after-image 714
3/11/72   13:14:25   14   before-image 934
                          after-image 934
3/11/72   13:14:32   14   before-image 1117
                          after-image 1117
3/11/72   13:15:01   14   result text, thread =
                          R1508.4 R1347.3 W1117.5
                          R934.3 W714.3 R516.7
                          W934.3 W1117.1;
```

Section of transaction log
(other entries for other transactions
may be interspersed)

File

Block#

516
Read rec. 7

714
Write rec. 4   Write
                    rec. 3
934
Read rec. 3
              Write rec. 1   Activity thread
1117
Write rec. 5   Message 14

1347
            Read
Read rec. 3 rec. 4
              1508   Result 14

Figure 11-7 Activity log for a transaction.

In some applications transaction input logging may be very difficult. If the messages are long, it may be desirable to copy them on the log by a separate preprocessor before letting them enter the system proper. Communication pre-processors are a feature of many larger systems and can help provide backup. To increase the chance of correct execution the actual transaction processing should be initiated only when the complete message has been received and logged.

In some scientific applications, data are acquired directly from instruments at high rates. Logging of all the data received may exceed available computer resources. In these instances, backup can be provided by collecting a copy of the data near the source, possibly on analog tape recorders. This method, though, will not allow the level of automatic recovery which we can design for the commercial system where messages can be completely copied by the system onto the transaction log.

Transaction output When a transaction is completed and has left the system, another entry on the transaction-log should be made to note the completion of the transaction. This information can be used to prevent the sending of duplicate output generated by correct but reexecuted transactions during a recovery operation. If the full text of the output result is kept, the transaction log can also be used for the correction of output communication failures, which will contribute indirectly to improved maintenance of files.

If, for instance, only the output message text has been lost, the result can be replayed without executing a new transaction request which might cause a duplicate update. A general capability for a user to inquire what happened to a transaction submitted to the system improves the user interface and leads to increased system reliability.

Before-images In order to preserve the prior state of the database for use in rollback, any block acquired with the intention to update and rewrite it must be copied to the log prior to writing of the updated version. The old block written is referred to as the *before-image*. All before-images should be written before the commit point. They are also marked with the identification of their transaction.

Even though only a field or a record may be changed, the entire block may be copied to the transaction log. This done for two reasons: simpler restoration and better protection. If only the record or field to be changed is logged, the restoration requires a merge of new and old records. This merge can be complex if records vary in size, and could even create block-overflow situations. Logging field changes only can reduce the logging load significantly and is used where performance or storage problems are expected.

These before-images can be used to undo the effects of any erroneous transaction. If there have been no subsequent transactions which have further updated the bad blocks, such a transaction can be cleared, as far as the database is concerned, by replacing all the affected blocks with their before-images.

If subsequent transactions may have used the data, all subsequent before-images may be restored in order to recreate an earlier version of the database; this process is called *rollback*. In order to avoid a complete rollback, the transaction thread presented below must be known.

After-images The use of rollback or of a backup can restore an earlier correct state. To restore a current state, the transaction input can be replayed but reexecution of all earlier transactions will cause intolerable delays. Even if a backup version is available which is perhaps a day or a week old, the processing time required for restoration can seriously affect all database use. We therefore also write on the log the complete result of all transactions as *after-images* and can restore a file from its initial or an intermediate state by copying into the database all after-images. Transactions which accessed bad data will of course not be restored using after-images, since this would restore secondary errors. These must be replayed or the submitters must be advised of their undoing.

After-images are especially useful when files have been destroyed independent of any specific transaction. No transactions have to be reexecuted. The cost of restoration can be reduced by sorting the after-images into the file sequence and omitting all older copies. Since some blocks are rewritten quite frequently the number of blocks to be replaced during restoration can be greatly reduced.

Transaction progress thread The combination of a transaction-log file and before- and after-images provides the capability to recover the files from the current version or from a past version, except where the subsequent use of erroneous stored data by other transactions has further contaminated the file. Results presented to users can also have been wrong if the queries referred to bad data.

In order to determine which transactions were indirectly affected by a file error, it is necessary to keep a record of every block that was read as well as the blocks that were written by every transaction. Since the written blocks have already been copied as after-images and the blocks only read did not change, a simple list of all the affected blocks will suffice. The progress of the transaction is recorded as if a thread were drawn from affected block to affected block. A list defining this activity thread is written out on the transaction log at the same time the transaction-complete message is written, as shown in Fig. 11-7. No other transactions should have had access to the data written between the commit point and completion of the faulty transaction.

The activity thread permits listing all subsequent transactions which read data from blocks generated by the faulty transaction. Any such transaction found is added to a list of affected transactions LA, as shown in Fig. 11-9. The activity threads of affected transactions will also be processed to find yet more affected transactions. The list of affected transactions also indicates which output messages may have been wrong because data from blocks containing errors were used.

Load Due to Logging of File Changes The volume of both the before- and after-images depends on the frequency of updates versus simple read requests to the file. In a typical environment, this ratio is approximately one to four so that the writing of two blocks to tape with every update may still be tolerable. The blocks containing the before-image are already available in memory for processing and record insertion. They can be written from memory before they are changed rather than be copied separately from disk to log file. The after-image is, of course, available in memory for copying to the log when the data file is being written.

Size of Protected Units We have used a block as our basic unit of protection. The smaller a basic unit we choose, the more manageable the problems associated with interference, copying, and restoration become. A record or field, however, is apt to move within blocks and may vary considerably in size. More bookkeeping is required to refine the unit of protection to less than block size. The log may, however, indicate which record of a block was the object of the access to avoid unnecessary restoration. The activity thread should always identify the record, or even the segment or field, so that the set of affected transactions will be kept minimal.

If an error found in a record is due to a system or device failure, it is best to check and restore the entire block, since other records of the block may also have been affected. A software system or transaction fault can destroy adjoining records within a buffer. Section 11-2-7 described a scheme which is especially useful if only field or record images are logged. In Chap. 13 more discussion of the protection unit size or *granularity* will take place.

11-4-3 Backup

The use of replay of transaction input or the restoration via after-images relies in practice on availability of a backup copy of an older version of the database. If versions are used backup copies may be constructed by resetting of the current high-water mark; otherwise backups are created by copying. Backup copies may be periodically generated, and a series of past versions may be kept. Each backup copy will be identified by time and date, and by the last transaction included. A backup copy should be generated while the database is quiescent, since updates during copying may cause the copy to be inconsistent. In a *very large database* there may never be a quiescent period long enough for making a backup copy. The transaction log can help here too.

Consistent Backup File Snapshot A sorted list of after-images, with older versions of duplicates eliminated, will in effect be a copy of a version of the entire database. Such a copy can be created separately from the database processing itself by using collected transaction logs, and will provide a backup for the entire database. This copy can be made consistent to any point in time by eliminating blocks which were changed because of transactions submitted beyond the cutoff point. The transaction-complete entry on the log can be used to determine that all transactions entered previous to the cutoff point had been completed.

Such a condensed list of after-images comprises a snapshot of the database in a form that actually never existed at any point in time. The copy will be *internally consistent*; that is, any transaction will be represented either completely or not at all. In a busy system with a very large database, as discussed in Sec. 9-7-4, there may never be a time where the database is internally consistent. This snapshot is actually more useful for backup than a true and complete instantaneous image during a time when the file was in active use. DL/1, for instance, provides facility to generate *backup* files in this manner.

Program Checkpoints In systems which process large computations, it may be undesirable to repeat the entire computation if a problem is encountered which makes progress impossible. To solve this problem the computation can include *checkpoints* which are initiated by the program. At a checkpoint, the past activity thread is written to the log as well as the entire state of the computation. When a computation has to be restarted from its checkpoint record, the state of the computation is restored and all file devices are reset to their state and position at checkpoint time, so that currency indicators remain valid. The cost of resetting such devices as tapes, and input units is so high that the placing of checkpoints requires great care.

11-4-4 Protection and Debugging

The development of new programs requires testing, and this can place a database at great risk. While it is possible to obtain a copy of the system for purposes of checking out programs, such a copy, especially if it requires many disk units, can be expensive to use. Often the debugging of changes in a large system will disable normal operation of the system. Earlier generations of programmers have tolerated the resulting impositions and often have worked at extremely awkward hours.

When we design a system today with the reliability features discussed above, we can include some features which can make it possible for programmers to rejoin the human race. First we install a separate log file, a *debug-log*, on which transaction information about all debugging transactions is written. Then we disable any output to permanent files or to regular user terminals for transactions being tested. The needed output for checkout will be found on the debug-log. When a transaction of a program in debug status requests a block, a list or hash table is checked to determine if this block was placed onto the current debug log, and if it was, the most recent copy is retrieved from the log by reverse scanning. This debug-log approach is now available to IDS users. While this practice will cause a slower response time for the debugging user, especially if the debug-log is maintained on tape, the system and human cost of such an approach will be immeasurably more reasonable.

It is possible to use the transaction log also for the debug log when testing. Interference with normal operations will occur when a block written in debug mode has to be retrieved. Any restoration has to ignore test transactions.

11-5 A SCENARIO FOR RECOVERY

In the preceding sections we have discussed some of the methods which can be used to collect data to protect the reliability of the database. We now will describe a sequence of actions which could be employed when a system failure occurs. We will assume that we are using a system which provides the logging facilities discussed earlier. Our task is made simpler by the fact that we do not consider the effects of the interaction of simultaneous programs at this point.

The following steps will be discussed:

    Error detection
    Error-source determination
    Locating secondary errors
    Application of corrections

11-5-1 Detection and Error Source Determination

The recovery process starts when the existence of an error is detected. A variety of entry points into the recovery process can be distinguished. We will consider system failures, detected by lack of system action or by unrecoverable redundancy checks, and incorrect output, noted by a user.

There may be a *system crash*, either immediately observed by computer operating personnel, who notice that equipment has stopped, or brought to their attention by users whose terminals no longer respond in the expected fashion. A crash has the advantage that the cause of the error is often obvious and that the time period of incorrect operation has been small.

If an error has been detected through one of the *redundancy*-based mechanisms, the error also has had little chance to propagate. If the error is due to an erroneous data record obtained from the file, a backward search through the transaction can locate the point where the data was put on the file. Such an error has had time to propagate. Manual correction of the erroneous element has to be performed if the error is an input-source error. If the error is due to malfunction of the storage device itself, it is sufficient to locate the after-image which was saved when the block was written and initiate restoration by replacing the bad block. If failures are caused by *access-path* errors, it may be possible to reconstruct the file structure without reference to data portions of the records. An index chain which has been damaged can be reconstructed from the data. If data records themselves are chained, the damage requires reconstructions from the log tapes.

Much more insidious is the failure which is detected only by the appearance of *incorrect output*. There may be a very long time interval between occurrence and detection of the error. Considerable detective work may be required to locate the cause. A search backward through the transaction log can determine all updates and thus find suspicious transactions.

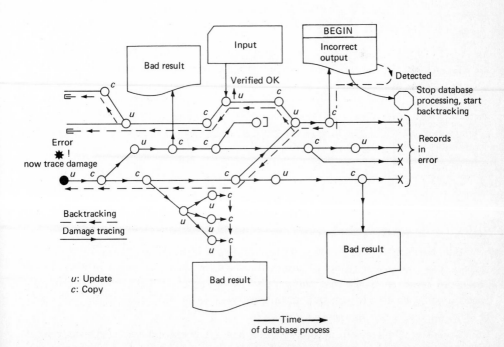

Figure 11-8 Error tracking and propagation.

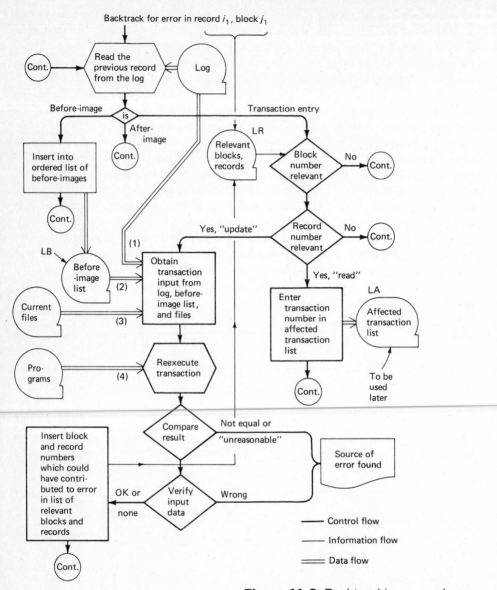

Figure 11-9 Backtracking procedure.

Backtracking becomes even more complex when an erroneous value in the database is the actual result of some computation rather than an original input value. In order to verify that the computation was carried out correctly, it may have to be repeated. To recreate an output, we need

1 The input to the transaction
2 Current images of any block which has not been updated in the interval
3 Before-images of blocks which have been updated in the interval
4 The program used to execute the transaction

The correctness of any input data entering the transaction has to be verified. This verification may also require manual assistance. To determine the conditions for 3 and 4 requires the creation of a list of before-images encountered while the transaction tape is processed in reverse order (**LB** in Fig. 11-9). Reexecution of a transaction may result in a different output or in a value which is found by inspection to be in error. The determination will probably require human interaction. If no error is found in the update procedure, we will have to continue backtracking.

All data which contributed to the value in error have to be verified. It is rare that we will have available a description of the computation in reversible form, so that we will assume that all records read during the processing of the transaction become candidates for further backtracking (**LR**).

The automatic backtracking process may proceed in parallel and collect all possible inputs. The lists of relevant records (**LR**), before-images (**LB**), and transactions which may have been affected (**LA**) will grow quickly as we walk backward in time. There will come a point where this process has to be discontinued even though the source of the error has not been found. We may compare the status of the file at that point with the status of a backup copy. If a comparison with the backup file does not indicate an error, an audit or other verification procedure has to be used to determine which data element is wrong and its correct value.

If bad data is found, but determination of the correct value would take an excessive amount of time, it may be easier to delete the input, proceed with the restoration procedure, and apply a correcting transaction later. The ability to apply corrections is basic to most systems, since some human errors will always occur.

Determination of Extent of Damage　In order to decide which corrective action is best, the extent of the damage has to be determined. This effort is, of course, closely related to finding the time and the cause of the error. After a *crash*, or when processing has been interrupted because of an error signal, we need to determine both which areas of the data file are suspect and which transaction did not complete. Blocks recently written may be checked for redundancy errors and may be compared with their after-images. If any errors are found, the related transactions are marked incomplete.

The backward search through the log can provide a list of any transactions started and not completed. If they performed any file updates, before-images can restore the files to their previous state.

When errors extend back into the file, a subsequent forward pass through the log can be used to collect all possibly affected transactions. The table (**LA**) collected during the backtracking procedure illustrated provides the initial entries for this search.

11-5-2 Locating Secondary Errors

When an error which caused an improper change to a file has been detected, a scan through the activity lists will find the transactions which used the bad block. The affected transactions can be then reentered automatically and correct results can be produced. If blocks were updated by transactions which read bad blocks prior to the write, further restoration of the file is required. The identification of all blocks and all messages affected can be produced by an iterative search of the transaction log. Comparison of the block or the result which was written with the correct version, to ensure that there was indeed an error, can avoid needless duplication and prune the search tree for secondary errors.

Since a transaction which uses internal data, in general, updates only a few records, the list of secondarily affected transactions should be small, especially when an error is detected early. If the damage is extensive, rollback restoration by replacing blocks using before-images may not be practical, and a forward restoration starting from a previous file snapshot which uses after-images may be a better procedure. The decision of rollback versus forward restoration may be automated, although one should hope that the decision is not frequently required.

The activity thread created for file-restoration purposes not only provides the means to recreate the file, to notify users, and to correct erroneous messages but also can aid in the maintenance of file integrity, as will be discussed in Sec. 13-2.

11-5-3 Application of Corrections

If the extent of damage is limited, a rollback process can be used. The damaged portions of the file are restored by first applying any before-images to the blocks in error and then replaying the incomplete transactions. The output from these transactions is suppressed, if possible, to avoid duplicating results that have previously been sent to the users. If this capability to select output does not exist, this output is marked as being due to an error-correction procedure and the user will have to determine its relevancy.

If the damage is great, one may have to start from a backup copy of the file and apply all after-images to it in chronological sequence, except those associated with incomplete transactions. Incomplete transactions are again replayed.

An overview of the process is sketched in Fig. 11-10. A program for the recovery process should be *idempotent*, that is, be able to restart itself at any stage, so that failures during recovery will not become disasters. During recovery the systems tend not be stable, and failure rates higher than during routine operations. If the restoration is major, it may be wise to copy the portion of the database to which corrections will be applied since restoration procedures, being rarely used, have a substantial chance of failure.

11-5-4 Recovery in Distributed Systems

We considered up to now program and input errors, as well as problems due to processor failures. In distributed systems we also have to consider communication failures. These change several assumptions made earlier.

> **Systemwide operation** A part of the distributed system may have failed. Transactions can still be submitted at some nodes, and some may be able to complete while others cannot.
>
> **Failure knowledge** A block may be transmitted over a communication line for writing or a remote file. The sending transaction may not know for a long time if the block has been correctly and safely stored.

The increased parallel activity from multiple nodes and from the longer times needed

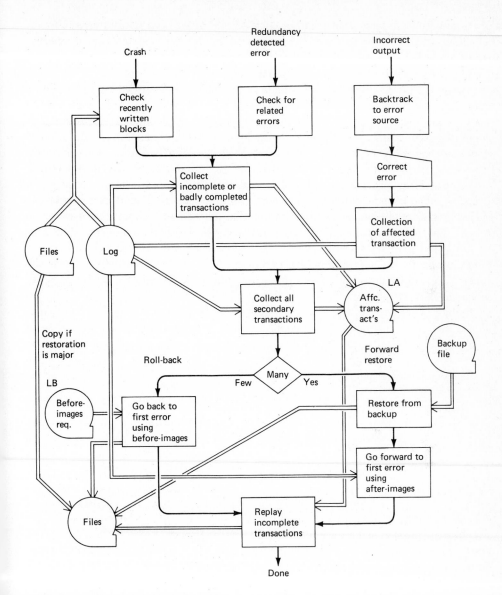

Figure 11-10 Correction process.

to complete transactions increases failure risks in distributed databases. A further consideration is the greatly increased use of replicated data in distributed databases (Sec. 7-5-1).

Operating an Incomplete Distributed Database A motivation for distribution is autonomy of operation in the distinct nodes. Having replicated data permits some continued operation when a node has failed or if the database has been partitioned into independent parts because of communication breakdowns. The independence of read operations is enhanced by having replicated data but update operations to replicated data on disabled nodes are blocked.

Local data elements of a distributed database can be updated if no other conflicting updates to replicated elements can occur. Any subtransactions to update inaccessible remote nodes can be held on a local transaction log. When the remote sites become available again, the transaction can be completed. Often the *primary copy* of a data element can indeed be defined to be local, and many distributed databases have only a few data elements which require distributed update privileges.

Protecting Stored Updates If distributed update privileges are required, a *primary token scheme* can be employed. The database is divided into fragments, each fragment will have an identical replication pattern and be associated with one token. The primary token identifies which copy of a fragment of replicated data currently has primary status. The primary copy token may be transferred between nodes. Updates to a fragment are permitted only at the node which holds the token. To avoid delays and errors due to communication failures; all updates are made initially to primary copies at the local sites. When another node requires an update of its copy of the fragment at its site, it has first to request the token. The transfer of a primary copy token will be held up until confirmation has been received that all replicated copies have been brought up to date. In order to deny access to conflicting users, the token is implemented as a type of *semaphore*, as further described in Sec. 13-1.

Recovery When a node recovers, it must first restore its own state. This may be done via transaction logging or versioning mechanisms if they are available. Nodes which have recovery capability are defined to have *stable storage*.

Small nodes may not be able to recover on their own. Nodes having had damage so severe that they were perhaps replaced cannot recover either. If, however, all the data fragments are replicated somewhere in the distributed system, a new local database may be recovered from those copies. If those copies hold a *primary copy token*, they should be directly usable for recovery, but if some primary copies are also lost the participating databases should first be brought to an earlier, consistent state. The use of transaction identifiers with time-stamps can identify such a state. Then recovery proceeds again by forward restoration of missed transactions.

If a node which held a primary-copy token is damaged so that its version is no longer available then a new primary copy must be elected. In order to find the latest version of a copy we use the identification numbers. The identification number is included with every subtransaction and also with each data unit updated. The copy with the highest identification number is the candidate for becoming the new primary copy.

To assure that the most recent primary copy can indeed survive, the original transaction cannot commit until there is a high confidence of permanency. Survival may be taken for granted when either a node with stable storage has indicated its readiness to commit or when sufficiently many simple nodes have indicated their readiness to commit a copy to their data storage. Since even stable storage systems are subject to some risk of total disaster the commitment decision may be based on a count $C = 3 \times \#(\texttt{stable nodes}) + \#(\texttt{storage-only nodes})$ with perhaps $C > 4$.

Once the damaged node is restored, the transactions and subtransactions which could not be fully completed because of network damage must now be restarted to achieve consistency throughout the database.

Although restoration of a distributed database appears complex, a careful allocation of update privileges can greatly reduce the degree of interdependence of the nodes, so that only few, and perhaps no update conflicts occur. We will see in Sec. 12-3 that the use of database schemas can provide a precise specification of update privileges in terms of update types and update objects. It is more costly in terms of conflict resolution to control simultaneous access to entire files. Problems due to simultaneous conflicting updates are considered in Sec. 13-2.

11-5-5 Problems

Unfortunately, it is true that errors rarely occur singly. Especially serious is a situation where the log or the backup itself cannot be read properly. Most vulnerable are the most recent records. In a crash some of these may be lost in buffers which have not yet been written. In other cases there may be undetected failures in the unit, typically a tape drive, used to write the backup and log files. The latter condition can be largely prevented by forcing regular reading of the log file; such use will provide feedback on the quality of the written file. A log file can also be used by the database administrator to collect data for detailed usage and accounting information, for system-optimization data, and for evaluation of developing equipment needs.

It is especially easy to lose recent transaction input when a failure occurs. When intelligent terminals or a communication network with buffering capability is used, provisions can be made to request retransmission of recent transaction initiating messages as of a given point in time.

The major cause of the tendency for multiple errors to occur is inadequate attention to single errors. Weak operating practices not only encourage errors but also will often leave the systems unprotected because of lack of adequate backup procedures. Ad hoc fixes, poor definition of responsibilities, and assignment of maintenance duties to staff which works also on urgent development tasks have made many database operations a sham. Lack of documentation is often exacerbated by personnel loss. Where efforts were made to avoid these problems, however, database systems have worked for many years without any failure affecting end users. In an operation which wishes to provide a high-level service, a very careful analysis is worthwhile to obtain confidence that reliability is adequate in specific areas, and that all areas have been covered.

Even when full logging capability cannot be provided, the use of adequate detection techniques can limit the propagation of errors to an extent that is manageable. When transaction inputs cannot be retained, it may be possible to clarify the system capabilitites with the users so that they can retain records of their transactions for some period. Users cannot be expected, though, to keep more than a week's worth of backup available.

A usable description of expected practical reliability can help optimize the efforts expended by users and system staff to provide a productive environment. Neither the attitude of *"our computers are perfect"* nor the doomsday attitude *"beware, all ye who enter data here"* is helpful when trying to get work done.

BACKGROUND AND REFERENCES

Reliability was the greatest concern of the users of early computers; problems were always run several times to verify correctness. After the programming systems stabilized, users began to trust them with large quantities of data, and demands of reliability became more stringent. Protection and integrity became a major concern with the development of multiuser systems, where one failure can impact dozens of users simultaneously, early contributions to understanding of the issues are by Ware[67] and Wilkes[72]. The occasional failures continue to have a major impact on database users. The relationship of load and failure rates is convincingly demonstrated by Iyer[82].

Physical security is stressed in guidelines for federal installations (NBS[74]) and is an important aspect of an AFIPS sponsored report and checklist (Browne[79]). A major study was sponsored by IBM(G320-1370 to 1376)[74] and contains many suggestions and experiences, as well as a very detailed bibliography, but does not provide a consistent model. Fernandez[81] provides a text.

The field of error-correcting codes is very well developed. TMR was proposed already by Von Neuman; the low cost of processors makes this solution increasingly practical, as seen in the space shuttle (Sklaroff[76]). A basic textbook is Petersen[72]; for recent references a collection of papers on coding theory, Berlekamp[74], may be consulted. Brown[70] presents the method used for tape-error control and Tang[69] covers decimal input checking schemes. Reliability measures for data input are stressed by Stover[73].

Techniques to keep files secure are presented by Barron[67] for ATLAS, Fraser[69], Weissman[69] for ADEPT, a military prototype, and Frey[71].

Yourdon[72] and Martin[73] present security techniques. Karsner in Kerr[75] presents experience at the Netherlands PTT. Often reliability measures are discussed with the objective of improving the protection of privacy (Conway[72] and others in Chap. 12). The frequency with which back-up files or checkpoints should be taken has been considered by Vold[73].

Many current DBMSs provide rollback capability. Appendix B lists several. The extent of reliability coverage can be hard to ascertain from manuals, but practical experience has been quite favorable. Verhofstad[78] provides a thorough analysis. Recovery-procedure concepts are presented by Lockeman[68], Oppenheimer[68], and Droulette[71] for IBM OS VS, Fichten[72] for WEYCOS, Smith[72], and Thomas[77] for pointers in EDMS.

The model used here was influenced by work of Iizuka[75], as applied to FORIMS. Severance[76] uses differential files to maintain backup versions incrementally. A technique for creating backups suitable for very large, active databases is presented by Rosenkrantz in Lowenthal[78]. Recovery using cooperation among processes is defined by Kim[82]. Recovery in SYSTEM R is described by Gray[81]. The block-level recovery scheme, using checkpoints in multiple timeframes, and its performance, was detailed by Lorie[77]. Audittrails are discussed by Bjork[75]; Sayani in Rustin[74], Menasce[79], and Bhargava[81L] have evaluation models for recovery actions.

Access to prior database versions is developed by Adiba[80].

The two-phase model of transaction processing is due to Eswaran[76]. It is evaluated by Menasce in Aho[82]. Undo of transactions is supported by an algorithm of Reuter[80].

Reliability in distributed databases is the focus of a series of conferences sponsored by the IEEE (Bhargava[81], Wiederhold[82]). Fischer[82] sets proper checkpoints in multiple sites. The primary copy token scheme is due to Minoura[81]. Reliability in various distributed system implementations is considered by Dadam[80], Hammer[80R], Borr[81], and Andler[82].

Journals Articles on database issues are found in nearly every scientific publication. In Chap. 8 we listed some specific database publications. General computer science journals which frequently carry papers on database topics include the *Communications* (*CACM*, since 1961) and *Journal* (*JACM*, since 1968) of the ACM. Survey articles appear in the ACM *Computing Surveys* (since 1969) and in *Computer* (since 1970) of the IEEE Computer Society. Some database papers also appear in the IEEE *Proceedings* and the *Transactions on Software Engineering* (since 1975).

The British Computer Society's *Computer Journal* (since 1962) and *Software Practice and Experience* (since 1973) often have pragmatic papers. The Australian Computer Society has a *Journal* which carries also database articles. *BIT (Nordisk Behandlings Informations Tidskrift)*, published since 1976 by the Regnecentralen (Copenhagen Denmark) and *Acta Informatica* (since 1971) often have relevant algorithmic papers. Papers on computational topics are found in SIAM *Journal on Computing* and also in *Information Processing Letters* (since 1971).

The ACM-SIGIR produces a newsletter for information retrieval. Oriented towards commercial data-processing is the *ACM-SIGDB Data Base*, produced since 1969 by the SIG on Business Data Processing and the *EDP Analyzer*, produced since 1964 by Canning Publications, Vista CA.

Many applications areas have journals which emphasize issues of data management. Management oriented papers are published in the Journal of the Society for Management Information Systems (Chicago IL). In the medical area we find *Methods of Information in Medicine* (Schattauer Verlag, Stuttgart FRG) and the *Journal of Medical Systems* (Plenum Publishing). The library field uses the *Annual Review of Information Science and Technology*, published by Knowledge Industry Publications, White Plains NY, under sponsorship of the American Society for Information Science. Butterworth, London, has begun publication in 1982 of *Information Technology: Research and Development*.

EXERCISES

1 Investigate the type of protection provided at your computer facility. Is it adequate for current use? Is it adequate for a permanent database? Can users augment the services to provide more protection for their work? How would the costs compare for user-managed protection versus system-managed protection?

2 Devise a check-digit method suitable for

   a Dates encoded as month/day/year

   b Sequentially assigned identification numbers

   c Dollar amounts

3 Design a method to provide TMR for some vital part of a database system. Use flowcharts or a procedural-language description to document the design.

4 Simulate the TMR design of Exercise 3 using randomly occurring errors at several rates.

5 Obtain a description of the recovery procedures from a database or file-system supplier, describe the approach in simple and general terms, and evaluate its effectiveness.

Chapter 12

Protection of
Privacy

Balyard had stopped off at the local personnel office for the name of a representative American in the neighborhood.

The personnel machines had considered the problem and ejected the card of E. R. B. Hagstrohm, who was statistically average in every respect save for the number of his initials: his age (36), his height (5'7"), his weight (148 lbs.), his years of marriage (11), his I.Q. (83), the number of his children (2: 1 m.9; 1 f.6), his car (3 yr. old Chev. 2 dr. sed.), the number of his bedrooms (2), his education (h.s.grad., 117th in a class of 233 ... .

Kurt Vonnegut, Jr.
Player Piano

There are two aspects to the issue of protection of data. We will try to cope with both of them in this chapter.

The first, and commonly understood, aspect is that we wish to *deny access* to data to those people who do not have a right to access these data. This is also commonly referred as the *protection of privacy* for personal data and *maintenance of security* for governmental or corporate data.

The second, but equally important, aspect of protection is that we have to *guarantee access* to all relevant data to those people who exercise their access privilege properly. This means that owners of databases also have the responsibility to protect the data entrusted to them. Part of this responsibility means that there has to be a reliable computer operation. The other aspect is that data has to be protected from exposure, vandalism, or alteration.

Some examples may help to define the scope of the protection problem.

Individual Privacy   In order to estimate the next month's operational cost at the Consolidated Iron Works, a program is written which uses personnel data to extrapolate costs from wages, normal working hours, and outstanding vacation days. Lucy Brown, who prepares the report, should not have access to the staff's psychiatric histories, which are kept on-line with the personnel data.

Professional Privacy   Fred Fierce, a manager of the Widget Division of Everything International Corporation, has access to all operational data of the Widget factory which have been collected into the corporate database. Fred is in personal competition with the manager, Shelley Smart, of the Gadget Division, since he feels a promotion is imminent. Should they have access to each other's data? How can we distinguish similar data from different sources? If we cannot guarantee that we can keep divisional data separate, there will be the temptation to withhold data from the corporate database.

Completeness of Data   Victor Velocity is stopped on the highway for speeding. An inquiry into the central police computer reveals that he is listed as *absent without leave* from his army unit. He is promptly arrested. Only after a few days can his lawyer prove that Victor rejoined his army unit after a week's absence and has since then been properly discharged. The later data had not been entered into the police files.

Audit Trail   A credit inquiry by an oil company to determine whether to issue a credit card to Sam Salesman determines that he frequently has been late in settling his accounts with Hal's Haberdashery, even though now he is in the clear. When Sam himself inquires into his credit standing, he is told that all is okay, and that the credit bureau cannot understand why he did not get his credit card from Global Energy Inc.

Vandalism   A programmer who has just been fired from Wholesome Wholesalers goes back to his terminal and deletes the accounts receivable file of the company.

Fraud   The president of Super Innovative Systems modifies the data in the company database so that results for this year look very good. This is accomplished by moving committed expenses into next year so that auditors fail to note the discrepancy. The resulting increase in the price of SIS stock enables the president to sell his equity at a high profit and quit.

A Counterargument   There is a question about privacy which goes beyond the problems posed in the examples above. We will present the argument, but its resolution is outside the scope of this book. The question concerns the social value of protecting privacy by mechanical means. The aspect of privacy which we attempt to protect here concerns itself only with access to facts, so that the more sensitive issue of privacy of thoughts should be kept separate.

We consider first that the restriction of access to facts will provide more benefits to those persons who have facts to hide, and second that any mechanism to protect privacy will be easier to defeat by those with great political or economic power than by average members of the population. A completely open society, without secrets, without privacy of facts, would provide an incentive to a great straightforwardness in human interaction, and would avoid the augmentation of existing centers of power with the power that results from differential access to data.

Data in such an environment would no longer have the questionable information value associated with secrecy. Databases would still be important for daily decision making and long-range planning.

12-1 COMPONENTS OF THE PROTECTION PROBLEM

Three types of elements combine to form the system which we use to discuss methods of protection:

1 The accessors
2 The type of access desired
3 The objects to be accessed

Each of these elements has to be propeerly identified in order to achieve control of access to data. It is also necessary to consider the *envelope*, or the boundary of the area within which the protection system is valid. Sections 12-2 to 12-5 will define these aspects one by one. This section will discuss various general topics in more detail.

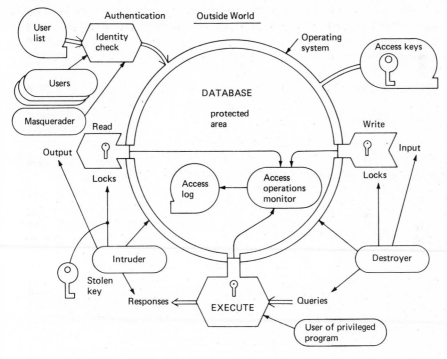

Figure 12-1 Elements of the protection problem.

Definitions We define a number of terms to clarify subsequent discussion of the mechanisms for achieving protection:

Envelope There is an area with a well-defined perimeter known as the database system.

Users and Intruders Within this area there may be active properly identified, *authenticated* individuals, individuals masquerading as valid users, and intruders.

Limited Scope The identity of individuals in the outside world is not known to the system.

Privileges Related to an individual's identification are various privileges of data access. The description of these is maintained as part of the database system.

Protection All data objects are protected to a specified extent while inside the database system area, and lose all system-provided protection when moved out of the area.

Reliability A high level of system reliability is a prerequisite to achieve protection of the database.

Protection, Privacy, and Secrecy Protection of data requires control over the reading, writing, and use of the data. Many of the methods which we will discuss do not distinguish between the protection of data, the maintenance of privacy, and the assurance of secrecy. Secrecy is achieved when there is no unauthorized access at all to data. Adequate privacy may be achieved when data that are obtainable cannot be linked to specific individuals or cannot be used to impute facts about them. The final section of this chapter will discuss approaches to privacy protection that are supplemental to other protection methods.

12-1-1 Value of Protection

In the area of protection, there are cost considerations similar to those we encountered in our discussion of reliability. Protection of data is always limited. The more protection is implemented to reduce accidental and deliberate access violations, the higher the cost of the system will be. When the cost of protection exceeds the value of the data elements protected, we have reached a limit.

The protection value of a data element can be determined by the benefit gained by a deliberate intruder or by the loss suffered by the owner in the case of an accidental disclosure. In the case of an inability to gain access to data, this value is again dependent on the gain obtained by the withholder or on the loss suffered by the accessor due to willful or erroneous omission of data.

Table 12-1   Protection Value of Data Elements

	Deliberate	Accidental	
Data revealed	Value of effect of information gain to intruder	Value of benefit of privacy of information to owner	
Data withheld	Value of effect of information loss to withholder	Value of benefit of use of information to owner	

The rules summarized in Table 12-1 are based on the assumptions that any deliberate attempts on privacy are limited by the potential payoff, but that accidental release of information is not so limited. If the manager of the database has the responsibility to maintain the data, costs will be incurred when damaged or lost data have to be replaced. We can assume that the cost the manager will have to bear is limited by the value of the data to the owner.

It is obvious that the substitution of dollars into these value categories may be considered impossible. This problem of value measurement occurs in any area where decisions have to be made involving trade-offs between humanistic values, or utilities, and mechanical values, or costs. In order to achieve quantitative measures of the value of a data item to its owner or to an intruder, interrogation techniques have been used. By comparing the loss of items which have an assessable value with the loss felt due to a violation of privacy, an approximate value for data can be established.

A typical question in such a process could be

"Would you request credit to buy this automobile if it revealed
to the public your record of alcoholism?"

For many people, this choice would be simple and affirmative; to some people, however, it would be negative unless the financial loss becomes too great. To give a value to privacy protection for the category of alcoholism information, the maximum value determined will have to be used. These techniques have been applied in a major study by the State of Illinois [IBM G320-1373] during a project which demonstrated the use of a secure operating system, IBM RSS.

The relationship between the quantity of data items lost in a violation of privacy and the information loss may be highly nonlinear. In one instance, the loss of a single fact might be highly incriminating in one instance, and loss of additional data may not matter much afterward. In other cases, the more traditional assumptions that the information value increases with the number of data items released will be valid. The calculation of expected loss aggregates all types of risks and their probable costs for a given system approach. This then provides a basis to assess the cost-to-benefit ratio. In the study a loss reduction by a factor of 50 was feasible, but the optimum was at a factor of 30.

Responsibility It is not clear who, in a legal sense, is responsible for losses suffered because of violation of rules of protection of privacy. In many operations the reponsibility rests on top management, although specific areas may be delegated to data-processing management.

If programming is to be regarded as a professional activity, some responsibility will have to be borne by the members of the profession. The extent of responsibility eventually assigned to data processing and its management will depend on the public perception of the behavior of this group in the operation of database systems. The development of ethical standards for data-processing personnel is an on-going concern for the professional societies.

12-1-2 Cost of Protection

To achieve protection there will be costs to create physical security (building, personnel supervision), costs to develop adequate software, and increased operational cost. We will consider here mainly the operational cost.

The cost of providing operational protection is high in traditional computers because computer hardware design has stressed capability and efficiency rather than protection. This preoccupation has had the result that costly software mechanisms are required to implement even marginal levels of security.

An example of lack of protection is the degree of accessing freedom accorded to operating systems. Processes executed by the operating system kernel have often unlimited accessing privileges so that they can control other processes efficiently.

Since resource control is a responsibility of the operating system, many services for the users' computations are performed by the operating system. In systems where kernel and service routines are not separated, a very wide path of information flow exists between protected and unprotected areas. Such a path may be misused through interspersion of inappropriate information into the stream of data. To protect this path, many validation procedures are required, measurably reducing computer performance. The complexity of the protection mechanism causes unreliability without assuring *confinement* of a malicious and knowledgeable intruder.

The value of adequate protection in commercial systems has been estimated at 10 to 20% of basic data-processing cost. One experiment within RSS [IBMG320-1376] caused an increase of 4.2% in file access cost but also limited flexibility and sharing. The total cost of implementation of a truly secure database is today larger by an order of magnitude than its benefit, since it requires development of substitute system programs and the training of personnel to monitor operations. Additional equipment may be needed for redundancy and logging.

Protection of privacy and system security have now been recognized as important concerns, so that we can expect that new systems will be designed with better support for protection. The cost to the user should then become less so that the benefits of a reasonable protection level outweigh the costs.

12-2 THE ACCESSOR

The external identification of accessors is primarily the name, as entered by them into the system. An accessor may also be identified by a *password*, which has to be typed in on request, or perhaps by a machine-readable key or badge. Methods have been proposed and tested which depend on the biological uniqueness of human beings. Manifestations of this unique coding of individuals are voice prints, fingerprints, and signatures. The database system, as defined here, will not be responsible for the primary decoding and validation or *authentication* of the presented information. Since access to operating-system services is a prerequisite to use of the database, the authentication task is left to modules of the operating system. The method used for authentication of an individual's identification depends very much on the technology available in a specific instance. The authentication subsystem will present to the database system a string of bits which we will consider the access key. This module has to prevent a *masquerader* from obtaining a key. All authorization and privileges given to accessors will depend on the access key.

12-2-1 Keys

To assure that access keys are not available to unauthorized accessors, the *individual's identification* has to be very difficult to mimic or copy. While an individual's name may be unique, this name is easy to mimic by anyone who can observe those who have access to the system, and is hence not suitable for a key. Once a system provided key is obtained this access key is used to enter the database system from the operating system. The responsibility for manipulating the key rests with both the accessor and the operating system.

To protect the process of obtaining a key the system, when the user logs in, requests a password with the users' name. The password is entered without displaying it to protect it from observers. The password will generally consist of a few letters, chosen by the user. A trial-and-error method of entering possible passwords could be used by an intruder to gain access. The time required to carry out a systematic trial is the principal discouragement to potential intruders. The expected time to open a specific lock without any prior knowledge is

$$T(\text{getin}) = \tfrac{1}{2} c^d \, t(\text{try}) \qquad\qquad 12\text{-}1$$

where c^d is the number of possible combinations and $t(\text{try})$ the time required to try a combination. For a three-letter password, $d = 3$ and $c = 26$ and the time for the interaction with the system may be $t(\text{try}) = 3$ seconds, so that $T(\text{getin}) \approx 7$ hours. If the authentication process is required only infrequently, an artificial delay in the opening process can increase the safety of the lock. An equivalent method is to allow only two or three attempts to enter a password. An intruder then has to go again through a full access procedure, maybe requiring about 20 seconds. The procedure can be more strict for access to critical data. When the security-control officer using RSS fails to provide his password correctly twice, the entire computer system is shut down. Extending the number of combinations is the other alternative to increase safety. A practical problem is that long passwords are harder to remember and will be frequently written down; another problem is that passwords are frequently chosen to be initials, middle names, friends' names, or other *aides-mémoire* and hence are easily guessed.

In order to establish legal responsibility, the accessors who have received a password giving them valuable privileges may be required to sign an agreement to keep the password confidential, and to promptly report any suspected loss of confidentiality. A frequent change of passwords can help limit the improper use of leaked passwords. Changing passwords puts an additional burden on users unless they are equipped with some automatic password generator which is matched by the receiving system. If we invent such a device, we also will have to protect its use.

Methods beyond passwords are used to increase protection. An *active authentication* procedure is provided by NCSS. A user can place an interrogation routine in the system which requests parameters during the authentication process. A possible query presents a number to the accessor, who is expected to multiply the number by 3 and add 12. This procedure is the "password" the user has to remember. Authentication methods based on keycards, badges, and so on can positively identify the card and hence the accessor, unless the card is copied, lost, or stolen. A card in combination with a password can be very effective.

An individual who has valid access to the system may, after initial entry, use the identification key to gain access to inappropriate privileges. An accessor may also be defined as a member of two projects. It may not be desirable that this user can have both corresponding access rights at the same time. These problems requires careful management of access privileges.

The existence of masquerading intruders may be determined a posteriori by reporting all access attempts in a given period to the owner of a file. To achieve faster detection, the file user can be informed on every access of the date, time, and a sequence number of the previous access.

Up to this point, we have characterized the accessor as an individual. Sometimes access authority is given to classes of individuals. Clerical personnel, for instance, may not be individually identified. Authentication by class is not very secure, since there is no individual responsibility.

Additional parameters may be added to authenticate the accessor more completely. The database system proper may remain relatively innocent of these further specifications, since these will be translated into separate access keys; the number of valid access keys may become much greater.

12-2-2 Programs as Accessors

Among the additional accessor attributes to be considered is the *program or process* that is used to access the data. There may be protected programs that are maintained and controlled by one set of accessors, and used by others. Use of such a program may confer unto the user some of the privileges accorded to the controller of such programs. The transfer of privilege is appropriate if the program acts as a filter of the information. Typical of such filters are programs which perform statistical analysis on data. A program which reads data from a set or subset of records and produces only an average of the data performs such a filtering function. The average value may well be appropriate for a general audience, whereas the details of the data are confidential. This program should refuse to produce a result if the number of records selected to provide data for the resulting average is so small that the result can be associated with an individual data record.

A query by a clerk of the United Tamale Corporation to obtain *"the average salary of all employees with a Beverly Hills zipcode in their address"* should be aborted since it would provide, in effect, the salary of the president of the company.

The concerns of *statistical access* to individual records arise mainly in the maintenance of larger demographic databases, such as health records or census data. It remains possible that, through multiple intersecting queries, some confidential data is retrievable. The result obtained directly by the above query can also be obtained from the average salary of all employees and the average of all employees who do not live in Beverly Hills. The transaction-log which was discussed in the previous chapter provides at least an ex post facto audit trail for such access attempts. We will discuss in Sec. 12-4 other aspects associated with programs as accessors.

12-2-3 Access Parameters

The *location* of the accessor, or more precisely the destination where the results are to be returned, can be another parameter of the access description. Confidential data are not to be shipped into areas that are not secure. The location also may define the type of device. Access to a check- or ticket-writing device may be made especially secure.

Sometimes it may not be desirable that a permanent paper record be created which could cause later confusion. An example might be an unverified clinical test result that is made available on a display to aid in quick diagnosis but should not become part of the permanent medical record. It may be more advisable to identify such preliminary information specifically rather than to devise separate access keys for hard and soft devices.

The *time and day* of access may be a necessary adjunct to the destination parameter in the accessor description. A location may be considered secure only during normal office hours. There also may be a time component to the value of data, so that data of a certain age may be more liberally accessible than very current information.

The *frequency* with which an element is accessed may be of concern. A sales total may be requested quarterly for the public stockholders report; the same value produced every hour could be correlated with specific sales activity which a company might wish to keep confidential. An unusually high access frequency would generally be indicative of an unusual situation and possibly reveal foul play.

12-2-4 Access Key Management

To lessen the possibility of theft within the system of accessor keys, a transformation which is not uniquely reversible can be applied to the keys. Within the system only the transformed keys are stored and used for access privilege verification, so that the original key is visible within the system only for a short time. The hashing techniques discussed in Sec. 3-5 provide this type of transformation.

The full number of access keys could be as large as:

$$\#(\text{accesskeys}) = \#(\text{individuals}) \times \#(\text{access procedures})$$
$$\times \#(\text{distinct devices or locations}) \times \#(\text{time categories}) \qquad 12\text{-}2$$
$$\times \#(\text{frequency categories})$$

We will discuss in Sec. 12-6 methods which can be used to map this set of access keys into a more manageable set of accessor categories or *cliques*.

12-3 TYPES OF DATA ACCESS

Accesses to data can be categorized by type. Distinctions are commonly made between authorization to read and authorization to write data. Magnetic-tape reels, cartridges, and some disks have inserts which, when removed, make writing physically impossible. Some disk drives have write-protect switches. Many shared operating systems have added an execute-only privilege. Here one can allow an accessor to use a program without allowing reading or copying the program. Such a facility provides a protection for the products of programmers. The execute-only privilege may in turn protect the data used by a protected program, since its access mechanism and identification key is hidden.

Computer systems limited to these three types of authorization still provide fairly unsatisfactory protection. The procedures which are part of the operating system are in general authorized to read or write anything, anywhere, and could not function if this privilege were removed. The read privilege is frequently available to any user and only a knowledge of the structure of another user's data is required to gain access. Various systems have implemented additional protection privileges. We will not survey these in detail but rather will summarize implemented and suggested types of access categories below.

Seven Access Types We will present in the remainder of this section a set of seven distinct access privilege types which in combination allow a great degree of protection control.

READ access grants the privilege of copying data into the accessor's environment. Once the data are copied, the copy can be manipulated by the accessors as they please. This type of access privilege protects the stored data, but not the information they contain.

EXECUTE access grants the privilege of use of a program or a procedure to the accessor. With the use of the privilege may be associated privileges of extended data access as discussed earlier. The text of the procedure and data read by the procedure are not made available, nor can the program be modified without additional privileges. Using this privilege information can also be selectively protected.

CHANGE access provides the accessor with the conventional write access. This access privilege provides capability to destroy stored data. In view of the *extend* privilege discussed below, it may be appropriate to restrict this privilege to the updating or changing of existing data items.

The **DELETE** access privilege is closely related to the privilege of write access. This privilege allows destruction of the information that a data object existed, and of course also destroys the data in the object itself.

Change access allows only destruction. It is not clear whether the fine distinction between these two access types is worth the addition of this access type. A delete access causes a change of file size; for this reason it may be desirable to distinguish the delete and change privileges.

The **EXTEND** access allows the addition of data to a file without the capability to destroy other data in the file and without the privilege to read previous stored data unless those privileges also were conferred. A file thus referenced will grow.

Files where only extend access is appropriate are the files which contain system accounting data or audit trails. Most data-entry operations also fall into this category. Many conventional write privileges combine change and extend.

The concept of **MOVE** access provides another privilege which is not commonly available. This privilege provides the capability to move data fields without the privilege to read their contents. Many operations within computing and data-processing systems involve the movement of passive data elements associated with key data elements. In order to make decisions, the key has to be read, and read access to the key has to be granted. The need to read the key does not imply that all associated data should be available.

Specific examples where the move privilege is appropriate and adequate for the tasks can be found in many operating system functions. The movement of users' data to output buffers for blocking as well as the movement of data pages in virtual memory systems requires only move access. The transposition program in Sec. 4-2 provides an example of no requirements to *read* the data whatsoever. In most commercial operations such as banking, public utility, and medical data processing, records are continuously being sorted or moved based on identification keys. The fact that the programmer who writes the programs that move the data also obtains read and write privileges has aided both intentional fraud and unintentional alteration of other data fields. Not all such errors can be prevented by protection but the additional detection capability obtained will help in minimizing problems.

The move privilege can also be used to place data on high- or low-performance devices in order to optimize overall system performance. System tuning is frequently aided by outside specialists who should not need read access to data in order to carry out their business.

The control of access for **EXISTENCE VERIFICATION** completes the set of privilege types to be considered. Without this privilege an accessor cannot determine if an object, say a specific record or an attribute value, exists. It frequently is necessary to determine whether a specific data element exists in order to make decisions on the invocation of further processes. A program to which this privilege has not been granted cannot even determine the existence of the record.

There is a need for two distinct alternate responses when data are accessed to which read privileges have not been granted. A program constructing an index of records has a valid need to determine existence and location of a record, and other programs should obtain such data.

An example might be a request for a psychiatric health record. An intruder who attempts to read a psychiatric record of an individual might receive the message `'No such record'` if the person does not have a psychiatric record. If there exists such a record, the intruder who does not possess read privileges would be denied access to the information and might receive a message from the computer stating `'Improper access request'`. These innocuous responses actually provide valuable information. Lack of existence verification privilege would result in a message `'Thou shalt not attempt to look for such data'`. In many implementations, this privilege may be closely related to the privilege of access to the index to the data, which we will discuss in the next section.

Summary The privileges given can be conveniently coded by single bit indicators; say `'0'` disallowing and `'1'` granting access. The seven distinct access types recognized above provide $2^7 = 128$ combinations as shown in Table 12-2.

Table 12-2   Bit Assignment for a Protection Key Byte

Bit 0	Key byte itself is valid
Bit 1	Read access is granted
Bit 2	Execute access is granted
Bit 3	Change access is granted
Bit 4	Delete access is granted
Bit 5	Extend access is granted
Bit 6	Move access is granted
Bit 7	Existence Verification access is granted

It is probable that the no-access code ('10000000') and the all-access code ('11111111') combinations will occur most frequently. System programs will refer to users' data with '10000011'. Access keys themselves can be manipulated with this protection level. The validity bit provides safety during manipulation. An understanding of the combinations that these access types provide is necessary in order to be able to specify the access level of a data object for an accessor.

12-4 THE OBJECTS TO BE LOCKED

The data space, addressed by an accessor for a specific type of access, contains the objects to be provided or defended. Various types of such objects can be distinguished: *data objects, access paths, database programs*, and *schema entries*. Each of these objects can have multiple versions over time. We will discuss all of these in turn.

Data First of all, there are the recorded facts themselves. A fact becomes interesting to the accessor only when it is bound to a set of attributes which will identify it so that the fact can be related to a real-world person or object. These attributes may have been used as the access path to the element, and hence may be known. On the other hand, there is little probability that a random exposure of a single data field will do much harm. If it could, we should not allow visitors to our computer installation to take a photograph of the console of the shiny machine with its lights displaying some current value of some object.

The size of an object is of greater concern. It is very conceivable that each element of a record has a distinct usage, so that accessor and access type should be specified for one element alone. More practical is that identical access constraints are assigned to all attribute values of the same attribute.

Gathering of attribute types which have common access constraints, say **street address** and **city**, creates protection segments. In many systems segments defined for protection and record segments defined for manipulation have to be identical. Other systems limit protection boundaries to records, so that the entire file is the data object to be protected.

Access Paths In addition to the data elements which represent data values, there are elements in database which indicate relationships and which appear as pointers in the files. Other pointers exist in indexes to the data. These pointers present a separate class of objects to be locked. In many instances there is the need for distinct protection privileges for pointers to objects and for the value of objects.

Let us consider some instances.

1 A data entry has to be updated: the pointer is read, but the data are read and rewritten.

2 A survey wants to know the number of alcoholics on the staff but should not be able to determine who they are. The pointer is read and counted if valid; the data are not accessible.

3 A file-maintenance program reorganizes the file; new pointers are created and written, but the data are only to be moved and are supposedly of no interest to the writer or executor of this task.

In each of the three examples of access to data via a path using pointers, it seems desirable to protect the pointers to a different degree than the data themselves.

There is some conceptual overlap between pointers as protection objects and the availability of existence verification as an access type. Complete omission of either may, however, leave some gaps in a protection system.

Programs Programs are also objects which already have generated a need for a specific protection type. Since programs can be active elements in a database system, their protection is of equal concern. Where protection for data is reasonably complete, programs, if put under the same rules, also will be protected. The classification of data objects as records with attributes, however, does not apply. The existence of program text has to be specifically recognized. The other aspect of a program, that of an active accessor, was discussed in Sec. 12-3-1. Programs will have to be treated as distinct names units if use of a specific program can convey extended access privileges.

Schemas The database schema, if one exists, is another object of protection. Here a concern is one of adequate object naming in a database schema environment, where protection is provided through the schema itself. Some systems may keep the schema again in a schema-controlled file and apply protection through this upward recursion. A proper termination of this nesting of schemas will have to be provided. If the schema is relatively static, it is possible to include the schema file in a single schema description.

The allocation of schema access privileges is very critical. Many accessors will have read privileges to the descriptors, but very few will have change or write privileges. An error when modifying a schema can make the entire database inaccessible. If the schema file is itself controlled by the same schema, the use of these modify privileges is awkward to control.

Stronger schema access protection may include a requirement that more than one accessor assigns a change access privilege to a process which will modify the schema task. Both will receive reports of all activities. This joint authorization is equivalent to the double signature requirement in many companies for writing of large checks. An alternate method of control is to maintain two schemas that control each other and that which are assigned to different accessors at the top level so that again joint control exists.

Time The age of a data object may be of concern in the assignment of access privileges. Data can lose information value over time and be made more generally available outside the system. There are other circumstances where information should not be made available after a legal statutory time limit, in order to protect individuals from continuing embarrassment or damage.

Summary The number of data objects that are candidates for protection is the sum of the counts of the object categories (data, access paths, programs, schemas) multiplied by a number of time-division categories. Section 12-6 discusses how to deal with this large number.

12-5 ENVELOPE OF PROTECTION

Since database and file services are an integral part of computer-system facilities, we cannot limit protection consideration to the database system alone, and yet there will be a area beyond which the responsibility for protection is no longer in the hand of the database management. The definition of the *envelope* where protection is maintained is frequently neglected. The omission of a statement defining the envelope, coupled with specifications of the security designed into the internal operation of the system, can easily be misleading. Users of computing systems may be only too willing to believe that adequate protection exists.

Protection-System Components We frequently will have to include in our considerations the operating system, the input and output subsystems, the authentication subsystem, as well as the staff involved in the operation. In the ideal case, we can protect the database as a separate unit. If the operating system is included, there is likely to be a lower reliability because of the large part counts and greater number of accessors. The state of security provisions in existing computer systems is such that genuinely secret work is carried out on unshared computers, and in protected buildings, by checked and bonded personnel.

We assume throughout that the database is accessed only through the database or through a file system which recognizes the protection boundaries. In systems where no transaction-log is part of the system, backup files will be created by using *utility* programs which often ignore protection conventions. The backup tapes as well as output from unauthorized execution of utility programs provide convenient opportunities for the breach of protection boundaries.

Loss of Control over Data Another problem in the definition of the protection envelope is due to routine exchange of information.

An example of a privacy leak is the movement of medical record data to insurance carriers and beyond, where the data is used to determine eligibility for insurance coverage and to evaluate claims for health care services provided. An extensive study [Carrol72] has shown that this is one of the largest leaks of private information. This transfer proceeds directly from provider to insurance company and then to centralized reference files so that potential loss of privacy is hard to perceive by outsiders.

Another case which has been cited is caused by law-enforcement support systems which service more than one state while these states operate under different legislative rules concerning privacy. The multinational companies, frequently with centralized computing facilities, are difficult to control legally by courts of the countries where they do business and on whose citizens they may keep records.

Rigorous definition of files, control of input and output, and identification of personnel entering the protected envelope are the most important tools currently available to prevent unauthorized access. Logging of all attempts, successful or not, to gain access helps in ex post facto analysis of violations. Genuine concern by management is needed to make the staff aware of the importance of protection.

Response to Violations The action to be taken when a violation of the protection mechanism is detected has to be carefully considered.

Not everybody who attempts to access the wrong record has to be thrown instantly into jail. A large number of access violations are due to programmer debugging or inquiry clerk typing errors. A system that exhibits an excessively paranoid behavior is likely to frustrate legitimate use as well. On the other hand, there should be adequate logging of deviant access behavior to allow detection of illicit action and eventual entrapment of perpetrators.

It has been recommended that, with the current level of protection provided by data-processing systems, commercial firms employ one data-processing oriented auditor for every 10 to 20 programmers on the staff [Browne[79]]. The high cost of such an approach, as well as the historic failures of auditors to detect glaring instances of computer abuse, should provide an impetus to make improvements in protection systems.

12-6 ACCESS KEY ORGANIZATION

In order to implement the requirements stated in the preceding section, the protection requirements have to be categorized and organized. A three-dimensional access matrix which is the product of the number of accessors, the number of access types, and the number of data elements and links will be excessively large.

12-6-1 Cliques

The effect of a large number of users can be reduced by establishing user categories or cliques. For example, all data entry personnel may be identified as a member of the same clique. Thus there will be a table which maps the individual user identification into a clique identification. A further reduction of number of cliques required is possible if an individual can be a member of more than one clique, since fewer special categories may be needed. On the other hand, unexpected privileges may be the result of multiple, concurrent clique memberships. To avoid this problem, an accessor may have to state the database area to which access is desired, so that only one clique membership is active at a time.

A clique-identification number is assigned internally. Once a clique member is authenticated, this number is hard to forge and will provide a better protection than user-identification keys. It may be desirable to periodically reauthenticate the submitters of clique-identification numbers. A monitoring process can check if the user's identification is appropriate for a legitimate member of the clique or would suggest that a stolen clique number exists. Clique numbers which have been compromised can be withdrawn and new numbers assigned.

12-6-2 Data Objects

The organization of the protection objects depends greatly on the type of database control which is provided in the system. For an object to be protected, it has to be accessed through a *naming* mechanism. Objects on levels where actual addresses are used cannot be identified for protection.

If the system provides detailed descriptions of record contents and linkages (i.e., a schema), quite detailed protection is possible. If no facilities of this type are provided, protection generally is limited to the file level.

Files Virtual-memory systems (see Sec. 4-8) can provide a hardware definition of files through the use of named storage segments, so that protection is easier to enforce. In other cases files are defined by software and control information, obtained by the operating system when a file is opened. In either case, files are the smallest units which have symbolic names or symbolic numbers. The method used for file protection is always determined by the operating system. To identify files uniquely within a system, their names will be prefixed automatically by a qualification term, constructed from the user name.

Example 12-1   User Authentication and File Names

Login:	NAME? Gio Wiederhold
	PROJECT? DataBase
	. . .
Execution:	. . .
	OPEN FILE(mine) UPDATE;
will define a file named	G_Wieder.DataBase.mine

This method is augmented to enable users to access common system files and to enable sharing of files to the extent desired. To access files other than one's own is made possible by specifying the fully qualified names of files such as

SYSTEM.Library.Regression or JCOther.DataBase.Observations

The operating system can check whether Joe Carlos Other has given anybody, or specifically someone with the system name G_Wieder, the privilege to access his data. A list of authorized users can be kept with the file directory and will indicate the type of privilege accorded. Once READ access privilege has been given, the original user has lost control over the data, since the reader can again permit another reader to access the files.

A project name, as DataBase used above, can be used to imply sharing of data files for all members of a project. A project becomes an external manifestation of a clique organization. A higher level of authorization can be required for access by users outside of the project.

12-6-3 System Support for Protection

Protection is largely a system function, and knowledge of the available capabilities, or the lack thereof, is necessary to equip database systems appropriately. File systems can rarely provide much protection beyond the facilties of the operating system and the underlying hardware.

Hardware Mechanisms The services provided by computer systems can be considerably enhanced by hardware mechanisms which can limit access at the point of data-element fetch or store. Hardware mechanisms are based on matching a protected access key provided by a user with a key field associated with data storage. Two types of methods are in use.

Rings A hierarchical assignment of access privileges has been used in some systems. Figure 12-2 illustrates the concept of protection rings where the degree and type of access available is dependent on a level number assigned to the accessor. Such a system is modeled on the basic military secrecy hierarchy of

> Unclassified
> Confidential
> Secret
> Top secret

In practice, only few levels are usable, since a single privacy hierarchy of data has to be established appropriate to all accessors. The MULTICS system [Graham[68]] associates ring privileges specifically with processes and storage segments. Systems with rings are effective in protecting operating systems and subsystems, and can contribute much to reliability. For databases the hierarchical constraints of rings have to be combined with control over files, record segments, and access paths.

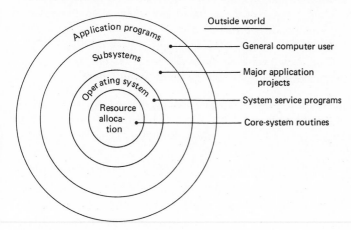

Figure 12-2 Protection rings.

Capabilities An allocation not based on a predetermined hierarchy of access privileges has been provided in so-called *capability-based computer systems*. Here the access control is provided through access keys which are shown and verified when data objects are accessed. Capabilities for access are initially given to a user when new objects are created. To avoid that access keys are copies or assembled by intruders, they are kept in a separate mechanism. In order to share data, the owner of the data can give an access key with selected capabilities to another user. To implement capability management in hardware, a machine architecture with virtual storage segments will be chosen.

Computer systems may combine access lists, rings, and capabilities to provide the basic protection mechanism.

Software Mechanisms No hardware system provides protection adequate for all circumstances, so that operating systems carry much of the responsibility for file protection. We find the two approaches used for hardware mirrored in operating systems.

Common to all software mechanisms is the use of catalogs which relate accessors to file names. Granting any type of access to a combination of user and file will in operating systems provide access to all data in the file.

Much implicit protection used to exist when access to computers was difficult. Now a large fraction of the population knows how to use computers and many computers are available on nationwide networks. This aspect of protection is no longer viable and should be discounted.

User-Based The information which files the user is permitted to access may be stored with the user's directory. The names of files which may be accessed by more than one user will appear in multiple directories; the entries will contain the access codes authorized by the user. The system has to protect these codes, so that the users cannot change entries in their own directory.

Excessive duplication of file entries may be avoided by having a hierarchical file directory structure. An entry in the directory as `Database→Database.Directory` can provide a link to a sharable subdirectory in which all the files associated with some database are entered. Multiple users with the same access privilege to the database may have such a link. Now access conflicts can occur. Issues dealing with the maintenance of integrity in this situation will be analyzed in Chap. 13.

File-Based The information which files the user is permitted to access is stored with the files. The file directory of every file contains the names of all the users who are authorized to access the file. If many users are authorized to use a file, the list might become excessive.

By now organizing users with similar access privileges into a *clique* those users can be authorized by having a single clique name in the file directory.

12-6-4 Schemas and Protection

The system-methods presented above are restricted to files as their unit of protection. A database system can distinguish much finer data units.

In a schema-oriented environment, privacy constraints for data elements can be kept with the data element descriptions in the database schema. We mentioned this in Sec. 8-1-3. Since we can expect many element types to have similar requirements, a reference to a data-privilege table can be used in the data-element description, so that duplication of access lists is avoided. Figure 12-3 illustrates this organization. This approach, while it keeps the access matrix relatively small, gives access to all or to no data values associated with a given attribute name.

By controlling access to index elements or selected rings of records, this organization can be extended to provide access to selected data elements of a certain name according to hierarchical requirements. Figure 12-4 expands on this notion in relation to one of the examples in the introduction to this chapter.

Fred Fierce can protect working data of his division by protecting an object used to define the access path to these data. Another manager can protect his portion of the database similarly.

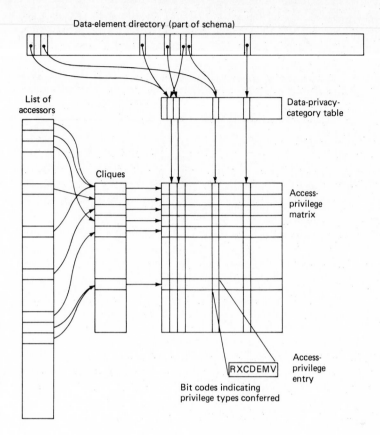

Figure 12-3 Schema-oriented access matrix.

The access path is probably defined via an index. Protection of *horizontal fragments* of files via access paths is associated with the use of hierarchically structured files. Network and relational structures are more difficult along the access path. In a relational system, INGRES, *constraint statements* (see Sec. 9-2-5) can be given for that purpose. These disallow retrieval based on values found in the tuples. The system will access these data before being able to apply the constraint.

A more general means of providing checks on accesses to subgroup information is provided through protective database procedures. An access verification program can look at system variables such as **user**, **date**, and **time**, and the database variables being accessed to determine if access is permissible. These routines are specified in the the schema and will be automatically invoked.

The use of a program allows checking of the originator of a request and the path by which the request arrives, and can also write an audit record to register the accesses. This approach is, however, costly in execution time and open to subversion. The verification program must have access privileges to the user area being verified, to the area where the access criteria are stored, and to the log file. Such extensive privileges are inherently dangerous.

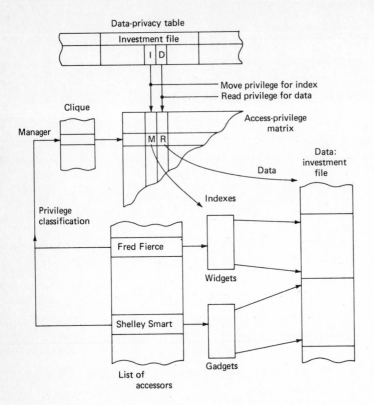

Figure 12-4 Vertical access segregation through limited index privileges.

The CODASYL specifications include most aspects of privacy protection. Access to data items, a record, an area, as well as the schema, can be protected by using statements as shown in Fig. 12-5. Here the accessor is assumed to be submit either a fixed password, which is specified in the schema itself (`literal`), or a password kept as a variable (`lock_name`), or is checked by means of a procedure (`data_base_procedure`). Such a procedure is invoked when the element is accessed and will not only have the ability to request the accessor's password but can also check on the terminal location, the access history, and other relevant material.

The access type can be made dependent on the operation being performed, i.e., `GET`, `MODIFY`, or `STORE`, for access to individual data elements, or may apply to all three operations on the elements. A `PRIVACY LOCK` on `LOCKS` refers to all locking operations in an area and would typically be very securely assigned to the database administrator.

Often the smallest data element that can be protected is the record. Elements that belong logically together but need separate `PRIVACY` constraints have to be kept in separate, parallel records segments.

Database procedures are also provided in general, and can be specified for execution under similar access conditions. In that case they can be use to maintain *integrity constraints*, for instance, disallow deletion of a referenced record.

12-6-5 Summary

We have reviewed in this section in a general sense the protection mechanisms which are available in operating systems. Current developments in operating systems are increasingly cognizant of the existence and needs of databases. We notice in the examples shown the interrelationship between protection methods and file system design. Such a feedback is difficult to avoid, and makes the design of secure systems an iterative undertaking.

It remains important for a database designer to review the available facilities and understand their weaknesses. Saltzer[75] has collected 10 principles to be considered in the analysis of protection systems.

Economy of Mechanism An excessively complex protection system does not allow verification of correctness and completeness.

Fail-Safe Defaults If something goes wrong, access should be denied. Even conscientious users will not report unexpected access privileges.

Complete Mediation Every access path to the database has to go via the protection mechanism.

Open Design Protection is not enhanced by keeping the mechanism used for protection secret. A secret mechanism can also install an unwarranted level of faith in the users.

Separation of Privilege Critical data should be protected, so that even a single authorized user cannot subvert the mechanism.

Least Privilege A program should be granted only the essential access privilege.

Least Common Mechanism Avoid all unnecessary sharing. We note that in an operating system sharing is perceived as a burden often incurred for economy of storage or computing facilities. In databases sharing is the major benefit, so that this principle is best restated as: avoid keeping data that cannot be shared in a database.

Psychological Acceptability The mechanisms must match the user's data model and the protection required for it. Failure to do so creates usage errors and an incentive to bypass the system.

Work Factor The effort to subvert the mechanism must be greater than the benefit which could be gained. The intruder will probably also have access to a computer so that he can exert much effort at little cost.

Compromise Recording Logging of accesses can create the audit trail necessary to correct problems and trap the perpetrators. Intruders into the innards of a system may, of course, be able to avoid creating a trail or can erase the evidence.

Where systems are found inadequate, the database designer may augment the facilities but should also provide to the users a realistic assessment of the available level of protection. If storage of critical data can be avoided, privacy protection is simplified. If the atmosphere of a database operation is open, vandalism will be less of a problem. Since the objective of a database is to enable the sharing of information, the removal of barriers to sharing is important.

/∗ Specifications for Privacy Protection of data, RECORDs, and AREAs. ∗/

[level_number] data_name

$$
\begin{bmatrix}
\text{ACCESS-CONTROL LOCK} \begin{bmatrix} \text{FOR \{GET\}\{MODIFY\}\{STORE\}} \end{bmatrix} \\
\text{IS} \begin{Bmatrix} \text{literal\_password} \\ \text{lock\_name} \\ \text{PROCEDURE p\_name} \end{Bmatrix} \begin{bmatrix} \text{OR} \begin{Bmatrix} \text{literal\_value} \\ \dots \\ \dots \end{Bmatrix} \end{bmatrix} , \dots
\end{bmatrix}
$$

RECORD NAME IS recordname

$$
\begin{bmatrix}
\text{ACCESS-CONTROL LOCK} \begin{bmatrix} \text{FOR \{FIND\}\{GET\}\{INSERT\}\{STORE\}} \\ \text{\{MODIFY\}\{DELETE\}\{REMOVE\}} \end{bmatrix} \\
\text{IS} \quad \dots \text{ as above } \dots
\end{bmatrix}
$$

AREA NAME IS area_name

$$
\begin{bmatrix}
\text{ACCESS-CONTROL LOCK} \begin{bmatrix} \text{FOR \{ALTER\}\{COPY\}\{DISPLAY\}\{LOCKS\}} \end{bmatrix} \\
\text{IS} \quad \dots \text{ as above } \dots
\end{bmatrix}
$$

Figure 12-5 DBTG privacy clauses.

12-7 CRYPTOGRAPHY

An alternate protection technique is provided by transformation of data into a form that does not provide information when intercepted. Such methods can provide privacy in otherwise insecure environments and can provide effective secrecy in conjunction with the methods which were discussed previously.

Three basic techniques are available:

1 Encoding of information

2 Transposition of codes representing data

3 Substitution of codes representing data

The encoding of data is a common process even without privacy consideration. Letting the value "1" mean **male** and the value "2" stand for **female** is a form of encoding, which will protect that field to someone who does not have access to a code book or schema. We will discuss methods of encoding in detail in Chap. 14.

Operations where basic symbols are transposed or substituted in order to garble the data are referred to as *enciphering*. Such a transformation creates *cipher text* from *plain text*.

In order to understand the message, the recipient will have to *decipher* the cipher text, according to rules and a key used in the enciphering operation. The intruder, who wishes to understand the text, will have to resort to *decrypting* techniques. Figure 12-6 shows the components of cryptography.

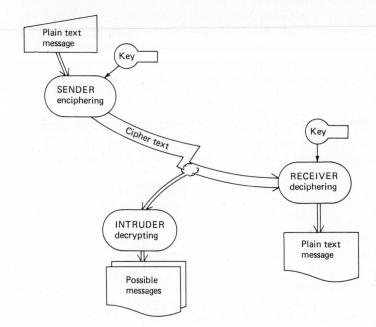

Figure 12-6 Elements of cryptography.

We will consider mainly operations on data consisting of alphabetic messages. It should be noted that in fields outside of cryptography, the term "code" is commonly used for processes regarded as a "cipher" within the field. Only in this section will we be careful and make the appropriate distinction.

The effectiveness of cryptography depends on the plain text to be enciphered. Natural-language text has very distinctive patterns, and also provides much redundancy which promotes both comprehensibility of garbled text in day-to-day use, and the decrypting of enciphered data by analytical methods. We first will present the two basic enciphering methods and then discuss the security which they provide.

12-7-1 Ciphering

A *transposition cipher* operates on a group of characters. A key indicates the rearrangement pattern, as shown in Fig. 12-7. If the block length is N there are $N!$ possible rearrangement patterns.

```
N:  1  2  3  4  5  6  7  8  9 10 11 12 13 14 15 16 17 18 19 20 21 22 23 24 25 26 27 28 29 30 31 32 33 34 35

P:  W  h  o  '  s     g  o  i  n  g     t  o     d  o     t  h  e     j  o  b     o  n     E  P  I  A  C  ?

K: 34  6  2 10 23 27  9 29 25 18 32  7 20 24 22 30 11 14  3 13  5 15 28 26  4  1 35 19 18 17 31 12 21 16 33

C:  C     h  n  j  o  i     b     I  g  h  o     E  g  o  o  t  s        n     '  W  ?  t  o  o  P     e  d  A
```

N: character number, P: plain text, K: transposition key, C: cipher text.

Figure 12-7 Transposition cipher.

Some of the $N!$ enciphering-key combinations will be undesirable, since they leave parts of the message in the same sequence as the plain text, but many acceptable alternatives remain, especially when N is large. The example shows that the use of infrequent uppercase letters exposes a critical part of the message. A large key presents a problem in itself, since it can be difficult to transmit the key required for deciphering to the intended recipient.

In order to obtain a larger effective N and yet operate on shorter messages, individual bits or small bit sequences may be scrambled through transposition. Figure 12-8 gives an example using a short message in the ASCII character encoding. Figure 14-1 provides the bit-pattern table to be used. In the example the transposition key used is very short ($N = 5$) and repeatedly used.

Plain text	D	—	1	7	(ETX)
ASCII* encoding	1000100 0101101	0110001	0110111	0000011	
Regrouping into 5-bit sections	10001 00010	11010	11000	10110	11100	00011
Key	45231 45231	45231	45231	45231	45231	45231
Cipher text sections	01001 00100	10101	00101	10011	00111	11000
Regrouping into ASCII	0100100 1001010	1001011	0011001	1111000	
Cipher text	$	J	K	(EM)	X	

*See ASCII table, Fig. 14-1.

Figure 12-8 Transposition ciphering using a 5-bit transposition key.

A *substitution cipher* provides replacement of characters of the source message by one or more characters of a cipher alphabet. A *constant substitution cipher* provides an alternate unique character for every character of the source alphabet. The number of alternatives here is again N. The cipher can be described by a substitution table, or alternatively by the number of positions in the alphabet between the source and cipher character. The substitution must be chosen so that it is reversible; i.e., two different characters from the plain text should not map to the same cipher text character.

A very simple constant substitution cipher is the *Caesar cipher*. The substitution is defined by a displacement of a fixed number of positions, and hence offers only 27 choices for a compact alphabet, of which the "0" displacement is of course unsuitable. The choice of "1" has achieved fame in Arthur Clarke's movie script for "2001" by its use in naming the HAL computer.

A Gronsfeld substitution cipher is not constant. The key specifies the number of steps taken through the alphabet to obtain the cipher character. The number of steps can vary from zero to the number of characters which comprise the plain-text alphabet. The key can be produced by random permutation generator. Figure 12-9 provides an example of such a Gronsfeld cipher for an alphabet of 27 characters. The number of alternative encodings is now N^2 for an N-character alphabet, with very few choices that are unadvisable. A key containing many zeros would not provide satisfactory enciphering.

```
P:  A T   N O   E X P E N S E   T O   B R A T P U H R   A M E R I C A     I L L

O:  1 20  0 14 15  0  5 24 16  5 14 19  5  0 20 15  0  2 18  1 20 16 21  8 18  0  1 13  5 18  9  3  1  0 23  9 12 12
                                                                                         repeat
K:  6  2 10 23 27  9 25 18  7 20 24 22 11 14  3 13  5 15 26  4  1 19  8 17 12 21 16 *6  2 10 23 27  9 25 18  7 20 24

S:  7 22 10 10 15  9  3 15 23 25 11 14 16 14 23  1  5 17 17  5 21  8  2 25  3 21 17 19  7  1  5  3 10 25 14 16  5  9

C:  G vv J   J O I   C O W Y K N P N W A E Q Q E U H B Y C U Q S G A E C J Y N P E I
```

P: plain text, O: ordinal numbers of plain text, K: key, S: sum of O and K, mod 27, C: cipher text.

Figure 12-9   Gronsfeld cipher.

Instead of using random key numbers, another message can be used. The ordinal values of the characters of the key message provide the amount of displacement in the alphabet value. This technique is called the *Vignere cipher*. The key text, of course, can be of any length, even as long as the message to be enciphered. Blanks in the key may be ignored. For instance, the key string 'AMERICA OF THEE I SING' will generate a sequence $K = 01\,13\,05\,18\,09\,01\,15\,06\,20\,08\,05\,05\,09\,17\,09\,14\,07$. A Vignere procedure for a larger alphabet is shown in Example 12-2. Ordinal numbers representing the characters are added modulo the size of the alphabet, to determine the ordinal number of the cipher character.

Example 12-2   **Vignere Ciphering Procedure**

```
/* Input is the linein, key, and option = true for enciphering,
   false for deciphering.  The result is in lineout */
cipher: PROCEDURE(linein,key,option,lineout) EXTERNAL;
     DECLARE (linein,lineout,key) CHAR;
     l_line = LENGTH(linein); l_key = LENGTH(key); lineout = '';
                                 /* the typewriter alphabet */
     DECLARE abc CHAR(89) INITIAL(' 0123456789AaBbCcDdEeFf...
  /* Use one character to define the beginning of the key   */
     k = INDEX(SUBSTR(key,l_key,1),abc); l_key = l_key-1;
     DO i = 1 TO l_line;
          ord = INDEX (SUBSTR(linein,i,1),abc);
          kod = INDEX (SUBSTR(key,k,1),abc);
          IF option THEN kod = -kod;
          cord = MOD(ord+kod,89)+1;
          SUBSTR(lineout,i,1) = SUBSTR(abc,cord,1)
          k = MOD(k,l_key)+1;
     END;
     RETURN; END cipher;
```

An alternative to the addition of ordinal numbers, modulo the size of the alphabet, to determine the ordinal number of the cipher character can be used when the characters use a fixed-bit space. The **exclusive-OR** operation, used in Sec. 3-5 for hashing, provides an operation which is symmetric for both enciphering and deciphering, as shown in Fig. 12-10.

Plain text		A	0	0	7
ASCII encoding		1000001	0110000	0110000	0110111
Key		H	I	H	$\bar{\text{O}}$
ASCII encoding		1001000	1001001	1001000	1001111
Exclusive-OR of text and key		0001001	1111001	1111000	1111000
Cipher text		(HT)	Y	X	X

Enciphering   Deciphering

Figure 12-10 Ciphering with the exclusive-OR operation.

More sophisticated methods can be developed based on the two transformations discussed, but we first will describe common procedures of decrypting so that we can evaluate the weaknesses of the basic enciphering techniques.

12-7-2 Decryption

The ease with which a message can be decrypted depends on a number of factors:

- Is the method known?
- Is the source language known?
- How many alternative encipherings did exist?
- How much enciphered text using the same key is available?
- Is any matching plain text available?

A basic tool to aid in the decrypting of a cipher text is the generation of a *tableau*. If the method is known and the number of keys is limited, a tableau can be simply a listing of all possible decipherments. The tableau is scanned by eye and the plain text message will probably stand out.

If many, but yet a reasonably finite number of decipherments are possible, a *heuristic selection* of deciphered text can reduce the volume of the tableau to be listed. Simple heuristic algorithms might be that a vowel should exist in nearly all words, and that capitals and punctuation appear with certain regularity. Tableaus which do not show unreasonable pattern are not presented.

If the source language is known, substitution ciphers can be attacked using known *statistics* of letter frequencies. A simple substitution will generally yield the source text directly if the most frequent letter is replaced by E, the second most frequent letter by T, and so on, according to Table 12-3. Similar tables have been prepared for digrams (combinations of two letters), trigrams, initial and ending letters, and many other features of a language.

Even if such tables do not exist, as is the case when we have enciphered programs in a computer language, it may be possible to generate frequency tables from available source language samples. Programming language text also will be relatively easy to decrypt for a knowledgeable cryptologist, since the syntax is limited and the original variable names do not have to be reconstructed. Sequences of data digits will not provide much frequency information for decryption.

Table 12-3   Relative Frequency of Letters in English Written Text

E	133	D	43	G	14
T	93	L	38	B	13
O	85	C	31	V	10
A	81	F	29	K	5
N	75	U	28	X	3
I	71	M	27	J	2
R	70	P	22	Q	2
S	65	Y	15	Z	1
H	61	W	15	Total	1032

In the examples shown for the transposition ciphers and the Gronsfeld ciphers, *random-digit sequences* have been used that were obtained from a random number generator. Computer-software random-number generators, as well as hardware generators built from shift registers, have perfectly predictable sequences based on a few parameters. The parameters are

- The initial condition
- The multiplicand and shift amount
- The length of the register

The assumption that a random-number generator provides protection equivalent to its cycle length, which for a 21-bit generator can be up to 2^{21}, is not true for someone who has insight into its mechanism. Since, in practice, these random-number generators use parameters which have been carefully selected to give a maximal-length cycle without repeats, the number of alternatives is considerably less. For the 21-bit generator, the number of full cycle sequences is only 84672 out of the 2^{21}, or more than 2 000 000 sequences.

Long keys provide more protection than shorter keys but may not be effectively used in retrieval from databases. For every block or record stored on a file the key is reset to its begin point to enable key synchronization on random retrieval. The key is then always limited to the length of the data unit. Only the first terms of random-number sequences are used in this case, but this allows more choices of random-number-generation parameters.

When the *key changes* decryption has to start over. Changing keys frequently implies more transmission of keys between the enciphering point and the deciphering station, and this increases the susceptibility to having the keys intercepted or stolen.

Determination of the *key length* is important to the cryptographer who needs to reduce the search space. If enough cipher text is available relative to the key length, statistical tests on various groupings of the cipher text can provide clues. It has been stated that a ratio of twenty is adequate. The key length is estimated by generating descriptive parameters of various groupings of the cipher text. The greater cohesiveness of statistical results on the groups which match the original key length versus the groups which are unrelated provides key-length information to a computer-equipped cryptographer. Large amounts of cipher text in a database help to reveal the key patterns.

A considerable effort is required for decryption of nontrivial enciphered text. There is hence a great inducement to obtain some helpful extra information.

If the cryptoanalyst obtains a *matching segment* of cipher and plain text, the task is considerably simpler. If the segment is longer than the key, the key used can be determined in most cases where the enciphering method is known. A method to obtain matching text can be the use of index and goal records of sorted data, which allow the conjecture of data values by linkage or position.

If the intruder (gallantry presumes him male) has the capability to use the enciphering process, then he can submit data and key himself to obtain matching plain and cipher text and guess the method. If he can masquerade as a legitimate user of entry facilities, he may be able to obtain matching plain- and cipher-text based on the legitimate key, and guess both method and key.

12-7-3 Countermeasures

Having looked at the tools of the well-equipped cryptoanalyst we can survey countermeasures against attacks to these vulnerable spots. The countermeasures are listed in the same sequence that the decrypting devices were presented.

To minimize the effectiveness of the use of *tableaus*, we ensure that the number of encipherings is very high. The parameters for the basic methods have been given; combinations of the basic methods may produce the product or the sum of the individual alternatives. For instance, two successive Vignere ciphers — a so-called *two-loop system* — provides only the sum of the two ciphering options, although the key length will be increased if the loops are not of equal length. We always assume that the method is known to the intruder; after all, he may be using the same computer.

Reducing the redundancy of the source text will aid in disguising the message. In general, blanks and other punctuation will be omitted, and only uppercase characters may be used, transforming an 89-character typewriter alphabet to a 36- or 26-character set. By restricting enciphering to material which truly requires protection, the volume of available cipher text will be less and the analysis will be more difficult.

A number of approaches can be used to hide statistical features of cryptographic text. The use of *homophonic enciphering* can be very effective and relatively easy in a computer-based database. This method makes use of the fact that frequently there are more bit positions available in a computer code than are actually used.

If eight bit positions are available so that there are 256 possible characters for our cipher text, and our source alphabet consists of only 26 characters, we can map the frequent characters into multiple cipher characters. Given the relative frequencies of Table 12-3, we can assign to the letter "E" $133 \times 256/1032 \approx 33$ different substitution characters in any kind of order and hide the frequency of this particular character. The character "Z", on the other hand, would require $\lceil 1 \times 256/1032 \rceil$ or one character position. Some adjusting is needed to assign an integer number of code positions to each character within the total of 256. The letter "U" would receive seven positions. We might assign then to "U" the code values: (17, 30, 143, 145, 173, 225, 249). A random choice of these seven values would be transmitted when enciphering. The receiver would substitute "U" for any of these values. The other characters translate similarly into nonintersecting subsets of the code.

The decrypter is robbed of all single-character frequency information. A more complex homophonic cipher attempts to avoid frequency information not only for all the single characters in the source alphabet but also for other linguistic features which might be useful to a cryptoanalysis. Digrams and trigrams are effectively hidden by providing a transposition in addition to the other techniques. Data which have been encoded prior to enciphering also provide artificial and misleading frequency information.

Random-number sequences used for key generation can become much harder to detect if only a portion of the random number is used in the actual enciphering method. The generators can be restarted from a key value associated with the user to obtain many alternate sequences.

In a database environment, keys can be well protected if the generator of the enciphered record is the same person as the receiver, since then the key itself resides in the system for only a short time. The remainder of the time the key is stored in the user's mind, purse, or wallet. A change of key to foil a suspected intrusion is, however, very costly, since all the data stored under a previous key has to be deciphered and reciphered. Such a process in itself opens opportunities to the intruder.

In order to make the determination of the key from data text more difficult, more than one key might be used. Selection from a number of keys, possibly based on a record number, can weaken statistical analysis operating on large amounts of cipher text.

Varying the key length can cause great difficulty to algorithms which an intruder may use in his initial attempts to crack cipher text. The expansion of short messages with data designed to provide noise in the decrypting process also can disturb cryptoanalysis. The additional characters should follow neither random nor natural patterns but should have purposely obfuscating frequencies.

To avoid release of matching plain text and cipher text, the need for enciphering should always be carefully considered. For instance, if in address records the city, but not the zipcode, is enciphered, a large volume of matching text can become available. The problems of system access by intruders in order to obtain matching text are best handled by the existing identification and access logging methods. Since decryption takes time, there is a good chance to catch an intruder when an unusual access pattern has been detected during a periodic review of the access log.

12-7-4 Summary

The previous two subsections have illustrated a cops and robbers game which can be continued ad infinitum. At some point, the effort required to decrypt data will be greater than the cost of other subversion tactics. Literature on cryptology rarely discusses alternative methods of gaining access, so that an overall security trade-off will have to be made by the system designer. Cryptography has been widely applied to data transmission, so that some factors which distinguish data storage from communications should be listed.

In data transmission, there is a continuous stream of characters over a line. The effective message length can be very long and can use a continuous enciphering sequence, subject only to resynchronization in order to cope with transmission errors. In data storage, we want to access records in random order, and frequently encipher only small, critical items of the data record. This places a limit on the key length. The intruder may be willing to gather many such fields from a file to obtain decrypting information equivalent to a long continuous tap of a phone line.

Cryptographic methods also provide tools for joint access control to critical data. Either two successive keys can be applied by two individuals or parts of a key can be allotted, which have to be joined to become useful. Individual and project security can also be accomplished by use of multiple encipherment.

Where data are not generated or analyzed in the processor, but simply entered, stored, and retrieved, the ciphering mechanism can be in the remote data terminal. Such devices have been developed and are becoming increasingly feasible because of the increased sophistication of terminals. With such an approach, ciphering methods have to be used that are both transmission- and storage-oriented.

In database stored on computer systems cryptographic techniques provide only one aspect of the required access protection. Protection from destruction, intentional or accidental, is not obtained by enciphering; in fact, data will be lost if either the cipher text is destroyed or the key is lost.

Enciphering provides the capability to destroy selected data from backup files by destroying the key. This is often the only tool users have to assure that their data do not become available to someone who happens to reuse a tape which was used for system backup. The implementation of a combination of protection methods, of which cryptography is an important component, can yield a high level of security.

12-8 ANONYMITY AND POLLUTION

This section will concern itself with approaches to provide privacy in data banks which are used primarily for research, rather than for individual fact retrieval. When it is important to the suppliers of sensitive data that they cannot be traced, a researcher collecting such data may wish to provide such assurance, but then has to protect the individual's data from dissemination by coworkers, data-processing personnel, and possibly from inspection by government investigators with powers to subpoena records.

Many data banks exist to which these considerations apply. The reason for creation of large databases is the power they provide to spot trends and relationships. For individual data paper records are often more convenient.

12-8-1 Anonymity

Separation of the individual's identification from the data can provide the required anonymity but may impair aspects of the research. If, for instance, responses are gathered without identification data, the lack of a respondent's profile can make interpretation of the responses difficult.

An example of the desirability to have respondent information occurs when only educated individuals return a mailed query about the value of a certain TV program, because of some erudite language used in the questionnaire.

A separate data response and identification response, which cannot be linked, allows determination of who answered, and allows followup to rally participants who did not respond. However, no recourse exists to correct incomplete or inconsistent responses once the identification has been separated.

A reference number can be used with the data which link data responses to an individual, allowing determination of individuals through the responsible researcher only for followup. To protect the respondents, at least the reference numbers on the identification responses are destroyed when the collection is completed. If a long-term study requires multiple occasions of data entry by respondents, the identification file remains a liability.

If the participant in a study has the option to reinitiate followup, the participant can keep the reference number. The participant will be warned that if the number is lost no further followup is possible. To avoid the problem of loss a randomization procedure can create a reference number from an arbitrary identification sumbitted by the person. Hashing does not allow tracing of the individual from the reference number kept with the data. The identification string invented by the participant must not be traceable and must be destroyed after the reference number is obtained. Some consistency of the individual is required here, and there is always a finite chance of conflicting reference numbers. Data for conflict resolution may not be available (see Sec. 3-5).

12-8-2 Protected Linkage

The methods summarized above provide techniques which are useful before critical information enters a data file. These tools have been extensively used because of the deserved distrust of computer security mechanisms.

In many studies the need exists for the researchers to contact participants, so that an identification file has to be maintained. At other times data required for processing can contain enough information to identify individuals, or identification data remains necessary to allow the merging of data from other sources than the respondent.

A solution to this problem is the removal of the identification file outside the scope of possible intruders. Such a removal has been carried out by contracting with a data-processing agency in another country on a study where government interference was feared. Instead of removing the identification itself, a linkage file of matching reference numbers of data records and reference numbers of identification records was created and removed. This concept is sketched in Fig. 12-11. Matching,

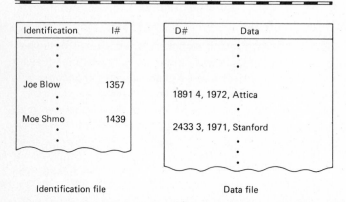

Figure 12-11   Remote linkage of data and identification.

when required, is carried out by the foreign operator, but the contract provides that only unidentified data are returned. The contract also specifies that the linkage file itself may not be returned, even to the contractees.

If data are to be matched at an insecure agency, but one is confident about one's own operation, enciphering of data other than the identification field may provide privacy.

12-8-3 Pollution

If the data are to be used only for statistical analysis, a systematic modification or *pollution* of the data may provide, if not privacy, at least protection from legal accountability. The modification should be such that statistical results remain valid but that individual data items cannot be ascertained.

A procedure of this type adds a normally distributed random number to a continuous observed data value. If the standard deviation of the normal is known, most statistical procedures can be used and their results adjusted. A lower level of confidence of the tested hypotheses is bound to occur because of the added degree of freedom in the data, but an increase in the number of observations can compensate for this loss. With binary data, such as yes/no responses, a certain number of the responses may be reversed on a random basis, which again can be accounted for in subsequent analyses. An individual record of such a file, while possibly embarrassing, is no longer of legal value.

The need to keep data private is an important responsibility in data-processing. The burden can be diminished by avoiding the collection of unnecessary data or unnecessary data elements. When data has lost its information value, it should be destroyed.

BACKGROUND AND REFERENCES

Westin[71] and Miller[71] survey history and legal issues of privacy protection. Petersen[67] describes the threats to computer security. Papers on abuse of privacy have been collected and analyzed (Parker[81]) at SRI International. VanTassel[72] also provides samples and guidelines. Carrol[72] shows how private data are used and misused. Many of the cases involve collusion and fraud; technical improvements to protect database access would not have prevented many of the abuses. An environment where reliability and protection is considered important might have discouraged many of the attempts. A professional code of ethics for computer professionals appears as part of a self-assessment procedure of the ACM in Weiss[82].

Data-processing practice and the use of RSS is described in IBM G320-1370–1376[74]. Two conferences sponsored by NBS (Renniger[74]) provide an overview of security and privacy concerns. Communication with a protected area is considered by Lampson[73]. Evans[74] and Purdy[74] decribes mechanisms to keep passwords secure. Authentication of users can be aided by cryptography as shown by Gifford[82] and Lindsay[79]. The problem of protecting individual data from statistical access has been frequently analyzed. Contributors are Schwartz[79], Denning[80], Beck[80], Chin[81], Schlorer[81], and Ozsoyoglu[82].

The move instruction is proposed by Lewin[69]. Hoffman[77] surveys access protection oriented toward privacy problems. Saltzer[75] provides a comprehensive summary of protection techniques in operating systems and includes a bibliography. Systems with protection features of interest are described by Weissman[69], Molho[70], Needham[72], Feustel[73], and Fabry[74].

Graham[68] presents an extensive model of accessors versus data objects and applies it to several systems. A simple model is formally analyzed by Harrison[76]. That the union of access privileges can be excessive is shown by Minsky[81]. The access model shown here was developed by a SHARE committee (Wiederhold[72]) as part of a requirements study.

MULTICS presents a major effort in the area of protection. Its development can be followed in Daley[65], Graham[68], Schroeder[72], and Saltzer[74]. Carrol[71] describes a system with adjustable object size for access control. Hoffman[71] protects data by procedures controlled by users. The accessor-object matrix is described by Conway[72]. How objects are managed is considered by Lindsay[79]. Owens in Codd[71] critically reviews many approaches and makes new suggestions.

Friedman[70] defines cliques. Access control rules for relational databases are given by Fernandez[81]. Stonebraker in King[75] uses integrity assertions (see Example 9-10 and Sec. 13-3) to assure privacy protection. Capabilities were introduced by Dennis[66], and were used by Fabry[74] in 1967. Access privileges are also granted to other users in a method developed by Griffiths[76] and improved by Fagin[78]. A schema-based approach with similar non-centralized privilege granting is developed by Arditi[78]. Recovery in distributed systems is surveyed by Kohler[81].

The basic book for cryptographers is Kahn[67]. Meyer[73] describes hardware. Mellen[73] surveys available methods; Stahl[73] presents homophonic enciphering. Friedman[74] evaluates the cost of ciphering. Feistel[73] and Diffie[76] present cryptology for computers. Gudes[80] develops the use for file systems. Bayer[76] applies enciphering to index trees and considers decryption and Davida[81] encrypts fields within records. Needham[78] applies encryption to users in distributed systems.

An implementation of DES for files is described by Konheim[80]. Bright[76] evaluated keys obtained from random-number generators. Gifford[82] considers both communication and databases. Pollution to protect privacy is considered by Reed[73].

EXERCISES

1 a Construct an example and evaluate the possible cost of accidental disclosure. Document the case as if to demonstrate current system weaknesses to a manager in a commercial computer installation.

    b Evaluate the loss for the case of Victor Velocity and of Sam Salesman in the introduction of the chapter.

    c Set up an interview protocol to determine the value of privacy of a juvenile police record for the members of a freshman college class.

2 A sign-on procedure consists of the entering of a name and the entering of a character password. Three trials at a password are allowed, and if no correct password is given, the accessor is logged off. Which provides more security: increasing the password from three to four characters or adding 1 minute to the logoff procedure? The following operational times are to be assumed:

$T(\text{name}) = 2$ s
$T(\text{password}) = 0.1$ s/character
$T(\text{response: "bad password"}) = 1$ s
$T(\text{basic logoff}) = 1$ s

96 different characters are allowed in the password.

3 a When is the above answer valid and when not?

    b What is the actual expected average time required for these alternatives?

4 A file has an internal 32-bit key. The call and test to open the file lock takes 20 μs. What is the expected safe time against trial-and-error entry?

5 Given the computer system you are currently using, investigate the types of access control available for user's data stored:

    a In primary memory

    b In secondary storage

6 How would you implement some of the access types listed in Sec. 12-3 that are not now available on the equipment you are currently using?

7 Rewrite the file-transposition program of Example 4-1 with a MOVE operation so that the privacy remains protected. Is this adequate?

8 How do the DBTG specification satisfy Saltzer's criteria in Sec. 12-6.

9 Augment Fig. 3-39 with procedures and tables required to achieve privacy for the work history of the employees.

10 Determine the key used and decrypt the source plain-text message for the following cryptogram. You know that the encoding is a 3-character Vignere cipher.

KMIRLLFXXRXL⊔WXRXSUNIKCDDJIKXD⊔SD⊔QMLQD

11 Write a program to do homophonic enciphering and deciphering. Then make a ranked frequency graph or table on the observed character frequency of some enciphered text.

Chapter 13

Integrity of Databases

Integrity is praised, and starves.

Juvenal
Satires, vol. 1 (A.D. 110)

Throughout the previous chapters we have implied that a well-structured database system, using careful data entry and update procedures, and operating reliably and free from unauthorized access, will be a secure depository for the data. There is, however, one area where failures can be generated while everything else seems to be proceeding satisfactorily. This problem area exists because of interference among the multiple transactions which are active within one computer system. The interference can be related to competition as well as to cooperation.

Integrity of a database means absence of inconsistent data. While an update transaction is in progress, the consistency of a database can be temporarily disturbed. One data element will reflect the update, while another element has not yet been changed. A low level of redundancy reduces potential integrity violations, since one fact will appear only rarely in more than one place. We have designed our databases with that objective, and yet find that they contain redundancies.

An error in a single transaction can cause a failure if a database update is not carried to completion, but the techniques presented in Secs. 11-3 and 11-4 deal with this problem successfully. However, even error-free update transactions can cause problems when they access shared data in a time period where there is other activity. Accessors sharing the data can pick up temporary inconsistencies caused by a concurrent update and spread the inconsistency through the database or to the output sent to the users.

Redundancy In order to achieve rapid access we create structures which are redundant. We also maintain connections between relations which employ redundancy. Less obvious are redundancies due to derived data, and due to externally imposed integrity constraints.

An index is a redundant access structure. The department name appears in each employee record and in one record of the department relation. The departmental salary expense is equal to the sum of all its employees' salaries. The total number of employees on the payroll should not change when an employee transfers from one department to another.

Many of the issues of integrity maintenance are also of concern to developers of operating-system services. We will in fact assume the availability of basic operating–system facilities and restrict our discussions to the interactions caused by database usage. An operating system will concentrate on controlling the competition for system resources due to interfering processes.

Competition Performance degradation due to competing multiple processes was seen in Sec. 5-4, and in Sec. 6-3 multiple processes were spawned by a single computation so that devices could be activated independently. Computations within a system may remain conceptually independent, and yet affect each other.

For databases we will deal again within the framework of *transactions*, as defined in Secs. 1-7-5 and 11-3-1. Although transactions may spawn multiple processes, we have to consider only cases of interference among processes which are initiated independently or, equivalently, by different transactions. We recall that a transaction is a computation that is initiated by a user, allowed to complete as rapidly as the available hardware permits, and then terminated.

The primary task of a transaction-oriented operating system is to keep one transaction as much as possible unaffected by the presence of other transactions. This independence is not completely realizable. There will be competition for the use of processors (especially if there is only one), for the use of disks and the channels to access them, and for the use of devices for input and output. Older devices for input and output (tape drives, readers, printers) are especially awkward to share since manual intervention is required to select the tapes to be mounted and to keep the paper going in and out in the proper order.

In a database operation there are additional resources to be shared. All users will want to access the schema, many may select a particular file, or index, or hierarchical level, and several may wish to access the same data item. Data are perfectly sharable, until one or more transactions want to make changes. Then some users may be denied access to the data to avoid the dissemination of inconsistent information; Figs. 13-1 and 13-2 will illustrate the problem. Now competition for **data** resources ensues.

Cooperation When a transaction has spawned multiple processes, their activities have to be coordinated (see Fig. 6-9). These processes may consist of multiple sections and spawn new processes themselves. In Example 8-8 database procedures were initiated to create **ACTUAL** results in storage, after an update or insertion of new source data in a file. Often transactions initiated by distinct users may have to be similarly coordinated.

An example where explicit cooperation is required can be found in the generation of salary checks by a payroll department. The transaction should be executed only after all `hours_worked` and salary raises have been entered for the period.

Locking, as described in Sec. 13-1 below, provides the means to keep transactions from interfering with each other. Locking is presented using examples of the various cases to be considered and the mechanisms which can deal with them. All the mechanisms have their own liabilities and must be considered with care. An especially serious problem due to locking is the possibility of mutual lock-out or deadlock, the topic of Sec. 13-2. We review data integrity in Sec. 13-3.

13-1 LOCKING

The basic problem of competition for apparently sharable resources can be illustrated by the interaction of the two transactions illustrated in Fig. 13-1. When more than one transaction obtains a copy of some data element for updating, the final database value for that element will be the result of the last transaction to write the updated value. The result of the other transaction has been overwritten. The database does not reflect the intended result, here 230 `Widgets`.

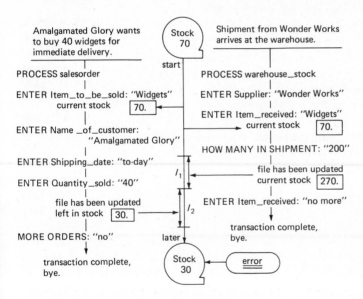

Figure 13-1 Update interference.

The integrity of results must also be protected. Figure 13-2 shows a case where a read transaction, executed while an update is in progress, produces an erroneous result. We also use Fig. 13-2 to illustrate other aspects of locking.

The solution to integrity problems is the provision of a *locking* mechanism which assures mutual exclusion of interfering transactions. The transaction which is the first to claim the nonsharable object becomes temporarily the owner of the object. Other transactions which desire access to the object are blocked until the owner releases the claim to the object.

13-1-1 A Lock Mechanism

The claim to an object is made by setting a *semaphore*. A simple binary semaphore is a protected variable **x**, which indicates if the associated resource is **free** or **occupied**. A semaphore can be set to indicate **occupied** only if it indicated before that the resource was **free**. The transaction which sets the semaphore becomes its owner, and only it is permitted to reset the semaphore to **free**.

In order to implement a semaphore which can be tested and set in this manner we need a primitive, indivisible computer operation. A typical instruction is shown in Example 13-1.

Example 13-1   Semaphore Machine Instruction

Label	Operation	Address	Comment
alpha	TEST_AND_SET	x	*If* x=0 *set* x:=1 *and skip to* alpha+2;
	JUMP	to_wait	*otherwise continue at* alpha+1
	OPEN	resource_x	*Go on and grab the resource*

Waiting may mean calling the system for later scheduling of this transaction; scheduling and queuing was described in Sec. 6-3.

We assume that any computer has some instruction which can perform the semaphore function. Some versions permit setting **x** with a code identifying the current owner; other versions can count the number of requests that are being held. An identifier or count data field can always be implemented by protecting a data field itself with a semaphore.

Locking is achieved by forcing all transactions which wish to access a protected object to check the semaphore. This checking is typically enforced by the system during the execution of update requests. When we talk about *locks* we mean some means to limit and delay access, typically implemented by the system through one or several semaphores.

13-1-2 Objects to Be Locked

In Fig. 13-1 only a single field had to be locked. Another field in the same record could have been modified independently. A schema-oriented database system is able to know what data fields may be altered by an update transaction and can lock only those fields. Since a **REWRITE** operation, however, specifies an entire record, and since file systems will in general write the entire block from the file buffers, it is difficult to make use of this detailed knowledge.

Granularity   The choice of size of objects to be locked is referred to as the *granularity* of locking. The smallest unit which can be identified for locking through a schema is a field or a segment as defined in Sec. 8-3-1; for file access it is a record, and the smallest unit available for buffer management is typically a block. Many operating systems provide locks only for entire files.

Having small granules will considerably enhance system performance since the probability of interference will be less. For read operations we can manage small granules; for update we may be limited to blocks. Small granules means having more locks, so that they are more difficult to manage. The management of locks is presented in Sec. 13-1-7. All granules have to be positively identified so that, if they are locked, they will be associated with only one lock.

Identification of Objects The identification of the granules, for instance, records, is a function of some supervisory system. Each granule most be positively identified. The users may not be able to recognize synonymous record names and will be even less aware about any shared blocks.

Example 13-2   Identifying an Object

In a complex file structure, the same record may be accessed via multiple paths, and hence may seem to have multiple names. Three alternate path-names for the data element which contains the inventory count of Widgets, stored in a warehouse for a customer may be:

```
supplier = 'Wonder Works',  part = 'Widget';
warehouse = 'Centreville',  shelfno = '321005';
customer = 'Grandiose Co',  account_item = 14.
```

One candidate for a unique identification is the TID, presented in Sec. 4-2-3. If the lock applies to blocks, the relative block number provides the required identification. To identify fields a catenation `block_number.record_number.field_number` may be used. The record number in a block is found through the marking scheme shown in Fig. 2-11 and the field number may be based on the schema entry. When a record spans blocks, multiple blocks have to be managed as one object.

Lock Interval Locking also has a time dimension. A protective approach is to lock each object read or needed for later update as early as possible. When the transaction is completed all locks will be freed.

The lock interval can be shortened by releasing locks from an object as soon as the update is performed. This means that each object to be read has to be locked if an update is contemplated. Locking during the READ_TO_UPDATE – REWRITE interval is typical when using the IMS system; the three GET operations seen in Sec. 9-6-2 have the alternate forms shown in Table 13-1.

Table 13-1   IMS Locking Commands

The operations
```
Get_and_Hold_Unique    segment_sequence
Get_and_Hold_Next      segment_sequence
Get_and_Hold_Next_within_Parent  segment_sequence
```
will lock the **segment_sequence** *until a writing, that is a*
```
REPLace   or   DeLETe
```
operation on the **segment_sequence** *is executed.*

A transaction may of course need to update several objects. Holding several records, updating and releasing them when done violates the rules defined for protection when using the two-phase transaction concept, introduced in Sec. 11-4.

No records should be written before the commit point. When the commit message is given to the transaction manager and accepted all writing takes place.

This means that the transaction locks data resources up to the commit point. Resources held by one user are not available to others. To get a high level of usage from a computer system it is desirable to exclude other users for as short a time as possible.

In the example of Fig. 13-1 the resource will have to be held for at least several seconds, since the READ and REWRITE operations are separated by an intermediate terminal activity. The time that other users are excluded can be reduced if we do not lock until ready to update the file. But the number of Widgets can be different now. Since within the transaction processing interval (I_1 or I_2 in Fig. 13-1), the Widgets in stock may have been sold by another transaction, a new READ_TO_UPDATE with a lock is executed before the REWRITEs. The value obtained by the second READ is checked again and, if found different and perhaps inadequate, the customer has to be informed and the transaction aborted. Data which dont contribute to the result do not have to be reread. The customer may have asked about other items, or there may been a check about previous Widget orders.

Deferring locking Extending the two-phase transaction concept to locking we can avoid actually locking resources until the transaction is completely defined. Not locking means there is some chance of another transaction having modified the data so that all data which contribute to the result have to be reread. When the transaction is ready to be committed all data are reread with locks. The time that other users are excluded is reduced, but at a cost: each record has to be read twice. If the result of the new read is not identical the transaction has to *release* the commit and redo its computation from the beginning. This mode of operation also has implications in avoiding deadlock, as will be discussed in Sec. 13-2-3.

Locking the devices to reduce the lock interval The cost of an extra READ_TO_UPDATE just prior to a REWRITE is small since little seek interference is expected. Even if only one READ is performed the lock interval may be much smaller if no other transactions access the devices being used and seeks are avoided. The assumption that seek interference is negligible has been made throughout the derivation of performance formulas (Eqs. 2-29 to 2-31). A transaction may be able to impose such a condition via a lock.

The possibility of a seek between READ_TO_UPDATE and the REWRITE can be avoided by letting the lock, which is set at the time of the READ_TO_UPDATE operation not only exclude other accesses to the object, but also exclude all other accesses to the entire device. In programming terminology the sequence of instructions between READ_TO_UPDATE and the completion of the REWRITE is made into a *critical section*.

13-1-3 Locking to Protect Transaction Results

We considered up to this point locks to protect the database. A temporary inconsistency introduced by an updating transaction can also create erroneous answers in transactions which report answers to the users. The example of Fig. 13-2 gives a scenario leading to a wrong result. This case appears not to be as serious, since the database will not be left in an erroneous state.

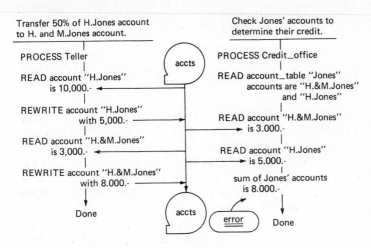

Figure 13-2 Read interference.

The **Jones**'s can probably set the record straight later if they get a lower than expected credit rating. If they are familiar with computing, they may realize that the poor rating was due to confusion created by other requests they made to their bank.

However, a system which produces erroneous results with any frequency will soon lose the confidence of the users. Locking is hence also appropriate in this case. Since no **REWRITE** will be given an explicit **UNLOCK** may be needed to release a lock once it is set. The update transaction should already be locked to prevent update interference. Read-only transactions which need to be correct, i.e., have to be able to stand up to an *audit*, should issue locks against simultaneous updates.

We note that erroneous results are only created due to interfering updates which modify multiple related data elements. In this example the lock interval extends over several update operations, but no intervening terminal operations occur in the interval.

Audit-reads and Free-reads While correct results from read-only queries are always preferable, we can envisage queries which do not require lockout of concurrent updates. A **READ NOLOCK** statement is available in PL/1 for that purpose. Queries which only fetch a single data value do not require protection by locks, although the single answer may be slightly out of date. If up-to-dateness is a problem, a second data element which contains the update time has to be fetched, transforming the single-element query to a multiple-element query. Now a decision to lock or not to lock has to be made.

Inquiries leading to a summarization of many values may also avoid the expense of locking and disabling concurrent updates and be allowed to proceed freely, and not test or set locks. If many values are aggregated in the query result, the effect of errors due to interference should be negligible. The use of locks to ensure audit-proof results to perform tabulations which require many accesses to a file can make shared database usage impossible. Audit-reads can be always be performed in systems which use versioning (Sec. 11-3-3) since the data elements will not be shared between reading and writing. We will call a query which needs to lock an *audit-read* and a query which can disregard locks a *free-read*.

13-1-4 Specification of a Lock

The database supporting system has to be made aware that a lock of an object is requested. One would not expect the end user, the salesperson or stockclerk, to request the locking action. The locking request is typically made by an applications programmer who defines the transaction, or by the transaction management system, or by the file system in response to the requested operations. A means to place the programmer in control of acquiring locks is a `CLAIM` operation, which exists in various forms on many systems.

When an object is *claimed*, the intention to use the object is noted by the system. The claim is acceptable if it cannot lead to problems. The claim is noted (using again a semaphore to avoid conflicting claims) and the transaction can proceed. If the claim is denied, the transaction has the choice of continuing with another task, maybe to return later, or to be placed into a waiting queue. Section 6-3 presented some examples of such queues.

When claimed objects are accessed then locks are set. There may be delays, but eventually a transaction waiting in the queue for an object is granted access to the claimed object and can proceed. The transaction sets a lock to gain exclusive access to the object, which will be held until the transaction executes a `RELEASE` command. Claims held by a transaction are also released when the transaction completes or aborts.

Transactions which terminate without releasing their locks are considered to be defective. If the system has the capability to undo the effects of defective transactions and to restore the database (Sec. 11-4), such a restoration is recommended. At a minimum the system administrator has to be informed when transactions halt without releasing all of their locks on resources. If locks are not released a part of the system becomes unavailable.

Table 13-1 showed some instructions which specify locks for segments of a hierarchical database file. When using operating systems other than transaction systems the control language may give a choice if a specific file can be shared among programs or cannot be shared. To prevent sharing a lock is associated with an entire file. The system will disallow any shared use of the file once it has been opened until it is again closed. Since `OPEN` and `CLOSE` operations tend to be costly, the lock interval tends to be long. The operating system, rather than the program controls any locking. For instance, the PL/1 statement

        OPEN FILE stock UPDATE

does not provide integrity protection. It permits `READ`, `REWRITE` sequences to be interrupted, and since execution of a `REWRITE` is not required no cue other than a `CLOSE` operation is available to release the object.

If sharing is permitted by the operating system, the programmed transactions or a transaction manager assumes some responsibility. The file, when it is initially defined or opened, is characterized to accept certain operations. The statement

        OPEN FILE(stock) EXCLUSIVE UPDATE

of PL/1 will cause any READ statement to set a lock on the record being read. Only one lock can exist per file. That lock will remain until either a REWRITE, a DELETE, or an explicit UNLOCK statement for that record is executed.

In systems using virtual memory support for files, some automatic protection exists for pages being updated. Either a single page will be shared among multiple processes, or the fact that a copy has been modified will force subsequent accessors to fetch the modified page. Problems can still occur if pages are modified, as was the case in Fig. 13-1, from data which are the result of calculations in the private region of a user. Since the paging system protects the access to the files, only the pages in memory need to be protected. If users share single copies of storage pages in memory, interference protection becomes simple and rapid. The transactions can set locks on the pages in memory, do the reread, check for interference, and, if the read values are still the same, do rewrite operations and release the locks. The same technique works if a file buffer managing program keeps only a single copy of each block in memory.

Regions to Be Locked Example 13-1 illustrated an interference problems due to concurrent updating of a single atomic object. While this problem certainly requires resolution, other interference problems may require locking of collections of objects, or *regions*.

A simple example was shown in Fig. 13-2, where data obtained by a read transaction are inconsistent because of a sequence of updates required to carry out a transfer of funds. In order to guarantee the correctness of other transactions a region comprised of two accounts (H.Jones, H.&M.Jones) has to be locked by the update transaction.

Regions have to be locked to avoid interference both from read and from update transactions. Figure 13-2 illustrated read interfence. A similar Credit_office transaction which computes and writes the credit rating of the Jones' would place an error into the database.

If very many or very large objects are included in the region to be locked for a transaction, the probability of other transactions being affected increases rapidly. In Sec. 13-1-5 we will discuss the extent of interference and in Sec. 13-1-6 the effect on performance. Section 13-1-7 will consider the management of locks.

The technique of holding objects until the update statement is executed fails when regions have to be considered. Regions either have to be defined by the programmer of the transaction or all resources accessed have to be held until the transaction is completed.

13-1-5 Interactions among Locks

We showed that it is necessary to provide lockouts among update transactions and between read-only queries which need results which can stand up to an audit and update transactions. Read-only queries do not interfere with each other. The use of lockouts makes a part of the database unavailable.

We also distinguished in Sec. 13-1-3 queries which needs to lock (audit-reads) and queries which can disregard locks (free-reads). The interaction rules are summarized in Table 13-2.

Blocking is achieved by having a locking semaphore set on the object of the operations. When the semaphore is freed the transaction scheduler can restart transactions which are queued because of that semaphore. The variable **flag** is a second semaphore to avoid *hibernation* of update transactions. This issue is discussed in Sec. 13-2-1.

Table 13-2   Data Access Interference

Request	Operation in Progress		
	Update	Audit-reads	Free-reads
Update	Block	Block and set **flag** on	Pass
Audit-read	Block	Pass unless **flag** on	Pass
Free-read	Pass	Pass	Pass

Serializability We have shown examples of interference among transactions. No interference would occur if each transaction would wait until its predecessor is finished. Such a schedule is called *serial*. The system performance, however, would be greatly impaired, since no computational or device overlap could occur. We wish to permit any overlap of transactions which will still give the correct answers and leave the database in some correct state. This will be true if the execution order of the primitive operations of the set of overlapping transaction gives a result which is equivalent to some *serial schedule*of the original transactions. The property of overlapping transactions having a corresponding serial transaction schedule is called *serializability*.

If we are conservative we assume that any transactions which share data are always sensitive to their excecution sequence, as defined in Sec. 11-3-4. Then we can consider only four cases of operations from two transactions on a shared data item.

Table 13-3   Cases for Serializability

Transactions A and B may each read or write the same data item X:				
case	rr	rw	wr	ww
transaction				
A:	read X	read X	write X	write X
B:	read X	write X	read X	write X
rearrangable	yes	no	no	yes

Serializability will be maintained if the operation sequence of any **rw** and **wr** cases is not interchanged. The **rr** case is not sensitive to order. In the **ww** case the value created by an overlapping transaction A is overwritten by transaction B and can be ignored if B has arrived. This case will occur rarely, since it actually indicates a poor transaction design. Transactions which independently write the same data element, without reading it first, to a file will produce results dependent on their relative time of execution. In practice some synchronization is required. There will be read operations to data or to some shared semaphore to control execution sequences.

Interference of Access Path Objects Access to intermediate objects often precedes access to goal data. Depending on the structure of the files in the database objects in the access path have to be locked as well. Typical access path objects are indexes, rings, or ancestors in a hierarchy. The access path can also involve intermediate data items, for instance, the Department record to find the Employee who is a 'Manager'.

In the locking of access paths a hierarchical structure is prevalent.

A transaction has to assign a task to an employee with suitable skills. While the task record is being analyzed any employee record is a candidate for further locking. When the required skills have been determined only the records of employees with those skills have to be held. When the appropriate employee is found only that one employee record has to be locked for an update.

If an update requires the change of one or more indexes, subsidiary index levels and records have to be locked out from concurrent updates. Audit-reads and free-reads can be permitted to make progress only if indexes and pointers to goal data remain valid. For audit-reads the goal object still requires locking.

Update transactions in a hierarchical structure require a lockout of all descendants. Audit-reads are also affected because goal data are qualified by the data values of their ancestors. Unless rings are updated very carefully, it may be wise to also lock out free-reads. When a tree is being updated, the possibility of rebalancing can make all or a large portion of the tree (a broom of the tree) inaccessible. If rebalancing is infrequent per update, it is advantageous to treat the rebalancing algorithm as a separate process. This avoids excessively large claims associated with update transactions which may cause rebalancing.

Table 13-4 summarizes the additional access constraints. It is important to note that the regions to which access is blocked are much larger than the goal objects considered in Table 13-2.

Table 13-4   Access Path Interference

Request	Operation in Progress		
	Update	Audit-reads	Free-reads
Update	Block	Pass if safe	Pass if safe
Audit-read	Pass if safe	Pass	Pass
Free-read	Pass if safe	Pass	Pass

The qualifier, *if safe*, has to be based on a thorough understanding of the file update transactions and of the sequence in which operations are scheduled. Section 13-1-6 illustrates some cases. Buffer queuing algorithms which reorder processing sequences to achieve optimal device utilization can also affect the safety of interacting transactions.

Explicit Claiming of Regions If the system does not support two-phase protocols, or if the transactions are so extensive that it is not acceptable to lock the required resources for the length of the transaction, explicit claiming becomes necessary. It can also be difficult to deal automatically with a wide variety of resources: records, blocks, rings, pointer-lists, files, devices, etc.

We use again the operating system concept of a *critical section* (Sec. 1-2-2). If all the objects comprising the region to be accessed are known at the beginning of the critical section, a multiple object claim can be presented to the system. A claim for multiple objects itself has to be processed as a single critical section by the supporting operating system to avoid claim conflicts from other transactions. The operating system can again use a semaphore to defer other requests.

The allocation of the object is not necessarily carried out when the object is claimed. Many objects are claimed because they may be of interest, but will not be actually needed. When a claim is granted, the system only promises to make the object available when needed. This allows a transaction which desires access to the claimed object, but which will not otherwise interfere with another transaction, to proceed. Deferral of allocation to the point of actual use can significantly decrease congestion in a system which requires regions to be claimed at one single time.

Incremental Claims It is not always possible, at the initiation of the transaction, to specify all objects which may be needed eventually. Intermediate analysis of data can define additional objects which have to participate in the claim. Some incremental claims may be avoided by initially claiming large regions, at the cost of making much of the database inaccessible. A capability to claim objects incrementally can hence be necessary in order to provide flexibility in transaction processing or in order to achieve adequate system performance.

When claims are submitted incrementally and a later claim is denied, the objects claimed previously by the transaction are tied up in an unproductive manner. Incremental claims also require extensive lock management.

13-1-6 Performance Issues of Locking

The use of locks has a great impact on database performance. Locks set by one transaction make the database unavailable to many other transactions. We already defined, in Sec. 13-1-3, the concept of a **Free-read** in order to create a class of uninvolved transactions.

The degree to which performance is affected depends on the size of the object or region being locked and the length of the locking interval. In Sec. 13-1-2 we considered reduction of the lock interval in a transaction by rereading the input data for a transaction, with a lock, just prior to the rewrite for the update operation. The cost incurred here is a duplicate read operation. A quantitative evaluation has to estimate the delays due to locking, using estimates of load, transaction lengths, and granularity versus the increase of read operations.

Deferred File Update The use of locks during daily processing can be avoided if file modifications, made due to updates, are not immediately reflected in the files. When updating is deferred the blocks or records generated by update transactions are identified relative to the main database, but held on an update-log file. The update-log file is merged into the database during periods of no or little simultaneous activity, typically at night. Implicit in this approach is a disregard of issues of serializability: read operations do not reflect recent writes.

Deferred update can be necessary in systems where locks are restricted to large objects (files) while update involves small objects (records or fields).

Reducing the Object Size There may also be opportunities to reorganize the granularity of a transaction to reduce the locking requirements. The redundancy existing in files permits breaking up of some complex operations, and this reduces extensive locking requirements.

Transactions which access many records of a file should be analyzed for granularity. Although locking of all records of a file is easy, sharing the file is made impossible. In some systems the cost of claiming and releasing all file records individually may be high; locking blocks may be optimal.

The critical section required to protect **Jones** in Fig. 13-2 extends from the first **READ** to the last **REWRITE** of the transaction, and the region to be locked involves two objects. In complex queries the region which has to be locked can involve many objects:

```
DEDUCT taxes FROM Employees.pay AND PUT SUM INTO tax_account.
```

Analysis shows that only one **Employee** record at a time and the one ledger record, namely **tax_account**, has to be locked.

In order to reduce the size of the large locked object, the **Employee** file, locks are set and released within the loop. Example 13-3 indicates the points with †. The number of **Employee** records specified by the DO-loop should be remain fixed. Setting a read-lock on **no_of_employees** will prevent insertion and deletion of entire **Employee** records, but other values in the file remain fully accessible during the **Withhold_tax** transaction.

Example 13-3   A Transaction with Locking Alternatives

```
Withhold_tax: TRANSACTION;
  tax_account = 0;
    DO FOR no_of_employees;
†      net_salary = gross_salary - tax;
       tax_account = tax_account + tax;          †
    END;
```

We note that the need to lock is again related to the existence of redundant derived information. The transitive functional dependency between an **employee**, **tax**, **gross_salary**, and **net_salary** is not obvious enough to be captured by a normalized view model.

Reliability and Performance of Simultaneous Transactions Interference in access paths can cause transaction programs to fail. Moving an object can cause a transaction trying to locate the object via pointer to pick up invalid data or, worse, garbage when further pointers are expected. These problems can be minimized or entirely avoided by careful design of the procedures which manipulate the paths.

When access methods use indexes, obsoleted pointers can be kept safe by not reusing the space that they point to, although the space is freed when records are deleted or updated. To avoid fetching bad data a *tombstone* is placed in the old spot. The space becomes safely reusable when a reorganization can assure that all pointers to this spot are gone. In Sec. 3-4-1 we considered how locking for update protection can be minimized in B-trees.

In ring structures (Sec. 3-6-1) the problems of losing a path through the database due to a simultaneous update become even more pronounced. Figure 13-3 sketches a problem which can occur with any form of linked records. If it is possible for one user to read the file while another user, or a system task, updates the chain, care has to be taken that the reader of the chain sequence is not thrown off the track, as indicated by the stars in the diagram. The safe procedure shown on the right of Fig. 13-3 unfortunately tends to use more buffers and more access time to execute, since READ and REWRITE operations for one block are not paired. If the entire ring is locked the left choice does become safe, the performance of the specific transaction increases, but other, simultaneous transactions may be held up.

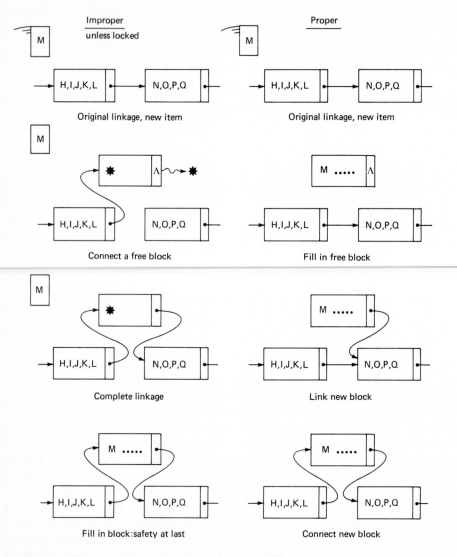

Figure 13-3 Insertion of a block into a chain.

13-1-7 Lock Management

Many operating systems only provide locks for entire files. Setting a lock means that all other updates or even all operations to the file are locked out. This can cripple system response time. A single lock per file does simplify the referencing mechanism. For every open file one lock is defined. When smaller granules are to be locked, the number of required locks is unpredictable, but often large.

Since shared databases require many locks, the management of the locks frequently becomes a responsibility of the database or the transaction management system. The semaphores used for locking have to be dynamically assigned to data items since it is not feasible to preassign a semaphore for every possible data item and its hierarchy. Locking schemes for databases, if implemented with care, can support the number of locks associated with a fine granularity.

A straightforward implementation to handle semaphores dynamically will use a linked list for the locked items. The identification of an item being locked and its temporary owner is entered into a list of locked items. When the lock is released the entry is removed from the list. On each reference which might conflict according to Tables 13-2 or 13-4 the list is checked to find if the object is locked. The search for locks requires a linear scan. Considerable CPU time will be used if many locks are active and have to be checked.

A more effective way to organize semaphores for locks is by using a hash table. Only one bit is needed to indicate that an object is locked, so that a modestly sized hash table can accommodate many locks. To minimize the number of collisions we choose a generous hash table size, say

$$m_s \approx 2 \,\#(\text{transactions}_{max}) \times \#(\text{number of locks a transaction may set})$$

A single additional semaphore is used to protect access to the hash table when setting or testing locks. The unique object identification is the key to be transformed into a bit address in the table, and the setting bit at that address indicates whether the object is **occupied** or **free**.

The important notion in using a hash table for the semaphores is that *collisions are not detected or resolved*. The collisions due to the use of hashing cause some false lock indications, but the rate of *false-locks* can be set very small by increasing m_s. A transaction is typically blocked without checking if the lock is true or false; the only check needed is that the **occupied** signal is not due to another lock request from the same transaction. The transaction progress thread defined in Sec. 11-4-2 contains the required data.

The rate of overall false lock indications will increase in busy times, but the time needed to deal with them remains constant, and this a considerable advantage over the list-processing scheme, which uses more time per check when the demand is already high. However, the probability of deadlock (presented in Sec. 13-2-3) increases at busy times, and if lexical ordering is used to avoid deadlock the key-to-address transformation should be of the sequence-maintaining type, as described in Sec. 3-5-1.

Using the same space to keep object names for collision resolution would greatly reduce m_s and increase the number of collisions. To regain the low number of collisions and have the capability to resolve them the hash table has to be made many times longer, for a 10-byte object name by a factor of 81, and this may cause paging, requiring another level of locking!

The blocking of transactions and resources will not only affect performance, but unfortunate interaction sequences can delay the system *forever*. These problems are the subject of the next section.

13-2 HIBERNATION AND DEADLOCK

The reader may have developed an uncomfortable feeling in the preceding section. Multiple transactions walk around a database, claiming ownership of objects and regions in order to block others from interfering with their intended activities. There is indeed a distinct possibility of trouble. The problems can be categorized into two classes:

Hibernation A transaction is blocked, or put to sleep, and the system is too busy to rouse the transaction within a reasonable time: *the transaction is in hibernation*.

Deadlock One transaction is blocked by another, and the other transaction is blocked in turn by the first one. The circle can involve multiple transactions, and none of them can be awakened without potential for integrity violations: *the transactions are mutually deadlocked*.

From the user's point of view the difference between hibernation and deadlock is small: *the system doesn't work again*. For a system designer the difference is major: deadlock can be understood and solved or its occurrence may be reduced to tolerable levels. Hibernation problems can be due to one-time activities, and by the time an analysis is done all transactions are awake and no evidence remains. Deadlock also has been more interesting to the computer scientist because it is more amenable to formal analysis, whereas analysis of hibernation requires showing that interference can lead to excessive delays relative to some performance specification.

Hibernation was already encountered in Table 13-2. The classic deadlock condition is associated with incremental claims; Fig. 13-4 illustrates the problem.

13-2-1 Hibernation

Hibernation occurs when a transaction does not receive resources for an exccessively long period. The user who submitted the transaction which is in hibernation has reason to believe that the system is not functioning.

Hibernation of a transaction H can occur because there is an apparently infinite chain of waiting transactions preceding H. Thhis can be caused because another transaction holding a claimed resource of H does not terminate, because H has a low scheduling priority relative to heavily used other transactions, or because the blocking priorities do not permit H to proceed.

An infinite chain of updates can be created if a circularity occurs in the transactions or in the database constraints. If the `sales_manager` gets 5% of the `department.profit` as a `salary` but the `salaries` are deducted from the `profit` then we have a case which will execute until round-off errors, a transaction manager, or the MTBF intercede. Such a transaction is in error, but the error will not be detected if it was tested on **employee**s who do not share in the profit.

Having transactions of differing priorities is obviously an invitation for hibernation of transactions which have low priority. Processes which have heavy file demands may be assigned a high priority to the CPU so that they will make acceptable progress. This rule also leads to an improved disk utilization. An excessive number of such processes can however starve all other users. A technique to deal with starvation due to priorities, if priorities cannot be avoided, is to increase the priority of a process by some amount periodically, so that eventually the delayed process will have an adequate priority to proceed. Transaction systems tend to avoid priority schemes.

An example of the third case, hibernation due to blocking, can be caused by the basic locking rules shown in Table 13-2. The addition of the **if flag** clause provides a solution.

The lock set by an **Audit-read** blocks subsequent interfering **Updates**, but not subsequent **Audit-reads**. Since there are no restrictions on multiple **Audit-reads** being processed, an **Update** can be permanently delayed if interfering **Audit-reads** are submitted continuously.

The solution shown in Table 13-2 uses an additional **flag** semaphore. The setting of the **flag** to **on** delays entry of further **Audit-read**s and enables access for waiting **Update** requests. Alternative means to assure access for waiting **Update**s and avoid hibernation use priorities or preemption.

Long-term blocking can still occur when one transaction issues updates at a high rate. Now all audit-reads will be delayed. It is hence necessary that the system not only considers integrity; when there are delays the system has also the task to allocate the use of resources equitably among the transactions.

A solution to the allocation problem [Dijkstra[65]] uses a semaphore to control a system variable which gives access to the object to each transaction in turn. An approach used in operating systems for page allocation may also be applicable: transactions which do not get their fair share of computing cycles receive an increased priority standing. Eventually the blocked transaction will be chosen from the queue.

A practical solution used by many transaction-oriented systems is to limit the length of time that a transaction is allowed to be active. This approach brings two new problems to the fore: The amount of time needed is influenced by system load, and a strict rule may cut off some valid transactions when the system is busy and let erroneous transactions proceed when the system is lightly loaded. This variablility can be controlled by more detailed accounting of CPU time; unfortunately, on many systems it takes a significant fraction of a CPU to account precisely for its use by multiple users.

The second, and more serious problem with killing a transaction which exceeds its time limit is: what does the system do within a transaction which did not finish? The fact that a lock was requested is an indication that an inconsistency could be expected. The only satisfactory solution is to attempt to undo the transaction. The logging and recovery facilities described in Sec. 11-4 are required to achieve this. The conditions for rollback will be further discussed in Sec. 13-2-4.

In systems which support extensive and short transactions the time limit is set according to time estimates specified by the programmer. This estimate may also be used for scheduling purposes. A long transaction can cause intolerably long blocking.

13-2-2 Causes of Deadlocks

Deadlocks occur when two or more transactions request resources incrementally and mutually block each other from completion. The transactions and resources form a cycle, seen in Fig. 13-4 and abstracted in Example 13-4. We will now also look at some other cases of deadlock and then treat the deadlock issue in general.

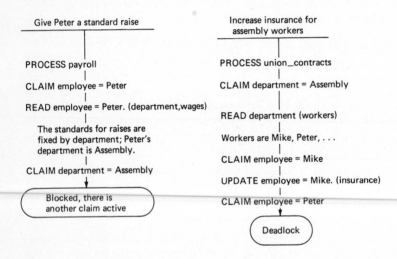

Figure 13-4 Circular deadlock.

A deadlock can even be created when a single object is accessed by two transactions and incremental claims are accepted. An example is shown in Fig. 13-5.

This type of deadlock has a higher probability of occurring if the objects being locked are large. When a file is the unit of locking, the first claim may be issued to gain access to one record and the incremental claim issued in order to update another record in the file. Both claims address the same unit.

Example 13-4   Deadlock Cycle

Transaction A	Object	Transaction B
payroll →	employee	
" →	department ←	union_contract
	employee ←	"

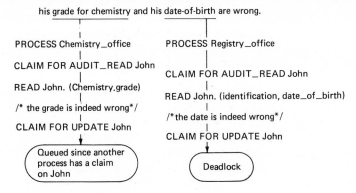

Figure 13-5 Deadlock on one object.

Deadlock Due to System Resource Sharing Deadlock can also be caused by competition for objects which are not specifically identified, but are members of a shared *resource class*. Temporary blocking occurs when resource limits are reached. A simple example is a system which has four tape units available to be allocated among the transactions. Let the claims of two transactions (P1,P2) for tapes be (3,3), and the initial allocation A1 be (2,1) as shown below. The sequence A2 leads to trouble, in the sequence A3 the blocking is only temporary.

Example 13-5   Deadlock in Resource Allocation

Transaction	Claim	A1	A2.1	A2.2	A3.1	A3.2	Limit
P1	3	2	2	$\to \cancel{3}$ Blocked	$\to 3$	Can Complete $\to 0$	$\Big\}\;4$
P2	3	1	$\to 2$	$\to \cancel{3}$ Dead	1	Blocked by P1	

At point A1 it is not safe to allocate (step A2) the remaining tape unit (#4) to transaction P2. If #4 were given to P2, a subsequent request for an allocation by P1, permitted by P1's claim, will be blocked (A2.2); P1 will not release its resources. Another request by P2 will cause deadlock since neither transaction can complete. Allocation step A3 is safe because it lets P1 complete, and then P2 can proceed. Other transactions with more limited claims, say one tape, may be scheduled for unused but claimed resources subject to the same constraints.

For the general case of resource sharing we have to consider multiple devices since deadlock can be caused by one transaction being blocked for, say, buffers from a finite buffer pool, while the other transaction is holding tape units. The algorithm to test for this occurrence is called the *bankers' algorithm* because it is similar to a simple view of commercial loan allocations. A program to decide if an incremental allocation can be safely made is presented in Example 13-6. The test is performed by iteratively simulating all transactions to eventual completion. Lack of success means the claimed unit should not now be allocated. In most successful cases only one iteration will be needed, one iteration of the algorithm requires on the order cases of #(transactions)×2#(number of device types) steps. This cost is still high.

Example 13-6   Bankers' Algorithm

```
/* This procedure is called when transaction tx wants to have one unit of dv allocated
   It returns 1 if ok, 0 if wait required, -1 if request exceeds earlier claim. */
Allocate_claimed_unit: INTEGER PROCEDURE(tx, dv);
/* There are tra transactions active and dev devices.
   Of each device type there are unit(d), d = 1 ... dev units.
   Given are also the claims made and prior allocations to each transaction: */
DECLARE unit(dev), claimd(tra,dev), allocd(tra,dev) EXTERNAL;
/* Working variables include the computed number of available units: */
DECLARE avail(dev), old_waitcount(tra), new_waitcount(tra), improved, t, d;
   IF allocd(tx,dv) + 1 > claimd(tx,dv) THEN RETURN(-1)    /* claim exceeded */
/* The procedure attempts the allocation and simulates then all transactions. */
   allocd(tx,dv) = allocd(tx,dv) + 1;    /* Try giving a unit of dv to tx */
   improved = 1;   old_waitcount = dev; /* Initialize to all tx waiting. */
   DO d = 1 TO dev;                                /* Add allocations to all */
      avail(d) = unit(d) - SUM(allocd(*,d));       /* transactions (*)   */
   END;                                            /* to compute avail.  */
   DO WHILE ( improved );              /* Simulate completion of all tras */
      improved = 0;                    /* as long as resources are freed.  */
      new_waitcount = 0;               /* Set computed number of blockages. */
      DO t = 1 TO tra;
         IF old_waitcount(t) ≠ 0 THEN  /* See if there are enough resources */
            DO d = 1 TO dev;           /* so this transaction     */
               IF avail(d) ≤ claimd(t,d) - allocd(t,d) THEN
                              new_waitcount(t) = new_waitcount(t) + 1;
            END;
         IF new_waitcount(t) = 0 THEN   /* can complete and eventually */
            DO d = 1 TO dev;            /* return its allocated units.   */
               avail(d) = avail(d) + allocd(d);
               improved = 1;           /* It did.      */
            END;
      END;
      IF SUM(new_waitcount) = 0 THEN RETURN(1) /* Go ahead, all can complete!*/
      old_waitcount = new_waitcount;                /* Try if the new avail helps */
   END;                                          /* by iterating again. */
   allocd(tx,dv) = allocd(tx,dv) - 1;    /* We can't do it, take unit back and */
   RETURN(0);                            /* Indicate that tx has to wait. */
END Allocate_claimed_unit;
```

Transactions which communicate in order to jointly process data are also subject to deadlock. An example of such cooperating transactions occurs when data are moved between files and buffers by one transaction and data are processed simultaneously by other transactions. A two-transaction example to accomplish double buffering was shown in Fig. 2-14. One transaction may generate data to be written to files at a high rate and acquire all buffers. Now a data-analysis transaction cannot proceed because the data-moving transaction cannot deliver additional data because of buffer scarcity. Since the data-analysis transaction will not give up its buffers until completion, there is again a classical deadlock situation.

Another problem to be addressed in communicating transactions is to avoid message loss when the arrival of a new message coincides with the clearing of an earlier message. This problem is solved using semaphores to introduce blocking of coincident arrivals and is not a primary database concern. The use of locks to resolve problems due to resource sharing does interact, however, with the management of locks in database systems.

Deadlocks Regions across Structural Levels Deadlocks can be caused by interfering demands on objects from distinct resources classes:

Transaction **P1** needs a tape drive to write results from its disk region.

Transaction **P2** cannot release a tape drive until it is no longer blocked from accessing a record in this same disk region.

Mechanisms to handle deadlocks hence must involve *all* lockable objects. This may include tape units, printers, and other devices, buffers and memory areas allocated by the operating system, and files, blocks, and records controlled by the file and the database system. This can cause problems in otherwise well structured systems, where devices are controlled on one system level and data objects are managed at higher system levels.

An unsatisfying solution is the use of potentially harmful global variables to communicate locking information. Strict rules regarding access privileges to these variables, and adequate documentation can avoid most problems.

Deadlock Conditions The potential for deadlock exists when all four conditions are true [Coffman[71]]:

1: Locks Access interference is resolved by setting and obeying locks.

2: Blocking An owner of an object is blocked when requesting a locked object.

3: Completion Guarantee Objects cannot be removed from their owners.

4: Circularity A circular request sequence, as shown in Example 13-4, exists.

All techniques to deal with deadlock attempt to change one of these conditions. Techniques which resolve deadlocks, however, will also affect hibernation. Any technique adopted should be analyzed to gain an understanding of its effect on system performance due to increased lock out and individual task response time due to blocking.

Frequency of Deadlock Occurrence Deadlock frequency will depend on the degree of interaction among transactions. When regions being locked consist of large and many objects, say multiple files are locked in various combinations, then deadlock will be frequent and will cause serious problems unless constraints are applied. Resolution involves isolation and duplicated files and is hence not well adapted to a database-oriented approach. In a very busy system deadlocks may yet be frequent where incremental claims specify small objects. A large system (WEYCOS), which has the capability to detect and recover from deadlock, experiences 100 deadlocks per hour [Bachman[73]].

Other published values range to as low as five [BrinchHansen[73]] or two per year [Frailey[73]] in systems which are programmed for limited deadlock prevention. Statistics of system failure due to deadlock are difficult to gather in an environment that fails to consider their existence. As shared systems increase in popularity and activity it will become more difficult to ignore deadlock.

13-2-3 Deadlock Avoidance

Prevention is the better part of valor. An ability to avoid deadlock can simplify many alternative choices. Deadlock avoidance schemes impose, however, restrictions on users which can be difficult to accept.

Given the list of four conditions allowing deadlock to occur, there are four approaches to avoid deadlock. A fifth approach avoids both blocking and circularity.

1: Postrepair Do not use locks and fix inconsistency failures later.

2: Dont Block Only advise requesters of conflicting claims.

3: Preempt Remove objects from their owners if there is a conflict.

4: Presequence Do not allow circular request sequences.

5: Two-phase locking Make all claims first and if none are blocked begin all changes.

Postrepair The first approach, repair problems due to not locking afterward, can be valid in experimental and educational systems, but is unacceptable in most commercial applications. If the systems has already some means to repair damage because of errors, the approach may be tolerable.

An airline, for instance, permits 15% overbooking on its routes. If lack of locking contributes, say, 1% cases of overbooking, reducing the planned rate to 14% and avoiding locks can greatly improve performance. Recording how a customer paid for the flight still requires locking payment files but here no or little interference is expected.

Dont block The second approach puts the responsibility on the transaction. The system will give a notification of potential interference by denying the request for exclusive access. Access is still permitted.

The transaction may proceed, taking the risk that data will be modified or it may decide to restart later. If the transaction wants to be sure then it will *preclaim* all needed resources before accessing them. Since this approach also avoids circularity we will discuss it below. If the transaction goes ahead it may simply warn the submitter of the fact that interference has been detected. The transaction cannot count on the validity of its previous claims. This choice may have to be made when systems do not have restoration or backup capabilities.

Whether the database is ever left in an inconsistent state depends on the programming algorithms and the types of interference encountered. A KEEP statement of the 1973 version of the COBOL proposals (CODASYL[78,⋯]) will interrupt transactions which access records modified by currently active transactions. The competing transactions have the same choice; go on or quit.

If auditable results are required, no interference can be tolerated; the transaction may decide to release its previous claims and restart itself after some delay or it may abort entirely and let an external restart mechanism take over.

Preempt The third approach, preemption of claims granted to transactions, requires a rollback capability. Either the transaction, when it is notified that it cannot proceed, has to restore the database and place itself in the queue for another turn, or the system has to kill the transaction, restore the database, and restart the transaction anew. Since this approach depends on deadlock detection, it will be further discussed in Sec 13-2-4.

Presequence The fourth choice is to avoid circularity in request sequences. There are three approaches here, monitoring for circularity, sequencing of objects to avoid circularity, and two-phase locking, treated, because of its importance, in a distinct subsection.

To avoid deadlock the request pattern of all the transactions can be monitored. If conditions of potential circularity which can lead to deadlock are detected the candidate transactions can be blocked. The *bankers' algorithm* of Example 3-6 provided a similar example.

If the request cannot be satisfied because of the potential for deadlock, the request is queued. As claims are released, the transactions waiting in the queue are checked to see if they can be restarted. A scheduling algorithm can be used to choose among multiple candidates for processing, but at least one request should be granted to prevent scheduler-caused deadlocks [Holt[72]]. In dynamic algorithms the transaction arrival order may have to be maintained.

Unfortunately the computation for the case of many resources, found when we deal with data elements instead of devices, becomes quite complex. A proper analysis also has to consider serializability and compatibility of interfering operations. The computation takes much longer when many transaction are active; an undesirable feature during busy times. References to such algorithms are found in the background section.

A simple algorithm, used in IBM OS, allows incremental claims only in ascending lexical sequence for the file name. The objects being locked are files. A proper pair of sequences to avoid deadlock is shown in Example 13-7.

Two ascending sequences cannot create a circular sequence so that deadlock problem seems solved. This technique, however, greatly limits flexibility for incremental requests. The IMS system operating under OS uses its own locking scheme, as seen in Table 13-1.

Example 13-7   Deadlock Avoidance by Lexical Ordering

Transaction P1	Transaction P2
File AA	File BA
File BA	File BB
File BC	File BC
File BD	File BM
File BZ	File BZ
File CX	

The ascending request rule can be relaxed by allowing requests to files lower in the lexical sequence to be made; but if such a request is denied the transaction is obliged to release all objects required up to this point and start over fresh.

This extension can be seen as combining approaches 3 and 4.

Two-phase Locking A simple approach to avoid circularity is to require preclaiming of all objects before granting any locks. Claiming resources before promising to grant access to them means that a transaction may not be able to complete the preclaiming phase. Once all claims have been made locks can be set to protect the transaction from interference by others. This technique is called *two-phase locking* and works well in an environment using a two-phase commit protocol for transactions.

Two-phase locking is hence characterized by a phase where resources are acquired and a phase where they are used and released. A failure to acquire resources in phase one can cause the transaction to be aborted without much pain. No resources may be acquired during phase two, since a failure to obtain them would require undoing of changes made to committed resources.

The major problem with two-phase locking is that preclaiming can lead to having to claim more and larger objects than will actually be needed. If a computation on part of the data determines what further object is needed, an entire file rather than a record may have to be preclaimed.

In Example 1-1 we determined from a `Department` file the name of the `manager` who was to receive a raise and found `'Joe'`. Preclaiming requires locking of the entire `Employee` file since we do not yet know which `Employee` will be updated. Not preclaiming and finding the `Employee.name = 'Joe'` record claimed could mean that an interfering transaction is just demoting `Joe` to a position which does not qualify him for the raise.

In order to reduce the granule size prereading may be used here, as presented in Sec. 13-1-2. The notification mechanism used in non-blocking schemes can warn the transaction of interference potential.

The simpler rule is that a transaction shall claim the entire region to be locked at one, and make no incremental claims. System primitives are used to lock out claims by other transactions until the availability of all objects in the· region is verified and the entire claim is recorded. To issue a comprehensive claim requires perfect foresight; the cost of failure is having to release all acquired resources in their original state, and initiating a new claim. A transaction, in order to reduce its probability of failure, will claim a generous region.

Summary   Deadlock avoidance methods suggest a familar theme, *binding* (Sec. 1-6). By imposing restrictions on the choices of the objects to be accessed, multioperation is made safe. This in turn allows a major improvement in the productivity of the system.

As stated earlier, the system may not allocate the claimed objects to the user until they are actually needed. Prior to allocating an object which is the subject of another claim, a check will be made if now a deadlock potential is created. Deferred allocation of claims is used in Burroughs 6500 systems.

Reserved Resources   Deadlock caused by competition for classified resources (tape units, disk drives, memory) is sometimes mitigated by not allowing any new transactions to be started when the utilization reaches a certain level. This technique will not assure deadlock avoidance unless the reserve is kept impractically large, enough to allow all active transactions to complete. This technique is used, for instance, by IBM CICS in its buffer management. Operational experience can be used to balance the amount of reserve against the deadlock frequency to achieve optimum productivity. The gathering of sufficient deadlock statistics for throughput optimization is an unpleasant task in systems which do not provide rollback.

13-2-4 Deadlock Detection

Deadlock detection is by definition too late. The only cure when deadlock is detected is to kill one transaction as gracefully as possible. Deadlock detection is, however, an important task in the maintenance of system integrity.

If deadlock avoidance is already part of the system, then deadlock detection provides a backstop which allows the correction of faults in programs or hardware. In an environment where the responsibility for deadlock avoidance is placed on the programmers, a deadlock detection facility is vital. Anyone who has ever attempted to debug a running on-line system which contains initially a few deadlocked transactions, but which slowly becomes paralyzed as another transactions attempt to access locked objects can recall the horror of working against time, knowing that at some point the debugging transaction itself will be blocked. The solution, canceling all transactions and restarting the system, leaves one waiting for the next occurrence. There are systems in operation which live with the expectation of occasional deadlocks, owing to the desire to optimize performance.

In systems which cannot legislate incremental claims out of existence, deadlock is unavoidable and has to be detected and, when detected, resolved. Deadlock detection algorithms are similar to deadlock avoidance algorithms. A circular chain of dependencies has to be found. In Fig. 13-6 transactions P1, P2, P4 create the circular deadlock (c, g, k, j, h, f, e, d).

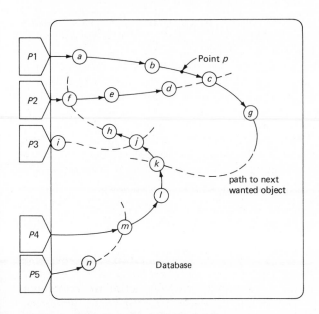

Figure 13-6 Deadlock and blocking.

Transactions P3 and P5, however, are also blocked until the deadlock is removed. The deadlock can be broken by application of approach 3: *remove owned objects from a transaction*. The least number of objects in the circle are owned by transaction P1 (c, g), but it is, in general, difficult to restart a transaction at an arbitrary point (p) unless a checkpoint was made. In a transaction-oriented system with recovery facilities an entire transaction can be restarted, so that transaction P2 is the candidate for assassination; it owns the least number of objects (f, e, d). Only objects which have actually been modified should be counted when the transaction to be killed is selected.

Deadlock detection by logical analysis is impossible if the desired object cannot be identified. A transaction which waits for a request from any of a number of terminals is an example. The transaction sleeps until awakened, and then it will check the reason for the alarm and do something appropriate. Figure 6-10 showed a file system process which can respond to user service requests, file operation completed signals, and time-exceeded signals. It is desirable that these processes do not themselves claim sharable resources so they can remain outside of the domain of deadlock management.

Time limits placed on transaction execution times provide another means to detect deadlock, blocking, or hibernation. The guilty party cannot be positively identified when a time limit is exceeded. In the example above, it is possible that transaction P5 exceeds its time allotment first. Killing P5, however, will not resolve the deadlock condition.

The action to be taken when a deadlock is detected will depend on the available recovery facilities. One popular multiuser system stops. This allows console diagnosis of the problem but leaves remote users quite unhappy.

Preemption If the transaction to be killed has not performed updates, it can be abandoned. If automatic restart is not possible, it is at least polite to notify the initiator of the transaction of the situation and request to please enter the request again. No satisfactory solution to resolve a deadlock where all transactions have performed updates exists unless rollback facilities are available.

If updates are infrequent, a requirement to perform a checkpoint before every lock involving an update can be imposed. A checkpoint would permit a rollback of transaction P1 to point p in Fig. 13-6. In a system which provides general recovery facilities, as described in Sec. 11-4, the before-images can be used to roll back any transaction to the point where it entered the database. The message which started the transaction can then be replayed from the transaction log. Some delay is desirable so that the other transactions have a chance to pass the object which caused the problem.

Correction If automatic rollback from a fault condition is not possible, human intervention is required to check for errors. A simple restart will leave the database inconsistent, and the reexecution of the update may introduce further errors. While Peter might appreciate a raise of 21% instead of 10%, the department budget totals may will not reflect this fact after an error.

All transactions blocked during the deadlock have to be traced for verification. Affected records have to be blocked from further access, listed, and manually verified and corrected. If blocking is not done, any inconsistencies introduced can further contaminate the database. A correction may require real world data, i.e., *"How many widgets do we really have in stock"* after an inventory file failure.

Where databases support financial data, the accountant's tradition of double entry bookkeeping can be helpful. Since any transfer of funds from one account to another is accomplished by matching pairs of debit and credit entries, manual correction of a damaged database is simplified. When the accounting entries are further properly identified with the name of the originator and the number of the transaction, a deadlock recovery system can present the request for correction in a simple form. Automatic correction (without rollback) may be possible but is not advisable since no adequate audit of data entry exists when transactions are not properly completed.

13-2-5 Techniques

The effort to avoid or detect deadlock can be significant. The time is affected by the number of transactions and the number of objects being locked. If both are small, a (transaction×object) matrix can describe the locking pattern. The matrix elements need only one or two bits (allocated, or claimed and allocated). For claims to resource classes, integers to denote the number claimed and received will be needed. If there are many objects (locking units are small: blocks or records), a static matrix becomes infeasible and dynamic lists have to be managed.

The better algorithms to detect deadlock, for instance, the bankers' algorithm of Example 13-6, require on the order of (#transactions × #objects) operations. In addition, all claims, allocations, and releases have to be noted. If the probability of deadlock is low, it may be feasible to test for deadlock only periodically. This may allow the deadlock to spread as other transactions attempt to use the blocked regions. It is important that the deadlock checking algorithm itself does not need to claim resources which might be blocked.

Transaction-oriented systems tend to mimimize potential interference by keeping the number of active transactions small. A high priority is assigned to transactions which hold resources so that they will leave the system as fast as possible. Two lists are adequate for deadlock detection, one to keep track of objects and one to record the state of each transaction. For each active transaction there is an entry in the lexically ordered object list. If an object when requested is found already in the list, and the owning transaction is blocked, there is a possibility of deadlock and the test for circularity is made.

13-2-6 Deadlock Management in Distributed Databases

Deadlock involving multiple nodes of distributed system can occur when transactions lock resources at multiple nodes. A deadlock in a distributed system can be localized to a single node. Subtransactions created by a remote transaction can be involved in a local deadlock. Except for the fact that the cost of aborting a subtransaction can be hard to evaluate and may well be high, the methods for handling local deadlocks remain unchanged.

In this section we consider deadlocks involving multiple nodes. The four principles of deadlock creation and resolution apply also when the deadlock involves more than one node. The risk and the cost of deadlock can be greater because the communication times increase the interval that resources may have to be held. The notion that a remote user can claim and block local computations is also in conflict with the concept of distributed authority and responsibility.

Deadlock and Replication The replicated elements we find more frequently in distributed databases also increase the chance for deadlock.

A change-of-address notice has been sent to two sites **A, B** by a customer who keeps accounts at multiple branches of a bank. The bank maintains an integrated database model and considers the customer a single entity having replicated data at **A** and **B**. At both sites the change-of-address is entered, at site **A** a subtransaction which will also update **B**'s copy is created, and at branch **B** a subtransaction for **A** is created. Each subtransaction finds its object busy. If the subtransactions lock their objects a deadlock is created.

We see all four conditions for deadlock (lock, block, hold, circularity) in this example. Not locking on a change-of-address is quite feasible, and the possible inconsistency from simultaneous updates may not harm much. If the date and time of any update is kept, a periodic validation can repair missed updates. In this example we used a data element whose consistency requirements can be relaxed.

The next scheme in terms of desirability addresses the fourth notion of deadlock prevention: avoidance of circularity. By designating one copy to be the primary copy, i.e., making only one node responsible for any one element, circularity in replicated copies is avoided. Here the rule might be that the nearest branch of the bank keeps the primary address. If a static assignment cannot be tolerated, a *primary-copy token scheme*, as presented in Sec. 11-5-4 will avoid deadlocks in replicated elements.

The remaining two strategies, avoidance of blocking or preemption, have a high cost in distributed systems and no special advantage in the replicated element case.

We considered in this example a data element which is not critical in terms of consistency, but the resolutions we found give a general direction.

Conflicts for many elements which have consistency constraints can be avoided by giving only one site update privileges. If this is not feasible, the primary copy token scheme will prevent deadlocks due to replicated data. These strategies address the second and fourth notions of deadlock prevention by having only one owner for a replicated element.

Deadlock Avoidance The general case of distributed deadlock is caused by transaction, which access several distinct objects. To avoid deadlock in the general sense in distributed systems again the avoidance of locking is most attractive. When locking can be avoided, first the frequency of deadlock is reduced and second the cost of deadlock resolution in the remaining cases becomes less. Having fewer elements participating in deadlock resolution reduces the communication and processing costs greatly.

A reasonable way to reduce locking in distributed systems is to restrict the claim privilege from remote nodes. A remote user may, for instance, not be given any right to claim local locks for read purposes. In that case the remote users can obtain data, perhaps with time and date stamps, and with an indication whether currently a local transaction had a claim on these data. Any decision on the validity of the data so obtained is made at the remote site, which can reissue the transaction if the value of the acquired data appears risky.

Preemption may be similarly modified by always giving priority to local transactions. This will reduce the effect of remote users on local transactions. The remote transaction has to reinitiate any canceled subtransaction. Since the remote transaction must in any case deal with communication failures, we can safely assume that a remote transaction has already the capability to restart its subtransactions.

The fourth solution, avoidance of circular request sequences, requires a global naming scheme. This scheme appears mainly of value in tightly controlled and strongly bound systems, since otherwise it is difficult to assume that all objects can be ordered, since the name to object correspondence may be a local option.

Distributed Deadlock Detection Distributed deadlock detection is initiated when a node finds that it is deadlocked. If the deadlock involves subtransactions submitted by remote nodes, a node has to collect information of all dependencies in the network, as shown for a local net in Fig. 13-6. The information needed can be always sent along when a subtransaction is submitted, or has to be obtained when a problem is detected by querying the other nodes. To resolve the deadlock a transaction involved in the chain has to be preempted. The selection of transaction can be based again on minimal loss, or on features of certain sites. Some sites may have good rollback capability or be deemed unimportant. If the information is available to all nodes, all deadlocked nodes can come to the same conclusion and resolve the deadlock identically. Queries for the information to resolve a deadlock after the deadlock has occurred must be answerable without access to any data which may be blocked.

These strategies are liable to fail if there is another system failure. The simple local priority scheme leading to preemption and avoiding deadlocks caused by remote transactions seems to be more robust.

13-3 MAINTENANCE OF INTEGRITY

The previous sections have shown how integrity can be violated, and how such violations can be avoided or their effect restored. These discussions are of necessity based on expectations of perfect hardware and software performance. Well managed system design and programming techniques can considerably improve system reliability.

A large multiuser on-line file system [Frey71] developed under management by the author operated for more than 6 years without loss of data stored on files. Control over reliability, security, and integrity was achieved by integrating access, access protection, and backup. The granule for all operations was the block; fields could be protected only by encryption (Sec. 14-3). Periodic monitoring was performed to locate errors. Backup procedures provided manually initiated rollback.

Continued integrity of a database is essential for successful operation. We would like to have assurance that the mechanisms used to protect shared data cannot fail. In practical systems today correctness of integrity protection is impossible to prove. Many levels of hardware and software have to work without failure to permit integrity protection mechanisms to do their work.

We covered in earlier Chaps. 11 and 12 the prerequisite reliability and access protection issues. Secs. 13-1 and 13-2 presented the locking mechanisms used to avoid problems due to shared access. We will now present some further considerations which can help designing and operating a database so that integrity is kept at a high level.

13-3-1 Programming Integrity

Most systems allow the programmers to make decisions regarding the use of locks. Problems may be caused by having one individual make decisions which affect programs written by others. A system organization to prevent update interference can be achieved if:

1 The *access protection system* allows only one user, the owner of the data, to modify a protected object or to set a lock for the object.

2 The *access security system* allows only one instance of the user to exist.

3 The *file management system* locks objects which are synonymous with the objects identified for ownership by the access protection system.

The last condition is rarely true. Ownership is allocated to logical entities: fields, records, files, databases, whereas physical control is exercised over physical objects: blocks, tracks, files, and devices. If interference problems can be resolved only on the common file level, shared database access is severely restricted. The rules outlined above do not solve read interference if query regions involve files of more than one user.

If the programmer is not restricted by the access system from potential interference with the activities of others, a higher level of control may be required. Update operations may be permitted only if a claim has preceded the operation. This removes the decision *to lock or not to lock* from the purview of the programmer, although it does not guarantee the locks will cover the correct region. Some system automatically precede update operations with a claim which will lock the object being updated, but an additional claim facility is required to let the programmer claim regions containing multiple objects. For the sake of programming consistency explicit claims are desirable.

The decision whether a read operation is of the *audit* or *free* type is local to a transaction and program. It is desirable to let the end user know which choice was made when the results are being transmitted.

The general problem of assuring the integrity of databases has not been solved. An initial step is the definition of the application requirements by collecting semantic constraints.

13-3-2 Integrity Monitoring

Since a single consistency failure can be gradually copied throughout the database, a strategy of regular monitoring of the database is essential wherever long term data are kept. If results based on data stored for many years are in error, the user's confidence in all the work of past years is suddenly lost.

Monitoring is possibly on two levels: structural and content-oriented. *Structural monitoring* can be carried out by the file system without user participation. *Content-oriented monitoring* requires the user to provide assertions regarding data relationships. In either case monitoring is possible only if there is some redundancy in a database.

Structural Monitoring Structural monitoring is often conveniently combined with periodic dumping operations. One of the areas to be verified is storage allocation: all blocks in the domain of the system should be owned by only one user or belong to the free space list. Some systems may also have a pseudo-owner for bad blocks – either physically damaged storage or blocks containing data which may be in error or are backup for data which may be in error.

Where pointers exist, their logic can be verified: rings should form circles, trees should not form circles, indexes should point only to their primary file. Where data are ordered the sequences can be verified. An entry in a key sequence which is out of order can make successor records unavailable or can make a binary search fail.

In Sec. 9-5 we indicated the desirability to avoid *essential links*. Redundant symbolic references can be used both for integrity monitoring as well as for restoration of the database. Symbolic references are less volatile and can be used to reset pointers if an object is found which corresponds to the reference argument.

Content Monitoring Some data-checking processes can be driven using information from the schema: high and low limits and code validity. The TOD system provides for the inclusion of checking database procedures, to be executed during database verification runs. This allows greater cross checking of database files than is possible at data entry time, and is applied to all database entries to assure equal integrity of old data. Data content summaries, presented graphically can be helpful to users who have a certain expectation regarding data.

Assertion statements, now being introduced for program verification, can also be used to verify the database. Possible assertions are

Example 13-8   Integrity Constraints

```
Department.salaries = SUM(Department.employee_salaries)
Apprentice.age < 30
COUNT(Children) ≤  12
Manager.salary > Employee.salary | Employee.manager=Manager.name
Employee.social_security_number ≠ UNDEFINED
```

Example 9-11 showed such statements from INGRES. Assertions which are too restrictive will cause excessive inconsistency reports, so that some tuning may be required.

Since data conditions are apt to change frequently, it is desirable that a content monitoring process can be table-driven by these statements. If continuous reprogramming is required, frustration will soon lead to disuse of integrity monitoring.

Summary The maintenance of database integrity is a major problem in any database operation. Unless the correct data are reliably available management cannot be expected to depend on database systems. If manual backup systems are kept in operation because of distrust of the computer operation, few economic benefits can be obtained. In databases which are intended for public benefits an unreliable operation will reap scorn and derision. Promises that the next version of the system will be better will be evaluated in the light of the promises made previously.

BACKGROUND AND REFERENCES

Integrity in a system has to be provided at many levels. The initial concerns about maintenance of integrity appeared in communication systems which had to manage multi-node message traffic, and later in operating systems which had to allocate resources to multiple users. Many of the initial applications were such that simple locks could solve the problem without causing deadlock. Only as locks became safe and common did deadlocks become an issue. We have described some problems in databases which require locks. Careful reading of the literature is often required to see which lock problem is being discussed. The principles are similar, but the validity of any method will depend on the application. Everest in Klimbie[75] distinguishes the lock types required in a database environment. Since locking is closely related to protection many references from Chapter 11, for instance Kohler[81], are also relevant.

We have assumed that secure lock primitives are available within the operating system. A seminal paper by Dijkstra[65] defines the tools and their application. The algorithms for processes which share data, presented by Dijkstra, were further developed by Knuth[66], deBruijn[67], Eisenberg[72], and Lamport[74] (*the baker's algorithm*). Hellerman[75] illustrates the problems. Dykstra also initiated the *banker's algorithm* for allocation of claimed resources; this was worked out in 1969 by Haberman[76] and improved by Holt[72], applying graph theory to the analysis.

BrinchHansen[73] and Bayer[78] consider many aspects of the management of locks in operating systems. Dennis[66] describes a locking mechanism. Coffman[71], Collmeyer[71], and develop the requirements for locking in concurrent database access. Locking in B-trees is developed in Bayer[77]. Gray in Kerr[75] and in Bayer[78] develops locking rules for regions of various granularity which combine claim and allocation protection. Interaction tables are provided for various file organization methods. Ries[77] looks at the performance tradeoff. Hawley[75], Everest in Klimbie[75], and Engles in Nijssen[76] provide more examples and the rules for CODASYL. Olle in Douque[76] reviews them critically. Locking and transactions are defined by Eswaran[76]. Mechanisms for a distributed system are described by Rosenkrantz[78] and in Bernstein[80S] and related papers.

Denning[71] provides a fine description of deadlock and Lamport[78] covers timing of events in distributed systems.

Mathematical and graphical techniques have been extensively developed to understand integrity problems in computer systems. Holt[72] and Genrich[73] present graphical approaches to deadlock algorithm development. Algorithms to locate cycles in graphs are found in Aho[74]. A survey for distributed systems is provided by Bernstein[81] and the performance of the protocols is analyzed by GarciaMolina[81]. An excellent overview of the basic mechanisms is given by Bernstein[82].

Dijkstra[71] develops in a very careful manner the algorithm (*the dining philosophers*) to allocate shareable resources. Deadlock can be prevented because the claim pattern is known beforehand. The byzantine generals algorithm (Pease[80] and Lynch and Dolev in Wiederhold[82]) addresses the problem of voting (Thomas[79], GarciaMolina[82E]) in the presence of faulty processors. Presser[75] summarizes deadlock problems and solutions.

A system which immediately allocates all claims is described by Reiter[72]. Havender[68] describes the allocation for resources held throughout successive computations in IBM OS. Frailey[73] developed a sparse matrix technique to avoid deadlock in Purdue's MACE operating system for the CDC 6500. Pirkola in Arden[75] uses a binary matrix to protect files in Michigan's MTS.

The concept of rollback used to be distasteful to many computer scientists (Yannakakis[82]) since it implies failure of prevention algorithms. Papadimitriou[79] defines serializability and Lynch[81] and Fischer in Aho[82] address the constraints imposed by it.

Bachman[73], reporting on WEYCOS (Fichten[72]), finds a major productivity benefit obtained from rollback of transactions versus greatly restricted access in a large database operation. These optimistic algorithms have been formalized and analyzed by Kung[81] and Schlageter[81].

Fossum in Klimbie[75] describes the facilities for deadlock management in UNIVAC DMS 1100. Chamberlin[75] describes the locking mechanism of SEQUEL. Deadlock detection is analyzed by Menasce[80] and Obermarck[81].

The distinction between audit-reads and free-reads (GarciaMolina[82W]) is not always explicitly stated in the literature, so that comparison of algorithms can be difficult. Audit-reads can be always be performed in systems which use versioning as shown by Adiba[80] and Fischer[82].

How timing problems lead to constraint violations is discussed by Morey[82]. Frey[71] describes several structural verification techniques for a file system. The (TOD) system by Wiederhold[75] includes schema directives for database audit. Buneman[79] defines *alerters* to monitor the database. Eswaran in Kerr[75], Gray in Neuhold[76], and Chamberlin[76] specify an integrity subsystem. In Andler[82] multiple processors are employed. Hammer in Kerr[75] and Stonebraker in King[75] apply integrity assertions at data entry time, but the concept is, of course, extendable to integrity monitoring. Lafue[82] considers the tradeoff. Hammer[78] and Bernstein[80B] improve the efficiency of integrity monitoring schemes.

EXERCISES

1 Determine the difference in access cost for the two update procedures shown in Fig. 13-3. Indecate where locks should be placed to make the left choice safe. If setting a lock is equivalent to a disk write and checking of a lock is equivalent to a disk read, which choice is preferable.

2 Draw a flowchart to avoid the deadlock illustrated in Fig. 13-4 using the preclaiming approach.

3 Program a deadlock detection scheme for Fig. 13-4. Estimate its running time given p processes and n objects.

4 a Devise some integrity assertion applicable to the sample problem you have been using since Exercise 1 of Chap. 1.

b Describe the size and quantity of the objects you use.

Chapter 14

Coding

We do not recommend the use of "Roman Numerals" in Western Electric Information Systems.

M. J. Gilligan
in McEwan[74]

The contents of a database is intended to be a representation of the real world. It is desirable to have an accurate and complete representation of our knowledge about reality so that decisions made on the basis of extracted information are applicable to the real world. It is, however, soon obvious that the model of the real world, as entered into a database, is both crude and incomplete.

While searching for a representation there is a reliance on abstraction: one speaks of a specific individual as an employee, a welder, a manager; and then this abstraction is encoded into numbers or characters, which are subsequently transformed into binary computer codes. Statements that *the database content represents reality* may indicate the goal of a system designer, but will be misleading to the user who has to reconstruct useful information from these codes.

During encoding and decoding a number of distortions and biases are introduced. The first section will investigate representation issues with particular regard to these problems. Standard codes will be presented in Sec. 14-2 and the chapter will close with a presentation of code-compression techniques.

646

This material is presented to provide guidance to applications designers when faced with the initial stages of a database problem. It is not unusual that a programmer is asked to *computerize* an information problem. Since a traditional computer science or engineering education has been concerned only with data-processing rather than with the transformation of knowledge to data, this facet of the database design effort may be neglected. Decisions implemented at the level of representation will bind the database to a specific content for many years of its operation. A designer of a database systems should be aware of alternatives of representation so that the system will support diversity and only restrict the unreasonable.

14-1 REPRESENTATION OF KNOWLEDGE

In this section we will present in a logical sequence the steps which are used to transform observations regarding the real world into data elements. In practice these steps can be combined, be ordered differently, or occur more than once.

The initial filter which reduces the capability of the database to represent the real world is the fact that we can only consider available knowledge, correct or wrong, verified or presumed, for representation. The fact that we don't know everything, or even very much, becomes clear when we have to act based on available information.

14-1-1 Taxonomy

Not all the available knowledge will be a candidate for incorporation into a database. Which aspects of our knowledge about an entity will be most useful is a decision that has important consequences on the eventual ability to reconstruct reality. The decisions leading to the categorization of observations have been formally studied by taxonomists, and their results have been applied to the selection of distinguishing characteristics in plants and animals. In database design the categorization is, in general, based on tradition and availability of data. In the traditional view the productivity of an enterprise is represented by its gross sales, and maybe by its tax contribution or payroll in the community. The satisfaction provided by the work to the employee or its effect on the environment has not been measured and collected, and hence will not appear in the database.

A similar decision concerns the level of aggregation of elemental data. Data can be collected in fine detail, or data collection can restrict itself to summarized data.

As an example we can take data collection regarding a patient. The medical diagnosis is an obvious data element. But when this data element is analyzed, one can see that a diagnosis in most cases is a convenient shorthand notation for a constellation of symptoms, complaints, and physical observations. These will not be identical for everyone who receives the same diagnoses; at the same time patients with several similar symptoms will be diagnosed differently. So one may decide to collect data at a lower level of aggregation and enter all the parameters which lead to a diagnosis. Some of these parameters themselves are results of aggregations. The appropriate level is determined by the intended purpose:

public health control measures, individual patient records, disease research, cell physiology, or molecular biology will require different levels of aggregation.

At a lower level of aggregation there will be more individual entries, increasing the cost of collection, storage, and processing. There may also be a greater variety of entities, and a greater variety of appropriate attributes. The benefit of having very detailed data may be hard to quantify. In the case of a bill-of-materials problem, there will be little benefit in obtaining control of minor standard parts: bolts, nuts, washers, and lubricants, so that these will only be registered as aggregate supplies. Other parts at the same hierarchical level may be expensive or specialized and warrant specific record keeping.

When a database is envisaged to serve the needs of users who need different levels of aggregation, data at the most detailed level has to be collected. Periodic or immediate updating of aggregate measures can be used to keep data at higher levels available.

When the entities and their attributes to be collected are defined, the specification of what constitutes membership of an entity class has to be further refined. It is, for instance, not obvious whether the paint on a bicycle is a part or an attribute value. Often there is an established basis which can be used to determine membership. Rules of auditing, for instance, specify in detail the types of income and expenses which are to be summed into ledger categories.

The outcome of a taxonomic decision requires documentation to be used at data entry:

"The number of children is based on the children of either parent, living in the same household, and less than 18 years old."

An alternative specification can be by reference:

"The number of children is as defined for federal tax purposes."

It is obvious that without such statements, different data collectors will record different information. An extended schema provides a central repository for these specifications.

14-1-2 Classification

When the entities and their attributes have been selected, the observation choices have to be classified. Sometimes the decision is simple:

"The number of children of a mother is specified by the integers 0, 1, 2, ... "

More frequently the observed data are not classified this simply. Classification of

" The weight of the children ... "

" The hair color of the children ... "

requires further decisions.

We will list some classification choices below and then comment on their usage. The classification of a type of observation is not always obvious. Once a data element type is classified, however, important aspects of the domain for the attribute values are established and an appropriate representation can be selected.

Whenever a *natural* order exists, the data values can be *ranked* into a sequence, which will be exploited in coding and data-processing. When there is no such natural order in the observations, an artificial order may be specified by convention.

Table 14-1   Classification of Attribute Values

Sortability	Measurability	Value choices	Sample domain
Ranked	Metric	Continuous	`weight`
		Integer	`number_in_stock`
	Ordinal	–	`friendliness`
Unranked	Nominal	Unlimited	`name`
		Limited	`haircolor`
	Existential	–	`female`

A schema which provides a ranking specification was shown in Example 8-6; SOCRATE allows a domain to be specified by a list, (e.g. `hair_color(black, brown, red, blond)`), and the order in the list defines the ranking. It remains, however, risky to formulate queries comparisons having GREATER or LESS operations unless the order definition or *collating sequence* is clear to the user.

If the values are *metric*, the data values are determined by measurement. Arithmetic operations can be applied to these data. The values within a domain `weight` can be added or subtracted as well as compared. This also means that operations which generate a mean or a standard deviation make sense. When data is *continuous*, decisions about range and accuracy have to be made. The limits imposed by computer hardware makes the choices often seem simple. The fact, however, that a computer retains six-decimal-digit precision does not mean that this degree of precision is warranted in data collection. Subsequent calculations can produce numbers of apparent accuracy which was not intrinsic to the original data.

The response to a query:

   `Joe weighs 68.0385 kg`

does not correspond in meaning with the data as they were entered:

   `Joe's weight is 150 pounds.`

Documentation in the schema of the accuracy of data entered can be used here to provide an appropriate truncation: `68.0 kg`.

For *ordinal* or *nominal* data, arithmetic operations should be restricted. An investigator may indeed develop a metric scale for data values which are intrinsically ordinal, but the results have to be taken with care. The measure used for intelligence (IQ) is such an example. An average is computed based on the assumption that intelligence has a normal distribution about the mean. With this assumption individuals can be assigned meaningful percentiles.

The statement

   `Proteus is twice as intelligent as Berringer.`

cannot be based on such an artificial metric. When there is no reason to assume a specific distribution, the use of averages themselves is also objectionable:

   `Joe was involved in an average car accident.`

The mode and the median remain computable in ordinal as well as in integer data since they can be obtained by comparison and counting.

When data values are strictly *nominal*, the most frequent occurrence, the mode, can still be found. "Lee" can be the most frequent name in an area, but no ranking is implied by the value "Lee". Joe's hair color cannot be considered less or greater than Mike's unless some ranking is introduced: perhaps light versus dark.

Nominal data values which have *unlimited* choices allow arbitrary text. Names of individuals, names of businesses, statements of opinion, etc., are data of this type. Accuracy becomes difficult to control and the values can only be used for comparison. Nominal data values cannot always be avoided, but if a limited domain can be established, many opportunities for data verification and control become available. The list of values may be so great that a lexicon will be required to define the domain. Sometimes a domain definition can be available as part of a coding convention, as shown in Sec. 14-2-2.

14-1-3 Encoding

Once the value domains to be collected have been classified, the selection of the actual data representation in the computer completes the conversion of knowledge to data specifications.

For values which have a metric classification the choice is straightforward. Continuous data can be represented by binary integers or fractions if the range of values permits. The position of a binary or decimal point can be noted in the schema. An alternative available on many computers is the use of a floating point notation. Occasionally a representation of values as rational fractions, using two integers for the dividend and the divisor, can be useful. An adequate representation of UNDEFINED or UNKNOWN values may prove difficult. On systems which use sign-magnitude representation for numeric values, the value "-0" has been used, but this convention can be recommended only where the generation of numeric values is controllable by the database-system designer.

Ordinal data are often given integer representation. A lexicon, internal or external to the system, is required for the translation. If ordinal data are not translated to integer or sortable alphabetic codes, a lexicon is required to carry out comparison operations:

Example 14-1   Encoding Table for a Domain

```
Grade: RELATION
    impression ⟨:⟩ value;
    Excellent        4
    Good             3
    Adequate         2
    Inadequate       1
    Failure          0
```

Nominal data of a limited domain is generally associated with a lexicon to verify correct data entry. The data may be represented in integer form for convenience in handling and storage. This will require another conversion, using the same lexicon in the opposite direction, whenever the value is to be produced as a result. Occasionally coded nominal data is not reconverted for output. This tends to be valid only where there is a standard encoding and where immediate intelligibility is not important. Medical diagnosis codes, for instance, can be part of the output from hospital billing systems, since they will be entered as such into the computers of the medical insurance companies. Better public relations and an integrity check is provided when the patient can also see whether the code on the communication signifies a tonsillectomy or a heart transplant. Both code and nominal value should be given in such cases.

If the encoded values carry a check digit or are otherwise redundant, some internal processing errors can be detected. Inadvertent computations will generate bad check digits, and when the lexicon is called upon to regurgitate the data value corresponding to the code, the error will be noted.

Unlimited nominal values can only be translated to an appropriate character code. These codes, in general, will have some redundancy which helps to locate errors. A listing of values in the database which occur only once or a few times can provide a tool to check on misspellings. Since unlimited nominal codes participate rarely in processing, some systems (RDMS, TOD) have replaced nominal values with reference codes. The actual character strings are kept on a remote file and accessed mainly during output procedures.

Bit positions 4321	000	001	010	011	100	101	110	111
0000	NUL	DLE	blank	0	@	P	`	p
0001	SOH	DC1	!	1	A	Q	a	q
0010	STX	DC2	"	2	B	R	b	r
0011	ETX	DC3	#	3	C	S	c	s
0100	EOT	DC4	$	4	D	T	d	t
0101	ENQ	NAK	%	5	E	U	e	u
0110	ACK	SYN	&	6	F	V	f	v
0111	BEL	ETB	'	7	G	W	g	w
1000	BS	CAN	(	8	H	X	h	x
1001	HT	EM	)	9	I	Y	i	y
1010	LF	SUB	*	:	J	Z	j	z
1011	VT	ESC	+	;	K	[	k	{
1100	FF	FS	,	<	L	\	l	|
1101	CR	GS	−	=	M	]	m	}
1110	SO	RS	.	>	N	^	n	~
1111	SI	US	/	?	O	_	o	DEL

Bit numbering is right to left within a character.

ACK	Acknowledge	ESC	Escape	NUL	Null
BEL	Audible signal	ETB	End of trans-	RS	Record separator
BS	Backspace		mission block	SI	Shift in
CAN	Cancel	ETX	End of text	SO	Shift out
CR	Carriage return	FF	Form feed	SOH	Start of heading
DCx	Device control	FS	File separator	STX	Start of text
DEL	Delete	GS	Group separator	SUB	Substitute
DLE	Data-link escape	HT	Horizontal tabulate	SYN	Synchronous idle
EM	End of medium	LF	Line feed	US	Unit separator
ENQ	Enquire	NAK	Negative	VS	Vertical tabulate
EOT	End of transmission		acknowledge		

American Standard Code for Information Interchange

Figure 14-1 ASCII character coding.

14-2 MACHINE REPRESENTATION

The representation of all categories discussed in the previous chapter is accomplished within a computer system by strings of bits. For all categories except unlimited nominal data, a data element can be coded as an integer or floating-point number. These data elements are typically of fixed size.

When data remain in character string form, the data element is represented by a sequence of binary coded characters, typically of varying length. Figure 14-1 presents the standard encoding for characters in the interchange of information, i.e., files and communication lines. Each character is represented by 7 bits; on machines with 8-bit character spaces, one bit will remain unused. Alternate character encoding methods in use for data storage are listed in Table 14-2.

Table 14-2   Character Codes and Their Sizes

Common name (organization)	Size	Number of symbols Data	Control	Undefined
Baudot (CCIT)	5 bits+shift	50	5	3+
BCD (CDC)	6 bits	64 or 48	0	0 or 16
Fieldata (US Army)	6 bits	48	16	0
ASCII (ANSI)†	7 bits	95‡	33	0
EBCDIC (IBM)	8 bits	133	64	59

† American National Standards Institute. A similar code has been adopted by ISO, the International Standards Organization.
‡ For international usage some characters can represent alternate symbols.

Control characters are used in data communication to designate empty spaces, to separate data units, and to control output device functions such as line feed, carriage return. In databases control characters are useful to delimit variable-length fields and to represent UNDEFINED. Such usage requires care to avoid conflict with assigned hardware functions. The ASCII symbols FS, GS, RS, US, and DEL may be suitable.

14-2-1 Conversion

Input data is converted to the binary representations when entered. Most common are computational procedures which take Hollerith character strings and convert the character representation to the desired values. Conversion is a costly procedure. Low error rates and reasonable cost are essential to database operation.

Coding during Data Entry Data-entry techniques can influence the choice of data representation. Of particular importance are the use of multiple-choice forms or display screens which allow nominal data to be selected as seen in Fig. 10-5. The code for the box checked is entered into the computer system. The table to translate from code to the intended term has to match the presented form precisely. Since forms and displays change over time, it is desirable that the code does not represent the position of the entry on the form, but is translated into a code which can be maintained over time.

These self-coding forms or multiple-choice questionnaires are seen in any application field. Digits or arbitrary characters are entered into designated spaces, which correspond in size to available space in the file records. It is possible to generate prototype forms by using data from the schema. This assures that data entered match the file specifications.

14-2-2 Standard Codes

The representation of nominal data by integer codes is a frequent occurrence. We have seen systems (PASCAL and SOCRATE) which provide definitional capability in order to relieve programmers of the task of assigning codes to words.

When data have to be shared among larger groups, the set of values to be encoded has to be agreed upon in order to ensure completeness, lack of ambiguity or redundancy, and appropriateness of level of aggregation. This can be an extremely time-consuming task.

Many organizations have found it necessary to define standard encodings for a large variety of data elements. Activities in the field have been led by groups in the Bell System, trade organizations, defense agencies, federal procurement agencies, and the Bureau of the Census. Some international standards are also developing. If a standard encoding can be used, a considerable amount of system-design effort can be saved. Further integration of the database with other areas is also simplified. The assignment of observations or concepts to the terms provided in a coding table can still cause some debate when an existing code is brought into a new environment. An example of a problem encountered has been the assignment of values to a currency code for countries which have different conversion regulations for investment and for tourism.

Table 14-3 provides some references to standard code tables. The list is by no means exhaustive. Many of these codes are available on tape to simplify their incorporation into data-processing systems.

14-2-3 Coding of Names of Individuals

The coding of names remains as one of the major problems in data-processing. The use of the social security number to identify individuals is restricted to files which relate to activities involving payments of taxes or disbursements from federal insurance or support programs. These are quite pervasive so that the social security number is used in many files, including some where its use is not appropriate. The use of names is hampered by two issues.

Clustering One problem with the use of names is the fact that some names appear very frequently. The Social Security Administration [SSA[57]] has found about 1 250 000 different last names in its files, but also that 48% of the people share the 1514 most common names. Thirty-nine names occur with a frequency greater than 0.1%. The use of first names can resolve the clusters to some extent, but 768 four-letter combinations comprise the four initial characters of more than 90% of the first names. Endings of first names show frequent changes (i.e., **Johnny** for **John**) and are hence not very reliable as identifiers. Duplication of entries for single individuals seems inevitable. When queries to name files are made in an interactive query situation, all collisions of the search key can be presented. A choice based on further data (**address, age**) can be made if the full name displayed is not yet adequate.

Table 14-3   A Sampler of Standard Codes

Subject area: Entities code name	Organization location	Number of entries: format of code†
GEOGRAPHY:		
States of the US	National Bureau of Standards	56:AA or :NN
USPS identifier	FIPS 5-1 Gaitherburg, MD	
Counties in states	NBS, FIPS 6-2	:NNN
Standard Metropolitan		
Statistical Areas	NBS, FIPS 8-3	:NNNN
Congressional Districts	NBS, FIPS 9	:NN
Countries	NBS, FIPS 10	
Place names in US and	Comp.&Bus.Equip.Manuf.Ass.	130000:AANNNNN C
a Class code for each	(CBEMA) Washington, DC	
Mailing Addresses, ZIP Code	US Postal Service	:NMMNN-MMM
	Canadian and British PO's	:ANA-NAN
ORGANIZATIONS:		
Businesses	Dun and Bradstreet, Inc.	>3000000
D-U-N-S	New York, NY	:NNNNNNNNN
Employers Identification	Internal Revenue Service	:XX-YYYYYYY
EIN	Washington, DC	
Occupations	Bureau of the Census	:XXXX
SUPPLIES:		
Automobiles	Consumers Union	{all cars since 1970}
Commodities (US Transp.)	Assoc. of Am. Railroads &	:NNNMMMMM
STC Code	DOT, Washington, DC	
Commodities (Internat. Trade)	United Nations	8 codes×350
SIT Classification	New York, NY	categories:NNNNN
Biologically active agents	College of Amer. Chemicals:	700:NNN
SNOP	Pathologists. Enzymes:	200:NNN
Electric Equipment & Parts	Western Electric, Inc.	various
WE standards	Newark, NJ	:hierarchical
Groceries	Distribution Codes, Inc.	:NNNNN MMMMM or
UPC (Bar code)	Washington, DC	XBBBBB BBBBBX
Publications	Library of Congress	(3 standards,
MARC	Washington, DC	100 elements)
Scientific Instruments	Am. Ass. Adv. of Science	:NNNNN
Guide to Sc. Instr.	Washington, DC	
MISCELLANEOUS:		
Data Processing Outputs	Hdq. US Army Material Command	9000:
AMC-DED	Alexandria, VA	
Device Failures	Western Electric, Inc.	:NNNMMM
WE Standard No. 10178	Newark, NJ	
Human Body	College of Amer. Topology:	2000:NNNN
SNOP	Pathologists Morphology:	1300:NNNN
(Systematic Nomenclature)	Skokie, IL Etiology:	1500:NNNN
	Function:	1200:NNNN
Motorists (accidents,insur-	National Highway	various
ance,vehicles,highway plan.)	Safety Administration	
ANSI-D20	Washington, DC	
Work-injuries ANSI Z16.2	Am. Nat. Stand. Inst.	7 categories

† A,C *denotes an alphabetic,* N,M *denotes a numeric,* X,Y *denotes a mixed, alphanumeric code.*

Name Spelling Variations An even more serious problem is the fact that the spelling of a name is not necessarily consistent. Whereas clustering leads to retrieval of too many names, variantion of spellings causes failure to retrieve information. Examples of common variations are listed on the left in Example 14-2. Cross referencing can be used to refer to frequent alternatives, but the synonym list soon becomes large.

Example 14-2   Name Variations and Soundex codes

McCloud, MacCloud, McLoud, McLeod, M'Cloud	M253,M253,M253,M253,M253,M253
Ng, Eng, Ing	N2,E52,I52
Rogers, Rodgers	R262,R326
Smith, Schmid, Smid, Smyth, Schmidt	S53,S53,S53,S53,S53
Wiederhold, Weiderhold, Widderholt, Wiederholdt, Wiederhout	
	W364,W364,W364,W364,W363

A technique to locate together all similiar sounding names which has seen intensive use is the Soundex method defined in Table 4-4. It can be viewed as a type of phonetic hashing.

Table 14-4   Soundex Procedure

All nonalphabetic characters (',-,⊔, etc.) are eliminated.
All lowercase letters are set to uppercase.
The first letter is moved to the result term.
The remainder is converted according to the next 4 steps:
   The frequently unvocalized consonants H and W are removed.
   The following replacements are made:

Labials	:	B,F,P,V	$\rightarrow$ 1
Gutterals, sibilants	:	C,G,J,K,Q,S,X,Z	$\rightarrow$ 2
Dentals	:	D,T	$\rightarrow$ 3
Longliquid	:	L	$\rightarrow$ 4
Nasals	:	M,N	$\rightarrow$ 5
Shortliquid	:	R	$\rightarrow$ 6

Two or more adjacent identical digits are combined;
    thus, LL$\rightarrow$ 4, SC$\rightarrow$ 2, MN$\rightarrow$ 5.
The remaining letters (the vowels: A,E,I,O,U, and Y) are removed.
The first three digits are catenated to the result.

For some names liable to inconsistent spelling this procedure will generate the Soundex codes shown in Example 14-2. It can be seen that many variations are completely merged, although some remain distinct. This scheme appears biased toward Anglo-Saxon names; other codes have also been constructed.

Use of Soundex codes as a primary key increases the number of collisions. This code provides at most $26 \times 7 \times 7 \times 7$ or 6734 choices, and the alternatives are not uniformly distributed. The first letter alone causes a poor distribution as shown in Table 14-5 [SSA[57]]. For comparison the occurrences of English words in a text of 4257692 words and the distribution of 5153 unique words in this same text are also shown [Schwartz[63]].

Table 14-5   Distribution of Names, Words and Word Types by Initial Letters

Initial Letter	Names(tokens) %	Rank	Text (tokens) %	Rank	Dictionary(types) %	Rank
A	3.051	15	12.111	2	6.229	4
B	9.357	3	4.129	9	5.550	7
C	7.267	5	3.916	10	9.722	2
D	4.783	10	2.815	13	6.016	5
E	1.883	17	1.838	18	4.386	11
F	3.622	13	3.911	11	5.162	9
G	5.103	8	1.960	16	3.086	16
H	7.440	4	6.937	5	3.842	12
I	0.387	23	8.061	3	3.707	13
J	2.954	16	0.427	23	0.776	21
K	3.938	12	0.576	21	0.602	22
L	4.664	11	2.746	14	3.474	14.5
M	9.448	2	4.429	8	4.560	10
N	1.785	18	2.114	15	1.844	18
O	1.436	19	6.183	7	2.271	17
P	4.887	9	2.897	12	7.801	3
Q	0.175	25	0.199	24	0.427	23
R	5.257	7	1.880	17	5.317	8
S	10.194	1	6.787	6	12.886	1
T	3.450	14	15.208	1	5.608	6
U	0.238	24	1.008	20	1.417	20
V	1.279	20	0.428	22	1.436	19
W	6.287	6	7.643	4	3.474	14.5
X	0.003	26	< 0.001	26	< 0.001	26
Y	0.555	21	1.794	19	0.369	24
Z	0.552	22	0.002	25	0.039	25

When the identity of an individual has to be resolved, secondary information, such as **address, birthdate, profession, birthplace, parents' names** may still be required. Which parameters are appropriate will differ according to circumstance. The month of one's birth, for instance, tends to be remembered more reliably (98%) than the day of birth (96%) or the year of birth (95%).

The relative freedom with which individuals in the United States can change their name makes positive identification of an individual difficult. The social benefits of this data-processing difficulty may outweigh the costs. Concerns about protection of privacy everywhere are discouraging the use of personal identification numbers. Some European countries are discontinuing their use.

The use of numbers as identifiers will not disappear. Individuals will have many numbers as identifiers: tax accounts, license numbers, bank accounts, employee numbers, etc.

14-3 COMPRESSION OF DATA

Data storage remains an important cost factor in many applications. Often the representation of the data causes unused space and redundant representation of data. While some redundancy may be part of schemes to improve reliability, significant opportunities for data compression remain. Compression is possible when any of the following conditions are true:

- High frequency of undefined or zero elements
- High frequency of small integers in fixed size words
- Low precision requirements for floating point numbers
- Values which range over a limited domain
- Values which change slowly
- Fixed length spaces for character strings
- Redundancy in character strings
- Character sizes in excess of character set needs

We will consider only schemes which allow complete reconstruction of the data when the compressed data are again expanded. In Sec. 4-2 we encountered *abbreviation* methods for index entries, which did not permit full reconstruction.

There is, of course, a trade-off between the degree of compression and the cost of processing time. Compression will also reduce data-transfer requirements so that file operations may become faster. The total trade-off to be considered is compression CPU time versus file access speed and storage cost.

14-3-1 Compression of Numeric Data Elements

For computational purposes, it is desirable that numeric values occupy full words. Frequently the data form matrices in order to allow rapid computation across rows and columns. Whenever these data represent observations of real world phenomena, it is not unusual that positions are allocated for values that have not been collected (u) or are of zero value.

By *storing only nonzero data values with their coordinates* the zero elements are compressed out of the file. The example below applies this idea to a record having $a = 20$ numeric data spaces.

Original record:

0,14,0,0,0,15,0,0,0,3,3,0,0,0,0,0,0,0,423,0,u;

Coordinate representation:

2:14,6:15,10:3,11:3,18:423,20:u;

Now the record requires $2a' = 12$ data spaces. This method is reminiscent of the record format shown for the pile-file organization presented in Sec. 3-1.

An alternative is the use of a descriptive *bit vector*. One bit is used per field, a 0 indicates the absence of a value. Now the same record is represented by

01000100011000000101_2: 14,15,3,3,423,u;

or, if the bit vector is shown as a single decimal integer

280068: 14,15,3,3,423,u;

If both zeros and undefined values occur, the bit vector can be used to describe the three choices:

```
 0   zero value
10   undefined value
11   actual nonzero value to be stored
```

The bit vector for the same record, now without u stored as data, becomes:

$$0110001\,100011\,110000011\,010_2:\ 14,15,3,3,423;$$

In this case there is no benefit; where **undefined** values are plentiful the effect will be felt. This last bit vector is more difficult to manage, since its size will change depending on the values in the record. In an application where values repeat frequently, four choices can be coded:

```
00   zero value           01   repeated value
10   undefined value      11   stored value
```

so that the fixed-size bit vector now reads

$$0011\,000\,000\,110\,000\,001\,101\,000\,000\,000\,000\,110\,010_2:\ 14,15,3,423;$$

This four-choice encoding for compression was applied to a file system which supported multiple databases using a total of more than three diskpacks and gave a reduction of 44% when applied to all files and 45% when applied only to records which became smaller. Some large statistical files were reduced by more than 80%.

When the *range of numeric values is small*, the numbers can be placed into a smaller space. It is unfortunately difficult to indicate boundaries within a bit string, so that the variable space assignment is awkward to implement. If numeric data are coded as decimal digits of four bits each, one of the $2^4 = 16$ codes can be used to provide a boundary. Such a code can be generated using the four low order bits of the ASCII character code (Fig. 14-1) for the ten digits, leaving space for six symbols, perhaps: * + - , . and US.

For binary values the conversion to fixed-size decimal digits does not make sense; it is better to use a fixed size for a record based on the values to be stored. A scan of the record can be used to determine the largest required space, and this size can be kept as another prefix with the record. Using again the same values we find that the largest data value fits into 9 bits, so that the record will have as contents

$$0011\,000\,000\ldots000\,110\,010_2:\ 9,014|015|003|423;$$

using | to indicate the boundaries of the 9-bit units. Here one word plus 36 bits is required instead of four words. The method is defeated by the presence of a single large value in the record.

An alternate input for compression can be a schema which specifies the range of values. Then the record can be formatted appropriate to the range in any column. In Example 8-7 the **years** were specified to range from 0 to 20, allowing storage of these values in fields of size $\lceil \log_2 20 \rceil = 5$ bits each.

Low-order positions of floating-point numbers can be truncated if the required precision is low. Such a decision would also depend on the specifications provided through the schema. Instrumentation data is often of low precision, and 16-bit floating-point formats with 10-bit or three-digit precision and a range up to $\pm 10^9$ have been devised. If floating-point numbers are used to represent integers or fractions with a known binary point, then a representation using binary integers may save even more space.

If data elements represent attribute values which *change slowly*, it can be attractive to store the differences of successive values. A capability to store small numeric values efficiently is required to make this scheme effective. A sequence,

$$854,855,857,856,859,860,863;$$

can be represented as

$$854,4,+1|+2|-1|+3|+1|+3;$$

Four bits are sufficient to store the successive differences. Unless we are dealing with transposed files, records containing sequential values tend to be rare. The method could be applied to selected columns over many records, but then the record cannot be processed unless it is sequentially accessed.

14-3-2 Compression of Character Strings

Compression of character strings is more frequent than compression of numeric values. One reason is that there are a number of large systems specifically oriented toward textual data, and a pragmatic reason is that systems which have to support text have had already to support variable-length data elements and records, so that the additional complexity introduced by compression is less.

Most schemes to compress text limit themselves to compression of the text representation. There is also a great deal of semantic redundancy within language sentences. It is estimated that 50% of English text is redundant. The redundant information, however, is not distributed in any regular fashion, so that automatic deletion of this redundancy is difficult.

In Sec. 4-2 techniques for abbreviation of words in indexes were presented. These techniques were effective because the keys appeared in sorted order, so that the redundancies were easily eliminated. The same techniques may at times be of use to compress data portions of files. Low-order abbreviation, however, causes loss of information. Abbreviations are frequently used independent of data-processing. They may range from

M for "Monsieur"

to   ADCOMSUBORDCOMAMPHIBSPAC for "Administrative Command,
        Amphibious Forces, Pacific Fleet, Subordinate Command."

Such abbreviations present a degree of data compression prior to data entry.

Abbreviations can reduce data-entry volume as well as storage costs. When abbreviations are developed specifically to deal with the database, their effect should be carefully considered. Compression of terms within the computer may be more economical than the abbreviations which simplify manual processing, but a reduction of manual data-processing errors is extremely worthwhile.

Recoding The most frequent technique used to compress textual data is the representation of the data in a character set of smaller size. Data may, for instance, be recoded from an 8-bit set to a 7- or 6-bit set. With 6 bits it is just possible to represent the digits, upper- and lowercase characters, a hyphen, and the blank, since $2^6 = 10 + 2 \times 26 + 2$. Most 6-bit codes do not retain the lowercase characters in order to provide a more complete set of special characters.

Recoding from 8 to 6 bits saves 25% of the space. This is often accomplished by deletion of the leading two bits of the ASCII code. Most modern output devices can present both upper- and lowercase characters; for much of the public the rule that *computer output is always uppercase* still holds. It seems unwise to remove the humanizing appearance of upper- and lowercase print to achieve data compression.

Single-case characters alone can be represented by 5 bits. If alphabetic and numeric characters appear mainly in separate sequences, the use of a method similar to Baudot coding, which uses a shift character to switch between sequences, can be used to represent text in an average of slightly more than 5 bits per character.

If the data represent digits, only the four low-order bits of most codes have to be retained. Starting from ASCII a blank (⊔) becomes a '0' but the 6 characters listed earlier (* + - , . and US) will be kept as distinguishable codes. Any other characters present will map into this set and probably cause errors.

Compression by recoding symbols into a specific number of bits will be optimal if the number of symbols to be represented is close to, but less than, a power of two. This is not the case for character sets containing only digits, or character sets containing upper- and lowercase characters, digits, and at least the 16 common special characters from ASCII column 010. These sets of 10, respectively 78 symbols, require 4 or 7 bits per character, adequate for 16 or 128 symbols. Recoding groups of a few characters into a single representation can produce a denser compression, as shown in Table 14-6. The limit for a group is, of course, 2^{bits}.

Table 14-6   Character Group Encoding Alternatives

Character set	Set size	Group	Group range	Bits	Limit	Saving, %
Digits	10	3 digits	1 000	10	1 024	16.6
Single-case alphabet	26	4 letters	456 976	19	524 288	5.0
Alphanumerics+28	90	2 characters	8 100	13	8 192	7.1
Alphanumerics+18	80	3 characters	512 000	19	524 288	9.5
Alphanumerics+22	84	5 characters	4.29×10^9	32	4.19×10^9	9.25

The saving is computed based on an ungrouped dense encoding. The bit sizes for the groups may not match word boundaries, so that multiword units have to be handled in order to exploit this type of compression. The grouping of 5 alphanumeric characters, however, allows a 32-bit word to be used to represent 5 characters, a saving of 20% over the common 8-bit-per-character encoding.

Deleting Blanks In formatted data there tend to be long sequences of blanks. A simple technique to compress such sequences is to replace a string of i blanks by a sequence of two characters '⊔i' as shown in Fig. 14-2. The value of i will be limited by the largest integer that can be kept in a character space (63, 127, or 255). In the scheme shown a single blank is actually expanded and requires two spaces. This can be avoided by letting single blanks remain and replacing longer strings of blanks by some otherwise unused character, followed by the count.

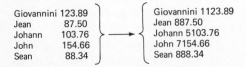

Figure 14-2 Compression of blank sequences.

Variable-Length Symbol Encoding As shown during decryption, using Table 12-3, characters do not occur with equal frequency. A technique, *Huffman coding*, takes advantage of this fact to compress data. The most frequent symbols are assigned to the shortest codes, and all longer codes are constructed so that short codes do not appear as initial bit sequences of the longer codes. No further marking bits are required to designate the separation of one character field and its successor.

Table 14-7   Algorithm for Constructing a Huffman Code

1	A list is initialized with an entry for each symbol, its frequency, and a space for its code.
2	Take the two entries of lowest frequency in the list; assign them the bits 0 and 1.
3	If an entry is a result of a previous combination, then catenate the new bit to the front of each code; otherwise initialize the code field with the bit.
4	Remove the two used entries from the list and insert a single, combined entry which has as frequency the sum of the two entries and attach the two used entries.
5	Repeat steps 2, 3, and 4 with the two entries which have now the lowest frequency, until all symbols have been processed.
6	The code values can be obtained from the tree of entries.

Using the frequency of single characters in English given in Table 12-3, the optimal space encoding begins as shown in Example 14-3.

Example 14-3   Construction of a Huffman Code

Next element	Encoding steps	Combined frequency	New code for previously encoded elements
fr(Z)=1			
fr(Q)=2	Z→ 0 Q→ 1	fr(ZQ)=3	
fr(J)=2	J→ 0 ZQ→ 1	fr(JZQ)=5	Z→ 10 Q→ 11
fr(X)=3	X→ 0 JZQ→ 1	fr(XJZQ)=8	J→ 10 Z→ 110 Q→ 111
fr(K)=5	K→ 0 XJZQ→ 1	fr(KJZQ)=13	X→ 10 J→ 110 ... Q→ 1111
fr(V)=10	V→ 0 KXJZQ→ 1	fr(VKXJZQ)=23	K→ 10 ... Z→ 11110 Q→ 11111
fr(B)=13			
fr(G)=14	B→ 0 G→ 1	fr(BG)=27	
fr(W)=15			
fr(Y)=15	W→ 0 Y→ 1	fr(WY)=30	
fr(P)=22	P→ 0 VKXJZQ→ 1	fr(PVKXJZQ)=45	V→ 10 ... Z→ 111110 Q→ 111111
fr(M)=27	M→ 0 BG→ 1	fr(MBG)=54	B→ 10 G→ 11
etc.			

The codes which are generated for this important case are given as Table 14-8. The encoding can also be represented by a tree as shown in Fig. 14-3. This tree construction can, in general, be used to minimize access to items of unequal frequency, as long as the access cost per link is equal.

Table 14-8   Huffman Code for English Text

E	100	D	11011	G	001111
T	000	L	11010	B	001110
O	1111	C	01110	V	001010
A	1110	F	01011	K	0010110
N	1100	U	01010	X	00101110
I	1011	M	00110	J	001011110
R	1010	P	00100	Q	0010111111
S	0110	Y	011111	Z	0010111110
H	0110	W	011110		

We find that for English text, given the frequencies of occurrence $fr(i)$ shown in Table 12-3, the average character length lc becomes

$$lc = \frac{\sum fr(i)\, len(i)}{\sum fr(i)} = 4.1754 \qquad \text{bits} \qquad\qquad 14\text{-}1$$

where $len(i)$ is the number of bits of symbol i in the Huffman code. This result can be compared with the $\log_2 26 = 4.70$ bits required for a minimal nonpreferential encoding of 26 symbols and the $19/4 = 4.75$ bits achievable with a grouping of four characters seen in Table 14-6.

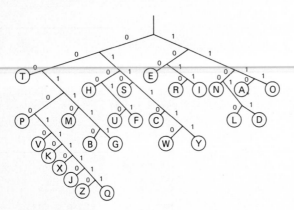

Figure 14-3 Huffman code tree.

Variable-Length String Handling An important factor in string compression is the support of variable-length strings. Names of individuals, organizations, titles of books, and references vary greatly in length, and to accommodate the maximum without truncation is rarely feasible using a fixed string length. A sampling of last names [SSA[57]] and a word list [Schwartz[63]] is shown in Table 14-9.

A marking scheme, as introduced in Fig. 2-11, is required. Most character codes provide a control character which is appropriate to terminate a character string. In the ASCII code (Fig. 14-1) US is in general appropriate. An alternative is the use of initial count field, although this imposes limits on the maximum string length. A count field of 8 bits limits strings to 255 characters, which is adequate for simple lines of text but is sometimes exceeded when formatting macros are included or when underlining is specified within the line. The use of a count field has computational advantages, since character strings move and catenation operations can be prespecified. When a US character is used, the string has to be scanned during processing.

Table 14-9　　Length of Names and Words in a Dictionary

Length	Names (tokens)		Words (types)	
	%	Cum.%	%	Cum.%
5 or less	29.53	29.53	40.44	40.44
6	24.22	53.75	17.37	57.81
7	21.56	75.31	14.96	72.77
8	12.81	88.12	10.23	83.00
9	6.10	94.22	7.03	90.03
10	2.87	97.09	5.05	95.07
11	1.15	98.24	2.66	97.73
12 or more	1.76	100.00	2.27	100.00

Replacement Although Huffman codes are easily docoded left-to-right, their use is awkward on most machines. The facilities for handling characters are often much better than bit-oriented operations. Schemes to use *free characters* to replace frequent long strings can be easy and effective. Both unassigned and unused control and data characters can be free. Table 14-2 shows that especially 8-bit codes, bytes, have many free characters. It is possible that about 150 of these character codes will not occur in the text.

Since blank sequences are frequent, some, say 4, free characters can be assigned to represent two blanks, three blanks, four blanks, or eight blanks. If other characters are expected to occur in long sequences, this technique can be extended to those characters. If many of the characters are apt to be repeated, the free characters can be used to indicate two, three, four, or eight repetitions of the preceding character.

If certain words appear with great frequency, they can also be replaced by single free characters. Which words occur most frequently in a text depends greatly on the universe of discourse. Words such as

　　　　THE OF A TO AND IN THAT IS IT FOR ON ARE

are universally frequent, and hence are, in general, candidates for replacement by single character codes.

Zipf's law In natural text, unfortunately, the shortest words occur already with the greatest frequency. A rule, *Zipf's law* provides an estimate for the relationship between frequency and size in many situations. If n words $w_i, i = 1 \ldots n$ are listed in the order of their size, from smallest to largest, we can expect that their frequency of occurrence $fr(w_i)$ will be

$$fr(w_1) = c/1, \ fr(w_2) = c/2, \ fr(w_3) = c/3, \ \ldots, \ fr(w_n) = c/n \qquad 14\text{-}2$$

The constant c is adjusted to generate the appropriate total. Words of equal size have to be ordered according to the frequencies observed.

If the frequencies fr are expressed as fractions, then $c = H$, the harmonic number for n. Knuth[73S] shows that for $n \gg 100$,

$$H_n \approx \ln n + \gamma \qquad\qquad 14\text{-}3$$

where γ or Euler's constant is $0.5772\ldots$.

One can consider replacing longer but yet frequent words by shorter multiple letter combinations, in a sense intensifying Zipf's law by inclusion of unpronounceable combinations. In a stored database textbook the replacement of "⎵database⎵" by "⎵db⎵" could be profitable. The lexicons required to effect this translation can become quite large. This approach has been used in files of names. Zipf's law can also be applied to estimate the progression of the type-token ratio for words in a text, ranked according to their frequency of occurrence, or individual type-token ratio. Knuth[73S] shows how a better fit to Zipf's law can be obtained by adding a parameter to the divisor in the sequence, so that

$$fr(\text{item}\,i) = \frac{c}{i^{1-\theta}} \qquad\qquad 14\text{-}4$$

With $\theta = 0.1386$ the sequence expresses Heising's 80-20 rule stated in Sec. 6-1-6, and with $\theta = 0.0$ the sequence expresses the type-token ratio for the words from the text by Schwartz[63] used for Table 14-5 for the words ranked from 5 to 4000. Extremely high and low frequencies do not quite match.

Since (as discussed in Sec. 14-2-3) a limited number of last names of individuals accounts for many of the names in files [SSA[57]], it is possible to replace these names by shorter representations. These short names can be made up out of the 20 consonants, giving, for instance, 8000 three-consonant combinations for more than half the names in use. Use of two letters and a digit in an arbitrary position of the representation would avoid the rare but possible confusion with an existing name and provide 20 280 combinations, beginning with "**1AA**" and ending with "**ZZ9**". The names with extremely high frequency can be represented by combinations of two characters, "**1A**" to "**Z9**". Lexicons to control replacement of names or words can be generated by analysis of the file or of a sample of the file.

If a fixed-field encoding is desirable, some of the codes can be used to refer to an overflow file for names which could not be encoded. A format **Zaa**, for instance, could use the digits **aa** to point to records containing unencodable names.

Dynamic Replacement   If adequate processor time at data-entry time is available, the selection of a lexicon to control replacement can be done dynamically. The lexicon which is specific to a record now has to be carried along with the record. An example from DeMaine[71] is shown in Fig. 14-4.

Compression of 40% to 60% is reported on strings ranging from 400 to 1500 characters using up to 10 patterns in the lexicon. The same technique is possible using arbitrary bit strings. In this case the record can contain numeric or string data, as well as results from previous compression algorithms.

A Huffman code could also be generated dynamically, but here the code tree would have to be appended to the record. The code tree is difficult to represent in a compact form. A general decoding program for variable character codes will also be larger and slower than a program oriented to a particular Huffman encoding.

"The string compresser compresses strings. " (41 characters)

"① string ② compresse: The ①2②2s①s."   (31 characters)

       ① and ② are control characters

Figure 14-4 Dynamic string replacement.

14-3-3 Implemention of Compression

Compression schemes can be best evaluated by applying them to a representative sample of the data. Several parameters have to be measured. The simplest measurement is the reduction of storage requirements. Changes in data transfer time are another benefit which should be evaluated. The processing cost for compression and expansion can be significant and should not be neglected. Since data retrieval is more frequent than update, complex compression schemes which generate encoding that are simple to expand are preferable. Evaluation requires that the retrieval to update ratio be known.

More than one method can be used in combination with others. In that case, the order in which compression algorithms are applied will make a difference. Replacement should precede Huffman coding, for instance, but if replacement leads to a more uniform use of character codes, subsequent Huffman coding will lose its advantage.

Processing Point for Compression Compression or expansion can be performed at various points in the data acquisition, storage, and retrieval process. If compression is done soon after data entry and expansion is done just before information presentation, the volume of data to be handled throughout the system is less. Data elements which only control selection of other data elements will not be expanded at all, so that processing time for expansion will be saved. On the other hand, extensive usage of compressed data will require that all processing routines can manage compressed data. If computational use of the data requires expansion, the data elements fetched may be expanded many times during processing. Especially statistical-analysis programs tend to require data elements that are of consistent size and cannot cope with compressed elements.

The alternative is to assign data compression entirely to the file system. File systems can be equipped with compression algorithms through the use of database procedures or file-system escape procedures, so that compression and expansion becomes fully transparent to the user. Now the degree of compression performed can be adjusted by a database administrator according to storage versus CPU cost ratios applicable to a particular system or system era.

The automatic management of compression by the system can lessen the involvement of the user with the hardware and reduce binding of programs to system features. A user who is worried about storage costs is apt to adopt the use of representation techniques which are not optimal from the human interface point of view.

Compression of numeric values in storage can be used to let all expanded numbers used in processing be of equal precision and size, without sacrificing storage space. The use of fixed data-element sizes in processing programs can increase the sharing of standard programs.

Hierarchical files, through their multiple record formats and lack of array structure, tend to benefit less from compression than files which are formatted as tables. There are instances, as shown in Sec. 4-5, where the benefits of dense storage are a major factor in the decision to use a hierarchical approach. The availability of compression can reduce the importance of this particular factor.

Compression and File Design   The compression of data has a significant impact on the file design:

Compressed files generate variable-length records. Updating of records in compressed files can cause these records to change size.

Since many current file systems do not support varying record lengths, the compression of data has been forced from the level of a file-system support option into the database system or into the user level.

The user without who is limited to fixed-lenghth records has also to create mechanisms to store the representation economically in addition to being burdened with the problem of finding an effective representation for the real-world data. The combination is frequently a difficult task for the user. There are important applications where the data are broken into many linked fixed-length records since variable-length records were not available.

In the opinion of the author this abdication of responsibility by file-system designers is the major reason why the use of file has remained a problem in computer systems. These same systems do provide compilers, editors, and libraries to attract users to their facilities. All these facilities provide a better match to the users processing concepts at the cost of some computing overhead. The provision of equally elegant file-support facilities is the next step.

BACKGROUND AND REFERENCES

The representation of knowledge by symbols is a basic human characteristic. Many of the ideas expressed in the initial section are from an excellent exposition by Feinstein[70]. Discussions on the topic are found in Brodie[81]. Pierce[61] provides background information and Reiter in Gallaire[78] considers the limits of encoding.

Coding conventions for computers can be commonly found in manufacturers' manuals. Loomis in Stone[75] summarizes codes used by computers to represent data. A state-of-the-art report of codes used in commerce is provided by McEwen[74].

The patterns of names and words have been studied; sources here are SSA[57], Schwartz[63], and Lowe[68]. SOUNDEX coding was introduced by Odell and Russel in 1918; it is described by Gilligan in McEwen[74]. O'Reagan[72] encodes verbal responses. Florentin[76] presents coding conventions for associative relations. Existing code conventions can also be found by looking at usage in available databases, a directory is Williams[82].

An extensive study and implementation of compression algorithms is presented by DeMaine[71] and abstracted in Codd[71]. The file system described in Wiederhold[75] includes compression. Bayer[77] places front-abbreviations into the B-tree. Numeric data files are considered by Alsberg in Hoagland[75]. Young[80] places extracted descriptors at higher levels and Eggers[81] places them into B-trees.

Hahn[74] and Martin[77] discuss character replacement. Huffman coding (Huffman[52]) is also presented in Martin[77], analyzed by Knuth[73S], and applied by Lynch[82]. Compression techniques are surveyed by Gotlieb[75]. Knuth[73S] points out the relation between Zipf's law (Zipf[49]), Heising's 80-20 rule (Heising[63]), and the data by Schwartz[63].

EXERCISES

1 Categorize data representations appropriate to the following data:
Car license-plate numbers
Miles driven per year
Driver-license numbers
Type of driver's license
Number of traffic violations
Severity of traffic violations
Location of accidents
Objects destroyed or damaged
Cost of repair and reconstruction

2 Locate the character-coding table for the computer you are using. How many data and control characters are available? Are there characters which are usable for compression algorithms? Are all characters usable in files, in terminal output, or on the printer? Can they all be generated from data input without special processing?

3 Locate a standard coding table, and describe size, format, density, susceptibility to errors, limitations, suitability for computing, and human-interface effectiveness.

4 Convert your name to Soundex. Do this also for misspellings of your name you have encountered.

5 Compress floating-point numbers for the case that only three-digits precision is required. Watch the normalization!

6 Test three algorithms for string compression on a body of text. This exercise can also be assigned as a competition. Discuss the result and the range of its applicability.

7 a Design a compact code for dates within this century.

   b Design a compact code for the time of day adequate for computer time accounting.

   c Design a compact code for time adequate for the resolution of synchronization problems in your computer.

8 Discuss when the abbreviation scheme used by VSAM (Sec. 4-3-3) is effective, and when it is not.

9 Locate another standard code, similar to those shown in Table 14-3, and describe its domain and utilty for databases.

Chapter 15

Database Operation
and Management

Donagon wiped his damp hands, opened the journal and began ... .
We decided not to abandon the attempt after all; to try once more to store a man digitally.
The last obstacle had been removed, i.e., storage. Previously we had estimated that many
thousands of miles of magnetic tape would be required, with complex retrieval problems.
The multiple storage paired redundancy tapes, developed by Müller-Fokker in Vienna...

Every datum will be recorded many times, to reduce error. At present surgeons are
removing tissue samples from the subject and determining cell structure data. We have
already encoded a DNA map, photographs, holographs, x-rays, resin casts, EKG's and so
on. There remains but one step, the mapping of all electrical and chemical activity of the
subject's brain. The press will be invited to this session ... .

From *The Müller-Fokker Effect*, a science fiction story
By *John Sladek*

The benefits of database systems are obtained only after the design and the implementation are completed, and after sufficient data has been collected so that the
user of the database can receive usable information. A large commitment of effort
is required to attain that stage. The remainder of the database cycle will involve
continuing assurance of reliability and quality, periodic adaptation to changing requirements, and eventually termination of the operation with transfer of valuable
data and procedures to a new system.

This final chapter will consider these issues and in the process summarize some
of the observations from earlier chapters.

669

15-1 DEVELOPMENT OF THE DATABASE

The development of a substantial database operation is invariably a task which requires the cooperation of a number of diverse individuals. The collection will include a large number of potential users, data-analysis specialists, information scientists, experts in various aspects of computing, communication specialists, the future database administrator, and representatives from management, who will be investing resources of the enterprise in the effort.

It is not unusual for potential vendors to be included in the initial discussions. They can bring considerable experience to bear on problems, but their opinions have to be validated at sites of prior implementations. A good deal of knowledge but relatively little experience is currently available in the academic world. Experimental research on large databases is difficult because of the large cost and long time scales associated with database system development.

Objective Setting The determining components of a database operation are the users and the data. The users determine the objectives of their applications and the semantics of the data determines how the objectives can be satisfied. The type, activity, and quantity of users and data have to be quantified before any specific system design can be done. The determination of these parameters is a management responsibility. A group associated with a specific system is apt to view users and data needs according to its capabilities, rather than according to the underlying user objectives. Documented feedback to management is required when imposed service demands are excessively costly. A constantly recurring problem is that programming staff venture opinions about cost and effectiveness of alternatives without analysis, often using a peremptory approach, sometimes basing opinions on personal interest.

In order to get a development group composed of diverse individuals moving in the same direction, a definition of the goal objectives is required. Both lower and upper levels of the operational parameters to be achieved have to be specified. Some quantified limits of system performance objectives for an application may be:

Response Time: 90% of single-element queries are to take less than 1 s between query entry-completion and begin of response.

Backup: Backup is to be available for all source data which have been entered more than 3 h ago. Backup is to be retained for all data which were deleted less than 3 months ago.

Deadlock: Less than one deadlock per year should occur.

Cost: A single element query should cost less than \$1.00. Successive data elements to be obtained at less than \$0.05 each.

Size: Capability to access 100 000 to 2 000 000 records of size as defined.

Objectives defined and understood at this level form the basis for mutual decision making and have to precede the exploration of the system alternatives. Objectives stated without restraint, as *instantaneous response, absolute reliability, perfect protection of privacy*, can lead to an unbalanced effort in system implementation.

Binding A decision criterion which appears throughout this book is the concept of binding. Binding measures the extent to which flexibility has been traded for efficiency. We have identified binding choices in file structures, in database models, in schema management, in information retrieval, and in the maintenance of data and integrity protection.

If much flexibility is required, the system will be loosely bound at many levels: the record structure will be variable, the access paths will be easily augmented or deleted, the schema will be able to accept changes, and the query-processing system will be able to interpret changes made at any time. If performance is important, constraints will be imposed on some of the levels, but at some other levels flexibility should be retained.

The concept of binding can promote a common understanding among the people involved in the system development process. A general problem in database design is that it involves the bringing together of people from many disciplines, both as users and as implementers.

Documentation   In a database the most important documentation is the database model. The database model will determine the processes required for file creation, file maintenance, and information retrieval. The schema, expanded with notes about real-world relationships, connection constraints, and the definitions of the variable domains and their representation becomes the formal repository for the database model documentation as the design is refined.

The technical aspects of the design process were described in Chap. 5. When the basic system choices have been formulated, more detailed specifications have to be developed. There will be many interfaces among the system components (see, for instance, the ANSI SPARC model of Fig. 8-16) which all require careful documentation. Human interfaces are difficult to visualize by documentation alone, and examples or pilot operations may be desirable. Particular care is required for interfaces using visual display units or graphics if their full power is to be exploited.

The extent and detail of program documentation required will vary according to scope and complexity of the system. If higher-level languages are used, an external description of the function of a program module, and detailed documentation of all variables used, is often adequate. Flowcharts have been of value where multiple processes interact.

A common vocabulary is important. In the beginning of a project, especially if multiple outside vendors are involved, terms will have a variety of meanings. People who recognize the problems will begin to talk in noun pairs: CODASYL-sets, LEAP-relationships, etc.; those who have read less will be confused. As the specific system design stabilizes, so does the vocabulary. During the development of this book much effort has been made to assure that definitions are consistent throughout, and most of the terms have been acceptable to the readers of the first edition; some definitions have been revised. Vocabularies adapted to a particular system will continue to be used, but a table of definitions, which may cross reference other work, such as CODASYL, will be helpful to outsiders.

The design of a *generalized database management system* is made much more complicated because of the absence of user objectives and specific database models. In practice certain types of users are postulated and artificial models are constructed. As was discussed in Chap. 10, there are some underlying concepts of an information methodology which can be applied when a new system is being considered. Since no system can be everything to all users an explicit boundary of the problem area to be addressed is required if conflicts during the design and the complexity of implementation of a generalized DBMS are to be kept tolerably low.

Programming Techniques of structured programming promise to aid in the construction of large programs. It is interesting to note that seminal work in this area was applied to information systems: the *chief-programmer* approach at the New York Times Information System [Baker[72]] and *formal modularization* for a KeyWord-In-Context generator [Parnas[72]].

The management of a critical section of code requires tools to manage locking mechanisms. The fact that locks transcend structural levels (Sec. 13-2-2) makes locks error-prone. A large amount of programming effort can be wasted if these issues are not addressed prior to implementation. The trade-offs among integrity control, performance, and flexibility in the applications are not well understood by most programmers. Papers that promise that these problems have been solved have misled many uncritical readers.

The separation of data structures from programs is another tool which is important in the development and maintenance of systems. The use of schemas provides this facility for the database, but similar facilities are also useful for access to other shared system resources.

The use of a top-down approach to program design is feasible when there are reasonable expectations about capabilities at lower levels. This book presented the material of the database world in a bottom-up fashion, so that at each step up it was possible to verify that the ground below was solid. Abstraction of alternatives at the lower level are the building blocks of the higher levels; these abstraction have to be based on realizable constructs.

15-2 MAINTENANCE OF A DATABASE

When a system is completed, adequately debugged, and populated with data, the real work begins. We stress again that the value of a database to the user is not in the database system but the data content and particularily, the results from queries entered by users and users' programs. Of course, a bad system can frustrate all other positive aspects.

There will be the need for modifications due to changes which came along while the system was being implemented. To avoid without serious disturbances changes are best not considered during the latter part of a development effort. Changes will be tested on a copy of the database so that ongoing use will not be affected until the changes are well checked out.

Then there will be the need for additional facilities or data, as users find that they cannot quite do everything they had expected. The gap between expectations and delivered product can be especially great for users that did not participate in the development effort. If participation in development is not possible, it is wise to warn the user that the installation of a database system will not provide all the possible benefits. The delays which a user can expect will depend on the divergence of the needs with the architecture of the sytem.

Stages, seen once a database system has been developed, include:

Operational shakedown of the database system The hardware and software is tested using pilot data.

Functional shakedown of data entry procedures It is difficult to have reliable data entry while the system is not perceived to be itself reliable, but at that point we have to assure ourselves that the input flows smoothly and error free into the database.

Verification of data content The benefits of integration of data can be proved only if the quality of the data stored is perceived by the users to be as good as their local data collections.

Report generation Use of the database to generate reports suitable for the environment provides initial operational experience and feedback of data.

Statistical analysis of data content Where data represents observations, descriptive statistics and graphs can present the contents in a form which leads to questioning and further inquiry.

Model building As the contents of the database matures, it becomes finally the intended resource. Hypotheses can be tested and projections made which are based on past data. This is the stage where the system actually generates information data useful to decision making and planning.

The time required to achieve the final operational stage can be many years. The various stages require increasingly sophisticated personnel and tools. The investment in these resources will be made only if earlier stages have provided the confidence that the effort is worthwhile. Disappointment due to expectations of rapid or massive benefits can cause a loss of confidence, and may make a system, which works technically reasonably well, a failure.

15-2-1 Tuning and Monitoring

An adequate performance-to-cost ratio will be of constant concern to the system administrator. An administrator will be developing continuously tools to measure system productivity. It may be difficult for users to formulate reasons for dissatisfaction with aspects of the systems performance, so that lack of use can be a signal to look for a problem. Sensitivity to the needs of the users is important.

Nearly all performance improvements increase the redundancy and the binding of the system. Access paths are generally easier to manipulate than replication of actual data. A system which allows the creation of new access paths can be tuned quickly to improve fetch behavior. Improving transactions which access many elements tends to be more difficult and may require considerable data redundancy. Increased redundancy, of course, decreases update performance. Increased duration and complexity of updates increases the probability of deadlock.

It is clear that the solutions which seem expedient are not always desirable. A good understanding of which system resources are heavily used and which are lightly used is necessary to make the correct decision.

Among the most difficult decisions to make is the unbinding of a previously bound relationship. This can involve the splitting of a collection of tuples into two separate relations, either by attribute or by ruling part. In Sec. 7-5-2 we combined a `highschool_record` and a `college_record` into a single relation `education`. This may have made the model simpler and more consistent. Unfortunately, as a file gets bigger, the time to process the file increases more than linearly. If we take that processing time as generally proportional to $n(\log n)$, we find that processing the same file split in two requires less time, namely, $2(\frac{1}{2}n \log \frac{1}{2}n)$. This example of a case where bigger is not better can be demonstrated in other facets of database systems. In general, database fragments that appear not strongly related to each other can be beneficially separated. Such a divorce, if it takes place after the data have been living together for a long time, is apt to be traumatic, since it may reveal the existence of relationships which were not documented.

Distribution of databases is best based on a partitioning into fragments that are not strongly bound, since this will minimize autonomy and integrity problems. There are cases where a single relation in a model may be split into *horizontal fragments*, namely tuples that are used mainly at different nodes. An example is where the employees work at at different locations and their data are kept on the local node. **Vertical fragments** are created when attribute usage differs among nodes. The employees' skill data may be kept on the **Personnel** computer, while salary data are kept on the **Payroll** machine.

Monitoring Measures of system utilization that can be profitably monitored include:

Statistics of device utilization. The percentage activity times of processors, channels, controllers, and disks. It is desirable to have both average values as well as values which pertain to the busy periods of system operation.

Statistics of file utilization. A matrix of user process versus file activities is the basic measure. The relative ratios of type of access such as fetch, get next, and update are important for decisions about the file organization. File density (space used versus space allocated) is another measure.

Statistics of record utilization. The frequency with which records are accessed for read or update provides a measure which can be used to provide optimization in systems where records are chained. The dates and times of last access and update are important for the maintenance of integrity, as is the identification of the process which updated the records.

Statistics of attribute utilization. The frequency with which attribute values are requested, updated, used as keys, or used as further search arguments provides the data for optimal tuple membership selection.

The measures can be obtained by continuous monitoring or by selective sampling. The best repository for data obtained from monitoring depends on the system design. It can be difficult to bring all the measurements together for automated analysis. A regular logging tape provides the most obvious repository.

Data on device utilization may be provided by the operating system. File utilization data can be saved in a file directory when a file is closed. Record activity logging was essential for comprehensive backup, but many systems do not provide this service. Data on record activity can be collected with the record when records are written or updated, but the cost of rewriting a record which has been read in order to collect access monitoring data is excessive. Attribute activity can be recorded with the schema, and recorded when the associated file is closed or when a process terminates.

The monitoring data listed above do not provide information regarding in-dividual data elements but do provide activity data for the record and the attribute, which together describe the activity of any element in terms of averages.

The availability of monitoring information not only provides data for tuning. A data administrator can now also justify expansion when needed, and can provide data when there are service conflicts among user groups. The job of a database administrator is already difficult. Without tools it is impossible. A person willing to undertake database administration without tools will be self-selected on the basis of political adroitness rather than on the basis of technical competence.

15-2-2 The Lifetime of Data and Database Systems

Both data and the systems lose value with age. It is hard to predict what becomes obsolete first, so that both effects have to be considered.

Data Archiving As data ages it becomes of less value. Eventually its value will not warrant continued on-line storage. The low cost of dense off-line tape storage makes it possible to retain old data as long as there is any probability that the data will be of eventual interest. Optical disks promise new alternatives for archiving old versions.

The procedures used during transaction logging have produced extensive back-up capability, but the contents of the logs and checkpoints is closely related to the status of the system when the backup was generated, so that these files may be difficult to utilize. For long-term archival storage, it is best to generate tapes in an output format, which can be read by input procedures when needed. If the schema entries for the attributes saved on the files are also written on the archival tapes, much of the file documentation will be retained with the files. In large and very dynamic systems, i.e., very large databases, it may not be possible to generate adequate archival tapes from the database, since the database as a whole is never consistent. Then the archival tapes can be generated from the logging files.

If preservation of auditability is important, archive files can be generated continuously in a database system. A **database_procedure**, specified in the schema, can state

ON DELETE, UPDATE CALL archival_recording

so that archiving responsibility is assumed by the manager of the schema.

It is important to read archival files, first immediately after creation, and later at least on a random sample basis. This avoids the embarrassment of finding that one's archives are useless, either due to an error when they were generated or due to incompatibilities introduced as the system was further developed.

System Life Cycle It is very hard for a developer to visualize the point where the operation of a particular system will be terminated. Even where the database remains of value, there will be a time when it is better to transfer the data and programs than to continue an operation which has become obsolete.

Obsolescence is often associated with hardware which is no longer up to date, but more serious is inadequate software. The maintenance cost of hardware and software tends to decrease initially as the bugs are shaken out, but eventually begins to increase again if an effort is made to keep old hardware and software facilities compatible with new developments.

External developments which require adaptation may be technical or organizational; for instance, changes in communication facilities or a company reorganization can force a database change. While a number of adaptations can be made, especially in systems which are not rigorously bound, eventually a required adaptation will cost more than a reimplementation, which also can take advantage of improved technology.

We can hence speak of a system *life cycle*, beginning from design, development, implemenation, loading with data, operation and enhancement, operation and maintenance only, terminating with a transfer of services to new a new system. Once the expected *life cycle* of a system is determined, other decisions can be made objectively. Investments in system improvements which will not realize adequate benefits over the remaining lifetime can be rejected.

15-3 THE DATABASE ADMINISTRATOR

The final word in this book belongs, quite properly, to the database administrator. The role of a database administrator (DBA) is not yet well defined, and the exact definition varies from one operation to the other. A possible role for the database administrator is the position sketched in Fig. 15-1.

The position of database administrator may be taken by several individuals or may be considered a part-time duty. The choice depends on the number of functions which are assigned to the DBA.

Function of the Database Administrator The DBA acts formally as the control mechanism of a system which manages information loops of the users. The inputs to the control function are the results of the monitoring activity and requests by unsatisfied users. In order to carry out the control function, the DBA can restructure the database or obtain additional facilities for analysis, processing, or communication. The inertia in the various control activities can differ considerably. Additional resources require allocation of investment capital which the DBA has to obtain from management.

The database administrator controls a resource which is important to a variety of users. The users will look toward the DBA whenever they wish to obtain more services from this resource. In order to provide the services, two components of the database operation have to be considered:

1 The database system

2 The database content

Given technical resources and time, it should be possible to satisfy all reasonable technical requests. If the DBA cannot satisfy a user, the user may go to management to request that allocations be increased so that the needs may be satisfied.

If the data contents of the database is inadequate, the DBA has to find the potential source of good data. Source data are often in the domain of other users. The DBA may be able to obtain the data freely or may have to provide a reimbursement for data-collection costs. There will be users who feel that they are already providing more than their share of data. A DBA may have to go to management to present the need if the data is not easily obtained. Management may itself be a major contributor and user of the database system.

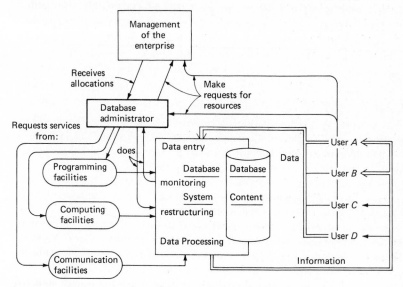

Figure 15-1 A place for the database administrator.

The principal tool that the DBA has available to allocate resources is the schema. The internal schema provides control over the efficiency and responsiveness of processes and the associated protection matrix controls access. The selection of the external schema determines the operational view that a user has of the database model. The conceptual schema, the description of the database model, is constrained by reality and not easily modifiable because of specific needs.

In addition the DBA will have monitoring tools and means to restructure the database. Automatic restructuring is an attractive concept which has up to now been applied only in limited and experimental situations.

Qualifications for a DBA The role of the DBA presented here requires primarily an understanding of the user's needs and a capability to deal with these needs. A DBA who cannot effectively deal with the majority of user requests does not fulfill the responsibility of the position since too much detail will require attention of management. The DBA needs sufficient authority to deal with the majority of user's needs. This implies a capability to obtain or allocate data collection, programming, computing, and communication resources. This capability implies the presence of two conditions: the command over adequate resources and the competence to manage and balance the use of these resources.

The fact that there are only a small number of true database administrators in industry today may be traced to the fact that people who have an adequate background are not easy to find. The technical competence of people engaged in database administration has to be at a level which enables them to judge the efforts of programmers. They may not be directly managing any programming projects but will depend on programming talent for system maintenance and tool development.

The persons who take on the functions of a DBA have to educate themselves continuously so that they will remain organizationally and technically competent. The material in this book may comprise a level of technical knowledge appropriate to the database administrator's role. Technical specialists in the database organization will have a deeper knowledge in their subject areas but will share the level of knowledge presented here to allow effective communication in a group effort.

BACKGROUND AND REFERENCES

Gruenberger[69] has an early evaluation of the role of data systems in data management; Sanders[74] includes some case studies. Jefferson[80] provides an inventory example. The objectives and data requirements for decision making in management applications are defined by Sprague[82]. Scientific applications are presented in Streeter[74].

The place of the database in the organization is presented in Davis[74]; the book contains many references. Spewak[80] considers the users; Sterling[75] provides some guidelines. The papers in Murdick[75] also stress the applicability of systems.

Brooks[75] presents an unusual degree of insight into the process of system development and should be read by anyone contemplating a project involving more than one programmer. Dolotta[76] and Freilich[80] present many management issues. A study by the General Accounting Office (GAO[79]) shows the need for proper planning. Lucas[81] defines the planning process for management-oriented systems. Case studies are included in Riley[81].

Donovan[76] gives an example of the dynamics of database usage. Archiving experiments are described by Smith[81] and Lawrie[82]. Data are given by Satyanarayanan[81].

Jardine[74] contains a discussion about the role of the database administrator, and an attempt to define the role is made in Steel[75]. Some theoretic approaches (Sundgren[75]) assign a very powerful role to the administrator, included is the design of the database system. Experience with the concept (DeBlasis in Lowenthal[78]) gives cause to consider a more limited function. Formal design techniques and system improvements (as Arditi[78]) will also affect the role of the DBA. Many other articles in the trade literature reflect on the function of the database administrator and the background required to manage database operations. A self-assessment procedure of the ACM in the area was developed by Scheuermann[78].

Index for
Alternate Terminology

... Behold, the people is one, and they have all one language; and this they begin to do: and now nothing will be restrained from them, which they have imagined to do.

Go to, let us go down, and confound their language, that they may not understand one another's speech.

Genesis 11, 6 to 7

This list is intended to provide assistance when reading about files and databases. Since there is a great deal of variation of meaning of the terms used in the literature, it is impossible to make this index truly comprehensive. The appropriateness of the provided cross references has to be verified in each case by careful reading of the source material and the corresponding section of this book. Often there will be no exact match and the concept or technique described in a reference will have to be circumscribed in a few sentences. Whenever references are used to present material for classroom discussion or evaluation, it is essential to use the standard terminology which has been introduced in this book to avoid misunderstandings and the associated waste of time.

Term Found in the Literature: Term Used Here

A-strings (DIAM): attribute column
absolutes: essential data or essential links
abuse: violation of protection
accept: get currency

Database Systems

The systems in this list were chosen because of their ubiquity, their historical interest, their potential for experimentation, or their significance for further study. Other sources for references to database and file systems can be obtained from commercial software catalogs (DATAPRO, Auerbach, ICP Quarterly) or from surveys in computer magazines, for example, Krass[81]. CODASYL[71A] contains a detailed review of GIS, MARKIV, NIPS/FFS, TDMS, UL/1, COBOL, DBIG, IDS, IMS, and SC-1; Martin in Nance[75] surveyed STAIRS, DIALOG, DATA CENTRAL, ORBIT used for MEDLINE, BASIS, SPIRES, LEADER, RECON, RIQS, INTREX, and NASIS. Kim[79] surveyed relational DBMS' and Brodie[82] includes a survey of relational systems: IDM, INGRES, MRDS, MRS, NOMAD, ORACLE, PASCAL/R, PRTV, RAPPORT, SYSTEM R, QBE, RAPID, and cites a total of 60. Wiederhold[82] includes descriptions of distributed DBMS efforts. CODASYL[76] provides guidelines for system selection. Landau[79] produces a listing of on-line databases.

The commercial systems included below vary in price from several hundred dollars total to several thousand dollars per month.

Name	Year	Developer location	Computer	Type and features
ACCENT R	1981	National Information Syst, Cupertino CA	DEC10/20	Com DBMS slc rel stq sch
ADABAS	1971	software ag Darmstadt FRG	IBM360/370 Siemens	Com DBMS hlc stq sch drf cip pri rec Atre[80]
ADEPT	1969	System Dev Corp Santa Monica CA	IBM360-50	Exp DBMS slc nlq(CONVERSE) pri Weissman[69]
ADMINS	1966	MIT&ADMINS inc Cambridge MA	DEC 11, VAX	DBMS slc sch rel trf McIntosh[68]
ALPHA	1971	IBM Research San Jose CA		Pro DBL slc rel Codd in Codd[71]

Name	Year	Developer location	Computer	Type and features
AMBASE	1979	Amcor Computer Corp Louisville KY	DEC 11 (RSTS)	Com DBMS sch isf
AMIGOS	1970	Comress Inc Rockville MD	IBM360/370	Com FMS hlc isf
APPEL IV	1974	SIS Paris France	IBM360/370 Burr.500/700	Com DBMS hlc hie drf isf
ASI/INQ	1975	Applications Softw. Torrance CA	IBM360/370	Com QUS for DL/1 slc hie stq
ASI/ST	1969	Applications Softw. Torrance CA	IBM360/370 Univac70	Com QUS slc rpg tbq sch *for* sqf, isf, IMS, TOTAL
Ass.PL	1967	General Motors Warren MI	IBM360-67	Inst DBMS hlp(PL/1) rnf gra Dodd[66]
AUTONOTE	1969	Univ of Michigan Ann Arbor MI	IBM360/370 (MTS)	Exp SATDBMS slc txt sch sqf drf Reitman[69]
BASIS	1970	Batelle Mem Labs Columbus OH	CDC6400 DEC 10/20,VAX IBM 370 UNIVAC1100	Inst IRS stq bib rpg Fried in Walker[71]
BEAST	1968	Brookings Inst Washington DC	DEC PDP10	Inst SATDBMS slc sch sqf Kidd[69]
BIS	1967	Am Tel &Tel New York NY	IBM360	Inst DBMS hlc hie sch Benner[67]
CAFS	1976	ICL Stevenage UK		Dev DBCMP rel Babb[79]
CASSM	1975	Univ of Florida Gainesville FL		Exp DBCMP Su[79] Hawthorn[82]
CDMS	1969	System Dev Corp Santa Monica CA	IBM360/370	Com DBMS service slc irq ixf *see* TDMS
CDMS	1974	Digital Eq Corp Maynard MA	DEC 11	Com DBMS slc hie trf *see* MUMPS
CFS	1980	Carnegie-Mellon U. Pittsburgh PA	DEC LSI-11s	Exp DFMS
CIA	1982	Computer Invest.Adv. Sewickley PA	Apple	Com DBMS 1-rel alg hlc(BASIC) rpg sch isf
COGENT	1969	Comp Sciences Corp Los Angeles CA	IBM7090, 370 Univac1100	Com DPG hlp(COBOL) sch hie isf ixf
CONVERSE	1967	System Dev Corp Santa Monica CA	IBM360-67 ANFSQ32	Exp QUS net nlq vrf Kellogg[68], in SIGIR[71]

Name	Year	Developer location	Computer	Type and features
COSTAR	1978	Mass Gen Hospital Boston MA	DEC PDP15,11 Tandem	SATBMS slc trf(MUMPS) Barnett[79]
CREATE	1975	Complete Computer Sys, Horsham PA	DataGeneral	Com DPG ixf pri
CREATE/3000	1977	CRI Inc Mountain View CA	HP 3000	Com DBMS hlc rel stq ixf
CZAR	1970	Crown Zellerbach San Francisco CA	IBM360/370	Inst QUS hlc sch isf Palmer[75]
DATA ANALYZER	1971	Program Prod. Nanuet NY	IBM360/370	Com IRS slc rpg sch sqf isf
DATACATALOG	1974	Synergetics Bedford MA	IBM370 OS,DOS UNIVAC	Com DDICT slc rpg sch isf DMS1100 IDMS IMS S2000
DATACOM	1970	Aplied Data Res. Dallas TX	IBM360/370	Com DBMS hlc sch sqf ixf cpr
DATA COMPUTER	1971	Comp Corp of Am Cambridge MA	PDP10 (TENEX)	Dev DBMS hlc hie stq vrf *for* ARPAnet
DATAMAN	1975	Dataman Ltd Calgary Alberta	IBM360/370	Com FMS slc rpg sch sqf
DATAMANAGER	1976	MSP London UK & Lexington MA	IBM360/370	Com DDICT slc rpg sch ADABAS IMS MARKIV SYSTEM 2000 TOTAL
DATAMASTER	1980	Microsoft Seattle WA	Apple 8080	Com FMS rpg sch sqf
DATASAAB	1974	Saab-Scania AB Linkoping Sweden	SAAB D22/D23	Com DBMS hlp(COBOL) net sch rnf pri Bubenko[75]
dBASE II	1981	Ashton-Tate Culver City CA	Z-80 CP/M	Com FMS, Join stq rpg ixf(1 *updated*)
DBC	1978	Ohio State&UNIVAC Columbus OH		Dev DBCMP sch ixf Banerjee[79], Hawthorn[82]
DBMS	1977	Prime Computer Inc Wellesley Hills MA	Prime	Com DBMS hlp net sch stq(IQL) rnf rec pri
DBMS10/20	1973	Digital Eq Corp Marlboro MA	DEC 10/20	Com DBMS hlc net(1973) sch stq(IQL) rnf rec pri
DBMS11	1979	Digital Eq Corp Marlboro MA	DEC 11	Com DBMS hlc net(1973) sch rnf
DBMS990	1980	Texas Instruments Austin TX	Ti990	Com FMS hlc(PASCAL CO-BOL FORTRAN) hie-tbq isf

Name	Year	Developer location	Computer	Type and features
DBMS1900	1974	ICL London England	ICL 1903	Com DBMS hlc sch isf pri rec
DBOMP	1970	IBM White Plains NY	IBM360/370	Com BOMP net stq DL/1 files; CFMS *for* isf
DBS90	1972	Sperry Rand GmbH Frankfurt a/M FRG	Univac90	Com BOMP hlc(COBOL) net
DB/DC	1975	IBM White Plains NY	IBM360/370 IMS	Com DDICT slc sch rpg (CMIS *for manufacturing*)
DIALOG	1967	Lockheed Res Corp Palo Alto CA	IBM360	Com IRS *service* slc irq hie bib Walker[71]
DIRECT	1977	Northwestern Univ Evanston IL		Pro DBCMP DeWitt[79] Hawthorn[82]
DISAM	1975	Four Phase Systems Cupertino CA	4phase70	Com FS *for* DDBMS hlp(COBOL) isf ixf
DL/1	1968	IBM White Plains NY	IBM360/370	Com FMS hlc sch hie sqf isf drf stq(CICS)
DM1, 5 *also* SC-1	1966	Auerbach Philadelphia PA	Univac418 IBM360/370	Com DBMS slc hie rpg sch ixf CODASYL[71A]
DMS1100, 90	1971	Univac Minneapolis MN	Univac1100 Univac90	Com DBMS hlp(COBOL) net(1969) rnf rec vie
DMS170	1977	Control Data Corp Minneapolis MN	Cyber170	Com DBMS hie sch sqf *derived from* (MARS) isf drf
DMS/1700	1975	Dedicated Systems Chicago IL	Burr.1700	Com FMS ixf
DMS II	1972	Burroughs Pasadena CA	B1700 *to* 7700	Com DBMS hlp(COBOL, ALGOL) net sch sqf isf ixf cpr rec
DMS IV *based on* IDS	1972	Honeywell Inf Sys Phoeniz AZ	H60	Com DBMS hlp(COBOL) net(1973) rpg rnf rec
DPL *also* IPL	1976	National Information Syst, Cupertino CA	DEC10/20	Com DBMS hlc(FORTRAN COBOL) sch isf pri
DYL250	1971	Dylakor Comp Syst Encino CA	IBM360/370	Com FMS slc rpg stq sqf isf
EDEN	1982	Univ of Washington Seattle WA	DEC VAX	Exp DFMS obj Jessop in Wiederhold[82]
EDMS	1969	Control Data Corp Brussels Belgium	CDC6400 Cyber	Com DBMS hlc(FORTRAN) stq sch(ANSII) isf Nijssen[77]

Name	Year	Developer location	Computer	Type and features
FACETS *was* PRISM	1981	Synergistics Bedford MA	IBM 370	Com DDICT slc rpg
FOCUS		Information Builders New York 10001 NY	IBM 370 CMS,TSO	Com QUS irq rpg isf,DL/1,IDMS pri
FORDATA	1974	CSIRO Canberra Australia	CDC CYBER76	Inst DBMS hlp(FORTRAN) net sch
FORIMS	1970	Nippon Univac Tokyo Japan	Univac1100	Dev DBMS hlc(FORTRAN) net ixf rec
FORTE	1959	Burroughs Corp Paoli PA	B2500/3500 B1700-7700	Com FMS hlc(COBOL) sqf isf drf ixf rnf Chapin[69]
FRAMIS	1977	Lawrence Liv.Lab. Livermore CA	CDC 7600 CRAY DEC VAX(VMS)	Dev DBMS rel alg stq rnf(CODASYL)
GIM	1967	TRW Systems Redondo Beach CA	IBM7094,360/ 370 Univac1100 Honeywell6000	Com QUS slc stq sch rec drf rng Nelson[67]
GIS	1966	IBM White Plains NY	IBM360/370	Com QUS hlc(COBOL, PL/1) hie stq sch sqf isf
GMIS	1975	MIT Sloan School& IBM, Cambridge MA	IBM370 (XRM)	Dev SATDBMS(Dec.supp.) rel vrf Donovan[76]
iDBP 86/440	1982	Intel-MRI Austin TX	*links to* IEEE 488, ETHERNET	Com DBCMP rel pri rec
HOPS	1975	Technicon Haifa Israel	Burroughs 126	Exp DBMS hie trf Reiter in Kerr[75]
IDM 500	1981	Britton-Lee Los Gatos CA	VAX *on* IEEE-488 *or* intlgnt.term.	Com DBCMP rel isf,ixf pri
IDMS	1972	Cullinane Corp Westwood MA	IBM360/370 ICL1902 Univac70,90 Siemens4004	Com DBMS hlp(COBOL) nlq(ROBOT) rpg (CULPRIT) net(1973+) sch DDICT drf rec
IDS I, II	1962	Honeywell Inf Sys Phoeniz AZ	H200, H60, H6000	Com DBMS hlp(COBOL) net(73) rnf rec Bachman[66]
IDP EDMS	1978	Honeywell *was* XDS Los Angeles 45 CA	H66 Sigma 6,7,9	Com DBMS hlc(COBOL) net rnf ixf sch rec
IFIP *also* RIM	1978	Boeing Computer Co (IPAD) Seattle WA	DEC VAX IBM	SATDBMS *for* CAD/CAM net(1978) hlp(FORTRAN)
IMAGE	1974	Hewlett-Packard Santa Clara CA	HP3000, HP2100	Com DBMS hlc sch pri stq net(2 level: drf, rnf)

Name	Year	Developer location	Computer	Type and features
IMARS	1971	Computeria Inc Braintree MA	DEC PDP10	Com QUS slc stq rpg rec
IMS-2/VS	1968	IBM White Plains NY	IBM360/370	Com DBMS hlc *multi*-hie sch(DL/1) stq rec(-VS)
INFOS	1975	Data General Southboro MA	DG Nova, Eclipse	Com FMS hlc hie isf ixf stq
INGRES	1973	Un.of CA&Relational Technology, Berkeley	DEC 11, VAX (UNIX, VMS)	Dev DBMS slc hlp(C, ao.) rel stq gra pri Held[75]
INQUIRE	1969	Infodata Systems Falls Church VA	IBM360/370	Com IRS hlc rpg stq sch pri; Dev DDBMS(IQNET)
INTREX	1966	Mass Inst. Tech Cambridge MA	IBM7094, IBM360	Inst IRS irq/stq bib ixf Walker[71]
IS/1 *later* PRTV	1971	IBM UK Research Peterlee UK	IBM360/370	Dev DBMS hlp(PL/1) rel alg vie com stq Todd[76]
ISAM70	1974	Software70 Anaheim CA	Any FORTRAN system	Com FS hlc(FORTRAN) isf
LADDER	1977	SRI International Menlo Park CA	DEC PDP10	Exp IRS nlq net(DBMS20) Hendrix[78]
LEADER	1967	Lehigh Univ Bethlehem PA	CDC6400	Inst IRS irq bib ixf Hillman[69]
LEXICON	1976	Arthur Anderson Chicago IL	IBM360/370, System 3	Com DDICT slc IDMS IMS TOTAL
LEXIS	1978	Mead Data Central Lexis: New York NY	IBM370	Com IRS *service* slc *legal, economic databases*
LUNAR	1972	Bolt Beranek Newman Cambridge MA	DEC PDP10 TENEX	Inst IRS nlq sqf ixf Woods[73]
MADAM	1970	MIT MacAIMS Proj. Cambridge MA	H6000 (MULTICS)	Dev DBMS *first* rel hlp (PL/1) stq rpg vrf Strnad[71]
MAGNUM	1975	Tymshare Cupertino CA	DEC PDP10	Com DBMS slc rel stq sch
MARKIV	1967	Informatics Canoga Park CA	IBM360/370 Univac900	Com FMS slc rpg tbq hie isf CODASYL[71A]
MARS	1969	Control Data Corp Sunnyvale CA	CDC6400	Com DBMS hie sch hlc(FORTRAN) sqf isf
MDBS	1980	Micro Data Base Syst Lafayette IN	Z80,8080-*based systems on* CP/M	Com DBMS slc stq net sch

Name	Year	Developer location	Computer	Type and features
MEDLARS *also* ELHILL	1963	National Lib Med Bethesda MD	IBM360	Inst SADBMS slc irq sqf isf bib Katter[75], *also* ORBIT
MICRO-SEED	1980	Microsoft Bellevue WA	Z80,8080-*based systems*	ComDBMShlc(FORTRAN) net sch *based on* SEED
MODEL204	1972	Comp Corp of Am Cambridge MA	IBM360/370	Com DBMS hlc stq sch plf ixf(IFAM)
MORIS	1972	Polytechnico Milano Italy		Pro DBMS rel cal sch stq(COLARD) Bracchi in Klimbie[75]
MUMPS	1966	Mass Gen Hospital Boston MA	DEC PDP15,11 8080 ao.	Com FMS slc hie trf Greenes[69]
MRDS *based on* RDMS	1978	Honeywell Inf Sys Minneapolis MN	H6000 L68 (MULTICS)	Com DBMS hlp(PL/1) rel stq(LINUS) rpg vrf
NOMAD	1975	National CSS Norwalk CN	IBM370-CMS	Com DBMS slc,hlc hie stq sch rpg
NYTIS	1970	New York Times New York NY	IBM360	Inst IRS slc txf ixf Baker[72]
OASIS	1971	Stanford Adm DP Stanford CA	IBM360/370	Inst SATDBMS hlc(COBOL) hie irq isf
ORACLE	1979	Relational Software Inc., Menlo Park CA	DEC VAX, IBM VM MVS DOS	DBMS hlc(COBOL PL/1 C) rel stq ixf cpr pri vie
OSIRIS	1973	Survey Res.Ctr.,Univ. of Michigan, Ann Arbor	IBM360/370	Inst SATDBMS sch sqf,isf rpg Rattenbury[74]
PLUS/4	1979	Century Analysis Pacheco CA	NCR 101 etc.	Com FMS hlc
POLYPHEME (SIRIUS)	1977	I. N. Polytechnique Grenoble France	CII & IBM	Exp DDBMS pri LeBihan[80]
RAMIS	1967	Mathematica Princeton NJ	IBM360/370	Com DBMS hlc stq rpg
RAP	1975	Univ of Toronto Toronto Canada		Exp DBCMP rel Ozkarahan[77] Hawthorn[82]
RAPPORT	1978	Brit.Min.Def. & LOGICA,New York NY	*Any* FORTRAN-*based system*	Com DBMS hlc stq rpg rec
RDF	1967	Rand Corp Santa Monica CA	IBM360	Exp IRS slc nlq rel Levien[67]
RDMS *based on* MADAM	1971	Mass Inst of Tech Cambridge MA	H6000 (MULTICS PL/1)	Inst DBMS hlp rel stq rpg vrf Steuert in [Rustin:74]

Name	Year	Developer location	Computer	Type and features
REGIS *early name:* RDMS	1972	General Motors Warren MI	IBM360-67	Dev DBMS hlp(PL/1) rel stq Joyce[76]
REL	1969	Calif Inst of Tech Pasadena CA	IBM360	Dev IRS nlq rel *extendible* Thompson[69]
RELGRAF	1982	Adv.Rel.Techn.Inc. Menlo Park CA	PRIME OS *or* MPX	Com IRS stq rel cal vie txt gra sch ixf
RETRIEVE	1970	Tymshare Cupertino CA	XDS940	Com DBMS service slc stq 1-sqf; FMS(IML) *for >2*
RFMS	1971	Univ of Texas Austin TX	CDC6400	Dev DBMS hie stq sch Hardgrave[80]
RISS	1974	Forest Hosp.& MIT Des Plaines IL	DEC 11	DBMS 1-rel sch rpg sqf McLeod[75]
ROBOT	1973	Software Sciences Farnborough UK	ICL 1906 Univac9400	Com DBMS slc rpg tnf Palmer[75]
RS/1, *based on* PROPHET	1980	Bolt Beranek Newman Cambridge MA	DEC 11, VAX	SATDBMS slc *with* PL/1 tbq rpg grf sch
SAM *basis for* RM, XRM	1968	IBM Scientific Center Cambridge MA	IBM360 *modified* 370	Exp FMS rel vrf Symonds[68] *later* RSS(SYSTEM R)
SAS	1972	Univ. N. Carolina & SAS Inst., Raleigh NC	IBM360/370	SATDBMS(*statistics*) slc stq rpg sqf
SBA *uses* QBE	1975	IBM Research Yorktown Heights NY		Dev DBMS rel tbq(*by example*) Zloof[77]
SCORE	1969	Programming Methods, New York NY	Any COBOL system	Com FMS hlp(COBOL) hie tbq sqf isf
SDD-1	1978	Comp Corp of Am Cambridge, MA	DEC 10/20	Exp DDBMS slc rel sch DAPLEX Bernstein[81]
SEED	1978	Internat'l Data Base Syst., Philadelphia PA	DEC 11,10/20 IBM370 CDC6000	Com DBMS hlp(COBOL) hic(FORTRAN) sch rpg net(1973) rnf
SEQUITUR	1981	Pacific Software Berkeley CA	DEC-11,VAX Z-8000 systems	Com DBMS slc,hlc(C) rel tbq ixf rpg txt
SESAM	1973	Siemens München FRG	S4004	Com FMS stq rpg sqf isf
SHOEBOX	1970	MITRE Corp Bedford MA	IBM360	Exp SATDBMS slc txt plf stq Glantz[70]
SIBAS	1974	Shipping Res Svc Oslo Norway& Houston TX	IBM360/370 Univac1100 DEC PDP10	Com DBMS net hlp(COBOL) hlc sch Palmer[75]

Name	Year	Developer location	Computer	Type and features
SIR	1977	Scientific Information Retrieval, Evanston IL	IBM360/370 CDC 6000,Cyber	Com IRS stq stat.interface sch net pri
SOCRATE	1970	Univ of Grenoble, CII Louveciennes, France	IBM360-370 CII Iris45,80	Dev, Com DBMS slc sch net stq vrf
SOLID	1967	Penn State Univ University Park PA	IBM360-40 -67	Exp DBMS slc cpr rec DeMaine[71]
SOURCE	1979	Telecomputing Co McLean VA	*multiple*	Com IRS *service* slc *business, consumer info, ads*
SPIRES	1967	Stanford Univ Stanford CA	IBM360-67, 370-168	Inst IRS, DBMS slc hie irq bib trf ixf pri Schroeder in Kerr[75]
SQL/DS	1981	IBM San Jose CA	IBM370 (DOS)	DBMS hlp(PL/1) rel stq ixf(VSAM) pri vie
STAIRS	1972	IBM Stuttgart FRG	IBM360/370 *with* CICS	Com IRS slc stq txt sqf drf isf pri
SWALLOW	1980	Mass. Inst. Tech. Cambridge MA		Exp DFMS obj
SYSIF	1970	CAP-SOGETI Paris 15 France	IBM360/370, CII Iris, Univac1100	Com IRS slc nlq sqf isf
SYSTEM 1022	1978	Software House Cambridge MA	DEC 10/20	Com DBMS slc,hlc ixf *timeshared services*
SYSTEM 2000 *or* S2000, S2K	1970	Intel-MRI Austin TX	IBM360/370 Univac1100 CDC6000	Com DBMS hlp(COBOL PL/1) hie stq isf Kroenke[78]
SYSTEM C	1981	Software Clearing House, Cleveland OH	NCR, Criterion	Com DBMS hlc net(1978) sch stq rnf rec pri
SYSTEM-R	1975	IBM Research San Jose CA	IBM370	Exp DBMS hlp(PL/1)rel stq (SEQUEL) vie Astrahan[76]
SYSTEM-R*	1981	IBM Research San Jose CA	IBM370 VMS	Exp DDBMS hlp rel sch stq vie
TDMS	1966	System Dev Corp Santa Monica CA	IBM360-50 (Adept)	Dev DBMS slc hie irq sch Bleier[68], CODASYL[71A]
TOD	1973	Stanford Univ. Stanford CA & ITTRI Chicago 16 IL	IBM360-50,67, 370 DEC VAX	Inst SATDBMS hlc(PL/1) sch irq gra ixf tnf cpr cip Wiederhold[75]
TOOL-IR	1974	Univ of Tokyo Tokyo Japan	HITAC8800	Inst IRS slc stq bib pri Yamamoto[75]

Name	Year	Developer location	Computer	Type and features
TOTAL	1971	Cincom Inc Cincinnati OH	IBM360/370 Univac 90,V70 CDC Cyber	Com DBMS hlc sch net (2 level:drf,rnf) DDICT Cagan[73]
		also on Siemens4004 Honeywell200 NCR Century		
TRAMP	1967	Univ of Michigan Ann Arbor MI	IBM360-67	Exp DBMS nlq rel Ash[68]
UCC TEN	1976	University Comp. Dallas TX	IBM360/370 IMS	Com DDICT slc rpg sch IMS
UNIDATA	1970	United Computing Kansas City MO	CDC6400	Com DBMS hie sch rpg gra
VISIFILE	1982	Visicorp San Jose CA	IBM PC, Apple	Com FMS slc ixf stq
WOODSTOCK	1979	Xerox Research Lab Palo Alto CA	Xerox Altos	Dev DFMS Swinehart[79]
ZETA *also* TORUS	1974	Univ of Toronto Toronto Ontario	IBM360/370	Exp DBMS hlc(PL/1) rel stq vie drf Tsichritzis[77]

Legend for type and features of database systems

alg relational algebra
bib bibliographic data
BOMP bill-of-materials processor
cal relational calculus
cip ciphering
Com commercial
cpr compression
DBCMP database computer
DBL database language
DBMS database-management system
DDBMS distributed DBMS
DDICT data dictionary system
Dev developmental
DFMS distributed FMS
DPG database program generator
drf direct or immediate file organization
Exp experimental
FMS file-management system
FS file system
gra graphic data support
hie hierarchical database organization
hlc host-language system accessed by CALL
hlp host-language system with preprocessor
Inst institutional
irq interrogative query processor
IRS information-retrieval system

isf indexed-sequential file
ixf indexed files
net network database organization,
        (year indicates CODASYL standard)
nlq natural language query capabilty
obj object based
plf pile file organization
pri privacy protection
Pro proposed
QUS query and update system
rec recovery support
rel relational database organization
rnf ring or chain file organization
rpg report generator
SADBMS single-application DBMS
SATDBMS single-application type DBMS
sch schema
slc self-contained system
sqf sequential file organization
stq statement-oriented query processor
tbq tabular query processor
tnf transposed files
trf tree-structured files
txt textual data
vie support for multiple user views
vrf virtual file support

Symbols Used

Mathematical Symbols Used

$\lceil\ \rceil$	CEIL, next higher integer
$\lfloor\ \rfloor$	FLOOR, next lower integer
$\approx$	approximately equal
$\gg$	much greater than
$!$	factorial
$\#$	number of
$\log_y x$	logarithm base y of x
$\log x$	natural logarithm of x, base $e = 2.71828182846$
$\sum_k f(k)$	sum of all $f(k)$ for the integer k's specified
$\ominus$	one of the comparison operators $> \geq = \neq \leq <$
$\wedge$	and, true if both sides are true
$\vee$	or, true if either side is true
$\mid$	where, precedes a conditional clause
$\cap$	set intersection
$\cup$	set union
$-$	set difference
$\times$	cartesian product
$\subseteq$	select tuples from a relation
π	project a value from a tuple
Π	project attributes from a relation
$\underset{a=b}{\bowtie}$	join two relations based on equality of the attributes a, b
$\longrightarrow$	reference connection
$\longrightarrow\!*$	ownership connection
$\longrightarrow\!\!\!\!\Rightarrow$	subset connection
$\subseteq$	subset of
$\in$	member of
$\forall$	for all
$\Rightarrow$	becomes
$\{\ \}$	enclose a set
$[\ \ ]$	enclose a reference

Programming and Syntax Symbols As Used

a + b	addition
a - b	subtraction
a * b	multiplication
a / b	division
MOD(a,b)	modulo, integer remainder of division
a ** b	exponentiation, a to the power b
a = b	depending on context in PL/1, assignment or equality comparison
a > b	greater than comparison, true if a greater than b
a ≥ b	greater or equal comparison, true if a greater than or equal to b
a ∧ b	and, true if both a, b true (& in PL/1)
a ∨ b	or, true if either a, b true (| in PL/1)
¬c	not, true if c false and vice versa
s ‖ w	catenation, string s connected to string w to form a single new string
s | c	where, do s if the predicate (conditional) clause c is true
R ∪ S	union of relations R and S
R ∩ S	intersection of relations R and S
R × S	cross product of relations R and S
R − S	difference, remove tuples matching S from R
⊆R.ex	select tuples of R according to expression ex
∏ R.a	projection of attributes a of R
R.a⋈S.b	Join R and S, on equality of attribute values in a and b
R.a⋈S.b	Outerjoin, join which includes all tuples
,	field separator
:⟩	key and goal fields separator
;	statement separator
.	termination of computational section
ss, ...	section ss may be repeated
[ss]	section ss is optional
{ ss/tt }	sections ss, tt are alternatives
::=	is defined by
/* Note */	explanatory comments
a.b	qualification of variable b by a higher-level variable a, i.e., employee.name
'Word'	character string constant
_	(underline) pseudo-alphabetic character without syntactic meaning used for legibility within variable names. (In COBOL - is used for this function.)

Variables Used in Performance Formulas

A	average space required for attribute name; attribute name	Sec. 3-1-3; 7-1-1
a	number of different attributes in a file	Sec. 3-1-1
a'	average number of attributes in a record	Sec. 3-1-1, 3-6-3
B	blocksize	Sec. 2-2
b	blockcount	Sec. 2-2-2
btt	block transfer time $= B/t$	Eq. 2-13
Bfr	blocking factor $\approx B/R$	Eqs. 2-5, 2-6, 2-7, 2-20
C	Cost factors	Sec. 5-4-6, 5-5-2
c	computational overhead per record, when not negligible	Sec. 2-3-4
D	space required for data	Eq. 5-1, Sec 5-3-3
d	number of records that have been invalidated	Sec. 3-1-3
F	subscript denoting a fetch for a specific record	Sec. 3-0-2
G	space required for an interblock gap	Sec. 2-2-3
h	classification variable	Sec. 5-4-3
I	subscript denoting insertion of a record	Sec. 3-0-2
j	number of cylinders	Sec. 2-2-1
K	projection list	Sec. 7-3-2
K	kilo or thousand (1024) times	
k	number of tracks per cylinder	Sec. 2-2-5, Table 2-1
L	load frequency factors; selection list	Sec. 5-1; 7-3-3
M	multiprogramming factor	Eq. 5-19
M	mega or million (1 048 576) times	
m	number of available slots for records	Sec. 3-5-1
N	subscript denoting getting the next serial record	Sec. 3-0-2
n	number of records in a file	Sec. 3-1-3
o	number of records that overflow	Secs. 3-1-3, 3-2-3, 3-3-3, 3-5-3
P	space required for a pointer	Sec. 2-3-3
p	collision cost, also probability	Eqs. 3-73, 3-74, 3-79, Fig. 3-23
q	production demand by a file application	Eq. 5-2, 5-4 to 5-6
R	space required for a complete record; relation	Sec. 3-0-2; 7-1-1
RW	subscript indicating rewriting	Sec. 2-3-6
r	rotational latency time	Eq. 2-3
S	set of attributes in a relation-schema	Sec. 7-3
SI	storage space for index	Eq. 3-52
s	average seek time	Eq. 2-2
s'	effective seek time	Eqs. 2-15, 2-16
T	the time required for various operations; set of tuples	Sec. 3-0-2; 7-3
T_{sort}	the time required to sort a file	Eq. 3-11
t	transfer rate from a storage unit to processing memory	Sec. 2-2-5
t'	bulk transfer rate	Eqs. 2-17, 2-18, 2-19
U	subscript denoting an update of a record	Sec. 3-0-2
u	utilization	Eqs. 5-3, 5-7 to 5-18, 5-20
uf	utilization factor	Eqs. 6-25, 6-29
V	average space for value part of an attribute	Sec. 3-1-3
v	number of records updated	Sec. 3-2-3
w	wait time in queues	Eq. 6-26
W	wasted space due to gaps per record	Eqs. 2-9, 2-10, 2-11, 2-21
X	subscript denoting an exhaustive search	Sec. 3-0-2
x	number of levels in an index structure, master level	Eq. 3-27, 3-49, 3-97
Y	subscript denoting a reorganization of a file	Sec. 3-0-2
y	fanout ratio	Eq. 3-26, 3-48

Bibliography

Abbreviations used in the bibliography:

ACM	Association for Computing Machinery (ACM), New York NY.
AFIPS	American Federation of Information Processing Societies, Arlington VA.
ASIS	American Society for Information Science, Washington DC.
BIT	*Nordisk Behandlings Informations Tidskrift*, Copenhagen Denmark.
CACM	*Communications of the ACM*, ACM, New York NY.
Comp. J.	*Computer Journal* of the British Computer Society, London UK.
FJCC	*Fall Joint Computer Conference* (sponsored by AFIPS).
IBM JRD	*IBM Journal of Research and Development*, Armonk NY.
IEEE	Institute of Electrical and Electronics Engineers, NY.
IEEE CS	IEEE Computer Society, Silver Spring MD.
IFIP	International Federation for Information Processing, Geneva Switzerland.
JACM	*Journal of the ACM*, ACM, New York NY.
NCC	*National Computer Conference* (sponsored by AFIPS).
SIGMOD	ACM Special Interest Group on Management of Data.
SJCC	*Spring Joint Computer Conference* (sponsored by AFIPS).
TODS	*ACM Transactions on Database Systems*, ACM, New York NY.
VLDB	*Conferences on Very Large Data Bases*.

Some information on these and other periodicals in the database area is provided in the background sections of Chap. 8 and 11.

Acton, Forman S. (**70**): *Numerical Methods That Usually Work*; Harper and Row, 1970, 541 pp.

Adiba, M.E. and Lindsay, B.G. (**80**): "Database Snapshots"; in *VLDB 6*, Lochovsky and Taylor(eds.), 1980, pp.86–91.

Adiba, M. (**81**): "Derived Relations: A Unified Mechanism for Views, Snapshots and Distributed Data"; in *VLDB 7*, Zaniolo and Delobel(eds.), 1981, pp.293–305.

Agarwala, A.K. (**70**): "Learning with a Probabilistic Teacher"; *IEEE Trans. on Information Theory*, vol.IT16 no.4, May 1970.

Aho, A.V., Hopcroft, E., and Ullman, J.D. (**74**): *The Design and Analysis of Computer Algorithms*; Addison-Wesley, 1974.

Aho, A.V. and Ullman, J.D. (**79U**): "Optimal Partial-Match Retrieval When Fields Are Independently Specified"; *TODS*, vol.4 no.2, June 1979, pp.168–179.

Aho,A.V., Sagiv,Y., and Ullman,J.D. (**79S**): "Efficient Optimization of a Class of Relational Expressions"; *TODS*, vol.4 no.4, Dec.1979, pp.435–454.

Aho, A.V.(ed.) (**82**): *Proceedings of the ACM Symposium on Principles of Database Systems*; ACM, 1982, 305 pp.

Alford,M.W. (**77**): "A Requirements Engineering Methodology for Real-Time Processing Requirements"; *IEEE Trans. Software Eng.*, vol.SE-3 no.1, 1977, pp.60–69.

Allen,A.O. (**75**): "Elements of Queuing Theory for System Design"; *IBM Sys. J.*, vol.14 no.2, 1975, pp.161–187.

Allen, Roy P. (**68**): "Omnibus, A Large Data Base Management System"; *Proc. 1968 FJCC*, AFIPS vol.33, Thompson Books, pp.157–164.

Allen,S.I., Barnett, G.O., and Castleman,P.A. (**66**): "Use of a Time-shared General Purpose File Handling System in Hospital Research"; *Proc. IEEE*, vol.54, 1966, pp.1641–1648.

Amble,O. and Knuth,D.E. (**74**): "Ordered Hash Tables"; *Comp. J.*, vol.17 no.2,May 1974, pp.135–142.

Anderson,H.D. and Berra,P.B. (**77**): "Minimum Cost Selection of Secondary Indexes for Formatted Files"; *TODS*, vol.2 no.1, Mar.1977, pp.68–90.

Andler,S., et al (**82**): "System-D: A Distributed System for Availability"; in *VLDB 8*, McLeod and Villasenor(eds.), 1982, pp.33–44.

Anzelmo, Frank D. (**71**): "A Data Format for Information System Files"; *IEEE Trans. on Computers*, Jan.1971, vol.C20, pp.39–43.

Arden, Bruce W.(ed.) (**75**): "Interactive Computer Systems"; *Proc. of the IEEE*, vol.63 no.6, Jun.1975, pp.883–979.

Arditi, J. and Zukovsky,E. (**78**): "An Authorization Mechanism for a Data-Base"; in *Databases*, Shneiderman(ed.), Academic Press, Aug.1978, pp.193–213.

Armstrong,W.W. (**74**): "Dependency Structures of Database Relationships"; *Information Processing 74*, North-Holland, Amsterdam, 1974, pp.580–583.

Aron, J.D. (**69**): "Information Systems in Perspective"; *ACM C. Surveys*, vol.1 no.4, Dec.1969, pp.213–235.

Arora,S.R. and Dent,W.T. (**69**): "Randomized Binary Search Techniques"; *CACM*, vol.12 no.2, Feb.1969, pp.77–80.

Arora, S.R. and Gallo,A. (**71**): "Optimal Sizing, Loading and Re-loading in a Multi-Memory Hierarchy System"; *Proc. 1971 SJCC*, AFIPS vol.38, pp.337–344.

Ash, W. and Sibley, E.H. (**68**): "TRAMP, An Interpretive Associative Processor with Deductive Capabilities"; *Proc. ACM 23rd Nat. Conf.*, 1968, pp.5–12.

Ashenhurst, R.L.(ed.) (**72**): "Curriculum Recommendations for Graduate Professional Programs in Information Systems"; *CACM*, vol.15 no.5, May 1972, pp.303–398.

Astrahan,M.M., et al (**76**): "System R: Relational Approach to Database Management"; *TODS*, vol.1 no.2, Jun.1976, pp.97–137.

Atre,S. (**80**): *Structured Techniques for Design Performance and Management*; Business Data Processing: A Wiley Series, 1980, 442 pp.

Atwood,R.C. (**72**): "Effects of Secondary Storage I/O Contention on the Performance of an Interactive Information Management System"; *Proc. of the ACM 1972 Conf.*, Aug.1972, pp.670–679.

Austing,R.H., Barnes,B.H., Bonnette,D.T., Engel,G.L., and Stokes,G. (**79**): "Curriculum '78 Recommendations for the Undergraduate Program in Computer Science"; *CACM*, Vol.22 No.3, Mar.1979, pp.147–166.

Babb,E. (**79**): "Implementing a Relational Database by Means of Specialized Hardware"; *TODS*, vol.4 no.1, Mar.1979, pp.1–29.

Baber,R.L. (**63**): "Tape Searching Techniques"; *JACM*, vol.10 no.4, Oct.1963, pp.478–486.

Bachman, C.W. and Williams, S.B. (**64**): "A General Purpose Programming System for Random Access Memories"; *Proc. 1964 FJCC*, AFIPS vol.26, pp.411–422.

Bachman, Charles W. (**66**): "On a Generalized Language for Organization and Manipulation"; *CACM*, vol.9 no.3, Mar.1966, pp.225–226.

Bachman, C.W. (**72**): "The Evolution of Storage Structures"; *CACM*, vol.15 no.7, Jul.1972, pp.628–634.

Bachman, C.W. (**73**): "The Programmer as a Navigator"; *CACM*, vol.16 no.11, Nov.1973, pp.653–658.

Bachman, C.W. (**75**): "Trends in Data Base Management - 1975"; *Proc. 1975 NCC*, AFIPS vol.44, pp.569–576.

Badal, D.Z. (**80**): "The Analysis of The Effects of Concurrency Control on Distributed Data Base System Performance"; in *VLDB 6*, Lochovsky and Taylor(eds.), 1980.

Baer, J-L. (**75**): "Weight-Balanced Trees"; *Proc. 1975 NCC*, AFIPS vol.44, pp.467–472.

Baker, F.T. (**72**): "Chief Programmer Team Management of Production Programming"; *IBM Sys. J.*, vol.11 no. 1, 1972, pp.56–72.

Banerjee, J., Hsiao, D.K., and Kannon, K. (**79**): "DBC–A Data Base Computer for Very Large Data Bases"; *IEEE Trans. on Computers*, vol.C-28 no.6, Jun.1979.

Barnett, G.O., et al (**79**): "COSTAR: A Computer-Based Medical Information System for Ambulatory Care"; *Proc. of the IEEE*, vol.67 no.9, Sep.1979, pp. 1226–1237.

Baroody, A.J., jr. and DeWitt, D.J. (**81**): "An Object-Oriented Approach to Database System Implementation"; *TODS*, vol.6 no.4, Dec.1981, pp. 576–601.

Baroody, A.J. jr. and DeWitt, D.J. (**82**): "The Impact of Run-Time Schema Interpretation in a Network Data Model DBMS"; *IEEE Trans. Software Eng.*, vol.SE-8 no.2, Mar.1982, pp.123–137.

Barron, D.W., Fraser, A.G., Hartley, D.F. and Needham, R.M. (**67**): "File Handling at Cambridge University"; *Proc. 1967 SJCC*, AFIPS vol.30, pp.163–167.

Barth, John (**66**): *Giles Goat-Boy*; Fawcett, Greenwich CN, 1966, 766 pp.

Baskett, F. and Smith, A.J. (**76**): "Interference in Multiprocessor Computer Systems with Interleaved Memory"; *CACM*, vol.19 no.6, Jun.1976, pp.327–334.

Batory, D.S. (**79**): "On Searching Transposed Files"; *TODS*, vol.4 no.4, Dec.1979, pp.531–544.

Batory, D.S. (**82**): "Optimal File Designs and Reorganization Points"; *TODS*, vol.7 no.1, Mar.1982, pp.60–81.

Batteke, J.P.H., Heaps, D.M., and Mercier, M.A. (**74**): "Canadian Water Resources Information – A Network Approach"; *Inf. Stor. and Retr.*, vol.10 nos.3, 4, March 1974, pp.85-99.

Bayer, R. and McCreight, E. M. (**72O, S**): "Organization and Maintenance of Large Ordered Indexes"; "Symetric Binary B-trees: Data Structure and Maintenance Algorithms"; *Acta Informatica*, vol.1 no.3, Feb.1972, pp.173–189; no.4, Nov.1972, pp.290–306.

Bayer, R. (**74**): "Storage Characteristics and Methods for Searching and Addressing"; *Information Processing-74*, North-Holland 1974, pp.440-444.

Bayer, R. and Metzger, J.K. (**76**): "On the Encipherment of Search Trees and Random Access Files"; *TODS*, vol.1 no.1, Mar.1976, pp.37–52.

Bayer, R. and Schkolnick, M. (**77**): "Concurrency of Operations on B-trees"; *Acta Informatica*, vol.9 no.1, 1977, pp.1–21.

Bayer, R. and Unterauer, K. (**77**): "Prefix B-trees"; *TODS*, vol.2 no.1, Mar.1977, pp.11–26.

Bayer, R., Graham, R.M., and Seegmüller, G.(eds.) (**78**): *Operating Systems, an Advanced Course*; Lecture Notes in CS, vol.60, Springer, 1978, 593 pp.

Bays, Carter (**73**): "The Reallocation of Hash-Coded Tables"; *CACM*, vol.1 no.1, Jan.1973, pp.11–14.

Beck,L.L. (**80**): "A Security Mechanism for Statistical Databases"; *TODS*, vol.5 no.3, Sep.1980, pp.316–338.

Beeri,C., Bernstein,P., and Goodman,N. (**78**): "A Sophisticate's Introduction to Database Normalization Theory"; in *VLDB 4*, Bubenko and Yao(eds.), 1978, pp.113–124.

Benci,E., et al(eds.) (**75**): *Data Structures Models for Information Systems*; Presses Universitaires de Namur, 1975, 250 pp.

Benner,F.H. (**67**): "On Designing Generalized File Records for Management Information Systems"; *Proc. 1967 FJCC*, AFIPS vol.31, pp.291–304.

Bentley,J.L. (**75**): "Multidimenional Binary Search Trees Used for Associative Searching"; *CACM*, vol.18 no.9, Sep.1975, pp.509–517.

Berlekamp,E.R.(ed.) (**74**): *Key Papers in the Development of Coding Theory*; IEEE Press, 1974, 296 pp.

Bernstein,P.A.(ed.) (**79**): *Proc. of the ACM SIGMOD Int. Conf.*; ACM NY, 1979.

Bernstein,P.A., Shipman,D.W., and Rothnie,J.B.jr. (**80S**): "Concurrency Control in a System for Distributed Databases (SDD-1)"; *TODS*, vol.5 no.1, Mar.1980, pp.18–51.

Bernstein,P.A., Blaustein,B.T., and Clarke,E.M. (**80B**): "Fast Maintenance of Semantic Integrity Assertions Using Redundant Aggregate Data"; in *VLDB 6*, Lochovsky and Taylor(eds.), 1980, pp.126–136.

Bernstein,P. and Goodman, N. (**81**): "Concurrency Control in Distributed Database Systems"; *ACM C. Surveys*, vol.13 no.2, Jun.1981, pp.185–221.

Bernstein,P.A. and Goodman, N. (**81**): "Power of Natural Semijoins"; *SIAM J. of Computing*, vol.10 no.4, 1981, pp.751–771.

Bernstein,P.A. and Goodman,N. (**82**): "A Sophisticate's Introduction to Distributed Database Concurrency Control"; in *VLDB 8*, McLeod and Villasenor(eds.), 1982, pp.62–76.

Bhargava, B.(ed.) (**81**): "Symp. on Reliability in Distributed Software and Database Systems"; *IEEE Cs Pub. no.81CH1632-9*, 1981, 205 pp.

Bhargava, B. and Lillien, L. (**81L**): "Feature Analysis of Selected Database Recovery Techniques"; *Proc. 1981 NCC*, AFIPS vol.50, May 1981, pp.543–554.

Bhattacharya,C.C. (**67**): "A Simple Method of Resolution of a Distribution into Gaussian Components"; *Biometrics*, Mar.1967.

Bisco,R.L.(ed.) (**70**): *Data Bases - Computers and the Social Sciences*; Wiley, 1970.

Biss,K., Chien,R. and Stahl,F. (**71**): "R2 - A Natural Language Question-Answering System"; *Proc. 1971 SJCC*, AFIPS vol.38, pp.303–308

Bjork,L.A.jr. (**75**): "Generalized Audit Trail Requirements and Concepts for Data Base Applications"; *IBM Sys. J.*, vol.14 no.3, 1975, pp.229–245.

Bleier, Robert E. and Vorhaus,A.H. (**68**): "File Organization in the SDC TDMS"; *Information Processing-68*, 1968 IFIP Congress, North-Holland, pp.F92–F97.

Blum,R.L. (**80**): "Automating The Study of Clinical Hypotheses on a Time-Oriented Database: The RX Project"; *MEDINFO 80*, Lindberg and Kaihara(eds.), IFIP, North-Holland 1980, pp.456–460.

Bobeck,A.H. and DellaTorre,E. (**75**): *Magnetic Bubbles*; North-Holland, 1975, 222 pp.

Booth,A.D. and Colin,J.T. (**60**): "On the Efficiency of a New Method of Dictionary Construction"; *Information and Control*, vol.3, 1960, pp.327–334.

Booth,G.M. (**73**): *Functional Analysis of Information Processing*; Wiley, 1973.

Borr,A.J. (**81**): "Transaction Monitoring in ENCOMPASS: Reliable Distributed Transaction Processing"; in *VLDB 7*, Zaniolo and Delobel(eds.), 1981, pp.155–165.

Bosak, Robert, et al (**62**): "An Information Algebra"; *CACM*, vol.5 no.4, Apr. 1962, pp.190–204.

Bose, R.C. and Koch, Gary G. (**69**): "The Design of Combinatorial Information Retrieval Systems for Files with Multiple Valued Attributes"; *SIAM J. Appl. Math.*, vol.17 no.6, Nov.1969, pp.1203–1214.

Boyce, R.F., Chamberlin, D.D., King, W.F.III, and Hammer, M.M. (**75**): "Specifying Queries as Relational Expressions: SQUARE"; *CACM*, vol.18 no.11, Nov.1975, pp.621–628.

Boyd, D.F. and Krasnow, H.S. (**63**): "Economic Evaluation of Management Information Systems"; *IBM Sys. J.*, March 1963, pp.2–23

Bracchi, G. and Nijssen, G.M.(eds.) (**79**): *Data Base Architecture*; North-Holland 1979.

Brainerd, W.(ed.) (**78**): "FORTRAN 77"; *CACM*, vol.21 no.10, Oct.1978, pp.806–820.

Bright, H.S. and Enisa, R.L. (**76**): "Cryptography using Modular Software Elements"; *Proc. 1976 NCC*, AFIPS vol.45, pp.113–123.

BrinchHansen, Per (**73**): *Operating System Principles*; Prentice Hall, 1973, 366 pp.

Brodie, M.L. and Zilles, S.N.(eds) (**81**): "Proc. Workshop on Data Abstraction, Databases and Conceptual Modelling"; *ACM-SIGMOD Record*, vol.11 no.2, Feb.1981.

Brodie, M.L. and Schmidt, J.W.(eds.) (**82**): "Final Report of the ANSI/X3/SPARC DBS-SG Relational Database Task Group"; in *ACM-SIGMOD Record*, vol.12 no.4, Jul.1982, pp. 1–62.

Brooks, F.D.jr. (**75**): *The Mythical Man-Month: Essays on Software Engineering*; Addison-Wesley, 1975, 195 pp.

Brown, D.T. and Sellers, F.F.jr. (**70**): "Error Correction for IBM 800-bit-per-inch Magnetic Tape"; *IBM JRD*, vol.14 no.4, Jul.1970, pp.384–389.

Brown, D.T., Eibsen, R.L., and Thorn, C.A. (**72**): "Channel and Direct Access Device Architecture"; *IBM Sys. J.*, vol.11 no.3, 1972, pp.186–199.

Browne, P.S.(ed.) (**79**): *Security Checklist for Computer Center Self-Audits*; Best Practices Series, AFIPS, Arlington VA, 1979.

Bubenko, J.A.jr. (**75**): "Some Theoretical and Practical Observations in a Data Base Case"; in *Systemeering-75*, Ludeberg and Bubenko(eds.), Student Litteratur, Lund Sweden, 1975.

Bubenko, J. and Yao, S.B.(eds.) (**78**): *Proc. of VLDB 4, Berlin*; IEEE CS 78 CH 1389.6C, Sep.1978, 555 pp.

Buchholz, W. (**63**): "File Organization and Addressing"; *IBM Sys. J.*, vol.2 no.2, Jun.1963, pp.86–111.

Buchholz, W. (**69**): "A Synthetic Job for Measuring System Performance"; *IBM Sys. J.*, vol.8 no.4, 1969, pp.309–318.

Buneman, O.P. and Clemons, E.K. (**79**): "Efficiently Monitoring Relational Databases"; *TODS*, vol.4 no.3, Sep.1979, pp.368–382.

Buneman, P., Frankel, R.E., and Nikhil, R. (**82**): "An Implementation Technique for Database Query Languages"; *TODS*, vol.7 no.2, Jun.1982, pp.164–186.

Burge, W.H. and Konheim, A.G. (**71**): "An Accessing Model"; *JACM*, vol.18 no.3, Jul.1971, pp.400–404.

Burkhard, W.A. (**76**): "Hashing and Trie Algorithms for Partial-Match Retrieval"; *TODS*, vol.1 no.2, 1976, pp.175–187.

Burkhard, W.A. (**79**): "Partial-Match Hash Coding: Benefits of Redundancy"; *TODS*, vol.4 no.2, June 1979, pp.228–239.

Cagan, Carl (**73**): *Data Management Systems*; Melville Publ., Los Angeles, 1973, 141 pp.

Cammarata, S. (**81**): "Deferring Updates in a Relational Data Base System"; in *VLDB 7*, Zaniolo and Delobel(eds.), 1981, pp.286–292.

Canaday, R.H., Harrison, R.D., Ivie, E.L., Ryder, J.L., and Wehr, L.A. (**74**): "A Back-end Computer for Data Base Management"; *CACM*, vol.17 no.10, Oct.1974, pp.575–582.

Cannellys, Nicholas (**67**): "Automation and Computers in Commercial Lending"; *The Journal of Commercial Lending*, Sep.1967, pp.21–27.

Cardenas, A.F. (**73**): "Evaluation and Selection of File Organization - A Model and a System"; *CACM*, vol.16 no.9, Sep.1973, pp.540–548.

Cardenas, A.F.(**79**): *Data Base Management Systems*; Allyn and Bacon, 1979, 519 pp.

Carrol, J.M., McHardy, L., Martin, R., and Moravec, H. (**71**): "Multi-Dimensional Security Program for a Generalized Information Retrieval System"; *Proc. 1971 FJCC*, AFIPS vol.39, pp.571–577.

Carrol, John M. (**72**): "Snapshot 1971 - How Canada Organizes Information About People"; *Proc. 1972 FJCC*, AFIPS vol.41, pp.445–452.

Ceri, S. and Pelagatti, G. (**82**): "Allocation of Operations in Distributed Database Access"; *IEEE Trans. on Comp.*, vol.C-32 no.2, Feb.1982, pp.119–128.

Chamberlin, D.D., Gray, J.N., and Traiger, I.L. (**75**): "Views, Authorization, and Locking in a Relational Data Base System"; *Proc. 1975 NCC*, AFIPS vol.44, pp.425–430.

Chamberlin, D.D. et al (**76**): "SEQUEL2: A Unified Approach to Data Definition, Manipulation, and Control"; *IBM JRD*, vol.20 no.6, Nov.1976, pp.560–575.

Chamberlin, D.D., et al (**81**): "Support for Repetitive Transactions and Ad Hoc Queries in System R"; *TODS*, vol.6 no.1, Mar.1981, pp.70–94.

Chamberlin, D.D., Gilbert, A.M., and Yost, R.A. (**81G**): "A History of System R and SQL/Data System"; in *VLDB 7*, Zaniolo and Delobel(eds.), 1981, pp.456–465.

Chan, P. and Shoshani, A. (**81**): "SUBJECT: A Directory Driven System for Organizing and Accessing Large Statistical Databases"; in *VLDB 7*, Zaniolo and Delobel(eds.), 1981, pp.553–563.

Chang, C.C. and Lee, R.C.T. (**82**): "Symbolic Gray Code as a Perfect Multiattribute Hashing Scheme for Partial Match Queries"; *IEEE Trans. Software Eng.*, vol.SE-8 no.3, May 1982, pp.235–249.

Chang,, H. (**78**): "On Bubble Memories and Relational Data Base"; in *VLDB 4*, Bubenko and Yao(eds.), Sep.1978, pp.207–229.

Chang, J.M. and Fu, K.S. (**81**): "Extended K-d Tree Database Organization: A Dynamic Multiattribute Clustering Method"; *IEEE Trans. on Software Eng.*, vol.SE-7, no.3, May 1981, pp.284–290.

Chang, S.K. and Cheng, W.H. (**78**): "Database Skeleton and Its Application to Logical Database Synthesis"; *IEEE Trans. Software Eng.*, vol.SE-4 no.1, Jan.1978, pp.18–30.

Chang, Shi-Kuo and Ke, J.S. (**78**): "Database Skeleton and its Application to Fuzzy Query Translation"; *IEEE Trans. Software Eng.*, vol.SE-4 no.1, Jan.1978, pp.31–44.

Chapin, Ned (**68**): *360 Programming in Assembly Language*; McGraw-Hill, 1968, 532 pp.

Chapin, N. (**69**): "Common File Organization Techniques Compared"; *Proc. 1969 FJCC*, AFIPS vol.35, pp.418–422.

Cheatham, T.E.jr. and Warshall, S. (**62**): "Translation of Retrieval Requests Couched in a 'Semi-formal' English-like Language"; *CACM*, vol.5 no.1, Jan.1962, pp.34–39.

Chen, Peter P. S. (**73**): "Optimal File Allocation in Multi-Level Storage Systems"; *Proc. 1973 NCC*, AFIPS vol.42, pp.227–282.

Chen, P.P.S. (**76**): "The Entity-Relationship Model - Toward a Unified View of Data"; *TODS*, vol.1 no.1, Mar.1976, pp.9–36.

Chen, P.P.S. and Sprowls, R.D.(eds.) (**80**): *ACM-SIGMOD 80 Proceedings*; ACM, Santa Monica(Los Angeles), May 1980.

Chen, P.P.S.(ed.) (**80**): *Entity-Relationship Approach to System Analysis and Design*; North-Holland, 1980, 663 pp.

Chen, P.P.S. and Akoka, J. (**80**): "Optimal Design of Distributed Information Systems"; *IEEE Trans. on Computers*, vol.C-29 no.12, Dec.1980, pp.1068–1081.

Chen,P.P.S.(ed.) (**81**): *Entity-Relationship Approach to Information Modeling and Analysis*; ER Institute, Los Angeles, 1981, pp.49–72.

Cheng,P.S. (**69**): "Trace Driven System Modelling"; *IBM Sys. J.*, vol.8 no.4, 1969, pp.280–289.

Chi,C.S. (**82**): "Advances in Computer Mass Storage Technology"; *IEEE Computer*, May 1982, pp.60–74.

Childs,D.L. (**68**): "Feasibility of a Set Theoretical Data Structure - A General Structure Based on a Reconstructed Definition of Relation"; *Information Processing-68*, Proc. IFIP 1968, North-Holland, pp.162–172.

Chin,F.Y. and Ozsoyoglu,G. (**81**): "Statistical Database Design"; *TODS*, vol.6 no.1, Mar.1981, pp.113–139.

Chu,W.W. (**69**): "Optimal File Allocation in a Multiple Computer System"; *IEEE Trans. on Computers*, vol.C18 no.10, Oct.1969, pp.885–888.

Chu,W.W. and Hurley,P. (**79**): "A Model for Optimal Processing for Distributed Databases"; *Proc. 18th IEEE CS Compcon*, Spring 1979.

Clark,R.A. (**67**): "LOGIC: The Santa Clara County Government Information System and It's Relationship to the Planning Department"; *Planning*, May 12, 1967.

Clark,W.A. (**66**): "The Functional Structure of OS/360: Part III Data Management"; *IBM Sys. J.*, vol.5 no.1, 1966, pp.30–51.

Clifton,J.A. and Helgeson,D.(eds.) (**73**): *Computers in Information Data Centers*; AFIPS Press, 1973, 109 pp.

CODASYL Data Base Task Group (DBTG) (**69S**): *A Survey of Generalized Data Base Management Systems*; ACM, May 1969.

CODASYL DBTG (**69R;71**): *Report of the* CODASYL DBTG; ACM, Oct.1969; Apr.1971.

CODASYL Systems Committee (**71A**): *Feature Analysis of Generalized Data Base Management Systems*; ACM, NY, May 1971.

CODASYL COBOL Committee (**73,75,78,...**): *Journal of Development*; Canadian Gov. Publishing Centre, Supply and Services Canada, Ottawa Ont. 1973, 1975, 1978.

CODASYL (**74**): *Data Description Language*; U.S. Dept. of Commerce, National Bureau of Standards Handbook no.112, Jan.1974.

CODASYL System Committee (**76**): *Selection and Acquisition of Data Base Management Systems*; ACM, Mar.1976, 276 pp.

CODASYL Data Description Language Committee (**78L**): *Journal of Development 1978*; Canadian Gov. Publishing Centre, Supply and Services Canada, Ottawa Ont, 1978.

CODASYL Systems Committee (**78D**): "Distributed Data Base Technology–An Interim Report of the CODASYL Systems Committee"; *Proc. 1978 NCC*, AFIPS vol.47, pp.909–917.

Codd,E.F. (**70**): "A Relational Model of Data for Large Shared Data Banks"; *CACM*, vol.13 no.6, Jun.1970, pp.377–387.

Codd,E.F. and Dean,A.L.(eds.) (**71**): *Data Description, Access, and Control*; ACM-SIGFIDET, 1971.

Codd,E.F. (**74**): "Recent Investigations in Relational Data Base Systems"; *Information Processing-74*, North-Holland, pp.1012–1021.

Codd,E.F. (**79**): "Extending the Database Relational Model to Capture More Meaning"; *TODS*, vol.4 no.4, Dec.1979, pp.397–434.

Codd,E.F. (**82**): "Relational Database: A Practical Foundation for Productivity"; *CACM*, vol.25 no.2, Feb.1982, pp.109–117.

Coffman,E.G.jr. (**69**): "Analysis of a Drum Input-Output Queue under Scheduled Operation in a Paged Computer System"; *JACM*, vol.16 no.1, Jan.1969, pp.73–90.

Coffman, E.G., Elphick, M.J., and Shoshani, A. (**71**): "System Deadlocks"; *ACM C. Surveys*, vol.3 no.2, Jun.1971, pp.67–78.

Coffman, E, G.jr., Klimko, L.A., and Ryan, B. (**72**): "An Analysis of Seek Times in Disk Systems"; *SIAM J. on Comp.*, vol.1 no.3, 1972, pp.269–279.

Cohen, L.J., Burr, W.E., Del'Marmol, G.M., Grodman, L.K., and Kerr, E.F. (eds.) (**75**): *Data Base Management Systems, a Critical and Comparative Analysis*; QED Information Sciences, Wellesley Hills MA, 1975, 420 pp.

Collmeyer, A.J., and Shemer, J.E. (**70**): "Analysis of Retrieval Performance for Selected File Organization Techniques"; *Proc. 1970 FJCC*, AFIPS vol.37, pp.201–210.

Collmeyer, A.J. (**71**): "Data Management in a Multi-Access Environment"; *IEEE Computer*, vol.4 no.6, Nov.1971, pp.36–46.

Comer, D. (**78**): "The Difficulty of Optimum Index Selection"; *TODS*, vol.3 no.4, Dec.1978, pp.440–445.

Comer, D. (**79**): "The Ubiquitous B-tree"; *ACM C. Surveys*, vol.11 no.2, Jun.1979, pp.121–137.

Connors, T.C. (**66**): "ADAM - A Generalized Data Management System"; *Proc. 1966 SJCC*, AFIPS vol.28, pp.193–203.

Conway, R.W., Maxwell, W.L., and Morgan, H.L. (**72**): "On the Implementation of Security Measures in Information Systems"; *CACM*, vol.15 no.4, Apr.1972, pp.211–220.

Cooper, W.S. (**76**): "Fact Retrieval and Deductive Question Answering Systems"; *JACM*, Apr.1976, vol.11 no.2, pp.117–137.

Copeland, G. (**82**): "What If Mass Storage Were Free"; *IEEE Computer*, vol.15 no.7, Jul.1982, pp.27–35.

Craig, J.A., Berezner, S.C., Carney, H.C., and Longyear, C.R. (**67**): "DEACON, Direct English Access and Control"; *CACM*, vol.10 no.11, Nov.1967, pp.715–721.

Cuadra, C.R. (ed.) (**66-75**): *Annual Review of Information Science and Technology*; Wiley 1966–1970, vol.1–4; Encyclopedia Brittanica 1971–1973, vol.5–7; with Lake(ed.): ASIS 1973–1975, vol.8–11.

Curtice, R.M. (**81**): "Data Dictionaries: An Assessment of Current Practice and Problems"; in *VLDB 7*, Zaniolo and Delobel(eds.), 1981, pp.564–570.

Dadam, P. and Schlageter, G. (**80**): "Recovery in Distributed Databases Based on Non-synchronized Local Checkpoints"; *Information Processing 80*, Proc. IFIPS 1980, North-Holland 1980, pp.457–461.

Dahl, O-J., Dijkstra, E.W., and Hoare, C.A.R. (**72**): *Structured Programming*; Academic Press, 1972.

Dahl, V. (**82**): "On Database Systems Development through Logic"; *TODS*, vol.7 no.1, Mar.1982, pp.102–123.

Daley, R.C., and Neuman, P.G. (**65**): "A General Purpose File System for Secondary Storage"; *Proc. 1965 FJCC*, AFIPS vol.27, pp.213–229.

Dana, C. and Presser, L. (**72**): "An Information Structure for Data Base and Device Independent Report Generation"; *Proc. 1972 FJCC*, AFIPS vol.41, pp.1111–1116.

Date, C.J. (**80**): "An Introduction to the Unified Database Language (UDL)"; in *VLDB 6*, Lochovsky and Taylor(eds.), 1980, pp.15–29.

Date, C.J. (**81**): *An Introduction to Data Base Systems, 3rd ed.*; Addison-Wesley, 1981, 575 pp.

Date, C.J. (**82**): *An Introduction to Data Base Systems, volume II*; Addison-Wesley, 1982, 383 pp.

Davida, G.I., Wells, D.L., and Kam, J.B. (**81**): "A Database Encryption System with Sub-keys"; *TODS*, vol.6 no.2, Jun.1981, pp.312–328.

Davidson,J. and Kaplan,S.J. (**80**): "Parsing in the Absence of a Complete Lexicon"; *Proc. of the 18th Annual Meeting of the Assoc. for Computational Linguistics*, Philadelphia PA, Jun.1980, pp.105–106.

Davies,D.W. et al(eds.) (**81**): *Distributed systems – Architecture and Implementation*; Lecture Notes in CS, vol.105, Springer-Verlag, 1981, 510 pp.

Davis,G.B. (**74**): *Management Information Systems, Conceptual Foundations, Structure, and Development*; McGraw Hill, 1974, 481 pp.

Davis,G.B. (**81**): "Strategies for Information Requirements Determination"; *IBM Syst. J.*, vol.21 no.1, 1981.

Davis, Lou (**70**): "Prototype for Future Computer Medical Records"; *Comp. and Biomed. Res.*, vol.3 no.5, Oct.1970, pp.539–554.

Dayal,U. and Bernstein,P.A. (**78**): "On the Updatability of Relational Views"; in *VLDB 4*, Bubenko and Yao(eds.), 1978, pp.368–378.

De, P., Haseman, W.D., and Kriebel, C.H. (**78**): "Toward an Optimal Design of a Network Database from Relational Descriptions"; *Operations Research*, vol.26 no.5, Sep.-Oct.1978, pp.805–823.

Dean,A.L.(ed.) (**72**): *Data Description,Access,and Control*; ACM-SIGFIDET,1972,420 pp.

Dearnley,P.A. (**74**): "A Model and The Operation of a Self Organising Data Management System"; *Comp. J.*, vol.17 no.1, Feb.1974, pp.13–16; no.3, Aug.1974, pp.205–210.

deBruijn,N.G. (**67**): "Additional Comments on a Problem in Concurrent Programming Control"; *CACM*, vol.10, no.3, Mar.1967, pp.137–138.

DeGreene, Kengon B. (**73**): *Socio-technical Systems: Factors in Analysis, Design and Management*; Prentice Hall, 1973, 416 pp.

Deheneffe,C., Hennebert,H., and Paulus,W. (**74**): "Relational Model for a Data Base"; *Information Processing-74*, Proc. 1974 IFIP Congress, North-Holland.

Delobel,C. and Casey,R. (**73**): "Decomposition of a Data Base and the Theory of Boolean Switching Functions"; *IBM JRD*, vol.17 no.5, Sep.1973, pp.374–386.

DeMaine,P. A. D. (**71**): "The Integral Family of Reversible Compressors"; *IAG Journal*, vol.4 no.3, 1971, pp.207–219.

DeMarco,T. (**79**): *Structured Analysis and System Specification*; Prentice Hall-Yourdon Inc., 1979.

Demolombe,R. (**80**): "Estimation of the Number of Tuples Satisfying a Query Expressed in Predicate Calculus Language"; in *VLDB 6*, Lochovsky and Taylor (eds.), 1980, Montreal, pp.55–63.

Denning,D.E. (**80**): "Secure Statistical Databases with Random Sample Queries"; *TODS*, vol.5 no.3, Sep.1980, pp.291–315.

Denning, Peter J. (**67**): "Effects of Scheduling on File Memory Operations"; *Proc. 1967 SJCC*, AFIPS vol.30, pp.9–21.

Denning,P.J. (**71**): "Third Generation Computer Systems"; *ACM C. Surveys*, 1971, vol.3 no.4, pp.145–216.

Denning,P.J. (**72**): "A Note on Paging Drum Efficiency"; *ACM C. Surveys*, vol.4 no.1, Mar.1972, pp.1–3.

Denning, P.J. and Buzen, J.P. (**78**): "The Operational Analysis of Queueing Network Models"; *ACM C. Surveys*, vol.10 no.3, Sep.1978, pp.225–261.

Dennis, J.B. and vanHorn, E.C. (**66**): "Programming Semantics for Multiprogrammed Computations"; *CACM*, vol.9 no.3, Mar.1966, pp.143–155.

Desmonde,W.H. (**64**): *Real Time Data Processing Systems*; Prentice Hall, 1964.

Deutscher, R.F., Tremblay, J.P., and Sorenson, P.G. (**75**): "A Comparative Study of Distribution-Dependent and Distribution-Independent Hashing Function"; *Proc. of the ACM Pacific-75 Conf.*, S.F. 1975, pp.56–61.

DeWitt,D.J. (**79**): "DIRECT - A Multiprocessor Organization for Supporting Relational Data Base Management Systems"; *IEEE Trans. on Computers*, vol.C-28 no.6, Jun.1979, pp.395–405.

Diffie,W., and Hellman,M.E. (**76**): "New Directions in Cryptography"; *IEEE Trans. on Information Theory*, vol.IT-22 no.6, Nov.1976, pp.644–654.

Dijkstra, Edsger W. (**65**): "Solution of a Problem in Concurrent Programming Control"; *CACM*, vol.8 no.9, Sep.1965, pp.569.

Dijkstra,E.W. (**71**): "Hierarchial Ordering of Sequential Processes"; *Acta Informatica*, vol.1 no.2, Oct.1971, pp.115–138.

Dimsdale,J.J. and Heaps,R.S. (**73**): "File Structure for an On_Line Catalog of One Million Titles"; *Journal of Library Automation*, vol.6 no.1, Mar.1973, pp.37–55.

Dixon, Wilfrid J. and Massey, Frank J.jr. (**69**): *Introduction to Statistical Analysis, 3rd ed.*; McGraw-Hill, 1969, 638 pp.

Dodd,G.G. (**66**): "APL - a Language for Associative Data Handling in PL/1"; *Proc. 1966 FJCC*, AFIPS vol.29, pp.677–684.

Dodd,G.G. (**69**): "Elements of Data Management Systems"; *ACM C. Surveys*, vol.1 no.2, Jun.1969, pp.117–133.

Dolotta, T.A., Bernstein, M.I., Dickson, R.S.,jr, and France, N.A., (**76**): *Data Processing in 1980–1985*; Wiley, 1976, 191 pp.

Donovan, J.J. (**76**): "Database System Approach to Management Decision Support"; *TODS*, vol.1 no.4, Dec.1976, pp.344–369.

Doty,K.L., Greenblatt,J.D., and Su,S.T.W. (**80**): "Magnetic Bubble Memory Architectures for Supporting Associative Searching of Relational Databases"; *IEEE Trans. Computers*, vol.C-29 no.11, Nov.1980, pp.957–970.

Douqué,B.C.M. and Nijssen,G.M.(eds.)(**76**): *Data Base Description*; North-Holland, 1976.

Droulette,D.L. (**71**): "Recovery through Programming System-360–System-370"; *Proc. 1971 SJCC*, AFIPS vol.38, pp.467–476.

Du, H.C. and Sobolewski, J.S. (**82**): "Disk Allocation for Cartesian Product Files on Multiple-Disk Systems"; *TODS*, vol.7 no.1, Mar.1982, pp.82–101.

Earley, Jay (**71**): "Towards an Understanding of Data Structures"; *CACM*, vol.14 no.10, Oct.1971, pp.617–627.

Earley, Jay (**73**): "Relational Level Data Structures for Programming Languages"; *Acta Informatica*, vol.2 no.4, Dec.1973, pp.293–309.

Easton,A. (**73**): *Complex Managerial Decisions Involving Multiple Objectives*; Wiley, 1973, 421 pp.

Easton,M.C. (**69**): "A Streamlined Statistical System for a Medical Computer Center"; *Proc. of the 24th National ACM Conference*, 1969, pp.494–475.

Eggers, S.J., Olken, F., and Shoshani, A. (**81**): "A Compression Technique for Large Statistical Databases"; in *VLDB 7*, Zaniolo and Delobel(eds.), 1981, pp.424–433.

Eisenberg,M.A. and McGuire,M.R. (**72**): "Further Comments on Dijkstra's Concurrent Programming Control Problems"; *CACM*, vol.15 no.11, Nov.1972, pp.999.

Ellis,C.A. and Nutt,G.J. (**80**): "Office Information Systems and Computer Science"; *ACM C. Surveys*, vol.12 no.1, Mar.1980, pp.37–60.

Ellis,M.E., Katke,W., Olson,J., and Yang,S.C. (**72**): "SIMS - An Integrated, User-Oriented Information System"; *Proc. 1972 FJCC*, AFIPS vol.41, pp.1117–1132.

ElMasri, R., and Wiederhold, G. (**79**): "Data Model Integration Using the Stuctural Model"; in *ACM-SIGMOD 79*, Bernstein(ed.), 1979, pp.191–202.

ElMasri, R., and Wiederhold, G. (**80**): "Properties of Relationships and Their Representation"; *Proc. 1980 NCC*, AFIPS vol.49, May 1980, pp.319–326.

ElMasri, R. and Wiederhold, G. (**81**): "GORDAS: A Formal High-Level Query Language for the Entity-Relationship Model"; in *Entity-Relationship Approach to Information Modeling and Analysis*, Chen(ed.), ER Institute LA, 1981, pp.49–72.

Epstein, R. and Hawthorne, P. (**80**): "Design Decisions for the Intelligent Database Machine"; *Proc. 1980 NCC*, AFIPS vol.49, pp.237–241.

Epstein, R. and Stonebraker, M. (**80**): "Analysis of Distributed Data Base Processing Strategies"; in *VLDB 6*, Lochovsky and Taylor(eds.), 1980, pp.92–101.

Eswaran, K.P. (**74**): "Placement of Records in a File and File Allocation in a Computer Network"; *Information Processing 74*, Proc. IFIP Congress, North-Holland, 1974.

Eswaran, K.P., Gray, J.N., Lorie, R.A., and Traiger, I.L. (**76**): "The Notions of Consistency and Predicate Locks in a Data Base System"; *CACM*, vol.19 no.11, Nov.1976, pp.624–633.

Evans, A.jr., Kantowitz, W., and Weiss, E. (**74**): "A User Authentication Scheme Not Requiring Secrecy in the Computer"; *CACM*, vol.17 no.8, Aug.1974, pp.437–442.

Everest, G. (**82**): *Management Information Systems*; McGraw-Hill, 1982.

Fabry, R.S.(**74**): "Capability Based Addressing"; *CACM*, vol.17 no.7, Jul.1974, pp.403–412.

Fagin, R. (**77**): "Multivalued Dependencies and a New Normal Form for Relational Databases"; *TODS*, vol.2 no.3, Sep.1977, pp.262–278.

Fagin, R. (**78**): "On an Authorization Mechanism"; *TODS*, vol.3 no.3, Sep.1978, pp.310–319.

Feinstein, A.R. (**70**): "Taxonorics"; *Archives of Internal Medicine*, vol.126, Oct.1970, pp.679–693; Dec.1970, pp.1053–1067.

Feistel, H. (**73**): "Cryptography and Computer Privacy"; *Scientific American*, vol.228 no.5, May 1973, pp.15–23.

Feldman, J.A. and Rovner, P.D. (**69**): "An Algol-Based Associative Language"; *CACM*, vol.12 no.8, Aug.1969, pp.439–449.

Feller, William (**68**): *An Introduction to Probability Theory and Applications*; Wiley: vol.1, 3rd ed., 1968; vol.2, 2nd ed., 1971.

Fernandez, E.B., Summers, R., and Wood, C. (**81**): *Data Base Security and Integrity*; Addison-Wesley, 1981, 320 pp.

Feustel, E.A. (**73**): "On the Advantages of Tagged Architecture"; *IEEE Trans. on Computers*, vol.C-22 no.7, Jul.1973, pp.644–656.

Fichten, J.P. (**72**): "The Weyerhaeuser Information System, A Progress Report"; *Proc. 1972 FJCC*, AFIPS vol.41, pp.1017–1024.

Files, John R. and Huskey, Harry D. (**69**): "An Information Retrieval System Based on Superimposed Coding"; *Proc. 1969 FJCC*, AFIPS vol.35, pp.423–432.

Findler, N.V.(ed.) (**79**): *Associative Networks: Representation and Use of Knowledge by Computers*; Academic Press, NY, 1979.

Finkelstein, S.J. (**82**): "Common Expression Analysis in Database Applications"; in *ACM-SIGMOD 82*, Schkolnick(ed.), Orlando FL, Jun.1982, pp.235–245.

Fischer, M.J., Griffeth, N.D., and Lynch, N.A. (**82**): "Global States of a Distributed System"; *IEEE Trans. Software Eng.*, vol.SE-8 no.3, May 1982, pp.198–202.

Fishman, George S. (**67**): "Problems in the Statistical Analysis of Simulation Experiments"; *CACM*, vol.10 no.2, Feb.1967, pp.94–99.

Florentin, J.J. (**76**): "Information Reference Coding"; *CACM*, vol.19 no.1, Jan.1976, pp.29–33.

Floyd, R.W. (**74**): "Permuting Information in Idealized Two-Level Storage"; in *Complexity of Computer Computations*, Miller et al (eds), Plenum, NY 1974.

Frailey, Dennis J. (**73**): "A Practical Approach to Managing Resources and Avoiding Deadlock"; *CACM vol.16 no.5*, Mar.1973, pp.323–329.

Frank, H. (**69**): "Analysis and Optimization of Disk Storage Devices for Time-Sharing Systems"; *JACM*, vol.16 no.4, Oct.1969, pp.602–620.

Franks, E.W. (**66**): "A Data Management System for Time-Shared File Processing Using a Cross Index File and Self Defining Entries"; *Proc. 1966 SJCC*, AFIPS vol.28, pp.76–86.

Fraser, A. G. (**69**): "Integrity of a Mass Storage Filing System"; *Comp. J.*, vol.12 no.1, Feb.1969, pp.1–5.

Fredkin, E. (**60**): "Trie Memory"; *CACM*, vol.39, 1960, pp.490–499.

Freiberger, W.(ed.) (**72**): *Statistical Computer Performance Evaluation*; Academic Press, 1972, 514 pp.

Freilich, L. and Sadowski, P.J. (**80**): "Managing Systems that Manage Data"; in *VLDB 6*, Lochovsky and Taylor(eds.), 1980, pp.155

Freund, J.E. (**62**): *Mathematical Statistics*; Prentice Hall, 1962.

Frey, R., Girardi, S., and Wiederhold, G. (**71**): "A Filing System for Medical Research"; *Bio-Medical Computing*, vol.2 no.1, Elseviers, Jan.1971, pp.1–26.

Friedman, T. D. (**70**): "The Authorization Problem in Shared Files"; *IBM Sys. J.*, vol.9 no.4, pp.258–280, 1970.

Friedman, Theodore D. and Hoffman, Lance J. (**74**): "Execution Time Requirements for Encipherment Programs"; *CACM*, vol.17 no.8, Aug.1974, pp.445–449.

Fuller, S.H. (**75**): *Analysis of Drum and Disk Storage Units*; Lecture Notes in CS, vol.31, Springer Verlag, 1975, 283 pp.

Fulton, R.E. (**80**): "National Meeting to Review IPAD Status and Goals"; *Astronautics and Aeronautics*, July-Aug.1980.

Furtado, A.L. and Morgan, H.L.(eds.) (**79**): *Proc. VLDB 5, Rio de Janeiro*; IEEE CS 79CH1406-8C, Oct.1979, 450 pp.

Gallaire, H. and Minker, J.(eds.) (**78**): *Logic and Data Bases*; Plenum Press, 1978.

Gallaire, H., Minker, J., and Nicolas, J-M.(eds.) (**81**): *Advances in Database Theory*; Plenum Press, vol.1, 1981.

Gambino, T.J., and Gerritsen, R. (**77**): "A Database Design Decision Support System"; in *VLDB 3*, Merten(ed.), 1977, pp.534–544.

GAO (Comptroller General) (**79**): *Data Base Management Systems — Without Careful Planning There Can Be Problems*; Report to Congress FGMSD–79-35, 1979.

GAO (**80**): *Continued Use of Costly, Outmoded Computers in Federal Agencies Can Be Avoided*; Report to the Congress of the United States AFMD-81–9, Dec.15, 1980.

GarciaMolina, H. (**81**): *Performance of Update Algorithms for Replicated Data*; UMI Research Press, Ann Arbor MI, Aug.1981, 320pp.

GarciaMolina, H. (**82E**): "Elections in a Distributed Computing System"; *IEEE Trans. on Computers*, vol.C31 no.1, Jan.1982.

GarciaMolina, H. and Wiederhold, G. (**82W**): "Read-Only Transactions in a Distributed Database"; *TODS*, vol.7 no.2, Jun.1982, pp.209–234.

Gaynor, Jerry (**74**): "Determining Access Time for Moving Head Disks"; *Digital Design*, Sep.1974.

Genrich, H.J. and Lautenbach, V. (**73**): "Synchronisationsgraphen"; *Acta Informatica*, vol.2 no.2, Aug.1973, pp.143–161.

Gentile, Richard B. and Lucas, Joseph R. (**71**): "The TABLON Mass Storage System"; *Proc. 1971 SJCC*, AFIPS vol.38, pp.345–356.

Germain, C.B. (**67**): *Programming the IBM 360*; Prentice Hall, 1967.

Ghosh,S.P. and Senko,M.E. (**69**): "File Organization: On the Selection of Random Access Index Points for Sequential Files"; *JACM*, Vol.16 No.4, Oct.1969, pp.569–579.

Ghosh,S.P. and Astrahan,M.M. (**74**): "A Translator Optimizer for Obtaining Answers to Entity Set Queries from and Arbitrary Access Path Network"; *Information Processing-74*, 1974 IFIP Congress, North-Holland, pp.436–439.

Ghosh,S.P. and Astrahan,M.M. (**76**): "A Translator Optimizer for Obtaining Answers to Entity Set Queries from and Arbitrary Access Path Network"; *Information Processing-74*, North-Holland, pp.436–439.

Ghosh,S.(**76**): *Data Base Organization for Data Management*; Academic Press NY, 1976.

Gifford,D.K. (**82**): "Cryptographic Sealing for Information Secrecy and Authentication"; *CACM*, vol.25 no.4, Apr.1982, pp.274–286.

Gildersleeve,T.R. (**71**): *Design of Sequential File Systems*; Wiley, 1971.

Glantz,R.S. (**70**): "SHOEBOX, A Personal File Handling System for Textual Data"; *Proc. 1970 FJCC*, AFIPS vol.37, pp.535–545.

Glinka,L.R., et al (**67**): "Design through Simulation of a Multiple Access Information System"; *Proc. 1967 FJCC*, AFIPS, vol.31, pp.437–447.

Goldberg,R.P., and Hassinger,R. (**79**): "The Double Paging Anomaly"; *Proc. 1979 NCC*, AFIPS vol.48, 1979, pp.195–199.

Goldstein,B.S. (**81**): "Constraints on Null Values in Relational Databases"; in *VLDB 7*, Zaniolo and Delobel(eds.), 1981, pp.101–111.

Gordon,G. (**69**): *System Simulation*; Prentice-Hall, 1969.

Gotlieb,C. and Borodin,A. (**73**): *Social Issues in Computing*; Academic Press, 1973.

Gotlieb,L. (**75**): "Computing Joins of Relations"; in *ACM-SIGMOD 75*, King(ed.), 1975, pp.55–63.

Gould,I.H. (**71**): *IFIP Guide to Concepts and Terms in Data Processing*; North-Holland Publishing Co., 1971, 161 pp.

Graham,G.S.(ed.) (**78**): "Queueing Network Models of Computer System Performance"; *ACM C. Surveys*, vol.10 no.3, Sep.1978, pp.219–352.

Graham,R.M. (**68**): "Protection in an Information Processing Utility"; *CACM*, vol.11 no.5, May 1968, pp.365–369.

Graham,R.M. (**75**): *Principles of Systems Programming*; John Wiley Sons, 1975, 422 pp.

Gray,J., McJones,P., Blasgen,M. et al (**81**): "The Recovery Manager of the System R Database Manager"; *ACM C. Surveys*, vol.13 no.2, Jun.1981, pp.223–242

Green,C. and Raphael,B. (**68**): "The Use of Theorem Proving Techniques in Question Answering Systems"; *Proc. 23rd ACM Conf.*, pp.169–181, 1968.

Greenes,R.A., Pappalardo,A.N., Marble,C.M., and Barnett,G.O. (**69**): "A System for Clinical Data Management"; *Proc. 1969 FJCC*, AFIPS vol.35, pp.297–305.

Griffiths,P.P. and Wade,B.W. (**76**): "An Authorization Mechanism for a Relational Datbase System"; *TODS*, vol.1 no.3, Sep.1976, pp.242–255

Groner,Leo H. and Goel, Amrit L. (**74**): "Concurrency in Hashed File Access"; *Proc. 1974 IFIP Congress*, North-Holland.

Gruenberger,F.(ed.) (**69**): *Critical Factors in Data Management*; Prentice-Hall, 1969.

GSA (**57**...): *Authorized Federal Supply Schedule Price List*; FSC Class 7440, Electronic Data Processing Machines.

Gudes, Ehud (**80**): "The Design of a Cryptography Based Secure File System"; *IEEE Trans. Software Eng.*, vol.SE-6, Sep.1980, pp.411–420,

Guibas,L. and Sedgewick,R. (**78**): "A Dichromatic Framework for Balanced Trees"; in *ACM-FOCS 78*, Proc. 1978 FOCS Conf.

Gurski, Aaron (**73**): "A Note on the Analysis of Keys for Use in Hashing"; *BIT*, vol.13 no.1, 1973, pp.120–122.

Habermann, A.N. (**76**): *Introduction to Operating Systems Design*; SRA, 1976, 372 pp.

Hahn, Bruce (**74**): "A New Technique for Compression and Storage of Data"; *CACM*, vol.17 no.8, Aug.1974, pp.434–436.

Hainaut, J-L. and Lecharlier, B. (**74**): "An Extensible Semantic Model of Data Base and Its Data Language"; *Proc. 1974 IFIP Congress*, North-Holland, pp.1026–1030.

Hall, P.A.V. (**76**): "Optimization of a Simple Expression in a Relational Data Base System"; *IBM JRD*, vol.20 no.3, May 1976, pp.244–257.

Hammer, M. (**77**): "Self-Adaptive Data Base Design"; *Proc. 1977 NCC*, AFIPS vol.46, pp.123–129.

Hammer, M. and Sarin, S.K. (**78**): "Efficient Monitoring of Database Assertions"; in *ACM-SIGMOD 78*, Lowenthal and Dale(eds.), 1978, pp.159–168.

Hammer, M. and Niamir, B. (**79**): "A Heuristic Approach to Attribute Partitioning"; in *ACM-SIGMOD 79*, Bernstein(ed.), 1979, pp.93–100.

Hammer, M. and Zdonik, S.B.jr. (**80K**): "Knowledge-Based Query Processing"; in *VLDB 6*, Lochovsky and Taylor(eds.), 1980, pp.137–147.

Hammer, M.M. and Shipman, D.W. (**80R**): "Reliability Mechanisms for SDD-1: A System for Distributed Databases"; *TODS*, vol.5 no.4, Dec.1980, pp.431–466.

Hammer, M. and McLeod, D. (**81**): "Database Description with SDM: A Semantic Database Model"; *TODS*, vol.6 no.3, Sep.1981, pp.351–386.

Hanan, M. and Palermo, F.P. (**63**): "An Application of Coding Theory to a File Address Problem"; *IBM JRD*, vol.7 no.2, Apr.1963, pp.127–129.

Härder, T. (**78**): "Implementing a Generalized Access Path Structure for a Relational Database System"; *TODS*, vol.3 no.3, Sep.1978, pp.285–298.

Hardgrave, W.T. (**80**): "Ambiguity in Processing Boolean Queries on TDMS Tree-Structures: A Study of Four Different Philosophies"; *IEEE Trans. Software Eng.*, vol.SE-6 no.4, Jul.1980, pp.357–372.

Harris, L.D. (**77**): "User Oriented Data Base Query with the ROBOT Natural Language System"; in *VLDB 3*, Merten(ed.), 1977.

Harrison, M.S., Ruzzo, W.L., and Ullman, J.D. (**76**): "Protection in Operating Systems"; *CACM*, vol.19 no.8, Aug.1976, pp.461–471.

Havender, J.W. (**68**): "Avoiding Deadlock in Multitasking Systems"; *IBM Syst. J.*, vol.7 no.2, 1968, pp.74–84.

Hawley, D.A., Knowles, J.S., and Tozer, E.E. (**75**): "Database Consistency and the CODA-SYL DBTG Proposals"; *Comp. J.*, vol.18, 1975, pp.206–212.

Hawthorne, P.B. and DeWitt, D.J. (**82**): "Performance Analysis of Alternative Database Machine Architectures"; *IEEE Trans. Software Eng.*, vol.SE-8 no.1, Jan.1982, pp.61–75.

Heaps, H.S. and Thiel, L.H. (**70**): "Optimum Procedures for Economic Information Retrieval"; *Inform. Stor. and Retrieval*, vol.6 no.2, 1970, pp.137–153.

Heising, W.P. (**63**): "Note on Random Addressing Techniques"; *IBM Sys. J.*, vol.2 no.2, Jun.1963, pp.112–116.

Held, G., Stonebraker, M.R., and Wong, E. (**75**): "INGRES: A Relational Data Base System"; *Proc. 1975 NCC*, AFIPS vol.44, pp.409–416.

Hellerman, H. (**73**): *Digital Computer System Principles*; McGraw-Hill, 1973, 245 pp.

Hellerman, H. and Conroy, T. F. (**75**): *Computer Systems Performance*; McGraw-Hill, 1975, 380 pp.

Hendrix, G.G., Sacerdoti, E.D., Sagalowicz, D., and Slocum, J. (**78**): "Developing a Natural Language Interface to a Complex System"; *TODS*, vol.3 no.2, Jun.1978, pp.105–147.

Herot, C.F. (**80**): "Spatial Management of Data"; *TODS*, vol.5 no.4, Dec.1980, pp.493–514.

Hertz, D.B. (**69**):   *New Power for Management-Computer Systems and Management Science*; McGraw-Hill, 1969.

Hevner, A.G. and Yao, S.B. (**79**): "Query Processing in Distributed Data Bases"; *IEEE Trans. Software Eng.*, vol.SE-5 no.3, May 1979.

Hibbard, Thomas N. (**62**):   "Some Combinatorial Properties of Certain Trees with Applications to Sorting and Searching"; *JACM*, vol.9 no.1, 1962, pp.13–28.

Hill, F.J. and Peterson, G.R. (**73**): *Digital Systems: Hardware Organization and Design*; Wiley, 1973.

Hillier, F.S. and Lieberman, G.J. (**67**): *Introduction to Operations Research*; Holden Day Inc. 1967.

Hillman, Donald J. and Kasarda, Andrew J. (**69**):   "The LEADER Retrieval System"; *Proc. 1969 SJCC*, AFIPS vol.34, pp.447–455.

Hoagland, A.S., and Rice, R.(eds.) (**75**): "Large Capacity Digital Storage Systems"; *Proc. of the IEEE*, vol.63 no.8, Aug.1975, pp.1092–1240.

Hoagland, A.S. (**79**):   "Storage Technology: Capabilities and Limitations"; *IEEE Computer*, vol.12, May.1979, pp.12–18.

Hoffman, L.J. (**71**): "The Formulary Model for Access Control"; *Proc. 1971 FJCC*, AFIPS vol.39, pp.587–601.

Hoffman, L.J. (**77**): *Modern Methods for Computer Security and Privacy*; Prentice Hall, 1977.

Holt, G.A. and Stern, H.C. (**75**):   "Cost-Benefit Evaluation of Interactive Transaction Processing Systems"; *Proc. 1975 NCC*, AFIPS, vol.44, pp.687–694.

Holt, Richard C. (**72**):   "Some Deadlock Properties of Computer Systems"; *ACM C. Surveys*, vol.4 no.3, Sep.1972, pp.179–196.

Hsiao, D.K. and Harary, F.D. (**70**):   "A Formal System for Information Retrieval from Files"; *CACM*, vol.13 no.2, Feb.1970, pp.67–73, corrigenda, no.3, Mar.1970, pp.266.

Hsiao, D.K. (**71**):   "A Generalized Record Organization"; *IEEE Trans. on Computers*, Dec.1971, pp.1490–1495.

Hu, T.C. and Tucker, A.C. (**71**): "Optimal Computer Search Trees and Variable-Length Alphabetic Codes"; *SIAM Jour. Appl. Math.*, vol.21 no.4, Dec.1971, pp.514–532.

Huang, Sheng-Chao and Goel, Amrit L. (**74**):   "An Analytical Model for Information Processing Systems"; *Proc. 1974 NCC*, AFIPS vol.43, pp.41–44.

Hubbard, G.U. (**81**): *Computer Assisted Data Base Design*; Van Norstrand Reinhold DP series, 1981.

Huff, Darrel (**54**): *How to Lie with Statistics*; Norton, 1954.

Huffman, D.A. (**52**): "A Method for the Construction of Minimim Redundancy Codes"; *Proc. of the IRE*, vol.40, Sep.1952, pp.1098–1101.

Hume, J.N.P. and Holt, R.C. (**75**): *Structured Programming Using PL/1 and SP/K*; Reston Publishing, 1975, 340 pp.

IBM F20-7(**71**): *Analysis of Some Queuing Models in Real Time Systems, 2nd ed.*; IBM Data Processing Division, White Plains NY, F20-0007, 1971.

IBM G320-1370 (**74**): *Data Security and Data Processing*; IBM Data Processing Division, 6 Vols., G320-1370 to 1376, 1974.

Iizuka, S. and Chiba, Y. (**75**): "GERM: General Error Recovery Model of a Shared Database"; *Soken Kiyo*, vol.5 no.1, Nippon Univac, Tokyo, 1975, pp.211–225.

Imielinski, T. and Lipski, W. jr. (**81**):   "On Representing Incomplete Information in a Relational Database"; in *VLDB 7*, Zaniolo and Delobel(eds.), 1981, pp.388–397.

Inglis, J. and Dee, E. G. (**73**): "Flexibility of Block-length for Magnetic Files"; *Comp. J.*, vol.16 no.4, Nov.1973, pp.303–307.

Inglis,J. (**74**): "Inverted Indexes in Multi-list Structures"; *Comp. J.*, vol.17 no.1, Feb.1974, pp.54–63.

Inmon,W.H. (**79**): *On-Line Data Base Design: Standard Work Unit Concept*; Amdahl Systems Consulting Pub. No.T1009.0, Sunnyvale CA, 1979.

Inmon,W.H. (**80**): *Effective Data Base Design*; Prentice-Hall, 1980, 228 pp.

Iyer,R.K., Butner,S.E., and McCluskey,E.J. (**82**): "A Statistical Failure/Load Relationship: Results of a Multicomputer Study"; *IEEE Trans. Comp.*, vol.C-31 no.7, Jul.1982, pp.697–706.

Jardine,D.A.(ed.) (**74**): *Data Base Management Systems*; North-Holland 1974, 279 pp.

Jardine,D.(ed.) (**77**): *The* ANSI/SPARC *DBMS Model*; North-Holland, 1977, 226 pp.

Jefferson,D.K. (**80**): "The Development and Application of Data Base Design Tools and Methodology"; in *VLDB 6*, Lochovsky and Taylor(eds.), 1980, pp.153–154.

Jewell,W.S. (**67**): "A Simple Proof of $L = \lambda \times w$"; *Operations Research*, vol.15, 1967, pp.1109–1116.

Johnson,Clayton T. (**75**): "IBM 3850/Mass Storage System"; *Proc. 1975 NCC*, AFIPS vol.44, pp.509–514.

Johnson,L.R. (**61**): "An Indirect Chaining Method for Addressing on Secondary Keys"; *CACM*, May 1961, pp.218–222.

Joyce,J.D. and Oliver,N.N. (**76**): "REGIS: A Relational Information System with Graphics and Statistics"; *Proc. 1976 NCC*, AFIPS vol. 45, pp.839–844.

Judd,D. R. (**73**): *Use of Files*; American Elseviers, 1973, 164 pp.

Kahn, David (**67**): *The Codebreakers*; Macmillan NY 1967.

Kaiman,R.A. (**73**): *Structured Information Files*; Wiley-Becker/Hayes, 1973, 161 pp.

Karlton, P.C., Fuller, S.H., Scroggs, R.E., and Kaehler, E.B. (**76**): "Performance of Height-Balanced Trees"; *CACM*, vol.19 no.1, Jan.1976, pp.23–28.

Karpinski,R.H.S. and Bleich,H.C. (**71**): "MISAR: A Miniature Information Storage and Retrieval System"; *Comp. and Biomedical Res.*, vol.4 no.6 Dec.1971, pp.655–660.

Kasarda, Andrew J. and Hillman,Donald J. (**72**): "The LEADERMART System and Service"; *Proc. 1972 Nat. ACM Conference*, pp.469–477.

Katter,R.V. and Pearson,R.M. (**75**): "MEDLARS II: A Third Generation Bibliographic Production System"; *Journal of Library Automation*, vol.8 no.2, Jun.1975, pp.87–97.

Katz,R.H. and Wong,E. (**79**): "Performance Enhancement for Relational Systems through Query Compilation"; *Proc. 1979 NCC*, AFIPS vol.48, 1979, pp.741–747.

Keller,A.M. (**82**): "Updates to Relational Databases through Views Involving Joins"; *2nd Int. Conf. on Databases: Improving Usability and Responsiveness, Jerusalem Israel*, Academic Press, Jun.1982, pp.363–384.

Kellogg, C.H., Burger,J., Diller,T., Fogt,K. (**71**): "The CONVERSE Natural Language Data Management System: Current Status and Plans"; in *ACM-SIGIR Proc. of Conference on Information, Storage, and Retrieval*, 1971, pp.33–46.

Kendrik, J.R. (**80**): "Management Information for Agriculture"; *Perspectives in Computing*, Oct.1980, pp.35–42.

Kent,A. (**71**): *Information Analysis and Retrieval*; Wiley-Becker/Hayes, 1971.

Kent,W. (**78**): *Data and Reality, Basic Assumptions in Data Processing Reconsidered*; North-Holland, Amsterdam, 1978.

Kent, W. (**80**): "Splitting the Conceptual Schema"; in *VLDB 6*, Lochovsky and Taylor(eds.), 1980, pp.10–14.

Kerr, Douglas S.(ed.) (**75**): *Proc. of VLDB 1, Framingham MA*; ACM, Sep.1975, 592 pp.

Kidd, Stephen W. (**69**): "Incorporating Complex Data Structures into a Language for Social Science Research"; *Proc. 1969 FJCC*, AFIPS vol.35, pp.453–462.

Kim,K.H. (**82**): "Approaches to Mechanization of the Conversation Scheme Based on Monitors"; *IEEE Trans. Software Eng.*, vol.SE-8 no.3, May 1982, pp.189–197.

Kim,W. (**79**): "Relational Database Systems"; *ACM C. Surveys*, vol.11 no.3, Sep.1979, pp.185–212.

King, J.J. (**81**): "QUIST: A System for Semantic Query Optimization in Relational Databases"; in *VLDB 7*, Zaniolo and Delobel(eds), 1981, pp.510–517.

King,J.L. and Schrems,E.L. (**78**): "Cost-Benefit Analysis in Information Systems Development and Operation"; *ACM C. Surveys*, vol.10 no.1, Mar.1978, pp.19–24.

King,J.M. (**81**): *Evaluating Data Base Management Systems*; Van Nostrand Reinhold, New York NY, 1981, 275 pp.

King,W.F.(ed.) (**75**): *International Conference on Management of Data*; ACM-SIGMOD 75, ACM 1975.

King,W.F.,III (**80**): "Relational Database Systems, Where Do We Stand Today?"; *Information Processing 80*, North-Holland 1980.

Kiviat,P.J., Villanueva,R., and Markowitz,H.M. (**69**): *The Simscript II Programming Language*; Prentice Hall, 1969.

Kleinrock, Leonard (**75**): *Queuing Systems, 2 Vols.: Theory* and *Computer Applications*; Wiley 1975, 1976; 417, 549 pp.

Klimbie,J.W. and Koffeman,K.L.(eds.) (**75**): *Data Base Management*; North-Holland, 1975.

Knight,K. (**68**): "Evolving Computer Performance"; *Datamation*, Jan.1968, pp.31–35.

Knott, Gary D. (**75**): "Hashing Functions and Hash Table - Storage and Retrieval"; *Comp. J.*, vol.18 no.3, 1975, pp.265–278.

Knuth,D.E. (**66**): "Additional Comments on a Problem in Concurrent Programming Control"; *CACM*, vol.9 no.5, pp.321–322, May 1966.

Knuth,D.E. (**69**): *The Art of Computer Programming, vol.2: Seminumerical Algorithms*; Addison-Wesley, 1969, 634 pp.

Knuth,D.E. (**73S**): *The Art of Computer Programming, vol.3: Sorting and Searching*; Addison Wesley, 1973, 722 pp.

Knuth,D.E. (**73F**): *The Art of Computer Programming, vol.1: Fundamental Algorithms*; Addison-Wesley, 2nd ed., 1973, 634 pp.

Knuth,D.C. (**79**): TEX and METAFONT, *New Directions in Typesetting*; Digital Press, 1979, 201+105 pp.

Kobayashi,H. (**78**): *Modeling and Analysis: An Introduction to Performance Evaluation Methodology*; Addison-Wesley, 1978, 446 pp.

Kobayashi,I. (**75**): "Information and Information Processing Structure"; *Information Systems*, vol.1, pp.39–49, 1975.

Kochen,M. (**74**): *Principles of Information Retrieval*; Wiley, 1974, 203 pp.

Kohler,W.H. (**81**): "A Survey of Techniques for Synchronization and Recovery in Decentralized Computer Systems"; *ACM C. Surveys*, vol.13 no.2, Jun.1981, pp.149–184.

Kollias,J.G., Stocker,P.M., and Dearnley,P.A. (**77**): "Improving the Performance of an Intelligent Data Management System"; *Comp. J.*, vol.20, 1977, pp.302–307.

Konheim,A.G., Mack,M.H., McNeill,R.K., Tuckerman,B., and Waldbaum,G. (**80**): "The IPS Cryptographic Programs"; *IBM Sys. J.*, vol.19 no.2, 1980, pp.253–283.

Kral,J. (**71**): "Some Properties of the Scatter Storage Technique with Linear Probing"; *Comp. J.*, vol.14 no.2, May 1971, pp.145–149.

Krass,P. and Wiener,H. (**81**): "The DBMS Market Is Booming"; *Datamation*, vol.27 no.10, Sep.1981, pp.153–170.

Krinos,J.D. (**73**): "Interaction Statistics from a Data Base Management System"; *Proc. 1973 NCC*, AFIPS vol.42, 1973, pp.283–290.

Kroenke,D. (**78**): "Database: A Professional's Primer"; *SRA*, 1978, 323 pp.

Kronwal,R.A. and Tarter,M.E. (**65**): "Cumulative Polygon Address Calculation Sorting"; *Proc. of the 20th National ACM Conf.*, 1965, pp.376–384.

Kuehler,J.D. and Kerby,H.R. (**66**): "A Photo-Dibital Mass Storage System"; *Proc. 1966 FJCC*, AFIPS, vol.28, pp.753–742.

Kung,H.T. and Robinson,J.T. (**81**): "On Optimistic Methods for Concurrency Control"; *TODS*, vol.6 no.2, Jun.1981, pp.213–226.

Kunii,T.L., Amano,T. Arisawa,H., and Okada,S. (**75**): "An Interactive Fashion Design System INFADS"; in *Computer and Graphics*, vol.1, Pergamon Press, 1975.

LaCroix,M. and Pirotte,A. (**76**): "Generalized Joins"; in *ACM-SIGMOD Record*, vol.8 no.3, Sep.1976, pp.14–15.

Lafue, Gilles M.E. (**82**): "Semantic Integrity Dependencies and Delayed Integrity Checking"; in *VLDB 8*, McLeod and Villasenor(eds.), 1982, pp.292–299.

Lamport,L. (**74**): "A New Solution of Dykstra's Concurrent Programming Program"; *CACM*, vol.17no.8, Aug.1974, pp.453–455.

Lamport,L. (**78**): "Time, Clocks and the Ordering of Events in a Distributed System"; *CACM*, vol.21 no.7, Jul.1978, pp.558–565.

Lampson, Butler W. (**73**): "A Note on the Confinement Problem"; *CACM*, vol.16 no.10, Oct.1973, pp.613–615.

Lancaster,F.W. (**69**): "Evaluation of the MEDLARS Demand Search Service"; *American Documentation vol.20 no.2*, Apr.1969, pp.119–142.

Lancaster,F.W. (**79**): *Information Retrieval Systems, 2nd ed.*; Wiley-Becker-Hayes, 1979, 378 pp.

Landau,R.N., Wanger,J., and Berger,M.C. (**79**): *Directory of Online Databases, Vol.1 No.1*; Cuadra Associates, Santa Monica CA, Fall 1979.

Landauer,W.I. (**63**): "The Balanced Tree and its Utilization in Information Retrieval"; *IEEE Trans. Comp.*, vol.EC12 no.6, Dec.1963, pp.863–871.

Lang,C.A. and Gray,J.C. (**68**): "ASP: A Ring Implemented Associative Structure Package"; *CACM*, vol.2 no.8, Aug.1968, pp.550–555.

Langdon,G.G.,jr.(ed.) (**79**): "Data Base Machine, An Introduction"; *IEEE Trans. Comp.*, vol.C-28 no.6, Jun.1979.

Langefors, Borje (**61**): "Information Retrieval in File Processing - I and II"; *BIT*, vol.1, 1961, pp.54–63 and 103–112.

Langefors, Borje (**63**): "Some Approaches to the Theory of Information Systems"; *BIT*, vol.3, 1963, pp.229–254.

Langefors, Borje (**73**): *A Theoretical Analysis of Information Systems*; Auerbach, Philadelphia 1973.

Larson,P-A. (**81**): "Analysis of Index-Sequential Files with Overflow Chaining"; *TODS*, vol.6 no.4, Dec.1981, pp.671–680.

Lawrie,D.H., Randal,J.M., and Barton,R.R. (**82**): "Experiments with Automatic File Migration"; *IEEE Computer*, vol.15 no.7, Jul.1982, pp.45–55.

LeBihan,J., Esculier,C., LeLann,G., Litwin,W., Gardarin,G., Sedillot,S., and Treille,T. (**80**): "SIRIUS: A French Nationwide Project on Distributed Data Bases"; in *VLDB 6*, Lochovsky and Taylor(eds.), 1980, pp.75–85.

LeDoux,C.H. and Parker,D.S.jr. (**82**): "Reflections on Boyce-Codd Normal Form"; in *VLDB 8*, McLeod and Villasenor(eds.), 1982, pp.131–141.

Lefkovitz,D. (**69**): *File Structures for On-Line Systems*; Spartan Books NY, 1969, 215 pp.

Lefkovitz, David (**74**): *Data Management for On-line Systems*; Hayden Book Co., 1974, 289 pp.

Levien, R.E. and Maron, M.E. (**67**): "A Computer System for Inference Execution and Data Retrieval"; *CACM*, vol.10 no.11, Nov.1967, pp.715–721.

Levin, K.D. and Morgan, H.L. (**78**): "A Dynamic Optimization Model for Distributed Databases"; *Operations Research*, vol.26 no.5, Sep.-Oct.1978, pp.824–835.

Levy, M.R. (**82**): "Modularity and the Sequential File Update Problem"; *CACM*, Vol.25, No.6, Jun.1982, pp.362–369.

Lewin, M.H. (**69**): "A Proposed *Background Move* Instruction"; *Computer Group News of the IEEE CS*, vol.2 no.12, Nov.1969, pp.20–21.

Lide, D.R. jr. (**81**): "Critical Data for Critical Needs"; *Science*, vol.212 no.4501, Jun.1981, pp.1343–1349.

Lien, Y.E. (**81**): "Hierarchical Schemata for Relational Databases"; *TODS*, vol.6 no.1, Mar.1981, pp.48–69.

Lien, Y.E. (**82**): "On the Equivalence of Database Models"; *JACM*, vol.29 no.2, Apr.1982, pp.333–362.

Lin, C.S., Smith, D.C.P., and Smith, J.M. (**76**): "The Design of a Rotating Associative Array Memory for a Relational Database Management Application"; *TODS*, vol.1 no.1, Mar.1976, pp.53–65.

Lin, J.J. and Liu, M.T. (**82**): "System Design and Performance Evaluation of a Local Data Network for Very Large Distributed Databases"; in *IEEE CS SRDSDS 2*, Wiederhold(ed.), Jul.1982, pp.134–143.

Lindgreen, P. (**74**): "Basic Operations on Information as a Basis for Data Base Design"; *Proc. 1974 IFIP Congress*, North-Holland, pp.993–997.

Lindsay, B. and Gligor, V. (**79**): "Migration and Authentication of Protected Objects"; *IEEE Trans. Software Eng.*, vol.SE-5, Nov.1979, pp.607–611.

Lipski, W. (**79**): "On Semantic Issues Connected with Incomplete Information"; *TODS*, vol.4 no.3, Sep.1979, pp.262–297.

Litwin, W. (**80**): "Linear Hashing: A New Tool for File and Table Addressing"; in *VLDB 6*, Lochovsky and Taylor(eds.), 1980, pp.212–223.

Litwin, W. (**81T**): "Trie Hashing"; in *ACM-SIGMOD 81*, 1981, pp.19–29.

Litwin, W. (**81L**): "Logical Model of a Distributed Data Base"; *Proc. of the Second Seminar on Distributed Data Sharing Systems, Amsterdam*, Jun.1981, North-Holland.

Liu, Ho Nien (**68**): "A File Management System for a Large Corporate Information System Data Bank"; *Proc. 1968 FJCC*, AFIPS vol.33, pp.145–156.

Lochovsky, F.H. and Taylor R.D.(eds.) (**80**): *Proc. of the 6th VLDB, Montreal*; IEEE CS pub. 80 CH-1534–7C, Oct.1980, 435 pp.

Lockemann, P.C. and Knutsen, W.D. (**68**): "Recovery of Disk Contents after System Failure"; *CACM*, vol.11 no.8, Aug.1968, pp.542.

Lockemann, P.C. and Neuhold, E.J.(eds.) (**77**): *Systems for Large Data Bases*; Proc. of VLDB 76, North-Holland, 1977.

Lohman, G.M. and Muckstadt, J.A. (**77**): "Optimal Policy for Batch Operations: Backup, Checkpointing, Reorganization, and Updating"; *TODS*, vol.2 no.3, Sep.1977, pp.209–222.

Lomet, D.B. (**75**): "Scheme for Invalidating Free References"; *IBM JRD*, vol.19 no.1, Jan.1975, pp.26–35.

Long, P.L., Rashogi, K.B.L., Rush, J.E., and Wycoff, J.A. (**71**): "Large On-Line Files of Bibliographic Data. An Efficient and a Mathematical Prediction of Retrieval Behavior"; *Information Processing-71*, North-Holland, 1971, pp.473.

Loo, John, O'Donald, B.T., and Whiteman, I.R. (**71**): "Real Time Considerations for an Airline"; *Proc. 1971 SJCC*, AFIPS vol.38, pp.83–92.

Lorie, R.A. (**77**): "Physical Integrity in a Large Segmented Database"; *TODS*, vol.2 no.1, Mar.1977, pp.91–104.

Lowe, T.C. (**68**): "The Influence of Data Base Characteristics and Usage on Direct Access File Organization"; *JACM*, vol.15 no.4, Oct.1968, pp.535–548.

Lowenthal, E. and Dale, N.B.(eds.) (**78**): *Proc. of the ACM-SIGMOD International Conf. on Management of Data*; ACM, New York 1978, 180 pp.

Lucas, H.C.jr. (**75**): "Performance and the Use of an Information System"; *Management Science*, vol.21, Apr.1975, pp.908–919.

Lucas, H.C. (**81**): *The Analysis, Design, and Implementation of Information Systems*; McGraw-Hill 1981, 419 pp.

Lum, V.Y. (**70**): "Multi-Attribute Retrieval with Combined Indexes"; *CACM*, vol.13 no.11, Nov.1970, pp.660–665.

Lum, V.Y. and Ling, H. (**71**): "An Optimization Problem on the Selection of Secondary Keys"; *ACM Proceedings*, 26th Annual Conference, 1971, pp.349–456.

Lum, V.Y., Yuen, P.S.T., and Dodd, M. (**71**): "Key-to-Address Transformation Techniques: A Fundamental Performance Study on Large Existing Formatted Files"; *CACM*, vol.14 no.4, Apr.1971, pp.238–239.

Lum, V.Y. (**73**): "General Performance Analysis of Key-to-Address Transformation Methods Using an Abstract File Concept"; *CACM*, vol.16 no.10, Oct.1973, pp.603–612.

Lum, V.Y., Senko M.E., Wang, C.P., and Ling, H. (**75**): "A Cost Oriented Algorithm for Data Set Allocation in Storage Hierarchies"; *CACM*, vol.18 no.6, Jun.1975, pp.318–322.

Lutz, Theo and Klimesch, Herbert (**71**): *Die Datenbank im Informationssystem*; Oldenburg Verlag, München 1971.

Lynch, C. and Brownrigg, E.B. (**81**): "Application of Data Compression Techniques to a Large Bibliographic Database"; in *VLDB 7*, Zaniolo and Delobel(eds.), 1981, pp.435–447.

Lynch, N.A. (**82**): "Mulilevel Atomicity"; in *ACM-PODS 1*, Aho(ed.), ACM, Mar.1982, pp.63–69.

MacDougall, M.H. (**70**): "Computer System Simulation: An Introduction"; *ACM C. Surveys*, vol.2 no.3, Sep.1970, pp.191–209.

Madnick, S.E. (**69**): "A Modular Approach to File System Design"; *Proc. 1969 SJCC*, AFIPS vol.34, pp.1–13.

Madnick, Stuart E. (**75**): "INFOPLEX: Hierarchical Decomposition of a Large Information Management System Using a Microprocessor Complex"; *Proc. 1975 NCC*, AFIPS vol.44, pp.581–586.

Maier, D., Mendelzon, A.O., Sadri, F., and Ullman, J.D. (**80**): "Adequacy of Decomposition of Relational Databases"; *J. Comput. Syst. Sci.*, vol.21 no.3, Dec.1980, pp.368–379.

Major, J.B. (**81**): "Processor, I/O Path, and DASD Configuration Capacity"; *IBM Syst. J.*, vol.20 no.1, 1981, pp.63–85.

Mallmann, F.P. (**80**): "The Management of Engineering Changes Using the Primus System"; in *ACM-SIGDA 17*, Jun.1980, pp.348–366.

Mallison, J.C. (**76**): "Tutorial Review of Magnetic Recording"; *Proc. of the IEEE*, vol.64 no.2, Feb.1976, pp.196–208.

Mantey, Patrick E. and Carlson, Eric D. (**75**): "Integrated Data Bases for Municipal Decision-Making"; *Proc. 1975 NCC*, AFIPS vol.44, pp.487–494.

March, S. and Severance, D. (**77**): "The Determination of Efficient Record Segmentations and Blocking Factors for Shared Files"; *TODS*, vol.2 no.3, 1977, pp.279–296.

Marill, T. and Stern, D. (**75**): "The Data-Computer – A Network Data Utility"; *Proc. 1975 NCC*, AFIPS vol.44ß, pp.389–395.

Marron,B.A. and deMaine,P.A.D. (**67**): "Automatic Data Compression"; *CACM*, vol.10 no.11, Mar.1967, pp.711–715.

Martin,James (**67**): *Design of Real-Time Computer Systems*; Prentice Hall, 1967, 640 pp.

Martin,J. (**72**): *Systems Analysis for Data Transmission*; Prentice Hall, 1972, 896 pp.

Martin,J. (**73**): *Design of Man-Computer Dialogues*; Prentice Hall, 1973, 496 pp.

Martin,J. (**76**): *Principles of Data-Base Management*; Prentice Hall, 1976, 352 pp.

Martin,J. (**77**): *Computer Data-Base Organization, 2nd ed.*; Prentice Hall, 1977, 576 pp.

Maruyama,K. and Smith,S.E. (**76**): "Optimal Reorganization of Distributed Space Disk Files"; *CACM*, vol.19 no.11, Nov.1976, pp.634–642.

Maryanski,F.J. (**80**): "Backend Database Systems"; *ACM C. Surveys*, vol.12 no.1, Mar.1980, pp.3–25.

Maurer, W. D. and Lewis, T. G. (**75**): "Hash Table Methods"; *ACM C. Surveys*, vol.7 no.1, Mar.1975, pp.5–20.

McCreight,E.M. (**77**): "Pagination of B∗-trees with Variable-Length Records"; *CACM*, Sep.1977, pp.670–674.

McEwen,H.E.(ed.) (**74**): *Management of Data Elements in Information Processing*; U.S. Dept. of Commerce, COM 74-10700, NTIS, Springfield VA, Apr.1974.

McFadden,F.R. and Suver,J.D. (**78**): "Costs and Benefits of Data Base System"; *Harvard Business Review*, vol.56 no.1, Jan.-Feb.1978, pp.131–139.

McGee, W. C. (**59**): "Generalization - Key to Successful Electronic Data Processing"; *JACM*, vol.6 no.1, Jan.1959, pp.1–23.

McGee, W.C. (**77**): "The Information Management System IMS/VS Part 1: General Structure and Operation"; *IBM Syst. J.*, vol.16 no.2, 1977, pp.84–168.

McIntosh,S and Griffel,D. (**68**): "ADMINS from Mark III to Mark V"; *Proc. 1968 IFIP Congress*, North Holland, pp.1260–1266.

McLeod,D. and Meldman,M. (**75**): "RISS: A Generalized Minicomputer Relational Data Base Management System"; *Proc. 1975 NCC*, AFIPS vol.44, pp.397–402.

McLeod, D. and Villasenor, Y.F.(eds.) (**82**): *Proc. of VLDB 8, Mexico City*; VLDB Endoment, Saratoga CA, Sep.1982, 387 pp.

Meadow,Charles T. (**73**): *The Analysis of Information Systems*; Wiley-Melville, 1973.

Mealy, George H. (**67**): "Another Look at Data"; *Proc. 1967 FJCC*, AFIPS vol.31, pp.525–534.

Mellen,G.E. (**73**): "Cryptology, Computers, and Common Sense"; *Proc. 1973 NCC*, AFIPS vol.42, pp.569–579.

Menasce,D.A., Muntz,R.R. and Popek,G.J. (**79**): "A Formal Model of Crash Recovery in Computer Systems"; *Proc. 12th Hawaii Intl. Conf. on System Sciences*, vol.1, 1979, pp.28–35.

Menasce,D.A., Popek,G.J., and Muntz,R.R. (**80**): "A Locking Protocol for Resource Coordination in Distributed Databases"; *TODS*, vol.5 no.2, Jun.1980, pp.103–138.

Mendelsohn, R.C. (**71**): "Data Banks and Information Systems for National Statistics"; *Information Processing-71*, North-Holland, Proc. 1971 IFIP Congress, pp.1483–1484.

Merrett,T.H., Kambayashi,Y., and Yasura,H. (**81**): "Scheduling of Page-Fetches in Join Operations"; in *VLDB 7*, Zaniolo and Delobel(eds.), 1981, pp.488–498.

Merten,A.G.(ed.) (**77**): *Proc. of VLDB 3, Tokyo*; IEEE CS pub. 77CH1268-2C, Oct.1977, 570 pp.

Meyer,C.H. (**73**): "Design Considerations for Cryptography"; *Proc. 1973 NCC*, AFIPS vol.43, pp.603–606.

Michaels,P.C. and Richards,W.J. (**75**): "Magnetic Bubble Mass Memory"; *IEEE Trans. on Magnetics*, vol.11, Jan.1975, pp.21–25.

Miller,A.R. (**71**): *The Assault on Privacy*; The Univ. of Michigan Press, Ann Arbor, 1971.

Miller, J.R. (**70**): *Professional Decision Making: A Procedure for Evaluating Complex Alternatives*; Praeger Publisher, NY 1970.

Minker, J. (**78**): "Search Strategy and Selection Function for an Inferential Relational System"; *TODS*, vol.3 no.1, Mar.1978, pp.1–31.

Minoura, T. and Wiederhold, G. (**81**): "Resilient Extended True-Copy Token Scheme for a Distributed Database"; *IEEE Trans. Software Eng.*, vol.SE-8 no.3, May.1981, pp.172–188.

Minsky, N. (**81**): "Synergistic Authorization in Database Systems"; in *VLDB 7*, Zaniolo and Delobel(eds.), 1981, pp.543–552.

Molho, L. (**70**): "Hardware Aspects of Secure Computing"; *Proc. 1970 SJCC*, AFIPS vol.36, pp.135–141.

Montgomery, Christine A. (**72**): "Is Natural Language an Unnatural Query Language"; *Proc. 1972 ACM Nat. Conf.*, pp.1075–1078.

Morey, R.C. (**82**): "Estimating and Improving the Quality of Information in a MIS"; *CACM*, vol.15 no.5, May 1982, pp.337–342.

Morgan, Howard Lee (**74**): "Optimal Space Allocation on Disk Storage"; *CACM*, vol.11 no.3, Mar.1974, pp.139–142.

Morgan, H.L. and Levin, K.D. (**77**): "Optimal Program and Data Locations in Computer Networks"; *CACM*, vol.20 no.5, May 1977, pp.315–322.

Moroney, M.J. (**56**): *Facts from Figures, 3rd ed.*; Pelican Books, 1956, 472 pp.

Morris, R. (**68**): "Scatter Storage Techniques"; *CACM*, vol.1 no.1, Jan.1968, pp.38–44.

Mott, T.H.jr, Artandi, S.A., and Struminger, L. (**72**): *Introduction to PL/I Programming for Library and Information Science*; Academic Press, 1972, 239 pp.

Mullin, James K. (**71**): "Retrieval-Update Speed Trade-offs Using Combined Indexes"; *CACM*, vol.14 no.12, Dec.1971, pp.775–776.

Mullin, James K. (**72**): "An Improved Indexed-Sequential Access Method Using Hashed Overflow"; *CACM*, vol.15 no.5, May 1972, pp.301–307.

Mulvany, R.B. (**74**): "Engineering Design of a Disk Storage Facility with Data Modules"; *IBM JRD*, vol.18 no.6, Nov.1974, pp.489–505.

Murdick, R.G. and Ross J.E. (**75**): *MIS in Action*; West Publishing Co., St. Paul MN and San Francisco, 1975, 724 pp.

Mylopoulos, J., Bernstein, P.A., and Wong, K.T. (**80**): "A Language Facility for Designing Database-Intensive Applications"; *TODS*, vol.5 no.2, Jun.1980, pp.185–207.

Nance, Richard E. (ed.) (**75**): *Proc. of ACM-SIGPLAN-SIGIR Interface Meeting: Programming Languages - Information Retrieval*; ACM SIGPLAN Notices, vol.10 no.1, Jan.1975.

Navathe, Shamkant B. and Fry, James P. (**76**): "Restructuring for Large Data Bases: Three Levels of Abstraction"; *TODS*, vol.1 no.1, Mar.1976, pp.138–158.

Navathe, S.B., and Schkolnick, M. (**78**): "View Representation in Logical Database Design"; in *ACM-SIGMOD 78*, Lowenthal and Dale(eds.), Jun.1978, pp.144–156.

Navathe, S.B. and Gadgil, S.G. (**82**): "A Methodology for View Integration in Logical Database Design"; in *VLDB 8*, McLeod and Villasenor(eds.), 1982, pp.142–164.

NBS (**74**): *Guidelines for Automatic Data Processing Physical Security and Risk Management*; NBS-FIPS pub.31, Jun.1974, 92 pp.

NBS (**80**): *Prospectus for Data Dictionary System Standard*; Application Systems Division, NBS IR 80-2115, Sep.1980.

Needham, R.M. (**72**): "Protection Systems and Protection Implementation"; *Proc. 1972 FJCC*, AFIPS vol.41, pp.571–578.

Needham,R.M. and Schroeder,M.D. (**78**): "Using Encryption for Authentication in Large Networks of Computers"; *CACM*, vol.21 no.12, Dec.1978, pp.993–999.

Nelson,D.B., Pick,R.A., and Andrews,K.B. (**67**): "GIM-1: A Generalized Information Management Language and Computer System"; *Proc. 1967 SJCC*, AFIPS vol.30, pp.169–173.

Neuhold,E.J.(ed.) (**76**): *Modelling in Data Base Management Systems*; North-Holland, 1976.

Newell,G.F. (**71**): *Applications of Queuing Theory*; Chapman and Hall, 1971.

Nielsen,Norman R. (**67**): "The Simulation of Time Sharing Systems"; *CACM*, vol.10 no.7, Jul.1967, pp.397–412.

Nievergelt,J. (**74**): "Binary Search Trees and File Organization"; *ACM C. Surveys*, vol.6 no.3, Sep.1974, pp.195–207.

Nijssen, G.M.(ed.) (**76**): *Architecture and Models in Database Management Systems*; North-Holland, 1976.

Nijssen, G.M.(ed.) (**77**): *Modelling in Data Base Management Systems*; North-Holland, 1977.

Nunamaker, J.F., Swenson, D.E.jr., and Whinston, A.B. (**73**): "Specifications for the Development of a Generalized Data Base Planning System"; *Proc. 1973 NCC*, AFIPS vol.42, pp.259–270.

Obermarck,R. (**81**): "Global Deadlock Detection Algorithm"; *TODS*, vol.7 no.2, Jun.1981, pp.187–208.

O'Connell,M. L. (**71**): "A File Organization Method Using Multiple Keys"; *Proc. 1971 SJCC*, AFIPS vol.38, pp.539–544.

Olle, T. William (Chairman), et al (**71**): "Introduction to 'Feature Analysis of Generalized Data Base Management Systems'"; *CACM*, May 1971, vol.14 no.5, pp.308–318.

Olle,T.W. (**78**): *The CODASYL Approach to Data Base Management*; Wiley, 1978.

O'Neill,J.T. (ed.) (**76**): MUMPS *Language Standard*; NBS Handbook 118, Government Printing Office, Washington DC, 1976.

Oppenheimer, G. and Clancy,K.P. (**68**): "Considerations for Software Protection and Recovery from Hardware Failures in Multi-Access, Multi-Programming, Single Processor Systems"; *Proc. 1968 FJCC*, AFIPS vol.33, pp.29–37.

O'Reagan, Robert T. (**72**): "Computer Assigned Codes from Verbal Responses"; *CACM*, vol.15 no.6, Jun.1972, pp.455–459.

Ouellette,R.P., Greeley,R.S., and Overby,J.W.II (**75**): *Computer Techniques in Environmental Science*; Petrocelli Books, 1975, 248 pp.

Overholt,K.J. (**73**): "Optimal Binary Search Methods"; *BIT*, vol.13 no.1, 1973, pp.84–91.

Ozkarahan, E.A., Schuster, S.A.,, and Sevcik, K.C. (**77**): "Performance Evaluation of a Relational Associative Processor" and "Analysis of Architectural Features for Enhancing the Performance of a Database Machine"; *TODS*, vol.2 no.2, Jun.1977, pp.175–195; no.4, Dec.1977, pp.297–316.

Ozsoyoglu,G. and Chin,F.Y. (**82**): "Enhancing the Security of Statistical Databases with a Question Answering System and a Kernel Design"; *IEEE Trans. on Software Eng.*, vol.SE-8 no.3, May 1982, pp.223–234.

Palermo,F.P. (**75**): "An APL Environment for Testing Relational Operators and Data Base Search Algorithms"; *Proc. APL 75 Conference*, Pisa, Italy, June 16-18, 1975, pp.249–256.

Palmer,I. (**75**): *Data Base Systems, A Practical Reference*; QED Information Sciences, Wellesly MA, 1975, 341 pp.

Papadimitriou,C.H. (**79**): "The Serializability of Concurrent Database Updates"; *JACM*, vol.26 no.4, Oct.1979, pp.631–653.

Parker,D.B. (**81**): *Ethical Conflicts in Computer Science and Technology*; AFIPS Press, Arlington VA, 1981.

Parker, Edwin B. (**67**): SPIRES, *Stanford Physics Information Retrieval System*; Institute for Communication Research, Stanford University, Dec.1967.

Parkin,A. (**74**): "Bringing Cost into File Design Decisions"; *Comp. J.*, vol.18 no.3, 1974, pp.198–199.

Parnas,D.L. (**72**): "On the Criteria to be Used in Decomposing Systems into Modules"; *CACM*, vol.15 no.12, Dec.1972, pp.1053–1058.

Parsons, R.G., Dale, A.G., and Yurkanan, C.V. (**74**): "Data Manipulation Language Requirements for Data Base Management Systems"; *Comp. J.*, vol.17 no.2, May 1974, pp.99–103.

Pease, M., Shostak, R., and Lamport, L. (**80**): "Reaching Agreement in the Presence of Faults"; *JACM*, vol.27 no.2, Apr.1980, pp.228–234.

Petersen,H.E. and Turn,R. (**67**): "System Implications of Information Privacy"; *Proc. 1967 SJCC*, AFIPS vol.30, 1967.

Peterson,W.W. (**57**): "Addressing for Random Access Storage"; *IBM JRD*, vol.1 no.2, Apr.1957, pp.130–146.

Peterson,W.W. and Weldon,E.J. (**72**): *Error Correcting Codes*; MIT Press 1972, 285 pp.

Piepmeyer, William F. (**75**): "Optimal Balancing of I/O Requests to Disk"; *CACM*, vol.18 no.9, Sept.1975, pp.524–527.

Pierce,J. (**61**): *Symbols, Signals, and Noise*; Harper and Row, 1961.

Premchand,V.K. (**74**): "Some Aspects of Buffering"; *Journal of the Computer Society of India*, vol.4 no.1, Jan.1974, pp.8–14.

Presser, Leon (**75**): "Multiprogramming Coordination"; *ACM C. Surveys*, vol.7 no.1, Mar.1975, pp.21–44.

Prywes, Noah S. and Gray,H.J. (**63**): "The Organization of a Multi-List Type Associative Memory"; *IEEE Trans. on Comp. and Elec.*, Sep.1963, pp.488–492.

Pugh,E. W. (**71**): "Storage Hierarchies: Gaps, Cliffs, and Trends"; *IEEE Trans. Magnetics*, vol.Mag-7, Dec.1971, pp.810–814.

Purdy, George B. (**74**): "A High Security Log-in Procedure"; *CACM*, vol.17 no.8, Aug.1974, pp.442–445.

Ralston, A and Shaw, M. (bf80): "Curriculum '78–Is Computer Science Really that Unmathematical"; *CACM*, Vol.23 No.2, Feb.1980, pp.67–70.

Ramamoorthy, C.V. and Chandy, C.V. (**70**): "Optimization of Memory Hierarchies in Multi-programmed Systems"; *JACM*, vol.17 no.3, Jul.1970, pp.426–445.

Ramamoorthy,C.V. and Wah,B.W. (**79**): "The Placement of Relations on a Distributed Relational Database"; *Proc. First Int. Conf. on Distributed Computing Systems*, Huntsville AL, IEEE CS 1979.

Rattenbury,J. and Pelletier,P. (**74**): *Data Processing in the Social Sciences with* OSIRIS; Survey Res. Center, Inst. for Social Research, Univ. of Michigan, 1974, 243 pp.

Ray-Chaudhuri, D. K. (**68**): "Combinatorial Information Retrieval Systems for Files"; *SIAM J. Appl. Math. vol.16 no.5*, 1968, pp.973–992.

Reisner,P., Boyce,R.F., and Chamberlin,D.D. (**75**): "Human Factors Evaluation of Two Data Base Query Languages - SQUARE and SEQUEL"; *Proc. 1975 NCC*, AFIPS vol.44, pp.447–452.

Reisner,P. (**77**): "The Use of Psychological Experimentation as an Aid to Development of a Query Language"; *IEEE Trans. Software Eng.*, vol.SE-3 no.3, May 1977.

Reiter,A. (**72**): "A Resource Oriented Time-Sharing Monito"; *Software Practice and Experience*, vol.2 no.1, Jan.1972, p.55.

Reitman, W.R. et al (**69**): "AUTONOTE, a Personal Information and Storage System"; *Proc. 1969 National ACM Conference P69*, pp.67–76.

Renniger, Clark R.(ed.) (**74**): *Approaches to Privacy and Security*; National Bureau of Standards, Wash. D.C., Spec. Pub. 404, Sep.1974.

Reuter, A. (**80**): "A Fast Transaction-Oriented Logging Scheme for UNDO Recovery"; *IEEE Trans. Software Eng.*, vol.SE-6 no.4, Jul.1980, pp.348–356.

Richardson, Gary L. and Berkin, Stanley J. (**75**): *Problem-Solving Using PL/C*; Wiley, 1975.

Ries, D.D. and Stonebraker, M.R. (**77**): "Effects of Locking Granularity in a Database Management System"; *TODS*, vol.2 no.3, Sep.1977, pp.233–246.

Riley, M.J.(ed.) (**81**): *Management Information Systems*; Holden-Day, 1981.

Rivest, R.L. (**76**): "Partial Match Retrieval Algorithms"; *SIAM J. on Computing*, vol.5 no.1, 1976, pp.19–50.

Robey, D. and Farrow, D. (**82**): "User Involvement in Information System Development: A Conflict Model and Empirical Test"; *Management Science*, vol.28 no.1, Jan.1982, pp.73–85.

Rosenberg, A.L. and Snyder, L. (**81**): "Time- and Space-Optimality in B-Trees"; *TODS*, vol.6 no.1, Mar.1981, pp.174–183.

Rosenkrantz, D.J., Stearns, R.E., and Lewis, P.M., II (**78**): "System Level Concurrency Control for Distributed Database Systems"; *TODS*, vol.3 no.2, Jun.1978, pp.178–198

Ross, D.T. (**77**): "Structured Analysis (SA): A Language for Communicating Ideas"; *IEEE Trans. Software Eng.*, vol.SE-3 no.1, 1977, pp.16–34.

Rothnie, J.B.jr. and Lozano, T. (**74**): "Attribute Based File Organization in a Paged Memory Environment"; *CACM*, vol.17 no.2, Feb.1974, pp.63–79.

Rothnie, J.B. (**75**): "Evaluating Inter-Entry Retrieval Expressions in a Relational Data Base Management System"; *Proc. 1975 NCC*, AFIPS vol.44, pp.417–423.

Rothnie, J.B.jr.(ed.) (**76**): *Proc. 1976 ACM-SIGMOD International Conference on Management of Data*; ACM NY 1976.

Rothnie, J.B. et al (**80**): "Introduction to a System for Distributed Databases (SDD-1)"; *TODS*, vol.5 no.1, Mar.1980.

Rubinoff, M., Cautin, S., Bergman, H., and Rapp, F. (**68**): "Easy English, a Language for Information Retrieval through a Remote Typewriter Console"; *CACM*, vol.11 no.10, Oct.1968, pp.693–696.

Rudolph, J.A. (**72**): "A Production Implementation of an Associative Array Processor - STARAN"; *Proc. 1972 FJCC*, AFIPS vol.41, pp.229–242.

Rustin, Randall(ed.) (**72**): *Data Base Systems*; Prentice Hall, 1972.

Rustin, Randall(ed.) (**74**): *Proc. ACM-SIGFIDET 74, Data Description, Access, and Control*; ACM, 1974.

Sadri, F. and Ullman, J.D. (**82**): "Template Dependencies: A Large Class of Dependencies in Relational Databases and Its Complete Axiomatization"; *JACM*, vol.29 no.2, Apr.1982, pp.363–772.

Sagalowicz, D. (**77**): "IDA: An Intelligent Data Access Program"; in *VLDB 3*, Merten (ed.), 1977, pp.293–302.

Salasin, John (**73**): "Hierarchial Storage in Information Retrieval"; *CACM*, vol.16 no.5, May 1973, pp.291–295.

Salton, Gerard (**62**): "The Manipulation of Trees in Information Retrieval"; *CACM*, vol.5 no.2, Feb.1962, pp.103–114.

Salton, G. (**75**): *Dynamic Information and Library Processing*; Prentice Hall, 1975.

Saltzer, Jerome H. (**74**): "Protection and the Control of Information Sharing in Multics"; *CACM*, vol.17 no.7, Jul.1974, pp.388-402.

Saltzer, J.H. and Schroeder, M.D. (**75**): "The Protection of Information in Computer Systems"; *Proc. of the IEEE*, vol.63 no.9, Sep.1975, pp.1278–1308.

Sanders, Donald H. (**74**): *Computers and Management in a Changing Society*; McGraw-Hill, 1974.

Satyanarayanan, M. (**81**): "A Study of File Sizes and Functional Lifetimes"; in *ACM-SOSP 8*, ACM Order no.534810, Dec.1981, pp.96–108.

Schank, R.C. and Colby, K.M. (eds.) (**73**): *Computer Models of Thought and Language*; W. H. Freeman, San Francisco, 1973, 454 pp.

Schay, G.jr. and Spruth, W.G. (**62**): "Analysis of a File Addressing Method"; *CACM*, vol.5 no.8, Aug.1962, pp.459–462.

Schay, G.jr. and Raver, N. (**63**): "A Method for Key-to-Address Tranformations"; *IBM JRD vol.7 no.2*, Apr.1963, pp.121–126.

Scheuermann, P. and Carlson, C.R. (**78**): "Self-Assessment Procedure V, Database Systems"; *CACM*, vol.21 no.8, Aug.1978

Schkolnick, M. (**75**): "The Optimal Selection of Secondary Indices for Files"; *Information Systems*, vol.1, 1975, pp.141–146.

Schkolnick, M. (**77**): "A Clustering Algorithm for Hierarchical Structures"; *TODS*, vol.2 no.1, May 1977, pp.27–44.

Schkolnick, M. (**78**): "A Survey of Physical Database Design Methodology and Techniques"; in *VLDB 4*, Bubenko and Yao(eds.), 1978, pp.474–487.

Schlageter, G. (**81**): "Optimistic Methods for Concurrency Control in Distributed Database Systems"; in *VLDB 7*, Zaniolo and Delobel(eds.), 1981, pp.125–130.

Schlorer, J. (**81**): "Security of Statistical Databases: Multidimensional Transformation"; *TODS*, vol.6 no.1, Mar.1981, pp.95–112.

Schmidt, J.W. (**77**): "Some High Level Language Constructs for Data of Type Relation"; *TODS*, vol.2 no.3, Sep.1977, pp.247–261.

Schneider, Ben Ross (**75**): *Travels in Computerland or Incompatabilities and Interfaces*; Addison Wesley, 1975.

Schneider, H-J.(ed.) (**79**): *Formal Model and Practical Tools For Information Systems Design*; North-Holland 1979, 296 pp.

Schneider, M.(ed.) (**82**): *Proceedings Human Factors in Computer Systems*; Institute for Computer Sciences and Technology, National Bureau of Standards, U.S. Dept. of Commerce, 1982, 399 pp.

Scholl, M. (**81**): "New File Organizations Based on Dynamic Hashing"; *TODS*, vol.6 no.1, Mar.1981, pp.194–211.

Schroeder, M.D. and Saltzer, J. (**72**): "A Hardware Architecture for Implementing Protection Rings"; *CACM*, vol.15 no.3, Mar.1972, pp.157–170.

Schwartz, Eugene S. (**63**): "A Dictionary for Minimum Redundancy Encoding"; *JACM*, vol.10 no.4, Oct.1963, pp.413–439.

Schwartz, M.D., Denning, D.E., and P.J. (**79**): "Linear Queries in Statistical Databases"; *TODS*, vol.4, no.2, Jun.1979; *corrigendum* vol.5 no.3, Sep.1980, pp.383.

Seaman, P.H., Lind, R.A., and Wilson, T.L. (**66**): "An Analysis of Auxiliary Storage Activity"; *IBM Sys. J.*, vol.5 no.3, 1966, pp.158–170.

Seaman, P.H. and Soucy, R.C. (**69**): "Simulating Operating Systems"; *IBM Sys. J.*, vol.8 no.4, 1969, pp.264–279.

Selbman, H.K. (**74**): "Bitstring Processing for Statistical Evaluation of Large Volumes of Medical Data"; *Methods of Inf. in Med.*, vol.13 no.2, Apr.1974, pp.61–64.

Semple, D.jr. (**67**): "GIS, A Tool for Design Automation"; *SHARE 4th Annual Design Automation Workshop*, Share Secretary Distr. C-4833, Sep.1967, pp.60–87.

Senko, M.E., Altman, E.B. Astrahan, M.M., and Fehder, P.L. (**73**): "Data Structures and Accessing in Data Base Systems"; *IBM Sys. J.*, vol.12 no.1, pp.30–93, 1973.

Senko, M.E. (**77**): "Data Structures and Data Accessing in Data Base Systems Past, Present, Future"; *IBM Syst. J.*, vol.16 no.3, 1977, pp.208–257.

Sevcik, K.C. (**81**): "Data Base System Performance Prediction Using an Analytical Model"; in *VLDB 7*, Zaniolo and Delobel(eds.), 1981, pp.182–198.

Severance, D.G. and Merten, A.G. (**72**): "Performance Evaluation of File Organizations through Modelling"; *Proc. 1972 National ACM Conference*, pp.1061–1072.

Severance, D.G. and Lohman, G.M. (**76**): "Differential Files: Their Applications to the Maintenance of Large Databases"; *TODS*, vol.1 no.3, Sep.1976, pp.256–367.

Shannon, C.E. and Weaver, W. (**62**): *The Mathematical Theory of Computation*; The Univ. of Illinois Press, reprint, 1962, 80 pp.

Sharpe, William F. (**69**): *The Economics of Computers*; Columbia Univ. Press, NY, 1969.

Shaw, D. (**80**): "A Relational Database Machine Architecture"; *SIGMOD Record*, vol.10 no.4, and SIGIR vol.XV no.2, Apr.1980, pp.84–95.

Shipman, D.W. (**81**): "The Functional Data Model and the Data Language DAPLEX"; *TODS*, vol.6 no.1, Mar.1981, pp.140–173.

Shneiderman, Ben (**73**): "Optimum Data Base Reorganization Points"; *CACM*, vol.16 no.6, Jun.1973, pp.362–365.

Shneiderman, Ben (**74**): "A Model for Optimizing Indexed File Structures"; *International Journal of Computer and Inf. Sciences*, vol.3 no.1, 1974, pp.93–103.

Shneiderman, B. (**77**): "Reduced Combined Indexes for Efficient Multiple Attribute Retrieval"; *Information Systems*, vol.1 no.4, 1977, pp.149–154.

Shneiderman, B. (ed.) (**78**): *Databases: Improving Usability and Responsiveness*; Academic Press, New York, 1978.

Shneiderman, B. and Thomas, G. (**82**): "An Architecture for Automatic Relational Database System Conversion"; *TODS*, vol.7 no.2, Jun.1982, pp.235–257.

Shopiro, J.E. (**79**): "Theseus–A Programming Language for Relational Databases"; *TODS*, vol.4 no.4, Dec.1979, pp.493–517.

Shortliffe, E., Axline, S.G., Buchanan, B.G., Merigan, T.C., and Cohen, S.N. (**73**): "An Artificial Intelligence Program to Advise Physicians Regarding Antimicrobial Therapy"; *Computers and Biomedical Research vol.6*, 1973, pp.544–560.

Shu, N.C., Housel, B.C. and Lum, V.Y. (**75**): "CONVERT: A High Level Translation Definition Language for Data Conversion"; *CACM*, vol.18 no.10, Oct.1975, pp.557–567.

Sibley, Ed H. and Taylor, Robert W. (**73**): "A Data Definition and Mapping Language"; *CACM*, vol.16 no.12, Dec.1973, pp.750–759.

Sibley, E.H. and Rabenseifer, A. (**74**): "Extremely Large Data Systems for National Statistics"; *Proc. 1974 IFIP Congress*, North-Holland, pp.1071–1074.

Sibley, E.H.(ed.) (**76**): *Special Issue on Data Base Management Systems*; ACM C. Surveys, vol.8 no.1, Mar.1976.

Sieworek, Daniel P., Bell, C. Gordon, and Newell, Allen (**82**): *Computer Structures: Principles and Examples*; McGraw-Hill Book Company, 1982, 926 pp.

Siler, K.F. (**76**): "A Stochastic Evaluation Model for Database Organizations in Data Retrieval Systems"; *CACM*, vol.19 no.2, Feb.1976, pp.84–95.

Simmons, R.F. (**70**): "Natural Language Question-Answering Systems: 1969"; *CACM*, vol.13 no.1, Jan.1970, pp.15–30.

Siwiec, J.E. (**77**): "A High-Performance DB/DC System"; *IBM Sys. J.*, vol.16 no.2, 1977, pp.169–174.

Skinner, C.E. (**69**): "Effects of Storage Contention on System Performance"; *IBM Sys. J.*, vol.8 no.4, 1969, pp.319–333.

Sklaroff, J.R. (**76**): "Redundancy Management Technique for Space Shuttle Computers"; *IBM JRD*, vol.20 no.1, Jan.1976, pp.20–30.

Sladek, J.M. (**71**): *The Müller Fokker Effect*; Pocket Books, Simon and Schuster, 214 pp.

Smith, A.J. (**81**): "Analysis of Long-Term File Migration Patterns"; *IEEE Trans. Software Eng.*, vol.SE-7 no.4, Jul.1981, pp.403–417.

Smith, J.L. and Holden, T.S. (**72**): "Restart of an Operating System having a Permanent File Structure"; *Comp. J.*, vol.15 no.1, Feb.1972, pp.25–31.

Smith, J.M. and Chang, P.Y. (**75**): "Optimizing the Performance of a Relational Algebra Data Base Interface"; *CACM*, vol.18 no.10, Oct.1975, pp.568–579.

Smith, J.M. and Smith, D.C.P. (**77**): "Database Abstractions: Aggregation and Generalization"; *TODS*, vol.1 no.1, Jun.1977, pp.105–133.

Snedecor, G.W. and Cochran, W.G. (**67**): *Statistical Methods*; Iowa State University Press, Ames IO, 1967, 593 pp.

Sockut, G.H. (**78**): "A Performance Model for Computer Data-Base Reorganization Performed Concurrently with Usage"; *Operations Research*, vol.26 no.5, Sep.-Oct.1978, pp.789–804.

Sockut, G.H. and Goldberg, R.P. (**79**): *Data Base Reorganization - Principles and Practice*; ACM C. Surveys, vol.11 no.4, Dec.1979.

Solomon, Martin B. (**66**): "Economics of Scale and the IBM System /360"; *CACM*, vol.9 no.6, Jun.1966, pp.435–440.

Spewak, S.H. (**80**): "A Pragmatic Approach to Database Design"; in *VLDB 6*, Lochovsky and Taylor(eds.), 1980, pp.151–152.

Sprague, R.H.jr. and Carlson, E.D. (**82**): *Building Effective Decision Support Systems*; Prentice Hall, 1982, 304 pp.

Sprowls, R. Clay (**75**): "Data Base Education for Students of Management"; *Proc. 1975 NCC*, AFIPS, vol.44, pp.907–911.

Sreenivasan, K. and Kleinman, A.J. (**74**): "On the Construction of a Representative Synthetic Workload"; *CACM*, vol.17 no.3, Mar.1974, pp.127–133.

Stacey, G.M. (**74**): "A FORTRAN Interface to the CODASYL Data Base Task Group Specification"; *Comp. J.*, vol.12 no.2, Feb.1974, pp.124–127.

SSA (**57**): *Preliminary Report of Distribution of Surnames in the SS Account Number File*; HEW, SSA, Bureau of Old Age and Survivors Insurance 1957.

Stahl, Fred (**73**): "A Homophonic Cipher for Computational Cryptography"; *Proc. 1973 NCC*, AFIPS vol.42, pp.565–568.

Stanfel, Larry E. (**70**): "Tree Structures for Optimal Searching"; *JACM*, vol.17 no.3, Jul.1970, pp.508–517.

Steel, T.B.jr. (**64**): "Beginnings of a Theory of Information Handling"; *CACM*, Feb.1964, pp.97–103.

Steel, T.B. (Chairman SPARC/DBMS Study Group) (**75**): *Interim Report of the ANSI-SPARC Study Group*; ACM-SIGMOD FDT, vol.7 no.2, 1975.

Stemple, D.W. (**76**): "A Data Base Management Facility for Automatic Generation of Data Base Machines"; *TODS*, vol.1 no.1, Mar.1976.

Sterling, T.D. (**74**): "Guidelines for Humanizing Computerized Information Systems, A Report from Stanley House"; *CACM*, vol.17 no.11, Nov.1974, pp.609–613.

Sterling, T.D. (**75**): "Humanizing Computerized Information Systems"; *Science*, vol.190 no.4220, Dec.19, 1975, pp.1168–1172.

Stocker, P.M. (**77**): "Storage Utilization in a Self-Organizing Data Base"; *Proc. 1977 NCC*, AFIPS vol.46, pp.119–122.

Stone, H. (**74**): *Introduction to Data Structures and Computer Organization*; McGraw-Hill, 1974.

Stone, Harold (ed.) (**75**): *Introduction to Computer Architecture*; SRA, Palo Alto 1975.

Stone, H.S. and Fuller, S.F. (**73**): "On the Near-Optimality of the Shortest-Access-Time-First Drum Scheduling Discipline"; *CACM*, vol.16 no.6, Jun.1973, pp.352–353.

Stonebraker, M. (**74**): "The Choice of Partial Inversions and Combined Indices"; *Journal of Computer and Information Science*, Jun.1974, pp.167–188.

Stonebraker, M., Wong, E., Kreps, P., and Held, G. (**76**): "The Design and Implementation of INGRES"; *TODS*, vol.1 no.3, Sep.1976, pp.189–222.

Stonebraker, M., et al (**79**): "Concurrency Control and Consistency of Multiple Copies of Data in Distributed INGRES"; *IEEE Trans. on Softw. Eng.*, vol.SE-5 no.3, May 1979.

Stonebraker, M. (**80**): "Retropection on a Data Base System"; *TODS*, vol.5 no.3, Sep.1980.

Stover, R.F. and Krishnaswamy, S. (**73**): "Ensuring Input Data Integrity in a High-Volume Environment"; *Proc. 1973 NCC*, AFIPS vol.42, pp.M54–M59.

Streeter, D.N. (**73**): "Centralization or Dispersion of Computing Facilities"; *IBM Sys. J.*, vol.12 no.3, 1973, pp.283–301.

Streeter, Donald M. (**74**): *The Scientific Process and the Computer*; Wiley 1974.

Strnad, Alois L. (**71**): "The Relational Approach to the Management of Data Bases"; *Information Processing 71*, IFIP 1971 Congress, North-Holland, pp.901–904.

Su, S.Y.W., et al (**79**): "The Architectural Fea-tures and Implementation Techniques of the Multi-Cell CASSM"; *IEEE Trans. on Computers*, vol.C-28 no.6, Jun.1979.

Su, S.Y.W., Chang, H., Copeland, G., Fisher, P., Lowenthal, E., and Schuster, S. (**80**): "Database Machines and Some Issues on DBMS Standards"; *Proc. 1980 NCC*, AFIPS vol.49, pp.191–208.

Sundgren, B. (**75**): *Theory of Data Bases*; Petrocell-Mason-Charter, New York 1975.

Sussenguth, E.H. (**63**): "Use of Tree Structures for Processing Files"; *CACM*, vol.6 no.5, May 1963, pp.272–279.

Swanson, W.E. (**80**): "Industry Involvement in IPAD Through the Industry Technical Advisory Board"; *Proc. of IPAD National Symposium*, NASA Conference Publication 2143, Sep.1980, pp.21–26.

Swinehart, D., McDaniel, G., and Boggs, D.R. (**79**): "WFS: A Simple Shared File System for a Distributed Environment"; in *ACM-SOSP 7*, ACM, Dec.1979.

Symonds, A. J. (**68**): "Auxiliary-Storage Associative Data Structure for PL/1"; *IBM Sys. J.*, vol.7 no.3, 1968, pp.229–245.

Taggart, W.M., jr. and Tharp, M.O. (**77**): "A Survey of Information Requirements Analysis Techniques"; *ACM C. Surveys*, vol.9 no.4, Dec.1977, pp.273–290.

Tanenbaum, A.S. (**81**): *Computer Networks*; Prentice Hall, 1981, 517 pp.

Tang, Donald T. and Chien, Robert T. (**69**): "Coding for Error Control"; *IBM Sys. J.*, vol.8 no.1, Mar.1969, pp.48–80.

Teichroew, D. (**66**): "Computer Simulation–Discussion of the Technique and Comparison of Languages"; *CACM*, vol.9 no.10, Oct.1966, pp.723–741.

Teichroew, Daniel(ed.) (**71**): "Education Related to the Use of Computers in Organizations"; *CACM*, Sep.1971, vol.14 no.9, pp.573–588.

Teichroew, D. and Hershey, E.A. (**77**): "PSL/PSA: A Computer Aided Technique for Structured Documentation and Analysis of Information Processing Systems"; *IEEE Trans. Software Eng.*, vol.SE-3 no.1, 1977, pp.41–48.

Teorey, Toby J. and Pinkerton, Ted B. (**72**): "A Comparative Analysis of Disk Scheduling Policies"; *CACM*, vol.15 no.3, 1972, pp.177–184.

Teorey, T.J. (**78**): "General Equations for Idealized CPU-I/O Overlap Configurations"; *CACM*, vol.21 no.6, Jun.1978, pp.500–507.

Teorey, T.J. and Fry, J.P. (**82**): *Design of Database Structures*; Prentice-Hall, 1982, 492 pp.

Terdiman, J.B. (**70**): "Mass Random Storage Devices and Their Application to a Medical Information System (MIS)"; *Comp. and Biomed. Res.*, vol.3 no.5, Oct.1970, pp.518.

Thiele, A.A. (**69**): "The Theory of Cylindrical Magnetic Domains"; *Bell System Journal*, vol.48, 1969, pp.3287–3335.

Thomas, D.A., Pagurek, B., and Buhr, R.J. (**77**): "Validation Algorithms for Pointer Values in DBTG Databases"; *TODS*, vol.2 no.4, Dec.1977, pp.352–369.

Thomas, J.C. and Gould, J.D. (**75**): "A Psychological Study of Query by Example"; *Proc. 1975 NCC*, AFIPS vol.44, pp.439–445.

Thomas, R.H. (**79**): "A Majority Consensus Approach to Concurrency Control for Multiple Copy Databases"; *TODS*, vol.4 no.2, Jun.1979, pp.180–209.

Thompson, F.B., Lockemann, P.C., Dostert, B.H., and Deverill, R.S. (**69**): "REL - A Rapidly Extensible Language System"; *Proc. 24th ACM National Conf. 1969*, pp.399–408.

Todd, S.J.P. (**76**): "The Peterlee Relational Test Vehicle"; *IBM Syst. J.*, vol.15 no.4, 1976, pp.285–307.

Tou, J.T.(ed.) (**74**): *COINS-IV*; Plenum Press, 1974.

Trivedi, K.S. and Sigmon, T.M. (**81**): "Optimal Design of Linear Storage Hierarchies"; *JACM*, vol.28 no.2, Apr.1981, pp.270–288.

Tsichritzis, D.C. and Bernstein, P.A. (**74**): *Operating Systems*; Academic Press, 1974.

Tsichritzis, D.C. and Lochovsky, F.H. (**77**): *Data Base Management Systems*; Academic Press, CS and Applied Mathematics, 1977, 388 pp.

Tsichritzis, D. and Lochovsky, F. (**81**): *Data Models*; Prentice Hall, 1981, 381 pp.

Tuel, W.G. jr. (**78**): "Optimum Reorganization Points for Linearly Growing Files"; *TODS*, vol.3 no.1, Mar.1978, pp.32–40

Uhrowczik, P.P. (**73**): "Data Dictionary/Directories"; *IBM Syst. J.*, vol.12 no.4, Dec.1973, pp.332–350.

Ullman, J.D. (**82**): *Principles of Database Systems, 2nd ed.*; Computer Science Press, 1982, 494 pp.

vandeRiet, R.P., Wasserman, A.I., Kersten, M.L., and DeJonge, W. (**81**): "High-Level Programming Features for Improving the Efficiency of a Relational Database System"; *TODS*, vol.6 no.3, Sep.1981, pp.464–485.

vanderPool, J.A. (**72,73**): "Optimum Storage Allocation"; *IBM JRD*, vol.16 no.6, Nov.-1972, pp.579–586; vol.17 no.1, Jan.1973, pp.27–38; no.2, Mar.1973, pp.106–116.

vanTassel, D. (**72**): *Computer Security Management*; Prentice Hall, 1972.

Vassiliou, Y. (**80**): "Functional Dependencies and Incomplete Information"; in *VLDB 6*, Lochovsky and Taylor(eds.), 1980, pp.260–269.

Verhofstad, J.S.M. (**78**): "Recovery Techniques for Database Systems"; *ACM C. Surveys*, vol.10 no.2, Jun.1978, pp.167–195.

Vold, Havard and Sjogren, Bjorn H. (**73**): "Optimal Backup of Data Bases: A Statistical Investigation"; *BIT vol.13 no.2 1973*, pp.233–241.

Vonnegut, K. jr. (**52**): *Player Piano, America in the Coming Age of Electronics*; Charles Scribner's Sons, 1952, 295 pp.

Wagner, H.M. (**75**): *Principles of Management Science*; Prentice Hall, 2nd ed., 1975, 562 pp.

Wagner, R.E. (**73**): "Indexing Design Considerations"; *IBM System Journal*, vol.12 no.4, Dec.1973, pp.351–367.

Walker, D.E.(ed.) (**71**): *Interactive Bibliographic Search : The User Computer Interface*; AFIPS Press, 1971, 375 pp.

Waltz, D.L. (**78**): "An English Language Query Answering System"; *CACM*, vol.21 no.7, Jul.1978, pp.526–539.

Wang, C.P. and Wedekind, H. (**75**): "Segment Synthesis in Logical Data Base Design"; *IBM JRD*, vol.19 no.1, Jan.1975, pp.71–77.

Ware, Willis (**67**): "Security and Privacy"; *Proc. 1967 SJCC*, AFIPS vol.30, pp.279–282, 287–290.

Waters, S.J. (**72**): "File Design Fallacies"; *Comp. J.*, vol.15, Feb.1972, pp.1–4.

Waters, S.J. (**74**): "Methodology of Computer System Design"; *Comp. J.*, vol.17 no.1, 1974, pp.17–24.

Waters, S.J. (**75**): "Estimating Magnetic Disk Seeks"; *Comp. J.*, vol.18 no.1, Feb.1975, pp.12–17.

Weingarten, Allen (**66**): "The Eschenbach Drum Scheme"; *CACM*, vol.9 no.7, July 1966, pp.509–512.

Weingarten, A. (**68**): "The Analytical Design of Real-Time Disk Systems"; *Proc. 1968 IFIP Congress*, North-Holland, pp.D131–D137.

Weiss, E.A.(ed.) (**82**): "Self-Assesment Procedure IX: Ethics"; *CACM*, vol.25 no.3, Mar. 1982, pp.181–195.

Weissman, Clark (**69**): "Security Controls in the ADEPT-50 Time-Sharing System"; *Proc. 1969 FJCC*, AFIPS, vol.35, pp.119–133.

Welty, C. and Stemple, D.W. (**81**): "Human Factors Comparison of a Procedural and a Nonprocedural Query Language"; *TODS*, vol.6 no.4, Dec.1981, pp.626–649.

Westin, A.F. (ed.) (**71**): *Information Technology in a Democracy*; Harvard University Press, Cambridge, 1971.

Weyl, S., Fries, J., Wiederhold, G., Germano, F. (**75**): "A Modular Self-Describing Databank System"; *Computers and Biomedical Research*, vol.8, 1975, pp.279–293.

Whang, K.-Y., Wiederhold, G., and Sagalowicz, D. (**81**): "Separability: An Approach to Physical Database Design"; in *VLDB 7*, Zaniolo and Delobel(eds.), 1981, pp.320–332.

Whang, K.-Y., Wiederhold, G., and Sagalowicz, D. (**82**): "Physical Design of Network Model Databases Using the Property of Separability"; in *VLDB 8*, McLeod and Villasenor(eds.), 1982, pp.98–107.

White, L.J. and Cohen, E.I. (**80**): "A Domain Strategy for Computer Program Testing"; *IEEE Trans. Software Eng.*, vol.SE-6, May.1980, pp.247–257.

Wiederhold, Gio, et al (**72**): "Report on the San Diego SHARE Data Base Committee on Technical Objectives meeting, Dec.1972"; *SHARE Proceedings*, 1972.

Wiederhold, Gio, Fries, J.F., and Weyl, S. (**75**): "Structured Organization of Clinical Data Bases"; *Proc. 1975 NCC*, AFIPS vol.44, pp.479–486.

Wiederhold, G. (**77**): *Database Design*; McGraw-Hill, Comp. Science Series, 1977, 658 pp.

Wiederhold, G. (**81**): *Databases for Health Care*; Lecture Notes in Medical Informatics, no.12, Lindberg and Reichertz(eds.), Springer-Verlag, 1981, 75 pp.

Wiederhold, G.(ed.) (**82**): *Second Symp. on Reliability in Distributed Software and Database Systems*; IEEE CS Pub. no.82CH1792-1, 1982, 171 pp.

Wiking, Donald (**71**): *The Evaluation of Information Services and Products*; Inf. Res. Press, Washington 1971.

Wilhelm, Neil C. (**76**): "An Anomaly in Disk Scheduling: A Comparison of FCFS and SSTF Seek Scheduling Using an Empirical Model for Disk Accesses"; *CACM*, vol.19 no.1, Jan.1976, pp.13–17.

Wilkes, M.V. (**72**): "On Preserving the Integrity of Data Bases"; *Comp. J.*, vol.15 no.3, 1972, pp.191–194.

Williams, Martha E.(ed.) (**76**): *Annual Review of Information Science and Technology (ARIST)*; American Society for Information Science, vol.12-16, 1976-1981.

Williams, M.E., Lannom, L. and Robins, C. (**82**): *Computer-Readable Databases: A Directory and Data Sourcebook*; Knowledge Industry Publications Inc., White Plains

NY, 1982, 1516 pp.

Winick, Robert M. (**69**):   "QTAM: Control and Processing in a Telecommunications Environment"; *Proc. of the 24th ACM National Conf.*, ACM 1969.

Wirth, Niklaus (**72**): "The Programming Language PASCAL"; *Acta Automatica*, vol.1 no.4, Dec.1972, pp.241–259.

Wong, C.K. (**80**): "Minimizing Expected Head Movement in One-Dimensional and Two-Dimensional Mass Storage Systems";   *ACM C. Surveys*, vol.12 no.2, Jun.1980, pp.167–211.

Wong, E. and Chiang, T.C. (**71**):   "Canonical Structure in Attribute Based File Organization"; *CACM*, vol.14 no.9, Sep.1971, pp.593–597.

Wong, E. and Youssefi, K. (**76**): "Decomposition–A Strategy for Query Processing"; *TODS*, vol.1 no.3, Sep.1976, pp.223–241.

Woods, W.A. (**73**):   "Progress in Natural Language Understanding, An Application to Lunar Geology"; *Proc. 1973 NCC*, AFIPS vol.42, pp.441–450.

Yamamoto, S., Tazawa, S., Ushio, K., and Ikeda, H. (**79**): "Design of a Balanced Multiple-Valued File-Organization Scheme with the Least Redundancy"; *TODS*, Vol.4 No.4, Dec.1979, pp.518–530.

Yamamoto, T. et al (**75**): "TOOL-IR, An On-line Information Retrieval System at an Inter-University Computer Center"; *Proc. of the 2nd USA-Japan Comp. Conf.*, 1975.

Yannakakis, M. (**82**): "A Theory of Safe Locking Policies in Database Systems"; *JACM*, vol.29 no.3, Jul.1982, pp.718–740.

Yao, A. (**78**): "Random 3-2 Trees"; *Acta Informatica*, vol.2 no.9, 1978, pp.159–170.

Yao, S.B., Das, K.S., and Teorey, T.J. (**76**):   "A Dynamic Database Reorganization Algorithm"; *TODS*, vol.1 no.2, Jun.1976, pp.159–174.

Yao, S.B. (**77**): "An Attribute Based Model for Database Access Cost Analysis"; *TODS*, vol.2 no.1, 1977, pp.45–67.

Yao, S.B. (**79**):   "Optimization of Query Evaluation Algorithms";   *TODS*, vol.4 no.2, Jun.1979, pp.133–155.

Yao, S.B., Navathe, S.B., Weldon, C.C. and Kunii, T.L.(eds.) (**82**):   *Data Base Design Techniques I: Requirements and Logical Structures*; Lecture Notes in CS, vol.132, Springer-Verlag, 1982, 227 pp.

Young, J.W. (**74**): "A First Order Approximation to the Optimum Checkpoint Interval"; *CACM*, vol.17 no.9, Sept.1974, pp.550–531.

Young, T.Y. and Liu, P.S. (**80**):   "Overhead Storage Considerations and a Multilinear Method for Data File Compression";   *IEEE Trans. Software Eng.*, vol.SE-6 no.4, Jul.1980, pp.340–347.

Yourdon, E. (**72**): *Design of On-line Computer Systems*; Prentice Hall 1972, 608 pp.

Yu, C.T., Lam, K. and Salton, G. (**82**): "Term Weighting Information in Informational Retrieval Using the Term Precision Model"; *JACM*, vol.29 no.1, Jan.1982, pp.152–170.

Yue, P.C. and Wong, C.K. (**78**):   "On a Partitioning Problem";   *TODS*, Vol.3 No.3, Sep.1978, pp.299–309.

Zadeh, L.A. (**72**): "A Fuzzy-Set-Theoretic Interpretation of Linguistic Hedges"; *Journ. of Cybernetics*, vol.2 no.3, July-Sep.1972, pp.4–34.

Zaniolo, C. and Delobel, C.(eds.) (**81**): *Proc. of VLDB 7, Cannes France*; IEEE CS pub. 81 CH1-701-2, Sep.1981, 570 pp.

Zaniolo, C. (**82**): "Database Relations with Null Values"; in *ACM-PODS 1*, Aho(ed.), Mar.1982, pp.27–33.

Zipf, G.K. (**49**): *Human Behavior and the Principle of Least Effort*; Addison-Wesley 1949.

Zloof, M.M. (**77**): "Query-by-Example: A Data Base Language"; *IBM Syst. J.*, vol.16 no.4, 1977, pp.324–343.

Index

This index contains entries for all defined terms and their principal occurrences. Page numbers in *italic* refer to the major discussion of a topic. Not included in the index are names of systems only listed in Appendix B and names of secondary authors appearing in the bibliography. Use of Appendix A, the alternate terminology index, can help to locate synonyms.

80/20 rule, 309, 664.
Abbreviation in indexes, 179, 182.
Abbreviation of terms, 657.
Abort a transaction, 202, 555, *557*, 637.
Access, 79.
    key for protection, 584, 587, *594*.
    load, 265.
    methods, 16, 90.
    paths, 106, 464, *591*.
    -path model, 402.
    privilege, 414, 580, *587*, 596, 600.
    protection and security, 579, 587, 642.
    ,sequential vs. serial or random, 77, 230.
    structures, 187, *515*.
Accessor, 581, 584.
Active authentication, 585.
Activity logging, 560, *562*, 674.
Acton, F., 341, 703.
ADABAS, 224, 484, 518, 689.
Addressing, 9, 13, *195*, 352.
Adel'son-Vel'skiĭ, 244.
ADEPT, 576, 689.
Adiba, M.E., 403, 447, 576, 645, 703.
AFIPS, 71, 69.
After entry, 260.
After-images, 557, 563, *565*, 567, 572.

Agarwala, A.K., 341, 703.
Aggregate system capability and demand, 267.
Aggregation functions, 459, 484.
Aho, A.V., 162, 401, 518, 644, 703.
Alford, M.W., 289, 704.
ALL quantifier, 462.
Allen, A.O., 342, 704.
Allen, R.P., 25, 162, 704.
Allen, S.I., 26, 244, 704.
Allocation of free storage, 337.
Alternate-block reading, 60.
Amble, O., 163, 704.
Ampex, 29, 36.
Anchor point, 95.
Ancestor, 211.
Anderson, H.D., 244, 704.
Andler, S., 577, 645, 704.
Anonymity, 609.
ANSI, 210, 439, 447, 652, 654, 689.
ANSI-SPARC, *439*, 447, 671, 730.
ANY quantifier, 462.
Anzelmo, F., 26, 71, 704.
APL, 470, 518, 679.
Appending of records, 589.
Append privilege, 589.
Application load distribution, 274.

735